CERTIFIED COURSE IN VISUAL BASIC 4

STEPHEN PRATA

WAITE GROUP PRESS™

Corte Madera, CA

Publisher . **Mitchell Waite**
Editor-In-Chief . **Charles Drucker**
Acquisitions Editor . **Jill Pisoni**
Editorial Director . **John Crudo**
Managing Editor . **Joanne Miller**
Content Editor . **Harry Henderson**
Technical Reviewer . **James D. Moore**
Copy Editor . **Jan Jue**
Production Director . **Julianne Ososke**
Production Manager . **Cecile Kaufman**
Design . **Tina Quarequio and Karen Johnston**
Production . **Jude Levinson, Tom Debolski, Karen Johnston**
Illustrations . **Larry Wilson**
Cover Design/Illustration . **Karen Johnston**

Published by Waite Group Press™, 200 Tamal Plaza, Corte Madera, CA 94925.

Waite Group Press is distributed to bookstores and book wholesalers by Publishers Group West, Box 8843, Emeryville, CA 94662, 1-800-788-3123 (in California 1-510-658-3453).

Printed in the United States of America
95 96 97 98 10 9 8 7 6 5 4 3 2 1

Library of Congress Cataloging-in-Publication Data

Prata, Stephen.
Certified Course in Visual Basic 4.0 / Stephen Prata.
p. cm.
Includes index
ISBN 1-57169-056-5
1. BASIC (Computer program language) 2. Microsoft Visual BASIC.
I. Title.
QA76.73.B3P68 1995
005.265—dc20

95-37676
CIP

DEDICATION

I dedicate this book to those who have made computers such wonderful toys and tools.

Message from the **Publisher**

WELCOME TO OUR NERVOUS SYSTEM

Some people say that the World Wide Web is a graphical extension of the information superhighway, just a network of humans and machines sending each other long lists of the equivalent of digital junk mail.

I think it is much more than that. To me, the Web is nothing less than the nervous system of the entire planet—not just a collection of computer brains connected together, but more like a billion silicon neurons entangled and recirculating electro-chemical signals of information and data, each contributing to the birth of another CPU and another Web site.

Think of each person's hard disk connected at once to every other hard disk on earth, driven by human navigators searching like Columbus for the New World. Seen this way the Web is more of a super entity, a growing, living thing, controlled by the universal human will to expand, to be more. Yet, unlike a purposeful business plan with rigid rules, the Web expands in a nonlinear, unpredictable, creative way that echoes natural evolution.

We created our Web site not just to extend the reach of our computer book products but to be part of this synaptic neural network, to experience, like a nerve in the body, the flow of ideas and then to pass those ideas up the food chain of the mind. Your mind. Even more, we wanted to pump some of our own creative juices into this rich wine of technology.

TASTE OUR DIGITAL WINE

And so we ask you to taste our wine by visiting the body of our business. Begin by understanding the metaphor we have created for our Web site—a universal learning center, situated in outer space in the form of a space station. A place where you can journey to study any topic from the convenience of your own screen. Right now we are focusing on computer topics, but the stars are the limit on the Web.

If you are interested in discussing this Web site or finding out more about the Waite Group, please send me e-mail with your comments, and I will be happy to respond. Being a programmer myself, I love to talk about technology and find out what our readers are looking for.

Sincerely,

Mitchell Waite

Mitchell Waite, C.E.O. and Publisher

200 Tamal Plaza
Corte Madera, CA 94925
415-924-2575
415-924-2576 fax

Website:
http://www.waite.com/waite

CREATING THE HIGHEST QUALITY COMPUTER BOOKS IN THE INDUSTRY

Waite Group Press
Waite Group New Media

ACKNOWLEDGEMENTS

Many have contributed to this book. Mitch Waite originated the concept, and Jill Pisoni helped develop it. Joanne Miller presided over the book's development, and Harry Henderson provided his usual helpful and informed editing. John Crudo and Mark Pruett devoted time and energy to the completion of the book. Mitch Waite, Gregg Irwin, Mark Pruett, Noel Jerke, and Don Kiely contributed programs for the advanced modules. I thank them all.

FOREWORD

The University of Phoenix is excited to work with Waite Group Press and Stephen Prata in presenting *Certified Course in Visual Basic 4,* an innovative approach to learning Visual Basic. This approach makes it possible for you, upon completion of certain requirements, to be rewarded with college-level credit. While self-paced tutorial approaches are not new, the combination of two tiers of certification and the awarding of a certificate with credit is new. (Appendix F, "Certification and Course Credit," explains how the two-tier testing procedure works.)

Approximately five years ago, the University of Phoenix began offering a Masters-level degree in Information Systems at its Denver campus. Since that time, the degree program has been expanded to include a Bachelor of Science in Business with a major in Information Systems. The degrees are offered at a number of campuses throughout the western U.S. The program started with an enrollment of 70 in 1991, and is up to nearly 1,200 students now.

In addition, the Technology Programs department of the University of Phoenix has been converting its courses to an online format. We are currently enrolling students in the Bachelor of Science and Business/Information Systems degree program through the University of Phoenix Online division.

The University of Phoenix recognizes that computer and information systems continually evolve. Visual Basic represents the evolution into a viable tool of many earlier programming trends. When Visual Basic became available, its popularity spread quickly, and it has enjoyed success throughout its several versions. As both a tool and a way to develop application programs, Visual Basic is an interesting and useful addition. The University is excited to help introduce students to this viable and accessible application development tool.

As you complete *Certified Course in Visual Basic 4,* you will have the opportunity to explore the topics presented in the book through laboratory exercises included in each chapter. As instructors, we encourage you to work each of the exercises and think about the results of your investigations into Visual Basic. As with most learning, the time you invest will be repaid many times over in your understanding of the material. We encourage you to take the time necessary to explore the flexible capabilities of Visual Basic.

After you have completed and submitted the final exam and received a passing score (as explained in Appendix F), we hope you will submit a request for Level II certification. The exam for this level provides you with an opportunity to apply your knowledge of Visual Basic by creating program code in response to questions. Upon achievement of Level II certification, you will be awarded three advanced placement credits in the University of Phoenix's undergraduate Visual Basic course.

We hope to receive requests from you for both levels of certification. We look forward to returning a certificate to you for each level.

Greg Temple
The University of Phoenix

TABLE OF CONTENTS

CONTENTS

PREFACE

For many years, the quickest, easiest way to get into programming an IBM-compatible PC was to learn Microsoft Basic or its successors QuickBasic and QBasic. However, these languages are rooted in the MS-DOS environment. To deal with the much richer Windows environment, something new is needed, something that lets you create Windows programs without burying you in the complexity that underlies Windows. That something is Visual Basic.

The latest incarnation of Visual Basic, Visual Basic 4, opens the world of Windows 95 to programmers and would-be programmers. It solves the complexity problem by providing Windows elements as fundamental building blocks. You want a window with a scrolling list box and a check box? Just open a new Visual Basic form, and use your mouse and the Visual Basic tool box to draw a scrolling list box and a check box on the form. You don't have to write code describing how to create these features; you simply use the features.

The great virtue of Visual Basic, then, is that it lets you program at the Windows level, using windows, command buttons, menus, and the like as your design elements. You don't have to deal with the messy underlying levels of operating-system function calls and hardware control. Thus, you can concentrate on high-level concerns, such as how your program will look and what it will do, rather than on low-level concerns, such as how to make the computer accomplish your high-level aims. In short, you can focus on design rather than on the underlying grunge work.

This book aims to be your guide to learning and using Visual Basic 4. It leads you in easy steps from your first simple program to a full exploration of the language. The book is organized into 20 lessons presenting the Visual Basic language and 3 advanced modules that explore some selected topics further. Here are some of the book's features:

- Assumes no prior programming knowledge
- Clear, detailed lessons presented in a light-hearted tone
- An introduction to each lesson and a list of the topics that will be covered
- Clear, detailed explanations of each topic, including step-by-step instructions, sample code, and numerous figures and illustrations to help you on your way
- A summary that quickly reviews what you've just learned
- A quiz to test your knowledge of the concepts. (The answers to the quiz are provided in an appendix.)
- Boxes with handy hints, rules, and reminders
- More coverage than the dumbed-down books and more fun than the encyclopedic tomes
- Programming projects to hone your skills

- Presents major language features, including code modules and class modules
- Instruction in program design
- A CD-ROM with all the example programs
- The opportunity to earn a certificate from the University of Phoenix

Visual Basic 4 is easily accessible, yet far-reaching in its capabilities. More than that, however, it is flat-out fun to use. *Certified Course in Visual Basic 4*, we hope, will help you experience all these aspects.

About the CD-ROM

The CD-ROM included at the back of this book contains the source code for the lessons and modules covered in *Certified Course in Visual Basic 4;* the final exam can also be found on the CD-ROM. A file named README.TXT provides an overview of the final exam.

Organization of the Contents

To view the contents of the CD-ROM, place it in your CD-ROM drive, then click on *My Computer* in the Windows 95 desktop. You can then click on the CD-ROM icon to see a list of 24 directories that correspond to the chapters in this book:

- Directories L01 through L20 contain the source code for the 20 lessons in the main body of the book.
- Directories M01 through M03 contain the source code for three advanced modules. Note that these three projects demonstrate high-end features of Visual Basic, and in some cases rely on controls that are found in the Professional or Enterprise Editions of Visual Basic 4, but are not included in the Standard Edition.
- The directory Finalex contains the running version of the final exam program, as well as the program's Visual Basic source code. You'll find more information about the final exam program and the certification process in Appendix F.

Copying Files to the Hard Disk

If you wish to copy any of the files or directories to your hard disk, you can move them easily using *Windows Explorer.* To start *Windows Explorer,* click on *Start* at the bottom of the Windows 95 desktop, then on the *Windows Explorer* icon. First, create a directory for your *Certified Course in Visual Basic 4* files and projects by clicking on *File* in the menu bar. Click on *New,* then on *Folder.* A new folder icon appears; type in a name for the new directory.

To move files from the CD-ROM to the hard disk, click on the CD icon in the directory tree on the left. The list at the right shows the contents of the loaded CD-ROM. Now you can drag folder icons, representing the CD's directories, to the newly created folder, which appears below the hard disk icon in the directory tree.

PROLOGUE

WINDOWS 95 TOUR

You probably are eager to start learning the fabulous Visual Basic programming language, so this prologue is a short one. But taking a look at Windows 95 is useful. The essence of Visual Basic 4 is Windows. Not only does Visual Basic run in the Windows 95 environment, it produces programs that run in the Windows 95 environment. The Visual Basic language—*command buttons, list boxes, mouse events,* and so on—is the language of Windows. Because the aim of Visual Basic is to make it easy for you to create Windows programs, it's useful to begin with a brief survey of Windows. This will remind you of some common Windows features and give them a name, and it will help identify some of the programming goals for a Windows application. Also, knowing how to use Windows helps you use the Visual Basic program. The primary goal for this tour is not to describe all the features of Windows but to introduce the elements that you will use in your own Visual Basic programs.

VISUAL BASIC EDITIONS AND WINDOWS

First, however, let's look at the relationship between Visual Basic 4 and the various versions of Windows. Visual Basic 4 comes in three editions:

- Standard Edition
- Professional Edition
- Enterprise Edition

The Standard Edition can run under Windows 95 and Windows NT 3.51 (or under later versions of these operating systems) but not under older versions of Windows, such as Windows 3.1. That's because the Standard Edition version of Visual Basic 4 is an example of a 32-bit program, and Windows 95 and Windows NT 3.51 are 32-bit operating systems. (That means these programs process instructions in 32-bit chunks.) The Professional and Enterprise editions each come with two versions of Visual Basic. One version is a 32-bit version that runs under Windows 95 and Windows NT 3.51. The second is a 16-bit version that runs under Windows 95 and Windows 3.1. You'll note that Windows 95 is the only version of Windows under which all versions of Visual Basic 4 run, and that's why Windows 95 will be surveyed.

THE START

Let's assume that you already are running Windows 95 (Win 95 among friends) and that you have installed Visual Basic 4. If you haven't done a lot of customizing, your Win 95 screen should look similar to Figure P-1. The background area is called the *desktop*. The little pictures along the left side are called *icons*. (Your screen may not have the Visual Basic shortcut icons yet, but perhaps it will by the time you finish this prologue.)

Something called the *taskbar* stretches across the bottom of the screen. At the far left of this bar is a rectangle labeled *Start*. This is an example of a *command button*. It's shaded to look slightly raised. The command button is a common Windows prop. To use it, you manipulate the mouse to move an arrow (the mouse *cursor*) across the screen until the cursor is over the button. Then, to perform the electronic equivalent of pressing the command button, you *click* on the left mouse button (that is, press and release the button in quick succession). The entire process of using the mouse to locate the cursor over the Start button and then clicking the left mouse button is subsumed in the phrase "click on the Start button."

Figure P-1 A sample Windows 95 opening screen

You and Your GUI

Before pursuing the exciting outcome of clicking on the Stop button, let's pause to appreciate the act. Clicking the mouse on a visual representation of a pushbutton is a classic example of using a *GUI,* or *g*raphical *u*ser *i*nterface. You respond to a visual cue (the command button) by using an input device (the mouse) to maneuver a graphic element (the cursor). Then you take decisive action and click the mouse button, generating what is known as an *event.* In this case, you generate a mouse-click event. Windows detects that event and responds to it. Here, in a nutshell, are the elements you need to provide when writing Windows programs—visual cues, mouse awareness, the ability to respond to events. These are precisely the elements that Visual Basic provides.

Now let's return to the consequences of clicking on the Start button, that is, to Windows' response to the mouse-click event. Windows displays a *menu* (see Figure P-2). A menu is a list of items from which you can select. This menu has two kinds of entries. One type has an arrowhead at the right (for instance, the Programs entry) and the other type doesn't (for instance, the Help entry). The ones with arrowheads are *hierarchical* menu items. Merely positioning the mouse over a hierarchical item *highlights* it (changes the background from light gray to dark blue and changes the lettering from black to white) and *activates* it. Activating a hierarchical menu item opens up a new submenu, which appears

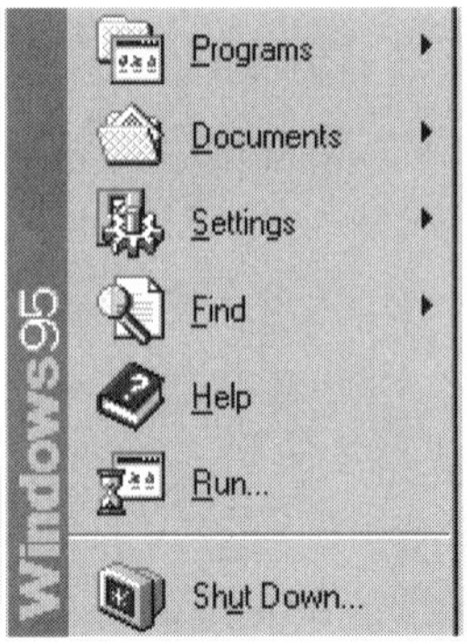

Figure P-2 The Start menu

in a new column to the right. To activate a nonhierarchical menu item, such as the Help entry, you have to click on it.

Let's see how you would use this system to start the Visual Basic program. First, you click on the Start button. Then you position the mouse over the Program entry, wait a moment, and get a submenu, one that lists the various *program groups* on your system. The setup program for installing most Windows applications establishes a program group for the product. A group may contain just one program or a set of related programs. The submenu shown in Figure P-3, for example, includes a program group for the 32-bit version of Visual Basic 4. Selecting this choice and waiting a moment opens another submenu, one which includes the name of the Visual Basic program (see Figure P-4). This final menu isn't hierarchical, so you then have to click on the program name to start the program.

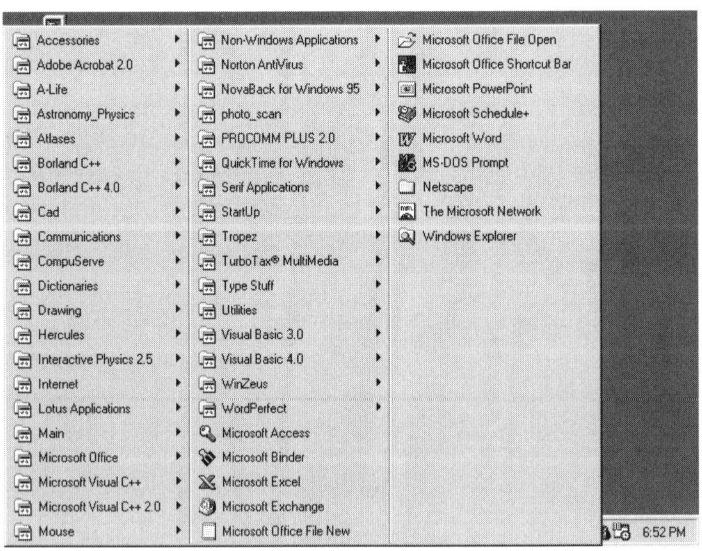

Figure P-3 The Programs submenu

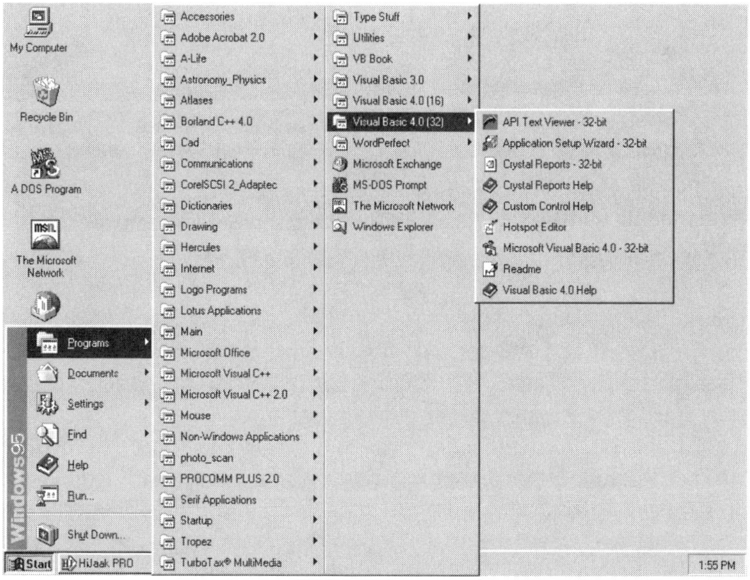

Figure P-4 The Visual Basic program group submenu

THE WINDOW

Navigating the Start menu is just one way to start a program. You could, instead, *double-click* on the My Computer icon at the top left of the screen. (To double-click is to locate the mouse cursor over an item, then click the left mouse button twice in quick succession. Double-clicking is another event that Windows recognizes.) This brings up an example of the most important visual element in Windows, the *window*. This particular window (see Figure P-5) exhibits icons representing important facets of the computer, such as the floppy drives and the

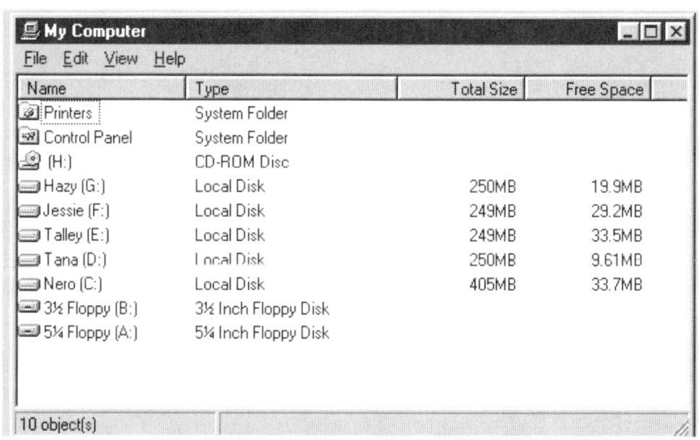

Figure P-5 The My Computer window

hard drives. You can double-click on a drive to get a list of directories and files on the drive. Depending on the settings, you might see the files and directories listed by name or represented by icons, with file folders representing directories. You can double-click on a directory to get a list of subdirectories and files in that directory, and so on. In this manner, you can navigate to the file that represents the executable file you want. Double-clicking on the file starts the program.

Rather than follow that path to the finish, however, let's contemplate the My Computer window itself. It illustrates common features of a window. Across the top it has a *title bar,* which bears a legend identifying the window. At the left end of the title bar is a small icon. This is the *control-menu icon.* In this case, the icon has been customized to represent a computer. Clicking on the control-menu icon brings up a menu of options, including the option of closing the window (see Figure P-6). To select a particular choice, click on it.

There are three interesting-looking boxes at the right end of the title bar (see Figure P-7). The leftmost member of the trio is the *minimize box.* Clicking on it minimizes the window, turning it into a command button that's added to the taskbar at the bottom of the screen. Clicking on the command button, in return, restores the window to it original size. The middle box, which bears the picture of a window, is the *maximize box.* Clicking on it puts the window in full-screen mode; that is, it resizes the window to fill the whole screen. The maximize box then converts to a *restore box,* which shows two overlapping windows instead of a single window. Clicking on the restore box puts the window back in its original form. The rightmost box, the one with the *X,* is the *close box* (not to be confused with a clothes box). Clicking on it closes the window. If the window represents an application, such as Visual Basic, clicking on the close box also terminates the application.

You can change the size of a window by positioning the mouse cursor over a border or corner of the window. The mouse cursor changes in appearance to a double-headed arrow. To change the border size, press down the left mouse button and move the mouse parallel to the double-headed arrow cursor. The border should move with the mouse. This process is called *dragging,* and yes, dragging is another special event that Windows detects and can respond to.

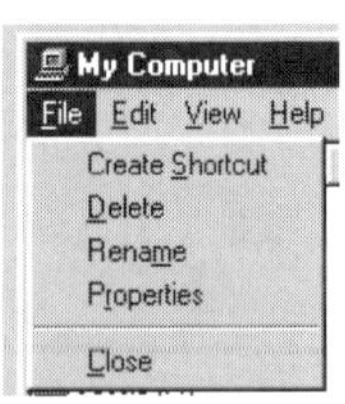

Figure P-6
A Window's control menu

Figure P-7
Title bar boxes

The My Computer window also displays a *menu bar,* which is an optional feature for a window. Clicking on a menu bar heading causes Windows to display the menu associated with the heading. As with the Start menu, you then can select a choice by clicking on it. Visual Basic makes it easy to add menus to programs.

Another way to start a program is to create a shortcut in the form of a desktop icon. Figure P-1, for example, shows shortcuts for starting two versions of Visual Basic. There are many ways to create shortcuts. One of the simplest is to locate the program by using the My Computer window and drag the program icon to the desktop. Win 95 will then place a Shortcut icon on the desktop. You then can start the program by double-clicking on the shortcut icon.

VISUAL BASIC AND THE GRAPHICS INTERFACE

You've just seen many typical features of a Windows program—windows, title bars, control icons, control boxes, resizeability, mouse awareness, and menus. You'll find that Visual Basic lets you provide these and other common Windows features with the greatest of ease. One of the keys to this ease is a Visual Basic Toolbox of common graphical interface elements that respond in standard ways to user actions. These elements are called *controls* and, as mentioned earlier, the user actions are called *events.* When you create a Visual Basic program, you start with a blank window on which you then place the controls you need to create the graphical user interface you want. Also, a *Menu Editor* lets you incorporate menus.

To give you a better idea of what you can expect to accomplish, let's take a longer look at common Windows elements that you'll be able to utilize in your own programs.

COMMON WINDOWS ELEMENTS

Let's look at more Windows elements, the kinds of things you might want to incorporate into Visual Basic programs you write. You've already glimpsed the following:

- Windows
- Menus
- Command buttons
- Icons

Figure P-8 The Visual Basic menu-bar window

Now let's add the following elements to the list:

- Option buttons
- Check boxes
- Text boxes
- Frames
- List boxes
- Scroll bars

These all are common components of Windows programs, and Visual Basic makes it easy to add them to programs you write. So let's find some examples to help familiarize you with the tools you'll soon have at your disposal.

Since you probably have Visual Basic installed, let's see what visual elements it can reveal to use. First, it displays a short but wide window containing a title bar and Toolbar, as shown in Figure P-8. Note the control-menu icon and the trio of control boxes. Each menu title in the menu bar can be clicked on to open a menu, as shown in Figure P-9.

These features you've seen. Clicking on Options from the Tools menu reveals some new features. Figure P-10 shows the dialog box that appears. At this point, don't worry about the meaning; just note the features. First, the dialog box has

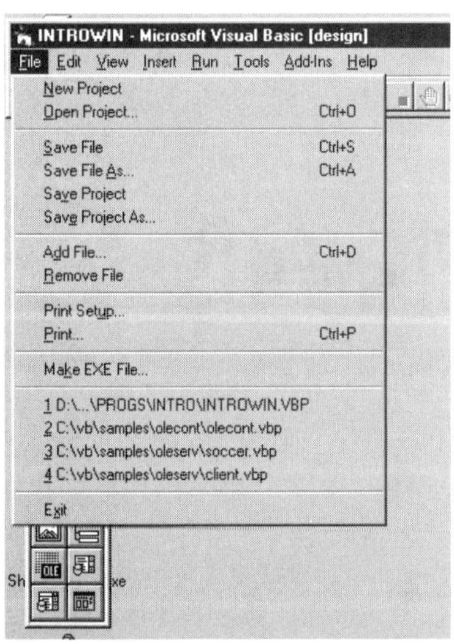

Figure P-9 A Visual Basic menu

several *check boxes*. These are small square boxes that can be toggled between a checked state (the box displays a ✔ symbol) and an unchecked state (empty box). Clicking on the box checks or unchecks it, providing a simple visual cue for turning particular features on or off.

Note that two sets of boxes lie within labeled rectangular outlines, one labeled "Form Design Grid" and one labeled "Windows On Top." These labeled rectangles are called *frames*. Frames are a device for grouping related items together visually.

Another frame, labeled "File Save," contains three labeled circles called *option buttons*. You can think of them as pushbuttons (some call them radio buttons), and they have the property that, at most, one option button in a group can be activated at a time. The active button shows a dark dot in its center; you can think of it as being pushed in. You can push an option button by clicking on it with the mouse. Activating an option button in a group automatically deactivates other buttons in the group. (All buttons in the same frame are in the same group.)

Then there are two rectangular boxes labeled "Width" and "Height." These are *text boxes*. Not only do they display text, but they also let you enter text. Just position the mouse cursor in the text box, and it turns into a vertical I-bar called a *text cursor*. Then you can use the keyboard to type in the text box.

Entities like text boxes, check boxes, and option buttons are examples of *controls*. Much of the Visual Basic program, as you'll see, consists of designing a visual interface by adding controls to a window. Incidentally, Figure P-10 also uses something called a *label control*. Some controls, such as option buttons and check boxes, come with their own labels, called *captions*, built in. Others, like text boxes, don't have built-in labels, but you add label controls next to them to identify the text box. For example, the word *Width* is part of a label control in Figure P-10.

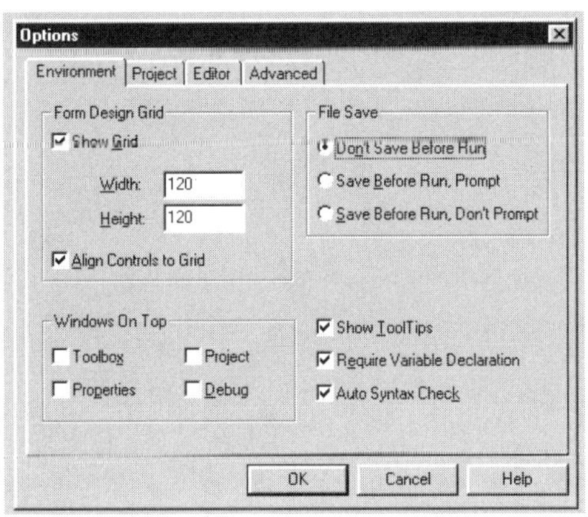

Figure P-10 A dialog box exhibiting check boxes, option buttons, text boxes, and frames

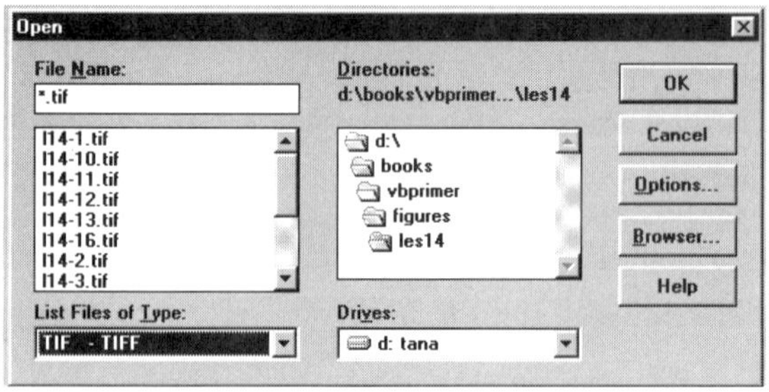

Figure P-11 A dialog box with list boxes

To get a look at a list, go to a Windows application File menu and try the Open choice. Most Windows applications use a standard *dialog box* like that shown in Figure P-11. A dialog box is a window that gives you a chance to enter information in response to inquiries posed in the dialog box. (Some 32-bit applications, including the 32-bit version of Visual Basic, use a different design for dialog boxes—see Figure P-12.) The dialog box in Figure P-11 shows two large side-by-side *list box controls,* one showing a list of files, and one a list of directories. Note that each list box has a vertical *scrollbar* on the right. If the list is too long to fit in the box, you can use the scrollbar to scroll through the list. The scrollbar is another example of a control. The list box control has a scrollbar built in, but you can use scrollbars as separate elements, too.

The bottom of the dialog box shows two instances of a second kind of list box. This kind is a *drop-down list box.* It shows just one item, but there is a button with a down arrow at the end of the list. Clicking on the arrow causes the complete list to drop down. This type of list box has the advantage of taking up little space until you need to use it.

SUMMARY

One of the strengths of Windows is its graphic user interface (GUI). The GUI provides a wealth of visual metaphors to guide the user to a successful interaction with a program. The central idea is the window, which acts as your view of a program. Visual controls such as command buttons, option buttons, check boxes, menus, text boxes, scrollbars, and list boxes, combine with the mouse control to provide a simple and consistent means to perform common actions.

If you write programs to run under Windows, you should support the users' expectations by employing these GUI features. That's where Visual Basic comes in. In Visual Basic, you don't have to build a window from scratch; Visual Basic automatically provides you with a fresh window, called a *form,* on which to base your program. You don't have to design list boxes, command buttons, and the

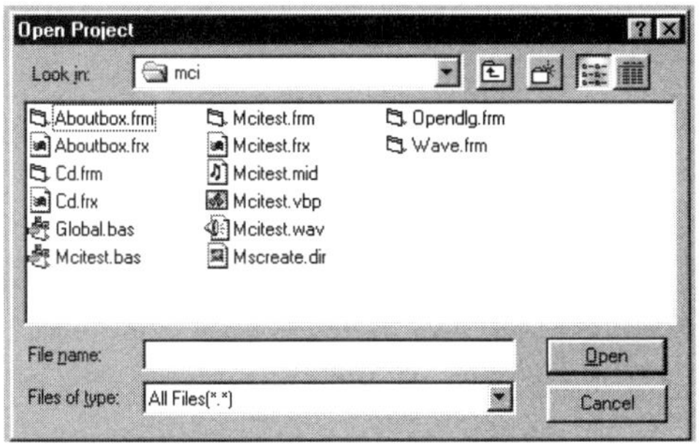

Figure P-12 The 32-bit version of a dialog box

like. Visual Basic lets you draw these controls on a form, and it takes care of the details, such as shading the appearance of a command button or making sure that clicking on an empty check box causes a check mark to appear.

LESSON

1

WHAT IS A VISUAL BASIC PROGRAM?

Before embarking upon the adventure of learning Visual Basic, you might like to have an idea of where you're headed. This lesson is your travel brochure. Actually, you'll get to the short answer very quickly, but the implications will take a bit longer to explore. In this lesson, you'll be introduced to the following:

- **A Visual Basic program**
- **A form**
- **A control**
- **An event**
- **A property**
- **An object**
- **How Visual Basic programming works**

A VISUAL BASIC PROGRAM IS A WINDOWS PROGRAM MADE EASY

A Visual Basic program is a Windows program. That is, you need Windows to run it, it looks like other Windows programs, and it works like other Windows programs. The wonderful thing about Visual Basic is that it makes it incredibly easy to create Windows programs. Instead of taking a few months to learn the C or C++ programming language and a few more months to learn Windows programming, you can create Windows programs with Visual Basic almost immediately. To programmers who have taken the longer route, Visual Basic almost seems unfair. This lesson provides you with background about Visual Basic programs, beginning with their appearance.

You start with that Windows keystone, the window itself. Visual Basic lets you fill the screen with them with just a mouse click or two, and you're off and running.

IN THE BEGINNING...FORMS

When you create a Visual Basic program, you begin with a form. But what is a form? The most obvious feature of a typical Windows program is the window. Visual Basic, being a Windows program, has several windows, such as the Properties window and the Project window, that help you create programs. More importantly, Visual Basic creates programs that have windows. Visual Basic calls those windows forms.

When you start Visual Basic, it automatically opens a form imaginatively named Form1. This form is a canvas upon which you can create a program. Initially, Visual Basic is in design mode, which lets you design a program. One way to tell you're in design mode is that the form shows a grid of dots to help you align visual elements. (You can turn the grid off if you like.) Another hint is

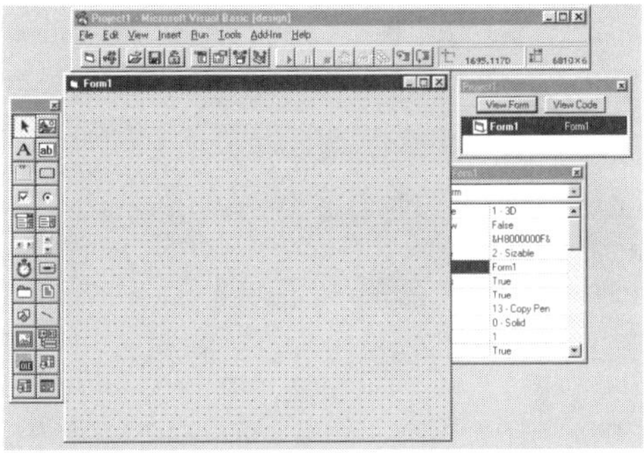

Figure L1-1 Visual Basic in design mode

that the Visual Basic menu bar is labeled "Microsoft Visual Basic [design]," as shown in Figure L1-1. (Its appearance will depend on whether you have the Standard Edition, the Professional Edition, or the Enterprise Edition.)

You don't have to do any designing to get a working Windows program, for even the empty initial form is a simple Windows program. You can go to the Visual Basic Run menu and select Start. Visual Basic switches to run mode (the "(design)" in the menu bar changes to "(run)"), then runs the program. A window labeled "Form1" appears onscreen, as shown in Figure L1-2. The grid points are gone. It's a blank window, possibly useful for Zen-like contemplation. Even though the content is minimal, you can do window-like things with the form. For instance, you can use the mouse to grab the lower-right corner of the window and resize it. You can click on the usual Minimize and Maximize boxes on the form to maximize or minimize the program. Maximizing, you recall, makes the window fill the whole screen, while minimizing a window reduces it to a minimized title bar just above the Windows taskbar (see Figure L1-3). If you minimize the program, you can click once on the button to restore the program to its previous appearance. You can click on the Close box to terminate the Form1 program and return to design mode. Then reflect upon the fact that you've created a simple (very simple) Windows program with a few mouse clicks.

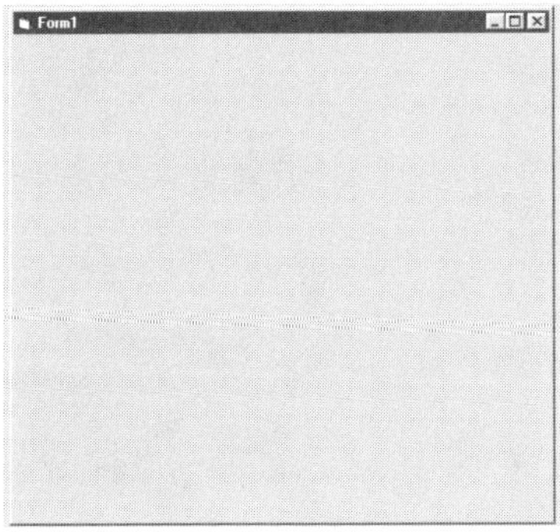

Figure L1-2 The default Form1 window

Figure L1-3 The minimized form

You may not find the empty Form1 program particularly fascinating, unless you've never seen a window before. But to a Windows programmer, Form1 is amazing. If you were programming from scratch in, say, assembly language or C or Pascal or C++, you would have to know a lot about Windows programming and you would have to put together a lot of code to draw a window, to give it the pretty and functional bar across the top, to make the window resizeable, to have the program recognize when the mouse cursor passes over the Close box, to have it react to mouse clicks, and so on. But Visual Basic delivers all this, and all you have to do is start the Visual Basic program. Also, once the program is started, you can create new forms by selecting New Form from the File menu. This is an example of the magic of Visual Basic—it lets you think conceptually ("I want a window") while it takes care of the grunge work.

CONTROLS—GOODIES FOR YOUR FORM

A Windows program usually has something in its windows. For example, it might have boxes in which you can enter information (*text boxes*), buttons to click (*command buttons*), *scrollbars* to adjust, lists of items to scan (*list boxes*), *labels*, boxes to check (*check boxes*), and so on. See, for example, the overly ambitious form in Figure L1-4. Visual Basic terms such items *controls*. It's quite easy to add controls to a program. Visual Basic provides a set of icons representing different controls. These are grouped together in a display called the *Toolbox*, which normally resides along the left side of the screen (see Figure L1-1). Just select a Toolbox icon representing a particular control, then use the mouse to draw the

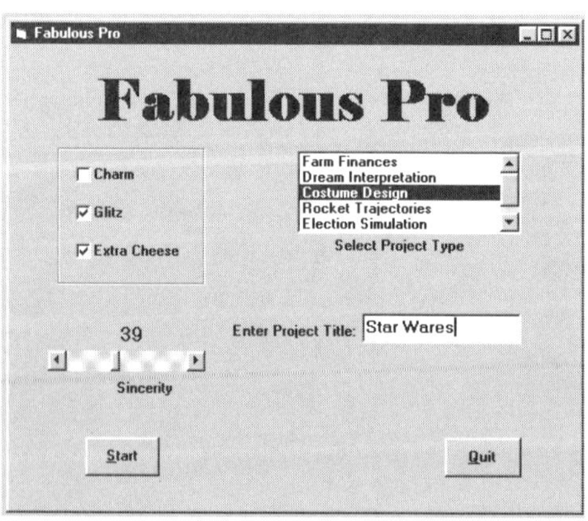

Figure L1-4 A form with controls

control on the form. (Lesson 2 will describe this process fully.) Again, Visual Basic takes care of the details, drawing the control correctly onscreen and providing it with the properties it needs. You then can alter those properties easily, choosing, say, a different caption or color.

Controls, like forms, can do a lot without any further effort on your part. For instance, you can use the mouse to grab the *slider* (also known as a *scroll box*) on the scrollbar and slide it back and forth. Also, you can use the mouse to scroll through the names in the list box and to select an item from the list.

Controls can do even more if you provide them with Visual Basic statements instructing them how to respond to various stimuli, such as mouse clicks or keystrokes. For example, you can create a button that beeps when you click on it by providing just one short instruction—*Beep*. (Making a button meow or bark, however, takes a bit more work.)

Table L1-1 lists some of the more common Visual Basic controls. With these and other built-in controls plus the options of creating your own controls and obtaining third-party controls, you needn't fear losing control of a Visual Basic program.

CONTROL NAME	SHORT DESCRIPTION
Check box	Lets you select a feature by checking a box
Command button	Executes commands when clicked
Frame	Collects other controls into a subunit
Image box	Displays images
Label box	Displays a text label
List box	Presents a scrollable list of choices for selection
Option button	Lets you select a feature from a mutually exclusive set of choices by clicking a button
Picture box	Displays images and otherwise acts like a mini-form
Scrollbar	Provides a graphic way of getting input or setting positions
Text box	Accepts text input
Timer	Executes instructions repeatedly at specified intervals

Table L1-1 Common Visual Basic controls

MENUS—CHOICES BY DESIGN

Menus are another way to get forms to work for you. By this time you should not be astonished to find that Visual Basic makes it simple to add a menu bar to a form. Just open a special menu-design window (see Lesson 8) and describe what should appear on the menu. Visual Basic does the rest, as shown in Figure L1-5.

The same design window also lets you specify the items that appear under the various menu headings, as shown in Figure L1-6.

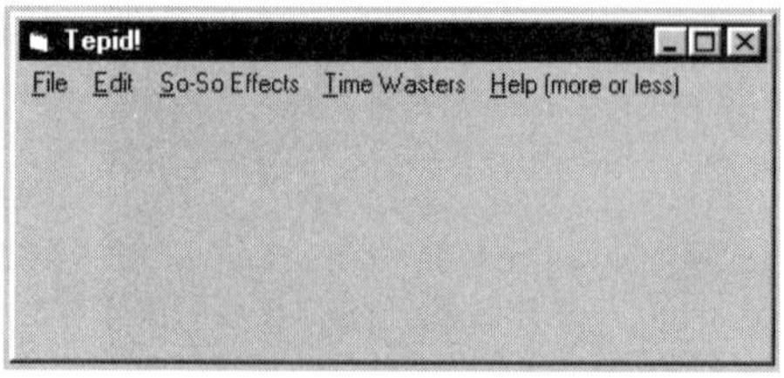

Figure L1-5 A form with a menu

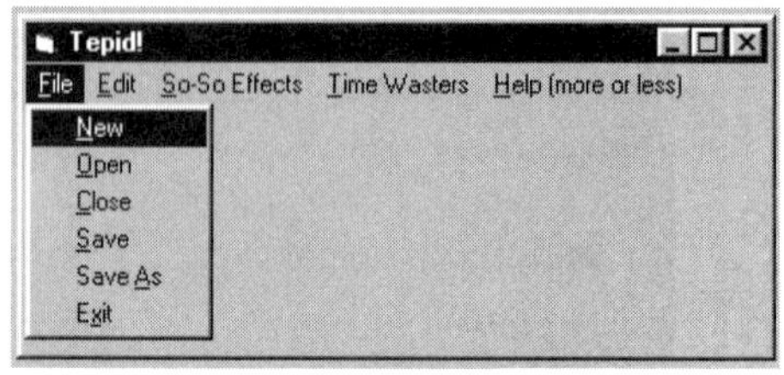

Figure L1-6 Items in a menu

The menu-design window only takes you so far, however. It lets you specify the menu appearance, and, when you run the program, it lets you select menu items. But you still have to provide Visual Basic program statements (*code,* for short) to implement the promise of the menu. That is, the menu may let you select Exit from the File menu, but you have to provide the code (the brief command *End*) that terminates the program once Exit is selected. As with controls, Visual Basic makes it easy to add such code.

EVENTS—SHAPERS OF DESTINY

As you've seen, Visual Basic creates programs that look like Windows programs. It also creates programs that act like Windows programs. Windows programs typically are *event-driven.* What are events? They are particular actions that take place when you use a computer. For example, clicking on a menu item or command button is an event. Double-clicking on a file name in a list box is an event, pressing a key is an event. Just about anything you do in a window is an event. Visual Basic programs detect and respond to events, and events control the flow of a Visual Basic program. Table L1-2 lists a few common events.

EVENT NAME	DESCRIPTION
Change	Control's value is altered
Click	Mouse button is pressed and released
DblClick	Mouse button is pressed and released twice in quick succession
GotFocus	Control gets the focus (becomes the control in charge because you clicked on it)
KeyPress	Key is pressed
Load	Program starts up
LostFocus	Control loses the focus (control loses being in charge)
MouseDown	Mouse button is pressed
MouseUp	Mouse button is released

Table L1-2 Some Visual Basic events

Most Visual Basic components, including forms, controls, and menus, recognize events. For instance, a control button recognizes the mouse-click event. But while

Visual Basic provides the recognition, you provide the response. That is, Visual Basic gives a control button the ability to detect a mouse click, and you provide the code that determines what happens after the button detects a mouse click. As you'll learn in the next lesson, Visual Basic makes it easy to provide such code.

PROGRAMMING THE VISUAL BASIC WAY

Visual Basic is a new way of programming. If you are used to programming in, say, QuickBasic, C, or Pascal, you may have some mental readjusting to do. Traditionally, programmers have been concerned primarily with two things:

- Data (information, which might be numbers or text)
- Algorithms (methods or recipes for processing data)

So a programmer would ask himself or herself questions like "how should I store five years of duck racing results?" and "how do I best sort all the racing ducks by performance?" Indeed, Niklaus Wirth, the creator of the Pascal programming language, once phrased this outlook as follows:

program = data + algorithms

Visual Basic adds a new term to the equation:

program = interface + data + algorithms

The *interface* is the part of the program that the user sees and uses. Ultimately, an interface, too, is composed of data and algorithms, so listing it as a separate item really is a matter of emphasis. Traditionally, programmers have tended to concentrate on the tasks a program had to perform and have worried about the interface only after the "important" parts of a program were working properly. With Visual Basic, however, you typically start with the interface. Thus, in Visual Basic programming, thinking about how you want a program to look and behave becomes as important as the data and algorithms it will use. After all, you want your program to look cool and be easy to use.

Visual Basic does more than increase the emphasis on the interface. It also alters the conceptual framework by making the programs event-driven instead of procedure-driven. What the heck does that mean? Let's look at an example. The example involves a formula, but if you don't like formulas, don't worry about it. What we're concentrating on is how a pre-Windows program and a post-Windows program look to a user.

Suppose, then, you want to write a program that calculates the number of gallons of water (or other liquid) in a rectangular swimming pool. Reading instructions on the label of some pool chemicals, you find the following formula:

```
gallons = width x length x average depth x 7.5      (dimensions in feet)
```

This formula is an example of an algorithm, and the various values involved are a sample of data. Gee, this program will use data and algorithms!

If you had to write such a program in pre-Windows days, you'd probably start by writing code to do the calculation. Consider that part done. Then you'd add some code to get the information from the user. You might come up with an interface that looked like this:

```
Enter pool width: 10
Enter pool length: 20
Enter average depth: 6
Pool volume = 9000
Do you wish to do another pool? <y/n> y
Enter pool width: 10
Enter pool length: 20
Enter average depth: 8
Pool volume = 12000
Do you wish to do another pool? <y/n> n
Bye!
```

Note how the program itself controls the actions of the user. You have to enter the data in the order that the program asks for it. If you want to do another calculation, you have to tell the program. And if all you want to do is change the depth, you still have to enter everything—width, length, depth—bummer! It practically takes all the fun out of calculating pool volumes.

Languages such as C, C++, Pascal, FORTRAN, and Basic (old style) are called *procedural* languages because they produce programs that are a set of procedures for the computer to follow. Procedural languages make a natural fit to the sort of programming style you just saw. The situation is quite different for a Visual Basic program. Visual Basic is *event*-driven rather than procedural, meaning it's designed around responding to mouse clicks and other such events.

The procedural programming style is akin to automated phone services. "If you have a question about animals, press 1. If you have a question about vegetables, press 2. If you have a question about minerals, press 3." You press 2. "If you have a question about invertebrates, press 1. If you have a question about vertebrates, press 2." And so on. With luck, you get to your final destination in fewer than 20 questions. The event programming style is more free form. "Hello, can I help you?" "I want to know about pigs." This triggers the pig event, and you get your information (see Figure L1-7).

The event orientation leads to a different approach to creating programs. For our example, you begin by thinking about the interface. First, you create a new form. Next, realizing that the program needs three numbers fed to it, you drag three suitable controls onto the form. For example, you might place three text boxes or three scrollbars on the form to let the user enter the three numbers. You'd add another box to show the answer. Next, you'd think about how the program will interact with the user. For instance, when should the program calculate and show the answer? Perhaps you want a Calculate button that you click to trigger the calculation. Or maybe you want the program to recalculate and display the new answer each time the user changes one of the pool dimensions.

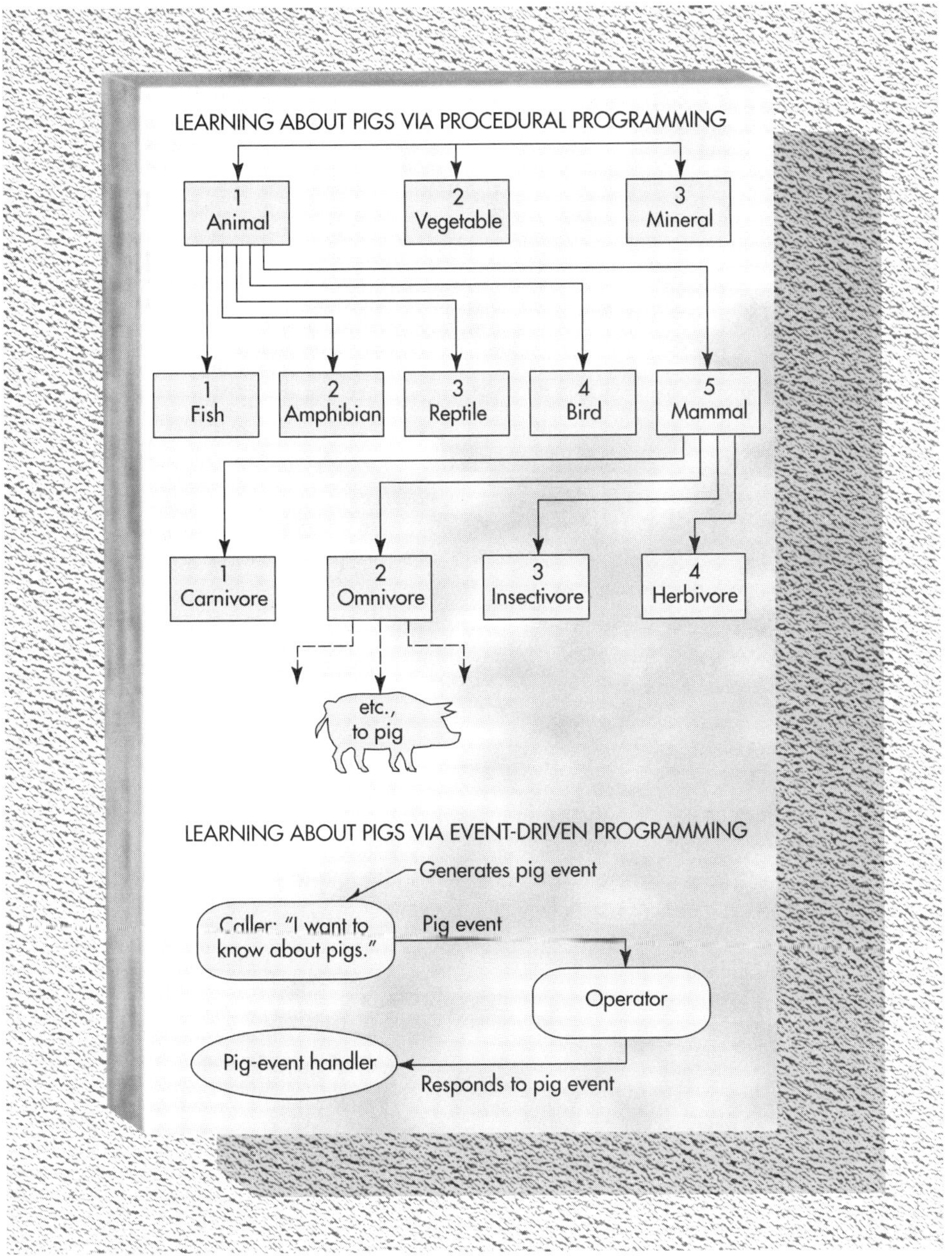

Figure L1-7 Procedural programming versus event programming

Visual Basic makes it simple to have the program detect and respond to such a change. Thus, your program might look like that shown in Figure L1-8. Finally, you'd write the code for the actual calculation.

The look and feel of this program is much different from the pre-Windows version. You can enter the data in any order you wish—height, width, depth, or width, depth, height, or some other order. Once you have the data entered, you can change just one dimension if that's all you need. You needn't keep telling the program you want to do another calculation. In short, you use events, such as dragging scroll boxes, to control the program flow.

OBJECTS—THE NEW MANTRA

If you hang out with Windows programmers (including Visual Basic programmers), you'll probably hear objects mentioned. And mentioned. And mentioned. You might soon conclude that objects are useful and desirable (objects of desire?), but you still might wonder about what they are. An object is a kind of programming unit that wraps data and code into a single entity. In Visual Basic, forms and controls are objects. Let's look at this in more detail.

Consider the Visual Basic form. What kind of data and code does it wrap together? A form has various characteristics, such as its height, width, color, caption, and position. These all are examples of data, and Visual Basic refers to data describing an object as its *properties*. All the properties of a particular form are saved in one place. A form also has some computer code associated with it that describes how a form responds to events. For instance, clicking the mouse in a form's Minimize box activates the code that minimizes the window. That code is predefined, but you can define code for other events, such as clicking on the form. The properties and code together define how a particular form object looks and behaves. They are the data and code associated with a form object.

Similarly, each command button has its own set of properties and its own set of programmed responses to events. Each command button is a separate object,

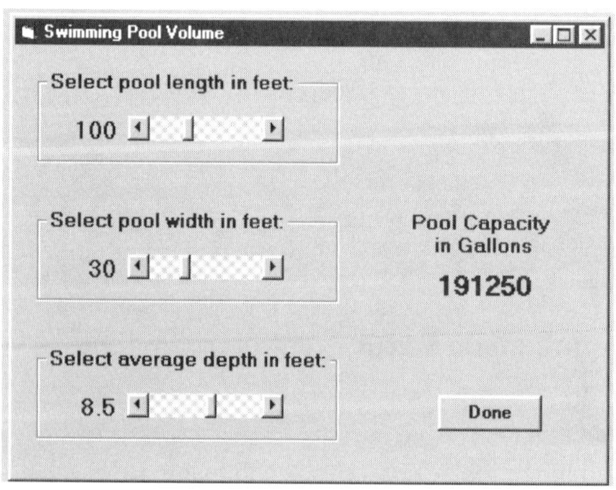

Figure L1-8 A Windows version of the pool program

but all command buttons have the same design. For example, command button Elsie may have a different size from the command button Elmer, but both have properties describing the width and height of the buttons. Clicking on Elsie may produce a different action from clicking on Elmer, but both have the capacity to recognize and react to a mouse click event. The simple act of creating a command button control creates an object with a whole set of potentialities built in.

In short, objects help make using Visual Basic simple. When you select the command button icon from the Visual Basic Toolbox and paint a command button on a form, you add an object with a predefined set of characteristics. Whump—there it is.

From this standpoint, creating a Visual Basic program is manipulating objects. You create a form object, and you drag various control objects onto the form. You modify the properties of these objects and add code to them to create the look and behavior you want for the program (see Figure L1-9). Thus,

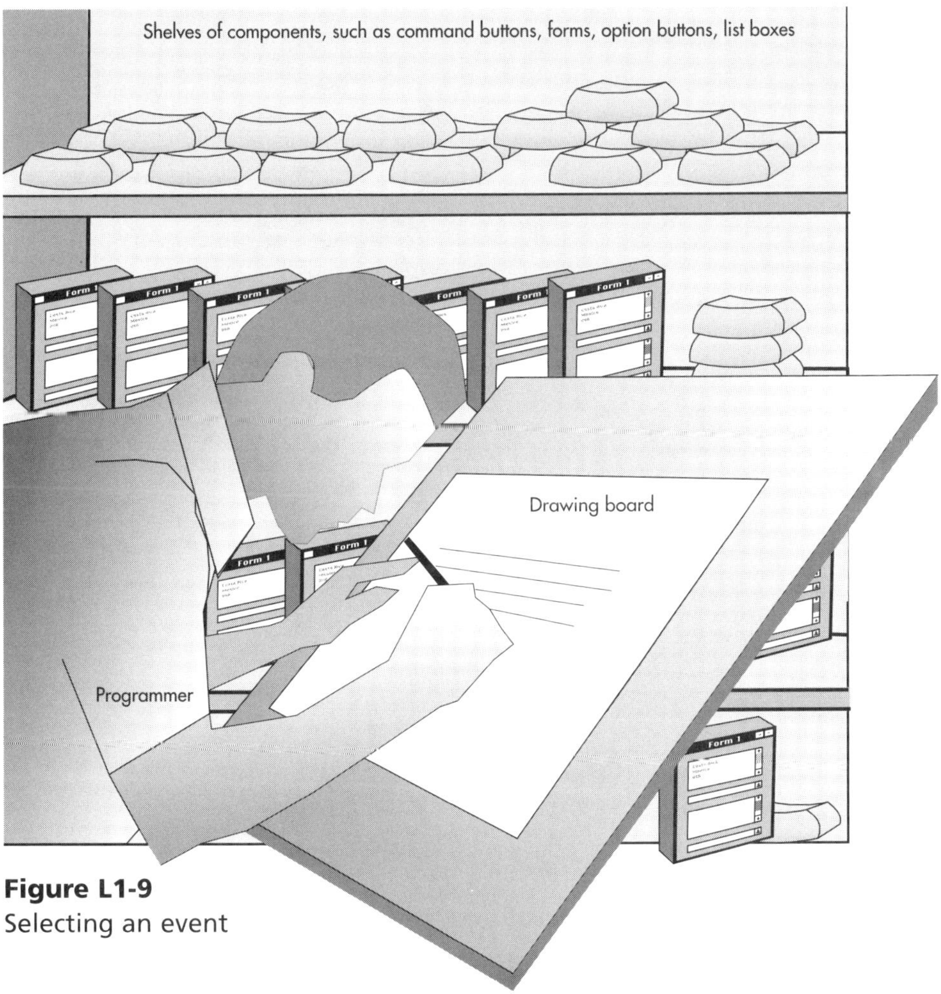

Figure L1-9
Selecting an event

Visual Basic is like a TinkerToy or Lego kit of various objects that you can play around with to create Windows programs. Part of learning Visual Basic is learning about the various kinds of objects you can use. More important, however, is learning how to use the Visual Basic arsenal of objects and how to integrate them into a program.

SUMMARY

Visual Basic programs are Windows programs. A simple Visual Basic program consists of a form (the Visual Basic term for a window) with a menu bar and some controls. Controls include things like buttons, text windows, and scrollbars. Visual Basic programs are event-driven, meaning that they respond to particular events such as clicking the mouse on a menu item or dragging the scroll box of a scrollbar. Forms and controls are examples of objects, which combine data and code into a single entity. Properties are the data that describe Visual Basic objects, for example, size, position, caption, and color. The code associated with a Visual Basic object determines which events an object recognizes and how it reacts to it.

Visual Basic programming starts with using forms, menus, and controls to design the program's interface with users, then adds code describing how components of the program respond to different events. This approach makes it much simpler to produce a friendly, accessible interface than did the older procedural approach.

QUIZ 1

Note: You probably didn't expect a quiz the first day in class. In deference to that, this quiz may not fully challenge your understanding of the lesson.

1. A Visual Basic program is a
   a. Component of Sensual Basic
   b. Windows program
   c. Systematic set of exercises designed to improve your eyesight

2. The word form in Visual Basic means
   a. A program
   b. A window
   c. A morf in disguise

3. A Visual Basic *control* is
   a. A dishonest troll
   b. A predefined programming interface element (an object) you can add to a Visual Basic program
   c. A kind of placebo used in comparing two programming approaches

4. Adding menus to a Visual Basic program
   a. Is difficult but barely possible
   b. Is simple
   c. Is a meaningless exercise of bravura programming

5. An *event* in a Visual Basic program is
   a. Getting the darn thing to work
   b. A particular happening in the program environment, such as a mouse click or a keystroke
   c. Nothing you should know about

6. Programming in Visual Basic
   a. Is pretty much like programming in a procedural language
   b. Is an interesting process emphasizing the user interface and responding to events
   c. Is an ineffectual process emphasizing a confused appeal to authority

LESSON 2

STEP BY STEP: YOUR FIRST VISUAL BASIC PROGRAM

Now that you have a general idea of what a Visual Basic program looks like and how you create a program, let's work through an example or two step by step. Here are some of the things you will learn in this chapter:

- **How to create a new form**
- **How to change the heading at the top of the form**

- **How to change the form color**
- **How to add Command button controls, Option button controls, and Label controls to a form**
- **How properties control the appearance of forms and controls**
- **How to set properties**
- **How to save a Visual Basic program**
- **How event procedures determine the behavior of controls**
- **How to provide code for event procedures**

Before starting, however, it's a good idea to create a directory in which to store your sample programs. This book will assume that you create a directory called VBPROGS on your Cdrive.

CREATING YOUR CANVAS—A FORM IS BORN

To begin, start Visual Basic. If you followed the usual installation procedure, you can start by clicking the Windows 95 Start button. Find the Programs entry on the pop-up menu, then find the Visual Basic submenu and select Visual Basic. The program should now start. (If you're using Windows 3.1, double-click on the Visual Basic program group to open the group window, and then double-click on the Visual Basic icon.) Visual Basic should then provide you with a blank form named Form1, as shown in Figure L2-1. The dots on the form, as Lesson 1 explained, are guides to help you align elements, and they don't show when you run the program. You'll also see a Project window, which will be dis-

Figure L2-1 Your first form

cussed later, and a Properties window, which will be discussed sooner. (They may be largely covered by the form, but you can click on one to bring it to the foreground, and you can move them around on your screen.)

A Windows 95 Shortcut

Windows 95 has an aliasing feature called a shortcut that lets you place a Visual Basic icon directly on the Windows 95 desktop. If you use this feature, you then can start up Visual Basic just by clicking the icon. Here's one way to do so. Double-click on the My Computer icon to open the My Computer window. Double-click on the icon representing the drive on which Visual Basic is installed. Navigate through the directory system until you find the executable file for Visual Basic. The 32-bit version is named Vb32.exe, and the 16-bit version is named Vb.exe. Use the mouse to drag the icon to the desktop. Because these are executable files, Win 95 doesn't actually move or copy the file. Instead, it creates a shortcut icon, which you then can use to start the program.

Properties and the Properties Window

Form1 has a rather drab look, but you can change that. The way a form looks depends on its properties, much as the way you look depends on your properties (height, clothing, panache, and so forth). For a form, properties are things like a form's height, background color, caption, and so on. Each form has a standard set of properties. In the spirit of "everyone has to be somewhere," every property has to have a value. To save you some trouble, Visual Basic automatically assigns reasonable values to every property (*default* values), but you can modify the settings. The Properties window should be peeking out from around the right side of the form, and you can click on it to bring it to the foreground. Or you can press the F4 function key–that will bring up the Properties window even if it has been closed. Either way, you should see a window like that shown in Figure L2-2. The window, called the Properties window, has several components. At the top is the label "Properties—Form1." Within the window are two components:

- The Object box
- The Properties list

The Object box is the top component. In it you'll find the name of the object whose properties are listed. At this point Form1 is the only object, so it's the one listed. Eventually you'll add other objects, and the Object box will display the name of the object you're currently working with. At the right end of the object box is a down-arrow icon. You click on it to get a list of all the objects associated with the form. The list drops down from the Object box, so it's called a *drop-list box*. (This kind of list is an example of a control you can add to your own

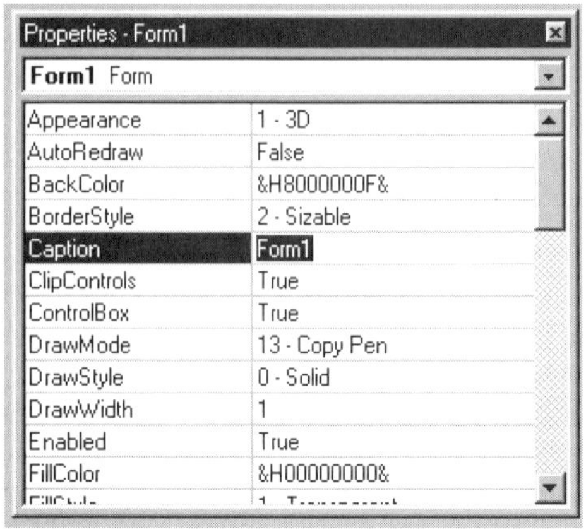

Figure L2-2 The Form1 Properties window

Visual Basic programs.) Right now Form1 is the only thing in the list. The entry *Form1 Form* means that this particular object is a form having the name Form1. As you add controls to the form, their names are added to the list. By selecting a different name from the list, you can change which object you're working on. But we're getting ahead of ourselves.

The second component (the Properties list) is a scrolling list of properties for the object identified in the Object box near the top of the window. The left side of the list provides the names for each property, while the right side provides the values. For instance, the AutoRedraw property has a value of False. The right side of each list item is called a *Settings box* because it shows the property setting and because you can use it to change the value of the property.

Learn these terms (Object box, Settings box, Properties list), for we'll be using them often in the rest of this lesson.

You have three ways to change the properties of a form or control:

- You can set them in the Properties window.
- You can change some properties by manipulating the object with the mouse when Visual Basic is in design mode.
- You can write code that changes object properties as the Visual Basic program runs.

All are much easier than changing your own properties, such as weight. Let's look at the first two methods now.

Taking Charge with the Properties Window

Form1 is not a very inspiring title for our form, so let's change it. The name Form1 appears in two places in the Properties list—as the value of the Caption property and as the value of the Name property. The Caption property represents the title that shows at the top of the form; this is what we want to change. The Name property is the name used to identify the form in Visual Basic program code; you'll use it in the next lesson. By default, the Name and Caption settings are the same, but they don't have to be kept identical.

To change the form's caption, first use the mouse to select Caption in the Properties window. Then type in the new caption, for instance, Wonder Window. The value of the selected property then appears in the Settings box (see Figure L2-3). As you type in the new name, you'll see it in the Properties list Settings box and at the top of Form1, too. To accept the new caption, press ENTER or else click the mouse outside the Settings box. Congratulations! You've changed your first property.

Incidentally, you also can edit the caption directly in the Settings box. It works a bit like a text editor in that you can use the mouse to position the text cursor in the Settings box, you can use the DELETE and arrow keys, and you can use the mouse to select part or all of the text in the Settings box. Some Settings boxes behave otherwise, but that's how the Caption Settings box behaves.

Changing Colors

Now let's change the form color. First, select BackColor in the Properties list. This property represents the background color for the form. You'll see that the color is described as being &H8000000F&. Hmmm, what color is that? Judging by the form's appearance, the background color is gray, but Visual Basic doesn't use simple words to describe colors. Instead, Visual Basic uses a numeric code. The &H prefix means the number is written in hexadecimal notation (see Appendix A), and the & suffix means that the number is a 4-byte number (see Appendix B). The default value corresponds to the current shade of white displayed by Wonder Window. Changing the 8-hexadecimal-digit number changes the color. Unfortunately, fewer than 0.4 percent of the possible 8-digit values are

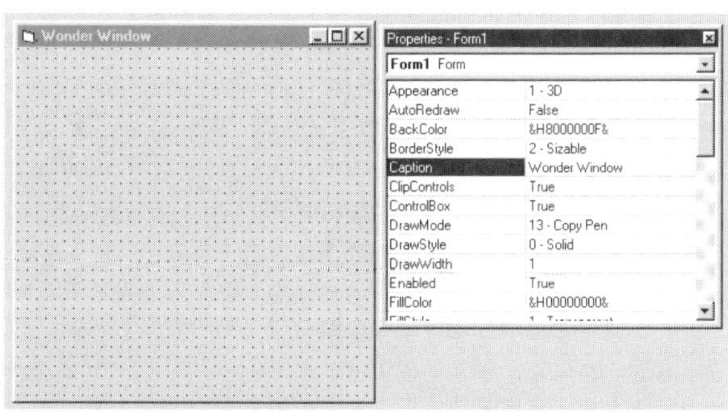

Figure L2-3 Changing a property in the Settings box

valid color codes, so picking a number at random doesn't work too well. You could learn how the color-coding scheme works in order to produce valid values (Lesson 10 goes into that), but the Settings box provides a much easier way. Look at the right side of the Settings box for the BackColor property. You'll find a button bearing a down arrow at the right end. This is a change from Visual Basic 3, which used a button with three dots (ellipses). When this button shows in the Settings box, you can click on it to display a selection of value choices. Try it. In this case, Visual Basic shows you a grid of color choices (see Figure L2-4). The exact contents depend on what color mode your computer system is using. For instance, some boxes may appear as solid colors in one mode but as colored patterns in another mode. Click on the color of your choice, and the corresponding numeric code appears in the Settings box. For instance, clicking on the white box in the upper-left corner of the color grid generates the &H00FFFFFF& color code. Also, the interior of Wonder Window turns this color. Click on another color box, and, again, the form will turn that color, and the corresponding color value will appear in the Settings box.

Color Values

Not too long ago, color PC systems could display up to 16 colors simultaneously. Before then, they could display up to four colors simultaneously. In those days you could have gotten away with using names like "blue" and "light blue" to represent color settings. But now most systems display up to 256 colors simultaneously. This is called *8-bit* color because 8 bits of memory can store 256 distinct values (see Appendix B). Many systems show up to 65,536 colors *(16-bit,* or *high color*) or even 16,777,216 colors *(24-bit,* or *true color*). It's a bit difficult to come up with over 16 million names for colors (demi-light-cat-eye-yellow-with-a-bit-of-pea-green?), which is why Visual Basic uses a numeric code instead. This code consists of a 32-bit number, which can represent over 4 billion values. Only 16,777,216 of them are valid color values, and Visual Basic protests if you try to use an invalid value. Fortunately, you can use the color grid to select a color visually.

The special down-arrow button only shows up in the Settings box for certain properties. Often, as with the Caption property, there is no button. More typically, if there is a down-arrow button, clicking on it displays a drop list. For example, select the MousePointer property in the Properties list. (You may have to use the scrollbar to locate it.) This property controls the appearance of the mouse cursor when it's in the form. When you select the MousePointer property, the right button in the Settings box turns into an icon with a down arrow. Click on it, and the Settings box expands into a scrolling list of possible mouse cursors (see Figure L2-5). Select the Up Arrow cursor (choice #10).

If you now move the mouse back to the form, it won't look any different from before. This is because the MousePointer setting takes effect only when the Wonder Window program runs. We'll check that out in a moment.

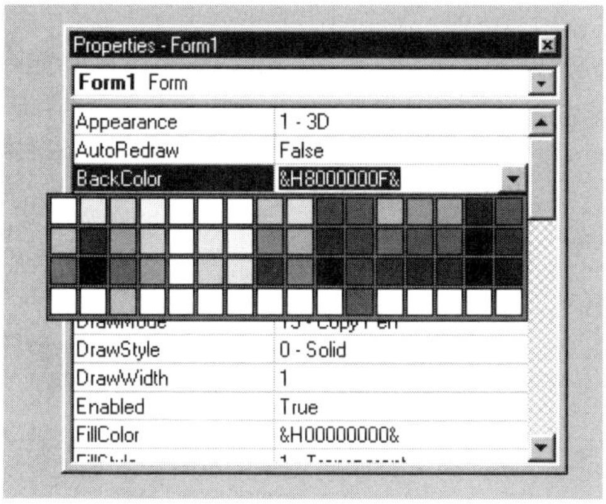

Figure L2-4 A special Settings box for BackColor

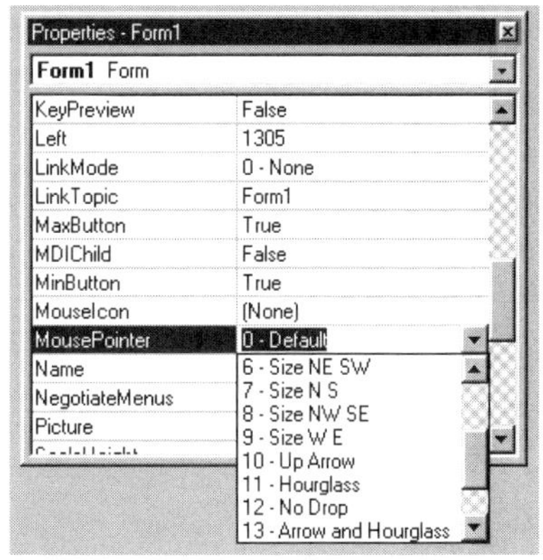

Figure L2-5 A Settings box with a list

Tip

Each kind of Visual Basic object has lots of properties, and this book won't discuss all of them. That encyclopedic task is for reference books like Waite Group Press' *Visual Basic Objects and Classes SuperBible.* Also, if you select a particular property in the Properties list and press the F1 function key, Visual Basic Help will come onscreen and describe that property. Or you can click on the Help button and use the Help Search feature to look up terms and topics.

Saving Your Work

Before going further, you should save your work. You never know when the power will suddenly fail or when a cat or child will decide that a keyboard is a toy. Saving your work involves saving two files. One file saves information about the form you're working on, and one saves information about your *project*. A *project file* lists all the components of a program, while a form is just one of those components. In general, a project can involve several forms, plus other files, too. For instance, a Visual Basic project can also include standard modules, class modules, resource files, and custom controls. We won't be using these program components yet, so let's not worry about what they are now. However, when you do use them, they show up along with any forms in the Project window, which appears when you start Visual Basic, and which you can bring up at any time by selecting Project from the Visual Basic Windows menu.

Here's what you do the first time you save your program. Select Save Project from the File menu. This initiates a sequence that first saves the form, then saves the project. It begins by opening the Save File As dialog box. Visual Basic suggests (in this case) a file name of *Form1.frm*. The *Form1* refers to the name of the current form (we changed the form caption, recall, but not the form name), and the *.frm* suffix means you're saving information about a form. You can use the suggested name or one of your own, as long as it ends in *.frm*. Since you'll be saving the first form in Lesson 2, call the file *Les2-1.frm*. Next, use the Drive box and the Directory box in the dialog box to navigate to your chosen program directory, the one we suggested you create at the beginning of this lesson. (If you don't change directories, Visual Basic will save the files in the Visual Basic directory, so you would be mixing your files with the standard Visual Basic files.) Now click on the OK button. Visual Basic saves the file, then moves on to the Save Project As dialog window, suggesting *Project1.vbp* as the name for the project file. The *vbp* suffix indicates a *V*isual *B*asic *p*roject file. You can accept this project name or choose your own. For consistency, enter *Les2-1.vbp* as the project name and click on the OK button.

Now that you've saved your work, you may as well see how the save process works. Quit Visual Basic and restart it. Once again, you should see the default Form1 window. If *Les2-1.vbp* is one of the last four projects you worked on, it should be listed at the bottom of the File menu. In that case, you can open the project by clicking on the name. Alternatively, you can select Open Project from the File menu, navigate to your project file, and select *Les2-1.vbp*. Click on the OK button, and Visual Basic opens your project. Either way, you should see the Project window (see Figure L2-6). If the window doesn't show at first, select Project from the Window menu.

The Project window should list the form you saved, and the form should be highlighted. Note the button labeled "View Form" at the upper left of the Project window. Click on it to reopen the Wonder Window form you worked on earlier.

What about saving the project in the future? You'll need to select Save Project only when you start a new project or if you change which files you want to belong to the current project, for example, if you add a second form to the project. But as

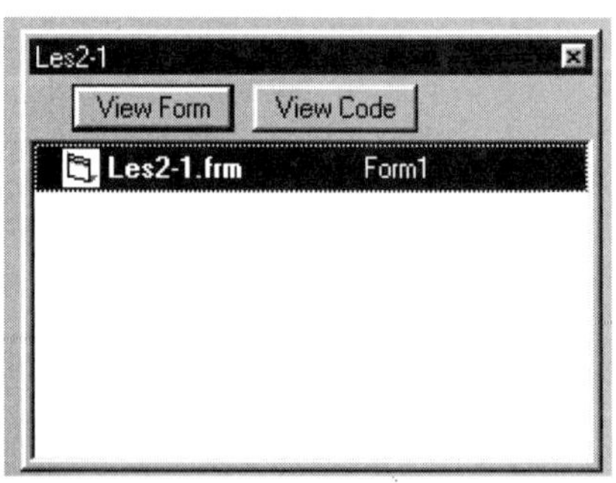

Figure L2-6 A Project window

you work on a particular form, changing its properties and adding code, you should save your work periodically by saving the form file. You can do so by selecting Save File from the File menu or by using the CTRL-S keystroke combination. Saving a form saves the current values of all the form properties.

Tip

The first time you save a project, choose Save Project from the File menu. You'll be prompted to save the form you're working on, then to save the project. Subsequently, as long as you don't add any new files to the project, use Save File or CTRL-S to save changes in the form you're working on.

Running and Quitting Wonder Window

To test what you've accomplished so far, select Start from the Run menu. This puts Visual Basic into run mode and begins the Wonder Window program. At this point, all it does is display a white window (unless you chose another color) bearing the Wonder Window label. Move the mouse so that the mouse cursor moves into Wonder Window. Note that the mouse cursor changes into an up arrow. As promised, the MousePointer property controls the mouse cursor appearance when the program runs.

You can quit Wonder Window a couple of ways. One is to double-click on the Control box at the left end of the Wonder Window menu bar. (If you're using Windows 95, you also can single-click on the rightmost box in the menu bar.) Another way is to select End from the Run menu. Either way, you return to design mode.

Alternatively, you can use the Visual Basic Toolbar to start and end the program. Figure L2-7 shows the Toolbar and identifies the Start and End icons. (It also identifies the Menu Editor button, which you will use in Lesson 8.) You can click on them to start and stop the program. Incidentally, if you position the mouse cursor over a Toolbar button and wait a moment, a short description of what the button does appears under the button as a pop-up caption. This is a convenient way to jog your memory.

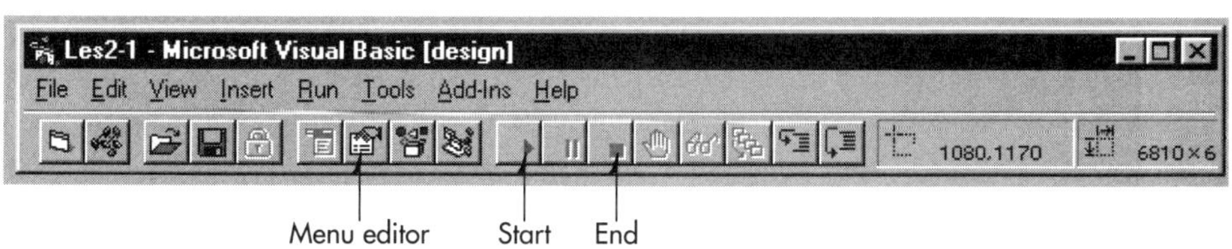

Figure L2-7 The Visual Basic Toolbar

Back to the Design Board

Let's continue playing with properties. Be sure that your program is stopped, that you are back in design mode, and that the Wonder Window form is showing. If necessary, press F4 to bring up the Properties window. This time, let's change properties by manipulating the form directly. Find the Height property in the Properties list. It measures the height of the form in *twips*. There are 1440 twips to a *logical inch*. So a form that is 5760 twips high is 4 logical inches high.

Note

Why have 1440 twips to a logical inch? Why not 1000, for example? The reason is that 1440 can be divided evenly by many values. For example, a 10th of an inch is 144 twips, a 16th of an inch is 90 twips, a 24th of an inch is 60 twips, a 30th of an inch is 48 twips, and a 72nd of an inch (also called a *point*, as in a 12-point font) is 20 twips.

Well, the term "logical inch" probably triggers some questions. Is the logical inch a Vulcan measurement? Are there illogical inches? If so, are they dangerous? The truth is pretty mild—a *logical inch* is the size on the screen that prints an inch long if you print the screen. The size that prints an inch long may be longer or shorter than an inch onscreen, depending on your monitor size and resolution. So a logical inch might be 0.8 true inch on one screen and 1.25 inches on another, but in either case it prints as 1 true inch (see Figure L2-8). Using logical inches scales measurements to the screen size. This will be taken up in more detail in the graphics discussion. For the nonce, the important point is that twips measure size.

To change the height, you can select the Height property and enter a new value in the Settings window. For example, enter 1440, and you get a form 1 logical inch tall. But you also can manipulate the form size directly. Maneuver the mouse until its cursor straddles the bottom boundary of the form window. The mouse cursor should change to a double-headed arrow. Then drag the border down. That is, depress the left mouse button, move the mouse so the cursor and border move down, and then release the left mouse button. Now look at the Height property in the Property list. It will show the new height.

Similarly, you can drag the right edge of the form to change its width, or drag the lower-right corner to change the width and height simultaneously. The Width property tracks the form width. To reposition the form, position the mouse over the title bar and drag the form around. The Top and Left properties track the position of the upper-left corner (just inside the boundary) of the form.

Practice moving the form around and resizing it. When you are done, save the form to save your choices. To abandon your changes, you can quit Visual Basic, choosing No when you're asked if you want to save your changes.

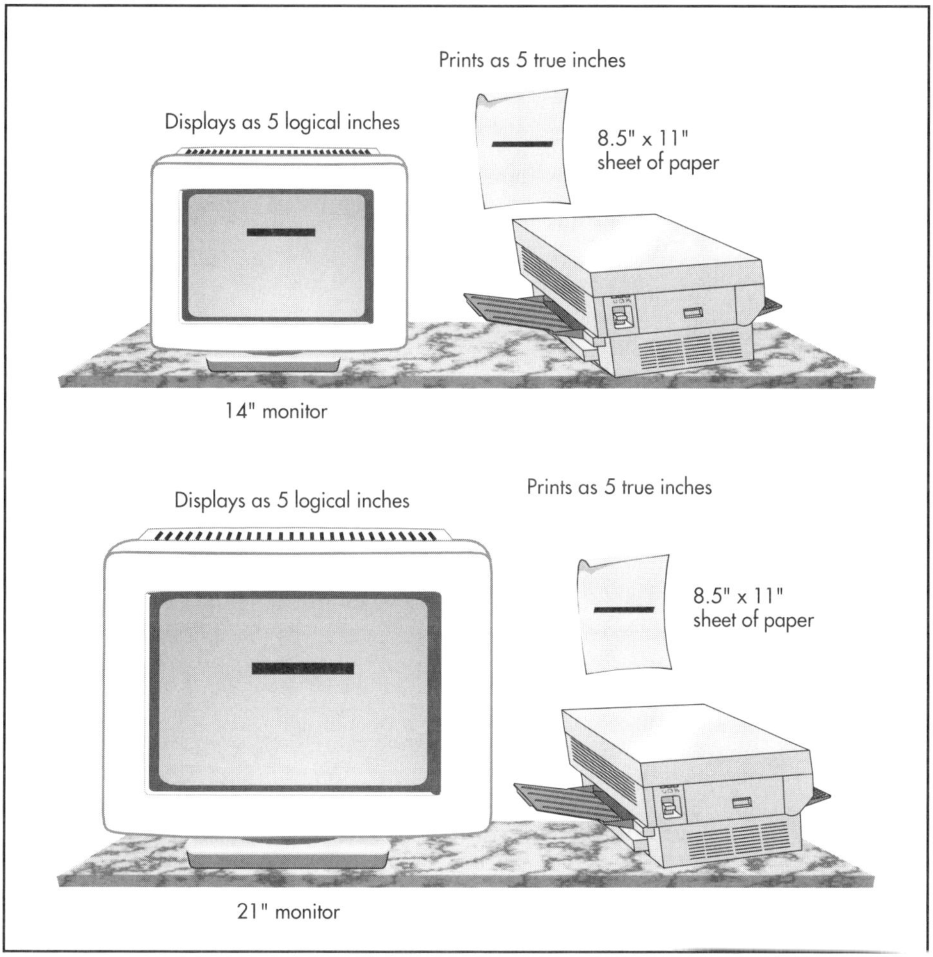

Figure L2-8 Logical inches

PROGRAMMER EMPOWERMENT—ADDING CONTROLS

Wonder Window still has nothing on it. Let's take a big step forward and add some controls. The Visual Basic Toolbox along the left side of your screen contains icons representing the various controls available to you as shown in Figure L2-9. (Don't confuse the *Toolbox*, which is a collection of icons representing controls, with the *Toolbar*, which is a collection of buttons representing commands.) This figure shows the default configuration for the Standard Edition. The appearance of your Toolbox will depend upon the edition and upon settings made in the Custom Controls and Reference dialog boxes in the tools menu. Each kind of control has its own special characteristics, but the process of adding a control to a form is pretty much the same for all controls:

1. Choose a control from the Visual Basic Toolbox by clicking on it.
2. Move the mouse cursor into the form (the cursor changes to a cross hair).
3. Depress the left mouse button, and then drag the mouse to produce a rectangular outline representing the size and location of the control.
4. Release the mouse button.
5. Gaze in astonished wonder at the control that appears on the form.

Eventually, you'll be able to skip step 5.

Your Wish Is the Button's Command

Let's apply these steps to place a command button control on Wonder Window. First, make sure that you are in design mode. That is, check to see that the Visual Basic title bar says "Microsoft Visual Basic [design]." If you're in run mode, select Stop from the Run menu. Then use Figure L2-9 or some other means to identify the Toolbox icon representing the Command button. (For example, you can let the mouse cursor linger over an icon, and a yellow pop-

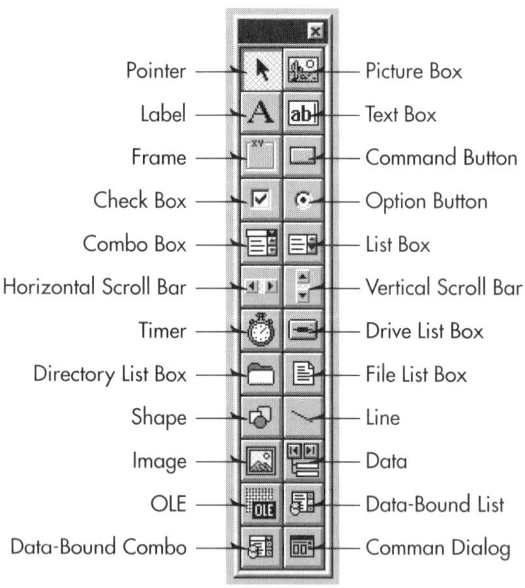

Figure L2-9 The Visual Basic Toolbox

Figure L2-10 A command button

up caption will appear identifying the icon.) Click on it, and then use the mouse as described earlier to create a command button on the Wonder Window form. Note that the button boundaries align with the dotted grid that appears in design mode. This simplifies aligning objects to each other. You should wind up with something like Figure L2-10. The black boxes, called *handles,* along the button perimeter indicate that this button is the currently selected object. That means, for example, that the Properties window, if visible, would show the properties for this object. (Remember, press F4 to bring up the Properties window.) Also, you can resize the selected button by using the mouse to grab the handles, and you can move the button around by dragging it.

By default, this button is captioned Command1. What does it do? Select Start from the Run menu, and then click on the button. How about that! The button appears to depress when you press the left mouse button, and it rises up when you release the button! But that's all it does. It's a functioning control button, but it's not yet connected to any action. Let's remedy that.

First, let's change the button caption to Beep. Stop the Wonder Window program and go to the Properties window for the command button. You can do this by selecting the button and pressing F4 or by clicking on the Properties window if it is visible. The Object box (one of the Properties window components that you were supposed to remember) should say *Command1 CommandButton.* If you've somehow deselected the button, perhaps by clicking elsewhere on the form, you can click on the down arrow at the right of the Object box and scroll to the command button. Command button properties work like form properties. Select the Caption property and type the name Beep in the Settings box. That just changes the caption on the button. The button name is still Command1.

Our Button Gets a Brain: Adding Code to a Control

Each command button has the potential to make something happen when you click on it; that's how it earned the title of command button. Defining that "something" is your job; you have to provide Visual Basic programming code that describes what the program should do when the button is clicked. You have to shift from your role as visual designer to a new role as programmer.

Let's ease into that role by adding Visual Basic code to the control so that clicking on the button in run mode will cause the program to produce a beep. Visual Basic, recall, is event-driven, so the code you provide should respond to particular events. Visual Basic handles this need by providing empty code units called *event procedures* for various events. For instance, there is a *Click* procedure that corresponds to a mouse click. It's an empty procedure, but you can fill it with code that produces a beep. Once you do that, clicking on the button in run mode will cause Visual Basic to run that code, producing a beep. The simplest

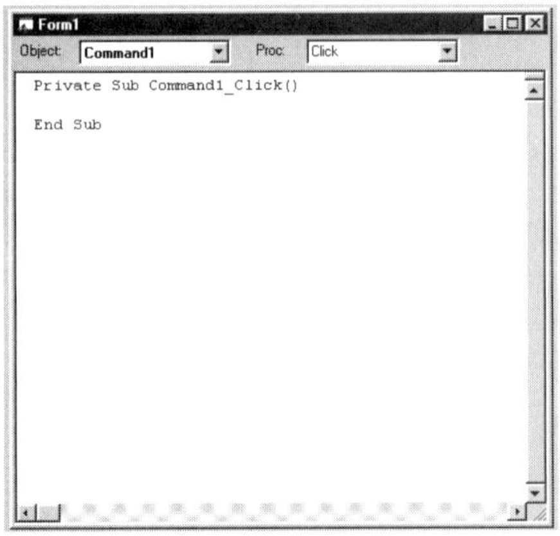

Figure L2-11 The Visual Basic Code window

way to begin is to double-click on the Beep button while in design mode. This brings up the *Code window,* as shown in Figure L2-11.

The Code window has three major elements. At the top left is the *Object* list box. It shows the name of the object for which you're writing code. It's a scrolling list box, so you can click on the down arrow and change to another object if you like. At this point, you should have just two objects: the form and the command button. As you add other objects to the form, their names will be added to this list.

The second element is the *Procedure* (Proc) list box. Because we've selected a command button control, the box lists procedures representing the events a button can respond to. The most common event a button responds to is a mouse click, so, by default, that's the procedure currently selected in the Procedure list box. You can click on the down arrow to see a drop list of event choices, as shown in Figure L2-12.

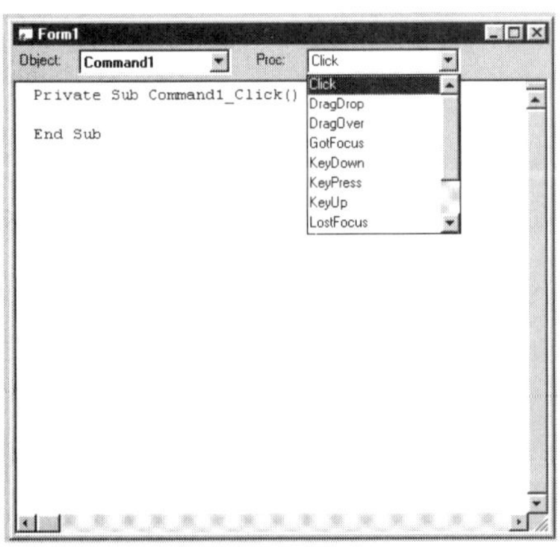

Figure L2-12 The Procedure list box

Subprocedures—Insert Brain Here

The third element of the Code window is a text window in which you can enter Visual Basic code. At this point the text window should contain the following:

```
Private Sub Command1_Click ()

End Sub
```

This is a skeleton *subprocedure*. Subprocedures (*SUBs*, for short) are Visual Basic programming units. *Sub* marks the beginning and *End Sub* marks the end of the subprocedure. This subprocedure is called an *event procedure* because it's designed to respond to the event. The subprocedure name is *Command1_Click*. Like other event subprocedure names, this name has two parts. The first part—*Command1*—shows that this SUB is attached to the Command1 object. The second part *_Click_* shows that this event subprocedure responds to the *Click* event, that is, to clicking the mouse in the Command1 command button. *Private* (a Visual Basic 4 addition) indicates that the procedure is private to the current form module. This concept only becomes important when you have programs with more than one module, so don't worry about it now.

Identifying Event Procedures

Visual Basic code identifies an event procedure for a given object with a two-part name that identifies both the object and event. The name has the following form:

object-name_event-name

For instance, the event procedure associated with clicking the mouse in the Command1 object is *Command1_Click,* and the event procedure associated with clicking the mouse in the Form1 object is *Form1_Click.* Note that Visual Basic uses an underscore character to separate the two parts of the name.

Our goal is to produce a beep when the button is clicked. To make that happen, you have to insert the proper code into this SUB. The code is very simple: Just add the command *Beep*. First, position the text cursor in the text window by clicking the mouse on the blank line in the SUB. Next, as a matter of style, press TAB to indent your entry. Now type in *Beep* so that the SUB looks like this:

```
Sub Command1_Click ()
    Beep
End Sub
```

Click the mouse anywhere outside the procedure to tell Visual Basic that you're done. That's all you need to do. However, sometimes it's useful to add comments to a program. Comments are lines preceded by a single-quote character. They are explanatory notes for people reading the program; Visual Basic itself ignores them. For instance, you can modify the procedure to read as follows:

```
Sub Command1_Click ()
' This line and the next line are comments to the reader
' CAUTION: STUDENT PROGRAMMER
    Beep
End Sub
```

By default, Visual Basic displays comments in green to make them easy to spot. Also, it automatically capitalizes Visual Basic commands like *Beep* when you quit or move to another line. Either version of the procedure works the same.

Running Your First Incredible Program

It's time to run your first program that uses code (that's what makes it incredible). Start the program using Start from the Run menu or by clicking the Run icon on the Toolbar. Locate the Beep button and click on it. Your computer should beep. Try this as often as you like, and then select End from the Run menu and save your work (choose Save File from the File menu).

At this point, you may decide you don't really need a Beep button, so let's make a couple of changes. First, go to design mode. If your form doesn't show, select Form from the View menu. Next, select the button and go to the Properties window. Because you selected the command button first, the Properties window should show the command button properties. If it doesn't (for instance, if you work too fast to be bothered with following every instruction step-by-step), you can click on the Object box in the Properties window and select the command button from the drop list that appears. Change the caption from Beep to &Quit. (The & is the ampersand character, usually found on the 7 key.) Note that on the button, the caption appears as Quit, not Quit. That's what an ampersand in a caption does—it makes the letter following it appear underlined on the object. You can put the ampersand anywhere in the caption. For example, a caption setting of Not No&w would appear on the button as Not Now. As your experiences with Windows programs probably have shown you, underlined letters in a control or menu indicate a shortcut. In this case, it means that typing ALT-Q when Wonder Window is running is the same as clicking on the command button. Visual Basic terms such shortcuts *access keys*. So here ALT-Q is the access key for the Quit button.

Before trying that, however, let's change the event procedure for the button to look like this:

```
Sub Command1_Click ()
    End
End Sub
```

That is, replace the *Beep* command with the *End* command. You can do this by double-clicking on the word *Beep* to select it, then typing *End* to replace the selection. The *End* statement is a Visual Basic command that terminates a program, so clicking on this button now has the same effect as selecting End from the Run menu or double-clicking on the Close box. The program doesn't really need a Quit button, but it makes for a more obvious, hence friendlier, user interface.

Run the program to try the new button. Note that you can terminate Wonder Window by clicking on the button or by typing the access key ALT-Q.

You've now learned the essentials of creating a simple Visual Basic program:

- Create a form.
- Add controls.
- Set form and control properties.
- Write event procedures.

Of course there are a lot more controls and events to learn about, so let's continue working on Wonder Window.

Make a Choice: Option Buttons

Option buttons are buttons that can be set to either On or Off, but only one in a set of option buttons can be on at one time. It's like a car radio with buttons set to various stations; you can only tune in one station at a time. That's why many people call option buttons radio buttons. Typically, you use option buttons to represent a set of mutually exclusive choices, such as choosing between a 12-hour clock and a 24-hour clock, or choosing to play a game in beginner mode, intermediate mode, or advanced mode.

Let's begin by creating three option buttons. Select the Option Button icon in the Toolbox (shown in Figure L2-9 or on the inside back cover of this book). Use the mouse to draw a button on the form. Repeat the process until you have three option buttons (see Figure L2-13). Visual Basic labels them "Option1," "Option2," and "Option3."

Now select Start from the Run menu. Initially, all three buttons are off. Click anywhere in one of the option buttons to turn it on. The button circle gets filled and a dotted outline appears around the caption (see Figure L2-14). Click on

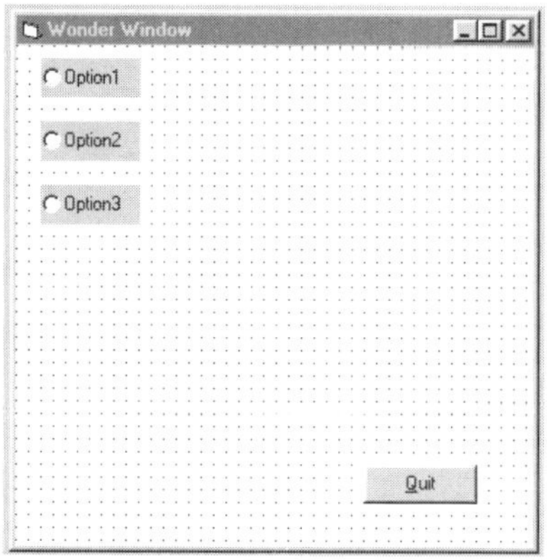

Figure L2-13 Three option buttons

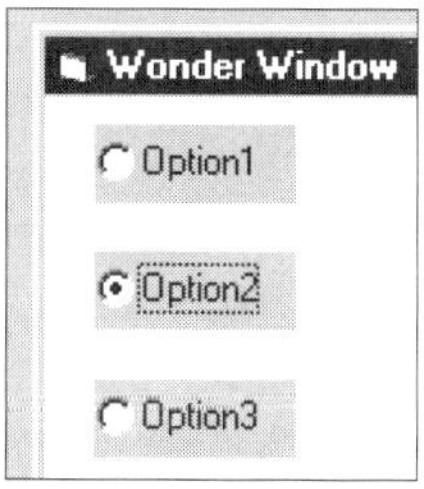

Figure L2-14 An on option button in a set of three

another button. It turns on, and the former on button automatically turns off. To get them to do more than turn on and off, you have to provide them with event procedures. That involves returning to design mode, so click the Quit button.

Exercising Your Options

Before programming the option buttons, you need to have something in mind for them to do. A colorful choice is having them change the color of the form. The BackColor property of the form controls the color, so that means you'll need to change the value of that property while the program runs. That is, you'll set the colors in run mode instead of design mode. That may sound hard to do, but it isn't. You merely need to place property-changing code statements in event procedures. Then, say, clicking on the second option button activates an event procedure, and that procedure then changes the form color.

Before doing that, let's do some prep work. For instance, you can make each option button's caption and color match the choice it represents. For example, you can change the Option1 caption to Red and set the button's BackColor property to a red color. Changing properties for an option button is just like changing properties for a form or for a command button. Rather than go through a blow-by-blow description, we can summarize the desired changes with a table listing the affected properties. Table L2-1, for example, lists the setting changes you should make now. They create red, blue, and green option buttons labeled with the names of the colors. Remember that you can do the color settings by using the color grid available in the Settings box.

OBJECT	PROPERTY	SETTING
Option1	Caption	Red
	BackColor	&H000000FF& (red)
Option2	Caption	Blue
	BackColor	&H00FF0000& (blue)
Option3	Caption	Green
	BackColor	&H0000FF00& (green)

Table L2-1 Option button settings

Runtime Action: Setting Properties with Events

Now that the option buttons are more attractive, let's give them some punch. The trick, as mentioned, is to set property values in an event procedure. Check that Visual Basic is in design mode and double-click on the Option1 button. The Code window should now display an empty *Option1_Click* event procedure:

```
Private Sub Option1_Click()

End Sub
```

Code Viewing Options

You can configure Visual Basic so that it shows just the current event procedure in the Code window or so that it shows all procedures. This book will assume that you display all procedures. To do so, select Options from the Tools menu, and click on the Editor tab. You should see a dialog box like that shown in Figure L2-15. Check the Full Module View check box and click on the OK button. The new setting will remain in effect until you change it.

However, it's more convenient to see all the procedures instead of one, so follow the steps in the Code Viewing Options box and configure Visual Basic to provide a full-module view. Then the Code window should look like this:

```
Private Sub Command1_Click()
' This line and the next line are comments to the reader
' CAUTION: STUDENT PROGRAMMER
  End
End Sub

Private Sub Option1_Click()

End Sub
```

The name *Option1_Click* means this procedure responds to a click event in the Option1 object. Thus, this code gets executed if you click on the Option1 object. To indicate the BackColor property of the Form1 object, use the following expression: *Form1.BackColor*. The name to the left of the period is the object

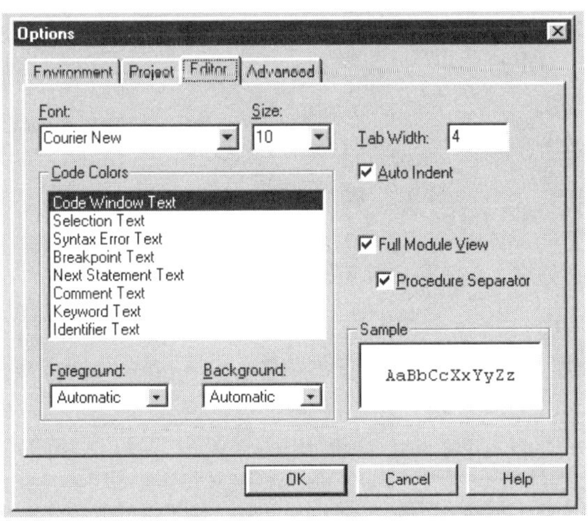

Figure L2-15 Getting a full view of your code

name, and the name to the right is the property name. So *Form1.BackColor* means the BackColor property of the Form1 object. So what would *Option1.Caption* mean? If you say it means the Caption property of the Option1 object, that's right! OK, then what's the code for setting the Form1 BackColor property to red? Here's one possibility:

```
form1.BackColor = &H000000FF&
```

Yes, this means set the form's background color to the color whose code is &H000000FF&. Not everyone will recognize this as the code for red, so you can clarify matters with a comment:

```
form1.BackColor = &H000000FF&   'code for red
```

However, as a true student of programming, you may be interested in a more sophisticated approach. Let's try this instead:

```
Private Sub Option1_Click ()
    form1.BackColor = Option1.BackColor
End Sub
```

This statement sets the form's background color to be the same as the background color for the Option1 button. This has three advantages. First, it gives you more practice with the object.property notation. Second, it eliminates the chance of making a typing error when typing in the numeric color code. Third, if you decide to set the option button to, say, cyan instead of red, you just have to change the option button properties and not the *Option1_Click* code.

Now make similar entries for the other two Option buttons. To get to the Option2 Code window, you can double-click on the Option2 button. Or, more quickly, you can click on the down arrow in the Code window Object box and scroll to the Option2 object. Give it this code:

```
Private Sub Option2_Click ()
    form1.BackColor = option2.BackColor
End Sub
```

Similarly, give the Option3 object this event procedure:

```
Private Sub Option3_Click ()
    form1.BackColor = option3.BackColor
End Sub
```

Now select Start from the Run menu. Wonder Window starts off white, if you've retained that choice from earlier in this lesson. Click on the option button captioned Red, and the form turns red. Click on the green option button, and the form turns green. Think about what the computer has to do—it has to identify all the screen dots (*pixels*) inside the boundary of Wonder Window, and then it has to set each one to green. But all you had to do was to write a single code statement that set a property to green. Once again, Visual Basic is doing most of the work for you.

Identifying Object Properties

Visual Basic code identifies an object property with a two-part name that identifies both the object and the property. The name has the following form:

object-name.property-name

For instance, Command1.Caption is the Caption property of the Command1 command button, and Form1.BackColor is the BackColor property of the Form1 object. Note that Visual Basic uses a period to separate the object name from the property name.

Note the distinction between property names and event procedure names. The first uses a period to combine an object name with a property name, while the second uses an underscore to combine an object name with an event name, as shown in Figure L2-16.

CREATING A NEW VERSION

There's a certain fascination in changing the form color with a mouse click, but we can add more character to the example by using a label control or two. Instead of modifying the example, however, let's modify a copy. It's often convenient to have two or more versions of a program, especially when you're trying

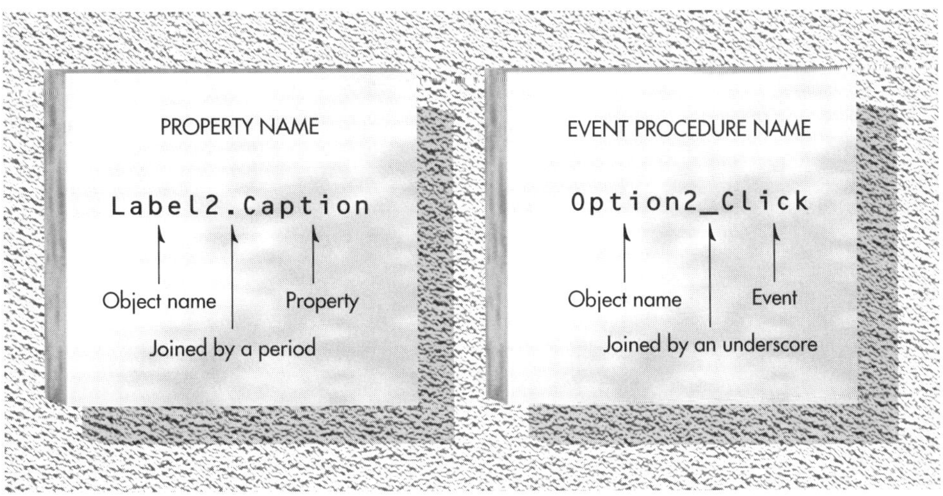

Figure L2-16 Property names and event procedure names

out new ideas, and it would be nice if you didn't have to start each version from scratch. Wonder Window involves both a project file and a form file, so you'll need new versions of both.

The simplest way to generate a copy is to use the Visual Basic File menu. If you've closed the *Les2-1.vbp* project, reopen it and the form. From the File menu, select Save Project As. Change to your program directory (C:/VBPROGS, we assume), enter *Les2-2.vbp* as the project name, and then click on OK. (If you're asked if you want to save the old *Les2-1.vbp* first, say yes.) The Save Project As choice creates a copy of the *Les2-1.vbp* file and names it *Les2-2.vbp*. It also makes the new project the current project, as you can see by looking at the Project window. It should be headed Les2-2. The first file in the project list should be *Les2-1.frm*. So right now you have a new project using the old form. Note that if you use the original project name (*Les2-1.vbp*), Save Project As merely saves the current project and doesn't make a copy.

Next, select Save File As from the File menu. For the file name, enter *Les2-2.frm* and click on the OK button. This creates a copy of *Les2-1.frm* and names the copy *Les2-2.frm*. It also replaces *Les2-1.frm* with *Les2-2.frm* in the Project window list. Note that if you use the original name (*Les2-1.frm*), Save File As merely saves the current project and doesn't make a copy. Assuming you do use a new name, you now have a new project and a new form and are ready to do business, as shown in Figure L2-17.

TRUTH IN LABELING: THE LABEL CONTROL

The *label control* lets you put text on a form. As with option buttons and command buttons, the text you see is set by the object's Caption property. What you'll do next is the following:

- Use a label control to phrase a question.
- Reset the option button captions to express possible answers.
- Use a label control to express the program's response to the answer selected.

First, select the label control icon from the Toolbox. It's the icon labeled *A*. Don't confuse it with the text box icon, which shows *ab* inside a box. (Text boxes let you enter text while a program is running, labels display text.) Use the mouse to draw a label on the form above the option buttons, moving the buttons first, if necessary. Then add a second label below the option buttons (see Figure L2-18). Since the labels are gray, reset the form's BackColor to gray (&H8000000F&) so the labels and form blend.

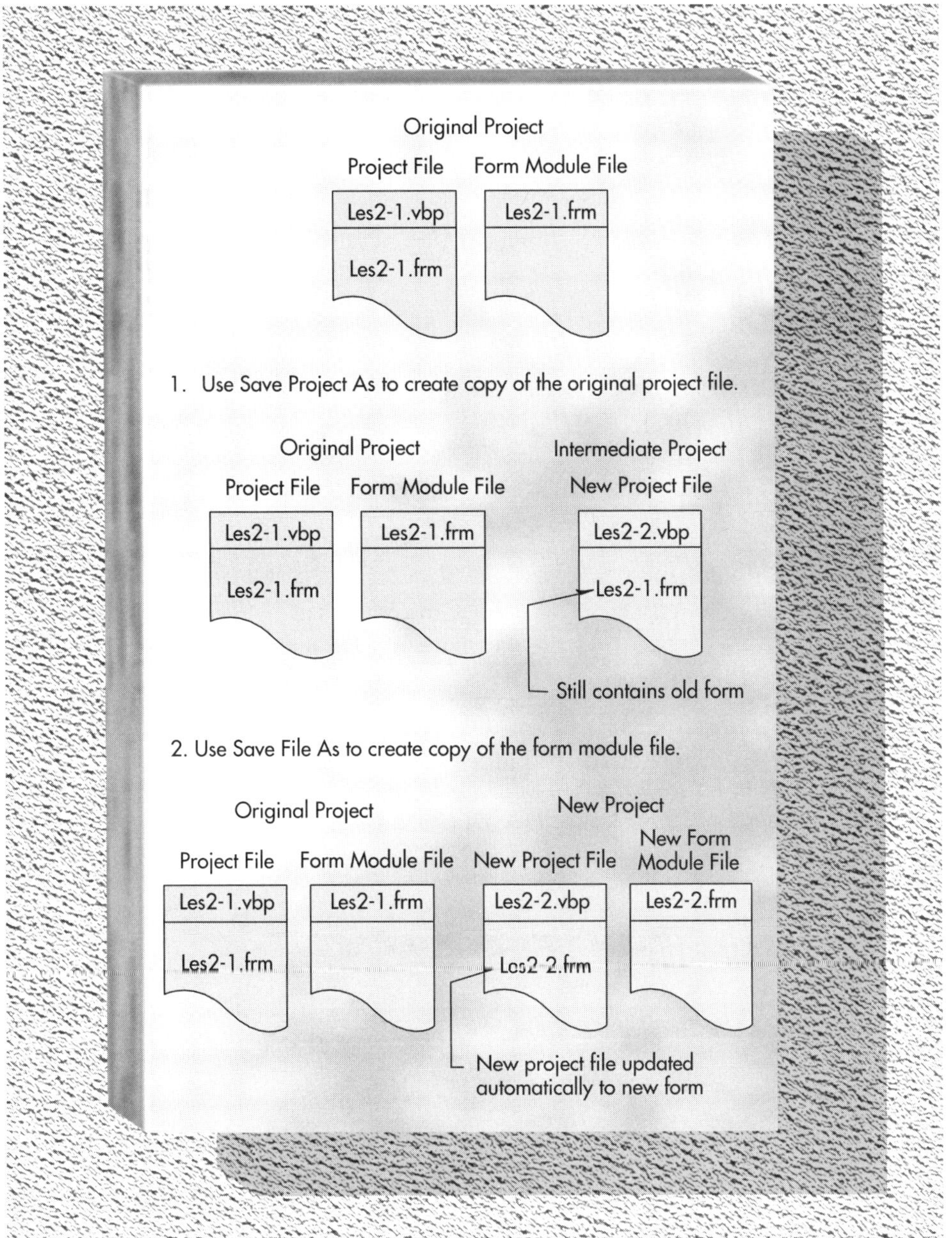

Figure L2-17 Copying a program

As you might expect, Visual Basic assigns the default captions Label1 and Label2. Next, set the label properties as shown in Table L2-2. Note that you delete the caption for Label2, making it appear blank. The program will use this blank space later.

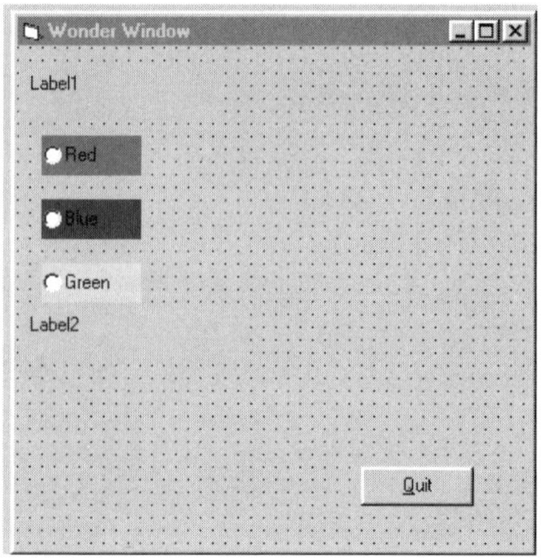

Figure L2-18 Label controls

OBJECT	PROPERTY	SETTING
Label1	Caption	This program is
	Font.Size	12
Label2	Caption	
	Font.Size	12

Table L2-2 Properties for the label controls

Setting the fonts is a bit more involved. First, select the Font property. If you click on the Settings box for the Font property, you'll get a button bearing three

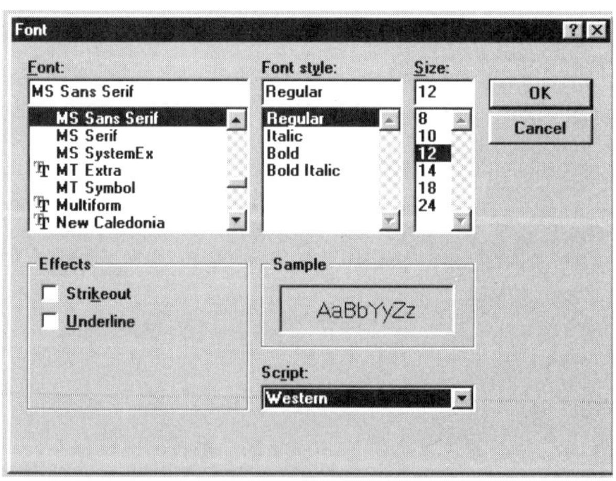

Figure L2-19 The Font dialog box

dots (...) at the right end. Click on that box, and you get a dialog box like that shown in Figure L2-19. Select 12 for the font size. What is happening here is that the Font property is itself an object, so it has its own properties. In essence, this dialog box shows properties of a property. That is, the Label1 object has a Font property, which is a Font object. The Font object has a Name property (the font name selected from the Font list), various style properties, such as Bold (selected from the Font Style list box), and a Size property, selected from the Size list. Just as you use a period to associate a property with an object (Form1.BackColor), you use a period to associate a property with a property object. So Label1 is an object, Label1.Font is a property which happens to be another object, and Label1.Font.Size is the Size property of the Label1.Font object. If you used this property in a code statement, you'd call it Label1.Font.Size. The Font.Size property controls the caption size. The default is 8 points (there are 72 points to a logical inch and 20 twips to a point). The font dialog box shows a list with the following six choices: 8, 10, 12, 14, 18, and 24. In doing so, it lies slightly. The true values are 8.25, 9.75, 12, 13.5, 18, and 24, which where the choices listed by previous versions of Visual Basic. Anyway, select 12.

Next, change the option button captions as shown in Table L2-3.

OBJECT	PROPERTY	SETTING
Option1	Caption	superb!
Option2	Caption	stupid.
Option3	Caption	no Excel.

Table L2-3 New option button captions

Now let's tailor the text in Label2 to fit the user's response. For instance, if the user completes "This program is" with "superb!", Label2 will display "I'm embarrassed!" in the second label as the form turns red. You can do this by setting the Label2.Caption property in the mouse-click event procedure for the Option1 button:

```
Private Sub Option1_Click()
    Form1.BackColor = Option1.BackColor
    Label2.Caption = "I'm embarrassed."
End Sub
```

Note that you use double quotation marks around the text when using a subprocedure to set a caption. Visual Basic calls such quoted text a *string*.

Now make similar entries for the other two option buttons:

```
Private Sub Option2_Click()
    Form1.BackColor = Option2.BackColor
    Label2.Caption = "I'm feeling blue."
End Sub

Private Sub Option3_Click()
    Form1.BackColor = Option3.BackColor
    Label2.Caption = "I'm envious."
End Sub
```

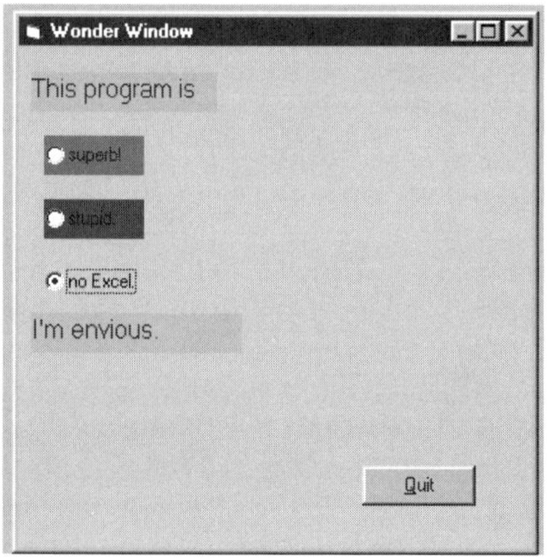

Figure L2-20 The new Wonder Window

Now run the new program. Click on any option and see the form color and label text respond to your choice (see Figure L2-20).

SUMMARY

A Visual Basic program consists of objects. A form object provides the window in which the program runs, and various control objects provide the interface. This chapter discusses three controls:

- Command buttons
- Option buttons
- Labels

A command button control provides a captioned button that you can click. Visually, the button depresses when you put the mouse cursor over it and press the left mouse button. When you release the mouse button, the control button goes back to its original appearance.

An option button control also provides a caption button that you can click. Visually, an option button shows a solid circle and an outlined caption when on. Only one of a set of option buttons can be on at any one time. Turning an option button on automatically turns the previously on button off.

A label shows text.

Each form and control is described by a set of properties. Properties control such things as the caption that appears onscreen, the background color, the size and location of a control, and font sizes. You can control the appearance of a form or control by manipulating it onscreen, by modifying its property settings in the Properties list, or by using Visual Basic code that modifies property settings while the program runs.

You can attach event procedures to forms and controls. An event procedure is a Visual Basic code module that gets executed when a particular event happens. For instance, if you click a mouse on a control, Visual Basic will execute a click event procedure defined for that control.

Event procedures associated with an object are named after the object and the event. For instance, clicking the mouse on an option button named Option1 triggers the event procedure named Option1_Click. You can use the Code window to provide code for event procedures.

Event procedures can change the property settings of objects. The code has to identify both the object and the property, and Visual Basic lets you do so with a two-part name made up of the object name and the property name separated by a period. For instance, Label2.Caption would mean the Caption property of the Label2 object.

Preparing a simple Visual Basic program involves the following steps:

1. Open a new project, which automatically opens a new form.
2. Use the Properties window or onscreen manipulation to modify the appearance of the form.
3. Add controls from the Visual Basic Toolbox to the form.
4. Use the Properties window or onscreen manipulation to modify the appearance and behavior of the controls.
5. Use the Code window to provide event procedures for controls.

QUIZ 2

1. Match the Properties window component with its purpose:

COMPONENT	PURPOSE
Object box	Lists each property and its current setting
Settings box	Identifies the object whose properties are listed
Properties list	Lets you enter new settings for a property

2. When you use a Properties window to change the Caption property of a form to Eyes Only!, what happens to the appearance of the form?

a. Nothing.

b. The form's title bar displays the phrase "Eyes Only!"
c. It self-destructs in 15 seconds.

3. Which of the following is not a standard way to terminate a Visual Basic program being executed in Visual Basic run mode?
a. Clicking the Close box in the form's title bar
b. Selecting Stop from the Visual Basic Run menu
c. Immersing your computer in a vat of acid
d. Clicking the Stop button on the Toolbar

4. A twip is
a. Short for "twit trip," as in "don't take a twip, Basil"
b. An acronym for techno-wimp inane prattle, as in "cut the twip, Frannie"
c. A unit of measurement, as in "1 logical inch is 1440 twips"

5. The Visual Basic Toolbox contains
a. Icons representing various Visual Basic controls
b. The Visual Basic wrench set
c. Itself

6. Visual Basic automatically names the first command button you create
a. Twipsy
b. Command1
c. Rambo

7. The way to make clicking on a Visual Basic command button (named Nick) initiate an action is to
a. Do nothing and hope for the best
b. Set the command button Action property to whatever you want done
c. Provide code for the *Nick_Click* procedure

8. Suppose a command button is named Nick. Which one of the following names can be used to identify the Caption property of Nick in an event procedure?
a. Nick_Caption
b. Nick.Caption
c. NickCaption

9. At most, how many option buttons in a set of five can be set to On at any one time?
a. One
b. Two
c. Five

10. The difference between Save File and Save File As in the Visual Basic file menu is that

a. Save File saves a form, while Save File As saves a project.

b. Save File saves the current form, while Save File As lets you save a copy under a new name.

c. Save File saves a form as a file, while Save File As saves a form as a banana.

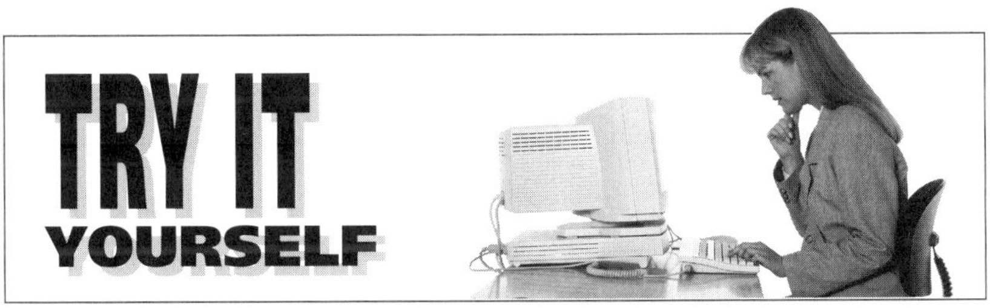

1. Create a new form. Give it the caption Canary and make the background color yellow.

2. Add a command button to the form. Make the button caption Quit and have clicking the button terminate the program.

3. Add two option buttons captioned English and Pig Latin. Clicking the Pig Latin button should change the command button caption from Quit to Itquay, while clicking the English option button should change the command button caption to Quit.

LESSON 3

INPUT AND OUTPUT: THE INS AND OUTS OF VISUAL BASIC

Humans wither in isolation. We need input and output to thrive. We have a rich variety of inputs, including food, ideas, music, stubbed toes, the smell of a sea breeze, and computer books. And we have a rich variety of outputs, including frowns, smiles, sighs, karate kicks, hugs, symphonies, body odor, and speeches. Computer programs, too, have input and output, although on a more modest scale. Simple DOS programs have rather simple input and output. Usually, the input is whatever you type at the keyboard, and the output is text displayed on the screen. Visual Basic I/O (short for input/output) is more versatile. Input can be keyboard input, but it also can be any of a variety of events, such as moving a mouse over a control, clicking the mouse, double-clicking the mouse, pressing the left mouse

button, releasing any key, and so on. The output can be text, but it also can be a sound, a display of color, or a picture. The fundamental point is that computer input conveys information from you to a computer program, while computer output conveys information from the computer program to you.

Of course, you've already used input and output in Lesson 2. Clicking the mouse on the Quit button was input, for example, and displaying "I'm embarrassed!" was output. This lesson will take you a bit further. In particular, you'll learn about the following:

- **Naming conventions for Visual Basic objects**
- **What a list box is**
- **How to add items to a list box**
- **How to obtain input from a list box**
- **What a string is**
- **How to combine strings to form text output**
- **How to use Visual Basic code to simulate an event**
- **The importance of a good interface**

THE TARGET PROGRAM

Let's begin by looking at the program that will be our goal this lesson. It's a window labeled Quick Author, and it looks like Figure L3-1. This program uses a control called a *list box*. A list box provides a scrollable list of items, and the user can select an item from the list by clicking on it. Quick Author uses three list boxes. The first lists some adjectives, the second lists some nouns, and the third lists some verbs. By choosing one word from each list, you provide Quick Author

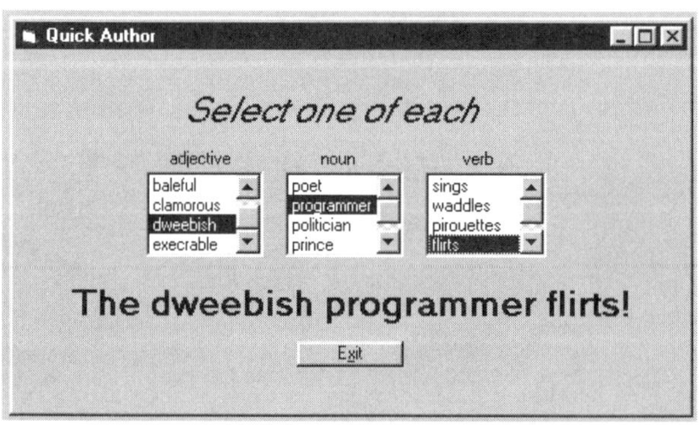

Figure L3-1 The Quick Author program

with input that it uses to construct a sentence that appears as output in a label control. As you can see, Quick Author provides a quick way to generate prose of an uncommon quality. Now let's look at how to put Quick Author together.

The Form

Begin Visual Basic and click on the default form. (If you already have Visual Basic running, select New Form from the File menu.) Next, set the two properties shown in Table L3-1.

OBJECT (INITIAL NAME)	PROPERTY	SETTING
Form1	Caption	Quick Author
	Name	frmQuickAuthor

Table L3-1 The new form

The first property, as you probably recall from Lesson 2, sets the title bar to display Quick Author. The new thing here is the form name. Initially it was Form1, and now it's renamed frmQuickAuthor. Thus, the Object box in the Properties window now reads *frmQuickAuthor form* instead of *Form1 form*.

Naming Conventions

Why make this name change? Default names like Form1 or Command1 are fine for small programs, but they don't tell you much about the intent of the form or control. When your programs get larger, you need all the help you can get to remind you of the purpose of a particular form or control. Suppose you have a program with five windows. The default names of Form1, Form2, Form3, Form4, and Form5 don't give much of a clue about what each form does. So it's good to include a reminder in the name. But the name should also tell you what kind of object you're dealing with. For instance, you couldn't tell from the name "Torus" whether it referred to a form, a command button, or to a mathematician's pet dog. Microsoft suggests a systematic system for naming objects. Each name consists of a three-letter prefix that identifies the type of object followed by a descriptive part. For instance, the three-letter prefix for a form is *frm*, leading to the frmQuickAuthor name. Table L3-2 lists Microsoft's guidelines for some of the more common controls.

CONTROL TYPE DESCRIPTION	PREFIX	EXAMPLE
Check box	chk	chkMail
Combo box and drop-list box	cbo	cboAgents
Command button	cmd	cmdHalt
Dir List box	dir	dirBackUp
Drive List box	drv	drvIn
File List box	fil	filDemos

continued on next page

continued from previous page

CONTROL TYPE DESCRIPTION	PREFIX	EXAMPLE
Form	frm	frmWonder
Frame	fra	fraStillLife
Horizontal scrollbar	hsb	hsbWidth
Image	img	imgCamera
Label	lbl	lblAnswer
Line	lin	linUp
List box	lst	lstMeals
Menu	mnu	mnuOptions
Option button	opt	optAdvanced
Picture	pic	picGoya
Shape	shp	shpCircle
Text/edit box	txt	txtAddress
Timer	tmr	tmrDone
Vertical scrollbar	vsb	vsbHeight

Table L3-2 Visual Basic object-naming conventions

Labels Again—More Properties

Labels, recall, are a handy way to display text on a form. Quick Author uses five label controls. The first, near the top of the form, provides instructions. The next three (adjective, noun, and verb) label the three list boxes. And the final label displays the magisterial output of the program. Use the mouse to draw five labels onscreen, positioning and sizing them to look like Figure L3-1. By default, they'll be named Label1, Label2, Label3, Label4, and Label5. Then set label control properties as shown in Table L3-3. Note that you rename the label objects following the standard conventions. The form should look like Figure L3-2 at this point.

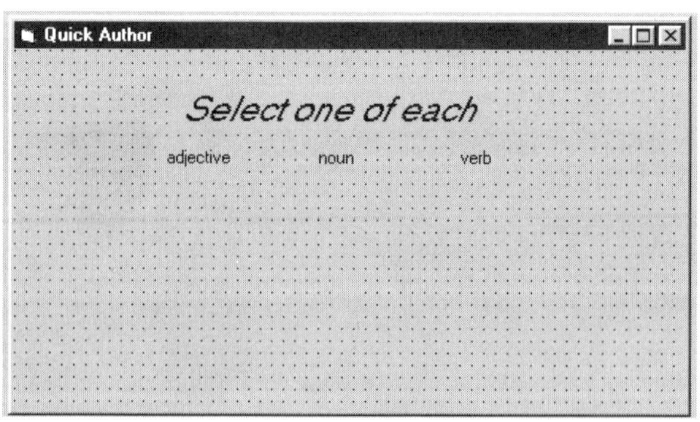

Figure L3-2 The form at an early stage

OBJECT (INITIAL NAME)	PROPERTY	SETTING
Label1	AutoSize	True
	Caption	Select one of each
	Font.Size	18
	Font.Italic	True
	Name	lblInstruct
Label2	Caption	adjective
	Name	lblAdjective
Label3	Caption	noun
	Name	lblNoun
Label4	Caption	verb
	Name	lblVerb
Label5	Alignment	2 - Center
	AutoSize	True
	Caption	
	Font.Size	18
	Font.Bold	True
	Name	lblSentence

Table L3-3 Label control settings

Sensational Shortcut—Using SHIFT

Suppose you wanted to give all five labels the same value for a particular property, such as BackColor. There's a shortcut you can use. Use the mouse to select the first label. Then hold down SHIFT and select the other four labels in turn. Keeping SHIFT down lets you select all five labels simultaneously. This process is called (watch your enunciation) *shift-clicking*. If you do this correctly, all five objects should show selection handles, except that they will be gray rather than the black that shows for single selections. Then go to the Properties window. The Object box will be blank because you have five objects selected. Now select the property you wish to set, say, the BackColor property, and use the Settings box to select a color. Your selection gets applied to all five labels.

Tip

If you use SHIFT and the mouse to select multiple objects (shift-clicking), you can use the Properties window to set a property for all the selected objects simultaneously.

You'll notice that Table L3-2 uses three new label properties:

- Alignment
- AutoSize
- Font.Style

Let's check them out.

New Property: Alignment

The Alignment property controls the horizontal location of the caption inside a label. It's one of those properties you can set by selecting from a list that appears when you click on the down-arrow button at the right of the Settings box. (That's a drop-list box, recall.) You get three choices.

- 0 - Left Justify
- 1- Right Justify
- 2 - Center

You can click on one of these selections or just type the number in the Settings box. Or you can double click on the property name to cycle through the choices one by one. This technique works for any property having the down-arrow icon in its Settings box. Left Justify means the caption will be snugged up against the left side of the label box. Right Justify means the caption will be snugged up against the right side of the label box. And Center means the caption will be centered. Figure L3-3 illustrates the differences.

New Property: AutoSize

The AutoSize box can be set to True or False. You can type T or F in the Settings box or select True or False from a drop-list box. If you select True, then Visual Basic automatically expands or contracts the width of the label box to fit the caption. Figure L3-4 shows the difference between having AutoSize set to True and set to False.

You may be wondering why both lblInstruct and lblSentence use the True setting for the AutoSize property, while only lblSentence uses the Center setting for Alignment. Indeed, since setting AutoSize to True makes the label box fit the caption exactly, the justification would seem to make no difference. After all, text that exactly fills a box is left-justified, centered, and right-justified all at once.

The tricky part is that the lblSentence caption length changes each time you select a new set of words for the sentence. With AutoSize set to True, the label box changes size each time the caption changes size. If you have Alignment set

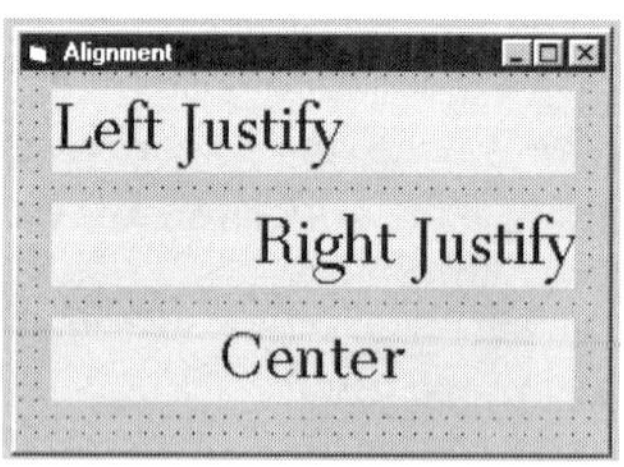

Figure L3-3 Alignment: Left Justify, Right Justify, and Center

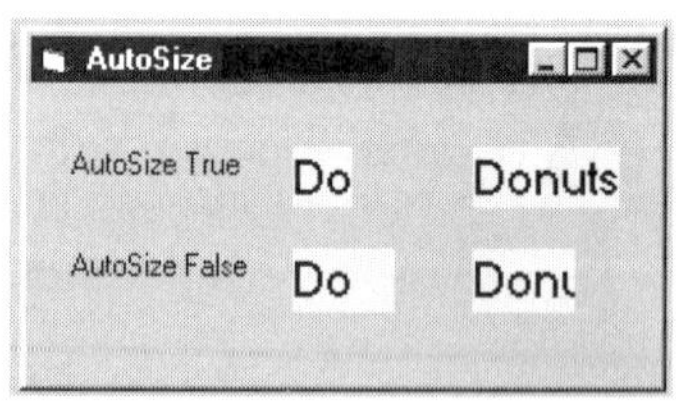

Figure L3-4 The AutoSize property

to Left Justify, the left end of the box stays fixed, while the right end adjusts to the caption size. Similarly, with the Right Justify setting, the right end stays fixed while the left end adjusts. But with the Center setting, the center stays fixed, while the left and right ends move in and out equally. Thus, the Center setting keeps the label centered in the form, and that looks better for this program (see Figure L3-5).

New Properties: Font.Bold and Font.Italic

As Lesson 2 revealed, when you click on the ... icon for the Font property, you get a Font dialog box. The Font Style list lets you a select style for the fonts. For example, selecting Bold from the list makes the text appear in boldface, and selecting Italic makes the text appear in italics. The list actually controls subproperties of the Font property. For example, choosing Bold sets the Font.Bold property to True, and deselecting Bold sets Font.Bold to False. Similarly, the Italic choice in the Style list controls the Font.Italic property, the Underline choice controls the Font.Underline property, and the Strikethru choice controls the Font.Strikethru property. You can mix style properties. For example, a caption can be both bold and italicized. But the entire caption has to be one style. That is, you can't italicize just one word out of several in a caption.

Changing Times

Earlier versions of Visual Basic didn't use subproperties of a Font property to control fonts. Instead, there was one property called FontSize, another called FontBold, and so on. For compatibility, Visual Basic 4 recognizes these older forms, but Microsoft recommends using the new system (Font.Bold, Font.Size, and so on) instead.

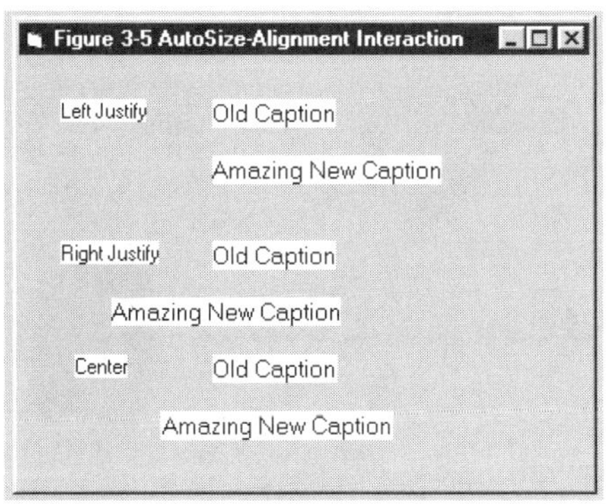

Figure L3-5 The AutoSize-Alignment interaction

The Usual Way Out

An Exit button is a nice touch, so select the command button tool and add one. Set the properties as shown in Table L3-4. Note that ALT-X is defined to be the access key for this control. Use Figure L3-1 to guide your placement.

OBJECT (INITIAL NAME)	PROPERTY	SETTING
Command1	Caption	E&xit
	Name	cmdExit

Table L3-4 The Exit command button

Next, add the *End* command to the button's click-event procedure:

```
Private Sub cmdExit_Click ()
    End
End Sub
```

Remember, you can double-click on the button to bring up the Code window and the *cmdExit_Click* event.

LIST BOXES—A NEW CONTROL

Now we get to the heart of the new program, using list boxes. The handy list box control is one of many controls designed to let you provide input to a program. It displays a list of items, and, when the program runs, you can click on an item to select it. If the list is long enough, such as the ones in Figure L3-1, the list box has a vertical scrollbar along the right side. Installing a list box control is simple enough. You select the list box icon from the Toolbox, then use the mouse to draw a list box on a form. Draw in three list boxes, locating them and sizing them approximately as shown in Figure L3-1. Then set properties as shown in Table L3-5.

OBJECT (INITIAL NAME)	PROPERTY	SETTING
List1	Name	lstAdjective
	Sorted	True
List2	Name	lstNoun
List3	Name	lstVerb

Table L3-5 List box control settings

Setting the Sorted property to True causes the list to appear in alphabetic order. The other settings rename the list boxes. But nothing here states what's in the lists! The reason for this is that Visual Basic doesn't include the list contents as part of the list box properties. One reason for that is that it's hard to set up a single property that might represent a list of three items one time and twelve items another.

The *AddItem* Method

So how do you get items into a list? You use a special Visual Basic command called *AddItem*. *AddItem* is an example of something called an *object method* because it applies to a particular object. That is, you can't just use *AddItem* by itself. Instead, the command also has to identify which list gets the item. For example, to add the word "addled" to the lstAdjective list, you give this command:

```
lstAdjective.AddItem "addled"
```

You also can describe this by saying that you're invoking the *AddItem* method for the lstAdjective object.

In general, you invoke a method by using the object name, then a period, then the method name (see Figure L3-6). How do you add the word "poet" to the noun list? That's right, you use the *AddItem* method for the lstNoun object:

```
lstNoun.AddItem "poet"
```

The next question is, where do you put these commands? Before answering that, answer another question: When do you want these commands to take place? Ideally, you'd probably want them to take place before the program starts, but that cannot be. Why? Because Visual Basic commands are executed during run time, not design time. In other words, you can't use commands to load words into the list until the program is running. Run time suggests putting the commands into an event procedure. What about using the *Click* event procedures for each list? Then each list would come up blank, and nothing would show until you clicked on the list. Nah. A better solution would be to place them in an event that happens automatically whenever you start the Quick

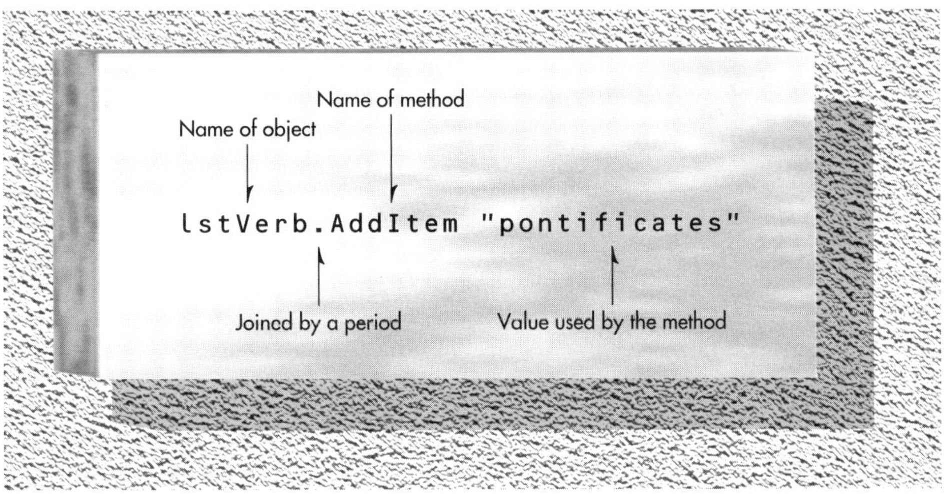

Figure L3-6 Invoking a method for an object

Author program. Rejoice! There is such an event. It's called *Form_Load*, and it's triggered when a form first opens.

The *Form_Load* Event

The *Form_Load* event procedure is the default event for forms, so if you double-click on the frmQuickAuthor form, you'll see the following:

```
Private Sub Form_Load ()

End Sub
```

Note that the event procedure is named *Form_Load* rather than *frmQuickAuthor_Load*.

> **Note**
>
> Control events are named after individual control names, as in *btnQuit_Click* or *lblSentence_Click,* but form events just use the generic term Form, as in *Form_Click,* regardless of a form's name.

It's now time to load adjectives, nouns, and verbs into the three lists. Just use the *AddItem* method with each of the lists, as shown in the following listing:

```
Private Sub Form_Load ()
    lstAdjective.AddItem "dweebish"
    lstAdjective.AddItem "addled"
    lstAdjective.AddItem "clamorous"
    lstAdjective.AddItem "baleful"
    lstAdjective.AddItem "execrable"
    lstNoun.AddItem "poet"
    lstNoun.AddItem "programmer"
    lstNoun.AddItem "politician"
    lstNoun.AddItem "prince"
    lstNoun.AddItem "pogoist"
    lstVerb.AddItem "sings"
    lstVerb.AddItem "waddles"
    lstVerb.AddItem "pirouettes"
    lstVerb.AddItem "flirts"
    lstVerb.AddItem "astounds"
End Sub
```

Now run the program. You should see something like Figure L3-7. All the words you added are there. That's good. Note that the words in the noun and verb lists appear in the same order that they did in the *AddItem* commands. But because the adjective list had the Sort property set to True, the words in that list are arranged alphabetically. Next, click on a particular word, and it gets highlighted. That's good. But nothing's highlighted when the program starts. That's bad. And highlighting a word doesn't seem to accomplish anything—the lblSentence label remains blank. Clearly, there's more to learn and more to do. Ah, such a great time to be a student!

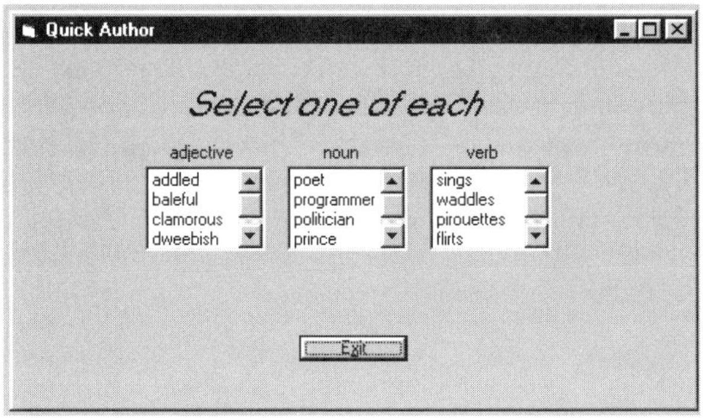

Figure L3-7 Three lists

Properties, Methods, and Event Procedures

You've now seen that Visual Basic controls and forms come with properties, methods, and event procedures, and you may want a little clarification on the differences between them. A *property* is a data value associated with a particular object, and you use a period to join the name of a particular object to a property name. For example, *lstToys.Sorted* represents the value of the Sorted property for the lstToys list. A *method* is an action associated with a particular object. As with properties, you use a period to join the name of a particular object to a method name. For example, the *lstToys.AddItem* method adds an item to the lstToys list. An *event procedure* associates an event with a particular object. You use an underscore to join the name of a particular object to a particular event. For instance, *lstToys_Click* represents the event procedure associated with clicking the mouse on the lstToys list. Methods and event procedures both perform actions, but a method's actions are predefined by Visual Basic, while you provide the code for an event procedure's actions.

List Box Runtime Properties

List box controls have lots of properties, and some of the most interesting ones don't appear in the Properties window. For example, the ListIndex property identifies the currently selected item, which is the item that got highlighted when you clicked on it. If the first item in the list is selected, the ListIndex property is 0; if the second item is selected, ListIndex is 1; and so on. If no item is selected, as is the case when our program starts, ListIndex is -1. Then there is the ListCount property, which equals the current number of items in a list. The Text property is set to the currently selected item.

The reason these properties don't appear in the Properties window is that they get set during runtime, not during design time. Remember, items don't get added to the list until you run the program, and they can be selected only then. Visual Basic Properties windows only list properties that can be set during design time, so ListCount, ListIndex, and Text don't show there.

You can use these properties during runtime, however. For example, you can add the following three commands at the end of the *Form_Load* procedure:

```
lstAdjective.ListIndex = 0
lstNoun.ListIndex = 0
lstVerb.ListIndex = 0
```

Setting the ListIndex properties to 0 for the three lists means that the first item in each list is the selected item and will appear in highlighted form. If you make these changes and restart Quick Author, you'll see that the top item in each list is highlighted now.

ListIndex and Text both refer to the currently selected item. ListIndex is the numeric index value, while Text is the item itself. For example, when *1stNoun.ListIndex* is 0, *lstNoun.Text* is the word "poet." Hey! You now have access to the selected items! The properties *lstAdjective.Text, lstNoun.Text,* and *lstVerb.Text* are just the items needed to make the sentence. The next problem is joining them into a single sentence. For that, let's take a short look at Visual Basic strings.

A Quick Peek at Strings

In Visual Basic, a string is a series of letters, digits, and punctuation marks (more generally, a series of characters) stored as a unit. When you set a Caption property in a Properties window, you enter a string. For instance, the Caption property for the frmQuickAuthor form is the string "Quick Author." Incidentally, one of the characters in this string is the space character between the two words. When you set a Caption property in a procedure, you indicate a string by enclosing it in double quotation marks:

```
lblPub.Caption = "The Goat and Throne"
```

Now both *lblPub.Caption* and "The Goat and Throne" are strings. The quoted string is called a *string constant* or a *string literal,* while *lblPub.Caption* is a *string variable* because it can be set to different values.

Now back to our demo program. To set the lblSentence caption to the item selected in the adjective list, you can do this:

```
lblSentence.Caption = lstAdjective.Text
```

However, the real goal is to combine the three selected words into a single string. Visual Basic makes this easy to do. Just combine (or *concatenate*) the strings using the & symbol. For example,

```
lblSentence.Caption = "do" & "or"
```

sets the caption to the string "door". This example combined string literals, but you also can concatenate string variables. For instance,

```
lblSentence.Caption = "The " & lstAdjective.Text
```

combines the string "The" with the selected adjective. If "addled" is selected, then the caption becomes "The addled". Notice the space in "The"; without it, the caption would become "Theaddled". If you want a space between words, you have to provide it. To build the whole sentence, you can do this:

```
lblSentence.Caption = "The " & lstAdjective.Text & " "
lblSentence.Caption = lblSentence.Caption & lstNoun.Text & " "
lblSentence.Caption = lblSentence.Caption & lstVerb.Text & "!"
```

This builds the string in three steps to make the code lines short enough to read easily. You could do it in one step, adding all seven strings in one command, but then the code line gets awkwardly long.

Visual Basic 4 has added a new feature that lets you spread a single long line over several screen lines. By typing a space followed by an underscore character (_), you can continue a single program line to the next line onscreen. For example, you can rewrite the last set of statements like this:

```
lblSentence.Caption = "The " & lstAdjective.Text & " " _
        & lstNoun.Text & " " & lstVerb.Text & "!"
```

In this context, the underscore character is called the *line-continuation character.* You can't use it for this purpose inside a string. That is, code like the following fails:

```
lblSample.Caption = "The surreal sea foamed in ambiguous eddies about _
     the edifice's complex foundations."      ' syntax error
```

Instead, to spread a long string over two code lines, use the line-continuation character in conjunction with the concatenation operator:

```
lblSample.Caption = "The surreal sea foamed in ambiguous eddies about " _
     & "the edifice's complex foundations."    ' okay way to handle long
                                                 string
```

Tip

Use a space followed by an underscore character to extend a single Visual Basic program statement over more than one line. Don't forget the space!

By the way, notice that assigning meaningful names to the controls makes this code easier to understand. That is, the names show that this code is combining an adjective, noun, and verb to form a sentence. Also, the names make it easier to program. If you used names like List1 and List3, you'd have to keep checking which label represented which kind of word.

Tip

Meaningful control names make it easier to write and understand code.

Incidentally, for backwards compatibility, Visual Basic lets you use the + operator instead of the & operator to concatenate strings. However, the & form is less confusing.

Strings have many other properties, but this is all you need to know for the task at hand, so let's get back to the program.

Making It Work

Finally, we have the code needed to create the sentence. The next question is where to put it. Let's try the *Click* event procedure for the lblSentence label:

```
Private Sub lblSentence_Click ()
    lblSentence.Caption = "The " & lstAdjective.Text & " " _
        & lstNoun.Text & " " & lstVerb.Text & "!"
End Sub
```

Now try running the program. As before, it starts up showing the top word in each list highlighted and with an empty lblSentence label. Now click on lblSentence. Finding the label is a little tricky because it blends into the background. But when you succeed, the label changes to "The addled poet sings!". Now select a new combination of words and click on the label. Hooray! It changes to a new sentence.

Making It Better

At this point you may have a couple of reactions—glee that it works, and annoyance that the label starts as a blank and that you have to click on the label before anything happens. So let's remove those annoyances.

There are several ways to get the sentence label to start up displaying something. We'll look at three methods, making an improvement each time. Then we'll use the best of the three.

Method 1 is to use the Property window to set lblSentence's Caption property to "The addled poet sings!" This is a simple solution, but has a problem. Suppose later you edit the lists so that some other words are at the top. Then you have to remember to change this property manually. It's better to come up with a scheme that updates the opening caption automatically.

Method 2 is to copy the code from *lblSentence_Click* to *Form_Load*. That is, copy the following code to the end of the *Form_Load* procedure:

```
lblSentence.Caption = "The " & lstAdjective.Text & " " _
    & lstNoun.Text & " " & lstVerb.Text & "!"
```

This sets up the Sentence label when the program starts. That's nice, but using the same block of code in several different places (*Form_Load* and *lblSentence_Click*, in this case) usually means you've overlooked a better approach.

Method 3 is that better approach. Suppose that starting the program automatically clicked the mouse on the lblSentence label. That would display the initial sentence. You can make this happen by placing the following code at the end of the *Form_Load* procedure:

```
lblSentence_Click
```

The command *lblSentence_Click* means "click on the lblSentence object." Giving this command has the same effect as actually clicking, so it activates the code in the lblSentence *Click* event procedure. This way you don't have to rewrite the code. Note that you add this code instead of the two lines of code mentioned in method 2.

Generating Events by Using Code

Visual Basic events, such as clicking a mouse in an object, can also be activated by invoking the event in Visual Basic code. The command should use the object name followed by an underscore followed by the event name. For instance, to simulate clicking a mouse on a cmdHello button, give the command *cmdHello_Click.*

Make this change and run the program again. This time the Sentence label shows "The addled poet sings!" immediately. However, when you change a list selection, you still have to click on lblSentence before the change shows up. Yucko! You can fix this by using the trick you just learned, this time in the *Click* procedures for the list boxes:

```
Private Sub lstAdjective_Click ()
    lblSentence_Click
End Sub

Private Sub lstNoun_Click ()
    lblSentence_Click
End Sub

Private Sub lstVerb_Click ()
    lblSentence_Click
End Sub
```

Now, if you click on a list box to change a selection, you also activate the lblSentence *Click* event, updating the display.

Interestingly, even though the sentence-making code is in the *lblSentence_Click* procedure, you never have to click on lblSentence. Placing the *lbl_Sentence_Click* command in the *Form_Load* procedure and in the list click procedures automates the program so that all the sentence-making takes place automatically when you start the program and when you change a word selection.

Make Your Interfaces Friendly

These days it's not enough to design a program that works. It also has to be easy to use. Let's look at three possible interfaces for Quick Author from this perspective.

Version 1 is the interface we began with before fixing it. It's the one in which no sentences appear until you click on the lblSentence control. Assume a user named Random Tester (RT, for short) walks in and starts up the program. RT will see three lists of words and the instructions "Select one of each:". If RT has any Windows experience, RT will probably click the mouse in the lists and select some words. But nothing happens. Nothing onscreen even hints at the next step, which should be to click on the invisible lblSentence control. Most likely, RT will lose interest and wander off, having accomplished nothing.

Variation 2 is a hypothetical variant in which we add a button labeled Update to Version 1. Clicking the button updates the lblSentence caption. This version supplies all the visual cues that Random Tester needs to make the program work. Select three words, click on the Update button, and behold the result. However, RT does have to take the extra step of clicking on the Update button. In some cases, that might be desirable, but it's just wasted effort here.

Variation 3 is the final version you saw earlier. Merely clicking on a word choice automatically updates the lblSentence caption. This version has all the visual information needed to show what to do, and it requires the least amount of user effort.

SUMMARY

Input and output are how you communicate with a program and vice versa. Visual Basic supports many forms of input and output, including keystrokes, mouse clicks, text, sound, and color. Visual Basic menus and controls provide you many communication choices.

Although Visual Basic provides default names for controls, Microsoft recommends a systematic convention for naming controls. In this convention each name begins with a three-letter abbreviation indicating the kind of control, then continues with a name indicating the location or function of the control.

The list box control is a particularly convenient form of input when the user has to select from a list of choices. Unlike the controls you used in Lesson 2, list box controls have several important properties that get set at run time instead of in design mode. In particular, you use the *AddItem* method to add items to a list, the ListIndex property to identify a list member by number, and the Text property to represent the selected value of a list. A method, by the way, is a command that has to be invoked for a particular object. You have to combine AddItem with the name of a particular list, for example, to add a word to that list:

```
lstGroceries.AddItem "mango chutney"
```

Strings are a series of characters treated as a unit. Visual Basic uses double quotation marks to indicate strings in code. Such strings are called string literals because each character is shown literally, that is, explicitly. For instance, "I am a Visual Basic string" is a string literal. Visual Basic lets you combine strings by adding them. For instance,

```
lblTitle.Caption = "The Fu" & "gitive"
```

sets *lbTitle.Caption* to "The Fugitive".

You can simulate particular events by invoking event procedures. For instance, the command

```
cmdUpdate_Click
```

has the same effect as clicking the mouse on the cmdUpdate button.

When designing programs, you should try to make the interface easy to understand and easy to use.

QUIZ 3

1. A good, convention-compliant name for an option button that sets a game to the Easy level would be
   a. Option3
   b. optEasy
   c. EasyOpt

2. A list box
   a. Tilts to one side
   b. Shows a list of items
   c. Show a column of boxes

3. To put items in a list, you usually
   a. Set the List property to the items you want.
   b. Use the AddItem method in the list's Click event.
   c. Use the AddItem method in the Form_Load event.

4. The code for highlighting the first item in the lstCat list is
   a. lstCat.ListIndex = 0
   b. lstCat.ListIndex = 1
   c. This is a trick question—the first item is highlighted automatically.

5. The expression *lstCat.Text* represents
   a. The caption that appears by the lstCat list box
   b. The name of the list box
   c. The currently selected item in the list

6. The expression *"the" & "me song"* is equivalent to the string
   a. "the me song"
   b. "theme song"
   c. "themesong"

7. What would be the effect of putting the *End* command in the *Form_Load* event?
   a. No effect.
   b. The program would quit when you tried to start it.
   c. Microsoft would go out of business.

8. You want clicking the cmdRelay button to automatically click the cmdGo button. You should
   a. Put the *cmdRelay_Click* command in the *cmdGo_Click* event code
   b. Put the *cmdGo_Click* command in the *cmdRelay_Click* event code
   c. Both a and b

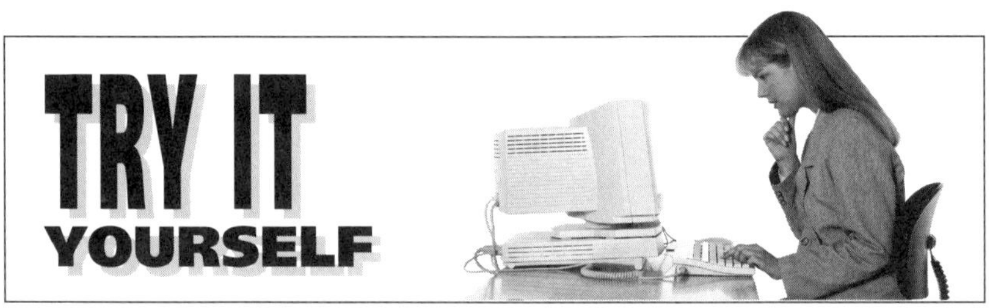

1. Implement the Version 2 interface discussed in the Make Your Interfaces Friendly section.

2. Prepare a program with two list boxes. The first should contain ten words, and the second should start empty. Selecting a word in the first list box should add that word to the second list box.

LESSON

4 EVENTS AND PROPERTIES

Suppose you are creating an artificial being, for instance, Robot Redford, Prince Android, or David Digitman. You would be concerned about your creation's appearance. You could describe the appearance with a table of properties: height, number of arms, top speed, and so on. You also would be concerned with the being's behavior. For instance, how does it respond to praise?

As a Visual Basic programmer, you have to deal with similar concerns. If you create a simple text viewer, as you will for Lesson 18, you'll be concerned about your creation's height, width, background color, foreground color, the

file types it will recognize, and so on. For describing properties, you have the Visual Basic form and control properties at your disposal. For prescribing behavior, you have Visual Basic event procedures to work with. So far, you've dealt with several properties, but the only events you've seen are the Form-load event and the Click event. There are many other events, and surely you want to know more about them. This lesson will expand your repertoire of Visual Basic tools, providing the groundwork for further development. You will learn about the following:

Text Display

- **The BorderStyle property**
- **The text control**
- **The Change event**

Managing Events

- **How to tell which events a particular control can recognize**
- **How to associate more than one event with a control**

Responding to Mouse Actions

- **The DblClick event**
- **The MouseDown event**
- **The MouseUp event**
- **The MouseMove event**

Responding to Keystrokes

- **The KeyDown event**
- **The KeyUp event**

Focus

- **The meaning of focus**
- **The GotFocus event**
- **The LostFocus event**

Using the TAB Key

- **The tabbing order**
- **The TabIndex property**
- **The TabStop property**

In short, you'll pick up lots of information that you'll be able to use in later lessons.

SETTING THE SCENE

Each kind of Visual Basic object has its own set of properties and its own set of events it recognizes. Many properties show up in most objects, but some are less common. For instance, all objects have a Name property, many (but not all) have a Caption property, and only some have a Text property. Similarly, most objects recognize several different events, but it depends on the kind of object.

There is rhyme and reason to the assignment of properties and events to a control. For instance, an object has to have a Name property so that you can refer to it by name when you write code. Controls that display read-only information, such as labels and command buttons, need a Caption property. Controls that let you enter text from the keyboard need a Text property. Controls that display text need a Font property. A control that is supposed to react to a mouse click should recognize mouse events. As you work with controls and get used to their purposes, you'll develop a feel for what properties and events they support.

Let's create a program that explores some of the possibilities. Once again, expertly guide your copy of Visual Basic into design mode and begin a new project. As usual, first set up the appearance of the form. Use the Toolbox to draw three labels, one text box, two command buttons, and two option buttons on the form. The Toolbox symbol for the text box is *ab* in a frame. Check Figure L2-9 to review the Toolbox icons, if necessary. Figure L4-1 shows how the form looks in design mode before you change properties. Then set properties as prescribed in Table L4-1. Figure L4-2 shows the form after you change properties. Use these figures as a guide as you create and modify the controls. You may need to resize and reposition some objects after changing the properties.

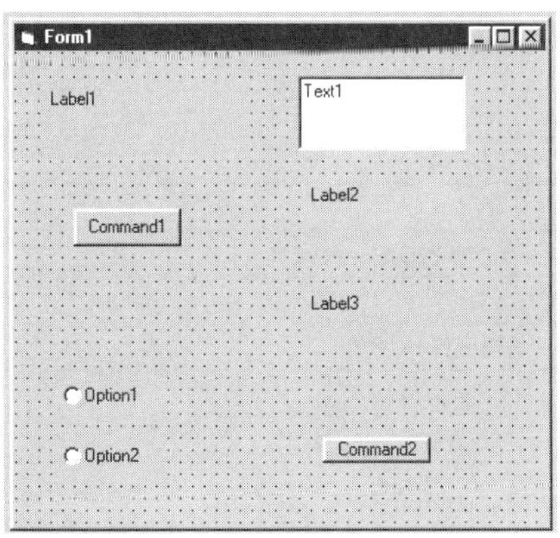

Figure L4-1 The initial form

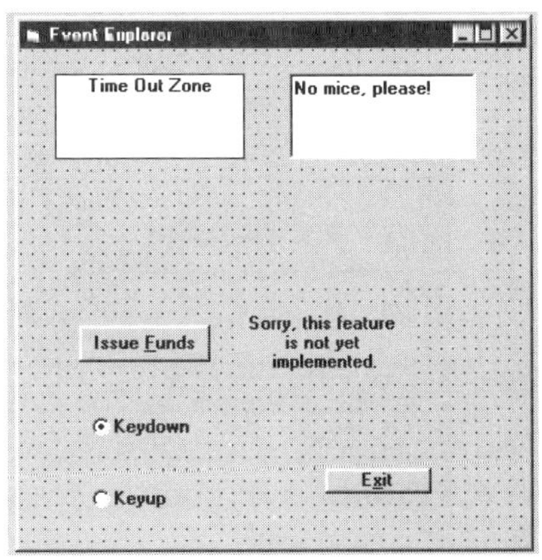

Figure L4-2 The form after setting properties

OBJECT	PROPERTY	SETTING
Form1	Caption	Event Explorer
	Font.Bold	True
	Name	frmEvent
Label1	Alignment	2 - Center
	Appearance	0 - Flat
	BorderStyle	1 - Fixed Single
	Caption	Time Out Zone
	Font.Bold	True
	MousePointer	11 - Hourglass
	Name	lblTimeOut
Label2	Caption	(blank)
	Font.Bold	True
	Name	lblEcho
Label3	Alignment	2 - Center
	Caption	Sorry, this feature is not yet implemented.
	Font.Bold	True
	Name	lblNotYet
	Visible	False
Command1	Caption	Issue &Funds
	Font.Bold	True
	Name	cmdIssue
Command2	Caption	E&xit
	Font.Bold	True
	Name	cmdExit
Option1	Caption	Keydown
	Font.Bold	True
	Name	optKeyDown
	Value	True
Option2	Caption	Keyup
	Font.Bold	True
	Name	optKeyUp
Text1	Font.Bold	True
	MousePointer	12 - No Drop
	Name	txtNotHere
	Text	No mice, please!

Table L4-1 Properties for the Event Explorer program

This program introduces one new control (the text box) and a few new properties. Let's begin by looking at the new properties.

Old Controls, New Properties

You've already dealt with labels and option buttons, but now you get to play with their BorderStyle, Appearance, Visible, and Value properties. The first three modify the appearance of controls, adding to the control you exert over the look of the final product.

The Interacting BorderStyle and Appearance Properties

Let's start with BorderStyle, with the lblTimeOut label (originally Label1). This property has two possible values for a label: 0 - None and 1- Fixed Single. The default value is None, which is why none of the labels to date have shown a border. But selecting Fixed Single causes Visual Basic to draw a border around the label. The Fixed part means you can't drag the boundary to a different size when the program is in run mode, and the Single part means the border is drawn with a single line. (Some objects, such as the form, have a wider range of choices for the BorderStyle property.)

The Appearance property currently has two possible values: 0 - Flat and 1 - 3D. When BorderStyle is None, the only apparent difference between the settings is that the label's background color is white for the Flat setting and gray for the 3D setting. But when you select the Fixed Single border, the 3D setting results in a shaded, three-dimensional look, while the flat setting results in a flat look. Figure L4-3 shows the interaction between the Appearance and BorderStyle properties for labels.

The Appearance property for a control interacts with the Appearance property for the whole form. To get a full 3D effect, both the form Appearance property and control Appearance property need to be set to 3D. Figure L4-4 shows how the four labels of Figure L4-3 look if you set the form's Appearance property to Flat. Note that the default color for the form changes from gray to white. (The gray color lends itself better to creating a 3D effect with shading.)

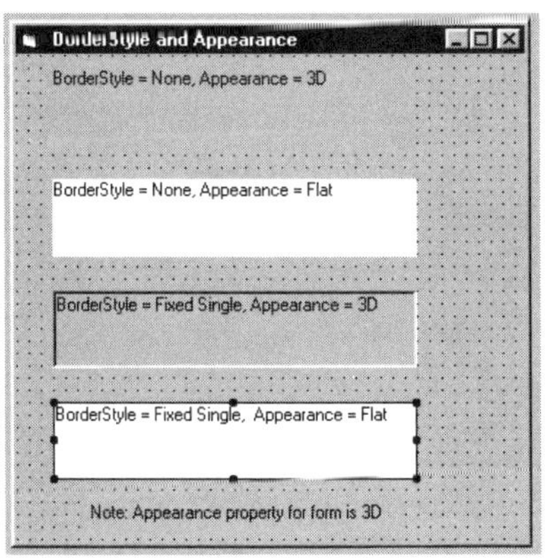

Figure L4-3 BorderStyle and Appearance properties for labels (3D form)

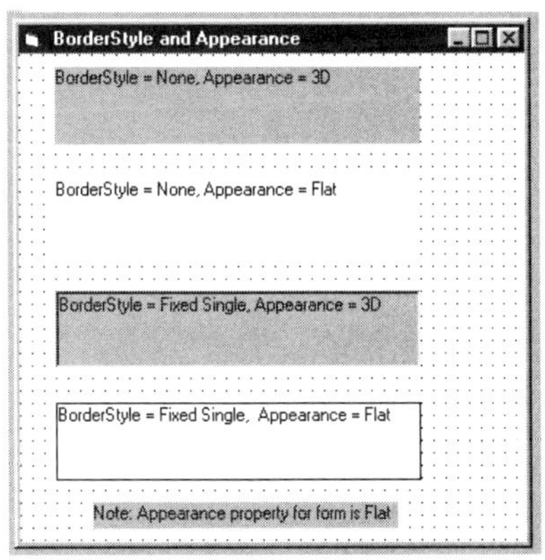

Figure L4-4 BorderStyle and Appearance properties for labels (flat form)

Tip

Forget what a property does? Highlight the property in a Properties window list and press F1. This brings up Visual Basic's built-in Help description of the property.

Now You See It, and Now You Don't—the Visible Property

Now let's look at the Visible property, which determines whether a control is visible. The lblNotYet label (originally Label3) sets the Visible property to False. This makes the label invisible when you run the program. It remains visible in design mode, however, because it would be difficult to manipulate a label if you couldn't see it. Try it. Run the program, and the label disappears. Quit the program, and the label reappears. Perhaps an invisible label seems less than totally useful (if a control is so ugly you want it to be invisible, perhaps you don't need it), but later you'll add an event procedure that makes the label visible under certain circumstances.

Objects with Value—the Value Property

The optKeyDown option button (originally Option1) sets the Value property to True. This engages the button, and you'll note that the black inner circle appears, indicating this button is depressed (physically, but not emotionally). Remember, at most one option button in a set can be engaged. By default, all option buttons start out disengaged, but the Value property gives you the option of selecting one preferred button. What happens if you set the Value property of the other option button to True, too? Try it. You'll find that Visual Basic lets you do so, but that setting the Value property of the second button to True automatically sets the Value property of the first button back to False. Either all the Value properties of a set of option buttons have to be False, or else exactly one can be set to True. Visual Basic checks to make sure you don't cheat.

Incidentally, a command button control also has a Value property, which is set to True when that button is selected and to False otherwise. Indeed, setting a command button's Value property is the same as clicking the button. The command button Value property is an example of a runtime property. It doesn't show up in the design mode Properties window, but you can use it in runtime code.

MousePointer Again

You've seen the MousePointer property before, but for the entire form. Using this property for a particular control is a bit more interesting. For instance, this example sets the MousePointer property for the lblTimeOut label and for the txtNotHere text box. Run the program and move the mouse cursor into the lblTimeOut label. Hey, the cursor turns into an hourglass! Move the cursor out, and it returns to its normal form. Now move it into the txtNotHere text box. This time, the cursor turns into the international Prohibited symbol, so get your mouse out of there! By the way, think about what the program has to do. It has to determine where the mouse pointer is, then determine if that position is inside or outside the control. If the pointer is inside, then the program has to redraw it. Once again, Visual Basic does a lot while the programmer does very little.

A New Control—the Text Box

Next, let's look at a new control, the text box. Could it possibly be a box with text in it? Yes. In many ways, the text box is like a label box. Both display text. Both have a BorderStyle property, but the default for the text box is Single Fixed instead of None. The fundamental difference is that the text box is designed to let you enter text while the program runs. That is, the label box basically is an output control, while a text box can be used both for input and output. One consequence is that the text box recognizes a couple of events that a label box control doesn't, and that is why Event Explorer has this particular control. Another consequence is that the text that appears in a text box is described by a Text property rather than a Caption property. Visual Basic uses the Caption property to describe text that a program user doesn't directly alter. So label boxes, command buttons, and option buttons all have Caption properties. The Text property, on the other hand, indicates text that a program user might alter directly. So you can change the Text property of a text box by typing in new text as the program runs. Or you can change the Text property of a list box by selecting another item from the list.

Let's try out a text box. Run the program and click the mouse in the text box. You should see the vertical bar text-insertion cursor appear where you clicked. Try typing something; the text you type should start appearing at the location of the text cursor. Use BACKSPACE to back up over what you just typed. Double-click on a word, and the word should be highlighted, as shown in Figure L4-5. Type in some new text, and it should replace the highlighted word, as shown in Figure L4-6. As you can see, a text box has the basic features of a simple text editor. You can add, delete, and replace text. You can move the text cursor through existing text. You even can use CTRL-C to copy selected text and CTRL-V to paste the copied text. Later lessons will discuss text boxes further, but that's all you need to know for now.

Figure L4-5 Selecting a word in a text box

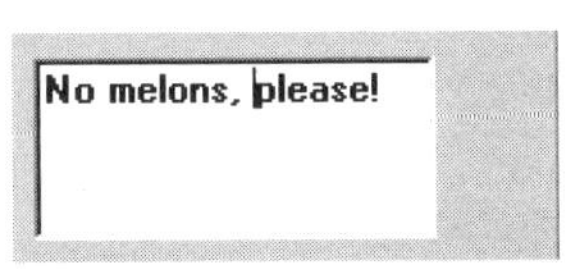

Figure L4-6 Replacing a word in a text box

ADDING EVENT PROCEDURES

The goal of Event Explorer is to explore events, so let's add some event procedures now, beginning with some familiar ones.

First, while Visual Basic is in design mode, double-click on the form. As before, this opens the *Form_Load* procedure, which you can use to initialize various controls. In this case, let's initialize the lblEcho caption to the text in the text window:

```
Private Sub Form_Load ()
    lblEcho.Caption = txtNotHere.Text
End Sub
```

You could have used the Properties list to set the lblEcho caption to the string "No mice, please!", but using the *Form_Load* event in the above fashion means that any changes you make in setting the txtNotHere Text property are tracked automatically when you start the program. That is, if you decide to change the textNotHere Text property to "Mice are nice!", you don't have to remember to manually change the lblEcho Caption property. Instead, it will be set automatically during run time when the program first starts.

Next, edit the *cmdExit_Click* procedure so that clicking on that command button terminates the program:

```
Private Sub cmdExit_Click ()
    End
End Sub
```

Now you're ready for the new stuff.

Expanding Your Mouse Repertoire: the *MouseDown* and *MouseUp* Events

Consider the button captioned "Issue Funds". As you might expect, there's no simple way to make this button actually issue funds to you. Rather than admit the button can't work, however, you can claim that this particular feature isn't ready yet. That, recall, is the message carried by the invisible lblNotYet label. There's no need to advertise this unreadiness until someone tries the feature, which is why the message is invisible. Honesty suggests showing that message if someone tries to use the feature, but it doesn't demand that we leave the message onscreen. Visual Basic's collection of events gives us a neat way to display and rehide the message, and we'll look at that now.

Clicking a mouse involves two actions—pressing the mouse button, then releasing the mouse button. The *MouseDown* and *MouseUp* events let you detect these two parts separately. So you can use the *MouseDown* event to make the message visible and the *MouseUp* event to make it invisible again. Thus, the warning message will appear only as long as you keep the mouse button depressed.

Let's set this up. First, with Visual Basic in design mode, bring up the Code window by (1) selecting Code from the View menu, or (2) pressing F7, or (3) clicking the View Code button in the Project window, or (4) double-clicking on the cmdIssue button. (The last choice generates a skeleton *cmdIssue_Click* event, which we won't use.) Select cmdIssue in the Object box. This generates a skeleton for the *cmdIssue_Click* event if you don't already have one. But we're not interested in that event. Instead, click on the down arrow in the Procedure box, and select *MouseDown* from the scrolling list (see Figure L4-7). This puts the *cmdIssue_MouseDown* event procedure in the text box. Add the code to make the warning message visible:

```
Private Sub cmdIssue_MouseDown (Button As Integer, Shift As Integer, _
    X As Single, Y As Single)
    lblNotYet.Visible = True
End Sub
```

The code making the message visible is simple; you just have to set the Visible property for the lblNotYet label to True. But what's all the *Button As Integer*, and so on, stuff following the event name? The good news is that you can ignore them for now. The even better news is that eventually (in Lesson 6), they will be quite useful to you.

Event Procedure Arguments—a Preview

Though we won't be using *Button*, *Shift*, and friends for a while, you probably would like at least an inkling of what they are. Each is an *argument* to the *Mouse_Down* event procedure. An argument represents information passed to

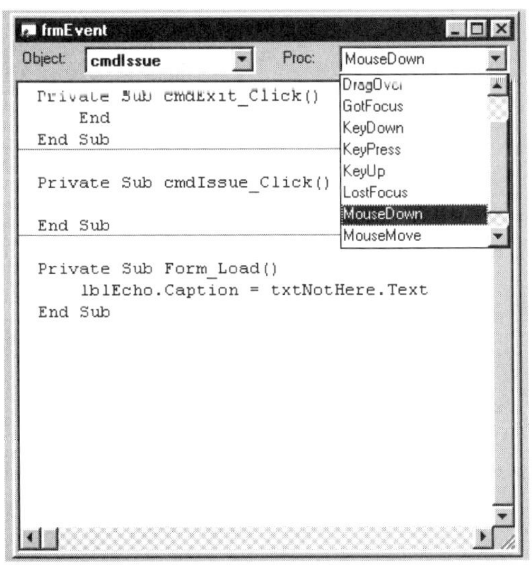

Figure L4-7 Selecting an event

the procedure when it's invoked. So when you invoke the *cmdIssue_MouseDown* event by pressing a mouse button, the four arguments *Button, Shift, X,* and *Y* each wind up as a symbolic name for a value, a lot like how properties are symbolic names for value. The phrase *Button as Integer* means *Button* is a symbolic name for an integer value. In particular, *Button* is 1 if the left mouse button is pressed, 2 if the right mouse button is pressed, and 4 if the center mouse button is pressed. (Of course, not all mice have three buttons. Not even all computer mice have three buttons.) You then can use the value of *Button* to determine which button was used. But you'll have to learn about some Visual Basic control statements (Lesson 6) before you can use this knowledge. Meanwhile, because our code doesn't mention any particular button, it works for all buttons. By the way, only one button can be active at a time, so if you press two buttons, the *Button* value will correspond to the first one pressed.

Similarly, the *Shift* argument indicates the state of the SHIFT, CTRL, and ALT keys. If *Shift* is 0, none of them is pressed. A value of 1 denotes a depressed SHIFT key, a 2 indicates a depressed CTRL key, and a 4 indicates a depressed ALT key. Combinations result in adding values. For instance, simultaneously depressing SHIFT and ALT produces a *Shift* value of 1 + 4, or 5.

The arguments *X* and *Y* describe the mouse position. The phrase *as Single* means that each is treated as a single-precision floating-point number, that is, a number with a fractional part. Lesson 5 will take up data types, including *Single*. By default, *X* and *Y* are measured in twips from the upper-left corner of the object. Lesson 12 will discuss some of the other possibilities.

As you can see, the *MouseDown* event "knows" a lot more about what's going on than does the *Click* event. It knows which button is pressed, what the states are of the SHIFT, CTRL, and ALT keys, and where the mouse is. Our program doesn't need to know any of that, so it doesn't use the values of *Button, Shift, X,* or *Y*. Later, you'll write programs that do use that information.

Back to Our Currently Scheduled Program

Now select the *MouseUp* procedure from the Procedure box and use it to make the label invisible again:

```
Private Sub cmdIssue_MouseUp (Button As Integer, Shift As Integer, _
    X As Single, Y As Single)
    lblNotYet.Visible = False
End Sub
```

As you can see, the *MouseUp* event knows the same information the *MouseDown* event does. Again, this program doesn't use that information.

By the way, check the scrolling list of the Procedure box while cmdIssue shows in the Code window Object box. You'll see that both *MouseDown* and *MouseUp* appear in boldface. This tells you that both events are active for the cmdIssue control.

Tip

You can provide code for more than one event for a given object. When that object appears in the Object box of the Code window, all events having code will show in boldface in the Procedure drop-list box.

Once you finish with these two events, try them. Run the program, position the mouse pointer over the Issue Funds button, and press the left mouse button. You should see the message "Sorry, this feature is not yet implemented." Release the button, and the message disappears. Neat! Try the same thing using the right mouse button. You get the same results, for the code didn't use the *Button* argument to limit the effect to one button.

The *DblClick* Event

The *MouseDown* and *MouseUp* events divide the *Click* event into two parts. The *DblClick* event combines two *Click*s into a single event. You've often used double-click events when using Windows programs. To generate a double-click event, you need to click the mouse button twice in quick succession. Figure L4-8 summarizes the differences between the mouse button events.

Historic Note

Had the rolling input device we call a mouse been called a hen originally, we could very well have wound up with the Cluck and DblCluck events.

You can use the Code window to add the double-click event to your own programs. Let's try it with the lblTimeOut control. With Visual Basic in design mode, double-click the lblTimeOut control to bring up the Code window. Scroll through the Procedure box, to find and select the *DblClick* event. Let's use it to change the label caption to italics:

```
Private Sub lblTimeOut_DblClick ()
    lblTimeOut.Font.Italic = True
End Sub
```

Notice the notation: *lblTimeOut.Font* is the Font property of the lblTimeOut object, and *lblTimeOut.Font.Italic* is the Italic property of the *lblTimeOut.Font* property. Also, note that, like the *Click* event, the *DblClick* event doesn't take any arguments. For some controls, such as the label, you can double-click any mouse button to trigger the *DblClick* event. For other controls, such as the textBox, only the left mouse button triggers the event.

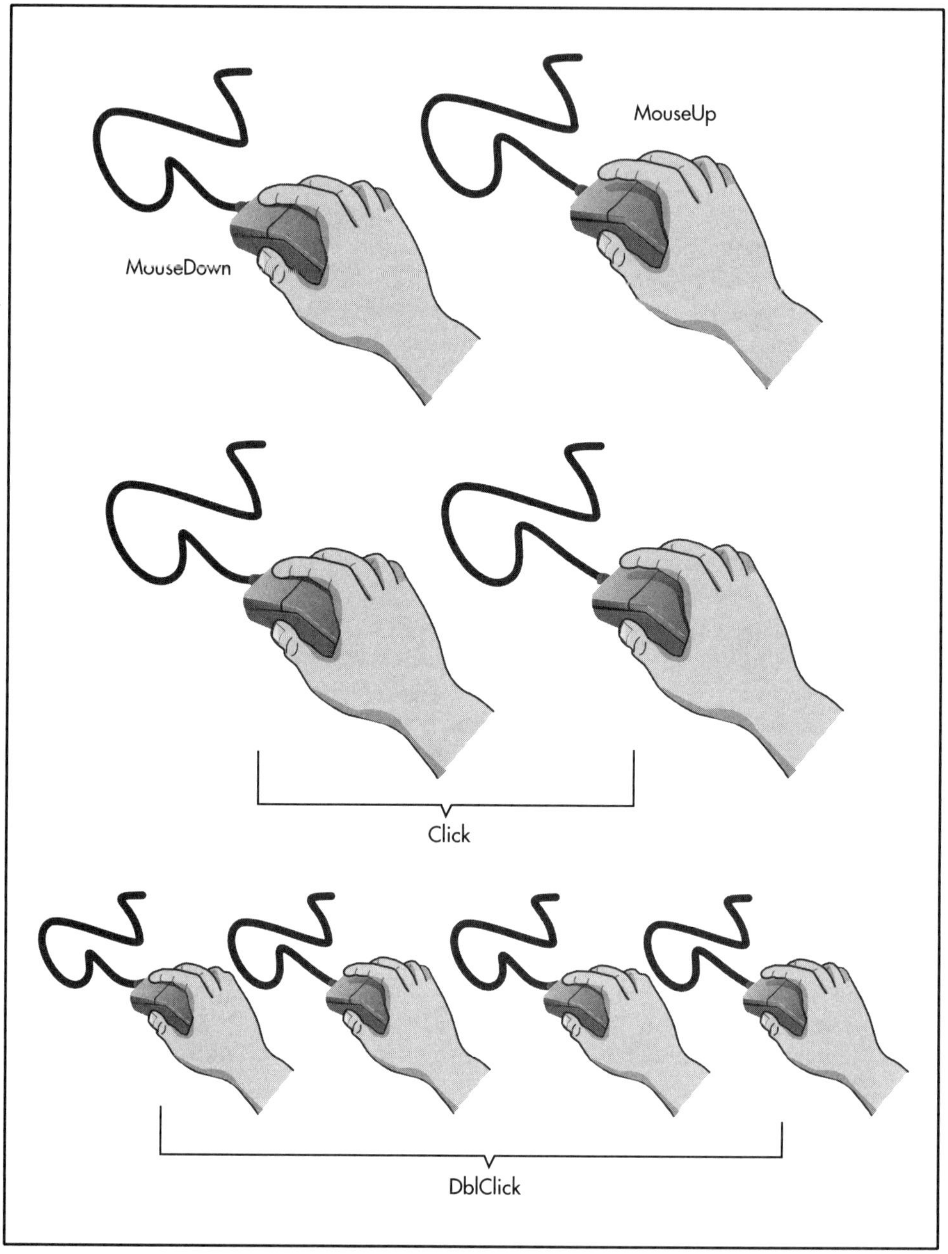

Figure L4-8 Mouse button events

Next, select the *Click* event and use it to reset the caption to non-italics:

```
Private Sub lblTimeOut_Click ()
    lblTimeOut.Font.Italic = False
End Sub
```

Now try the code. Run the program, moving the mouse pointer into the lblTimeOut control. Note the pointer turns into an hourglass because you earlier set the MousePointer property to 11. Double-click the mouse, and the Time Out Zone caption changes to italics (see Figure L4-9). Single-click, and the caption returns to non-italics. One thing to try is to double-click while the caption still is italicized. You may be able to see that the caption briefly turns to non-italics after the first click before reverting to italics. That's because a double-click looks like a single click until you get that second click in.

The *MouseMove* Event

The txtNotHere control pretty clearly wants mice to stay away. Moving the mouse into this text box already converts the mouse pointer to the international "Prohibited" symbol. Let's add some aural reinforcement. You don't have to click a mouse button to get a control's attention. Just moving the mouse pointer through a control is enough to trigger the *MouseMove* event. Each movement beyond a minimum threshold triggers a separate event, so as long as you keep the mouse moving in the text box, you generate *MouseMove* events. Let's check it out.

With Visual Basic in design mode, double-click on the txtNotHere object to open the Code window. Select the *MouseMove* event from the Procedure box and insert some mildly annoying code:

```
Private Sub txtNotHere_MouseMove (Button As Integer, Shift As Integer, _
    X As Single, Y As Single)
    Beep
End Sub
```

Note that the *MouseMove* event takes the same arguments as the *MouseDown* and *MouseUp* events, so the event procedure could use this information. For example, you could modify the procedure so that it beeps only if SHIFT is down while the mouse moves. Again, that requires techniques you'll learn in Lesson 6.

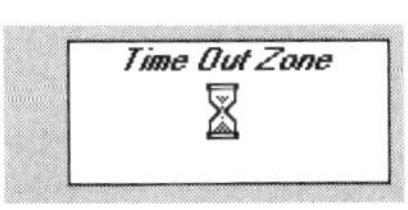

Figure L4-9 Result of double-clicking

Unlike the case for the *MouseDown* and *MouseUp* events, for which only one button can be active at a time, the *MouseMove* version of *Button* can indicate when two or more buttons are depressed. For instance, pressing the left button (a value of 1) and the right button (a value of 2) simultaneously sets *Button* to 3.

Let's run the program and experiment with this event. Move the mouse pointer at different speeds across the text box. The faster you move the mouse, the more closely spaced the beeps come. However, if you move the mouse fast enough across, say, a corner of the text box, you may not get any beeps at all. This is because a computer doesn't monitor the mouse position continuously. Instead, it checks in brief intervals. If you can move the mouse in and out of the text box in between two consecutive check times, you don't activate the mouse event. Similarly, if a movement is below a certain threshold in distance, it won't register. That's because mouse locations are measured in discrete units, the size of which depends on your software and hardware. For example, some mice have to move 15 twips before the movement is noticed.

A Couple of Key Events

Mice aren't the only source of events. Many controls also recognize key-generated events. For example, pressing a key generates a *KeyDown* event, releasing a key generates a *KeyUp* event, and pressing and releasing a key generates a *KeyPress* event. Let's use the two option buttons to try out the *KeyUp* and *KeyDown* events. First, open the Code window for the optKeyDown option button and select the *KeyDown* event from the Procedure box. Insert the *Beep* command:

```
Private Sub optKeyDown_KeyDown (KeyCode As Integer, Shift As Integer)
    Beep
End Sub
```

This event procedure has two arguments. The *KeyCode* argument reports a code that indicates which key was just pressed, and the *Shift* argument reports the states of the SHIFT, CTRL, and ALT keys. Lesson 6 will pursue that topic further. This example, however, merely beeps regardless of the key.

Next, choose the *KeyUp* event for the optKeyUp option button, and give it the same code:

```
Private Sub optKeyUp_KeyUp (KeyCode As Integer, Shift As Integer)
    Beep
End Sub
```

Now let's see how it works. Run the Event Explorer program and select the option button captioned "Keydown". Press a key. That generates a *KeyDown* event, and the computer beeps. If you hold the key down, the computer should beep a lot. That's because holding a key down eventually causes it to repeat. For instance, if you hold a key down too long when word processing, you suddenly get a string of identical characters. In this case, the repeat feature generates a series of *KeyDown* events. But if you release the key quickly enough, you get just the one beep as the key is pressed.

Next, select the option button captioned "Keyup" and begin pressing and releasing keys. This time you get a beep when a key is released.

Next, click the Issue Funds button, and then press a key. Nothing happens. It isn't enough that the optKeyDown option button be down. The control must also be *selected* before it responds to *KeyDown* or *KeyUp* events. This raises an important new topic—focus.

SELECTING CONTROLS—WHO'S GOT THE FOCUS?

Like some people, Visual Basic controls can compete to be the center of attention. In the Windows environment, only one object (including forms) can receive keystrokes at any one time. That object is said to *have the focus*. Typically, the object with the focus has its caption highlighted by an enclosing dotted rectangle. For example, if you created the Event Explorer objects in the suggested order, the program comes up with the cmdIssue button having the focus. Figure L4-10 shows the highlighting rectangle. A text box, on the other hand, doesn't have a caption to highlight. The way to tell if a text box has the focus is to see if the vertical text-insertion cursor appears in the box. If it does, then that text box has the focus, and you can type in the box. (If you check back to Figure L4-6, you'll see an example of the text-insertion cursor.)

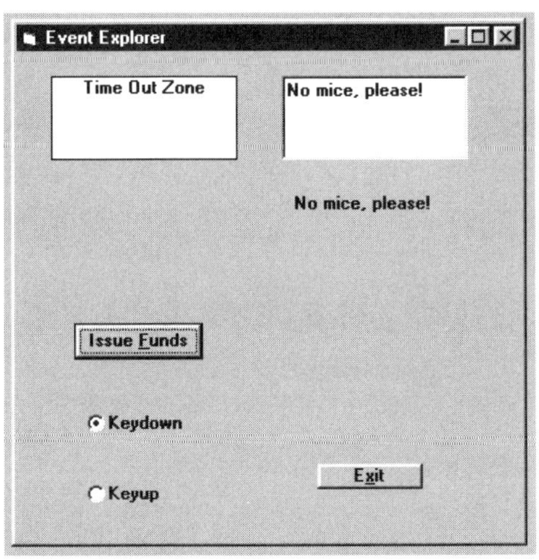

Figure L4-10 A dotted rectangle shows the control with the focus

There are several ways to change the focus:

- Click on the object you want to have the focus.
- Press the access key, if any, for the object.
- Press TAB to cycle through the various objects.
- Use the *SetFocus* method in a procedure to assign focus to an object.

An access key, recall, is one you define by placing an & before one of the letters in the Caption property. That letter gets underlined in the caption, and the access key is the key corresponding to that letter combined with the ALT key. So ALT-F is the access key for the cmdIssue button, for example.

Let's look at using *SetFocus* to set the focus. Like other methods, you have to combine the *SetFocus* method with an object name to use it. For example, you can modify the *optKeyDown_KeyDown* method to read as follows:

```
Project Sub optKeyDown_KeyDown (KeyCode As Integer, Shift As Integer)
    Beep
    optKeyUp.SetFocus
End Sub
```

If you press a key while the optKeyDown has the focus, this code sounds the beep, then shifts the focus to the optKeyUp control.

Focus and the *Click* Event—Related but Different

The *Click* event and getting the focus often go together, but they are two separate acts. Clicking on an object and pressing an access key for an object combine the two, both selecting the object and generating a *Click* event. For example, clicking on the cmdExit button selects it and triggers a *Click* event procedure, which terminates the program. Using the ALT-X access key has the same effect.

Using the TAB key or the *SetFocus* method, however, selects an object *without* generating a *Click* event. Try running the program and pressing TAB until the Exit caption is highlighted. The cmdExit button now has the focus, but the program is still running. With the cmdExit button selected, press ENTER or space bar. The program terminates! That's another aspect of having the focus—pressing ENTER or space bar sends a *Click* event to the control with the focus.

Restart the program. If the cmdIssue button doesn't have the focus, press TAB until it does. Now press ENTER. Nothing happens. Try the ALT-F access key. Again nothing happens. Click on the button. You see the invisible message appear and disappear. If pressing ENTER generates a *Click* event, why doesn't pressing ENTER have the same effect as clicking on this button? Similarly, why doesn't using the access key have the same effect? The answer is that the cmdIssue button *doesn't use* the *Click* event. We didn't define one. Instead, this button reacts to the *MouseDown* and *MouseUp* events. When you click the mouse on the button, you generate all three events: *MouseDown, MouseUp,* and *Click*. But pressing ENTER or ALT-F generates a pure *Click* event with no *MouseDown* and *MouseUp* involved. Define a *cmdIssue_Click* event procedure, and all three actions (clicking, pressing ENTER if the button has the focus, and pressing the access key) will trigger its execution. In general, if an object can accept the focus, the following rules apply:

- Mouse-clicking on an object gives it the focus and generates the MouseDown, MouseUp, and Click events.
- Pressing the access key for an object gives it the focus and generates the Click event.
- Pressing ENTER generates a *Click* event for the object currently having the focus.
- Pressing TAB or using the *SetFocus* command gives an object the focus without generating a *Click* event.

Of course, there are the occasional exceptions due to the requirements of particular controls. For instance, pressing ENTER when a text box has a focus generates a beep instead of a *Click* event.

Focus Restrictions

Not all objects can get the focus. Run the Event Explorer program and use TAB to move the focus from one control to another. You'll note the following:

- The command buttons can get the focus.
- The text box control can get the focus.
- The label controls never get the focus.
- Only the "on" option button gets the focus.

Of the controls discussed thus far, only the label control can't get the focus. Conceptually, labels shouldn't respond to keyboard input anyway, so this makes sense. If you examine the Procedure box list for a label control, you'll see that it doesn't even list the various keyboard events.

Here are some other restrictions on getting the focus:

- Controls with the Visible property set to False can't accept the focus.
- Controls with the Enabled property set to False can't accept the focus.
- A form can accept the focus only if it has no controls that take the focus.

The Enabled property determines whether you can use a control. Setting the Enabled property to False prevents a control from responding to any user-generated events. It also grays out the control's caption or text.

The Tabbing Order—Who's Next?

The *tabbing order* describes the order in which pressing TAB transfers the focus from one control to another. Each time you add a new control to a form, it's assigned an index representing its place in the order. The first control created is assigned an index of 0, the second an index of 1, and so on. This is true whether or not the control can accept the focus. The TabIndex property in the Properties list for a control shows you that object's index. The object having the index of 0 is the object that gets the focus when you start a Visual Basic program. However, if it is a control that can't accept the focus, Visual Basic goes through the tabbing order until it finds a control that can accept the focus. If there is no such control, then the form gets the focus.

Tip

You can change the tabbing order by changing the TabIndex properties. Visual Basic automatically prevents duplicate TabIndex properties, so if you change the TabIndex of a particular control to 0, the control that used to have a TabIndex of 0 gets it changed to 1, the one with a value 1 gets it changed to 2, and so on. The TabIndex values have to be consecutive.

Controls that can take the focus also have a TabStop property. If this value is True (the default), the control becomes part of the sequence that gets the focus as you press TAB. If you set the property to False for a particular control, tabbing through the controls will skip that control. You still can give that control the focus by clicking on it, however.

The *GotFocus* and *LostFocus* Events

The very acts of acquiring and losing focus are events. For example, if you open the Code window for the txtNotHere text box and examine the Procedure list, you'll see *GotFocus* and *LostFocus* listed. Moving the focus to a control generates the *GotFocus* event, and shifting the focus elsewhere triggers the *LostFocus* event. (The next time you explain something, see if you can spot the *GotFocus* and *LostFocus* events in the listener's eyes!) Let's try these events in Event Explorer. Use the Code window to create the following two event procedures:

```
Private Sub txtNotHere_GotFocus ()
   txtNotHere.Text = "No mice! No mice!"
End Sub

Private Sub txtNotHere_LostFocus ()
    txtNotHere.Text = "No mice, please!"
End Sub
```

Next, run Event Explorer and use the mouse or TAB to shift the focus to each control in turn. When the text box gets the focus, the text changes to *No mice! No mice!* When the focus moves to another control, the text changes back to *No mice, please!*

THE *Change* EVENT

Let's look at one more event. The act of changing some controls during run time generates a *Change* event. This is true, for instance, for the text box, label, and list box controls. For instance, if you change even a single character in a text box, you trigger a *Change* event. Let's try out this event with the textNotHere object. Use the Code window to create the following procedure:

```
Private Sub txtNotHere_Change ()
    lblEcho.Caption = txtNotHere.Text
End Sub
```

Earlier, the *Form_Load* procedure caused the lblEcho caption to duplicate the text in the txtNotHere box when the program started. The code here causes any changes in the text box to be duplicated, too. Try running the program after you make this addition. When you shift focus to the text box, both the text box and the label box change to displaying *No mice! No mice!* And if you type in the text box while it has the focus, the same text appears in the lblEcho label box, also. Each change you make to the text box triggers the *Change* event, which, in turn, updates the label box.

SUMMARY

Visual Basic programs are event-driven, and you have many events to choose from. Table L4-2 summarizes the events you've encountered thus far. Not all objects recognize all events. For instance, command button controls don't recognize the *DblClick* event.

EVENT	TRIGGERED BY
Change	Changing a control during run time
Click	Clicking the mouse on an object
DblClick	Clicking the mouse twice in quick succession
GotFocus	Getting the focus
KeyDown	Pressing a key
KeyPress	Pressing and releasing a key
KeyUp	Releasing a key
Load	Starting a program
LostFocus	Losing the focus
MouseDown	Pressing a mouse button down
MouseMove	Moving the mouse
MouseUp	Releasing a mouse button

Table L4-2 Some Visual Basic events

In a Visual Basic program, keyboard input can be directed to only one object at a time. That object is described as having the focus. Only some kinds of objects can accept the focus. Generally, they are the objects that accept some sort of input, such as the text box, the command button, and an "on" option button. Typically, you pass the focus to an object by clicking on it or by pressing its access key, if any. These two approaches both pass the focus *and* generate a *Click* event. Also, you can cycle through the various objects that can accept the focus by pressing TAB. Or you can use the *SetFocus* method in a procedure to shift the focus to a particular object. These two approaches give an object the focus, but without generating a *Click* event.

The order in which pressing TAB grants focus to objects is called the tabbing order. The tabbing order is determined by the TabIndex property. Each control, whether or not it can receive the focus, is assigned a TabIndex value in the order in which it was added to the form. By changing the TabIndex values in the Properties window, you can alter the tabbing order. Also, by setting the TabStop property of an object to False, you can cause the tabbing mechanism to skip the object.

QUIZ 4

1. Table L4-1 failed to set the Caption property for the text box because
   a. The default value was good enough.
   b. Someone forgot.
   c. Text boxes don't have a caption property.

2. The *most* significant difference between a text box and a label is
   a. The label can display text.
   b. Someone using a program can enter text into a text box during run time.
   c. The text box has a border.

3. Pressing and releasing a mouse button when the mouse pointer is over a label generates which events?
   a. Just the *Click* event
   b. The *Click* event, the *MouseDown* event, and the *MouseUp* event
   c. The *Click* event, the *MouseDown* event, the *MouseUp* event, and the *Squeak* event

4. Which one of the following does not have the same effect as clicking on a command button?

a. Pressing the access key for the button
b. Tabbing to the button
c. Tabbing to the button and pressing ENTER

5. Which of the following cannot receive the focus?

a. A command button
b. A text box
c. A label

6. Match the event to a possible cause:

EVENT	POSSIBLE CAUSE
MouseUp	Pressing M when a text box has the focus
LostFocus	Releasing a mouse button
Change	Pressing TAB when a text box has the focus

7. If you type "Estimated Taxes" while a Visual Basic program is running, this input necessarily is sent to

a. An appropriate government agency
b. The first text box in the tabbing order
c. The object with the focus

8. How can you tell what the access key is for a command button control?

a. Look up the predefined access key in a reference.
b. Note which letter in the caption is underlined.
c. Type 411 for access information.

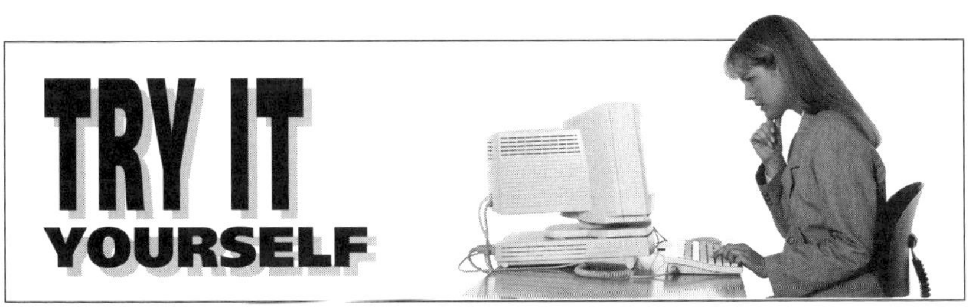

1. Modify Event Explorer so that pressing TAB cycles the focus through the following controls in the order shown: txtNotHere, cmdIssue, cmdExit.

2. Put together a Visual Basic program with the following features:

- A command button captioned "Click Here" changes its caption to "Ahh!" while you click it and reverts to "Click Here" when you release the mouse button.
- A text box for which the mere act of moving the mouse pointer into the box gives the focus to the box.
- A text box for which the computer beeps each time you alter the text.
- Two option buttons such that clicking on the second button makes the first button "on" and shifts the focus to the first button.
- A text box that becomes invisible when you try to type in it and a command button that makes the text box visible again.

LESSON 5 VARIABLES AND DATA TYPES

So far these lessons have concentrated on controls, which must be very satisfying to control freaks. Learning about a control consists of learning its properties, the events it recognizes, and its methods, such as *SetFocus* or *AddItem*. Knowing your controls is good, but it's also important to learn about what code you can place in event procedures. Otherwise your programs may have a pretty face but no brains. (And while that is good enough to succeed in some venues, it's not good enough in the computer world.) The brain material for Visual Basic programs is the Visual Basic programming language, which is pretty similar to its DOS ancestor, QuickBasic. So if you already know Basic in one of its older forms, you have a head start when it comes to writing Visual

Basic procedures. Your brain classifies and stores information. Visual Basic programs use properties for that role, for instance, storing words in a Caption property or a size in a Width property. More generally, Visual Basic can use *variables* to store information. A variable represents a value symbolically. That is, a variable lets you use a name to stand for a value. For instance, the variable *State* might represent the string "California". As the term "variable" suggests, the same variable can have different values at different times. For instance, you could have *State* represent "Rhode Island" or "frazzled" instead. You can use the = symbol to assign values to variables. For example, the following statement assigns the value 144 to the variable named *Gross:*

```
Gross = 144
```

In fact, you've already been using variables, for a control property is really a special case of variable, one that's attached to a particular control. For instance, *Label1.Caption* can represent different values symbolically, such as "Don't press the adjoining button" or "Free the Standard and Poor 500". Or *Option1.TabIndex* can have the value 3. Event arguments, such as the *Button* and *X* arguments to the *MouseDown* event procedure also are special forms of variables, ones that are tied to particular event procedures.

Note that the Caption property represents a string, while the TabIndex property represents a number. That is, these two properties represent different *types* of data. Variables have the same behavior. In general, you can characterize a variable by three things:

- **Its name**
- **Its data type**
- **Its value**

Learning to use variables is a vital step in learning Visual Basic. This lesson will introduce you to the following topics:

- **Naming conventions for variables**
- **Creating variables**
- **Visual Basic's intrinsic data types**
- **Simple arithmetic**
- **Type conversions**

By the time you finish this lesson, you should be comfortable creating and using variables.

NAMING AND CREATING VARIABLES

Visual Basic gives you a lot of flexibility in naming variables, but there are some rules to follow. Here they are:

- A variable name cannot be more than 256 characters long (up from 40 characters in Visual Basic 3).
- The only characters you can use are letters, digits, and the underscore (_) character.
- The first character in a name must be a letter.
- The name cannot be a keyword, that is, a word built into the language, such as *Sub, Beep,* or *End.* However, a name can contain a keyword, so *Beepman* and *Submarine* and even *EndBeep* are valid names.

Table L5-1 shows some examples of valid and invalid names.

VALID	INVALID
PrettyByte	ThisOneIsNotTooLongToBeAValidVi$ualBasicNameButStillIsInvalid
Cre8	4ever
See_more	_Seymour
BeepEnd	Beep

Table L5-1 Valid and invalid names for variables

The reason for allowing so many characters is to encourage you to choose self-explanatory names. For instance, use *YearBought* and *YearSold* rather than *Y1* and *Y2*. Visual Basic doesn't discriminate between uppercase and lowercase. That is, *WhyNot*, *whynot*, and *WHYNOT* all are considered to be the same name. However, the usual custom is to capitalize the first letter of each word in a name. This makes it easier to read. For instance, *YearsOld* suggests a different meaning from *YearSold*. However, because Visual Basic ignores cases in names, *YearsOld* and *YearSold* are the same name, and they represent the same variable. If you really need both versions, you can use the underscore to clarify the names. That is, you can create one variable called *Years_Old* and a second variable called *Year_Sold*.

Creating Variables the Easy Way—Implicit Declarations

Visual Basic offers you two ways to create variables—*implicit* declarations and *explicit* declarations. Implicit means something you do implies that the variable exists. More exactly, the implicit way is to assign a value to the variable. The implicit way is easier, and we'll start with it. However, the explicit way is more reliable, and it's the one the rest of the book will use. To see how the implicit way works, first create a form with a command button according to Table L5-2. Place the command button in the upper-right corner of the form.

OBJECT	PROPERTY	SETTING
Form1	Caption	Variables
	Font.Size	12
	Name	frmVariables
Command1	Caption	Show &Area
	Name	cmdShowArea

Table L5-2 Properties for the Variables program

The goal is to create a command button that calculates and displays the area of the form. That requires a bit of Visual Basic code. Select the command button and use the Code window to edit the *Click* event as follows:

```
Private Sub cmdShowArea_Click ()
    Area = frmVariables.Height * frmVariables.Width
    Print "The area of the form in square twips is"
    Print Area
End Sub
```

This code has some new elements, so let's look at it step-by-step.

How do you find the area of a rectangle? This is where we get to use an algorithm. An algorithm (see Lesson 1), remember, is a recipe to accomplish a particular goal. (An algorithm is not what Al Gore beats out on the bongo drums.) Here the goal is to calculate the area of a rectangular shape, and the recipe is that you multiply the rectangle's height times its width. The Height and Width properties of the frmVariables form give the form's dimensions (in twips), and the * is the Visual Basic symbol for multiplication. So the expression *frmVariables.Height * frmVariables.Width* represents the value of the area. *Area* is a new variable that we created by naming it and assigning it a value. So at this point *Area* is a variable whose value is the area of the form.

Print is a Visual Basic method. It's the standard command for displaying text. In the days of DOS-based Basic, the *Print* statement displayed text on the screen. In Visual Basic, the *Print* method displays text directly on the form. The first *Print* statement prints a string. The second *Print* statement prints the value of the variable *Area*. The fact that the word *Area* is not in quotes tells the program that it is a variable name, not a string. Each *Print* statement prints on its own line, so this procedure prints two lines.

The *Print* Method and Forms

Methods, recall, are invoked by objects. Because *Print* is a method, it should be invoked by a particular object. Logically, you should use statements like this:

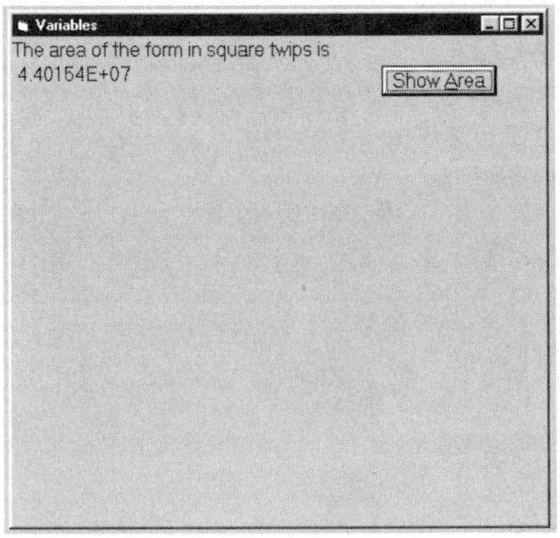

Figure L5-1 Showing the area

```
frmVariables.Print Area
```

However, if you just use *Print,* Visual Basic assumes the invoking object is the form whose Code window contains the code.

It's time to try this puppy out. Run the program and click on the button. You should see something like Figure L5-1. Now, while the program is running, use the mouse to grab the lower-right corner of the form. Resize the form, making sure the command button is still visible, and click the button again. This time the program should report the new area of the form, as shown in Figure L5-2.

What should you notice? For one thing, the output is in a larger font than the form's name in the title bar. That's because all the font properties for a form apply to text displayed in the form but *not* to the title bar. So setting Font.Size to 12 affects the *Print* statement output, but not the title bar. With Visual Basic 4 (but not with earlier versions), font-related settings for a form also become the default settings for any controls you subsequently add to the form. However, controls added before you change the form font settings are unaffected.

Second, clicking the Show Area button again doesn't replace the old text. Instead, it adds two additional lines of text. This kind of line-by-line output is a bit like using a typewriter with an automatic carriage-return feature. Each *Print* statement returns to the beginning of the next line upon completion.

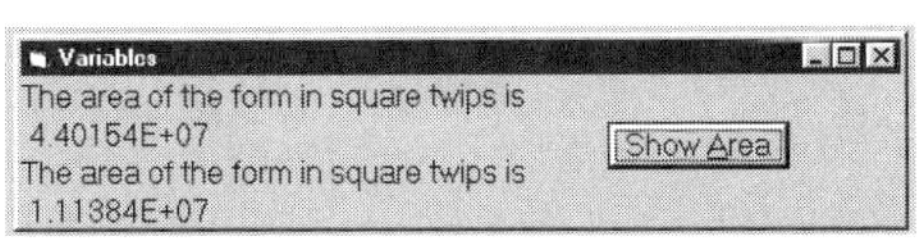

Figure L5-2 Showing the new area

Scientific Notation

If you're not familiar with how computers often express large numbers, you may be a bit taken aback by the value 4.40154E+07. This notation is an adaptation of something called *scientific notation*. The E+07 stands for 10^7, which means the product of 7 10s, or 10,000,000. So the actual value is 4.40154 times 10,000,000, or 44,015,400. (That's a lot of square twips, but a square twip, besides sounding silly, is pretty small.) You can think of E+07 as meaning, "move the decimal point 7 places to the right." Similarly, E-05 means, "move the decimal point 5 places to the left." Thus, 3.45E-05 is 0.0000345.

Problems with the Easy Way

Creating a variable just by using it is easy enough. In fact, it is too easy. Modify the button code so it looks like the following (including the typo *Arae*):

```
Private Sub cmdShowArea_Click ()
    Area = frmVariables.Height * frmVariables.Width
    Print "The area of the form in square twips is"
    Print Area
    Print "Repeat, the area is"; Arae
End Sub
```

The semicolon in the final *Print* statement lets you print a list of items on the same line. So it should print the area on the same line as the string "Repeat, the area is". However, running this version of the program produces output like the following:

```
The area of the form in square twips is
 4.65412E+07
Repeat, the area is
```

The problem is that the code misspells *Area* as *Arae*, so Visual Basic treats *Arae* as a brand-new variable. The program doesn't assign a value to that variable, so nothing is displayed when *Arae* is printed. The way around this kind of problem is to first supply a list of all the variables that you'll use so that the program can check if any unauthorized variables have crept in. Listing a variable in this fashion is called an *explicit declaration;* let's see how the process works.

Explicit Declarations

An explicit declaration announces a name to be a variable before the variable is used. In Visual Basic, you use the keyword *Dim* at the beginning of a procedure to declare variables. For example, here's how to declare the *Area* variable explicitly in the button click procedure:

```
Public Sub cmdShowArea_Click ()
    Dim Area
    Area = frmVariables.Height * frmVariables.Width
    Print "The area of the form in square twips is"
```

```
     Print Area
      Print "Repeat, the area is"; Arae
End Sub
```

The statement

```
Dim Area
```

is called a *declaration* because it declares, or announces, that you intend to use the word *Area* as a variable name.

Historic Note

The word *Dim* seems like an odd choice for this task. It's a relic from the old days of Basic when *Dim* was used to create arrays, data forms that can hold a list of values. *Dimensioning* an array meant declaring how many items it could hold. At that time, arrays were the only variable form you declared. When Basic extended declarations to ordinary variables, it co-opted the *Dim* keyword for the task.

To avoid the misspelled variable name problem, it's not enough to declare a variable explicitly. You also have to tell Visual Basic that you will honor only explicitly declared variables. The way to do this is to include the command *Option Explicit* in your program. You must place this command in a very special place called the Declarations section. This section is the very beginning of the Code window before any procedures are defined. So go to the Code window, select General from the Object box and Declarations from the Procedure box, and enter the *Option Explicit* statement. Your Code window should look like this now:

```
Option Explicit
Private Sub cmdShowArea_Click()
     Dim Area
     Area = frmVariables.Height * frmVariables.Width
     Print "The area of the form in square twips is"
     Print Area
     Print "Repeat, the area is"; Arae
End Sub
```

Next, try running the program with *Arae* still misspelled. This time, because only *Area* is declared and *Arae* isn't, Visual Basic displays a box exclaiming "Variable not defined!" Also, Visual Basic highlights the offending *Arae* in the code. Now that the error is obvious, you can correct the spelling to *Area*, and the program will work as expected.

Tip

Use *Option Explicit* and declare your variables to help make your Visual Basic programs more error-free. This bit of advice can save considerable debugging effort as your programs grow.

In short, using *Option Explicit* can help you catch errors. Microsoft recommends that you use this option in all your programming. To back up this advice, Visual Basic makes it possible to have *Option Explicit* added automatically to any new forms you create. To do so, first choose Environment from the Tools menu. Then select the Require Variable Declaration option in the dialog box and enter or select the word Yes. Thenceforth, Visual Basic will add *Option Explicit* to new forms automatically. However, it won't alter old existing forms. Those you would have to handle manually. The rest of this book will assume that you've taken the *Option Explicit* road.

Tip

Use the Environment dialog box from the Tools menu to set Require Variable Declaration to Yes. This causes Visual Basic to require you to declare all variables, which is a good idea.

Where's the Variable?

By default, a variable that you create in a procedure is *local* to that procedure. That means other procedures don't know about the variable. If you declare two variables of the same name in two procedures, then they are two separate variables independent of each other, much like Springfield in Ohio is independent of Springfield in Illinois. But a variable that you create on the module level (for example, in the Declarations section) is a *module-level* variable that can appear in any of the procedures defined in the module (see Figure L5-3). Let's experiment with these concepts.

First, create a module-level variable called *Diameter* by declaring it in the Declarations section just after the *Option Explicit* command. The Code window now should look like the following:

```
Option Explicit
Dim Diameter    ' module-level variable
Private Sub cmdShowArea_Click()
    Dim Area
    Area = frmVariables.Height * frmVariables.Width
    Print "The area of the form in square twips is"
    Print Area
    Print "Repeat, the area is"; Area
End Sub
```

The *Diameter* variable is available to all procedures in this module, while *Area* is available just to *cmdShowArea_Click()*.

Next, let's create a couple of controls that can share the *Diameter* variable. Create the objects described in Table L5-3 and arrange them to look like Figure L5-4.

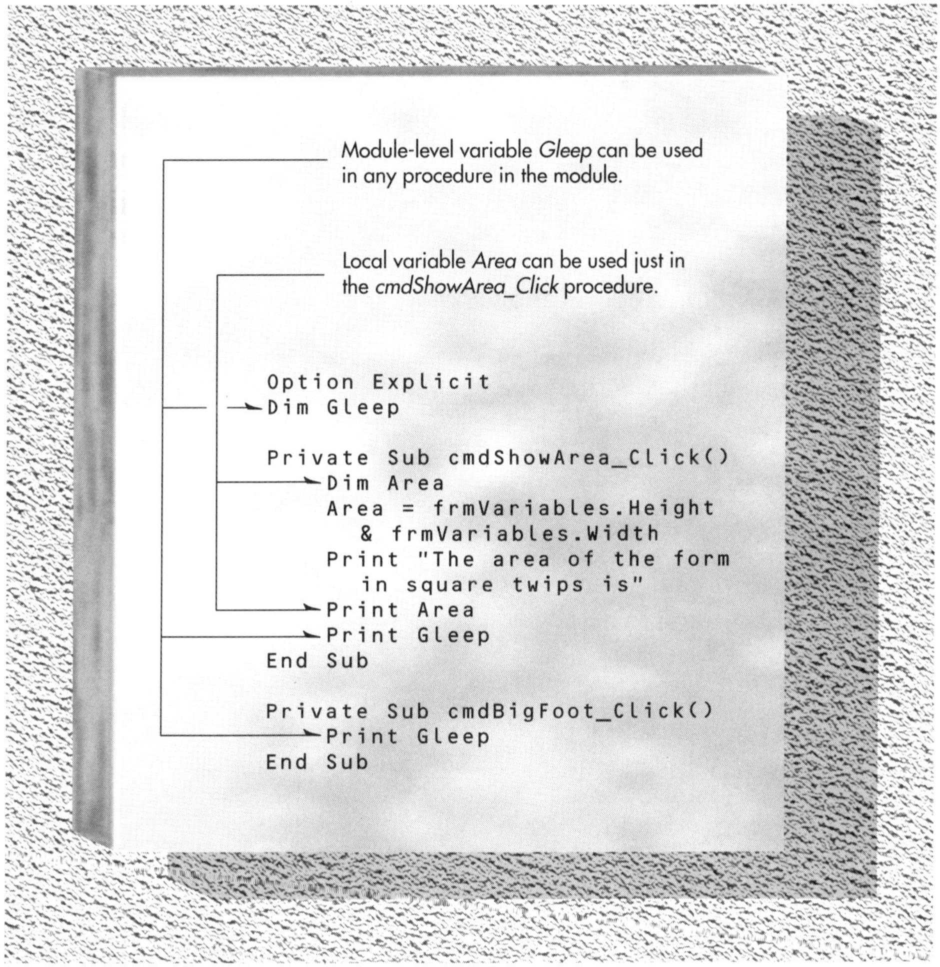

Figure L5-3 Module-level and local variables

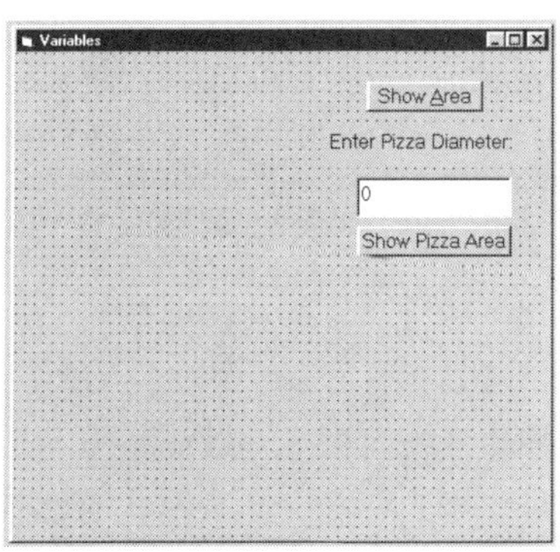

Figure L5-4 The revised form

OBJECT	PROPERTY	SETTING
Label1	Caption	Enter Pizza Diameter:
	Name	lblInstruct
Text1	Name	txtPizzaDiameter
	Text	0
Command1	Caption	Show Pizza Area
	Name	cmdPizzaArea

Table L5-3 Properties for the Variables program

We'll use the text control to set the value of the *Diameter* variable and let the new command button use the value. You can do this by adding the following event procedures to the Code window:

```
Private Sub txtPizzaDiameter_Change()
    Diameter = txtPizzaDiameter.Text
End Sub

Private Sub cmdPizzaArea_Click()
    Dim Area        ' local variable
    Area = 3.14159 * Diameter * Diameter / 4
    Print "Area = "; Area
End Sub
```

If you type a new number into the text box, that triggers the *Change* event, which sets the module-level variable *Diameter* to the new number. When you click on the new button, it triggers the *Click* event, and the event procedure uses *Diameter* to calculate the area of the pizza. (You'll find the formula in Euclido's *Handbook of Pizzametry*.) Try it. You'll like it.

Incidentally, please note that the program now has two independent *Area* variables. If you click the Show Area button, the program uses the *Area* defined in the *cmdShowArea_Click* procedure. But if you use the Show Pizza Area button, the program uses the *Area* defined in the *cmdPizzaArea_Click* procedure.

Duration

Another difference between module-level variables and local variables is in how long they remain in memory. A module-level variable in a form remains in memory until the form is terminated, which happens when you end the program. A local variable remains in memory only while the procedure using it is executing.

You Can, but Should You?

You may be delighted that using a module-level variable lets you share information among procedures, but the hard-earned lesson of years of software engineering is that it's usually better to stick to local variables. The problem is that shared variables open the way to hard-to-find errors in large programs. Suppose, for example, that you add a command button to the Variables form that deals with the diameters of coins and that you have code like this:

```
Private Sub cmdDime_Click( )
    Diameter = 18
    ....
End Sub
```

Because *Diameter* is module-level, this statement also makes the program think the pizza diameter is 18, too, even though the text box setting remains unchanged. The larger the program, the greater the chances are that you'll inadvertently reuse a module-level name for something else and thus mysteriously alter the module-level variable.

Incidentally, you can have local and module-level variables with the same name. For example, you can replace the previous code with this:

```
Private Sub cmdDime_Click( )
    Dim Diameter
    Diameter = 18
    ....
End Sub
```

The local definition hides the module-level definition inside the procedure. That means the program will use the local *Diameter* when executing the *cmdDime_Click()* procedure and the module-level *Diameter* elsewhere. Nonetheless, using the same name this way is a bad idea. First, it may be confusing to anyone reading your program. Second, if you forget to declare the local variable, you wind up using the module-level variable instead.

Tip

Don't use the same name for both a module-level and local-level variable. It's legal, and the local definition overrides the module-level definition. Nonetheless, it can lead to confusion.

Usually, try to avoid using module-level variables. For instance, the example had this code:

```
Dim Diameter
Private Sub txtPizzaDiameter_Change()
    Diameter = txtPizzaDiameter.Text
End Sub

Private Sub cmdPizzaArea_Click()
    Dim Area
    Area = 3.14159 * Diameter * Diameter / 4
    Print "Area = "; Area
End Sub
```

You can replace the module-level variable with a local one and do this:

```
Private Sub cmdPizzaArea_Click()
```

continued on next page

continued from previous page

```
    Dim Area
    Dim Diameter
    Diameter = txtPizzaDiameter.Text
    Area = 3.14159 * Diameter * Diameter / 4
    Print "Area = "; Area
End Sub
```

Or, in this case, you can dispense with the variable entirely and just use the expression *txtPizzaDiameter.Text*:

```
Area = 3.14159 * txtPizzaDiameter.Text * txtPizzaDiameter.Text / 4
```

However, that makes the code a little harder to read.

KINDS OF DATA

Just what kinds of data can you store in a variable? Let's take an experimental approach and add the controls described in Table L5-4. (They follow just as logically from the pizza set of controls as the pizza controls followed from the original area button. Incidentally, programming in this grab bag fashion may prepare you for a career in marketing.) Place the new controls under the existing controls, as shown in Figure L5-5. Then we can experiment by trying to enter various kinds of data.

OBJECT	PROPERTY	SETTING
Label1	Caption	Enter Meal Cost:
	Name	lblMeal
Text1	Name	txtMeal
	Text	
Command1	Caption	Add Tip and Tax
	Name	cmdMeal

Table L5-4 More properties for the Variables program

The plan is that you will enter the cost of a meal in the text box and that clicking on the cmdMeal button will display the total cost after adding in tip and tax. To accomplish this, add the following *Click* procedure:

```
Private Sub cmdMeal_Click()
    Dim Before, After
    Before = txtMeal.Text
    Print "Total bill for "; Before;
    After = 1.22 * Before
    Print " is"; After
End Sub
```

As you can see, this code sets the *Before* variable to the text box input, which represents the initial cost of the meal. Then the event uses *Before* to calculate the

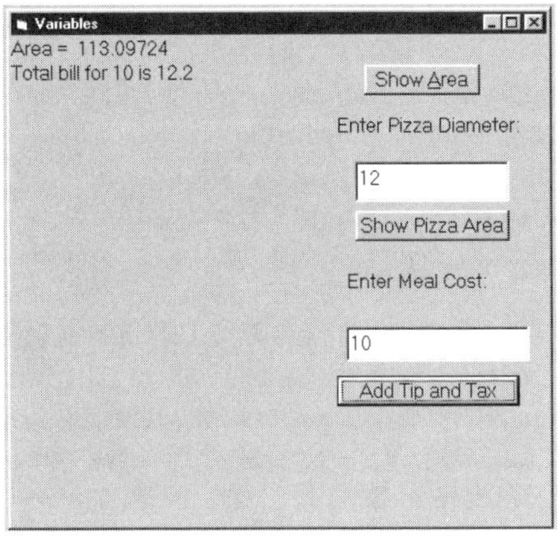

Figure L5-5 Using the program properly

value of the *After* variable. The procedure assumes that tax and tip together total 22% of the bill. The procedure then displays the result in the form window.

Once you've got the program ready, run it and enter a meal cost of 10. Clicking on the cmdMeal button then should produce a form looking like that shown in Figure L5-5.

That example used the program as intended. But now try confounding the program by responding inappropriately, entering *Too Much!* as the cost. This time you get results like that shown in Figure L5-6. (Actually, we cheated a bit by sliding the error message window over so that you can see the program output.).

What's this "Run-time error '13'" message about? The box tells us there is a type mismatch. To get more information, click on the Debug choice. This activates the

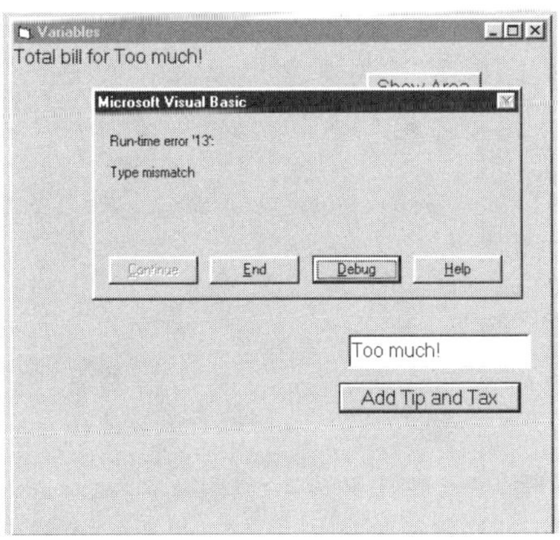

Figure L5-6 Using the program improperly

Visual Basic Debug facility, which highlights the problem by showing the offending line of code in the Code window (see Figure L5-7).

The error dialog box shown in Figure L5-6 gives two options other than Debug. Clicking on End terminates the program, and clicking on Help displays a Help window discussing the error you encountered. For instance, in this case, you'd get a description of Error 13—what the error is and some possible causes.

The first interesting point here is that the *Before* variable was able to hold a number (*10*) the first time and a string ("*Too Much!*") the second time. You can tell it held the string because the program printed the phrase "Total bill for Too Much!". The second interesting point is that the computer loved (or, at least, accepted) *1.22 * Before* when *Before* was *10* but hated *1.22 * Before* when *Before* was "*Too Much!*". Well, that's reasonable. Multiplying 10 by 1.22 makes sense (1220 cents, in fact), but multiplying a phrase by 1.22 is meaningless. The lesson here is that Visual Basic distinguishes among different kinds of data. You can do things to numbers that you can't do to strings, and vice versa. Visual Basic protests, as you just saw, if you attempt to do something unseemly with a particular kind of data.

Actually, most computer languages distinguish among different kinds of data. What's a bit unusual about Visual Basic is that it *doesn't* make you use separate types of variables for separate types of data. That is, most languages would have one type of variable that can just hold integers, another type that can just hold strings, and another type that can just hold numbers with fractional parts.

Although Visual Basic doesn't make you use different kinds of variables, it does give you that option. The most general type is also the default type, and it's called the *Variant* type because it can deal with a variety of data forms. If you have a *Variant* type variable, you can assign a variety of number types as well as strings. You pay a price for this convenience, however, for using a *Variant* type may be less efficient than using a type tailored to a specific need. For instance, if your program uses *Variant* variables for doing mortgage calculations, it will

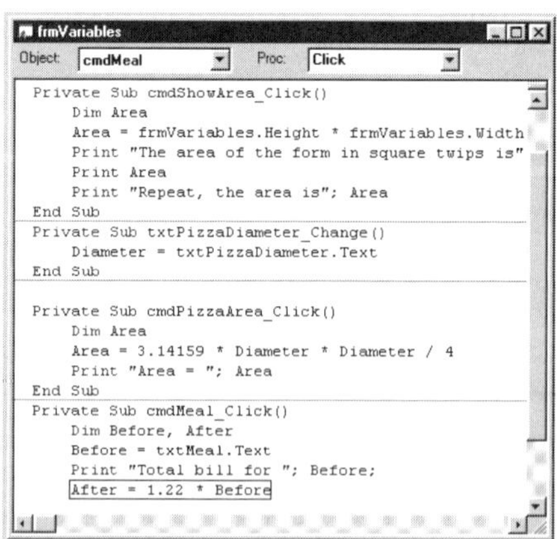

Figure L5-7 The problem

have to waste time converting the values to regular numbers when doing the calculations. You'd be better off using a type designed to hold just numbers. Or if you need to store, say, 100 numerical values, your program may require less memory storage if you store them as numbers rather than as *Variant* values.

The *Variant* Type

When you create a variable without saying what type it is, Visual Basic makes it a type *Variant* variable. That means it can hold a variety of kinds of information, such as numbers or strings. This versatility makes the *Variant* type convenient, but typically it is less efficient than a more specialized type of variable.

VISUAL BASIC'S FUNDAMENTAL TYPES

Because you often are better off using specialized data types instead of the default *Variant* type, let's survey the data types Visual Basic offers you. First, a *data type* is defined by two things:

- The kind of information stored in the computer
- The operations you can perform on it

Consider information. A string variable has to store a series of characters, while an integer variable has to store a single integer. Consider operations. You can add and multiply integers. You can search strings for particular substrings, such as looking for *oslo* in *Czechoslovakia*. (Oslo's in Norway? Czechoslovakia no longer exists? Both true, but the word "Czechoslovakia" still exists, and it still has the substring "oslo" in its middle.)

Visual Basic provided many built-in data types, known as *intrinsic types*, or *fundamental types*. Some types hold integers, others hold floating-point numbers, which are numbers with fractional parts. One type specializes in currency values. Another type holds logical values (True and False). Yet another holds strings. Appendix D summarizes these and other intrinsic types. For now, however, let's look at two types—*Integer* and *String*—to illustrate how data types work.

The *Integer* Type

Integers are whole numbers, and they are the most natural type of data for computers. Just as you can count by integers using your fingers, computers can count by integers using their memory bits. (Appendixes A and B can satisfy your curiosity about how that's done.) The amount of computer memory a computer uses to store an integer determines the upper limit for how big that number can be. Visual Basic uses 2 bytes to hold an *Integer* type, and that limits the integers to the range –32,768 to +32,767. So if you need to work with integers in that range, use the *Integer* type.

The way to make a type *Integer* variable is this:

```
Dim Marbles as Integer
```

This statement creates a variable named *Marbles*. This variable can be used to hold any integer in the range –32,768 to +32,767. It can't be used to hold your name, unless you go by something like 24812.

More generally, you can use the *as* mechanism for any of the intrinsic types. For instance,

```
Dim WorkMore as Boolean
```

makes *WorkMore* a *Boolean* variable, one that can be set to True or False.

The *Boolean* Type

The English mathematician George Boole demonstrated that problems in logic can be represented and solved with mathematics. Usually, mathematical expressions, such as 2 + 3, evaluate to a numerical value. But logical expressions, such as the statement "All Martians have four eyes," have a value of True or False. The *Boolean* type, named after George Boole, represents quantities that can be true or false. Several Visual Basic properties, such as the Visible property, use *Boolean* values.

Once you have an integer or two, what can you do with them? Visual Basic recognizes the following operations for integers:

+	(addition)
–	(subtraction)
-	(negation)
*	(multiplication)
\	(integer division)
/	(floating-point division)
Mod	(finding the remainder)
^	(exponentiation)

In short, you can do arithmetic.

You probably recognize addition, subtraction, and multiplication. Negation means changing the sign of a value. For instance, if *Marbles* is 58, then –*Marbles* is –58. Visual Basic has two kinds of division for integers. Integer division truncates the answer to an integer by dropping the fractional part, while floating-point division includes the fractional part, if any. For instance, 13 / 5 is 2.6, while 13 \ 5 is truncated to 2. The *Mod* operation shows the remainder that results from dividing the first number by the second. For instance, 13 Mod 5 is 3, since 5 goes into 13 twice with a remainder of 3 (see Figure L5-8). Integer

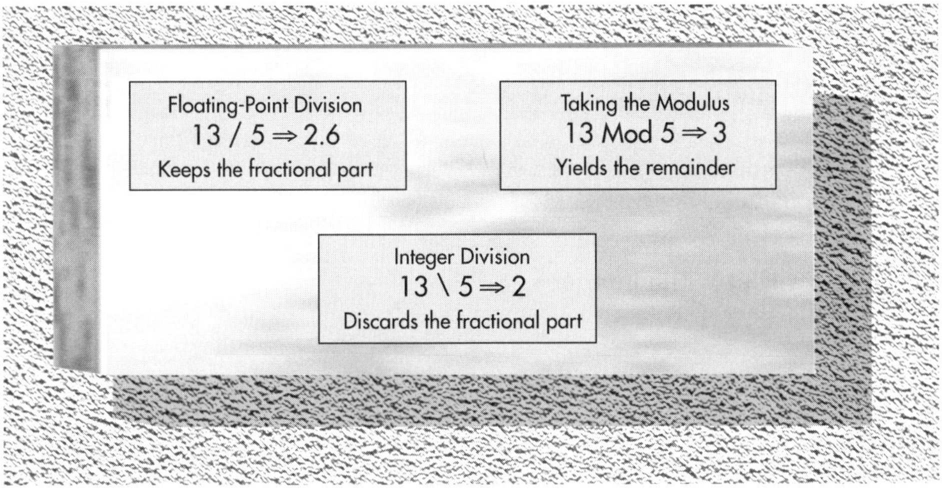

Figure L5-8 Floating-point division, integer division, and taking the modulus

division and taking the modulus are useful for dividing things that only come in whole units. For instance, if you deal out a deck of 52 cards to five people, you can use \ and Mod to compute that each person gets 10 cards, with 2 cards left over.

The exponentiation operator raises a number to a power. For example, 2^5 means 2^5, or 2 x 2 x 2 x 2 x 2, which is 32. A number to a negative exponent is the inverse of the number to a positive exponent. For instance, 2^–5 is 2^{-5}, or $1/2^5$, or 1/32.

An *Integer* Example

Let's look at an example that uses the *Integer* data type and integer operations. You can build a simple calculator for simple arithmetic. Lay out a form as shown in Figure L5-9.

Set the properties as shown in Table L5-5, resizing controls as necessary. When you finish, the form should look similar to Figure L5-10. Note that the

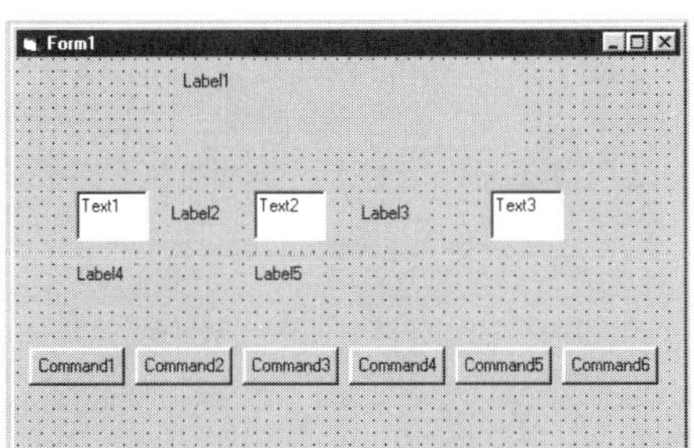

Figure L5-9 Initial form layout

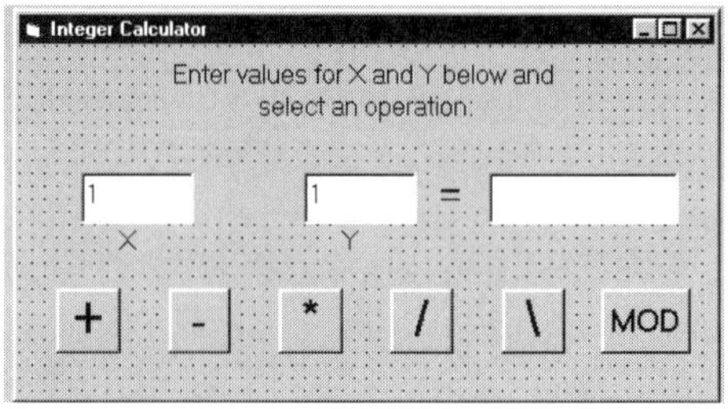

Figure L5-10 The Integer Calculator form

txtAns text box has its Locked property set to True. That means you can't type new text in the box while the program is running. You still can change the text property in the Properties window or by using txtAns.Text in code, however. Earlier versions of Visual Basic called this property ReadOnly instead of Locked. You could use a label instead of a locked text box, but the locked text box matches the two input text boxes in appearance.

OBJECT	PROPERTY	SETTING
Form1	Caption	Integer Calculator
	Name	frmInt
Label1	Alignment	2 - Center
	Caption	Enter values for X and Y below and select
		an operation:
	Font.Size	12
	Name	lblInst
Label2	Alignment	2 - center
	Caption	
	Font.Size	18
	Name	lblOperation
Label3	Caption	=
	Font.Size	18
	Name	lblEqual
Label4	Caption	X
	Font.Size	18
	Name	lblX
Label5	Caption	Y
	Font.Size	18
	Name	lblY
Text1	Name	txtX
	Text	1
Text2	Name	txtY
	Text	1

OBJECT	PROPERTY	SETTING
Text3	Font.Bold	True
	Font.Size	14
	Locked	True
	Name	txtAns
	Text	
Command1	Caption	+
	Font.Size	24
	Name	cmdAdd
Command2	Caption	–
	Font.Size	24
	Name	cmdSub
Command3	Caption	*
	Font.Size	24
	Name	cmdMult
Command4	Caption	/
	Font.Size	24
	Name	cmdDivFloat
Command5	Caption	\
	Font.Size	24
	Name	cmdDivInt
Command6	Caption	MOD
	Font.Size	18
	Name	cmdMod

Table L5-5 Properties for the Integer Calculator program

The next step is to provide *Click* events for the six command buttons. This is the approach we'll use for each operation:

1. Create two integer variables.
2. Assign the value of the first text box to the first variable.
3. Assign the value of the second text box to the second variable.
4. Set the lblOperation caption to the symbol for the selected operation.
5. Set the txtAns text to the result of the calculation.

For example, provide the following code for the cmdAdd button:

```
Private Sub cmdAdd_Click()
    Dim X As Integer
    Dim Y As Integer
    X = txtX.Text
    Y = txtY.Text
    lblOperation.Caption = "+"
    txtAns.Text = X + Y
End Sub
```

Actually, this could be done just by adding the Text properties directly instead of using the *X* and *Y* variables, but this way we get practice with variables. You can handle the other operations similarly. Listing L5-1 shows the complete code for the program. Notice that each event procedure has its own local *X* and *Y* variables. Also, when you change the contents of the txtX or txtY boxes, the program uses *Change* events to clear the operator box and answer box, making the form ready for a new set of operations with the new data.

Listing L5-1
The Integer Calculator code

```
Option Explicit

Private Sub cmdAdd_Click()
     Dim X As Integer
     Dim Y As Integer
     X = txtX.Text
     Y = txtY.Text
     lblOperation.Caption = "+"
     txtAns.Text = X + Y
End Sub

Private Sub cmdDivFloat_Click()
     Dim X As Integer
     Dim Y As Integer
     X = txtX.Text
     Y = txtY.Text
     lblOperation.Caption = "/"
     txtAns.Text = X / Y
End Sub

Private Sub cmdDivInt_Click()
     Dim X As Integer
     Dim Y As Integer
     X = txtX.Text
     Y = txtY.Text
     lblOperation.Caption = "\"
     txtAns.Text = X \ Y
End Sub

Private Sub cmdMinus_Click()
     Dim X As Integer
     Dim Y As Integer
     X = txtX.Text
     Y = txtY.Text
     lblOperation.Caption = "-"
     txtAns.Text = X - Y
End Sub

Private Sub cmdMod_Click()
     Dim X As Integer
     Dim Y As Integer
     X = txtX.Text
     Y = txtY.Text
     lblOperation.Caption = "MOD"
```

```
    txtAns.Text = X Mod Y
End Sub

Private Sub cmdMult_Click()
    Dim X As Integer
    Dim Y As Integer
    X = txtX.Text
    Y = txtY.Text
    lblOperation.Caption = "*"
    txtAns.Text = X * Y
End Sub
' Clear operator box and answer box when numbers are changed.
Private Sub txtX_Change()
    lblOperation.Caption = ""
    txtAns.Text = ""
End Sub

Private Sub txtY_Change()
    lblOperation.Caption = ""
    txtAns.Text = ""
End Sub
```

You can create these procedures faster by using Visual Basic's copy and paste editing features. For instance, copy the code for *cmdAdd_Click*, paste it into the *cmdSub_Click* procedure, and then edit a couple of lines.

Now you can use the form to see how the integer operations work. Figure L5-11 shows an example of the program in action.

Here are some other sample results:

```
29 \ 7 = 4
29 / 7 = 4.142857
29 Mod 7 = 1
```

As described, integer division (\) rounds to the nearest integer. Floating-point division gives a 7-digit answer. The MOD operator gives the remainder.

Integer Mishaps

What happens if you feed the program faulty values? For instance, enter a floating-point number instead of an integer:

```
12.6 / 2 = 6.5
```

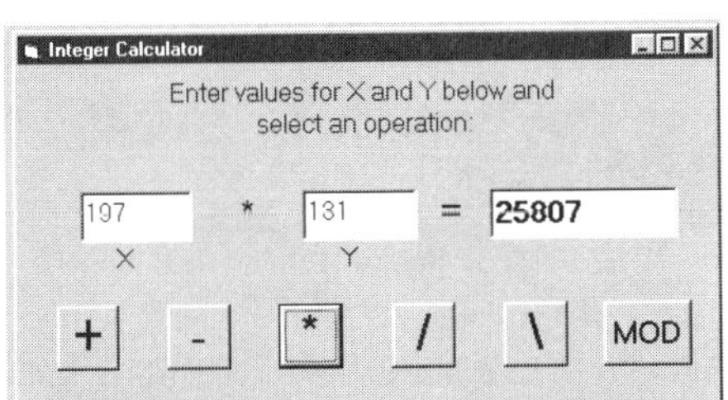

Figure L5-11 Integer Calculator at work

This doesn't look like good arithmetic! What has happened is that Visual Basic tries to accommodate you by converting data from one type to another, if feasible. Here, for instance, Visual Basic rounded the noninteger 12.6 value to the integer value of 13 when assigning it to the *X* variable, and 13 / 2 is 6.5. Note that the *txtX.text* property has no problem holding 12.6. That's because the text property is a string type. That is, it stores the number as the string "12.6". The conversion from string to integer takes place when *X* is set:

```
X = txtX.text
```

Truncating and Rounding

When doing integer division, Visual Basic *truncates* the answer. That means it discards the fractional part, whether it be 0.1 or 0.9. So 99 / 10 is 9.9, but 99 \ 10 is 9, with the .9 part truncated. When converting a noninteger number to an integer, however, Visual Basic rounds the answer. That means it converts the number to the nearest integer. So, if X is an Integer variable, then

X = 9.9

results in 9.9 being rounded to 10.

Next, try spelling out a number, entering, say, "ten" instead of "10". You get an error message like the following:

```
Run-time error '13'
Type mismatch
```

Although Visual Basic finds the conversion of a floating-point number to an integer obvious, it doesn't convert words to integers. Again the problem is with *X*, which is type *Integer*, and not with the *txtX.text* property (see Figure L5-12).

Now try multiplying 2000 by 500. You'll get a dialog box with the following message:

```
Run-time error '6'
Overflow
```

This is Visual Basic's response to the fact that 2000 * 500 is 1,000,000, which is bigger that the largest possible *Integer* value, which is 32,767. You'll get the same message if you enter a number outside the *Integer* range and attempt to use it.

Operator Precedence

Suppose you use more than one operator in an expression, as in the following:

```
InchHeight = Inches + 12 * Feet
```

Visual Basic needs a way to decide whether to do the addition first or the multiplication first, for the order makes a difference. For example, suppose *Inches* is 7 and *Feet* is 6. If you add before multiplying, you get the following:

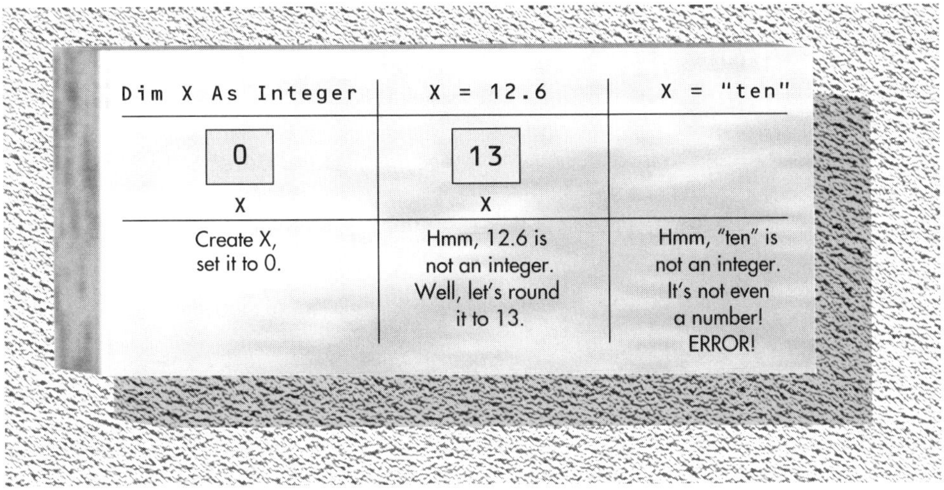

Figure L5-12 Adventures in *Integer* assignment

```
(7 + 12) * 6 = 19 * 6 = 114
```

If you multiply first, you get this:

```
7 + (12 * 6) = 7 + 72 = 79
```

Fortunately, Visual Basic has some simple rules. Multiplication, division, and taking the modulus are done before addition and subtraction. Table L5-6 shows the order of precedence for all the arithmetic operators. If two operators have the same precedence, they are used in left-to-right order. However, expressions within parentheses are evaluated first, so you can use parentheses to force the order you want. These points are illustrated in the following examples

```
7 + 12 * 6 = 7 + 72 = 89
12 * 8 / 4 = 96 / 4 = 24
144 / 4 * 3 - 36 ^ 3 = 108
144 / ( 4 * 3) = 144 / 12 = 12
2^5 + 3 = 32 + 3 = 35
2^(5 + 3) = 2^8 = 256
```

OPERATOR	MEANING
^	Exponentiation
-	Negation
*, /	Multiplication, division
\	Integer division
Mod	Modulus
+, -	Addition, subtraction

Table L5-6 Arithmetic Operators in order of decreasing precedence

Other Numeric Types

Visual Basic supports two other integer types. The *Byte* type, as its name suggests, uses just one byte of memory. A *Byte* variable can hold integers in the range 0–255. The *Long* type uses 4 bytes of memory and can store integers in the range from –2,147,483,648 to 2,147,483,647. You can use the *Byte* type to save memory if you're dealing with small values. You can use the *Long* type if you need integers larger than *Integer* can cope with. You can use *Dim* to create variables of these types:

```
Dim Toes As Byte         ' Create a Byte variable.
Dim MyVirtues As Long    ' Create a Long variable.
```

Visual Basic also provides two *floating-point* types, which support fractional values. The *Single* type uses 4 bytes of memory and offers 7 digits of precision. The *Double* type uses 8 bytes of memory and offers about 15 digits of precision:

```
Dim BattingAverage As Single      ' Create a Single variable.
Dim Distance As Double            ' Create a Double variable.
```

Floating-point numbers can be written two ways. The first way, called *fixed notation,* is the usual decimal-point notation, as in the following:

```
BattingAverage = 0.302
Distance = 1524835.94
```

Incidentally, notice that *Distance* uses 9 digits, all of them significant. If *Distance* had been *Single* instead of *Double,* the number would wind up rounded to the nearest 7 significant digits, or to 1524836.00.

The second way is to use scientific notation, as described earlier in this lesson:

```
Distance = 3.4E07    ' a distance of 34 million
```

Floating-point numbers cover a much larger range in values than do integers. For example, type *Single* values can range from about 1.4E-45 to 3.4E38, either positive or negative. A *Single* value also can be 0, but the 1.4E-45 represents the smallest nonzero positive value. Similarly, the *Double* range is from about 4.9E-324 to 1.8E308. (The latter number completely dwarfs the number of atoms in the known universe.)

Visual Basic also has a *Currency* type that's sort of a cross between integer and floating-point types. It supports up to 11 digits to the left of the decimal point and 4 digits to the right. Anything beyond the fourth decimal place is rounded. For example, consider the following:

```
Dim Debt as Currency
Dim Share as Currency
Debt = 200.00
Share = Debt / 3
```

Share will be exactly 66.6667. That is, if the units are dollars, then amounts are rounded to the nearest hundredth of a cent. If you take the currency unit to be 100 dollars, then calculations are rounded to the nearest cent.

The *String* Type

The *String* type is handy because any series of characters is a string. So "Hoopla", "That darn wombat", and "Zx$&72!!@ my foot" all are strings. Conceptually, a string is stored as a series of characters, one character to a byte. In practice, the computer stores numbers in binary form, so each character is represented by a numeric code called the ASCII code. For example, the number 65 represents the character A, 66 represents B, and so on. (Appendix C summarizes the code.) Thus, the computer really stores a series of 1-byte numeric codes, each code representing a character in the string (see Figure L5-13).

Note that the string "24282" is not the same as the integer 24282. The integer is stored as a number. In particular, it's stored as the 2-byte binary representation of that number. The string "24282", however, is stored as a sequence of five characters. More exactly, it's stored as the character code for the "2" character followed by the code for the "4" character, and so on. Visual Basic, however, is unusually forgiving for a computer language. While it rejects expressions like 2 * "moose", it accepts 2 * "128" and converts the string "128" to the integer 128 automatically.

Visual Basic has a host of facilities for strings, which Lesson 14 explores more fully. In the meantime, let's look at a simple example using strings.

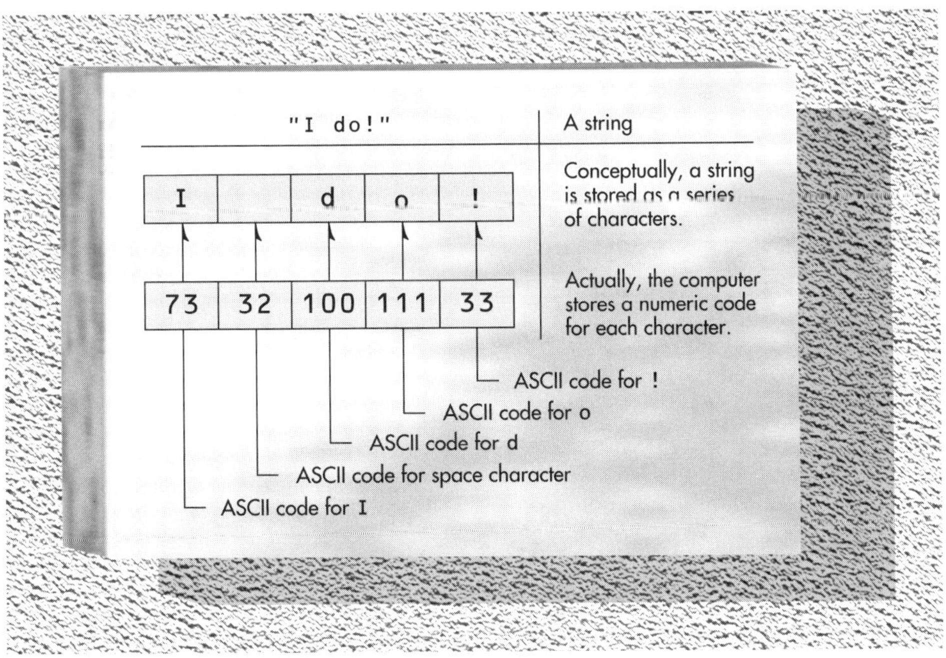

Figure L5-13 Storing a string in memory

Pigs of Doom—Developing an Interface

You're developing the opening screen for your Pigs of Doom game project. You want it to request the player's name and to make a suitable response. Both the name and the response are strings, so here's an opportunity to use String variables. Keeping things simple, create a new form as described by Table L5-7 and Figure L5-14.

OBJECT	PROPERTY	SETTING
Form1	Caption	Pigs of Doom
	Name	frmPigDoom
Label1	Caption	Enter your name:
	Font.Size	12
	Name	lblInstruct
Text1	Font.Size	12
	Name	txtName
	Text	
Text2	BackColor	&H8000000F& (gray)
	BorderStyle	0 - None
	Font.Size	12
	Locked	True
	MultiLine	True
	Name	txtBlurb
	Text	Then click here.

Table L5-7 Properties for the Pigs of Doom program

Setting the Locked property for txtBlurb means that the user can read the text in the box but can't type in new text. However, as you'll see, the program itself

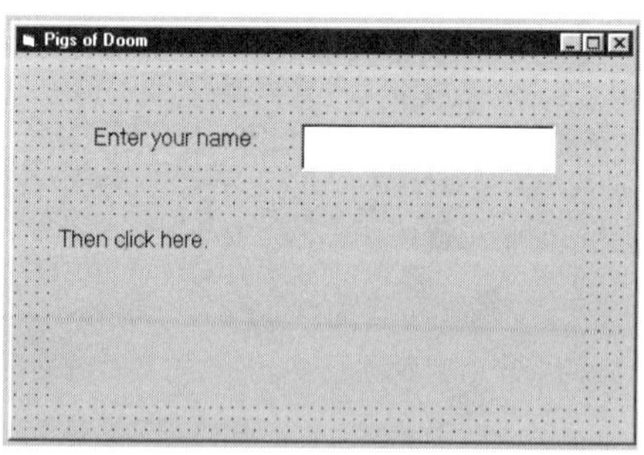

Figure L5-14 The Pigs of Doom form

still can change the text. Setting the MultiLine property to True allows the text property to display on more than one line if necessary.

Piecing Strings Together—Concatenation

Let's use a couple of string variables to help create a welcoming message when the user clicks on the txtBlurb box. One problem is that the message string will be a bit long to fit on one line. Also, we'll want to combine several strings. One way to deal with these problems is to build up the string a bit at a time using *string concatenation*. String concatenation means attaching one string to the end of another. Visual Basic uses the & symbol to indicate concatenation. For example, Visual Basic concatenates the expression *"fat"* & *"her"* into the single string *"father"*.

You can use + instead of & to concatenate strings. Note that + has quite a different meaning for strings than it does for integers. That is, *"cat"* + *"sup"* is the string *"catsup"* and "34" + "56" is *"3456"*, but *34* + *56* is not *3456;* it's the integer 90. You can see that it might get confusing if you use + to join strings that represent numbers; that's why & is preferred for string concatenation. When you see it, you know it means concatenation. Using concatenation, you can add the following event procedure to the Code window:

```
Option Explicit

Private Sub txtBlurb_Click()
    Dim Greeting As String
    Dim CoinCount As String
    Dim Coins As Integer
    Greeting = "Welcome, " & txtName.Text _
        & ", to the Pigs of Doom! "
    Coins = Len(Greeting)
    CoinCount = "You begin your adventure as a first-level" _
        & " Swine Master with" & Str(Coins) + " gold pieces."
    txtBlurb.Text = Greeting + CoinCount
End Sub
```

The code uses the continuation character (an underscore following a space) to fit long lines more easily into the code. Note how the code incorporates the user's name, obtained from the first text box, into the greeting.

The procedure uses a couple of Visual Basic's many built-in functions. The *Len* function returns the length of the string, that is, the number of characters in the string. In this case, the user gets a number of gold pieces equal to the length of the *Greeting* string. (People with longer names should get some reward for the extra typing they have to do!) The *Coins* variable is an integer, but we need to convert the value to a string in order to incorporate it into the *CoinCount* string. That's what the *Str* function does—it converts numbers to strings (see Figure L5-15). It also puts a blank space in front of the string if the number is positive and a minus sign if the number is negative. That is, *Str(22)* is " 22", while *Str(-273)* is "–273".

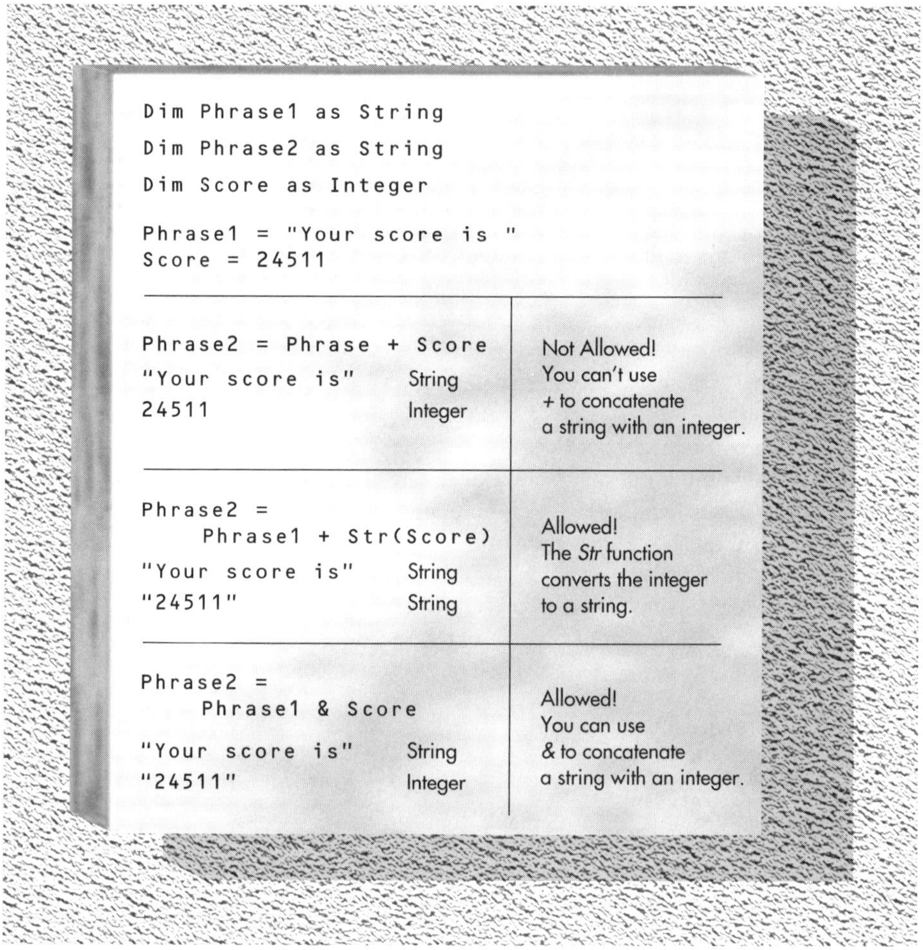

Figure L5-15 Using the Str function

Functions

Visual Basic functions are similar to Visual Basic procedures in that they can take arguments and you can call them from other procedures and functions. The distinguishing feature for a function is that it returns a value, which you can display or assign to a variable or otherwise use. Thus the *Len* function takes a *String* argument and returns an *Integer* value representing the number of characters in the string.

After the program constructs the two strings *Greetings* and *CoinCount,* it concatenates the two into the final text for the txtBlurb box, as shown in Figure L5-16.

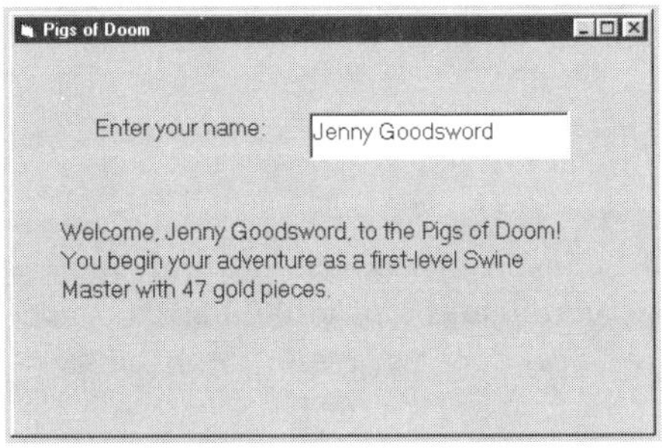

Figure L5-16 Jenny ventures into the world of computer gaming

GRACEFUL TRANSITIONS: TYPE CONVERSIONS

Visual Basic does try to convert from one type to another automatically if it thinks the operation makes sense. For instance, consider the following statements:

```
Dim IQ as String
IQ = 78 ' IQ is "78".
IQ = 100 + 25   ' IQ is "125".
IQ = "80" + "5" ' IQ is "805".
IQ = "80" + 5   ' IQ is "85".
IQ = "smart" + 10   ' Type mismatch!
```

The first assignment converts the integer 78 to the string "78" and assigns that string to IQ. The second assignment first adds the two integers together, converts the result to a string, and assigns the string "125" to IQ. In both cases Visual Basic thinks it's clear that you intend to convert an integer to a string. In the next case, both values are strings, so it's clear you mean concatenation. The next case is trickier. It might mean integer addition (80 + 5 = 85) or string concatenation ("80" + "5" = "805"). Visual Basic takes the first view. Finally, Visual Basic finds the final assignment statement so senseless that it reports a type mismatch.

These are just a few examples of conversion rules. Although, with self-discipline, you can learn all the automatic conversion rules, you are better off using special Visual Basic functions that convert data from one type to another. Using these functions documents your intentions and ensures that the conversion you want, not the ones Visual Basic thinks you want, get done. If you use Visual Basic Help to look up Conversion Functions, you'll find 18 conversion functions listed. One is the *Str* function we just used; it converts numbers to strings. Another is the *Format* function. It has several fancy capabilities, but if you just feed it a number, it acts like *Str* with one important difference—it doesn't leave a blank space in front of a positive number. For instance, "80" + *Str(5)* is "80 5", while "80" + *Format(5)* is "805".

Tip

Don't rely on automatic conversions except in the simplest of cases. If you have to convert values, use Visual Basic's conversion functions. That way, you document your intentions.

The *CInt* function goes in the other direction, converting strings and numbers to *Integer*. For instance, *CInt("383")* has the value 383, and *CInt(28.56)* has the value 29. To show that you really mean to add integers, use *CInt("80")* + *5* rather than "80" + *5*.

Rounding Numbers

CInt rounds numbers with a fractional part of 0.5 to the nearest even integer. That is, it rounds 12.5 to 12 and 13.5 to 14. This is the sensible way to do things, for it means that, on the average, 50 percent of such numbers get rounded up a half and 50 percent get rounded down a half, balancing round-off effects.

The Omnivorous *Variant* Type

The *Variant* type eliminates conversion problems by happily accepting values of any of the built-in data types:

```
Dim Anything            ' Variant by default
Anything = 225          ' Anything holds an Integer
Anything = "House"      ' Anything holds a String
Anything = -1.206       ' Anything holds a Single
Anything = "225"        ' Anything holds a String
```

The most interesting point is that no conversions are involved. If you assign an integer to a *Variant* variable, Visual Basic puts an integer into the variable. If you assign a string to a *Variant* variable, Visual Basic puts a string into it. Thus, *Anything* stores 225 differently than it stores "225".

What the Heck Is It? The *TypeName* Function

To see the *Variant* type's amazing ability to hold any kind of value, you can use Visual Basic's *TypeName* function, which returns the type of its argument as a string. Open a form, add a command button, name the button cmdTypeInfo, and try the following code:

```
Option Explicit
Private Sub cmdTypeInfo_Click()
```

```
    Dim Waist As Integer
    Dim Inseam           'Variant by default
    Print "Type of Waist = "; TypeName(Waist)
    Print "Type of Inseam = "; TypeName(Inseam)
    Waist = 28
    Inseam = 34
    Print "Waist = "; Waist
    Print "Inseam = "; Inseam
    Print "Type of Waist = "; TypeName(Waist)
    Print "Type of Inseam = "; TypeName(Inseam)
    Waist = "30" + "2"
    Inseam = "30" + "2"
    Print "Waist = "; Waist
    Print "Inseam = "; Inseam
    Print "Type of Waist = "; TypeName(Waist)
    Print "Type of Inseam = "; TypeName(Inseam)
End Sub
```

If you run the program and click the button, you get this output:

```
Type of Waist = Integer
Type of Inseam = Empty
Waist = 28
Inseam = 34
Type of Waist = Integer
Type of Inseam = Integer
Waist = 302
Waist = 302
Type of Waist = Integer
Type of Inseam = String
```

Let's see what we can learn from this output. First, an *Integer* is an *Integer* is an *Integer*... The *Waist* variable starts out as an *Integer* type before it's ever used. It remains an *Integer* when assigned the value *28*. And it remains an *Integer* when assigned *"30"* + *"2"*. In the last case, Visual Basic does string concatenation to get the string *"302"*, then converts that string to the number *302*.

But look at the *Variant Inseam* variable. Its type matches whatever value was last assigned to it. It even begins with a special type called *Empty*, indicating that *Inseam* really doesn't have a type until it gets a value assigned to it.

The *Variant* type is a great convenience, but it's not a cure-all. You still can't add a string to an integer, even if both are stored in *Variant* variables. Also, think about how Visual Basic can tell what type a *Variant* variable is. It has to store additional information in the variable indicating the type. This requires extra space. For example, an *Integer* occupies 2 bytes of memory, a *Double* uses 8 bytes, but a *Variant* holding a number uses up 16 bytes of memory. And a *Variant* holding a string uses up 22 bytes beyond the space needed just for the string. Finally, arithmetic with *Variant* variables also gets slowed down because Visual Basic has to check the type of each variable before using it.

In short, using the default *Variant* type is fine for simple programs such as those found in these lessons. But there are times you should explicitly choose appropriate types to promote slimmer, faster programs.

Type-Declaration Characters

In the olden days, before Visual Basic let you declare variables explicitly, it used a *type-declaration character* at the end of the name to indicate the variable type. For instance, if you used a variable named Volume#, the # indicated that the variable was type *Double*. Table L5-8 lists these special characters.

TYPE-DECLARATION CHARACTER	TYPE	EXAMPLE
%	Integer	Members%
&	Long	CityPop&
!	Single	Area!
#	Double	Volume#
@	Currency	Loan@
$	String	Rank$

Table L5-8 Type-declaration characters

It's better to declare variables explicitly. However, you can use this notation as a shortcut for explicit declarations. For example, the declaration

```
Dim Top!
```

is short for the following:

```
Dim Top as Single
```

In either case you can use *Top* as the variable name.

Using type-declaration characters is ingrained in many experienced Basic users, so you'll probably encounter them once you start reading other people's code.

SUMMARY

Variables are an important part of the Visual Basic programming experience; they are information carriers. A variable enables you to assign a symbolic name to a value and to change that value. For instance, the variable *YearSalary* could represent the value 45600, then be changed to 867000. (However, if *YearSalary* were type *Integer*, you would get overflow errors for these values.) Variables can represent different forms of data, including integers, floating-point numbers, and sequences of characters called strings.

You can declare variables using the *Dim* statement. For instance,

```
Dim Wit
```

declares that *Wit* is a variable. You can use the declaration to make the variable be a particular data type so that the type matches the intended use. For instance, if you're going to use a variable to count the number of dinner guests, use an *Integer* type, and if you're going to use a variable to represent a beloved pet's name, use a *String* type. You can use the *Dim ... As ...* syntax for this purpose:

```
Dim Guests as Integer
Dim TopPet as String
```

Visual Basic has a wide variety of data types, which we'll introduce as needed.

Each type has its own set of operations. For example, you can do arithmetic with integers, and you can concatenate (join) strings. Visual Basic allows some latitude in assigning values of one type to variables of another type. For instance, you can assign the string *"1492"* to the *Integer* variable *Date,* and Visual Basic will convert the string to the integer *1492*. But you can run into problems, too. For example, you can't assign the string *"Murphy Brown"* or *"Jean Luc Picard"* to the *Integer* variable *Date;* Visual Basic will protest that you've made a type mismatch. However, Visual Basic does provide a raft of conversion functions for converting types on a sensible basis.

The *Variant* type is Visual Basic's default type, and it generously accepts values of any of the built-in types. This type offers convenience at the cost of some efficiency, which may not be important in many applications.

1. Indicate whether each of the following is a valid variable name or not:

a. Bigfoot
b. 2Much
c. End
d. ThisIsALongName
e. ButThisIsEvenALongerName!AlbeitAVeryStupidOne
f. Hot-Pink
g. ClassOf99

2. Indicate whether each of the following is true or false:

You can create variables without declaring them explicitly.	True	False
Microsoft recommends declaring variables explicitly.	True	False
The default type for a new variable is *String*.	True	False
The *Option Explicit* statement converts implicit declarations to explicit declarations.	True	False

A variable declared in one procedure automatically is available to other procedures in the same module. True False

You must be over 17 to use explicit declarations. True False

3. Suppose we have the following declarations:

```
Dim Andy as Integer
Dim Bitsy as String
Dim Colinda
```

What is the result of each of the following statements? (One nice thing about computers is that if you get stuck with a question like this, you can just put the statements in a program and print the values.)

```
Andy = 1054
Bitsy = 1054
Colinda = 1054
Bitsy = TypeName(Colinda)
Andy = "10" + "54"
Bitsy = 10 + 54
Colinda = "10" + Str(56)
Bitsy = TypeName(Colinda)
Colinda = "The Crab Nebula"
Andy = "The Crab Nebula"
```

4. What would be an appropriate data type for each of the following quantities?

a. Your name
b. The number of computers you own
c. The number of bytes on your hard disk
d. Your height
e. The amount of money in your bank account
f. The number of atoms in your body
g. The distance from Chicago to New Orleans

1. Write a simple calculator program that uses the *Single* type instead of the *Integer* type. Note that integer division (\) and finding the remainder (Mod) are not valid operations for the *Single* type.

2. Write a simple program that lets you enter your name and favorite color and which composes a sentence from your input. For instance, if you enter "Deborah Bora" and "red", the program would display "Deborah Bora, would you like a red computer?"

LESSON 6

GETTING SMART WITH CONTROL STATEMENTS

Forms and controls give a Visual Basic program a pretty interface, properties and variables give a program its information buckets, and control statements give it its smarts. *Control statements* (no relation to Visual Basic controls) are language tools that let a program make choices and perform repetitive actions easily. For instance, a *MouseDown* event reports which button is pressed to the *MouseDown* event procedure. The Visual Basic *If Then* statement lets the procedure act one way for the left button and in a different way for the right button. Cool! The *If Then* statement and its relatives will open new vistas in programming for you.

In this lesson, you'll be enriched by the following:

- ***If Then*** **statements**
- ***If Then ElseIf Else*** **statements**
- ***Select Case*** **statements**
- **Symbolic constants**

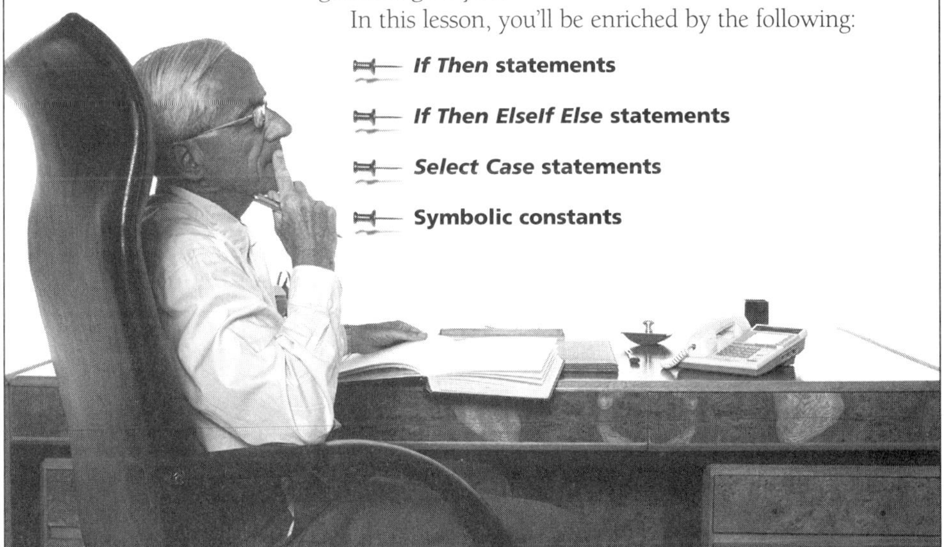

- **Comparison operators**
- **The *And* and *Or* logical operators**
- **Detecting ENTER**

There's a lot of information in this chapter, but you will be well-rewarded for learning it. (Note: Do not construe this as an offer of financial remuneration from the Waite Group Press.)

WHAT IF?—THE *IF THEN* STATEMENT

Often we try to make conditions about behavior. "You can have dessert *if* you eat your pickled cabbage." "You can get a 10 percent discount *if* your order is over $100." "I'll set you free *if* you can teach my horse to sing." Computer programs, too, may need to express conditions. "I'll let you proceed *if* you press the left mouse button." The *If Then* statement is the Visual Basic way to express such conditions. The *If Then* statement executes a command only if it determines a test condition is true. The simplest version has this form (*syntax,* in more technical terms):

```
If test-condition Then statement
```

Here *test-condition* is an expression that is evaluated as true or false, and *statement* is a Visual Basic statement. For example, the *If Then* statement

```
If lblCheese.Font.Size = 10 Then lblCheese.Font.Bold = True
```

sets the Font.Bold property to True only if the Font.Size property is 10. In this example, the test is for equality—is the value of *lblCheese.Font.Size* equal to 10? You also can test for different forms of inequality. Table L6-1 lists Visual Basic's *comparison operators,* that is, operators used to make comparisons. These comparisons relate to size. If you want to compare two people to see who is, say, the grungier, you first have to find a way to quantify grungines as a number.

OPERATOR	MEANS
=	Equal to
<>	Unequal to
<	Less than
>	Greater than
<=	Less than or equal to
>=	Greater than or equal to

Table L6-1 Visual Basic comparison operators

For example, if you wanted to set the font to bold only if the font size is 12 or greater, you would use this statement:

```
If lblCheese.Font.Size >= 12 Then lblCheese.Font.Bold = True
```

Comparison operators create expressions that have the value True or False. That is, the value of the expression 5 > 3 is True, while the value of the expression 10 = 12 is False. True and False, recall, are termed Boolean values (see Lesson 5).

The test condition for an *If* statement doesn't have to be a comparison. More generally, you can use any expression with a True-False (Boolean) value. For example, you can use a property that has a Boolean value:

```
If cmdIgor.Visible Then cmdInga.Caption = "Yo!"
```

This sets *cmdInga.Caption* to *"Yo!"* if the *cmdIgor.Visible* property is True.

Two Kinds of = Operators

Visual Basic uses the = symbol two ways. The first, called *assignment,* sets the value of a variable or a property:

```
Elves = 13
```

The second, called *comparison* for *equality,* compares two values, returning a value of True if the two compared values are the same and a value of False otherwise:

```
If Elves = 13 Then Print "Unlucky elves."
```

Assignment, in general, changes the value of something, while comparison examines a value without altering it. Visual Basic distinguishes between assignment and comparison by looking at the context.

Now let's look at a second, more versatile, syntax for *If Then*. It looks like this:

```
If test-condition Then
    statement(s)
End If
```

This form makes it easier to associate several statements with a single test, as in the following:

```
If txtInput.Text = "Yes" Then
    lblCheese.Visible = True
    lblYogurt.Visible = False
End If
```

Everything between the *If Then* line and the *End If* line is executed if the test condition is true (the text box contents are the word "Yes") and is skipped if the test condition is false. You can put multiple statements in the one-line form, but they have to be separated by colons, and the format is hard to read. The multiline format is easier to read, especially if you follow the standard convention of indenting the statements between the *If Then* line and the *End If* line.

Comparison Operators and Precedence

All comparison operators have the same precedence, and that precedence is lower than that of any arithmetic operator. So a comparison expression like Y > X + 5 means Y > (X + 5), which is convenient. That means you don't have to type parentheses.

Comparisons and Types

Visual Basic lets you compare strings as well as numbers. In the case of strings, > means "follows alphabetically." For instance, the comparison *Name* > *"Smith"* is true if the value of the *Name* variable is a string that comes after "Smith" alphabetically. Similarly, < means "precedes alphabetically," and so on. By default, characters are compared according to their ASCII codes. In this code, all the uppercase characters precede all lowercase characters. So *"Ferraro"* > *"Smith"* is false and *"ferraro"* > *"Smith"* is true. You can use the *Option Compare Text* command at the beginning of a module to cause comparisons to ignore case.

Can you compare a string to a number? Yes, you can if the string is a number in string form. In that case, Visual Basic converts the string to a number for the sake of comparison. For example, 20 > "150" is false. Note, however, that comparing two numbers in the form of strings compares them by the ASCII codes for the characters. For example, "20" > "150" is true because the character "2" follows the character "1" in the ASCII code.

Table L6-2 summarizes comparisons you can make. In it, *value1* and *value2* refer to the two items being compared. The real lesson here is not memorizing this table; rather it's that you're better off not creating mixed comparisons in the first place.

VALUE1	VALUE2	RESULT
Number	Number	Numeric comparison
String	String	String comparison
Number	Number in string form	Numeric comparison
Number in string form	Number in string form	String comparison
Number	String that's not a number	Type mismatch
Number	Variant holding a number	Numeric comparison
Number	Variant holding a string	Same as number-string comparison
String	Variant holding a string	String comparison
Variant	Variant	Determined by contents of variant, as described in the rest of the table

Table L6-2 Comparing mixed types

Which Button?—A Choice Example

Let's try the *If Then* statement using the *MouseDown* and *MouseUp* event procedures. These procedures (see Lesson 4) come with arguments that describe the states of the mouse buttons and of the SHIFT, CTRL, and ALT keys. We can use If Then to tailor the response of a command button to particular mouse button and key combinations. First, create the form shown in Figure L6-1 and described in Table L6-3.

OBJECT	PROPERTY	SETTING
Form1	Caption	Using If
	Name	frmIf
Command1	Caption	Click Me!
	Name	cmdIf
Label1	Caption	Left is Deft!
	Font.size	14
	Name	lblLeft
	Visible	False
Label2	Caption	Right is Might!
	Font.size	14
	Name	lblRight
	Visible	False

Table L6-3 Properties for the If program

This time the plan is to have pressing the left mouse button display the left message by setting *lblLeft.Visible* to True and pressing the right mouse button display the right-hand message. You can accomplish that with the following code:

```
Option Explicit

Private Sub cmdIf_MouseDown(Button As Integer, Shift As Integer, _
    X As Single, Y As Single)
    If Button = 1 Then lblLeft.Visible = True
    If Button = 2 Then lblRight.Visible = True
End Sub
```

Now that you've studied variables, you can understand the *MouseDown* event better. The stuff in parentheses declares four variables: *Button* and *Shift* are type

Figure L6-1 The If form

Integer variables, and *X* and *Y* are type *Single* variables. Variables declared this way are called arguments or *parameters*. Arguments convey information to a procedure. When a *MouseDown* Event is triggered, Visual Basic creates these arguments and assigns values to them. In particular, *Button* is set to 1 if you press the left mouse button and to 2 if you press the right mouse button. So the statement

```
If Button = 1 Then lblLeft.Visible = True
```

makes the Left is Deft! message visible if you position the mouse pointer over the command button and press the left mouse button.

Recall that Visual Basic sets the *Shift* parameter to 1 if SHIFT is down when the mouse button is pressed, 2 if CTRL is down, and 4 if ALT is down. We can make the button response more versatile by using those keys to change the font style. Modify the code to look as follows:

```
Private Sub cmdIf_MouseDown(Button As Integer, Shift As Integer, _
    X As Single, Y As Single)
    If Button = 1 Then lblLeft.Visible = True
    If Button = 2 Then lblRight.Visible = True
    If Shift = 1 Then lblLeft.Font.Size = 18
    If Shift = 2 Then lblRight.Font.italic = True
End Sub
```

Now, if you press the left mouse button while SHIFT is depressed, the left message appears in 18-point font. Similarly, you can use CTRL to make the right message appear in italics.

To complete the program, supply a *MouseUp* event procedure that restores the form to its original condition. To illustrate the multiline *If Then* syntax, we'll have releasing the mouse button initiate a beep in addition to restoring invisibility.

```
Private Sub cmdIf_MouseUp(Button As Integer, Shift As Integer, X As Single, _
    Y As Single)
    If Button = 1 Then
        lblLeft.Visible = False
        Beep
    End If
    If Button = 2 Then
        lblRight.Visible = False
        Beep
    End If
    If Shift = 1 Then lblLeft.Font. Size = 14
    If Shift = 2 Then lblRight.Font.Italic = False
End Sub
```

Events Again

The last program offers a good chance to investigate events further. Try the following experiments.

1. Press the left mouse button while the mouse pointer is outside the command button, move the pointer over the command button, and release the mouse button.
2. Next, locate the mouse pointer over the command button, press the left mouse button, move the pointer off the command button, and then release the mouse button.

For experiment 1, nothing happens. There is no beep, even though you released the mouse button over the command button. For experiment 2, the left message appears and disappears, and there's a beep even though you didn't release the mouse button over the command button. The lesson here is that a *MouseUp* event is sent to the object that received the prior *MouseDown* event (see Figure L6-2).

Who's Got the Button?

If you press a mouse button when the mouse pointer is over one object, then move the mouse pointer to a different object before releasing the button, the *MouseUp* event goes to the object that originally received the *MouseDown* event.

3. Now position the mouse pointer over the command button, hold down [SHIFT] press the left mouse button, pause, and release the key and the mouse button. Repeat, but this time hold down both [SHIFT] and [CTRL].

The first effort should show the *Left is Deft!* message in 18-point font, and the second effort should show no font change, even though [SHIFT] is depressed. That's because the value of *Shift* in this case is 3, the sum of 1 (for [SHIFT]) and 2 (for [CTRL]). If you held down the [SHIFT], [CTRL], and [ALT] keys simultaneously, Shift would be 1 + 2 + 4, or 7.

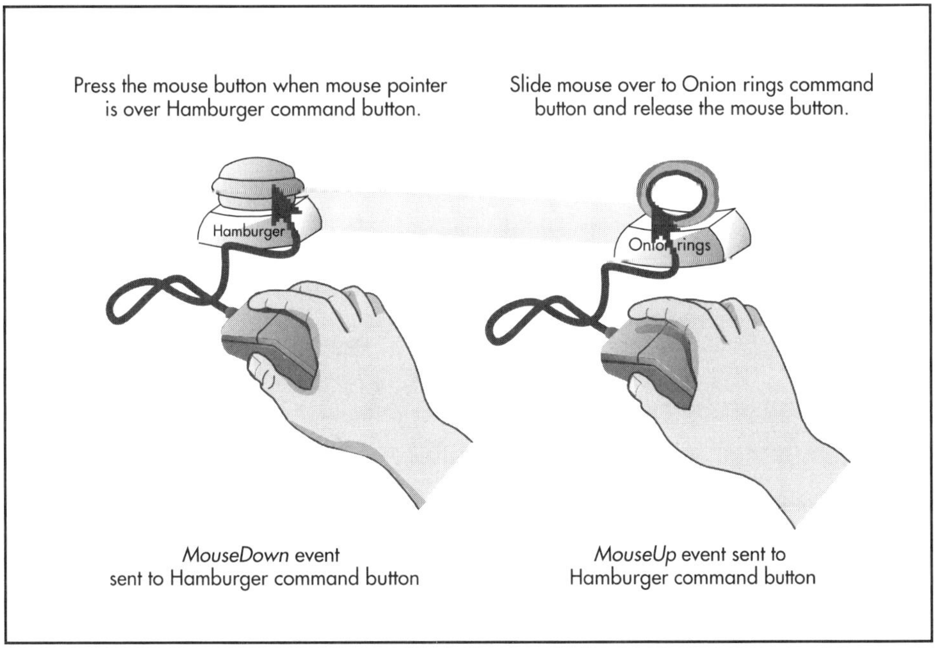

Figure L6-2 *MouseUp* follows *MouseDown*

One Key Combination, One *Shift* Value

A test like Shift = 1 tests for the SHIFT key and just the SHIFT key (out of the SHIFT, CTRL, and ALT keys) being pressed. Each combination of these three keys has its own numeric code. For instance, 3 means both SHIFT and CTRL are pressed.

If you want SHIFT to make the text bold regardless of the state of the other two keys, you have to be trickier. Later in this chapter you'll learn how to be that tricky.

Let's continue with our eventful experiments.

4. Position the mouse pointer over the command button, hold down SHIFT, press the left mouse button, pause, release SHIFT, then release the mouse button. Now press the left mouse button again. This time the Left is Deft! message starts out in 18-point font.

The point here is that the *MouseUp* event senses the SHIFT key state at the time the mouse button is released; it doesn't know about the *Shift* value from the *MouseDown* event. Thus, if you release SHIFT before releasing the mouse button, the two events will have different values for the *Shift* parameter.

THE *IF THEN ELSE* STATEMENT

The code in the last example is not (gasp!) perfect. For instance, if a test shows that *Button* is 1, the program wastes time by testing if *Button* is 2. (If *Button* is 1, it can't be 2.) It would be better to skip the second test if the result of the first test is true. The *If Then Else* statement lets you do just that. Here is its syntax:

```
If test-condition then
     statement(s)         ' Do these statements if test is true.
Else
     statement(s)         ' Do these statements if test is false.
End If
```

As the comments suggest, the program will execute the first block of statements if the test is true and the second if it's false. Figure L6-3 compares the two forms of *If* by showing two *flow diagrams*. The rectangles represent statements, the diamonds represent tests, and the arrows represent the program flow. The diamonds have two arrows leaving them because the program can flow two different ways, depending upon the result of the test.

Let's look at an example of *If Then Else*. Consider this code:

```
If State = "California" then
     print "Would you like avocado on your hamburger?"
Else
     print "Would you like catsup on your hamburger?"
End If
```

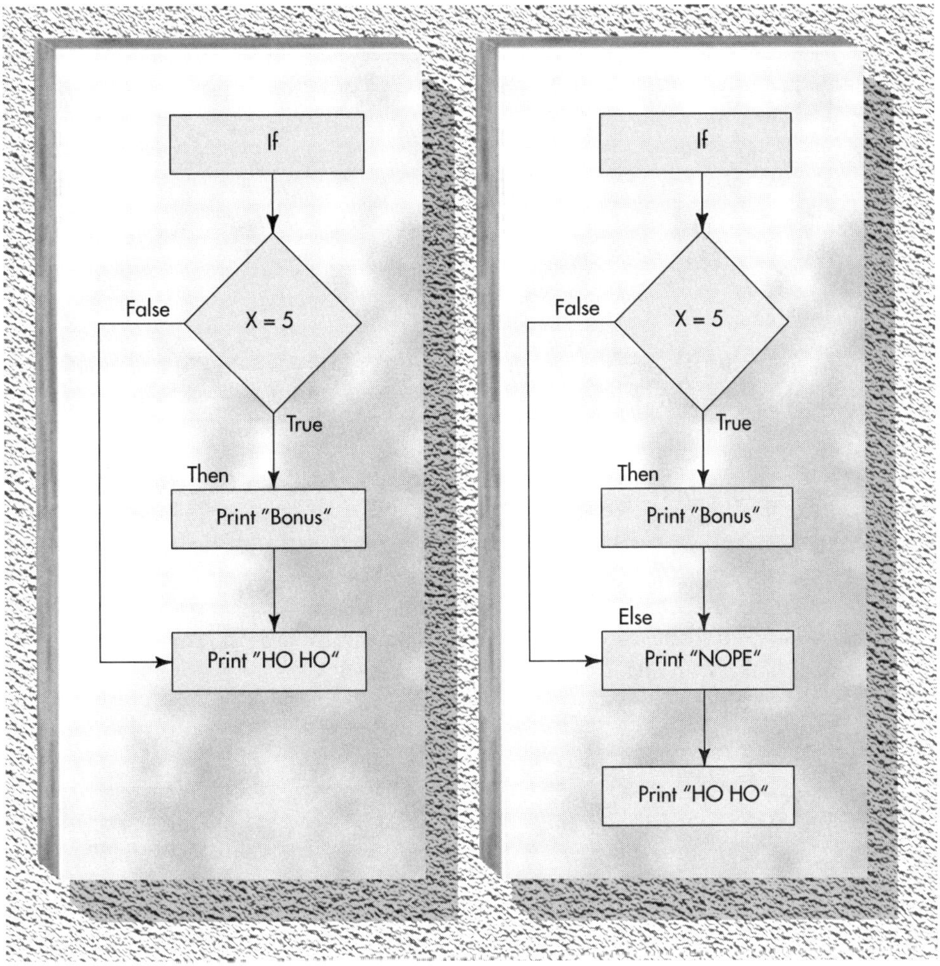

Figure L6-3 *If Then* versus *If Then Else* statement

It prints the first message if the *String* variable *State* is set to *"California"* and prints the second message otherwise.

Can you use new syntax with our last program? That is, can you do this?

```
If Button = 1 Then
    lblLeft.Visible = True
Else
    lblRight.Visible = True
End If
```

You can, but the results are not quite right if a person uses a three-button mouse. With a two-button mouse, *Button* must be 2 if it isn't 1. But with a three-button mouse, *Button* can be 2 or 4 (the middle button) if it isn't 1. So the *Else* part gets executed if you press either the middle or the right mouse button. We can fix that by putting another *If* statement in the *Else* part:

```
If button = 1 Then
     lblLeft.Visible = True
Else
     If button = 2 Then
          lblRight.Visible = True
     End If
End If
```

However, Visual Basic provides another syntax that shortens the code. You can rewrite the example this way:

```
If button = 1 Then
     lblLeft.Visible = True
ElseIf button = 2 Then
     lblRight.Visible = True
End If
```

The keyword *ElseIf* lets you put the test on the same line as the *Else,* and also lets you eliminate an *End If.* The general form is this:

```
If test-condition1 Then
     statement(s)
ElseIf test-condition2 Then
     statement(s)
Else
     statement(s)
End If
```

A program executes the first block of statements if *test-condition1* is true, the second block if *test-condition2* is true, and the third block if neither test is true. If a program finds a true statement, it skips the rest of the tests. That is, if both test conditions are true, then only the first block of statements is executed.

You can omit the final *Else* block if your program doesn't need it, and you can have more than one *ElseIf* if your program needs that. For instance, you set up a list of alternatives, as in the following:

```
If Score < 100 Then
     Print "Sorry! Better luck next time."
ElseIf Score < 200 Then
     Print "You've earned a free game!"
ElseIf Score < 400
     Print "You've earned two free games!"
ElseIf Score < 800
     Print "You've earned three free games!"
Else
     Print "Sorry, you're too good for this game!"
Endif
```

VISUAL BASIC CONSTANTS—NUMBERS WITH NAMES

Another deficiency in our first *If* example form is that the meaning of some of the code is less than obvious. For instance, when you read the code testing if *Button* is 1 or if *Shift* is 2, there's nothing to remind you what 1 and 2 mean. Fortunately, Visual Basic provides some symbolic constants you can use instead of 1 and 2. Symbolic constants are names that stand for particular values. For instance, Visual Basic defines the constant *vbLeftButton* as 1, so you can use *Button = vbLeftButton* instead of *Button = 1*. Symbolic constants make programs easier to read because the name indicates the meaning of the constant. Table L6-4 lists constants that you can use with the *MouseUp* and *MouseDown* events.

CONSTANT	VALUE	MEANING
vbLeftButton	1	Left mouse button is pressed or released
vbRightButton	2	Right mouse button is pressed or released
vbCenterButton	4	Middle mouse button is pressed or released
vbShiftMask	1	SHIFT is pressed
vbCtrlMask	2	CTRL is pressed
vbAltMask	4	ALT is pressed

Table L6-4 Constants to use with *MouseUp* and *MouseDown*

Note

These named constants are new with Visual Basic 4, and they are automatically available. Earlier versions of Visual Basic used constants with different names that were available only if you loaded a file called CONSTANT.TXT into your module or else coded them manually.

Visual Basic also lets you define your own constants. For instance, the statement

```
Const States = 50
```

creates an *Integer* constant having the symbolic name *States* and the value 50. Because it's a constant, you can't accidentally change the value elsewhere. That is, a statement like

```
States = 210
```

gets caught as an error. The symbolic name has two advantages:

- The name reminds you of the significance of the value.
- Changing the definition of the constant updates the value of the constant everywhere you've used it.

For instance, suppose you've written a program that uses the constant *States* in several places and that the United States adds another state (Northern California, for example, or, less likely, France). Then all you have to do is change the constant definition to the following:

```
Const States = 51
```

If you had just used the number 50 instead of the constant States, you would have to track down everywhere you've used 50 and change each occurrence to 51. Sure, you could use a global search-and-replace to convert each 50 to a 51, but some of the 50s in your program may have different meanings, such as the frequency of European power lines, and should remain unchanged.

Tip

Assign symbolic names to meaningful constants in your program. This makes the program easier to understand and to maintain.

By default, constants are of type *Variant*, but you can use the as syntax to specify some other type. For instance, here's a better way to define the *States* constant:

```
Const States as Integer = 50
```

Like variables, constants declared in a procedure are local to the procedure and constants declared at the module level are local (by default) to the module. Thus, defining *States* at the module level would make that constant available to all procedures in the module.

LOGICAL OPERATORS *AND* AND *OR*

The amusement park Rides of Passage admits only persons who are over 12 years old and who are taller than 45 inches. Gerbil Brothers Clothing Store lets you charge a purchase if the amount is over $25 or if you have a GerbilCharge card. Computer programming situations, too, often present circumstances for which you have to combine two or more tests. Visual Basic provides several *logical operators* (don't visualize Euclid or Descartes in flashy clothes) that let you combine tests logically. Let's look now at the two most commonly used logical operators, *And* and *Or*.

The *And* operator combines two expressions into a single expression that is True only if both subexpressions are True. For example, consider the following:

```
If Age > 12 And Height > 45 Then
    Print "You may ride the Mighty Herculator!"
End If
```

Here the *And* combines the comparison *Age > 12* with the comparison *Height > 45* to produce an expression that is True only if both the original expressions are True.

Similarly, the *Or* operator combines two expressions into a single expression that is True if at least one of the original expressions is True. For example, consider the following:

```
If Purchase > 25 Or Card = "GerbilCharge" Then
    Print "You may charge your purchase!"
End If
```

Here the *Or* combines the comparison *Purchase > 25* with *Card = "GerbilCharge"* to produce an expression that is True only if either or both the original expressions are True.

Figure L6-4 compares *And* with *Or*.

Exotica—Another Way of Using *And* and *Or*

The *Or* operator gives you one way to detect the SHIFT key regardless of the state of the CTRL and ALT keys. You can replace

```
If Shift = 1 Then lblLeft.Font.Bold = True
```

with the following:

```
If Shift = 1 Or Shift = 3 Or Shift = 5 Or Shift = 7 Then
    lblLeft.Font.Bold = True
End If
```

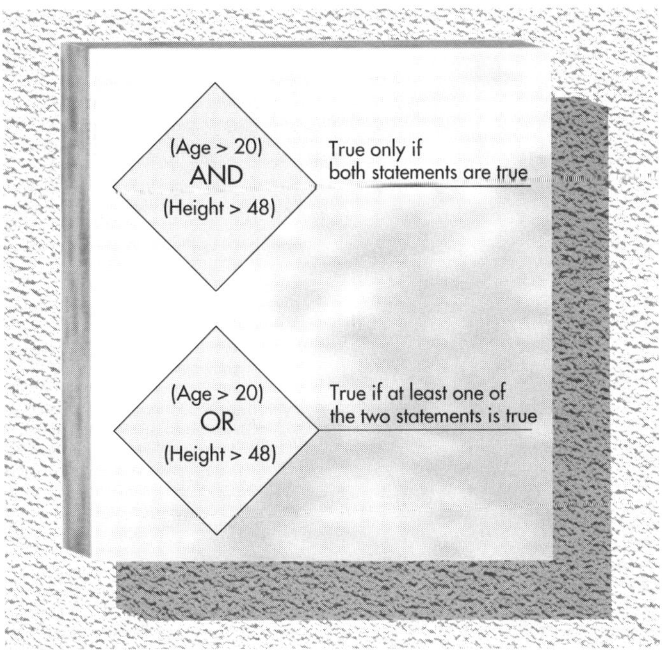

Figure L6-4 *And* and *Or*

This tests for all the possible combinations (SHIFT SHIFT-CTRL, SHIFT-ALT, and SHIFT-CTRL-ALT) that have the SHIFT key down. However, looking at this statement, it's not obvious what it means. You could replace 1 with *vbShiftMask*, 3 with *vbShiftMask + vbCntrlMask*, and so on, and make the meaning of the code clearer. But you also get a very long test condition. Fortunately, you have an alternative. You can use the following code:

```
If (Shift And vbShiftMask) = vbShiftMask Then
    lblLeft.Font.bold = True
End If
```

This code sets the bold property to true if SHIFT is pressed, regardless of the states of the other two keys.

Operator Precedence

Visual Basic requires the parentheses shown in the example above; otherwise it tries to *And* the wrong values. That is, Visual Basic grants higher precedence to evaluating comparison operators than it does to evaluating logical operators. Thus, Visual Basic evaluates the line

```
If Shift And vbShiftMask = vbShiftMask Then ...
```

as if you wrote the following:

```
If Shift And (vbShiftMask = vbShiftMask) Then
```

And that is not a particularly meaningful test.

This version is gratifyingly brief. Unfortunately, it also is quite mysterious looking. Explaining this idiom involves a more intimate acquaintance with binary numbers than you may care for, so you have some choices now.

1. You can ignore the matter, hoping it doesn't come up in your lifetime again.
2. You can accept this idiom on faith, perhaps arguing that a detailed explanation of how it works only tarnishes the magic of the method.
3. You can read the following discussion and learn what's going on.

To understand how the idiom works, you need to know two things:

- How the possible values of the *Shift* parameter look in binary number form
- How *And* works when used to combine integers instead of to combine True-False expressions

Binary numbers (see Appendix A) are numbers written using just two digits—0 and 1. Using this system (and showing just three places), 1 is 001, 2 is 010, and 4 is 100. You can visualize these three places as three light switches side by side. Pressing SHIFT flicks the right switch on (001), pressing CTRL flicks the middle switch on (010), and pressing ALT flips the left switch on (100). Pressing ALT and SHIFT simultaneously flips both switches on (101), and 101, not incidentally, is the binary representation of 5, the code for both ALT and SHIFT being pressed. In short, each switch (or each position in the binary number) indicates the state of a particular key. See Figure L6-5 and note how the binary value is a picture of key states. So if you know, say, that the rightmost digit is a 1, that means SHIFT is pressed, regardless of what the other digits are.

What we need, then, is a way to look at one particular binary digit. That's where *And* comes in. When you combine two integers with *And*, it looks at them in binary format. A computer stores integers one binary digit per bit, so *And* looks at each bit position individually. The resulting value has a bit set to 1 only if the corresponding bits in the two original values also are 1 (see Figure L6-6).

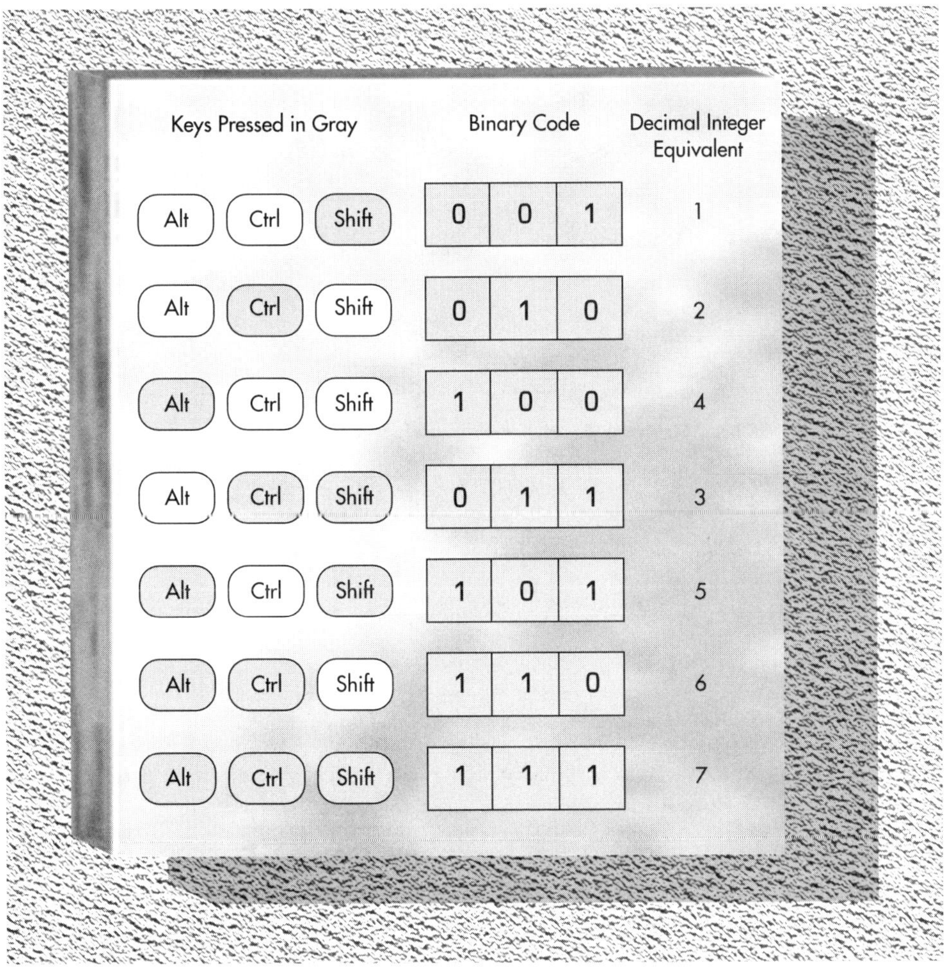

Figure L6-5 Key states and the binary code

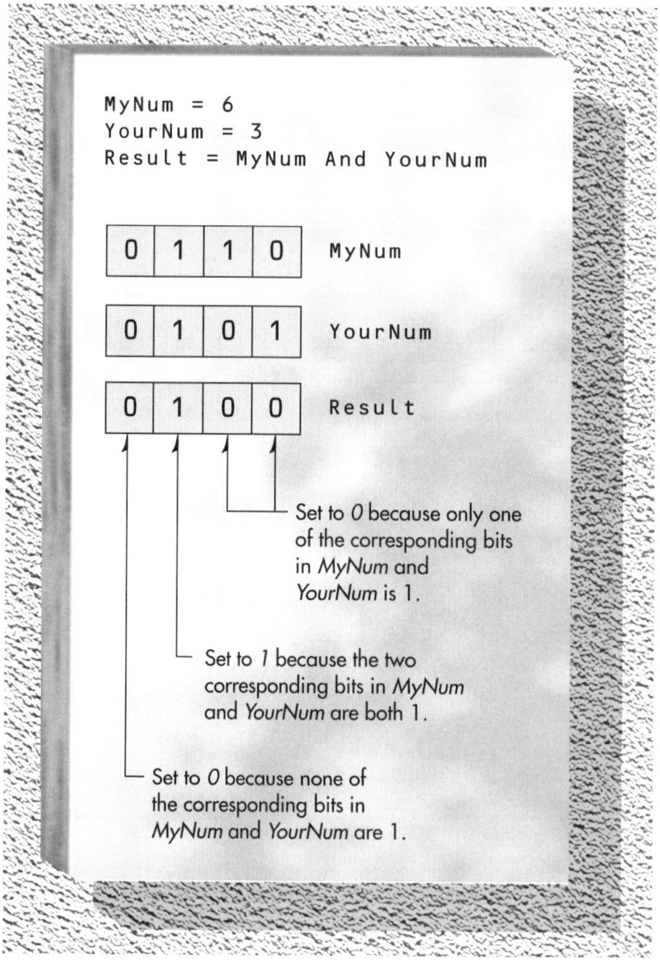

Figure L6-6 Combining two integers with *And*

Note

Using *And* to combine two True-False expressions produces a value of True or False. Using *And* to combine two integer produces a new integer in which each bit is set to 1 only if both corresponding bits in the original integers are set to 1.

Let's apply this knowledge to the expression *Shift And vbShiftMask*. The constant *vbShiftMask* is just 001. (Actually, Visual Basic uses 16 bits for integers, so it's really 0000000000000001, but we'll just look at the last three binary digits.) Suppose *Shift* is abc, where each of a, b, and c is a *0* or a 1. Then, because 0 *And* any bina-

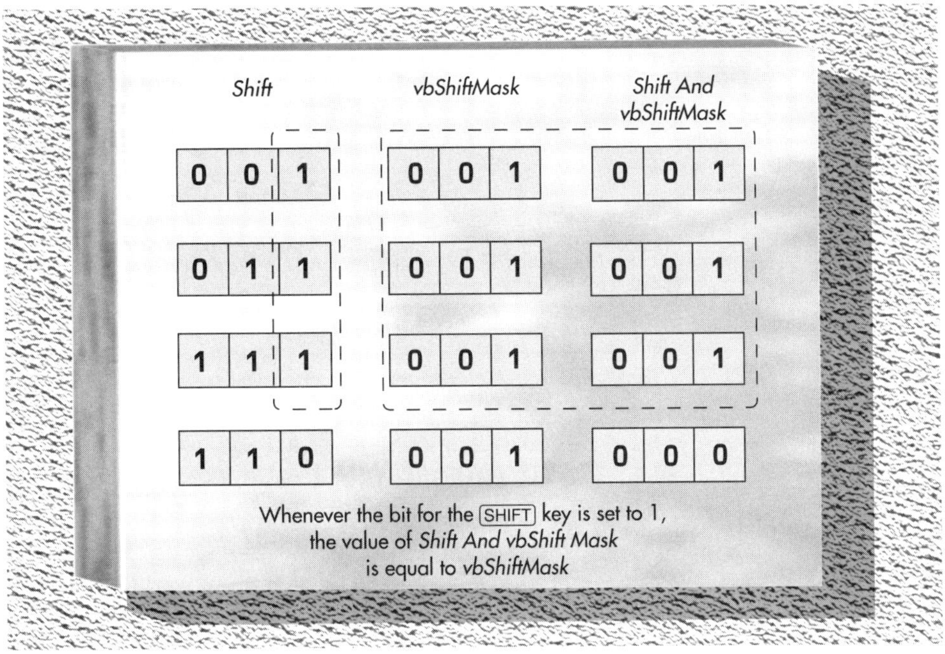

Figure L6-7 Masking the *Shift* parameter

ry digit is a 0, the expression *Shift And vbShiftMask* is 00c. That is, *vbShiftMask* "masks" all the digits in *Shift* except the one describing the state of the SHIFT key. That, of course, is why the name includes the word "Mask" (see Figure L6-7).

Thus, if SHIFT is pressed, the digit c is 1, and the result 001 is the same as the value of *vbShiftMask*. Hence the expression (*Shift And vbShiftMask*) = *vbShiftMask* is true if SHIFT is pressed. If SHIFT isn't pressed, c is 0, the result of the *And* operation is 000, which is not equal to *vbShiftMask*, and the test expression is wrong. Similarly, (*Shift And vbCtrlMask*) = *vbCtrlMask* tests for CTRL being pressed (see Figure L6-8).

This Is Useful—*Not*

Visual Basic has several logical operators. The three most often used with *If* test conditions are *And, Or,* and *Not*. The *Not* operator reverses the value of a Boolean expression. For instance, if *X = 28* is True, then *Not (X = 28)* is False. For relations, it's clearer to reverse the test. That is, don't say the following:

```
If Not (Feet = 6) Then Print "Not an insect."
```

Instead, use this:

```
If Feet <> 6 Then Print "Not an insect."
```

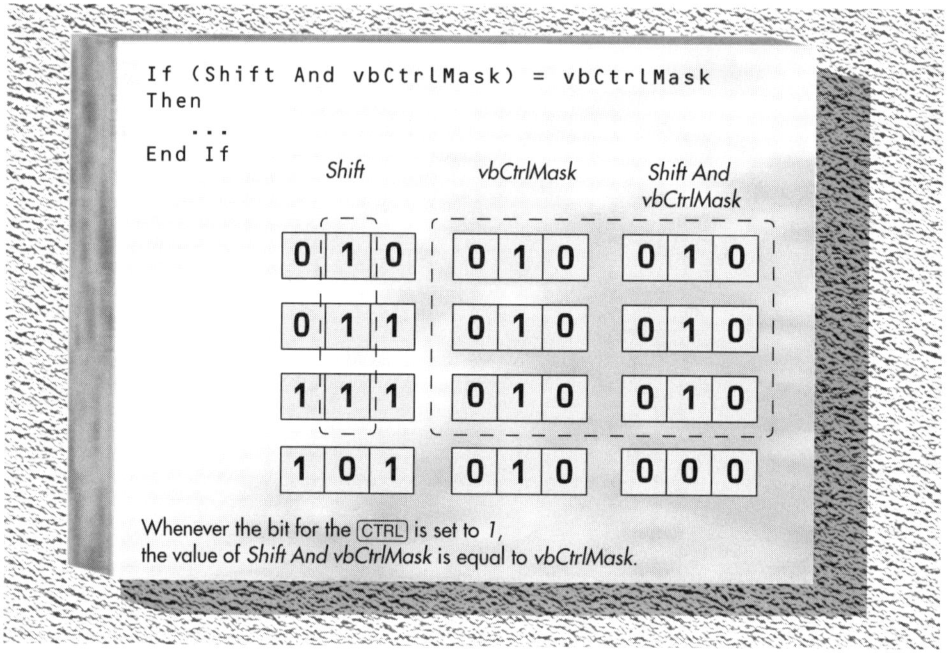

Figure L6-8 Testing for CTRL being pressed

However, *Not* is useful for functions and properties with Boolean values. For instance, the Font.Bold property is either True or False. If you want to check if text in a text box is not in bold, you can do the following:

```
If Not txtHorse.Font.Bold Then
     txtHorse.Font.Bold = True
Else
     txtHorse.Font.Bold = False
End If
```

This sets the Font.Bold property to True if it's False, and vice versa.

The *Toggle* Trick

An even trickier use of *Not* is to toggle a Boolean value from True to False and vice versa. For example, consider the following code:

```
txtHorse.Font.Bold = Not txtHorse.Font.Bold
```

If the Font.Bold property currently is True, this statement sets it to False. If the property is False, the statement sets it to True. This is cute enough that we'll use it in subsequent lessons.

XOR—the Exclusive *Or*

There are two kinds of "or." If you tell a friend to drop by if he feels sad or lonely, you probably mean to include the possibility that he is both sad and lonely.

This is an example of the *inclusive Or,* and it's what the *Or* operator means. But if a server tells you that you can have coffee or tea with your meal, he or she probably means you can have one or the other, but not both. This is an example of the *exclusive Or* and Visual Basic represents this interpretation with the *Xor* operator. So an expression like

```
X > 10 Xor Y > 10
```

is true if one or the other expressions is true, but not if both are true or both are false.

IMPROVING THE EXAMPLE AGAIN

You've just learned three techniques for improving the first example program—using *If Then ElseIf,* using defined constants, and using logical operators. So let's use these techniques to revise the example. Try replacing the original code with the code in Listing 6-1.

Listing 6-1

New code for the *If* program

```
Option Explicit

Private Sub cmdIf_MouseDown(button As Integer, Shift As Integer, _
    X As Single, Y As Single)
    If button = vbLeftButton Then
        lblLeft.Visible = True
        If (Shift And vbShiftMask) = vbShiftMask Then
            lblLeft.Font.Bold = True
        End If
        If (Shift And vbCtrlMask) = vbCtrlMask Then
            lblLeft.Font.Italic = True
        End If
    ElseIf button = vbRightButton Then
        lblRight.Visible = True
        If Shift = vbShiftMask Then
            lblRight.Font.Bold = True
        ElseIf Shift = vbCtrlMask Then
            lblRight.Font.Italic = True
        End If
    End If
End Sub

Private Sub cmdIf_MouseUp(button As Integer, Shift As Integer, X As Single, _
    Y As Single)
    If button = vbLeftButton Then
        lblLeft.Visible = False
        If Shift And vbShiftMask = vbShiftMask Then
            lblLeft.Font.Bold = False
        End If
        If Shift And vbCtrlMask = vbCtrlMask Then
            lblLeft.Font.Italic = False
```

continued on next page

continued from previous page

```
        End If
    ElseIf button = vbRightButton Then
        lblRight.Visible = False
        If Shift = vbShiftMask Then
            lblRight.Font.Bold = False
        ElseIf Shift = vbCtrlMask Then
            lblRight.Font.Italic = False
        End If
    End If
End Sub
```

This new version improves the readability and the functionality of the program, both commendable goals. In particular, you now can display either message in bold (SHIFT key down), or italic (CTRL key down). In addition, you can display the left message in bold-italic (SHIFT key and CTRL key down). The code that makes that possible is this:

```
If (Shift And vbShiftMask) = vbShiftMask Then
    lblLeft.Font.bold = True
End If
If (Shift And vbCtrlMask) = vbCtrlMask Then
    lblLeft.FOnt.ITalic = True
End If
```

Note that this code uses two separate *If* statements instead of an *If Else*. That's because the first test being true doesn't preclude the second from being true; it's possible for both SHIFT and CTRL to be pressed at the same time. The code for the right mouse button, however, does use an *If Else* for illustrative purposes. That results in allowing just italic or bold, but not both simultaneously.

Also, the code uses *If Else* for examining the mouse button state. In this case, it's necessary. That's because the *MouseDown* event recognizes the first button pressed. That is, the button parameter can be 1, 2, or 4 (left, right, or middle button), but it can't be, say 3 (both left and right).

Tip

Use an *If Else* statement for mutually exclusive tests, but use separate *If* statements for tests that are independent of one another.

MORE OPTIONS—THE *SELECT CASE* STATEMENT

Do you want to select one action from a list of several, but you're tired of using *If ElseIf* statements? Try *Select Case*, the lean, mean decision maker. A *Select Case* statement examines the value of a variable and tries to match it to a label. If the value matches the label, Visual Basic executes the statements at that label. Here's an example, where *TofuBurgers* is an *Integer* variable:

```
Select Case TofuBurgers
Case 0
    Print "You don't like my tofuburgers?"
Case 1
    Print "Have another tofuburger!"
Case 2
    Print "Ah, you like my tofuburgers!"
Case Else
    Print "Do you feel well?"
End Select
```

If *TofuBurgers* has the value 0, the program executes the statement following *Case 0*. Here there is only one statement, but you can have more. In general, the program will execute all the statements from the matching case to the next *Case* label. Similarly, if *TofuBurgers* has the value 2, the program executes the statement following *Case 2*. If *TofuBurgers* doesn't match any of the *Case* labels, Visual Basic executes the statement following *Case Else*. You can omit the *Case Else* if you want nothing done in the absence of a match (see Figure L6-9.)

Visual Basic's *Case* labels are pretty flexible. You can have any of the following:

- A single value, such as *Case 5*
- A range of values, such as *Case 6 To 9*
- A comma-separated list of values, such as *Case 1,3,5*
- A comparison, as in *Case Is > 50*
- A combination of the above forms, as in *Case 6,8,10 To 18, Is > 35*

Note that you use the keyword *To* to indicate a range and the keyword *Is* to indicate a comparison. With all these possibilities, you can wind up with more than one label matching, as in the following:

```
Select Case TofuBurgers
Case 0
    Print "You don't like my tofuburgers?"
Case 1,2
    Print "Have another tofuburger!"
Case 3 To 5
    Print "Ah, you like my tofuburgers! Have another!"
Case Is > 4 And TofuBurgers < 10
    Print "My, you are a good eater!"
Case Else
    Print "Do you feel well?"
End Select
```

Here a *TofuBurgers* value of 5 matches *Case 3 To 5* and the next case (*Case is > 4*) as well. In such instances, Visual Basic executes just the statements of the *first* matching case.

By the way, notice the following label:

```
Case Is > 4 And TofuBurgers < 10
```

Here *Case Is > 4* stands in for *TofuBurgers > 4,* but if you want to combine that comparison with another one by using *And* or *Or,* you have to use the variable name explicitly in the second test.

The test variable in a *Select Case* statement can be a string, too. In that case, the *Case* labels should be strings. For instance, *Case "crab" To "crow"* matches any string falling in that range alphabetically, such as *"crab"*, *"crass"*, and *"cretin"*.

Often you can use either an *If ElseIf* sequence or a *Select Case* statement. Usually, if you have a list of three or more choices, a *Select Case* statement is easier to read, and the computer may implement it more efficiently.

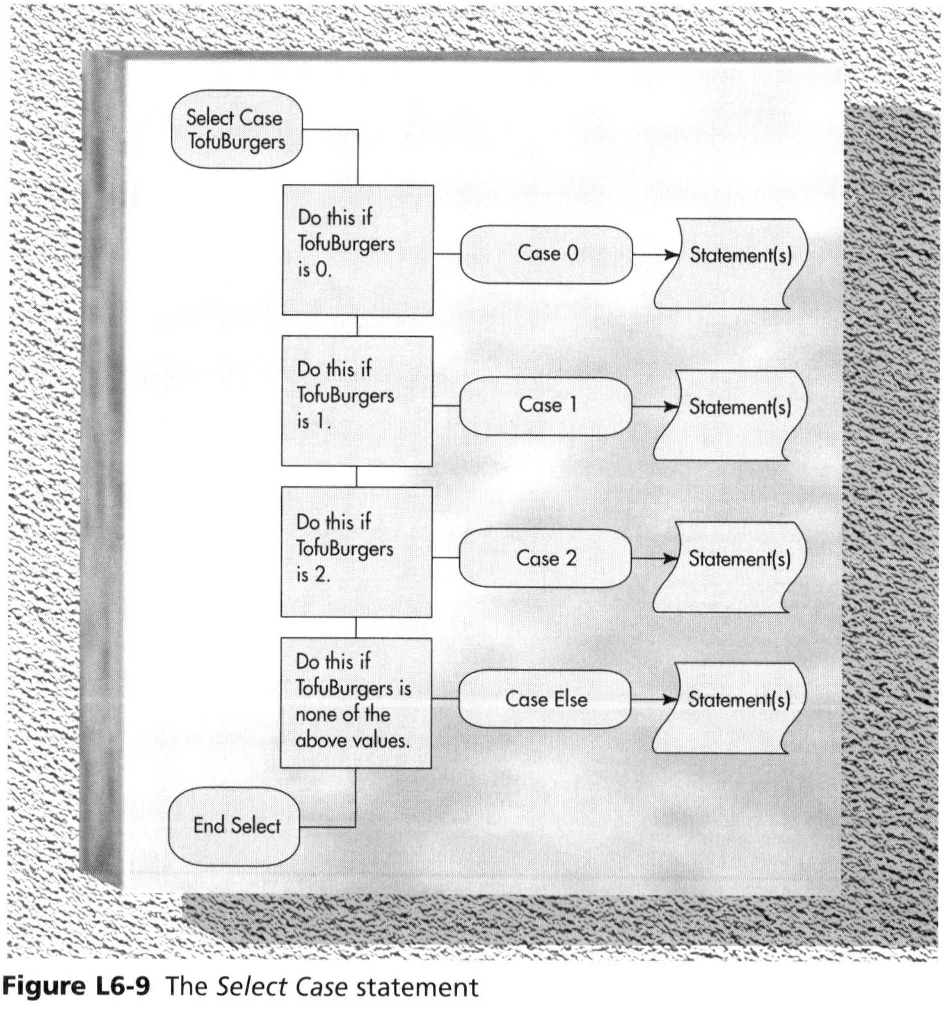

Figure L6-9 The *Select Case* statement

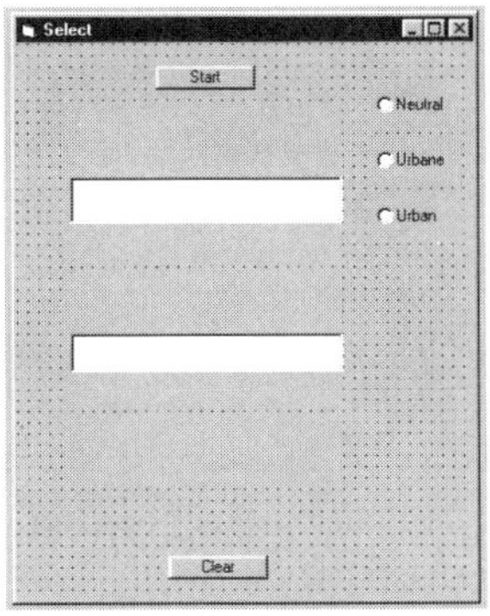

Figure L6-10 The Select form

A Select Example

It's time for another Visual Basic example. This one will illustrate the following points:

- Using the *Select Case* statement
- Using a module-level variable
- Using the *KeyPress* event with an argument
- Using option buttons (a review)
- Using user-defined constants

The example will be an interview form in which you use an option button to choose if you want the interview conducted in a neutral, urbane, or urban style. The option buttons will set the value of a module-level variable called *Style* that will be used by *Select Case* statements in some of the event procedures that manage the interview. (Sharing information among event procedures is the most common reason for using a module-level variable.)

Begin by laying out a form as shown in Figure L6-10. In it, the bordered boxes are text boxes, and the borderless boxes are labels.

Next, assign properties as shown in Table L6-5. The labels and text boxes are listed in the top-to-bottom order in which they appear on the form. As usual, feel free to add color and to change fonts to fit your tastes.

OBJECT	PROPERTY	SETTING
Form1	Caption	Select
	Name	frmSelect
Option1	Caption	Neutral
	Name	optNeutral

continued on next page

continued from previous page

OBJECT	PROPERTY	SETTING
Option2	Caption	Urbane
	Name	optUrbane
Option3	Caption	Urban
	Name	optUrban
Command1	Caption	Start
	Name	cmdStart
Command2	Caption	Clear
	Name	cmdClear
Label1	AutoSize	True
	Caption	
	Font.Size	12
	Name	lblName
	Width	3000
	WordWrap	True
Text1	Font.Size	12
	Name	txtName
	Text	
	Visible	False
	Width	3000
Label2	Caption	
	Name	lblEnter1
	Visible	False
	Width	3000
Label3	AutoSize	True
	Caption	
	Font.Size	12
	Name	lblTitle
	Visible	False
	Width	3000
	WordWrap	True
Text2	Font.Size	12
	Name	txtTitle
	Text	
	Visible	False
	Width	3000
Label4	Caption	
	Name	lblEnter2
	Visible	False
	Width	3000

OBJECT	PROPERTY	SETTING
Label5	AutoSize	True
	Caption	
	Font.Size	12
	Name	lblClose
	Visible	False
	Width	3000
	WordWrap	True

Table L6-5 Properties for the Select program

So much for the beauty—let's turn to the brains. First, create some constants and a variable:

```
Option Explicit
Const Neutral As Integer = 1
Const Urbane As Integer = 2
Const Urban As Integer = 3
Dim Style As Integer
```

The constants *Neutral*, *Urban*, and *Urbane* represent the three possible style choices, one of which will be assigned to the *Style* variable.

Tip

This example uses mutually exclusive values; *Style* can't be a combination, say, of *Urban* and *Urbane*. If you do want values that could be combined, then you should emulate *MouseDown* and use powers of 2 (1,2,4, and so on) for the constants. Then you can use the *And* operator to test for combinations, just as we did for the *Shift* parameter earlier.

When the program starts up, it would be nice if *Style* started out with a valid value. Initializing module-level variables is one of the tasks intended for the *Form_Load* event. You also can use that event to set up one of the option buttons as the default. That, you may recall, involves setting the button's value to True:

```
Private Sub Form_Load()
    Style = Neutral
    optNeutral.Value = True
End Sub
```

Next, let's have the option buttons set the *Style* value:

```
Private Sub optNeutral_Click()
    Style = Neutral
End Sub

Private Sub OptUrban_Click()
    Style = Urban
End Sub
```

continued on next page

continued from previous page

```
Private Sub optUrbane_Click()
     Style = Urbane
End Sub
```

Now let's use *Select Case* in the Start command button to adjust the program's behavior:

```
Private Sub cmdStart_Click()
     Select Case Style
     Case Neutral
          lblName.Caption = "Enter your name:"
          lblEnter1.Caption = "Press Enter when done."
     Case Urbane
          lblName.Caption = "Please enter your name, my friend:"
          lblEnter1.Caption = "Please press the Enter key when done."
     Case Urban
          lblName.Caption = "You're holding up the program! Enter your name!"
          lblEnter1.Caption = "Press the #*#$ Enter key when done."
     Case Else
          lblName.Caption = "Select Case error in cmdStart_Click!"
     End Select
     txtName.Visible = True
     lblEnter1.Visible = True
     txtName.SetFocus
End Sub
```

This code does several things:

- It sets the *lblName.Caption* property to instructions corrresponding to the current option button setting.
- It makes the txtName text box visible.
- It sets the proper instructions for entering one's name (the *lblName.Caption* property), displaying them under the txtName text box.
- It sets the focus to the txtName text box, thus displaying the text cursor in the box and preparing it for data entry.
- It demonstrates defensive programming by using a *Case Else* label to catch *Style* values that shouldn't occur.

Tip

Use the *Case Else* label to catch unexpected values.

Figures L6-11 and L6-12 show how the form looks before and after clicking the Start button.

The next programming step is to describe what happens when the user enters a name. There are two goals here:

- Constructing the next set of instructions, incorporating the user's name
- Making the instructions and the next text entry box visible once the user finishes

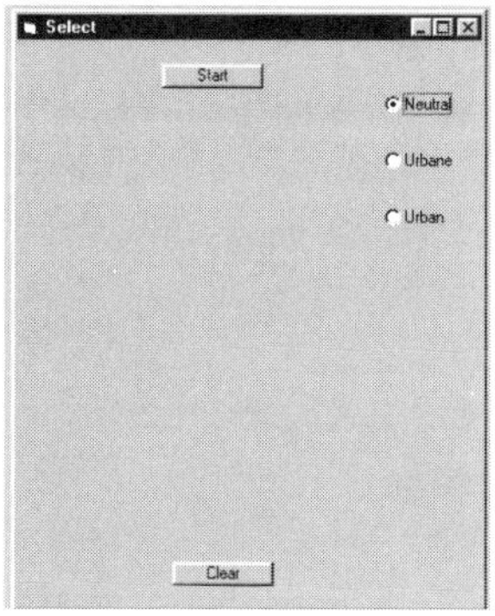

Figure L6-11 The Select form before clicking the Start button

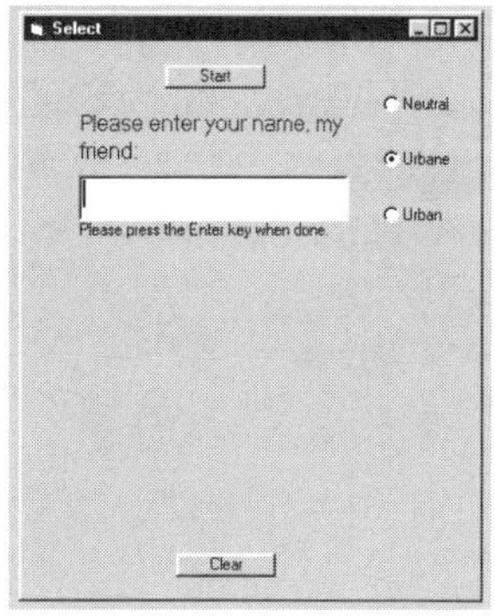

Figure L6-12 The Select form after clicking the Start button

We've already discussed (in Lesson 5) how entering text in a text box triggers the *Change* event. Unfortunately, each character you type triggers an event. So if you use the *Change* event to make the next set of controls visible, they become visible immediately after the first character is typed. Sometimes that's okay, but sometimes you want to wait until the last character is typed before responding. That raises a question. How can the program know when you've finished entering a name? One way is to ask the user to type a particular key, such as ENTER, when finished entering data. That's what this program will do, which is why it uses a label control to tell the user to press ENTER. You can use the KeyPress event to detect that keystroke, so that's the event we'll use.

Detecting the ENTER Key—The *KeyPress* Event

The *KeyPress* event has one argument, the integer parameter *KeyAscii,* which gets set to the ASCII code for the key that was pressed. For instance, if you press A with SHIFT down, *KeyAscii* gets set to 65, the ASCII code for the uppercase *A* character. ENTER generates the Carriage Return character (CR, for short), and that has an ASCII code of 13. So we can compare *KeyAscii* with 13 to detect when ENTER is pressed. To make the comparison clearer, we can use the Visual Basic constant *vbKeyReturn* instead of 13. That leads to the following code for the *txtName_KeyPress* event.

```
Private Sub txtName_KeyPress(KeyAscii As Integer)
    If KeyAscii = vbKeyReturn Then
        Select Case Style
        Case Neutral
            lblTitle.Caption = "Enter your title:"
            lblEnter2.Caption = "Press Enter when done."
        Case Urbane
            lblTitle.Caption = txtName.Text & ", please enter your title:"
            lblEnter2.Caption = "Please press the Enter key when done."
```

continued on next page

continued from previous page

```
        Case Urban
            lblTitle.Caption = "Got a title? Enter it NOW!"
            lblEnter2.Caption = "Don't forget the Enter key, dummy!"
        Case Else
            lblTitle.Caption = "Select Case error in txtName_Change!"
        End Select
        lblTitle.Visible = True
        txtTitle.Visible = True
        lblEnter2.Visible = True
        txtTitle.SetFocus
    End If
End Sub
```

While you enter text, the rest of the controls stay unchanged. But once you press ENTER, the *txtName_KeyPress* event sets the captions for lblTitle and lblEnter2, then makes the two labels and the txtTitle text box visible. It also moves the focus to the newly visible text box. So after the user enters a name and presses ENTER, the form might look like Figure L6-13.

Next, we can use the same technique to display the final label after the user enters a title:

```
Private Sub txtTitle_KeyPress(KeyAscii As Integer)
    If KeyAscii = vbKeyReturn Then
        Select Case Style
        Case Neutral
            lblClose.Caption = "Sorry, program is still under construction."
        Case Urbane
            lblClose.Caption = txtTitle.Text & " " & txtName.Text & _
               ", I'm sorry, but this program is not yet complete. Goodbye."
        Case Urban
            lblClose.Caption = "You screwed this one up!"
        Case Else
            lblClose.Caption = "Better send this program back!"
        End Select
        lblClose.Visible = True
    End If
End Sub
```

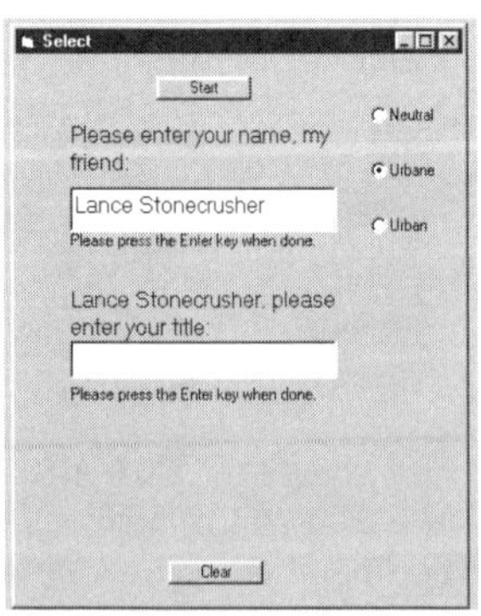

Figure L6-13 The Select form after entering a name

After the user enters a title and presses ENTER, the form might look like Figure L6-14.

Finally, let the Clear command button restore the screen to its initial condition so that you can use the program again without restarting it:

```
Private Sub cmdClear_Click()    'restore original screen
    txtName.Visible = False
    lblEnter1.Visible = False
    lblTitle.Visible = False
    txtTitle.Visible = False
    lblEnter2.Visible = False
    lblClose.Visible = False
    txtName.Text = ""
    txtTitle.Text = ""
    lblName.Caption = ""
End Sub
```

SUMMARY

The *If*, *If ElseIf*, and *Select Case* statements give Visual Basic programs the ability to make choices. Often these choices are based on comparison expressions, which use Visual Basic's comparison operators to compare two values. Comparison expressions have Boolean values, meaning the result is true or false.

You can use the logical *And* and *Or* operators to combine two comparison tests into one. For the *And* operator, the resulting expression is true only if both comparisons are true. For the *Or* operator, the resulting expression is true if at least one comparison is true.

Visual Basic provides symbolic constants, such as *vbLeftButton* for 1, that are clearer in meaning than the bare number. You, too, can define symbolic constants by using the *Const* keyword.

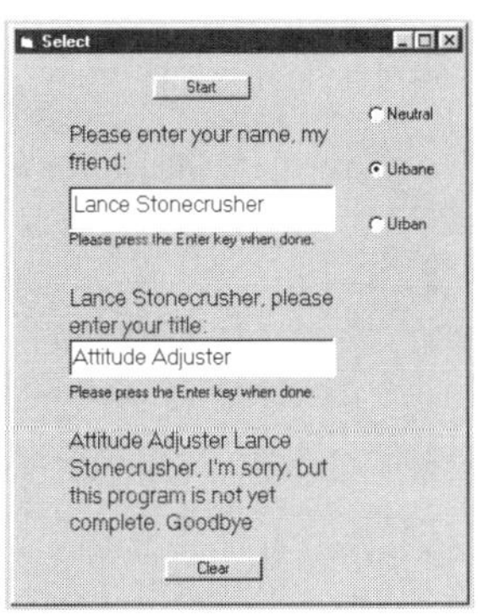

Figure L6-14 The Select form after entering a title

QUIZ 6

1. Indicate whether each of the following expressions is true or false:

```
3 = 4
3 < = 4
10 >= 6 + 4
10 > 5 And 10 < 12
10 > 5 Or 10 > 14
"house" > "castle"
Len("house") > Len("castle")
```

2. Find the error(s) in the following code excerpts (assume any variables are defined):

a.

```
If Guests > 12 Print "Too many!"
```

b.

```
If Computer = "Cray"
     Print "What's this program doing here?"
```

c.

```
If X = 7 then
     Print "Seven is correct!"
elseIf X <> 7 then
     Print "Sorry, that's wrong."
```

3. Define constants to represent the following values:

a. The number of inches (12) in a foot
b. The number of items (12) in a dozen
c. The constant pi (3.14159)
d. The number of people who live in the same building you do

4. Which one of the following best tests if ALT is depressed during a *MouseDown* event:

a. Alt = 4
b. Shift = 4
c. Shift = vbAltMask
d. (Shift And vbAltMask) = vbAltMask

5. How could you change the *Select* example in this lesson so that clicking an option button also restores the original screen?

TRY IT YOURSELF

1. Have a label box display the mouse position at the time a mouse button is pressed and also at the time the button is released. That is, if you press the mouse button when the pointer is in the label box, the caption shows the mouse position at that moment. If you then move the mouse and release the button, the caption shows the mouse position at the time the button is released.

2. Using *Select Case,* write a *MouseDown* procedure for a label box that displays "Left is Deft" if the left mouse button is pressed, "Right is Might" if the right mouse button is pressed, and "Center is the Implementer" if the center button is pressed. Use symbolic constants.

LESSON

7

LOOPS

Into each life some repetition must fall. You have to wash 20 dishes or do 30 sit-ups. If the repetition shows up in a programming problem, you may be in luck. Visual Basic provides several ways to create a *loop,* which is a programming structure that cycles, or loops, through a set of instructions several times. A loop lets you automate repetitive tasks. So instead of having to write 100

```
Print "I will declare my variables."
```

statements, you can accomplish the same result with a single *For Next* statement. In this chapter you'll learn about the following:

- **The *For Next* statement**
- **The *Exit For* statement**
- **The *Do Loop* statements**
- **The *Exit Do* statement**
- **The *DoEvents* function**
- **The horizontal scrollbar control**

When you finish this lesson, you'll have taken another remarkable step toward learning Visual Basic.

THE *FOR NEXT* STATEMENT

The basic *For Next* statement lets you repeatedly execute a set of statements. For instance, to print the same sentence ten times, you can do this:

```
For N = 1 To 10
    Print "The For Next loop is easy to use."
Next N
```

This causes the program to loop through the *Print* statement ten times. Visual Basic uses the variable *N* to keep track of the number of loops. In this case, *N* begins with the value 1, and the *Next N* part adds 1 to *N* each cycle. *N* has the value 10 for the last loop, and when the *Next N* statement increases *N* to 11, the loop terminates.

You can use any valid name for the counter variable, and you can use other values for the starting and ending values of the variable. Thus, the more general syntax is this:

```
For Counter = Initial To Final
    statement(s)
Next Counter
```

Here *Counter* is an integer variable that acts as a counter. When Visual Basic executes the *For Next* statement, it begins by setting *Counter* to the integer value *Initial*. If *Counter* is less than the integer value *Final,* Visual Basic then executes the statements between the *For* line and the *Next* line. When it reaches the *Next* line, Visual Basic increases *Counter* by 1. Then it returns to the *For* line and checks if the new value of *Counter* is less than *Final*. If so, Visual Basic again executes the statements and increases *Counter* by 1. This continues until *Counter* exceeds *Final*. Then the program skips the statements and goes to the line following *Next*.

You can use the counter variable in the statements, too. For example, the code

```
For I = 10 To 15
    Print I
Next I
Print "Done!"
```

will display the following output on the form:

```
10
11
12
13
14
15
Done!
```

As you can see, *I* starts with the value of 10, then increases by one each cycle of the loop. The last value printed is 15. After that, *I* is increased to 16, which exceeds the bounds for the loop, and the loop terminates (see Figure L7-1).

This looks simple enough. Let's try it in a Visual Basic program. First, create a form with a command button in the upper-right corner and use the properties shown in Table L7-1.

OBJECT	PROPERTY	SETTING
Form1	Caption	Top Ten
	Font.Font	Arial (or some other TrueType or PostScript font)
	Name	frmTop10
Command1	Caption	Click Me!
	Name	cmd10

Table L7-1 Properties for the Top Ten program

Note that the specifications call for you to select a TrueType or PostScript font. That's because these fonts are scaleable to different sizes, and the program will use the scaling feature. (Imagine the excitement!)

Next, let's produce some code:

```
Option Explicit

Private Sub cmd10_Click()
    Dim I As Integer
    Print "Ten top reasons for using Visual Basic:"
    For I = 1 To 10
        Print I & ": More fun, less work!" & _
            " [font size = " & frmTop10.Font.Size & "]"
        frmTop10.Font.Size = frmTop10.Font.Size * 1.1
    Next I
End Sub
```

The loop needs a counter, so the program declares *I* for that purpose. Just because it's a loop counter doesn't exempt it from needing to be declared when *Option Explicit* is in effect.

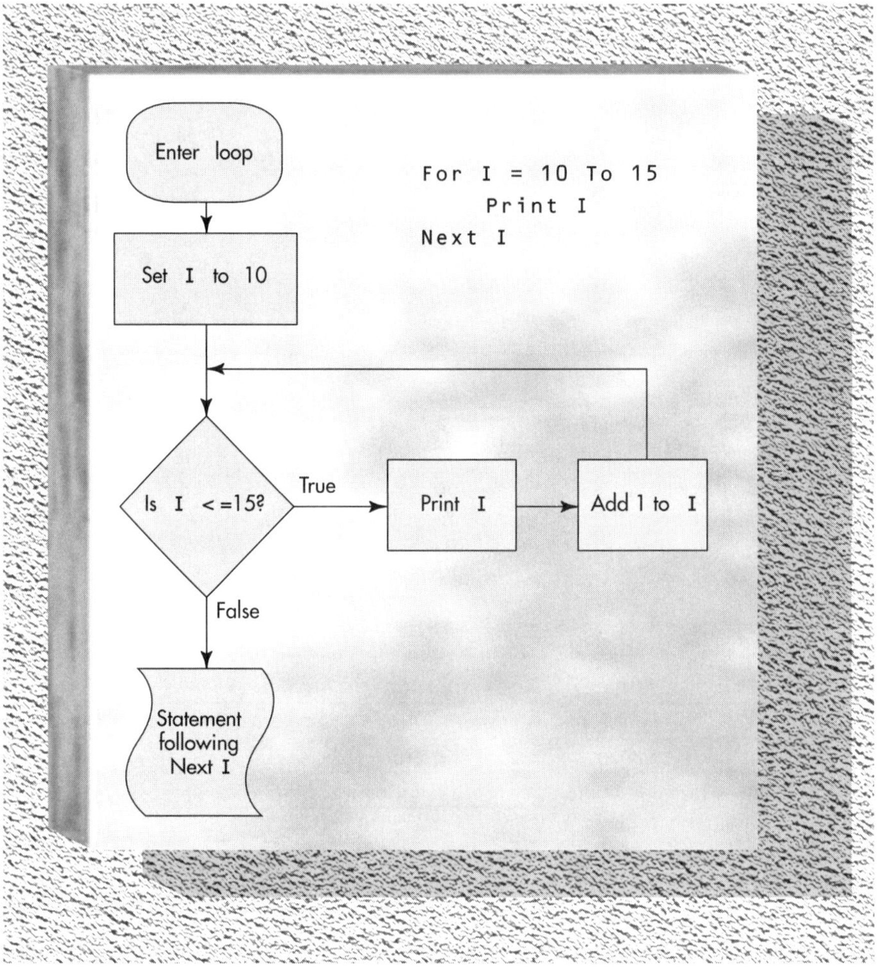

Figure L7-1 The *For Next* loop

The program uses the *Print* method to display *I* and a string. For instance, when *I* has the value 5, the printed string will begin with "*5: More fun, less work!*". Then the *Print* method adds information about the size of the font. For example, the second line printed in the loop will be this:

```
2: More fun, less work! [font size = 9]
```

The line

```
frmFor.Font.Size = frmFor.Font.Size * 1.1
```

increases the font size by a factor of 1.1 each cycle. Actually, that's not quite true. Visual Basic is a bit mendacious about font sizes. You can't really set a scaleable font to any size. You can't even set scaleable font sizes to the precise choices that appear in the font dialog box! Instead, Visual Basic increments scaleable font sizes in units of 0.75 point. That is, the allowable sizes go like this: 8.25, 9.0,

9.75, 10.5, 11.25, 12.0, 12.75, 13.5, and so on. Other sizes get dropped down to the nearest allowable size. For instance, if you select 14 in the font dialog box, Visual Basic really uses 13.5. And when the loop above calculates that 1.1 * 8.25 is 9.075, the actual value used is 9.0. The next cycle would multiply 9.0, not 9.075 by 1.1, yielding 9.9, which is dropped to 9.75, and so on. Figure L7-2 shows the output for a scaleable font. You can see how the font sizes behave.

The situation for nonscaleable types, like the default MS Serif, is different. Here the allowable sizes run 8.25, 9.75, 12, 13.5, 18, and 24. Here multiplying 8.25 by 1.1 yields 9.075, as before, but this is still smaller than the next step, so the result is dropped back to 8.25. That means 8.25 is the font size the next cycle, too, so the same thing happens again, and the size never changes. Try it. You probably won't like it.

Note

Visual Basic increments (and decrements) scaleable font sizes in units of 0.75 point. The 12-point size is exact, so the next two larger sizes are 12.75 and 13.50, and the next two smaller sizes are 11.25 and 10.50. Settings you make in the Font Settings box are converted to the nearest Visual Basic size that's no larger than your selection. So a setting of 11 is converted to 10.50, and so on.

Optional *For Next* Features—Free!

The *For Next* loop has a couple of optional features you can use. First, you can use the keyword *Step* to modify how the counter is changed each loop cycle. Second, you can use the *Exit For* command to terminate a loop. Let's look these options over.

You're not limited to incrementing the counter by 1. You can use the optional *Step* keyword to indicate the amount to add to the counter each cycle. For instance, the following loop counts from 8 to 80 by 8s:

```
For I = 8 To 80 Step 8
    Print I
Next I
```

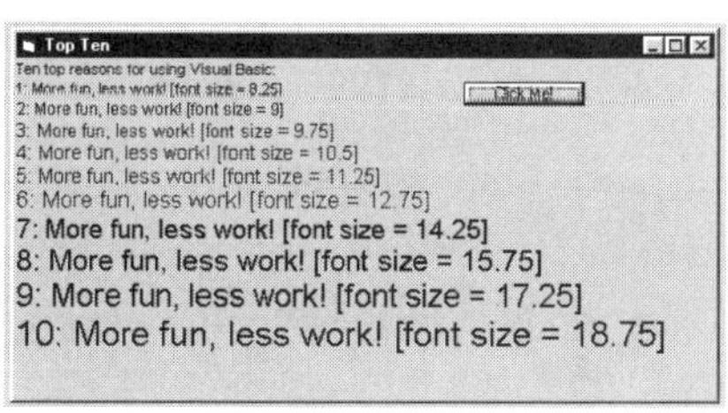

Figure L7-2 The result of running Top Ten

You can use a negative step to count backwards. For example, the following code counts down from 5 to 0:

```
For I = 5 To 0 Step -1
    Print I
Next I
```

Note that the following code does nothing:

```
For I = 5 To 0
    Print I
Next I
```

Note

If you omit *Step,* Visual Basic takes *Step* to be 1. If *Step* is positive, Visual Basic skips over any loop for which the starting value is greater than the ending value.

What if you do something like this?

```
For I = 1 To 40 Step 9
    Print I
Next I
```

Here the step size is such that *I* never hits 40 exactly. Instead, it jumps from 37 to 46. Well, the loop terminates when *I exceeds* the end value. So the loop prints 37, increases *I* to 46, and terminates without printing the value 46.

The *Exit For* statement lets you terminate a loop early. Sometimes conditions pop up when you might want to do so. For instance, if you click the Click Me! button a second time without restarting the program, it reprints the top ten reasons without resetting the font size to 8.25, so the fonts get even bigger. You might like that feature, but you might want to prevent the process from going past a font size of, say, 48. Then you could modify the loop to look like this:

```
For I = 1 To 10
    Print Str(I) + ": More fun, less work!"
    frmFor.Font.Size = frmFor.Font.Size * 1.1
    If frmFor.Font.Size > 48 Then Exit For
Next I
```

The *Exit For* command causes the program to jump immediately to the statement following the *Next*. Typically, you use the *Exit For* command in an *If* statement, as in this example.

There are a couple of other things you might like to know. In a simple *For Next* loop you can omit the counter name after the *Next;* Visual Basic knows it should be the same name that immediately follows the *For:*

```
For Tickets = 1 To 5
    ...
Next     'Visual Basic knows to increment Tickets by 1.
```

Second, since the counter variable is just another variable, you can change its value in a loop. However, it's a bad idea to do so, for it makes the code harder to understand:

```
For Counter = 1 To 10
     Print Counter
     If Counter > 3 Then Counter = Counter + 2 'bad programming style
Next I
```

This would print the following:

```
1
2
3
4
7
10
```

Once *Counter* exceeds 3, the *If* statement increases *Counter* by 2 and the *Next* part increases *Counter* by 1, so overall the loop increments *Counter* by 3 each cycle. Not easy to figure out, is it? That's why this is an example of what you shouldn't do.

> **Tip**
> Regard your programs as exercises in clear communication, not as puzzles to baffle readers.

Relaxing at the Horizontal Scrollbar Control

This heading looks like a complete change of topic, but it's just a prelude to using the control in another *For Next* example. The horizontal scrollbar control gives you a horizontal scrollbar like those you might see in the bottom of a word processor window except that the scrollbar is isolated. You can move it around on a form and size it as you desire. You can use the scrollbar as an input control, with the user sliding the scroll box (or *slider*) back and forth to select a value. This is handy for getting integer input, for you don't have to worry about the user somehow misunderstanding your clear instructions and entering a string by mistake.

Let's look at the basics. Create a new form, choose the horizontal scrollbar icon from the Toolbox, and draw a scrollbar on a form. Run the program and note how you can use the mouse to drag the scroll box back and forth. Very nice, you say, but what can you do with it? Quit the program and take a look at the Properties list for the scrollbar. The three most important properties for our purposes are these:

- *Value*—the integer value represented by the position of the scroll box
- *Min*—the minimum possible value, corresponding to the scroll box being at the far left of the scrollbar
- *Max*—the maximum possible value, corresponding to the scroll box being at the far right

As you slide the scroll box back and forth, you change the *Value* parameter. By default, *Min* is 0 and *Max* is 32767, so you can use the scroll box to select values anywhere in that range. For fine control, you can click on the arrows at the end of the scrollbar to increase or decrease the value by 1. Also, clicking on the bar just next to the arrows also changes the value by 1.

Click Management

You can change the effect of clicking on or near the arrows on a scrollbar by setting the SmallChange and LargeChange properties. If you click *on* an arrow, the Value property changes by an amount equal to the SmallChange property, which is 1 by default. If you click on the bar *next to* an arrow, the Value property changes by an amount equal to the LargeChange property, which also is 1 by default (see Figure L7-3).

Of course, it would be nice to see what the value is. One way is to create a Label box just above the scrollbar and use the horizontal scrollbar *Change* event to set the label's caption. That way, each change you make to the scrollbar updates the label display.

```
Private Sub HScroll1_Change()
    Label1.Caption = HScroll1.Value
End Sub
```

The Growing Window Program

Armed with your knowledge of the horizontal scrollbar control and of the *For Next* statement, you can undertake the challenge of the Growing Window. This program will feature a form with a command button and a scrollbar. When you click on the command button, the window will shorten to nearly no height, then grow back to its original size. The scrollbar will let you set how fast the screen grows. First, create a form according to the layout shown in Figure L7-4 and using the properties shown in Table L7-2.

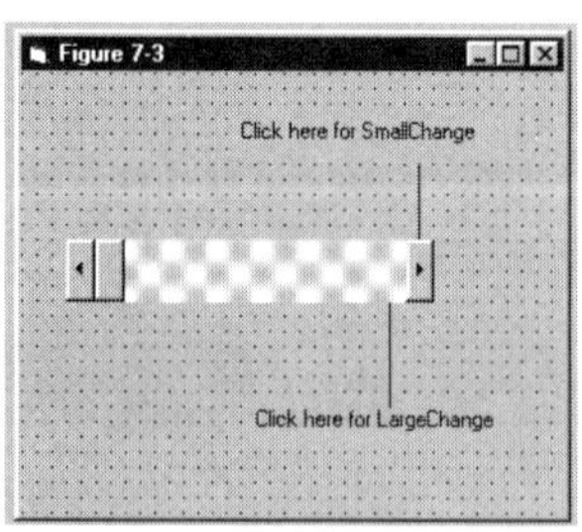

Figure L7-3 SmallChange and LargeChange

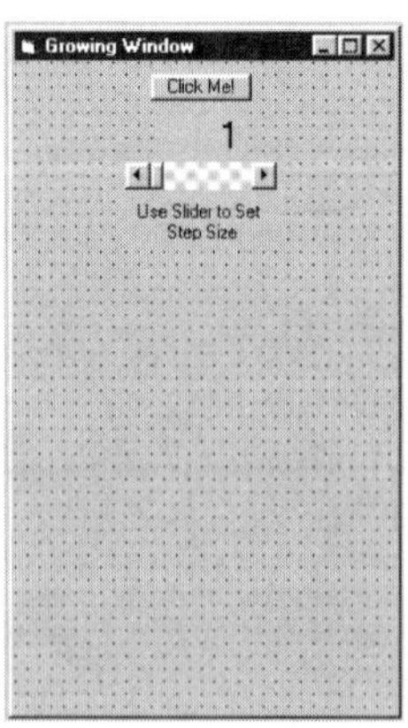

Figure L7-4 The Growing Window form

OBJECT	PROPERTY	SETTING
Form1	Caption	Growing Window
	Name	frmGrow
Command1	Caption	Click Me!
	Name	cmdFor
Label1	Caption	1
	Font.Size	18
	Name	lblStep
Label2	Alignment	2 - Center
	Caption	Use Slider to Set Step Size
	Name	lblSet
Hscroll1	max	100
	min	1
	Name	hsbStep

Table L7-2 Properties for the Growing Window program

One thing to notice is that Visual Basic automatically resets the *Value* parameter to whatever you set the *Min* property to. That way, the scrollbar starts with the scroll box at the far left.

Now let's proceed to the code. The *cmdFor_Click* event will run a *For Next* loop that changes the form's height. By using different values for the loop's *Step* value, you can control how fast the size changes. You can use the scrollbar to get a value for *Step* by using the *hsbStep_Change* event. The simplest way to communicate a value between the two events is to have them share a module-level variable, so that's what the code shown in Listing L7-1 does.

Listing L7-1
The Growing Window code

```
Option Explicit
Dim StepSize As Integer 'set in Change event, used in Click event

Private Sub cmdFor_Click()
    Dim H, Counter As Integer
    H = frmGrow.Height        'Save original height.
    For Counter = 100 To H Step StepSize
        frmGrow.Height = Counter
    Next Counter
    frmGrow.Height = H        'Restore to original height.
End Sub

Private Sub Form_Load()
    StepSize = 1              'Initialize variable.
End Sub

Private Sub hsbStep_Change()
    LblStep.Caption = hsbStep.Value 'Show value.
    StepSize = hsbStep.Value        'Set step size to value.
End Sub
```

Let's step through this code and see how it works.

1. Loading the form initializes the *StepSize* variable to 1.
2. Changing the position of the scrollbar scroll box resets *StepSize* to a new value and displays that value in the label above the scrollbar.
3. Clicking the button causes the *Click* event procedure to save the current height of the form in the variable *H*.
4. The procedure resets the height to 100 pixels, making the form small first so that it can grow.
5. The *For Next* loop proceeds to increase the form's height using the value of *StepSize* as its *Step* value. The bigger the step size, the faster the program grows the window.
6. If the step size is larger than 1, the *For Loop* may not hit the final value quite on the nose, so the last statement sets *frmFor.Height* to *H* exactly.

Try the program using different step sizes. If your computer is very fast or very slow, you may want to use a different value for *Max*.

THE OTHER CHOICE—THE *DO LOOP*

The *For Next* loop is an excellent choice if you need something repeated a definite number of times. But sometimes your needs may be more indefinite. For instance, you might want a button to flash Click Me! repeatedly until you click it. Or you might want a program to keep accepting input until the user gets it right. The user may need 1 try or 20 tries; you just don't know in advance how many loops will be needed. For situations like these, the *Do Loop* is the answer.

The versatile *Do Loop* comes in four varieties. Let's look at one variety first and see how it works. The *Do While Loop* has this syntax:

```
Do While test-condition
     statement(s)
Loop
```

The *test-condition* is the same sort of test condition an *If* statement uses, one that evaluates to true or false. In this case, the program repeatedly executes the statements between the *Do While* line and the *Loop* line as long as the test condition remains true. More exactly, a Visual Basic program starts by checking the test condition. If it's true, the program executes the statements up to the *Loop* line. Then the program returns to the *Do While* line and tests the condition again. If it's true, the program repeats the statements again. If *the test-condition* is false, even if this happens the first time the test is made, the program jumps to the statement following the *Loop* line (see Figure L7-5).

For example, here's a loop that prints integers and their squares until the squares get too big (bigger than 100):

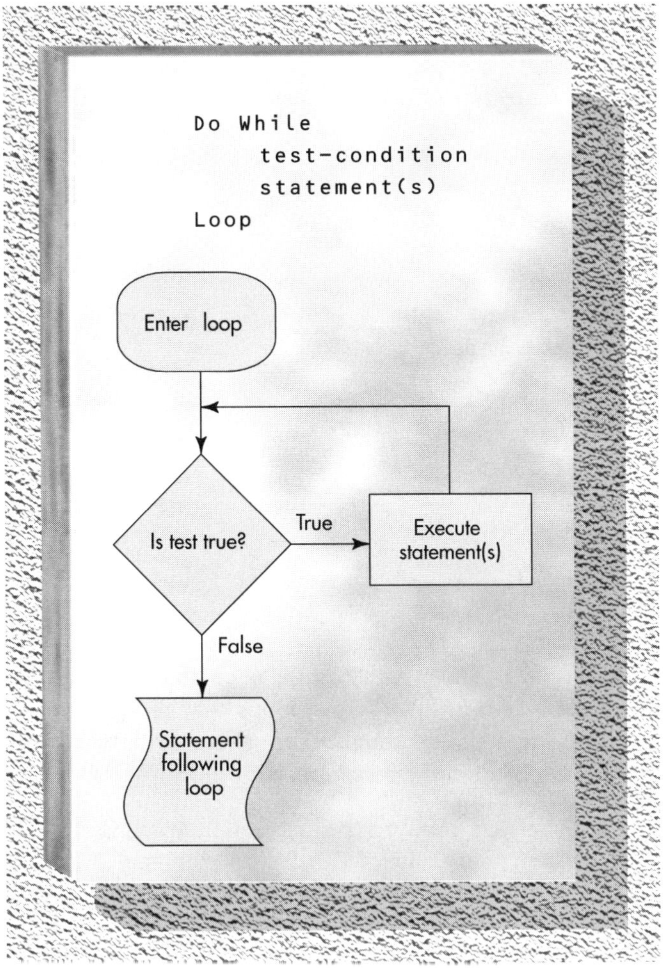

Figure L7-5 The *Do While Loop* structure

```
Dim N As Integer
N = 1
Do While N * N < 101
    Print N; N * N
    N = N + 1
Loop
```

The test condition is that *N* ∗ *N* is less than 101, so this loop prints the integers 1 through 10 and their squares. Note the following very important line:

```
N = N + 1
```

Without it, the variable *N* would remain with the value 1, so *N* ∗ *N* also would remain 1 * 1, the test condition would remain true, and the loop would repeat

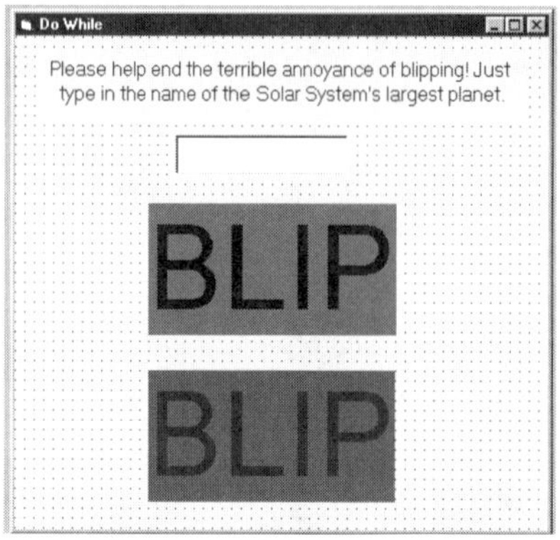

Figure L7-6 The Do While program

itself forever, printing 1 1. Now that is boring! Needless to say (but we'll say it anyway), you should design your loops so that the test condition will fail at some point, terminating the loop. (If you produce such a runaway loop, use CTRL-BREAK to halt the program.)

Tip

One potential problem with the *Do Loop* family of loops is that careless design can result in loops that repeat forever. Therefore, check to see that your program creates conditions that eventually terminate the loop.

Usually, it's the code in the loop that alters the values in the test condition. For instance, the last example changed the value of *N* each cycle of the loop. But event-driven programming creates other possibilities, as the next example illustrates.

Do While Loop Meets *DoEvents*

In some cases, loops need to use an interesting command called *DoEvents*. Before explaining what *DoEvents* does, let's develop a situation that requires the command.

The next project is a simple, one-question quiz in which the user has to type the answer in a text box. To add a bit of casino-type distraction, the form also will flash two label boxes off and on until the user enters the correct answer. As usual, begin by laying out the form. Figure L7-6 shows the three labels and one text box, and Table L7-3 lists the relevant properties.

OBJECT	PROPERTY	SETTING
Form1	BackColor	&H0000FFFF& (yellow)
	Caption	Do While
	Name	frmDoWhile

OBJECT	PROPERTY	SETTING
Label1	Alignment	2 - Center
	BackColor	&H0000FFFF& (yellow)
	Caption	Please help end the terrible annoyance of blipping! Just type in the name of the Solar System's largest planet.
	Font.Size	12
	Name	lblMessage
Label2	Alignment	2 - Center
	AutoSize	True
	BackColor	&H000000FF& (red)
	Caption	BLIP
	Font.Font	Arial (or some other TrueType or PostScript font)
	Font.Size	72
	Name	lblBlip1
Label2	Alignment	2 - Center
	AutoSize	True
	BackColor	&H00FF0000& (blue)
	Caption	BLIP
	Font.Font	Arial (or some other TrueType or PostScript font)
	Font.Size	72
	Name	lblBlip2
	Visible	False
Text1	Name	txtAnswer
	Text	

Table L7-3 Properties for the Do While program

To make things easy for the user, you should set up the form so that the text box has the focus. That way, the text box will have the text entry cursor active, and the user can enter an answer immediately. Normally, you could use a *SetFocus* method in the *Form_Load* procedure. But in this case, the text control is the *only* control of the bunch that can take the focus, so it automatically gets it.

Toggling Tricks

Next, let's look at the code. The *Do While Loop* statement can take care of blinking the two BLIP labels on and off by toggling the Visible properties between True and False. Here's a straightforward way to do that:

```
Dim Toggle As Integer
Toggle = 0
Do While txtAnswer.Text <> "JUPITER"
    If Toggle = 0 Then
        Toggle = 1
```

continued on next page

continued from previous page

```
        lblBlip1.Visible = False
        lblBlip2.Visible = True
    Else
        Toggle = 0
        lblBlip1.Visible = True
        lblBlip2.Visible = False
    End If
Loop
```

As you can see, the loop changes the value of the *Toggle* variable from 0 to 1 to 0 to 1, and so forth. When the value is 1, the form shows lblBlip2, and when the value is 0, the form shows lblBlip1. Thus the effect of this loop is to alternately blip each label. As the text condition shows, this action continues until the user enters (*txtAnswer.Text*) the correct answer of "JUPITER".

However, this is a case where you can use the *Not* operator (see Lesson 6) to shorten the code quite a bit. Remember, applying *Not* to a Boolean value, such as the Visible property, returns the opposite value—*True* for *False* and *False* for *True*. So you can reduce the code to the following, which converts a Visible property to its opposite each loop cycle.

```
Do While txtAnswer.Text <> "JUPITER"
    lblBlip1.Visible = Not lblBlip1.Visible
    lblBlip2.Visible = Not lblBlip2.Visible
Loop
```

Tip

If you need to toggle Boolean values, use the *Not* operator.

Where Does It Go?

One very interesting question is, where does this code go? Ideally, the blipping should start as soon as the program begins. That suggests putting this code in the *Load* event. But the *Load* event occurs *before* the controls even appear, so it doesn't accomplish anything useful to place this code in the *Load* event procedure.

Another choice is creating a control button, perhaps captioned "Start," to hold the code. But that adds an extra step to using the program, one that isn't needed.

The simplest solution is to place this code in the *txtAnswer_GotFocus* event. Remember, the txtAnswer control, being the only control on the form that can accept the focus, gets the focus when the program starts. Thus, the *txtAnswer_GotFocus* event is the first event triggered after the *Form_Load* event, so the loop begins executing as soon as the program finishes loading (See Figure L7-7).

The Need for *DoEvents*

Suppose you go ahead and place the code in the *txtAnswer_GotFocus* event. You then come up against a major flaw. Recall the loop test:

```
Do While txtAnswer.Text <> "JUPITER"
```

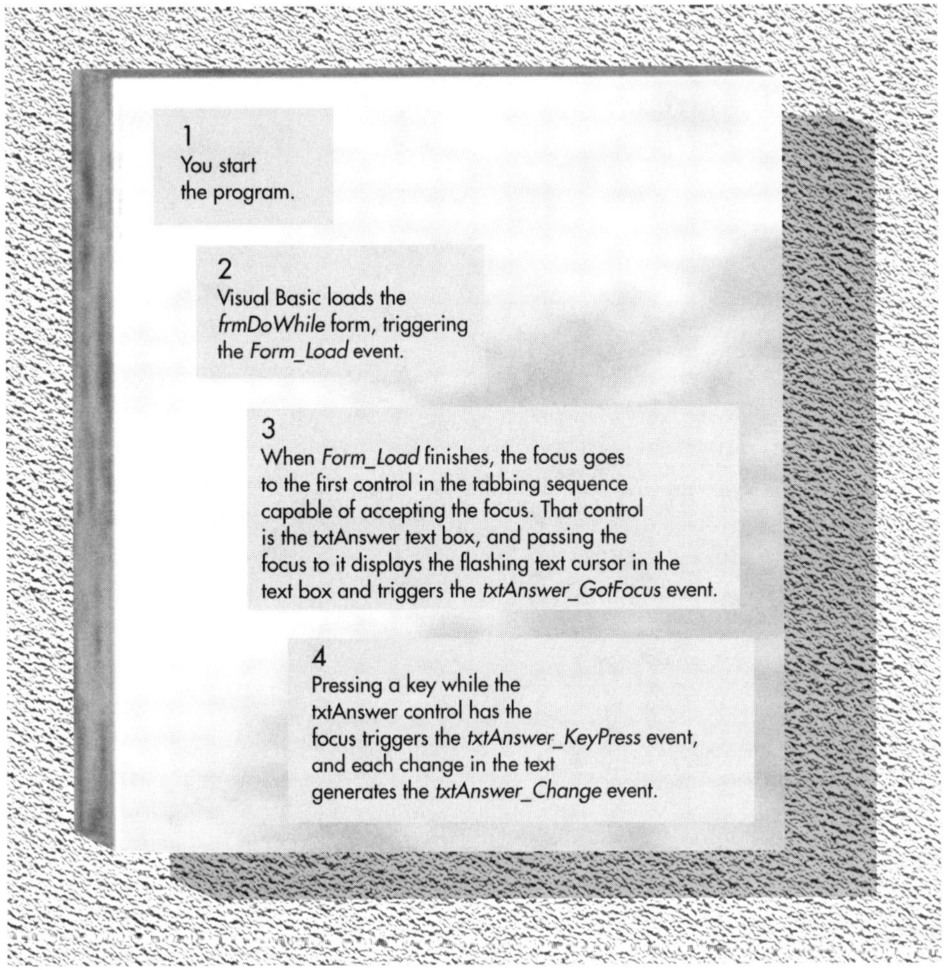

Figure L7-7 Event order for the Do While form

Typing an answer in the txtAnswer box generates the *txtAnswer_Change* event for each character you enter. Unfortunately, the Visual Basic program can't process another event until it completes the *txtAnswer_GotFocus* event. So you can't use the keyboard to alter the value of the *txtAnswer.Text* property until the *txtAnswer_GotFocus* event finishes. But the *txtAnswer_GotFocus* event can't finish until you correctly alter the value of the *txtAnswer.Text* property! See Figure L7-8.

What we need is for the loop to pause briefly, letting Visual Basic check for and process other events. What we get is a function by the name of *DoEvents*. The *DoEvents* command passes control to the operating system, letting it process any pending events, such as keystrokes and mouse clicks. When the operating

Figure L7-8 The fatal flaw

system finishes with that task, it passes control back to the procedure containing *DoEvents*. Thus, by placing *DoEvents* in the loop, you give the program the opportunity to update the value of the *txtAnswer.Text* property, as shown in Figure L7-9.

Tip

Use *DoEvents* in a loop if you want your program to be able to process other events while the loop runs.

Figure L7-9 The *DoEvents* function at work

Now you can complete the code for the program:

```
Option Explicit

Private Sub txtAnswer_GotFocus()
    Do While txtAnswer.Text <> "JUPITER"
        lblBlip1.Visible = Not lblBlip1.Visible
        lblBlip2.Visible = Not lblBlip2.Visible
        DoEvents
    Loop
    lblBlip1.Visible = True
    lblBlip2.Visible = True
    lblBlip1.Caption = "Thank"
    lblBlip2.Caption = "You!"
End Sub
```

This code also adds a few lines to alter the display to thank you once you enter the correct answer. Figure L7-10 shows the result of a successful response.

Incidentally, Visual Basic functions return values. So because *DoEvents* is a function, it returns a value. In particular, it returns the number of open forms in a Visual Basic program. In this example, for instance, it returns the value 1. However, this program didn't need that information, so we called the function without using its return value. If you wanted the return value for some reason, you could capture it using assignment:

```
FormsOpen = DoEvents
```

Uppercase, Anyone?

The program still has a shortcoming. To halt the loop, you have to enter "JUPITER". Alternative capitalizations, such as "Jupiter" or "jupiter" don't match the "JUPITER" string exactly, so they don't halt the loop. This is fixable. In fact, it is fixable in many ways.

The first method is the simplest. The Visual Basic *UCase* function takes a string as an argument and returns a string in which all the letters are uppercase. For example, the function call *UCase("Alistair Cooke")* would return the string *"ALISTAIR COOKE"*. This means we can solve the uppercase problem by replacing

```
Do While txtAnswer.Text <> "JUPITER"
```

with the following:

```
Do While UCase(txtAnswer.Text) <> "JUPITER"
```

The second method is more involved, but it illustrates some useful techniques. The idea is to use the *KeyPress* event to intercept each keystroke and convert it to uppercase. This way the typed answer always is uppercase.

Here's how to convert the input to uppercase.

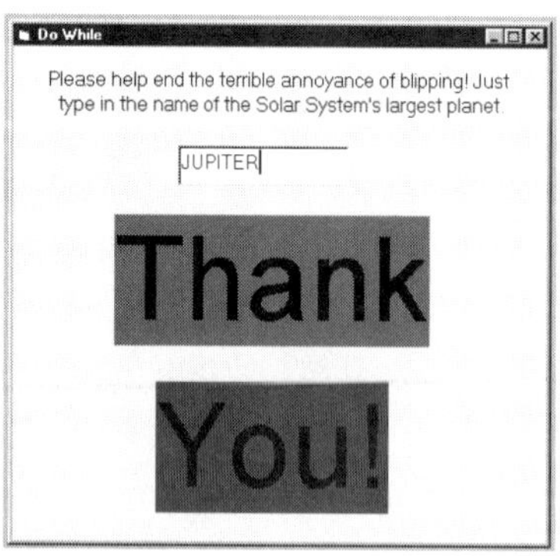

Figure L7-10 A successful completion

```
Private Sub txtAnswer_KeyPress(KeyAscii As Integer)
    Dim char As String
    char = Chr(KeyAscii)
    KeyAscii = Asc(UCase(char))
End Sub
```

The *KeyAscii* argument represents the character code for the key you press, and this code converts the code for lowercase characters, such as *j*, to the code for uppercase characters, such as *J*. This event procedure previews several string functions the lesson on text (Lesson 13) discusses later. The *Chr* function converts an ASCII code to a string. The *UCase* function converts a string to uppercase, and the *Asc* function returns the ASCII code for the first character in a string. Suppose, for example, that you press J. This sets *KeyAscii* to 106, the ASCII code for the *j* character. The line

```
char = Chr(KeyAscii)
```

assigns the string "*j*" to the variable *char*. The function *UCase(char)* then returns the uppercase version, the string "*J*". This makes the *Asc* function call equivalent to *Asc("J")*, which returns the value 74, the ASCII code for the *J* character. So now *KeyAscii* winds up with the ASCII code for *J* instead of for *j*, so the text box displays the character *J*.

Clearly, the first method is simpler. However, the second method illustrates that you can control user input. You could even do something like this:

```
If char = "j" Or char = "J" Then char = "L"
```

Everytime the user types a *J*, it appears onscreen as an *L*, making it impossible to answer the question correctly. Of course, you should not do something like that.

Other *Do Loop* Variations

There are two aspects you can vary in a *Do Loop*. One is the kind of test. You can use either *While* or *Until*. As the names suggest, a *Do While Loop* continues as long as a particular test remains true, while a *Do Until Loop* continues as long as the test is false, terminating when it becomes true. For instance, the loop

```
Do While X = 7
    ...
Loop
```

keeps going as long as the variable *X* has the value 7. But the loop

```
Do Until X = 7
    ...
Loop
```

keeps going *until* X is 7; that is, the loop continues as long as the variable *X* is not 7.

Choosing between *While* and *Until* is a matter of convenience, for you can convert one form to another by rewording the test. For example,

```
Do Until X <> 7
    ...
Loop
```

is the same as the following *While* version:

```
Do While X = 7
    ...
Loop
```

Test Placement

The second thing you can vary is the placement of the test. The test can come at the beginning, as in the examples so far, or it can come at the end, as it does for the next two examples:

```
Do
    ...
Loop While Cat <> "Sylvester"

Do
    ...
Loop Until Winner = "Me"
```

If the test is at the beginning, the loop is an *entry-condition* loop, meaning the test must be passed before the loop is entered. If the test is at the end, the loop is an *exit-condition* loop, meaning the test is the last step of the loop cycle instead of the first.

The most important difference is that an entry-condition loop has the option of terminating without ever executing any statements in the loop, while an exit-condition must execute at least one cycle before terminating. That's because the program can't examine the test condition without passing through the statements above it first.

Generally, an entry-condition loop is safer because it checks before doing anything rash. For instance, the entry-condition loop

```
Do While X <> 0
    Y = 1.0 / X
    ...
Loop
```

avoids the computer no-no of attempting to divide by 0. But the exit-condition loop

```
Do
    Y = 1.0 / X
    ...
Loop While X <> 0
```

will attempt to divide by 0 because it doesn't test the value of *X* until after the action.

The *Exit Do* Statement

Just as you can exit a *For* loop prematurely with an *Exit For* statement, you can exit any of the *Do* loops prematurely with an *Exit Do* statement. For instance, suppose the Do While program also had a command button labeled I Give Up that set a module-level *Boolean* variable called *IGiveUp* to True. You want that condition to terminate the loop. Then you could modify the *Do While* loop as follows:

```
Do While txtAnswer.Text <> "JUPITER"
    lblBlip1.Visible = Not lblBlip1.Visible
    lblBlip2.Visible = Not lblBlip2.Visible
    DoEvents
    If IGiveUp Then Exit Do        'Alternative exit to loop.
Loop
```

SUMMARY

Visual Basic offers two looping mechanisms—the *For Next* loop and the four varieties of the *Do Loop*. The *For Next* loop is best suited for loops that are executed for a predetermined number of cycles. For example, the loop

```
For I = 1 To 10
    Print "I'm some kind of programmer."
Next I
```

cycles exactly ten times.

More generally, you can specify a step size. For instance, the loop

```
For I = 0 To 100 Step 10
    Print I
Next I
```

prints the numbers 0, 10, 20, 30, and so on, through 100.

The *Do Loop* comes in four varieties. The *Do While Loop* and the *Do Until Loop* loops are entry-condition loops that perform a test before each loop cycle, while the *Do Loop While* and the *Do Loop Until* loops are exit-condition loops that perform a test at the end of each loop cycle.

A *Do Loop* is best suited for loops that cycle until some condition changes to meet a desired condition. For instance, the following loop exits when the integer *D* divides evenly into the integer *N*; thus it finds the smallest divisor of *N*:

```
N = 169
D = 2
Do Until N Mod D = 0
    D = D + 1
Loop
```

If one number goes into another evenly, then there is no remainder, so *N Mod D* would be 0. This loop goes until it finds the first divisor of *N*. If *N* has no divisor (that is, *N* is prime), the loop quits when *D* reaches *N*, because *N* divided by *N* yields 1 and no remainder.

You can exit a *For Next* loop prematurely by using an *Exit For* statement, and you can exit a *Do Loop* prematurely by using an *Exit Do* statement.

If you place a loop in an event procedure, the program won't be able to process any other events until the loop terminates and the event procedure terminates. By placing the *DoEvents* function call in a loop, however, you allow the program to process pending events before returning to the loop.

The horizontal scrollbar control provides a convenient way to get numeric input from a user. Because its Value property is an integer based on the position of the scrollbar slider, you don't have to worry about getting some other data type the way you do if you get input from a text box.

For all questions, please assume that all variables have been declared correctly.

1. What would the following loop display?

```
For I = 1 to 13 Step 5
    Print I
Next I
```

2. What would the following loop display?

```
For I = 10 to 1
    Print I
Next I
```

3. What would the following loop display?

```
I = 1
Do While I < 5
    Print I
    I = I + 1
Loop
```

4. What would the following loop display?

```
I = 1
Do
    Print I
    I = I + 1
Loop While I < 5
```

5. What would the following loop display?

```
I = 1
Do Until I = 5
    Print I
Loop
```

6. Expound in a knowledgeable yet lively manner on the differences between entry-condition loops and exit-condition loops.

7. Describe four useful properties of a horizontal scrollbar.

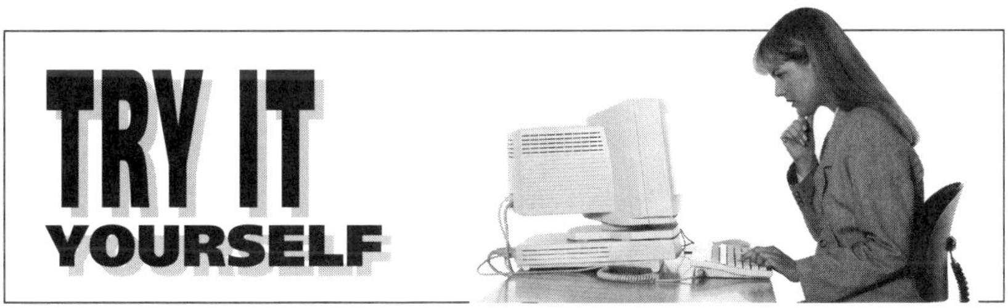

1. Rewrite the Top Ten program so that it counts in reverse—10, 9, 8, and so on. But still have the font get bigger each cycle.

2. Write a program that has the user provide integer input via a horizontal scrollbar. Have the program find the smallest integer that divides evenly (no remainder) into the chosen number.

3. Write a program that asks you to pick a number from 1 to 100. You use a horizontal scrollbar to select the number in that range. The program uses a loop to process your picks. If your pick is too high, a label displays "Too high!". If your pick is too low, a label displays "Too low!". If you pick the correct number, a label congratulates you, and the processing loop ends. For setting the secret number, you can use a Visual Basic function that returns a number randomly. You'll learn more about this function later. For now, just place the following code in the Form_Load event procedure:

```
Secret =  Int ( 100 * Rnd + 1)
```

This sets *Secret*, which should be a module-level variable, randomly to an integer in the range 1–100.

LESSON

8

SO WHAT'S ON THE MENU?

Certainly menus are among the most ubiquitous features of Windows programs, and Visual Basic makes it easy (of course) to add menus to a form. This lesson will explore those ways. While developing examples, the lesson also will introduce the Clipboard object, which makes it easy for you to cut and paste. And you'll meet up with the Screen object and the TypeOf test, which will help you manage forms and controls. In short, you'll learn about the following:

- **Creating menu items**

- **Creating submenu items**
- **Creating menu item arrays**
- **Programming menu *Click* events**
- **The Clipboard object**
- **Using the Windows Clipboard to cut, copy, and paste**
- **The Screen object**
- **The *TypeOf Is* test condition**

THE MENU EDITOR

Your main tool in creating menus is the aptly named Menu Editor. You can start it by selecting Menu Editor from the Visual Basic menu or by choosing the Menu Editor icon from the Toolbar, which runs horizontally under the menu bar. You should see the new window pictured in Figure L8-1.

As you can see, the Menu Editor has several parts. We'll start with the basics:

- The Caption text box
- The Name text box
- The arrow controls
- The menu-control list box

The simplest way to see how these parts work is to use them, so let's begin.

Start by creating a name that will appear on the menu bar. Such names are called menu titles. Use the Caption text box to enter the caption that will appear on the menu bar as a menu title. For example, enter the word "Dine". You'll notice the same word also appears in the *menu-control list box,* which occupies the bottom half of the Menu Editor.

Next, use the Name text box to enter a name for the menu title. Just like controls, each menu title needs a unique name which program code can use to identify the menu title. Unlike controls, however, menu titles don't come with default names. That is, if you create a label, it's named Label1 by default. But if you create a menu title, it doesn't have a name until you enter one in the Name text box. The Visual Basic convention is to use "mnu" as the beginning of menu title names, so enter *mnuDine* as the name. The Menu Editor should look like Figure L8-2.

Next, click on the OK button. The Menu Editor closes, and the word "Dine" appears at the left end of the form's menu bar. You now have the beginnings of a menu. Let's continue the work.

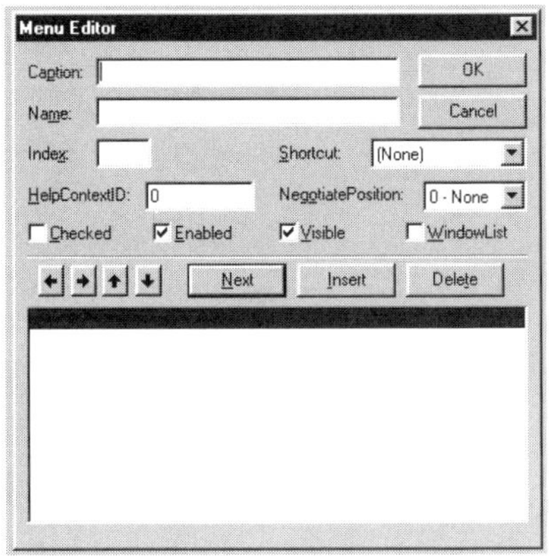

Figure L8-1 The Menu Editor

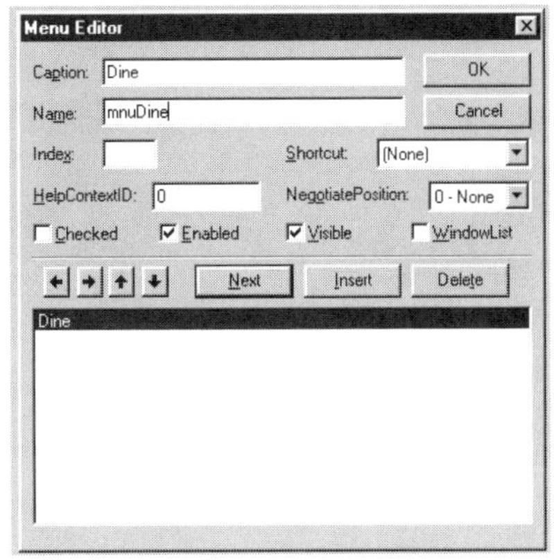

Figure L8-2 Adding a menu title with the Menu Editor

Open the Menu Editor again. First, modify the Caption to read "&Dine" instead of "Dine". Just as with ordinary controls, the & makes the following letter an access key. That is, now you can access the Dine menu by pressing ALT-D as well as by clicking on the menu item. It also causes the letter to be underlined in the menu.

Adding Menu Items to a Menu Title

For our next trick, let's create a *menu item,* that is, an item that shows up when you click on a menu bar title. Begin by clicking the Next button. The highlight bar in the menu-control list box moves down from &Dine to the next line. Now enter a new caption, &Figs. (Using the & here means you can access this menu item by pressing ALT-D to open the menu and F to select the Figs item.) Next, enter a name. You can call it anything, but the convention is to append a suitable name to the end of the main menu title name. For instance, use *mnuDineFigs*. This name identifies the item as being the &Figs item belonging to the Dine menu. You need to do one more thing to make &Figs a menu item—click on the right arrow control. This shifts the &Figs name to the right in the menu-control list box, which now should look like Figure L8-3. If you don't shift the name to the right, you would create another menu title.

Now extend the menu by clicking on the Next button and adding a new item. Enter &Duck for the caption and *mnuDineDuck* for the name. Note that the new item automatically aligns with the one above it, so &Duck also is a menu item under the &Dine menu. Using the same technique, add a third submenu item. Caption it &Corn and name it *mnuDineCorn*. The Menu Editor now should look like Figure L8-4.

Click on the OK box, run the program, and click on Dine in the menu bar. This will open the Dine menu, showing the three menu items you just added (see Figure L8-5).

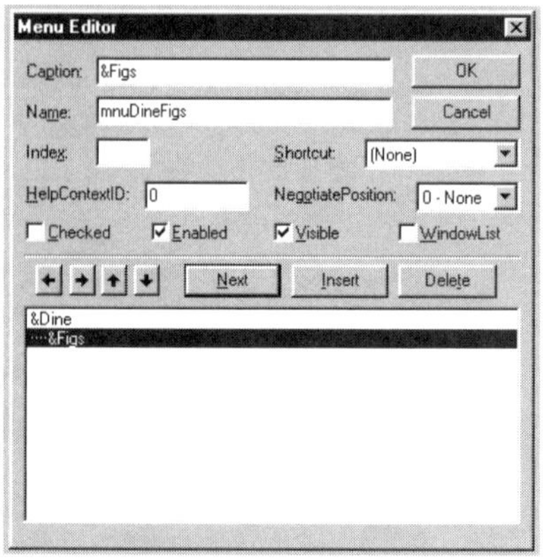

Figure L8-3 Adding a submenu item with the Menu Editor

Adding a Second Menu Title

Now add a second menu title and some menu items for it. First, click on Next again. Then, to get back to the menu title level, click on the left arrow control. Now enter &Wine for the caption. It appears all the way to the left in the menu-control list box, meaning that it will appear as a menu title in the title bar. Name it *mnuWine*. Then, using the Next button and the right-arrow button, add a few menu items, such as &Red, named *mnuWineRed;* &White, named *mnuWineWhite;* and &Expense Account, named *mnuWineExpenseAccount*. Then click on the OK button, run the program, and admire your menus.

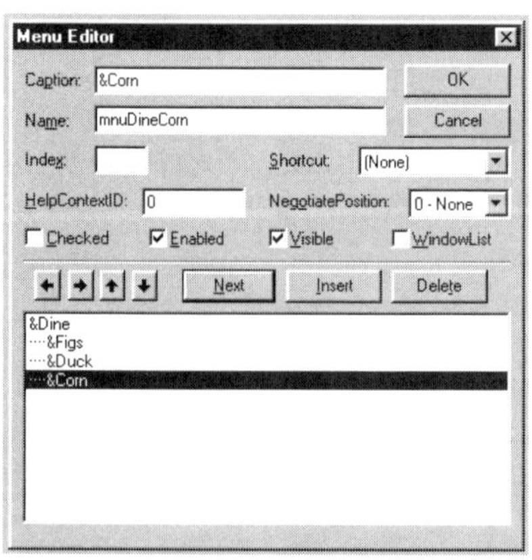

Figure L8-4 A menu title with menu items

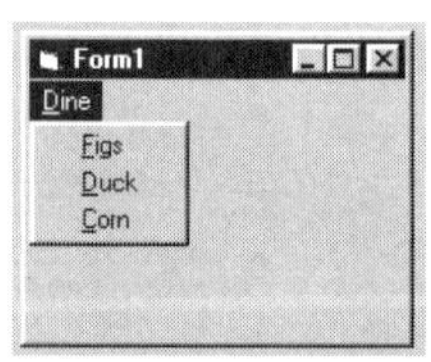

Figure L8-5 Opening a menu

Note

Unindented menu names in the menu-control list box appear as menu titles on the menu bar. Singly indented menu names become menu items listed under the menu titles.

WORKING MENUS

The Menu Editor only takes you so far. You can use it to design the appearance of a menu, but to get the menu to do something, you have to provide code. The method is a familiar one. In design mode, click on a menu title. That opens the menu, listing the menu items. Then double-click on a menu item. That opens the Code window and places the cursor in the *Click* procedure for that menu item. You then enter the code for what you want to happen when someone clicks on the menu item. Each menu item is, in essence, a control that recognizes just one event, the *Click* event.

To illustrate the process of empowering menu items, create a form with a large text box, as described in Table L8-1.

OBJECT	PROPERTY	SETTING
Form1	Caption	Try My Menus
	Name	frmMenus
Text1	Font.Font	Arial (or some other TrueType or PostScript font)
	Font.Size	10
	MultiLine	True
	Name	txtMenus
	Text	

Table L8-1 Properties for the Try My Menus program

Next, add two menu titles with menu items as described in Table L8-2. The List Box Entry column shows the indentation level by duplicating the row of dots that appears in the menu-control list box, so you can use it to discriminate between menu titles and menu items. Note the Hot Key feature. You can use the Hot Key list box in the Menu Editor to assign a hot key to a particular menu choice. Scroll down and select the hot key of your choice. The *hot key* is a keystroke that takes you directly to the choice without clicking the menu. Thus, to select Bold from the Fonts menu, you can click Fonts, then click Bold, or you can use ALT-T, B (the access key combination), or you can use CTRL-B (the hot key).

LIST BOX ENTRY	CAPTION	NAME	HOT KEY
&File	&File	*mnuFile*	
....E&xit	&Exit	*mnuFileExit*	
Fon&ts	Fon&ts	*mnuFonts*	
....&Italic	&Italic	*mnuFontsItalic*	CTRL-I
....&Bold	&Bold	*mnuFontsBold*	CTRL-B

Table L8-2 Initial menu entries for the Try My Menus program

Key Notation

You'll notice that the keys on your keyboard are labeled with uppercase letters. Following this tradition, computer literature identifies keystrokes using uppercase letters, even though pressing the key transmits a lowercase character. To indicate an uppercase keystroke, use the Shift modifier. Thus, "Press B" means press the B key, while "Press SHIFT-B" means press B while SHIFT is depressed. Similarly, ALT-B means pressing B when ALT is depressed, and CTRL-B means pressing B when CTRL is depressed. A comma indicates consecutive keystrokes, so "ALT-F, X" means first press F with ALT depressed, then press X with no other keys depressed.

Adding Code

The stage is set. Now, while remaining in design mode, go to the form, click on File in the form menu, and double-click on the Exit choice. The purpose of this menu choice is to end the program, so insert an *End* statement into the *Click* event code:

```
Private Sub mnuFileExit_Click()
    End
End Sub
```

To gain confidence that this works, run the program and select Exit from the File menu. You can use the mouse or the access key combination (ALT-F, X). Lo! The program terminates.

Next, go to the Fonts menu. We want these menu items to work like corresponding items in regular Windows programs. That is, clicking on Bold should set the Bold property for the txtMenus box to True. It also should put a check mark by the Bold menu item to indicate that Bold has been selected. If you click on Bold when the check mark shows, that should remove the check mark and turn off the Bold property. Our task now is to come up with the right code to make the menu work the way we like.

First, let's attend to the check marks. Conveniently, menu items have a Checked property. If the property is true, a check mark shows next to the item in the menu, and if the property is false, there is no check mark. This means you can use the check mark to tell a user whether Bold is in effect, and you can use the Checked property to tell the program whether Bold is in effect. The following code shows the straightforward way to set the Bold property and set the Checked property.

```
Private Sub mnuFontsBold_Click()       ' straightforward version
    If mnuFontsBold.Checked = True Then
        mnuFontsBold.Checked = False
        txtMenus.Font.Bold = False
    Else
        mnuFontsBold.Checked = True
        txtMenus.Font.Bold = True
    End If
End Sub
```

If the *mnuFontsBold.Checked* property is true, the code turns off Bold and removes the check mark. Otherwise (if the property is false), the code turns on Bold and adds the check mark. However, now is a good time to remember the trick about toggling Boolean values by using *Not:*

```
Private Sub mnuFontsBold_Click()       ' Not-toggling version
    ' toggle Checked property
    mnqFontsBold.Checked = Not mnuBontsBold.Checked
    ' toggle Bold property
    txtMenus.Font.Bold = Not txtMenus.Font.Bold
End Sub
```

This version does depend upon the Checked property and the Bold property starting out in synchronization; that is, both begin as True or else both begin as False.

Now do the same thing for the Italic menu item:

```
Private Sub mnuFontsItalic_Click()
    mnuFontsItalic.Checked = Not mnuFontsItalic.Checked
    txtMenus.Font.Italic = Not txtMenus.Font.Italic
End Sub
```

It's time to check your work. Insert the above code, run the program, and type some text into the text window. Select Bold from the Fonts menu, and the text becomes bold. Select Bold again, and the text reverts to normal. If you like, you can select both Bold and Italic, as Figure L8-6 shows.

SubMenus

Visual Basic lets you subdivide a menu choice further. For instance, you can add a Size menu item to the Fonts menu and have clicking on the Size choice open a new menu listing some type sizes, as shown in Figure L8-7. Such a subordinate menu is called a *submenu*.

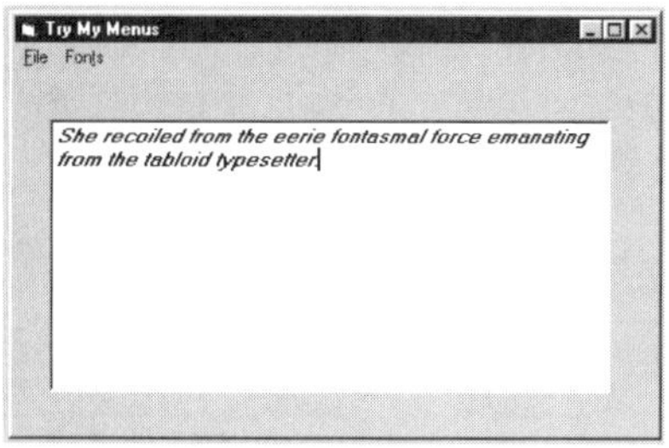

Figure L8-6 Setting text attributes

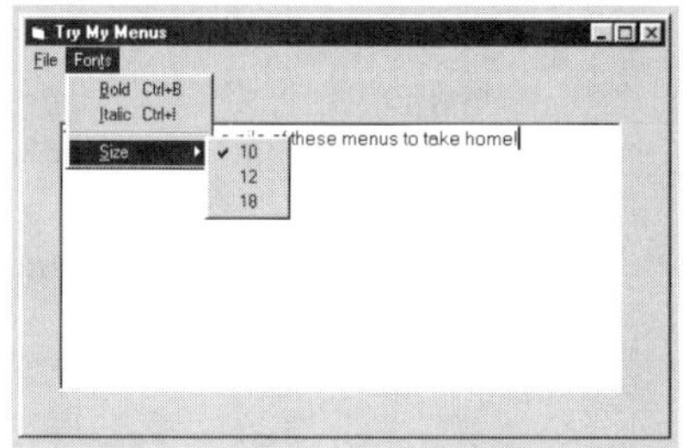

Figure L8-7 A submenu

Let's do it. Open the Menu Editor, select the ....&Italic line in the menu-control list box, and click the Next box. For the next entry, use - (a hyphen) as the Caption and *mnuFontsBar* as the name. This places a horizontal separator line in the menu separating the style items (Bold and Italic) from the Size section.

Next, click on the Next box and use &Size for the Caption and *mnuFontsSize* for the name. Once again, click on the Next box. This time click on the right-arrow control to indent the menu item one level farther to the right. This makes the new item a submenu item. For the Caption, enter 10, and for the name, enter *mnuFontsSize10*. Since 10 is the starting font size (*txtMenus.Font.Size* is 10), also click on the Checked button in the Menu Editor. This causes this item to appear initially with a check in the menu. Now add unchecked entries for point sizes of 12 and 18. The Menu Editor should look like Figure L8-8. Table L8-3 summarizes the new entries.

LIST BOX ENTRY	CAPTION	NAME
....-	-	*mnuFontsBar*
....&Size	&Size	*mnuFontsSize*
........10	10	*mnuFontsSize10*
........12	12	*mnuFontsSize12*
........18	18	*mnuFontsSize18*

Table L8-3 Additional menu entries for the Try My Menus program

When you finish, run the program, click the Fonts menu title, and then click the Size menu item. This opens the submenu, as shown previously in Figure L8-7. Note how the 10 is checked.

There's still the code to write. It will be a bit trickier than the code for the font styles because you can select only one font size at a time. That means that selecting a font size should do the following things:

- Set the font size to the new value.
- Check the new size setting.
- Uncheck the previously checked setting.

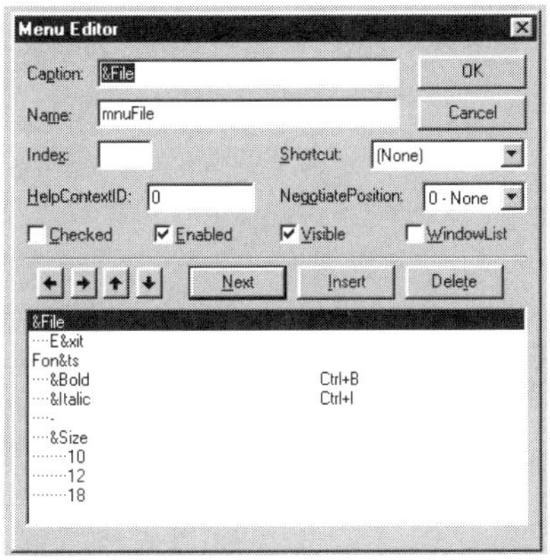

Figure L8-8 Submenu settings in the Menu Editor

The following code offers one approach, one we'll improve upon later:

```
Private Sub mnuFontsSize10_Click()
    'Set check marks.
    mnuFontsSize10.Checked = True
    mnuFontsSize12.Checked = False
    mnuFontsSize18.Checked = False
    'Set font size.
    txtMenus.Font.Size = 10
End Sub
```

Note that this code doesn't keep track of which submenu item was previously checked. It simply unchecks all the menu choices other than the selected one. It's actually quicker for the computer to do this than to examine the original values. That is, the following code avoids setting a Checked property to False if it's already False, but the time taken to make the test is more than the time saved by not resetting False properties to False.

```
Private Sub mnuFontsSize10_Click()
    'Alternative, but slower way to set check marks.
    mnuFontsSize10.Checked = True
    If mnuFontsSize12.Checked = True Then
        mnuFontsSize12.Checked = False
    ElseIf mnuFontsSize18.Checked = True
        mnuFontsSize18.Checked = False
    End If
    'Set font size.
    txtMenus.Font.Size = 10
End Sub
```

Let's follow the simpler approach for the other two *Click* events:

```
Private Sub mnuFontsSize12_Click()
    mnuFontsSize12.Checked = True
    mnuFontsSize10.Checked = False
    mnuFontsSize18.Checked = False
    txtMenus.Font.Size = 12
End Sub
```

continued on next page

continued from previous page

```
Private Sub mnuFontsSize18_Click()
    mnuFontsSize18.Checked = True
    mnuFontsSize10.Checked = False
    mnuFontsSize12.Checked = False
    txtMenus.Font.Size = 18
End Sub
```

MENU ARRAYS

As wonderful as the last example is, it has room for improvement. For instance, choosing from three font sizes involved three very similar event procedures. If you decided to add another dozen choices for font sizes, you'd have to add another dozen essentially identical event procedures. That seems like a lot of dull work. In programming, the need for a lot of dull work often is the sign that there must be an easier way. (Programmers have a strong lazy streak, which prompts them to expend great effort and enormous amounts of time to develop easier ways of doing things.) In this instance, the time-saver is the *menu array*. A menu array gathers several related menu items together so that they can share a single event procedure. To distinguish among the different items, they are assigned integer *indices* with the numbering starting at 0. To identify a particular menu item, you use the array name followed by the index enclosed in parentheses. For example, if you had a menu array named *mnuFontsArray,* then *mnuFontsArray(0)* would be the first menu item in the array, *mnuFontsArray(1)* would be the second menu item in the array, and so on.

Making a menu array will make all that much clearer, so let's do so. First, you have to get ready by doing the following:

1. Make a copy of the last project, recaptioning the form as Try My Menus 2.
2. Delete the three event procedures for the three font sizes from the Code window. (You can do this by selecting the text in the Code window and pressing DELETE or by selecting Delete from the Edit menu.)
3. Delete the three font size submenu items from the Menu Editor. (Select each submenu item in the menu-control list box, and then click on the Delete button.) The last item in the list box should be &Size.

Now you are ready to create your first menu array.

As usual, click on the Next button to create a new menu item. Then click on the right-arrow control to begin a submenu. As before, use *10* as the caption for the new menu. For the name, enter *mnuFontsSizeArray*. And now comes the new step—enter a *0* in the Index box in the Menu Editor.

For the next menu item, click Next, and repeat the process. This time use *12* for the caption and (this is *important*) use the same name—*mnuFontsSizeArray*—as you did for the preceding array member. This time enter 1 in the Index box.

Now add two more items, again using the same name. Use *18* for the first caption and *2* for the Index setting. Use *36* for the second caption and *3* for the Index setting. Table L8-4 summarizes the new entries.

LIST BOX ENTRY	CAPTION	NAME	INDEX
........10	10	*mnuFontsSizeArray*	0
........12	12	*mnuFontsSizeArray*	1
........18	18	*mnuFontsSizeArray*	2
........36	36	*mnuFontsSizeArray*	3

Table L8-4 The menu array for the Try My Menus 2 program

Next, let's add the code. In design mode open the Fonts menu, open the Size submenu, and click on one of the size entries. This opens a single event procedure for the entire menu array:

```
Private Sub mnuFontsSizeArray_Click(Index As Integer)

End Sub
```

Here the argument *Index* represents the index value for whichever menu item is clicked. For instance, if you click on the 10 item in the submenu, Visual Basic sets *Index* to 0. If you click on the 18 item, Visual Basic sets *Index* to 2. Your code then can use the *Index* value to determine what actions are performed. For example, you can use code like this:

```
Private Sub mnuFontsSizeArray_Click(Index As Integer)
    If Index = 2 Then
        mnuFontSizeArray(2).Checked = True
    End If
End Sub
```

This says, "if someone selects the third item in the menu array, set the Checked property for that menu array item to True." See Figure L8-9.

In our program the *Click* event has two duties—correctly positioning the check mark in the submenu and setting the font size for the text box. One approach for handling the check mark is to use a *For* loop (see Lesson 7) to process each array item in turn. If the index for the item matches the *Index* argument, set the Checked property to True. Otherwise, set the Checked property to False. The following code does that:

```
'Version 1
Dim Item As Integer
Const Items As Integer = 4      ' number of menu items
For Item = 0 To Items - 1
    If Item = Index Then
        mnuFontsSizeArray(Index).Checked = True
    Else
        mnuFontsSizeArray(Item).Checked = False
    End If
Next Item
```

Figure L8-9 A menu array and the *Click* event

As noted, the constant *Items* represents the number of items in the menu array. Because the number starts with 0, the loop runs from 0 to *Items - 1* instead of from 1 to *Items*. Note that if you decide to add another dozen items to the menu array, all you have to do in this code is change the value of *Items*.

Actually, you can save the effort of doing all those *If* tests (one per loop) by using the loop to set *all* the Checked properties to False, then resetting the proper Checked property to True after the loop:

```
'Version 2
Dim Item As Integer
Const Items As Integer = 4      ' number of menu items
For Item = 0 To Items - 1
     mnuFontsSizeArray(Item).Checked = False
Next Item
mnuFontsSizeArray(Index).Checked = True
```

This approach takes less typing and probably the computer handles it more quickly.

Next, to set the font size, you can use the *Select Case* statement (see Lesson 6), with the case labels matching the possible menu array index values:

```
Select Case Index
     Case 0
          txtMenus.Font.Size = 10
     Case 1
```

```
        txtMenus.Font.Size = 12
    Case 2
        txtMenus.Font.Size = 18
    Case 3
        txtMenus.Font.Size = 36
End Select
```

For instance, suppose a user clicks on the menu item captioned 18. That corresponds to the menu array item with an index value of 2 (that is, *mnuFontsSizeArray*(2)), which causes the argument *Index* to be set to 2, which causes the program to go to the Case 2 label.

The following event procedure combines the last two code segments. Isn't it nice to see that the time you spent learning about *For* loops and *Select Case* statements is useful?

```
Private Sub mnuFontSizeArray_Click(Index As Integer)
    Dim Item As Integer
    Const Items As Integer = 4   'number of items
'Set check mark in menu.
    For Item = 0 To Items - 1
        mnuFontsSizeArray(Item).Checked = False
    Next Item
    mnuFontsSizeArray(Index).Checked = True
'Set font size.
    Select Case Index
    Case 0
        txtMenus.Font.Size = 10
    Case 1
        txtMenus.Font.Size = 12
    Case 2
        txtMenus.Font.Size = 18
    Case 3
        txtMenus.Font.Size = 36
    End Select
End Sub
```

Tip

Select Case and *For Next* statements are useful tools for implementing events for menu arrays.

Other Menu Features

The Menu Editor has some features this book won't use but which you may be wondering about, so let's go over them briefly.

When you create an application, you have the option of creating a Help file to go with it. Each project has an *App* object, and the *App* object has a HelpFile property that identifies the particular file. Different objects in a project, such as forms, controls, and menus, have a HelpContextID property which can be used to identify a particular section of the Help file. If, say, you have the menu selected and press F1 for help, Help uses the HelpContextID property to identify which part of the Help file to display.

Visual Basic allows you to embed or link other applications, such as an Excel spreadsheet, in a Visual Basic application. Normally, when the embedded or linked application has the focus, its own menu replaces your application's menu, but the NegotiatePosition property provides other alternatives that let both menus appear on the menu bar. The NegotiatePosition property interacts with the form's NegotiateMenu property, which must be true for the NegotiatePosition property to have any effect.

Visual Basic supports a *Multiple Document Interface* (MDI) that lets you create a parent window with multiple child windows. In such a case, you can use the WindowList property to create a Windows menu title. Opening that menu will show a list of open child windows, showing a check mark by the currently active window and letting you use the menu to switch to another child menu. Lesson 19 will use this feature.

ADDING AN EDIT MENU

With its font style and font size menu choices, the txtMenus text box is beginning to look a bit like a simple word processor. You can enhance this uncanny resemblance by adding an Edit menu with the usual cut, copy, and paste features. The price for adding these features is that you must learn about two more topics: identifying selected text in a text box and accessing the Windows Clipboard. Visual Basic makes attaining these skills easy, and learning always is a joy, so the price is an easy one to pay.

Selections in a Text Box

Selecting text in an active text box is simple. You have three methods you can use:

- Press the left mouse button, drag across the text you wish to select, and release the mouse button.
- Double-click on a word you wish to select.
- Click the mouse once at the start of the desired selection, move the text cursor to the end of the desired select, hold down SHIFT, and click the mouse again.

The selected text then appears in highlighted form in the text box. Try these methods in the text box of the preceding program. You'll see (Figure L8-10) that Visual Basic already has built these facilities into the text box.

The highlighting lets you see which text is selected, but how does a Visual Basic program know what's selected? The answer is properties. A text box has three properties concerning selections. These properties, described in Table L8-5, do not appear in the Properties window. That's because you can't select text

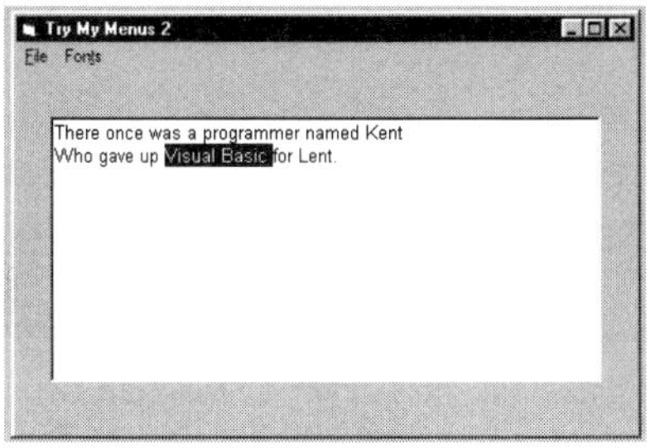

Figure L8-10 Selected text in a text box

until the program is running, so the selection properties only make sense in run mode, not in design mode.

PROPERTY	DATA TYPE	DESCRIPTION
SelLength	*Long*	Represents the length of the selected string. *SelLength* equals 0 if no text is selected, and setting it to 0 deselects any selected text.
SelStart	*Long*	Represents the location of the first character in the selected string or, if nothing is selected, the location of the character immediately following the text cursor. Numbering starts at 0 and is measured from the start of the text box.
SelText	*String*	Represents the selected string. *SelText* equals "", the empty string, if there is no selection. Setting *SelText* to a string replaces the selected text with the new string and also sets *SelLength* to 0.

Table L8-5 Run-time selection properties for a Textbox control

These properties let you identify and manipulate selected text. For instance, suppose *Temporary* is a type *String* variable and that txtMenus is a text box. Then the following code copies the selected text to the variable:

```
Temporary = txtMenus.SelText
```

To delete the selected text, you can do the following:

```
txtMenus.SelText = ""
```

This code replaces the selected text with the empty string. If you both copy and delete the string, you've cut the string.

To paste, say, the text "I'm new here!" into the text box, do the following:

```
txtMenus.SelText = "I'm new here!"
```

The text appears at the location given by *txtMenus.SelStart*. If no text is selected, the new text is inserted at that location, which would be just after the text cursor. If text is already selected, the new text replaces it.

Note

The properties describing selected text in a text box are run-mode properties which are set and altered while a program runs. These properties don't appear in the design-mode Properties window.

See! It is easy. The selection properties provide all the tools you need to cut, copy, and paste selected text. Next, you need a location to store cut or copied strings. You could just use a module-level string variable, and that would let you cut and paste from one part of the text box to another. But by using the Windows Clipboard to hold the cut or copied string, you can cut, copy, and paste between your program and other Windows programs, and that sounds much more interesting.

The Windows Clipboard

When you run a Windows application and cut or copy some text, that text is stored in the Windows Clipboard. When you paste, Windows copies the text currently in the Clipboard into the application you're using. Thus, the Clipboard lets you exchange information between any applications that can access the Clipboard.

Visual Basic gives your programs access to the Clipboard via an object called Clipboard. The Clipboard object is not like a control object in that it doesn't appear on a form. It can appear in your code, however, where it acts as an intermediary between your program and the Windows Clipboard. For instance, to copy text to the Windows Clipboard, you use a *Clipboard* method designed to do just that. Similarly, to get text from the Windows Clipboard, you fetch text with another *Clipboard* method. The Clipboard object also can deal with several graphics formats, but we just need its text abilities now. The text abilities are embodied in the three methods described in Table L8-6. Methods, recall, are invoked by appending them to an object name using a period separator. For instance, to invoke the *Clear* method for the Clipboard object, use the command *Clipboard.Clear*.

METHOD	DESCRIPTION
Clear	Clears the Clipboard
GetText	Returns a string containing the current text contents of the Clipboard. If the Clipboard contains no text, *GetText* returns "", the zero-length string.
SetText *string*	Places the type *String* argument *string* into the Clipboard, replacing any prior string contents.
GetFormat(*kind*)	Returns True if the Clipboard contains data of category *kind* and False

METHOD	DESCRIPTION
	otherwise. The argument *kind* is an integer, with different values corresponding to different kinds of data, such as different picture formats. Use a value of 1 (or the corresponding constant *vbCFText*) to test for text.

Table L8-6 Text-related methods for the Clipboard object

Objects Again

It's been a while since we've discussed objects. To remind you, an object is an entity composed of data and code and which you can treat as a unit. For instance, each control is an object. A control's properties hold the data describing the control, and a control's event procedures and methods are the code component. The methods are predefined code, while the event procedures are code that you define. The Clipboard is a predefined object having methods designed to let you communicate with the Windows Clipboard.

The Clipboard object methods along with the text box selection properties give you all the tools you need to implement the cut, copy, and edit facilities. For instance, to clear the Clipboard and to copy selected text from the txtMenus text box to the Clipboard, you can do the following:

```
Clipboard.Clear
Clipboard.SetText txtMenus.SelText
```

Setting Up the Edit Menu

Now that you've packed knowledge of the selection properties and of the Clipboard methods into your neurons, you're set to create the Edit menu. Make a copy of the preceding project and form (Try My Menus 2) and recaption the form Try My Menus 3. Open the Menu Editor. The standard convention for menu titles has File as the first title and Edit as the second title, so you should place the Edit menu title in between the File and Fonts menu titles. To do so, select the Fonts entry in the menu-control list box, and then click on the Insert button. This opens up a new line just above the Fonts line. Use the editor to create the menu title and menu items shown in Table L8-7. Note that it establishes the same hot keys that most Windows applications use for these functions.

LIST BOXENTRY	CAPTION	NAME	HOT KEY
&Edit	&Edit	*mnuEdit*	
....C&ut	C&ut	*mnuEditCut*	CTRL-X
....C&opy	C&opy	*mnuEditCopy*	CTRL-C
....&Paste	&Paste	*mnuEditPaste*	CTRL

Table 8-7 New menu title and items

Next, use the Code window to provide events procedures for each menu item:

```
Private Sub mnuEditCopy_Click(Index As Integer)
    Clipboard.Clear
    Clipboard.SetText txtMenus.SelText
End Sub

Private Sub mnuEditCut_Click()
    Clipboard.Clear
    Clipboard.SetText txtMenus.SelText
    txtMenus.SelText = ""      'Delete selected text.
End Sub

Private Sub mnuEditPaste_Click(Index As Integer)
    txtMenus.SelText = Clipboard.GetText()
End Sub
```

That's all it takes. You now should be able to copy text from the txtMenus text box and paste it elsewhere in the txtMenus box and also paste it in, say, a Word for Windows or WordPerfect or AmiPro document (see Figure L8-11). That's a lot of functionality for just a few lines of code.

Adding Sophistication

The Try My Menus 3 program is quite naive. By limiting itself to just one control (the text box) it avoided facing problems that arise in more complex forms. For example, suppose you add a second text box to the form. It would be nice to be able to cut and paste in that box, too, but the Try My Menus 3 code only deals with the txtMenus text box. Or suppose you add a control, such as a

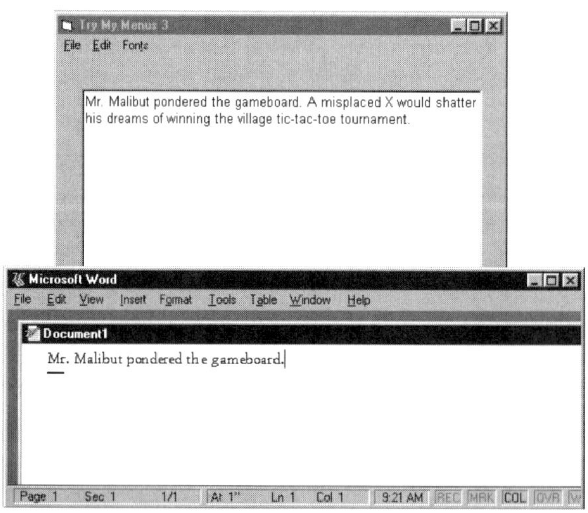

Figure L8-11 Cutting and Pasting

command button, that doesn't allow you to select text. In that case, operations such as copy and paste don't make sense and should be disabled when the command button has the focus. These are problems with solutions, and the key element to these solutions is something called ActiveControl, a property of the Screen object.

The Screen Object

Like the Clipboard object, the Screen object is predefined by Visual Basic. Like the Clipboard object, the Screen object is invisible. That is, you can use it in your code, but it doesn't have an icon that appears on your form. The Screen object, naturally, represents the screen on your monitor. The key to using the Screen object is to use its properties. Table L8-8 lists the Screen properties. As the name Screen suggests, the Height and Width properties describe the entire display screen, not just the form.

PROPERTIES	DESCRIPTION
ActiveControl	Specifies the control that has the focus
ActiveForm	Specifies the active form
FontCount	The number of fonts available to the current display or to the active printer
Fonts(id)	The name of the font having an index of *id;* the fonts are numbered from 0 to *FontCount* - 1
Height	The height of the screen in twips
MousePointer	The numeric code for the type of mouse pointer displayed
TwipsPerPixelX	The number of twips per pixel horizontally
TwipsPerPixelY	The number of twips per pixel vertically
Width	The width of the screen in twips

Table L8-8 Properties of the Screen object

Pixels

Two of the Screen object properties refer to *pixels.* Pixels (short for picture elements) are the small dots from which video images are built. A standard VGA monitor, for example, is described as having a resolution of 640 x 480. That means the picture is 640 pixels wide by 480 pixels tall. To display an image, the computer has to set each of these 307,200 pixels to the proper color and intensity. Similarly, the standard Super VGA (SVGA) resolution of 800 x 600 means the video image is composed of 480,000 pixels in a grid 800 pixels wide by 600 pixels tall.

The key property for our purposes is ActiveControl. The table says ActiveControl specifies the currently active control. Suppose, for example, that txtMenus is the active control. Then the expression *Screen.ActiveControl.Text* stands for *txtMenus.Text*. If you then shift the focus to, say, the txtMeToo text box, then the expression *Screen.ActiveControl.Text* represents *txtMeToo.Text*. In short, *Screen.ActiveControl* acts like a variable whose value is a particular control. If you write code using *Screen.ActiveControl*, that code will use whichever control is active when the code executes (see Figure L8-12).

Let's get a bit more specific. Remember this event handler?

```
Private Sub mnuEditCopy_Click(Index As Integer)
    Clipboard.Clear
    Clipboard.SetText txtMenus.SelText
End Sub
```

It copies selected text from the txtMenus text box to the Clipboard. Let's replace the specific control txtMenus with the general expression Screen.ActiveControl:

```
Private Sub mnuEditCopy_Click(Index As Integer)
    Clipboard.Clear
    Clipboard.SetText Screen.ActiveControl.SelText
End Sub
```

Now clicking on the Copy menu item will copy the selected text from whichever control is active to the Clipboard. If txtMenus has the focus, its selected text is copied. If some other text box is open, its selected text is copied. Suddenly, the event procedure is much more powerful!

In fact, it's a little too powerful. Suppose the control with the focus is a command button. The command button has no SelText property, so the expression *Screen.ActiveControl.SelText* now is invalid—there is no such critter! You can warn users not to use the Edit menu when a command button is selected, but that doesn't quite qualify as friendly or foolproof. The best thing to do is to make

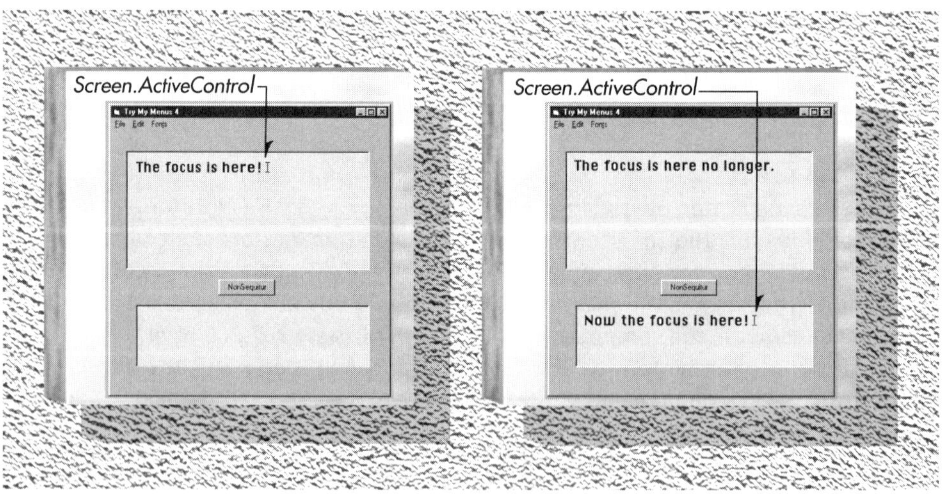

Figure L8-12 The *Screen.ActiveControl* property

the Edit menu command unavailable for such cases. If it can't be used at all, it can't be misused. Of course, this involves yet another Visual Basic feature, the *TypeOf Is* condition.

The *TypeOf Is* Condition

Visual Basic has a special *If* statement syntax that lets you determine what sort of object a control is. For instance, suppose you want to know if *Screen.ActiveControl* is a text box. You can use code like this:

```
If TypeOf Screen.ActiveControl Is TextBox Then Print "Text box!"
```

As the code suggests, if the active control is a text box, then *TypeOf Screen.ActiveControl Is TextBox* evaluates to True. More generally, the expression

```
TypeOf object-name Is object-type
```

is True if *object-name* identifies an object of *object-type* and is False otherwise.

Great! We can use this tool to activate Edit menu items if the active control is a text box and to deactivate them otherwise. Of course, we need a place to put the code. The simplest choice is to place it in the *Click* event for the Edit menu title. That is, you can have code like this:

```
Private Sub mnuEdit_Click()
    If TypeOf Screen.ActiveControl Is TextBox Then
        mnuEditCut.Enabled = True
        mnuEditCopy.Enabled = True
        mnuEditPaste.Enabled = True
Else
        mnuEditCut.Enabled = False
        mnuEditCopy.Enabled = False
        mnuEditPaste.Enabled = False
    End If
End Sub
```

When the Enabled property of a menu item is False, the item shows up in gray text instead of in black on the menu, and you can't select the item. We say the menu choice is *grayed out*. So this code makes the Edit commands available only if a text box has the focus.

There's a refinement you might like to add, and that is to gray-out the Paste menu item if the Clipboard is empty. The Clipboard object *GetFormat* method returns True if the Clipboard contains text, providing that you use 1 or the symbolic value *vbCFText* as an argument. That is, you can use code like this:

```
If Clipboard.GetFormat(vbCFText) = True Then
        mnuEditPaste.Enabled = True
    Else
        mnuEditPaste.Enabled = False
```

This enables the Paste menu item only if there is something to paste.

It makes sense to restrict the Font menu to text boxes, also. You can use the same technique:

```
Private Sub mnuFonts_Click()
    If TypeOf Screen.ActiveControl Is TextBox Then
        mnuFontsBold.Enabled = True
        mnuFontsItalic.Enabled = True
        mnuFontsSize.Enabled = True
    Else
        mnuFontsBold.Enabled = False
        mnuFontsItalic.Enabled = False
        mnuFontsSize.Enabled = False
    End If
End Sub
```

Putting It Together

Let's put together an example illustrating these ideas. Start with a copy of the Try My Menus 3 example, and recaption the new form Try My Menus 4. Add two more controls to the form—a control button and a second text box. Give them the properties shown in Table L8-9.

OBJECT	PROPERTY	SETTING
Command1	Caption	NonSequitur
	Name	frm NonSequitur
Text1	Font.Font	Times New Roman (or some other TrueType or PostScript font)
	Font.Size	10
	MultiLine	True
	Name	txtMeToo
	Text	

Table L8-9 Additional properties for the Try My Menus 4 program

The primary purpose of the command button is to provide a nontext box control that can accept the focus. It will be the guinea pig for testing deactivating the Edit menu. Still, you can give it something interesting to do. For instance, have it report the current screen resolution. The Screen object doesn't report that information directly, but it does let you calculate it. The Width property gives the width in twips, and the TwipsPerPixelX property tells how many twips make up a single pixel on screen. So dividing Width by TwipsPerPixelX yields the width of the screen in pixels. You can do the same thing with screen height. These considerations lead to the following code:

```
Dim Temp As String
Dim Hor As Integer
Dim Ver As Integer
Hor = Screen.Width / Screen.TwipsPerPixelX
Ver = Screen.Height / Screen.TwipsPerPixelY
Temp = " Screen Resolution =" & Str(Hor) + " x " & Str(Ver)
```

Now you have all the tools you need to complete the new version:

- Using the Screen.ActiveControl instead of txtMenus makes the various menu commands more general.
- Using the TypeOf Is test limits editing commands to the text boxes.
- Screen properties let you determine the screen size.
- Using the Clipboard GetFormat method lets you determine if there's any text in the Clipboard to paste.

A Slight Delay

However, there are a couple of niggling details to attend to. For example, suppose you enter text in the first text box and select Bold from the Font menu. Now you go to the second text box. The Font menu will still have Bold checked, even though the Bold property is False for the second text box. Similarly, you can have problems with the Italic menu item and the font size menu items not being in sync with the current text box.

The problem, then, is to bring the Font menu into accord with the currently active text box so that the Bold, Italic, and Size menu items match the corresponding text box properties. Such a problem is merely an opportunity to use your programming skills. Like many Visual Basic programming problems, this involves two levels of programming:

- Designing on the event level
- Programming at the code level

On the event level, you have to determine what event or events to use to bring the menu into accord with the currently active text box. On the code level, you have to figure out what code will actually accomplish the desired result.

So let's figure out what events to use. One approach is to ask, when should the menu settings change? Clearly, they should change when a particular text box becomes active. Is there an event associated with that? Yes, the *GotFocus* event is triggered for that text box. So we should use the *txtFonts_GotFocus* event and the the *txtMeToo_GotFocus* event to adjust the Font menu settings.

What code do we use? Previously, we've used menu settings to set text box properties. To initialize the menus correctly, we can use text box properties to set menu settings. Here, for example, is how we can bring the menu into accord with the txtMeToo text box:

```
Private Sub txtMeToo_GotFocus()
    Dim Item As Integer
    Const ItemMax As Integer = 3
    For Item = 0 To ItemMax
        mnuFontsSizeItem(Item).Checked = False
    Next Item
```

continued on next page

continued from previous page

```
    Select Case txtMeToo.Font.Size
    Case Is >= 36
        Item = 3
    Case Is >= 18
        Item = 2
    Case Is >= 12
        Item = 1
    Case Else
        Item = 0
    End Select
    mnuFontsSizeItem(Item).Checked = True
    mnuFontsBold.Checked = txtMeToo.Font.Bold
    mnuFontsItalic.Checked = txtMeToo.Font.Italic
End Sub
```

Handling the Bold menu item is simple—just set the mnuFontsBold.Checked property to the text box's Bold property. The same method works for the Italic menu item. The Size item is more involved, for you have to match a menu index to a font size while taking into account that the actual font sizes may be different from the menu selections. For example, the menu choice of 10 corresponds to a true size of 9.75.

Back on Track

Now we're ready for the final effort. Putting all these elements together yields the code shown in Listing L8-1. You may notice that Try My Menus 4 is considerably larger than Try My Menus 1. Indeed, if you had been faced with the prospect of developing Try My Menus 4 from scratch, you might have been tempted to find your fun elsewhere. But developing the program in a succession of steps wasn't all that bad.

Tip

Break up large projects into smaller, more easily achieved projects.

Listing L8-1
Try My Menus 4

```
Option Explicit

Private Sub cmdNonSequitur_Click()
    Dim Temp As String
    Dim Hor As Integer
    Dim Ver As Integer
    Hor = Screen.Width / Screen.TwipsPerPixelX
    Ver = Screen.Height / Screen.TwipsPerPixelY
    Temp = " Screen Resolution =" & Str(Hor) & " x " & Str(Ver)
    txtMeToo.Text = txtMeToo.Text & Temp
End Sub
```

```
Private Sub mnuEdit_Click()
    If TypeOf Screen.ActiveControl Is TextBox Then
        mnuEditCut.Enabled = True
        mnuEditCopy.Enabled = True
        If Clipboard.GetFormat(vbCFText) = True Then
            mnuEditPaste.Enabled = True
        Else
            mnuEditPaste.Enabled = False
        End If
    Else
        mnuEditCut.Enabled = False
        mnuEditCopy.Enabled = False
        mnuEditPaste.Enabled = False
    End If
End Sub
Private Sub mnuFonts_Click()
    If TypeOf Screen.ActiveControl Is TextBox Then
        mnuFontsBold.Enabled = True
        mnuFontsItalic.Enabled = True
        mnuFontsSize.Enabled = True
    Else
        mnuFontsBold.Enabled = False
        mnuFontsItalic.Enabled = False
        mnuFontsSize.Enabled = False
    End If
End Sub

Private Sub mnuEditCopy_Click()
    Clipboard.Clear
    Clipboard.SetText Screen.ActiveControl.SelText
End Sub

Private Sub mnuEditCut_Click()
    Clipboard.Clear
    Clipboard.SetText Screen.ActiveControl.SelText
    Screen.ActiveControl.SelText = ""
End Sub

Private Sub mnuEditPaste_Click()
    Screen.ActiveControl.SelText = Clipboard.GetText()
End Sub

Private Sub mnuFontsBold_Click()
    mnuFontsBold.Checked = Not mnuFontsBold.Checked
    Screen.ActiveControl.Font.Bold = Not Screen.ActiveControl.Font.Bold
End Sub

Private Sub mnuFontsItalic_Click()
    mnuFontsItalic.Checked = Not mnuFontsItalic.Checked
    Screen.ActiveControl.Font.Italic = Not
Screen.ActiveControl.Font.Italic
End Sub

Private Sub mnuFileExit_Click()
    End
End Sub

Private Sub mnuFontsSizeItem_Click(Index As Integer)
    Dim Item As Integer
```

continued on next page

continued from previous page

```
     Const ItemMax As Integer = 3
     For Item = 0 To ItemMax
          mnuFontsSizeItem(Item).Checked = False
     Next Item
     mnuFontsSizeItem(Index).Checked = True
     Select Case Index
     Case 0
          Screen.ActiveControl.Font.Size = 10
     Case 1
          Screen.ActiveControl.Font.Size = 12
     Case 2
          Screen.ActiveControl.Font.Size = 18
     Case 3
          Screen.ActiveControl.Font.Size = 36
     End Select
End Sub

Private Sub txtMenus_GotFocus()
     Dim Item As Integer
     Const ItemMax As Integer = 3
     For Item = 0 To ItemMax
          mnuFontsSizeItem(Item).Checked = False
     Next Item
     Select Case txtMenus.Font.Size
     Case Is >= 36
          Item = 3
     Case Is >= 18
          Item = 2
     Case Is >= 12
          Item = 1
     Case Else
          Item = 0
     End Select
     mnuFontsSizeItem(Item).Checked = True
     mnuFontsBold.Checked = txtMenus.Font.Bold
     mnuFontsItalic.Checked = txtMenus.Font.Italic
End Sub

Private Sub txtMeToo_GotFocus()
     Dim Item As Integer
     Const ItemMax As Integer = 3
     For Item = 0 To ItemMax
          mnuFontsSizeItem(Item).Checked = False
     Next Item
     Select Case txtMeToo.Font.Size
     Case Is >= 36
          Item = 3
     Case Is >= 18
          Item = 2
     Case Is >= 12
          Item = 1
     Case Else
          Item = 0
     End Select
     mnuFontsSizeItem(Item).Checked = True
     mnuFontsBold.Checked = txtMeToo.Font.Bold
     mnuFontsItalic.Checked = txtMeToo.Font.Italic
End Sub
```

Of course, you must try the program. You'll be able to copy and paste from one text box to the other. If you click on the command button, the current screen resolution is appended to the text in the txtMeToo box. If you click on Edit immediately after clicking on the command button, you'll find the three editing commands grayed-out. Clicking on one of the text boxes gives that box the focus, and the Edit commands become active again. Note that when you do choose a menu command, the currently active control remains active. So to cut and paste within one text box, you don't have to first click on the box to give it the focus. If you'd used command buttons, however, to handle the editing commands, you'd have to deal with the fact that clicking on a command button makes the command button the active control. Figure L8-13 shows a sample screen appearance.

Menus and Focus

Menus are a particularly good way to implement cutting and pasting because clicking on a menu item does not change the focus.

SUMMARY

The Menu Editor enables you to construct menus with ease. Menu titles are terms that appear in a program's menu bar. Menu items appear under a menu title when you click on the title. You can assign submenus to menu items in order to provide a hierarchical access to menu choices. You can use the Menu Editor to associate access keys and hot keys with menu items. To implement menu choices, you provide appropriate code for the menu item's *Click* event.

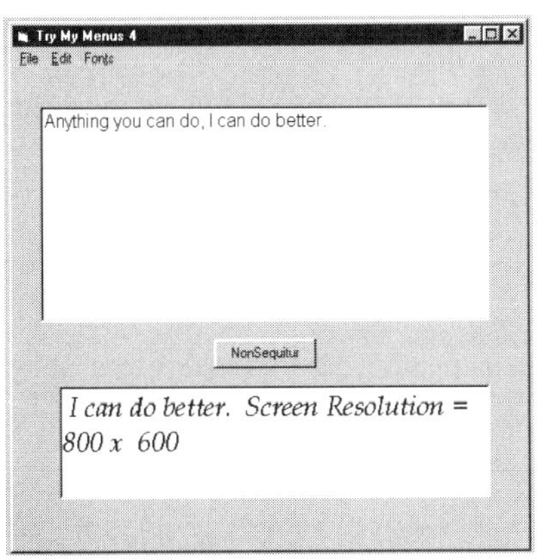

Figure L8-13 Try My Menus 4

Also, you can create menu item arrays. The menu items in an array share a common name and *Click* event, but use a numerical index to distinguish one item from another. Often the *Select Case* and *For Next* statements come in handy when you write code for the *Click* event procedure for a menu item array.

The Clipboard object is a Visual Basic object that mediates between your program and the Windows Clipboard. By using *Clipboard* methods, you can copy text to and from the Clipboard and ascertain if there's any text in the Clipboard.

The Screen object describes the state of the screen, such as its dimensions in twips. The ActiveControl property identifies which control currently is active, that is, which control has the focus.

The *TypeOf Is* condition lets you determine what type a control is. For example, you can use it to test if Screen.ActiveControl is a text box.

1. Suppose you give the name &Treats to a menu title. How will it appear in the menu?

a. Treats
b. &Treats
c. T̲reats
d. AndTreats
e. &$%@!

2. Suppose the &Treats menu title has a menu item named Son&g. You can access that item with which keystroke(s)?

a. Alt-T, S
b. Alt-T, Alt-G
c. Ctrl-G
d. Alt-G
e. Alt-T, G

3. What's the difference between an access key and a hot key?

4. What does the Checked property of a menu item control?

5. Suppose you want Pudding, Mousse, and Flan to be three components of a menu array under the Dessert menu title? What steps do you take?

6. Which of the following would hide the control having the focus?

a. *Control.Hide*
b. *Screen.ActiveControl.Hide*
c. *Screen.ActiveControl.Visible = False*
d. *Screen.ActiveControl.Focus = False*

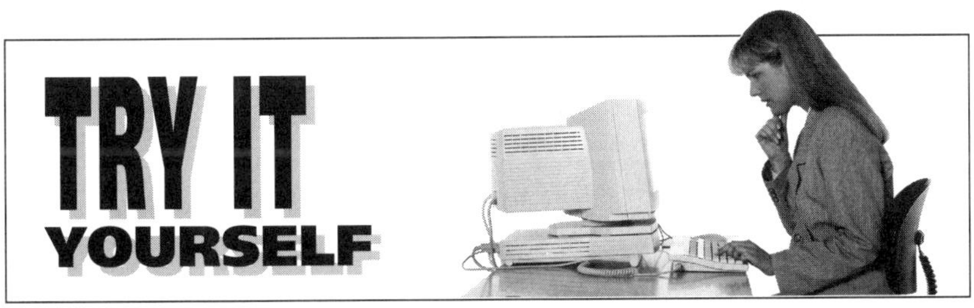

1. Revise the Select example in Lesson 6, replacing the Start and Clear buttons with menu items under a menu title of Run and replacing the three option buttons with three menu items under a menu title of Style.

2. Revise the Quick Author example in Lesson 3, replacing the three lists with menus. That is, there would be a Noun menu title whose menu items would be the word list of nouns, and so on.

LESSON

9 CONTROL ARRAYS AND DATA ARRAYS

Many things come in plurals—3 option buttons, 12 days of Christmas, 20 years of sales figures, 5 vice-presidents, and so on. The usual computer ploy to deal with multiple items is to use an array. For example, in Lesson 8, you learned about menu arrays. Visual Basic also lets you create control arrays and data arrays. In this lesson the array has the focus. In particular, you'll learn about the following topics:

- **How to create a control array**
- **How to use a control array**
- **The frame control**

- **The check box control**
- **The vertical scrollbar control**
- **How to create a data array**
- **How to use a data array**

CONTROL ARRAYS

Suppose you have a set of option buttons to control the background color for a form. A *control array* lets you lump such a set of related controls (all of the same type) into a single group. Normally, each control you add to a form has its own event procedures. But if you create a control array, all the controls in the array share the same procedures. As with menu controls, you use an index value to distinguish one control of an array from another. For example, suppose you created a control array called optPicks. The first member of the array has an index value of 0 and is written optPicks(0), the next member is optPicks(1), and so on. The *Click* event procedure for the array would be structured like this:

```
Private Sub optPicks_Click(Index as Integer)
    ...
End Sub
```

When you click on an option button in the array, Visual Basic sets the argument *Index* to the index value for the clicked option button. For instance, if you click on the second button in the array, *Index* is set to 1. As you can see, control arrays work just like menu arrays (see Figure L9-1).

Creating a Control Array

There are a couple of ways to create a control array. Let's step through one method—giving several controls the same name. First, open a new project with a new form. Next, place three option button controls along the right side of the form. See Figure L9-2 for approximate positioning. Give them the properties shown in Table L9-1. In particular, note that all the controls get the same name. That makes them part of an array. Also note the index values; these establish the order of the controls in the array.

OBJECT	PROPERTY	SETTING
Form1	Caption	Three Buttons in an Array
	Name	frmOptArray
Option1	Caption	Button 1
	Index	0
	Name	OptArray

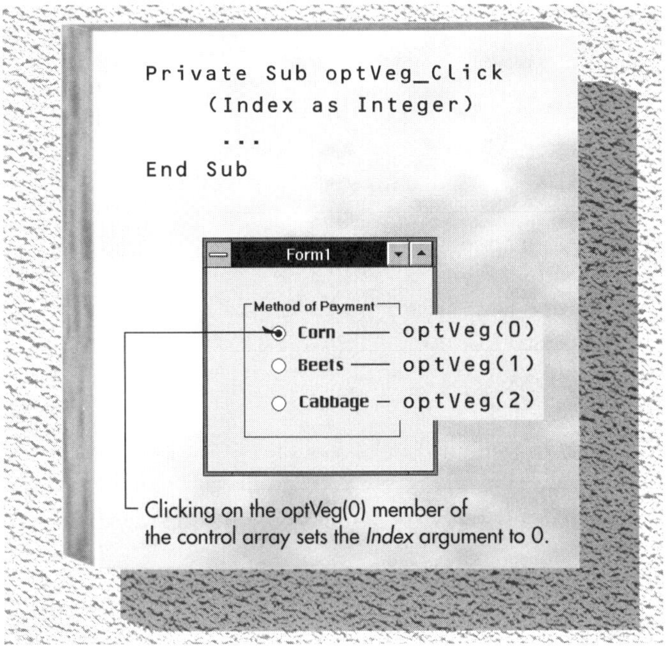

Figure L9-1 An array of option buttons and the *Click* event

OBJECT	PROPERTY	SETTING
Option2	Caption	Button 2
	Index	1
	Name	OptArray
Option3	Caption	Button 3
	Index	2
	Name	OptArray

Table L9-1 Properties for the Three Buttons in an Array program

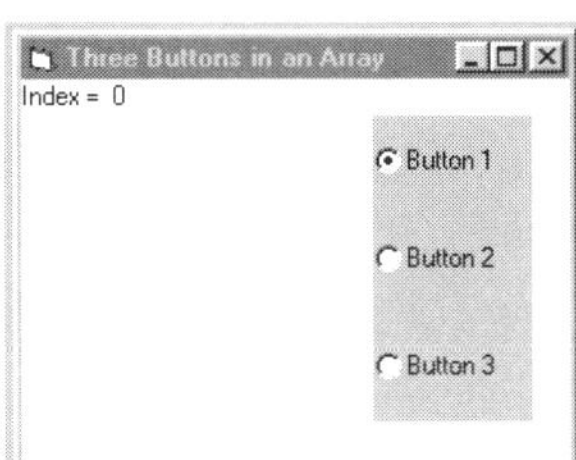

Figure L9-2 The Three Buttons in an Array form

Another way to create a control array is to create one control, select it, then use Copy and Paste from the Visual Basic menu. When you paste, Visual Basic displays a dialog box telling you that you already have a control by that name and asking if you want to make a control array (see Figure L9-3). If you respond by clicking on the Yes button, Visual Basic pastes a new control having the same name as the old control. It also automatically sets the Index properties for the two controls.

A third way is to create a control without setting an index value, then creating a second control and giving it the same name. That brings up the same dialog box that the copy-and-paste approach does. Click on the OK button, and Visual Basic automatically sets the Index properties for the two controls.

Tip

The key to creating a control array is to give the same name to each control in the array. You can do this manually using the Properties window or semi-automatically by using Copy and Paste.

Using a Control Array

You can write code that gets executed no matter which control in an array is clicked, and also can write code that depends on which control is clicked. Let's see how.

Click on any one of the three buttons in the new project while in design mode. This brings up the *optArray_Click* event procedure. It's easy to write code that gets executed exactly the same way regardless of which button is clicked during run time. For instance, the procedure

```
Private Sub optArray_Click(Index As Integer)
    Beep
End Sub
```

generates a beep no matter which button you clicked during run time.

You can use the *Index* variable to provide code whose behavior is modified by the button clicked. For example, the procedure

```
Private Sub optArray_Click(Index As Integer)
    Print "Index = "; Index
End Sub
```

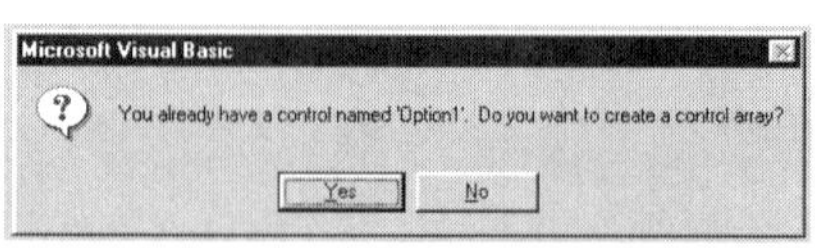

Figure L9-3 Control array dialog box

prints out the value 0 if you click the first button and a value of 2 if you click the third button.

By using an *If Else* or *Select* statement, you can provide different code for different buttons:

```
Private Sub optArray_Click(Index As Integer)
     Select Case Index
          Case 0
               frmOptArray.BackColor = vbYellow
          Case 1
               frmOptArray.BackColor = vbCyan
          Case 2
               frmOptArray.BackColor = vbMagenta
     End Select
End Sub
```

Here *vbYellow, vbCyan,* and *vbMagenta* are constants defined by Visual Basic 4 to represent the number code for the colors yellow, cyan, and magenta. They're a bit easier to remember than the number codes themselves.

To illustrate all these possibilities, enter the following code in the Code window:

```
Private Sub optArray_Click(Index As Integer)
'applies to all buttons equally
     Beep
'different code for different Index values
     Select Case Index
          Case 0
               frmOptArray.BackColor = vbYellow
          Case 1
               frmOptArray.BackColor = vbCyan
          Case 2
               frmOptArray.BackColor = vbMagenta
     End Select
'behavior modified by value of Index
     Print "Index = "; Index
End Sub
```

The *Print* statement follows setting the background color because resetting the background color redraws the form window, obliterating previous text. Figure L9-2 shows a sample of the program in operation.

Incidentally, you can override the default 0,1,2,... indexing by entering other values for the Index properties. For instance, you could assign the three option button indices of 20, 33, and 54. But for clarity it's much better to number them consecutively.

THE FRAME CONTROL AND THE CHECK BOX CONTROL

The option button control, recall, has the interesting property that at most one button can be activated at a time. That is, only one button shows up as "on," and only one option button has its Value property set to True. This behavior doesn't always fit the needs of a program. For instance, suppose you want to use one set of option buttons to control the background color of a text box and a second set of option buttons to control the foreground color. Ideally, you'd want these two sets of controls to function independently of one another. In practice, however, clicking on any one button turns it on and turns all the others off.

The frame control offers a way to modify that behavior. To create a frame, you select the frame icon from the Visual Basic Toolbox and draw a frame on a form. This creates a rectangle with a caption in its upper-left corner (see Figure L9-4).

If you create a set of option buttons inside a Frame control, their universe consists of just that frame. That is, the option buttons in a frame are linked by the usual "at most one on" rule, but they are independent of any option buttons outside the frame. So you can have two option buttons set to "on" at the same time providing one is in the frame and the other is outside the frame. By using several frames, you can create several sets of independent option buttons (see Figure L9-5).

You must create the frame first, and then use the option button tool from the Toolbox to create the button in the frame. If you create an option button elsewhere, then drag the button into the frame, it will look like it's in the frame, but it really isn't. It's just sitting on top of the frame visually. One way to tell if a control really is in a frame is to select and drag a frame. If the control comes along with it, it's in the frame. If you wish to create an array of controls in a frame, you have to be careful of the copy-and-paste method. That's because Visual Basic automatically pastes the copy in the upper-left corner of the form, not in the frame. Thus, the copy is in the wrong place. However, if you select a frame before pasting, the pasted control will go into the selected frame.

Tip

For a control to be in a frame, you must create the frame first, and then create the control inside the frame. Dragging a control to inside the frame doesn't work.

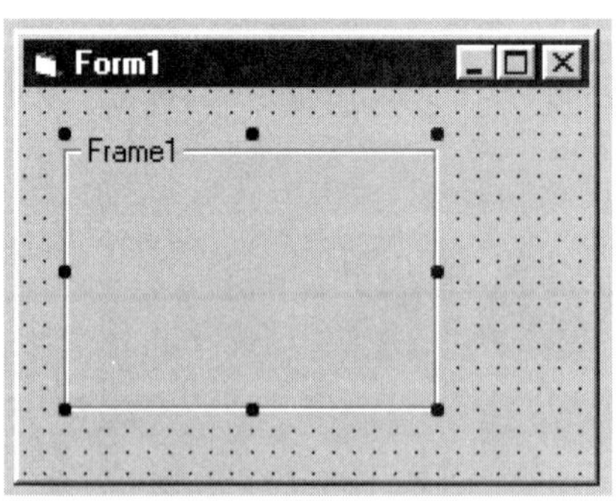

Figure L9-4 A Frame control

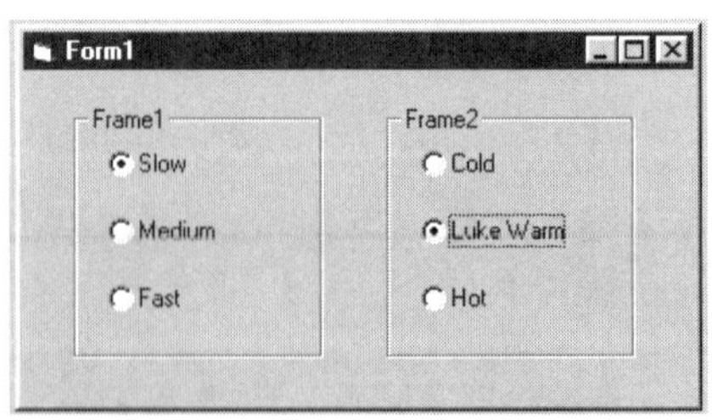

Figure L9-5 Independent option buttons in separate frames

Tip

To create a control array within a frame, you can create each control in the frame, giving the controls the same name. Or you can use copying and pasting provided you select the frame before pasting.

You also can use a frame as a design element to group controls visually. For instance, you can select a different background color for the frame, and you can use the frame's Caption property to label the set of controls in the frame.

CHECK BOXES

The check box control, like the option button control, is a two-state control. The option button is either on or off, while the check box control is either checked or unchecked. Aside from the different look, the main difference is that check box controls are independent of one another. You can have one, none, or all of the check boxes in the checked state (see Figure L9-6).

Check boxes are handy for sets of choices that are independent of one another. For instance, if check boxes represented a game character, you could click on the check boxes labeled "Big Feet," "Rotund," and "Sly," if those were the characteristics you desired. Option boxes are better suited for mutually exclusive choices, such as "Dwarf," "Giant," or "Elf."

Tip

Use option buttons for mutually exclusive choices and check boxes for independent choices.

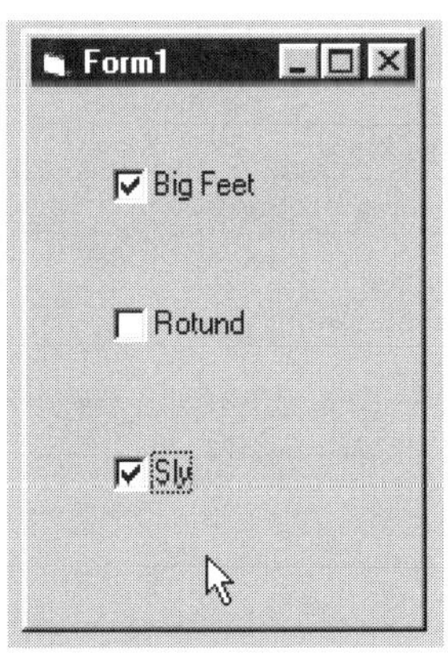

Figure L9-6 The check box control

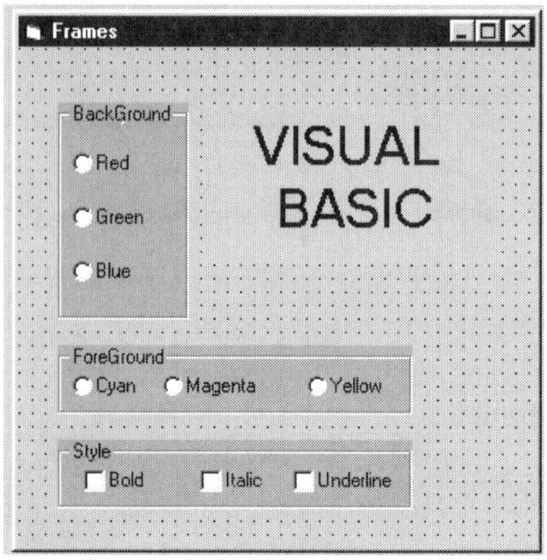

Figure L9-7 The Frames form

Let's try these new controls in a new example. Create a new form. Create a label box on it and three frames. Create an array of three option buttons in the first frame, another array of three option buttons in the second frame, and an array of three check boxes in the third. Arrange them as shown in Figure L9-7 and assign properties as shown in Table L9-2. Remember that you must create the option button and check box controls in the frames.

OBJECT	PROPERTY	SETTING
Form1	Caption	Frames
	Name	frmFrames
Frame1	BackColor	&H008080FF& (salmon)
	Caption	BackGround
	Name	frmBackGround
Frame2	BackColor	&H008080FF& (salmon)
	Caption	ForeGround
	Name	frmForeGround
Frame3	BackColor	&H008080FF& (salmon)
	Caption	Style
	Name	frmStyle
Option1	BackColor	&H008080FF& (salmon)
	Caption	Red
	Index	0
	Name	OptBackColor
Option2	BackColor	&H008080FF& (salmon)
	Caption	Green
	Index	1
	Name	OptBackColor

OBJECT	PROPERTY	SETTING
Option3	BackColor	&H008080FF& (salmon)
	Caption	Blue
	Index	2
	Name	OptBackColor
Option4	BackColor	&H008080FF& (salmon)
	Caption	Cyan
	Index	0
	Name	OptForeColor
Option5	BackColor	&H008080FF& (salmon)
	Caption	Magenta
	Index	1
	Name	OptForeColor
Option6	BackColor	&H008080FF& (salmon)
	Caption	Yellow
	Index	2
	Name	OptForeColor
CheckBox1	BackColor	&H008080FF& (salmon)
	Caption	Bold
	Index	0
	Name	chkStyle
CheckBox2	BackColor	&H008080FF& (salmon)
	Caption	Italic
	Index	1
	Name	chkStyle
CheckBox3	BackColor	&H008080FF& (salmon)
	Caption	Underline
	Index	2
	Name	chkStyle
Label1	Alignment	2 - Center
	Caption	VISUAL BASIC
	Font.Size	24
	Name	lblTest

Table L9-2 Properties for the Frames program

As the names suggest, this program will use the option buttons and check boxes to control the appearance of the label box and of the text in it. The program uses option buttons for the colors because the choices are mutually exclusive. If the background is blue, it can't also be red. The two option button arrays are in separate frames so that they will be independent of one another. Clicking on the Blue option button turns off the other buttons in the same frame, but has no effect on the buttons in the ForeGround frame.

The program uses check boxes for the style choices because the choices are independent of one another. The text can be both bold and underlined, for example. The check boxes are in a frame to match the visual appearance of the option buttons.

Now let's move to the code. First, there are things to do when the program starts. In particular, you should set the Value property to True for one option button in each frame; this establishes which button in each set is on initially, and that establishes the startup colors in the label.

```
Private Sub Form_Load()
    optBackColor(0).Value = True
    optForeColor(0).Value = True
End Sub
```

Next, provide code for each option button array to select the background and foreground colors for the label. You can use the *Select Case* statement to match the action to the option button clicked. (Thank heavens we covered *Select Case* before doing control arrays!)

```
Private Sub optBackColor_Click(Index As Integer)
    Select Case Index
        Case 0
            lblTest.BackColor = vbRed
        Case 1
            lblTest.BackColor = vbGreen
        Case 2
            lblTest.BackColor = vbBlue
    End Select
End Sub

Private Sub optForeColor_Click(Index As Integer)
    Select Case Index
        Case 0
            lblTest.ForeColor = vbCyan
        Case 1
            lblTest.ForeColor = vbMagenta
        Case 2
            lblTest.ForeColor = vbYellow
    End Select
End Sub
```

The code uses six Visual Basic constants (*vbRed*, *vbGreen*, *vbBlue*, *vbCyan*, *vbMagenta*, *vbYellow*) to identify colors. Red, green, and blue are the *additive primary colors*. You can blend light of these three colors together to reproduce other colors, which is what a color monitor does with its red, green, and blue phosphors. Cyan, magenta, and yellow are the *subtractive primary colors*. You can blend pigments of these three colors together to reproduce other colors, which is what color inkjet printers and comic books do. These six colors are special enough to earn symbolic constants representing their numeric color codes. Visual Basic also defines *vbBlack* and *vbWhite* to represent (you guessed it) black and white. Lesson 10 discusses color further.

Finally, the code for the check box array determines which style properties are in effect. Because the Value property of a check box is True if the box is checked, you can set the font style properties to the corresponding Value properties. For example, the statement

```
lblTest.Font.Bold = chkStyle(0).Value
```

sets the Bold property to True if the first check box is checked and to False otherwise. More generally, you can use the *Index* parameter for the *chkStyle_Click* event to identify which font property to set:

```
Private Sub chkStyle_Click(Index As Integer)
    Select Case Index
        Case 0
            lblTest.Font.Bold = chkStyle(Index).Value
        Case 1
            lblTest.Font.Italic = chkStyle(Index).Value
        Case 2
            lblTest.Font.Underline = chkStyle(Index).Value
    End Select
End Sub
```

Once you enter the code for these four events (*Form_Load, optBackColor_Click, optForeColor_Click*, and *chkStyle_Click*), you're in business. You can use the option buttons and check boxes to control the background color, foreground color, and text style of the label box.

DATA ARRAYS

Long before Basic became Visual Basic and gained control arrays, it had *data arrays*. A data array can hold several values of the same type. For instance, one array can hold 20 type *Integer* values, and another array can hold 12 *String* values. Arrays are convenient for storing related values. For example, to store the names of 48 prize-winning racing pigeons, you can use a single array of 48 strings instead of 48 separate string variables. As with control arrays and menu arrays, you use an index to identify individual array members. By default, the numbering starts with 0, so the first member of the array has an index of 0. Figure L9-8 shows what an array looks like.

To create an array, use the *Dim* statement with an additional element indicating the range of indices in the array. For instance, to create an array of eight integers, you can do this:

```
Dim Odds(1 To 8) as Integer     'create array of 8 Integers
```

This creates an array named *Odds*. The first element of the array is called *Odds(1)*, and so on. Figure L9-9 illustrates the basic format for creating arrays. Note that index values used in declaring an array should be constants. (There's a way to use variables for index values, and you'll learn about that later.)

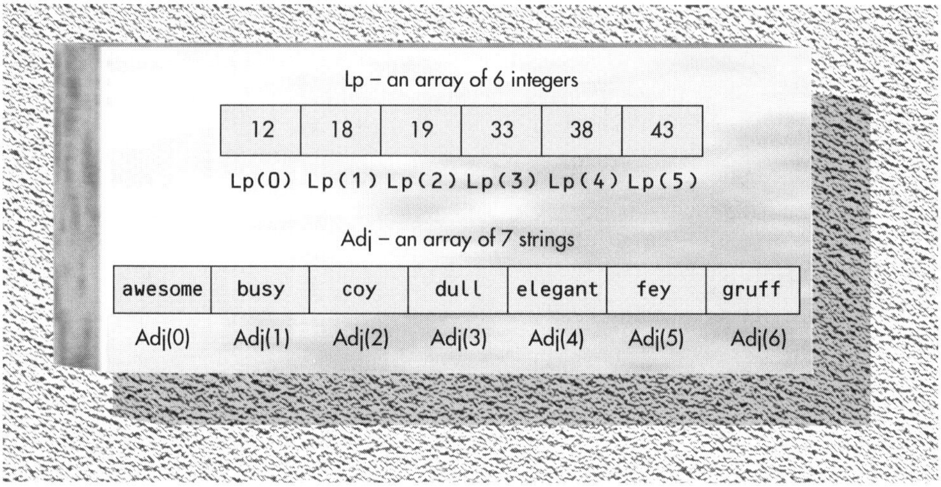

Figure L9-8 Data arrays

The *For* loop is just the thing to handle an array, for you can use the loop index to represent the array index. For example, suppose you want to store the first eight odd numbers in the *Odds* array. Assuming you've declared *Index* as type *Integer,* you can do this:

```
For Index = 1 to 8
    Odds(Index) = 2 * Index - 1
Next Index
```

The main point here is that you can use the *For* loop to process each element of an array in turn.

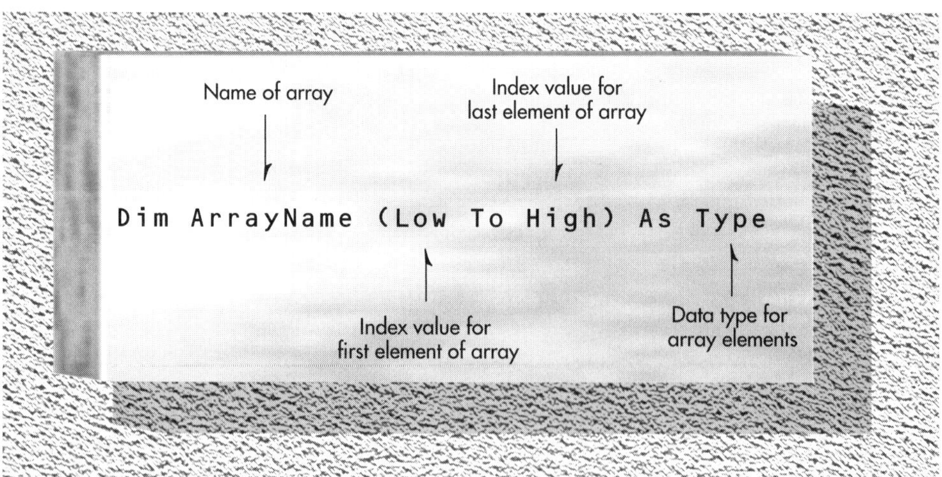

Figure L9-9 Using *Dim* to create an array

Ancient Basic history leaves us with a couple of idiosyncrasies concerning the *Dim* statement. First, you can use just a single number instead of a range. In that case, the number represents the upper limit for the array index. For instance, consider this array declaration:

```
Dim Relic(10) as Integer '10 is upper limit for array index
```

This means that the very last element in the *Relic* array is *Relic(10)*.

If that's the last element, what's the first element? That's another idiosyncrasy. By default, the first element is *Relic(0)*. Thus, the declaration above creates an array with 11 elements numbered from 0 to 10. However, you can override the default with the *Option Base* statement. This is a module-level statement that indicates how array numbering begins if a *Dim* statement just gives the upper limit. You have two choices:

```
Option Base 1   ' Default array numbering starts at 1.
Option Base 0   ' Default array numbering starts at 0.
```

All in all, rather than relying on these rules, you're much better off simply giving the index range explicitly when you declare the array.

Tip

As a matter of programming style, indicate the index range explicitly when declaring arrays.

A Modest Improvement to the Program

You can use arrays to make a modest improvement to the Frames program. Consider the following excerpt.

```
Private Sub optBackColor_Click(Index As Integer)
    Select Case Index
        Case 0
            lblTest.BackColor = vbRed
        Case 1
            lblTest.BackColor = vbGreen
        Case 2
            lblTest.BackColor = vbBlue
    End Select
End Sub
```

Here the value of *Index* indicates which option button was clicked. Suppose the color values were stored in an array instead of individual constants. For instance, suppose you stored *vbRed* in element 0, *vbGreen* in element 1, and *vbBlue* in element 2 of an array called *BackColors*. Then you could replace the above code with something much shorter:

```
Private Sub optBackColor_Click(Index As Integer)
    lblTest.BackColor = BackColors(Index)
End Sub
```

Here the contents of the data array are coordinated with the option buttons in the control array. The option button captioned "Red" has the same index as the array element containing the color code for red. You could also do something similar for the foreground colors:

```
Private Sub optForeColor_Click(Index As Integer)
    lblTest.ForeColor = ForeColors(Index)
End Sub
```

For this to work, you have to create the proper arrays and store the correct values in them. Note that the arrays that hold the color values need to be arrays of *Long* because the color values are 32-bit integers, while the Integer type is only 16-bit. The way to do this is to declare the arrays at the module level and to use the *Form_Load* event to assign proper values:

```
Option Explicit
Dim BackColors(0 To 2) As Long ' to hold color codes
Dim ForeColors(0 To 2) As Long ' to hold color codes

Private Sub Form_Load()
    optBackColor(0).Value = True
    optForeColor(0).Value = True
    BackColors(0) = vbRed
    BackColors(1) = vbGreen
    BackColors(2) = vbBlue
    ForeColors(0) = vbCyan
    ForeColors(1) = vbMagenta
    ForeColors(2) = vbYellow
End Sub
```

What Day Is It? (A New Project)

Let's create a program that uses arrays more extensively. The goal this time is a program that lets you select a month and a day in the month, and which reports the corresponding day in the year. For instance, if you select February 3, the program will display 34, since February 3 is the 34th day of the year. To keep things simple, the program will ignore leap years, but one of the exercises at the end of the chapter will give you the opportunity to overcome that limitation.

First, consider the interface. How should you get information from the user? A text box will do, but the problem with text boxes is that users don't always respond with a choice you expect. You ask for an age, and they respond with "Aquarius." You ask for the type of monitor, and they reply "Giant Lizard." If only certain answers will do, you often are better off letting the user select from a list. So for getting a month of the year, you can use a list box that shows the 12 months.

Getting the day of the month is a bit trickier because different months have different numbers of days. Ideally, you'd like to make it impossible for the user to enter, say, February 30. One way of accomplishing this is to use a vertical scrollbar control for setting the day value. With proper coding, you can key the Max property for the scrollbar to the month. That is, if the user selects May, the

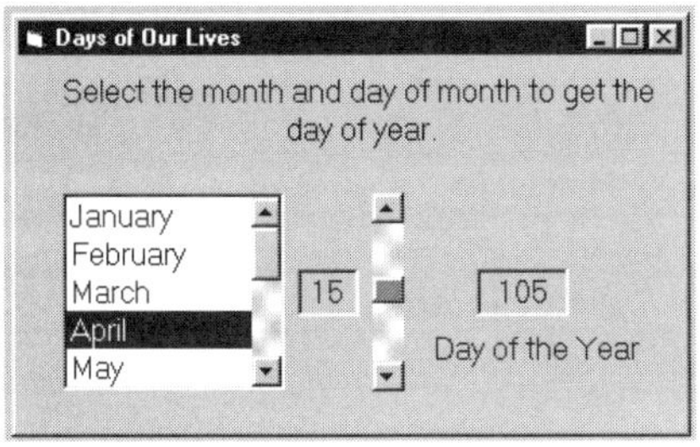

Figure L9-10 The Days of Our Lives form

program sets the Max property to 31, and if the user selects June, the program sets the Max property to 30. Also, you can set the LargeChange property to 7 so that clicking near the ends of the scrollbar will change the date a week at a time.

The program also should have a label box giving instructions, a second label box displaying the day of month the user selects, and a third label box displaying the resulting day of the month. This yields the appearance shown in Figure L9-10 and described by the properties given in Table L9-3. Note that the form size has been scaled down to fit the controls.

OBJECT	PROPERTY	SETTING
Form1	Caption	Days of Our Lives
	Font.Size	12
	Name	frmOptArray
List1	Name	lstMonths
VScroll1	LargeChange	7
	Min	1
	Max	31
	Name	vsbMonthDay
Label1	Alignment	2 - Center
	Caption	Select the month and day of month to get the day of year.
	Name	lblInstructions
	WordWrap	True
Label2	Alignment	2 - Center
	BorderStyle	1 - Fixed Single
	Caption	1
	Name	lblMonthDay
Label3	Alignment	2 - Center
	BorderStyle	1 - Fixed Single
	Caption	1
	Name	lblDayOfYear

continued on next page

continued from previous page

OBJECT	PROPERTY	SETTING
Label4	Alignment	2 - Center
	AutoSize	True
	Caption	Day of the Year
	Name	lblLabel

Table L9-3 Properties for the Days of Our Lives program

Where do arrays come in? They can serve as information holders. For example, the program needs to know how many days there are in each month. That information can be stored in an array with 12 elements. Another useful batch of information is the cumulative number of days in a year up to the beginning of a particular month. For instance, the number of days in a year up to the beginning of March is 31 + 28, or 59. If you want to know what day of year March 5 is, you can add the day of the month (5) to the number of days to the beginning of March (59) to find that March 5 is the 64th day of the year.

You can declare these arrays at the module level as follows:

```
Option Explicit
Dim DaysIn(0 To 11) As Integer  'days in month
Dim DaysTo(0 To 11) As Integer  'days to start of month
```

The reason for numbering the elements 0 to 11 instead of 1 to 12 is that the ListIndex property for list boxes starts its numbering with 0. Recall from Lesson 3 that the ListIndex property represents the index value for the currently selected item in the list. So if you select January in the list box, the ListIndex property is 0. Thus we've set things up so that a 0 index in the two arrays also corresponds to the first month, January, so the array indices and the list index are in sync.

The *Form_Load* event procedure has a lot to do for this program. As you may recall, you use the *AddItem* method in the *Form_Load* event to set up the items that appear in a list box. Also, the *Form_Load* event is a good place to fill the two arrays with the correct data. Finally, you can use the *Form_Load* event to set the Selected property to True for the first item in the list so that the program will begin with January already selected. Here is code to make it so.

```
Private Sub Form_Load()
    Dim Month As Integer
    ' Add month names to list box.
    lstMonths.AddItem ("January")
    lstMonths.AddItem ("February")
    lstMonths.AddItem ("March")
    lstMonths.AddItem ("April")
    lstMonths.AddItem ("May")
    lstMonths.AddItem ("June")
    lstMonths.AddItem ("July")
    lstMonths.AddItem ("August")
    lstMonths.AddItem ("September")
    lstMonths.AddItem ("October")
    lstMonths.AddItem ("November")
```

```
    lstMonths.AddItem ("December")
    ' Initialize DaysIn to number of days in each month.
    DaysIn(0) = 31 'January
    DaysIn(1) = 28 'February
    DaysIn(2) = 31 'March
    DaysIn(3) = 30 'April
    DaysIn(4) = 31 'May
    DaysIn(5) = 30 'June
    DaysIn(6) = 31 'July
    DaysIn(7) = 31 'August
    DaysIn(8) = 30 'September
    DaysIn(9) = 31 'October
    DaysIn(10) = 30 'November
    DaysIn(11) = 31 'December
    ' Calculate cumulative number of days to beginning
    ' of each month and initialize DaysTo array.
    DaysTo(0) = 0
    For Month = 1 To 11
        DaysTo(Month) = DaysTo(Month - 1) + DaysIn(Month - 1)
    Next Month
    ' Start with January selected.
    lstMonths.Selected(0) = True
End Sub
```

Note the scheme for calculating the cumulative days to the beginning of each month:

```
DaysTo(0) = 0
For Month = 1 To 11
    DaysTo(Month) = DaysTo(Month - 1) + DaysIn(Month - 1)
Next Month
```

The cumulative days to the beginning of January is 0, so the program sets DaysTo(0) to 0. Then it uses a *For* loop to handle the rest of the months. For each month, the cumulative number of days to the beginning of the month (*DaysTo(Month)*) is the cumulative number of days to the beginning of the previous month (*DaysTo(Month - 1)*) plus the number of days in the previous month (*DaysIn(Month - 1)*). For example, the cumulative number of days to the beginning of March (59) is the cumulative number of days to the beginning of February (31) plus the number of days in February (28).

The *Form_Load* event does most of the hard work in this program. The rest of the code is pretty short. The key calculation is that the day of the year equals the day of the month plus the number of days to the beginning of the month. In terms of properties and array values, that calculation looks like this:

```
lblDayOfYear.Caption = vsbMonthDay.Value + DaysTo(lstMonths.ListIndex)
```

When should this calculation be made? It should be done whenever the user uses the list box to change the month or uses the scrollbar to change the day. That suggests placing the calculation in the *Click* event for the list and in the *Change* event for the scrollbar.

The event procedures have two more tasks to do. First, each time the user changes the month setting, the program should reset the Max property of the scrollbar to match the number of days in the new month. Second, each time the user uses the scrollbar to change the day of the month, the program should update the number showing in the lblMonthDay label box. The following code takes care of these matters.

```
Private Sub lstMonths_Click()
    vsbMonthDay.Max = DaysIn(lstMonths.ListIndex)
    lblDayOfYear.Caption = vsbMonthDay.Value +
DaysTo(lstMonths.ListIndex)
End Sub

Private Sub vsbMonthDay_Change()
    lblMonthDay.Caption = vsbMonthDay.Value
    lblDayOfYear.Caption = vsbMonthDay.Value +
DaysTo(lstMonths.ListIndex)
End Sub
```

Once you have this code in place, the program should work fine, as shown earlier in Figure L9-10.

SUMMARY

Visual Basic lets you create control arrays, a convenient way of organizing a set of related controls, all of one kind. The members of a control array share the same Name property, but each has its own Index property. By default, Visual Basic assigns the first control an index of 0, the second control an index of 1, and so on. All the members of a control array share their event procedures in common. Each event procedure for a control array has an *Index* argument that is set to the Index value of the particular control that invoked the event. For instance, clicking on an option button that's part of a control array named optButtons invokes the following event procedure:

```
Private Sub OptButtons_Click(Index as Integer)
    ...
End Sub
```

If you click on the button having an Index property of 2, then the *Index* argument to *OptButtons_Click* is set to 2.

Within an event procedure for a control array, you can provide code that takes place no matter which array member gets the event, and you can use the *Select Case* statement to provide particular code choices for individual members.

A frame control provides a framework into which you can place other controls. You must create the control in a frame, not just drag a control into a frame. A frame lets you group a related set of controls. If you move the frame, all the controls in the frame move along with it. Option buttons within a frame act independently of other option buttons on the form.

A check box control can be toggled between being checked and unchecked. It's handy for setting and unsetting properties and features.

A vertical scrollbar control has the same properties as a horizontal scrollbar, except it scrolls up and down instead of from left to right.

A data array stores a series of values of one type. The general form for creating an array is this:

```
Dim ArrayName(LowIndex To HighIndex) as Type
```

Here *ArrayName* is the name of the array, *LowIndex* is the index value for the first element of the array, *HighIndex* is the index value for the last element of the array, and *Type* identifies the type of data stored in the array. Arrays are handy for storing related sets of data, such as yearly beet harvest statistics for a decade.

QUIZ 9

1. A control array is
   a. A device used by control freaks
   b. A set of controls sharing a common name but each having its own Index property
   c. A set of controls in the same frame

2. All members of a given control array share the same event procedures. How, then, can a program respond differently to different controls in the same array?

3. The main operational difference between option buttons and check boxes is
   a. You can turn on any number of option buttons in the same set, but only one check box in a set can be checked.
   b. You can check any number of check boxes in a set, but only one option button in a set can be set to on.
   c. You need a cross mouse to check a check box.

4. Why would you place option buttons in a frame?

5. Provide declarations that create the following:
   a. An array of integers with the indices running from 1 to 20
   b. An array of 15 strings with the first index being 0
   c. An array of 10 Boolean values with the first index being 1985

6. Suppose Scores is an array of 20 integers with the first index being 0. Write code that calculates the sum of all the elements in the array.

7. If you create a module-level array, where might you initialize that array?

TRY IT YOURSELF

1. Modify the Days of Our Lives program so that it can handle leap years. Use a check box to allow the user to choose whether it is a leap year.

2. The Snitdale High School football team has the following record over a 12-year span:

YEAR	WINS	LOSSES
1984	7	3
1985	8	2
1986	5	5
1987	6	4
1988	4	6
1989	3	7
1990	4	6
1991	2	8
1992	4	6
1993	5	5
1994	8	2
1995	9	1

Prepare a program that stores this information in arrays. The program should have a vertical scrollbar that lets you select the year, and it then should display the win-loss record for that year. An array of three option buttons in a frame should let you select black, blue, or red for displaying the number of wins, and a similar array in a second frame should offer the same choices for displaying the number of losses.

LESSON

10 COLOR PRIMER

Color is one of the most, well, colorful tools at your disposal. You can use it to soothe, to grab attention, to decorate, to guide the eye, and to waste time. This lesson will explore the Visual Basic view of color. In particular, you'll learn about the following:

- **The nature of color**
- **8-bit, 16-bit, and 24-bit color**
- **The RGB function**

- **The QBColor function**
- **BackColor, ForeColor, BorderColor, and FillColor properties**
- **The shape control and the line control**
- **The timer control**
- **The Rnd and Randomize functions**

Actually, the last two topics in the list don't have much to do with color directly, but they'll prove useful in creating some colorful examples.

THE NATURE OF COLOR

What does it mean to be blue? Ask physicists, and they'll tell you that blue light consists of electromagnetic waves lying in a particular range of wavelengths. Or they may say blue light consists of photons lying in a particular range of energies. (Physicists have this thing about the particle-wave duality of nature at the subatomic level.) In either case, blue, and other colors, correspond to measurable physical properties of light. Indeed, there is an instrument, the spectrograph, that lets you analyze just which wavelengths (or energies) are present in a sample of light and what the proportions are. So you can describe color by numbers.

But numbers (aside from painting by numbers) are not how we perceive color. We experience blue as a particular sensation. From the physiological standpoint, color is the body's way of identifying different wavelengths (or energies) of light. Our system is a bit crude. Human eyes have detectors (molecules in structures called *cones*) sensitive to three colors—red, green, and blue. If red light strikes the eye, it's absorbed by a red detector, which then uses the energy from the absorbed light to send a signal to the brain saying "Incoming red!" The detectors are broad-band detectors, meaning that each detector responds to a wide range of different wavelengths (or energies).

So you have detectors for red, green, and blue. Why aren't those the only colors we experience, then? The answer lies in your brain. Suppose a small spot on the back of your eyeball is hit by a mixture of red and green light. The red detectors send the "Incoming red!" message, and the green detectors send the "Incoming green!" message. The brain resolves these mixed messages with a new response—"Seeing yellow!" In short, the perception of yellow is your brain's response to receiving roughly equal amounts of red light and green light from the same location. Similarly, perceiving magenta is your brain's response to receiving roughly equal amounts of red light and blue light from the same location.

In general, you can match any color by adding red, green, and blue light to each other in appropriate proportions. For this reason, red, green, and blue are

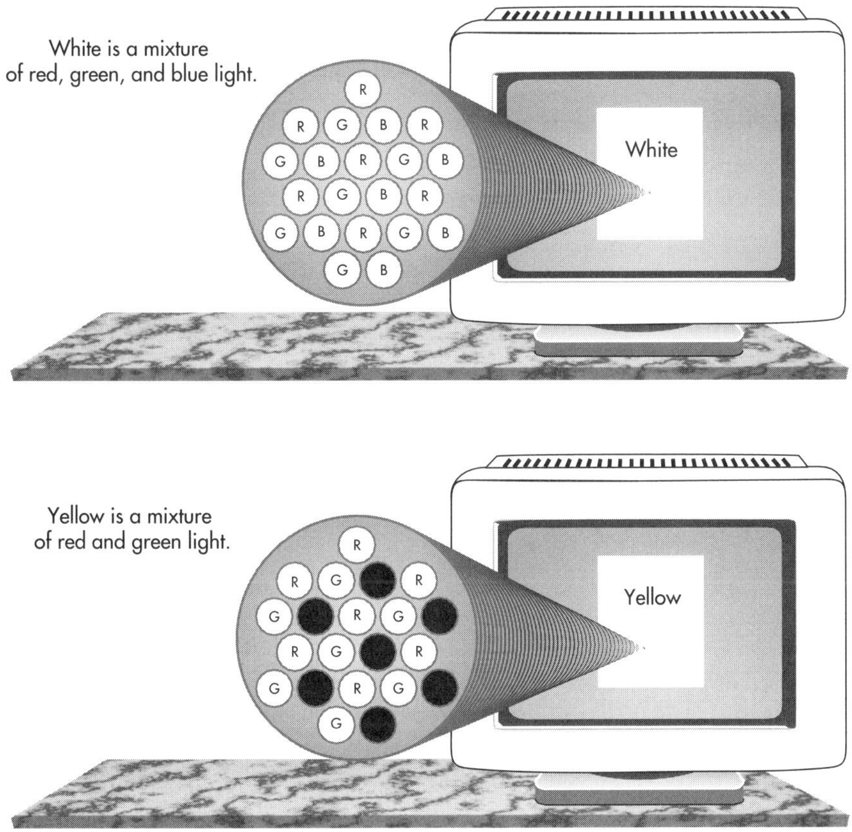

Figure L10-1 Colors on a monitor

called additive primaries. (There are three primary colors because our eyes have detectors for three kinds of color.) Color televisions and computer monitors use small adjacent dots of red, green, and blue phosphors to reproduce different colors. You can verify this by looking closely at a color screen with a sufficiently powerful magnifier. (Sony Trinitron tubes use stripes instead of dots.) White, for example, consists of all three colors of dots turned on with equal intensity. To make a region yellow, the monitor uses just the red and green dots (see Figure L10-1). From normal view distances, the light from adjacent dots or stripes blends together so that you see the blended color rather than the individual primary colors.

So what's this got to do with programming? Because screen colors are blends of red, green, and blue, they can be described in terms of the individual

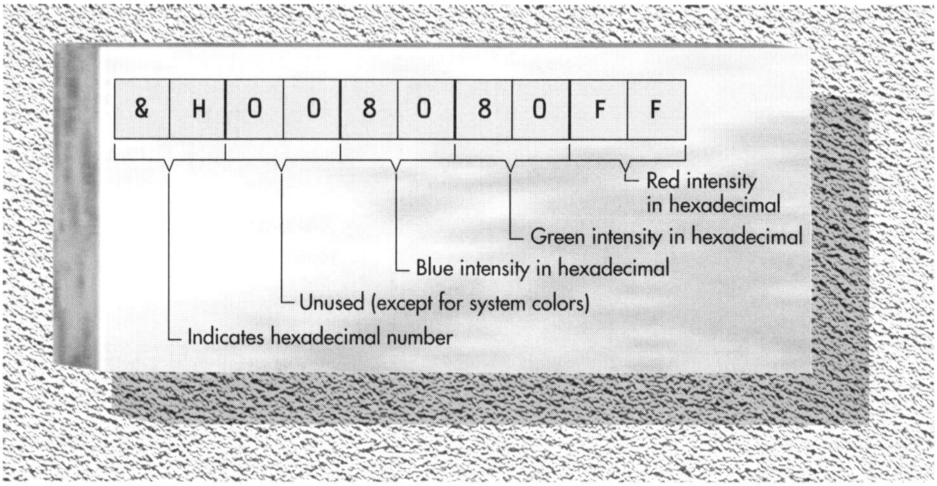

Figure L10-2 Color settings in hexadecimal

intensities of those three colors. And that is what the Visual Basic color representation system does.

Specifying Colors in Visual Basic

The Visual Basic color representation scheme dedicates 1 byte to each primary color to represent the color's intensity. Each color, then, can have an intensity value in the range 0 to 255, with 0 being off and 255 being maximum intensity. To get black, set all three intensities to 0. To get bright white, set all three intensities to 255. Other combinations produce the other colors. All together, there are 256 x 256 x 256 possible color settings, corresponding to a grand total of approximately 16.7 million distinct colors. The range 0 to 255 conveniently fits in 1 byte of memory, so you need 3 bytes to hold the settings for the red, green, and blue primary colors. This is too large to fit in an *Integer* value (2 bytes), but it fits with room to spare in a *Long* value (4 bytes). So Visual Basic uses the *Long* type to represent color values.

Viewing the color value in hexadecimal notation is very revealing because in that notation each byte corresponds exactly to two hexadecimal digits. In particular, the two rightmost digits are the red setting, the next two digits are the green setting, and the next two are the blue setting (see Figure L10-2). Table L10-1, which lists the Visual Basic color constants you used in Lesson 9, also shows the hexadecimal representation. Given that FF in hexadecimal is 255 in decimal, you can see, for example, that *vbRed* corresponds to maximum red intensity (&H0000FF), while *vbYellow* (&H00FFFF) is a mix of maximum red and maximum green intensities.

COLOR	SYMBOLIC CONSTANT	COLOR VALUE (HEX)
Black	vbBlack	&H000000
Red	vbRed	&H0000FF
Green	vbGreen	&H00FF00
Blue	vbBlue	&HFF0000
Cyan	vbCyan	&HFFFF00
Magenta	vbMagenta	&HFF00FF
Yellow	vbYellow	&H00FFFF
White	vbWhite	&HFFFFFF

Table L10-1 Visual Basic color constants

Suppose you want your code to use a color other than the eight in Table L10-1. For instance, perhaps you want to change the color of a control if it gets the focus. One thing you can do in design mode is go to the Properties window, select the BackColor property for a control, and open the color selection box. Select a color you like, then note the corresponding number code that appears in the Properties window. You then can use Visual Basic's Copy and Paste hot keys (CTRL-C, CTRL-V) to copy the value and paste it into the Code window.

But what if you want to construct a color? For example, suppose you want a color that's full intensity red (255), about 3/4 intensity green (192), and about 1/2 intensity blue (128). You could convert the intensity value to their hexadecimal equivalents (FF, C0, and 80), then combine them to form a hexadecimal color value (&H80C0FF), using the order blue, green, red, as indicated by Figure L10-2. But there is a much easier way. Use the Visual Basic *RGB* function. It takes three arguments—the red, green, and blue intensities—and returns the corresponding type *Long* color value. For instance, to set the background of a label to the color just described, you can do this:

```
lblWarning.BackColor = RGB(255,192,128)
```

A Property of Another Color

You may have noticed that some of the default color codes that appear in the Properties window don't match the previous description. For instance, most controls have a BackColor property of &H80000005. The RGB color description uses just the last 6 digits of an 8-digit hex value, so what's that 8 doing as the first digit? It's announcing that the code is a *system color code* instead of an RGB code. System color codes refer to color choices made by the Windows operating system. For example, the code &H80000005 means "use the system color for a window background." By default, that color is white, but you can use the Desktop choice in the Windows Control Panel to change the background color for windows. Similarly, you can use the Control Panel to adjust other color choices, too, such as the color of the desktop, the color of the title bar of an active window, and so on. Visual Basic has color codes for all these choices, and Table L10-2 lists them along with symbolic colors for the constants. The idea is that if someone resets the Windows desktop colors, programs that use colors from Table L10-2 will track the changes. So if you set the BackColor property for a form to &H80000005 and a user uses the Windows Control Panel to change the windows background color to light blue, then your program will follow suit automatically.

Color	Symbolic Constant Color	Value (Hex)
Scrollbar color	vbScrollBars	&H80000000
Desktop color	vbDesktop	&H80000001
Color of the title bar for the active window	vbActiveTitleBar	&H80000002
Color of the title bar for an inactive window	vbInactiveTitleBar	&H80000003
Menu background color	vbMenuBar	&H80000004
Window background color	vbWindowBackground	&H80000005
Window frame color	vbWindowFrame	&H80000006
Color of text on menus	vbMenuText	&H80000007
Color of text in windows	vbWindowText	&H80000008
Color of text in caption, size box, and scroll arrow	vbTitleBarText	&H80000009
Border color of active window	vbActiveBorder	&H8000000A
Border color of inactive window	vbInActiveBorder	&H8000000B
Background color of multiple-document interface (MDI) applications	vbApplicationWorkSpace	&H8000000C
Background color of selected items in a control	vbHighlight	&H8000000D
Text color of selected items in a control	vbHighlightText	&H8000000E
Color of shading on the face of command buttons	vbButtonFace	&H8000000Fl
Color of shading on the edge of command buttons	vbButtonShadow	&H80000010
Disabled (grayed) text	vbGrayText	&H80000011
Text color on push buttons	vbButtonText	&H8000012D

Table L10-2 Visual Basic Windows system color constants

Visual Basic Color Values and Your Monitor

Visual Basic can identify 16.7 million colors, but can your computer system do so? Some video cards support what's known as *true color* or *24-bit color*, meaning the card uses 8 bits (1 byte) per primary color for a total of 24 bits, or 3 bytes. These cards can display 16.7 million colors. In that case, each possible Visual Basic color setting corresponds to an onscreen color.

More typically, however, video cards support fewer colors. The usual choices are 8-bit color (256 color choices) and 16-bit color (65,536 color choices). Some older systems may just offer 4-bit color (16 color choices). In all these cases, the computer system can display far fewer than 16.7 million colors, so most color values can't be displayed as described.

For 256-color displays, Visual Basic resorts to *dithering,* that is, attempting to simulate an unavailable color with a pattern of pixels of available colors. For instance, dithering might match a lime green with a mixture of green and yellow pixels. (Each pixel itself contains a full complement of color phosphors, so the yellow pixel would have its green and red dots or stripes turned on.)

For 65,536 color displays, Visual Basic takes a less obtrusive approach. It matches the 32-bit RGB to the closest 16-bit value. The result is close enough to pass muster unless, possibly, you could place the two choices side-by-side.

Color Mode Differences

Generally speaking, 24-bit color offers "photo realism," reproducing colors with a degree of subtlety similar to that of a photographic color slide. 16-bit color comes close, and most people won't notice the difference between a color photograph reproduced in 16-bit color and one in 24-bit color. However, a color slide converted to 8-bit color is clearly different from the original.

Colors the Old Way

Visual Basic inherits an older color numbering system from the days of 16-color displays. At that time, IBM compatibles used a simple code for the colors, the code shown in Table L10-3. QuickBasic, for example, used this system. Visual Basic provides a function called *QBColor* that converts these colors to the new system. For instance, to set the background of a text box to blue, you could use this code:

```
Text1.BackColor = QBColor(1)
```

COLOR	NUMBER	COLOR	NUMBER
Black	0	Gray	8
Blue	1	Light blue	9
Green	2	Light green	10
Cyan	3	Light cyan	11
Red	4	Light red	12
Magenta	5	Light magenta	13
Yellow	6	Light yellow	14
White	7	Bright white	15

Table L10-3 QuickBasic color numbers

Figure L10-3 The Color Chooser form

The main uses for the *QBColor* function are to convert older Basic programs to Visual Basic, to provide a simple 16-color palette, and to support the habits of veteran Basic programmers. New Visual Basic programs should use the named color constants, the *RGB* function, and the color grid available from the Properties window.

Showing Your Colors

Now that you've seen the basics, let's move on to a program using color. The plan this time is to display a form with text in a text box. One array of three scrollbars will let you choose the red, green, and blue components for the background color, and a second array will let you choose the red, green, and blue components for the text color. Two label boxes will display the corresponding color values. This program will let you explore the color capabilities of your own system. If you can, try the program with 8-bit color, 16-bit color, and 24-bit color so you can see how the different levels of color support react to the Visual Basic color values. Figure L10-3 shows the layout for the controls, and Table L10-4 shows the properties. The table shows each control array as a single entry, with the Index property showing the values for the three members of each control array. Remember that you can use the Properties window color grid to select colors for the properties.

Object	Property	Setting
Form1	BackColor	&H00C0C0C0& (gray)
	Caption	Color Chooser
	Name	frmColors
Text1	Alignment	2 - Center

Object	Property	Setting
	Caption	CAN YOU READ ME?
	Font.FontSize	24
	MultiLine	True
	Name	txtColors
Frame1	Caption	Background Color
	Name	fraBackGround
Frame2	Caption	Text Color
	Name	fraTextColor
Label1	ForeColor	&H000000FF (red)
	Caption	Red
	Name	lblRed1
Label2	ForeColor	&H0000FF00 (green)
	Caption	Green
	Name	lbGreen1
Label3	ForeColor	&H00FF0000 (blue)
	Caption	Blue
	Name	lblBlue1
Label4	ForeColor	&H000000FF (red)
	Caption	Red
	Name	lblRed2
Label5	ForeColor	&H0000FF00 (green)
	Caption	Green
	Name	lbGreen2
Label6	ForeColor	&H00FF0000 (blue)
	Caption	Blue
	Name	lbBlue2
VScroll1	Index	0, 1, 2
	LargeChange	16
	Max	255
	Min	0
	Name	vsbBackColor
VScroll2	Index	0, 1, 2
	LargeChange	16
	Max	255
	Min	0
	Name	vsbTextColor
Label7	Alignment	2 - Center
	BorderStyle	1 - Fixed Single
	Index	0, 1, 2
	Name	lblVal1

continued on next page

continued from previous page

Object	Property	Setting
Label8	Alignment	2 - Center
	BorderStyle	1 - Fixed Single
	Index	0, 1, 2
	Name	lblVal2
Label9	Alignment	1 - Right
	BorderStyle	1 - Fixed Single
	Font.FontSize	11
	Name	lblRGB1
Label10	Alignment	1 - Right
	BorderStyle	1 - Fixed Single
	Font.FontSize	11
	Name	lblRGB2

Table L10-4 Properties for the Color Chooser program

The BackColor and ForeColor Properties

For most of the controls we've used so far, the BackColor property specifies the background color of the control and the ForeColor property specifies the colors of items that appear in the control, such as captions, text, and list box (see Figure L10-4). So a text box with a BackColor property set to red and a ForeColor property set to yellow shows yellow text on a red background. There are some exceptions. For instance, the scrollbar controls have neither a BackColor nor a ForeColor property; these controls use preset shades of gray. Command buttons only have a BackColor property, and it doesn't affect the color of the control. Instead, it controls the color of the highlighting rectangle that appears around a command button caption when the button gets the focus.

Now that the interface design is done, let's move on to the code. First, when the program starts, it should set up the initial values for the scrollbar settings. Each of the background color intensities should be set to 255 to get white, and each of the foreground intensities should be set to 0 to get black. The program also should set the captions for the labels tracking the intensities and the color values. The *Hex* function converts a number to the hexadecimal representation as a string, so we can use it to display the color values in hexadecimal form. All this can be done in the *Form_Load* event procedure.

```
Option Explicit

Private Sub Form_Load()
    Dim I As Integer
```

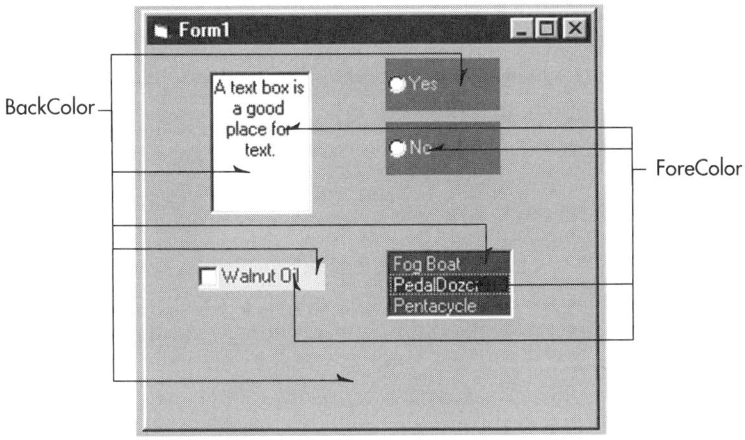

Figure L10-4 BackColor and ForeColor

```
    For I = 0 To 2
        vsbBackColor(I).Value = 255
        vsbTextColor(I).Value = 0
        lblVal1(I).Caption = 255
        lblVal2(I).Caption = 0
   Next I
   lblRGB1 = Hex(vbWhite)
   lblRGB2 = Hex(vbBlack)
End Sub
```

Next, changing the scrollbar settings should change the colors you see along with the labels describing the intensities and the color values. That can be done in the *Change* event procedures for the two control arrays.

```
Private Sub vsbBackColor_Change(Index As Integer)
    Dim BColor As Long
    lblVal1(Index).Caption = vsbBackColor(Index).Value
    BColor = RGB(vsbBackColor(0).Value, vsbBackColor(1).Value, _
        vsbBackColor(2).Value)
    txtColors.BackColor = BColor
    lblRGB1 = Hex(BColor)
End Sub

Private Sub vsbTextColor_Change(Index As Integer)
    Dim TColor As Long
    lblVal2(Index).Caption = vsbTextColor(Index).Value
    TColor = RGB(vsbTextColor(0).Value, vsbTextColor(1).Value, _
        vsbTextColor(2).Value)
    txtColors.ForeColor = TColor
    lblRGB2.Caption = Hex(TColor)
End Sub
```

And that's it! The main new elements in this program are using the *RGB* function to convert individual red, green, and blue intensities to a color number and using the *Hex* function to convert color numbers to a hexadecimal representation. The most important feature of the program is that it gives you a hands-on experience with the Visual Basic system of representing colors.

Tip

Use the RGB function to set colors in Visual Basic code.

Things to Do

Here are some things you might try.

If you have a 256-color display, set the green and blue components of the background color to 0, and then slowly reduce the red intensity. Notice that Visual Basic handles the background immediately around the text differently from the background below the text. The background below the text goes through a series of dithered patterns, occasionally hitting a solid color when the red value matches one of the available reds. The background around the text, however, is always solid, matching the closest available solid red. (A dithered background would make the text hard to read.) So the background around the text stays constant through a wide range of red intensities, then jumps to the next level.

If you have a 16-bit color display, set the text to a pure red with an intensity of 125. Also set the background to a pure red and find what range of background settings makes the text invisible. Of course, when the background has the same setting as the text, you can't see the text. But you'll find a narrow range on either side also obscures the text. This is because a range of 24-bit color values maps to the same 16-bit color value, so the color only changes when you move 8 units or so instead of 1 unit.

If you have a 24-bit color display, see how closely the background color and the text color have to match before you can't read the text. If you use one of the primary colors for both, you'll probably be able to discriminate between colors 2 or 3 units apart from each other. But mixed colors, depending on the proportions, will have a lot more leeway. For instance, if you use a red value of 250, a green value of 192, and a blue value of 20 for the background, you probably will be able to notice rather small differences in the red value. But because the faint blue component is overwhelmed by the more intense components, you should be able to vary it over a wide range without seeing a difference. In short, a lot of the 16.7 million possible colors will look pretty indistinguishable from one another.

THE SHAPE CONTROL

Visual Basic lets you add graphics shapes, such as rectangles and ovals, to forms and frames as design element controls. A shape control is relatively primitive. It doesn't use text or captions, it doesn't have a Value property, and it has no event procedures. Thus, a shape control doesn't respond to clicks, and it doesn't take the focus. Its primary attributes are that it has a shape, it has colors (which is why we're squeezing it into this chapter), and it has a fill pattern. In short, a shape is more a decorative feature than a programming feature.

Let's investigate the shape control. Open a new form and select the shape icon. (It shows three overlapping geometric forms.) Drag the mouse to draw a shape on the form. The shape turns out to be a rectangle. Open the Properties window. One of the properties of a shape control is called Shape. Opening the list box to the right of that property, you'll find the choices listed in Table L10-5.

SHAPE PROPERTY VALUE	DESCRIPTION
0	Rectangle
1	Square
2	Oval
3	Circle
4	Rounded rectangle
5	Rounded square

Table L10-5 Shape property choices

Try the various values. You'll find that the oval and rounded rectangle have the same dimensions as the original rectangle, while the square, circle, and rounded square have the same dimensions as the short dimension of the rectangle (see Figure L10-5). If you select the object, the handles correspond to the dimensions of the rectangle.

Next, try setting the BackColor property to, say, red. Interestingly enough, the shape control should appear unchanged. That's because there is a BackStyle property which, by default, is set to 0 - Transparent. That means you can see through the shape, hence you don't see the background color of the shape. Change the BackStyle property to 1 - Opaque. That makes the control opaque, and the background color of the shape becomes visible.

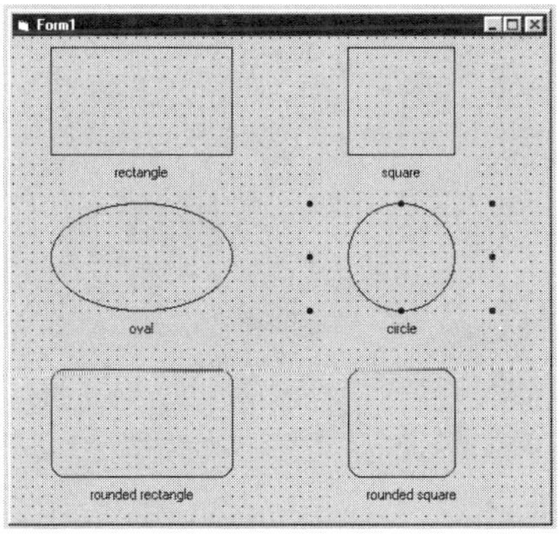

Figure L10-5 Some shapes

The shape control has two new color properties. One is called BorderColor. As you might guess, it controls the color used to draw the border for the shape. There also is a BorderStyle property. By default, it's set to solid, but you have other choices, including transparent (invisible), dotted, and dashed. A third border property, BorderWidth sets the width of the border in pixels, with the default being 1 pixel wide. If you set BorderWidth to more than 1, however, you can only use the Transparent, Solid, and Solid Inside border styles. Visual Basic will use Solid if you select a style other than these three.

The second new color property is called FillColor. Try picking a fill color of blue. Just as when you picked a BackColor, nothing seems to have happened. That's because the effect of picking a fill color depends on the FillStyle setting, which is 1 - Transparent by default. Set the file style to 0 - Solid, and the fill color fills the shape. The other style choices are geometric. For instance, try the 6 - Cross setting. This fills the shape with a grid pattern. The grid is drawn using the fill color, and the background uses the back color (see Figure L10-6).

The shape object has a really wild property called DrawMode. It controls how the colors used for a shape interact with the colors of the form and controls behind the shape. The default, Copy Pen, behaves simply. Opaque and solid colors hide whatever is behind the shape. But the other choices provide all kinds of variants. Lesson 12 on graphics will talk more about these choices. For the present, let's stick with the simple default behavior. To add a bit of interest to using shapes, let's introduce a new control.

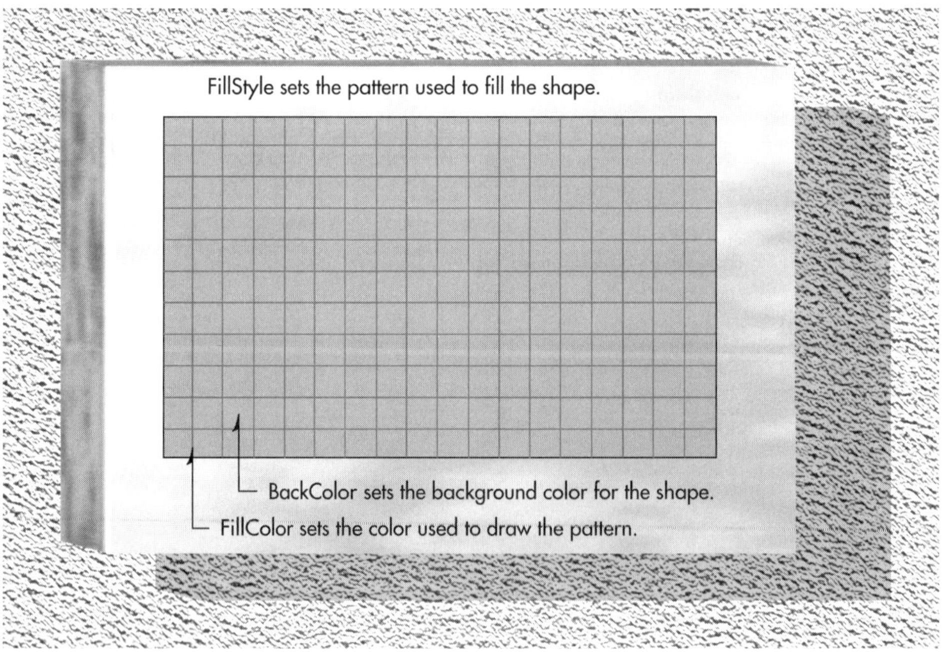

Figure L10-6 FillColor, BackColor, and FillStyle

THE TIMER CONTROL

The timer control is quite different from the other controls. It's kind of half control, half programming device. It appears on a form in design mode, but becomes invisible in run mode. It responds to only one event, the *Timer* event. Here's how the control works.

1. You select the timer control icon from the Toolbox and create a timer control on a form.
2. You set the control's Interval property to a time value, which is measured in milliseconds, so a value of 1000 represents 1 second, 500 represents half a second, and so on.
3. You provide code for the timer control's *Timer* event.
4. When you run the program, Visual Basic generates a *Timer* event for the control each time an Interval's worth of time elapses.

For example, if you set a timer control's Interval property to 2000, the program executes the code in the timer's *Timer* event procedure every 2 seconds.

Try it. Open a new form and place a timer control on it. By default, it will be named Timer1. Set the Interval property to 500 (a half-second). Double-click on the control to open the *Timer1_Timer* event procedure. Let there be beeps:

```
Private Sub Timer1_Timer()
    Beep
End Sub
```

Run the program. The form will be blank, but you'll hear a beep at the end of every half second.

Timer Timing

The timer control gets its timing from the PC's system clock. This clock "ticks" about 18.2 times per second, so the elapsed time between ticks is about 0.055 seconds, or 55 milliseconds. This means the timer really is limited to multiples of 55 milliseconds. So if you specify 1000 milliseconds, you really get the nearest multiple of 55, which is 990 milliseconds.

An active timer is like an infinite loop in that it keeps going as long as the program runs. However, setting the Interval to 0 deactivates the timer. For instance, set the Interval property to 1024 and try the following event procedure:

```
Private Sub Timer1_Timer()
    Beep
    Timer1.Interval = Timer1.Interval \ 2
    Print Timer1.Interval
End Sub
```

This code cuts the interval in half each time using integer division. Finally, it divides 1 by 2, getting 0, and the beeping stops. Also, you can deactivate the timer by setting its Enabled property to False.

The Timer Meets the Shape

Let's use a couple of timers to control the colors of some shapes. You can have two or more timers running at once using different intervals, as this example will illustrate. Also, the timers will use Visual Basic's random-number function to choose colors for the shapes randomly. Create a form with three shapes, two timers, and a command button as described by Figure L10-7 and Table L10-6.

OBJECT	PROPERTY	SETTING
Form1	Caption	Colorful Timers
	Name	frmColors
Shape1	BackStyle	1 - Opaque
	FillStyle	6 - Cross
	Name	shpOval
	Shape	2 - Oval
Shape2	BackStyle	1 - Opaque
	Name	shpHBar
	Shape	0 - Rect
Shape3	BackStyle	1 - Opaque
	BorderStyle	0 - Transparent
	Name	shpVBar
	Shape	0 - Rect
Timer1	Interval	750
	Name	tmrOval
Timer2	Interval	1000
	Name	tmrRect
Command1	BackColor	&H000000FF (red)
	Caption	Pause
	Name	cmdOnOff

Table L10-6 Properties for the Colorful Timers form

A key part of this project is choosing colors randomly. The *Rnd* function returns a random floating-point number in the range 0 to 1. More exactly, the number is equal to or greater than 0 and less than 1. Suppose, instead, you want a random integer in the range of 0–255. Then you can use the expression *Int(256 * Rnd)*. Multiplying *Rnd* by 256 gives a number equal to or greater than 0 and less than 256, and the *Int* function converts the result to an integer. Thus, any number in the range of 255.0 to 255.99999 becomes 255, and so on. We'll come back to random numbers a little later in this lesson.

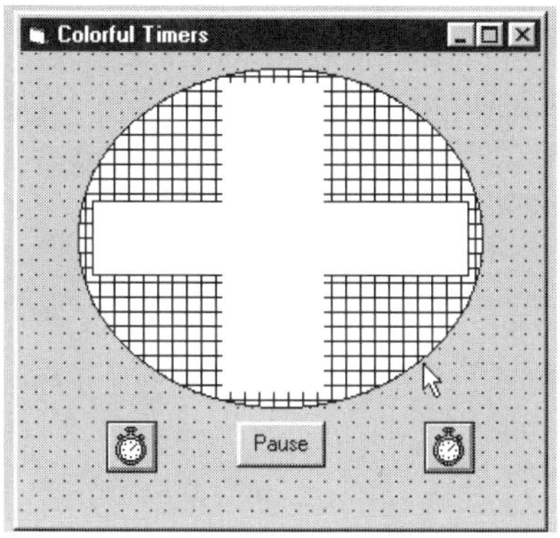

Figure L10-7 The Colorful Timers form

Armed with this knowledge, let's proceed to the code. The *Click* event for the command button shows how you can use either the Interval property or the Enabled property to turn a timer off and on. It also shows how to toggle the command button caption. In this case, it toggles the caption between "Pause" and "Resume."

```
Option Explicit

Private Sub cmdOnOff_Click()
    If cmdOnOff.Caption = "Pause" Then
        cmdOnOff.Caption = "Resume"
        tmrOval.Interval = 0
        tmrRect.Enabled = False
    Else
        cmdOnOff.Caption = "Pause"
        tmrOval.Interval = 750
        tmrRect.Enabled = True
    End If
End Sub
```

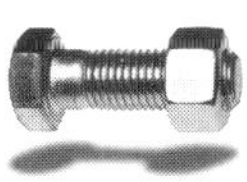

Tip

To deactivate a timer, either set its Interval property to 0 or its Enabled property to False.

Next, the *Timer* event for tmrOval selects random values for the red, green, and blue components, then uses the *RGB* function to construct the corresponding color value for the oval shape.

```
Private Sub tmrOval_Timer()
    Dim Red As Integer
    Dim Green As Integer
    Dim Blue As Integer
    Red = Int(256 * Rnd)
    Green = Int(256 * Rnd)
    Blue = Int(256 * Rnd)
    shpOval.BackColor = RGB(Red, Green, Blue)
End Sub
```

Finally, the timer control for tmrRect sets the color for the horizontal and vertical bars.

```
Private Sub tmrRect_Timer()
    Dim Red As Integer
    Dim Green As Integer
    Dim Blue As Integer
    Red = Int(256 * Rnd)
    Green = Int(256 * Rnd)
    Blue = Int(256 * Rnd)
    shpHBar.BackColor = RGB(Red, Green, Blue)
' set complementary color
    shpHBar.FillColor = vbWhite - RGB(Red, Green, Blue)
    shpVBar.BackColor = shpHBar.FillColor
    shpVBar.FillColor = shpHBar.BackColor
End Sub
```

Complementary Colors

The code refers to *complementary colors*. When you mix lights of two colors, the colors are termed complementary if they combine to produce white light. For instance, *vbBlue* (&HFF0000) and *vbYellow* (&H00FFFF) are complementary because combining them produces *vbWhite* (&HFFFFFF). In general, to find the complementary color for any Visual Basic color, subtract the color's color value from *vbWhite,* as the code above does. Incidentally, notice that the word is "complementary," as in supplying mutual lacks, making complete, not "complimentary," as in expressing praise or admiration.

If you're using a 256-color mode, you'll notice that Visual Basic does color dithering for the two bars but not for the oval. That's because when Visual Basic puts a foreground and background color in the same area, as with the cross pattern or with text, it avoids dithering. Instead, it picks the nearest solid color in order to avoid visual confusion.

More about Random Numbers

The *Rnd* function produces pseudorandom numbers instead of truly random numbers. The pseudo part comes from the fact that the *Rnd* function is predictable. Given the same starting conditions, it always produces the same sequence of numbers. For instance, try giving a command button this code:

```
Private Sub Command1_Click()
    Dim I As Integer
    For I = 1 To 10
        Print Int(10 * Rnd)
    Next I
End Sub
```

Start up the form, and you get this sequence:

```
7
5
5
2
```

```
3
7
0
7
8
7
```

Click on the button again, and you get this sequence:

```
0
4
8
7
3
9
8
0
9
3
```

As long as the program is running, *Rnd* "remembers" what it's done before, so the second sequence of ten random numbers continues from where the first ten left off. But if you quit the form, then restart it, you get the same sequence you did the first time. That's the pseudo part.

The random part is that if you make the loop, say, print 10,000 numbers, you'll get approximately equal numbers of each number. Hmmph, that sounds confusing. To put it another way, the number 2 will appear about as often as the number 9, which will appear about as often as the number 4, and so on. Randomness being what it is, the frequencies of the different numbers won't be exactly equal, but they will be close.

Visual Basic has a way to make the random sequence less predictable from the user's point of view, and that is to change the starting conditions for the *Rnd* function. To do so, call the *Randomize* function. It uses the current system time to set up the starting conditions for *Rnd*. Typically, you'd call the *Randomize* function in the *Form_Load* event procedure. Since the odds of starting the program at exactly the same time (to the nearest 0.055 seconds) are pretty small, using *Randomize* means the starting conditions are altered for *Rnd* each time you use the program, leading to a different sequence of random numbers each time. Try adding the following code to the last example:

```
Private Sub Form_Load()
    Randomize
End Sub
```

Trying this, we got the following sequence when starting up the program:

```
3
0
7
6
3
0
0
6
2
7
```

Note that it's different from the original starting sequence. If you try it, you should get yet another sequence.

Perhaps random numbers seem senseless to you, but they have many uses. You can use them to make games less predictable. A computer card game that always dealt the same sequence of cards would soon grow tiresome, but random numbers let you imitate shuffling the deck. Random numbers are useful for many kinds of simulations. For example, suppose you had to model traffic flow at a bridge tollgate. Random numbers can reproduce real-life phenomena such as the irregular flow of traffic. Or suppose you're doing a statistical study in which you are supposed to select some samples at random; again, random numbers can help do the job.

ANOTHER RANDOM EXAMPLE

Let's look into a game application of random numbers. You'll create a form that will show a large rectangle and eight smaller rectangles, except that only one of the small ones will be visible at a time. The color of the visible rectangle will change randomly, as will which small rectangle is visible. The object of the game is to click the small rectangle when its color matches that of the large rectangle. To keep things manageable, the game will limit itself to eight colors.

At first glance, you might be tempted to use a shape control for the rectangle. Unfortunately, shapes don't recognize events, so a shape can't tell if you've clicked on it. Therefore, the game uses captionless labels instead. *They* are smart enough to recognize a click! The example also will help keep your memory of data arrays and control arrays more vivid. Figure L10-8 and Table L10-7 describe the layout and properties for the game. Note that Label1 is a control array with eight elements.

OBJECT	PROPERTY	SETTING
Form1	Caption	Color Matching
	Name	frmMatch
Label1	BorderStyle	1 - Fixed Single
	Caption	
	Index	0,1,2,3,4,5,6,7
	Name	lblColor
Label2	Alignment	2 - Center
	BorderStyle	1 - Fixed Single
	Caption	Match This Color
	Name	lblMatch
Timer1	Interval	650
	Name	tmrBoxes

OBJECT	PROPERTY	SETTING
Timer2	Interval	3250
	Name	tmrMatch

Table L10-7 Properties for the Color Matching form

Moving on, the simplest way to limit the possible colors to eight possibilities is to create an array of eight color values. This array will be used in more than one procedure, so it should be a module-level array. Since color values are of the *Long* type, the array should be type *Long*. You can begin the code with this:

```
Option Explicit
Dim Colors(0 To 7) As Long
```

Next, you need to assign color values to the array elements. The place to do this is in the *Form_Load* procedure. (You also could use the *Form_Initialize* procedure, which Lesson 13 will discuss.) This is a good time to use the *Randomize* function and to set the initial color for the large label.

```
Private Sub Form_Load()
    Randomize
    Colors(0) = vbBlack
    Colors(1) = vbRed
    Colors(2) = vbGreen
    Colors(3) = vbBlue
    Colors(4) = vbCyan
    Colors(5) = vbMagenta
    Colors(6) = vbYellow
    Colors(7) = vbWhite
    lblMatch.BackColor = Colors(Int(8 * Rnd))
End Sub
```

Next, have the first timer select a member of the control array at random and assign it a color from the color array at random. This involves picking an index at random for each array. Each interval, the code sets all the boxes to invisible, then resets the selected box to visible.

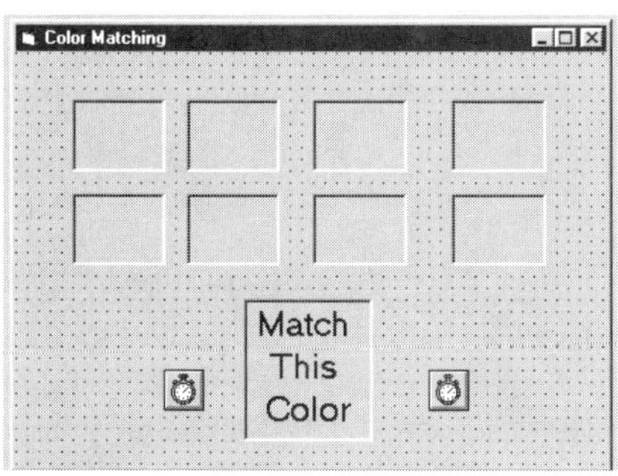

Figure L10-8 The Color Matching form

```
Private Sub tmrBoxes_Timer()
    Dim I As Integer
    Dim Index As Integer
    For I = 0 To 7
        lblColor(I).Visible = False
    Next I
    Index = Int(8 * Rnd)
    I = Int(8 * Rnd)
    lblColor(I).BackColor = Colors(Index)
    lblColor(I).Visible = True
End Sub
```

The second timer just has to change the color of one array.

```
Private Sub tmrMatch_Timer()
    lblMatch.BackColor = Colors(Int(8 * Rnd))
End Sub
```

Clicking on one of the small boxes should make it compare its current color with the current color of the large box. If they agree, the event procedure should disable the timers and change the big label box's caption.

```
Private Sub lblColor_Click(Index As Integer)
    If lblColor(Index).BackColor = lblMatch.BackColor Then
        tmrBoxes.Enabled = False
        tmrMatch.Enabled = False
        lblMatch.Caption = "Click to Restart"
    End If
End Sub
```

Finally, clicking on the large label box should restart the game.

```
Private Sub lblMatch_Click()
    tmrBoxes.Enabled = True
    tmrMatch.Enabled = True
    lblMatch.Caption = "Match This Color"
End Sub
```

How the program runs will depend upon the speed of your computer and video card, so you may have to adjust the timings up or down. (We'll resist the temptation of suggesting an impossible short interval as an easy starting value.)

THE LINE CONTROL

To round off the lesson, let's examine the line control. This control lets you draw a line on a form. It's a very simple shape described by just a few properties. The X1 and Y1 properties give the horizontal and vertical positions of the start of the line measured, by default, in twips from the top left corner of the object containing the line. The X2 and Y2 properties give the corresponding positions for the other end of the line. The BorderWidth property gives the line width, in pixels, and the BorderColor property gives the line's color. Figure L10-9 and Table L10-8 describe

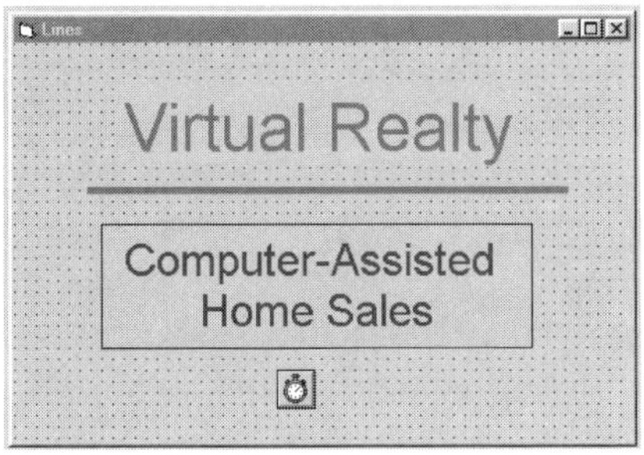

Figure L10-9 The Lines form

a simple example. It uses a thick line to highlight a company name, and it uses a timer to make a border in which four colors chase each other around the perimeter. The border itself consists of four elements of a line array.

OBJECT	PROPERTY	SETTING
Form1	Caption	Lines
	Name	frmLines
Label1	Alignment	2 - Center
	Caption	Virtual Realty
	Name	lblVR
Label2	Alignment	2 - Center
	Caption	Computer-Assisted Home Sales
	Name	lblBlurb
Timer1	Interval	250
	Name	tmrLines
Line1	BorderColor	&H000000FF& (Red)
	BorderWidth	5
	Name	linUnder
Line2	Index	0,1,2,3
	Name	linAround

Table L10-8 Properties for the Lines form

The code begins by defining an array to hold four color values and using the *Form_Load* event to assign color values to the array.

```
Option Explicit
Dim Colors(0 To 3) As Long

Private Sub Form_Load()
    Colors(0) = vbBlue
    Colors(1) = vbRed
    Colors(2) = vbGreen
    Colors(3) = vbYellow
End Sub
```

Then a timer control cycles each line in the control array through the four colors.

```
Private Sub Timer1_Timer()
    Dim I As Integer
    Static J As Integer      'automatically starts as 0
    For I = 0 To 3
        linAround(I).BorderColor = Colors((I + J) Mod 4)
    Next I
    J = (J + 1) Mod 4
End Sub
```

This code has a couple of tricks. Consider this part, for example:

```
For I = 0 To 3
        linAround(I).BorderColor = Colors((I + J) Mod 4)
    Next I
```

When *J* is 0, the four control array elements are assigned the colors having the same array index. That is linAround(0) gets Color(0), and so on. When *J* is 1, each line element gets the next color in the array, with *linAround(0).BorderColor* getting *Color(1)*, and so on. Here's one of the tricks. When *I* is 3 and *J* is 1, *I* + *J* is 4, which is out of bounds for the array. But the *Mod 4* part gives the remainder when dividing by 4, which always is an integer in the acceptable range of 0–3. In essence, *(I + J) Mod 4* causes the combined value to "wrap around" back to 0 when it reaches 4.

Similarly, the code

```
J = (J + 1) Mod 4
```

causes *J* to cycle through the values 0, 1, 2, 3, 0, 1, 2, 3, and so on. This code is shorter than the following, although it would have the same wrap-around effect in this example:

```
J = J + 1
If J = 4 then
    J = 0
End If
```

Tip

You can use the *Mod* operator to limit integer values to a particular range. For example, the expression *N Mod 8* results in a value of 0 through 7. In general, if both N and M are positive integers, the expression *N Mod M* results in a value 0 through M - 1.

The other trick is the new declaration form:

```
Static J As Integer      'automatically starts as 0
```

Normally, variables in procedures are discarded between events, but using *Static* instead of *Dim* tells Visual Basic to remember the value of the variable between events. Also, using *Static* causes the variable to start off with the value 0. So *J* is 0 the first time the *Timer* event procedure runs. At the end, the procedure increases *J* to 1, and that's the value *J* has the next time the procedure runs. Then *J* goes to 2, to 3, back to 0, and so on.

To see the difference between a normal variable and a static variable, open a new form, add a timer, and try this code:

```
Private Sub Timer1_Timer()
    Dim I As Integer
    Static J As Integer
    Print I; J
    I = I + 1
    J = J + 1
End Sub
```

The output will look like this:

```
0 0
0 1
0 2
0 3
```

Each time the *Timer* event runs, *I* gets reset to 0, while *J* builds upon its preceding value. Visual Basic remembers the value of *J*, but not of *I*.

Tip

A procedure retains the value of a *Static* variable between procedure calls. This property can be convenient for some *Timer* events.

Of course a module-level variable also retains its value between procedure calls, so both module-level variables and static variables last for the duration of the program. The difference is that a module-level variable can be used by any procedure in the module, while a static variable is still localized to the procedure in which it is defined. So if you need an enduring variable that is to be shared among procedures, use a module-level variable. If you need an enduring variable that is used in just one procedure, declare it in the procedure as a static variable.

SUMMARY

Color has a both a physical and a physiological basis. By mixing red, green, and blue light (the three additive primaries), you can reproduce the full range of colors. Each pixel of a color monitor contains color dots or stripes of the three primary colors, and this enables it to match other colors. However, the range is limited by how much memory the computer's video card devotes to describing colors. Display cards that use 8 bits of memory per pixel can display up to 256 colors simultaneously, while 16-bit display cards and 24-bit display cards can display up to 65,536 and 16.7 million colors simultaneously, respectively.

Visual Basic uses a color numbering system capable of describing 16.7 million colors. It does so by ascribing an intensity in the range 0–255 for each of the three primary colors. If you write the color value in hexadecimal notation, the rightmost two hexadecimal digits represent the red intensity, the next two digits represent the green intensity, and the next two digits represent the blue intensity.

The *RGB* function lets you construct a complete color number from the individual intensities of the three primary colors.

The BackColor property specifies the background color of a control, and the ForeColor property specifies the foreground color for a control. Visual Basic uses the foreground color for text and other elements, such as check boxes, that appear in the control. Some controls have a BorderColor property that specifies the color of the control's border. Also, some controls have a FillColor property, which specifies the color used for fill patterns, such as grids, that appear in the control.

A timer control provides a way to automate repetitive acts. Its Interval property specifies the time lapse between each execution of the control's *Timer* event procedure.

The *Rnd* function generates a random number, and the *Randomize* function alters the initial conditions for the *Rnd* function, changing the exact sequence produced by the *Rnd* function.

1. The three additive primaries are
   a. Red, white, and blue
   b. Red, yellow, and blue
   c. Red, green, and blue
   d. Cyan, yellow, and magenta
   e. Black, white, and gray

2. Suppose a color blend has a blue intensity of &H40, a green intensity of &H80, and a red intensity of &H60. Its Visual Basic color value is
   a. &H40806000
   b. &H00806040
   c. &H00408060
   d. &H80806040

3. What color is represented by RGB(0,0,0)?
 a. Red
 b. White
 c. Blue
 d. Black
 e. The color of zero

4. Explain what each of the following properties describes: BackColor, ForeColor, FillColor.

5. Explain the differences between 8-bit, 16-bit, and 24-bit color.

6. What are the six possible shapes for a shape control?

7. How do you make a timer repeat a Visual Basic command every two seconds?

8. What are two ways to deactivate a timer?

9. Which of the following produces a random integer in the range 0–19?
 a. 20 * Rnd
 b. Int (20 * Rnd)
 c. Int (20 * Rnd) + 1

10. Which of the following produces a random integer in the range 1–20?
 a. 20 * Rnd
 b. Int (20 * Rnd)
 c. Int (20 * Rnd) + 1

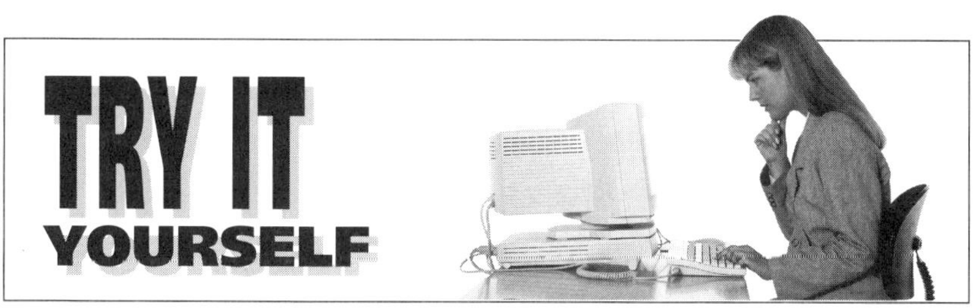

1. Make the Red, Green, and Blue labels above the scrollbars display the color value for that particular slider. That is, if the red scrollbar is set to 128, have the word "Red" displayed at an intensity of 128.

2. Modify the Color Matching program by adding a slider bar to control the timer intervals.

LESSON

11 THE BASIC ARTIST

Windows is a graphical interface, and people have come to expect graphical elements in the Windows programs they use. Toolbars abound—you only need to look at the Visual Basic program itself to see an example. Icons are part of the Windows way, and many programs have their own special graphic logos. One of Visual Basic's intents is to make it easy to add graphical elements to a program. These can be elements you create yourself, or they can be taken from graphics libraries. Visual Basic itself, for instance, supplies selections of icons and other images.

In this lesson, you'll learn about the following:

- **The image control**
- **Simple animation**
- **The PictureBox control**
- **The Picture object**

GRAPHICS FORMATS

Visual Basic forms and graphic controls can hold three kinds of images:

- Bitmaps, contained in files with a .BMP or .DIB extension
- Icons, contained in files with an .ICO extension
- Windows metafile images, contained in files with a .WMF extension

The file formats differ in that bitmap and icon images store a point-by-point description of an image, while the metafile can store vector images, that is, mathematical descriptions of the shapes in an image. Undoubtedly your thirst for knowledge wants more than this short explanation, so let's take a more thorough look.

Bitmapped Images

Bitmapped images, also called raster images, store information point-by-point. When a computer displays an image on a monitor, it does so by controlling the color of each screen pixel on the screen. In the early days, images were black and white (or black and green or black and orange). Thus, you could describe each screen pixel with a single bit of memory. (A bit, recall, is the smallest unit of memory and can be set to 1 or to 0.) If the bit were set to 1, the corresponding screen pixel would be turned on (white, green, or orange). If the bit were set to 0, the corresponding screen pixel would be turned off (black). Thus, the image could be represented, or mapped, by a pattern of bits in memory, hence the term "bitmapped" (see Figure L11-1).

Adding color means more memory is needed to describe the image. For instance, 256-color images require 8 bits, or 1 byte of information per pixel. As the size and number of colors increase, so does the amount of memory needed to hold the image. For instance, describing a 24-bit color 800 x 600 pixel image requires 1,440,000 bytes, which is a pretty big bite of memory. Bigger and more colorful image displays is why video cards need more memory than they used to. Now you can buy video cards with 1, 2, or even 4 MB of memory. Such images

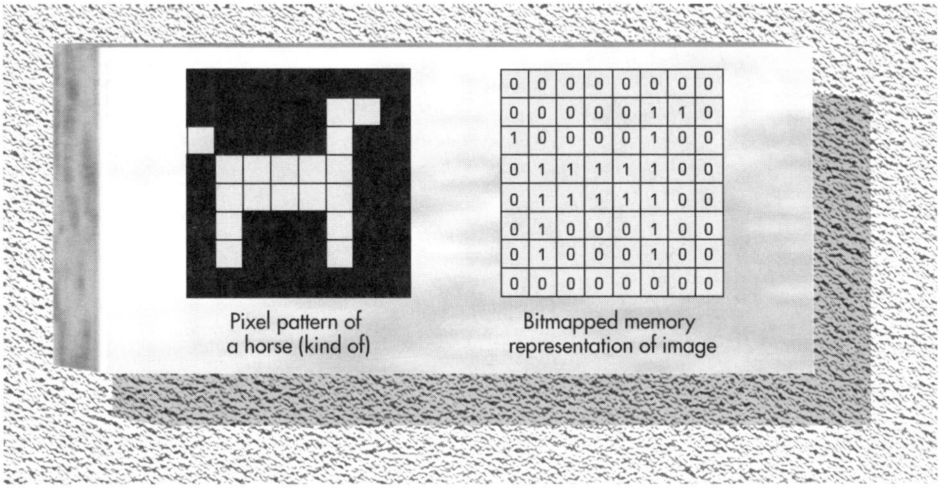

Figure L11-1 A bitmapped image

usually can be saved more compactly to disk, for you can use compression tricks, such as saying that the next 200 pixels are blue instead of storing the code for blue 200 consecutive times. There are many file formats around for bitmapped images, some of them unique to particular programs, others shared among many programs. Visual Basic uses the *BMP* and *DIB* file formats developed primarily for Windows applications. The standard Visual Basic installation creates a BITMAPS subdirectory in your Visual Basic directory. This directory contains further subdirectories, such as ASSORTED and GAUGE, containing BMP files.

Icons are bitmapped images restricted to a maximum size of 32 x 32 pixels and stored in files having the .ICO extension. The standard Visual Basic installation creates an ICONS subdirectory in your Visual Basic directory. This directory contains several subdirectories of icon files.

One problem with bitmapped images is that they scale poorly. For instance, suppose you want to make a picture 30 percent larger. Suppose that picture has a line 1 pixel wide. You can't make the line 1.30 pixels wide, for you have to work in whole pixels. So either you leave the line unchanged, or you widen it to 2 pixels. Either way, you change the way the picture looks. Also, if you make a picture 10 times bigger, you expand each pixel into 100 pixels (a block 10 pixels wide and 10 pixels tall), making the appearance very blocky. See Figure L11-2, which shows an enlargement of the Books05 icon shown later (in Figure L11-3).

A second problem with bitmapped images is that they can use large amounts of storage. The bitmapped images that come with Visual Basic are quite small, just a few hundred bytes, but more elaborate images can consume megabytes of hard disk space. Perhaps it's true that a picture is worth a thousand words, but a bitmapped image may require as much storage space as a few hundred thousand words!

Figure L11-2 Bitmap scaling problems

Vector Images

Vector graphic formats are more sophisticated. They represent images in terms of scaleable lines and shapes which are described by mathematical formulas. The upshot is that vector graphics scale much more smoothly than bitmapped graphics. There are many vector graphic formats, including PostScript EPS files. Visual Basic recognizes the Windows Metafile format (.WMF extension), which can, in fact, store both vector and bitmapped information. The standard Visual Basic installation creates a METAFILE subdirectory in your Visual Basic directory. It holds a couple of subdirectories containing .WMF files.

You may very well have other examples of these formats at hand. For instance, if you have Microsoft Word for Windows, check out its CLIPART subdirectory for .WMF files. Also, you can find graphics files of various sorts on online services, such as CompuServe, and from providers of clip-art libraries. CDs are a popular way of distributing graphics libraries today.

THE IMAGE CONTROL

The image control is an image holder. Let's try it. First, open a new form. Next, select the image control icon in the Toolbox. It's the picture frame with some mountains in it. Draw an image control on the form and go to its Properties window. Select the Picture property and click on the 3-dot button to the right. This opens the Load Picture dialog box with the usual Windows Directory and File list boxes. Let's start with an icon. Use the Load Picture dialog box to navigate to the Writing subdirectory of the Icons subdirectory in the Visual Basic directory. Select, say, the *Books05.ico* file, and click on the OK button. The icon image of a row of four books appears in the control, as shown in Figure L11-3.

Figure L11-3 An icon in an image control

The size of the control snaps to fit the icon size. Notice that the Picture property is set now to (Icon). That is, the Properties window identifies the type of picture in the control, but doesn't identify the picture selected. (The following table, however, shows the file name.)

What can you do with this icon? You can move it to different locations on the form. You can use the BorderStyle property to draw a border around the icon. You can use the MousePointer property to alter the mouse pointer's appearance when you maneuver the mouse pointer over the icon during run time. You can use the Visible property to make the icon visible and invisible.

Can you resize the icon? You can if you set the Stretch property to True. Otherwise, you can't, which is the default behavior. When Stretch is true, you can resize the image during design time (by dragging the control handles) and during run time (by using suitable code). In fact, let's make a short program in which you can use the left mouse button to double the icon size and the right mouse button to halve the size. You already have a form with the *Books05.ico* icon. (At least you do if you've been doing your part of the lesson.) Modify the properties to match those in Table L11-1.

OBJECT	PROPERTY	SETTING
Form1	Caption	The Resizer
	Name	frmResize
Image1	Name	imgResize
	Picture	*(Icon) Books05.ico*
	Stretch	True

Table L11-1 Properties for the Resizer program

You can use the *MouseUp* event to detect which button is pressed and to control the image size. The code is simple. If the left button is used (*button* = 1), then the program doubles the width and height of the image. If the right button is used (*button* = 2), the program cuts these dimensions in half. Figure L11-2 showed the result of magnifying the icon size a few times.

```
Private Sub imgResize_MouseUp(button As Integer, Shift As Integer, _
    X As Single, Y As Single)
    If button = 1 Then
        imgResize.Width = imgResize.Width * 2
        imgResize.Height = imgResize.Height * 2
    ElseIf button = 2 Then
        imgResize.Width = imgResize.Width / 2
        imgResize.Height = imgResize.Height / 2
    End If
End Sub
```

Other Images

You can also can place bitmaps and metafile images in image controls. Figure L11-4 shows a form with image controls containing an icon, two bitmaps, and two vector drawings in image controls. One bitmap comes from the *Dome.bmp* file supplied with Visual Basic in the GAUGE subdirectory of the BITMAP directory. The second bitmap (the face) was drawn using a Windows paint program and saved using the .BMP extension. (With enough dedication and training, you, too, may be able to produce works of similar merit.) The Properties window shows (Bitmap) for the Picture property when you select a bitmap.

The satellite comes from the *Satelit1.wmf* file that accompanies Visual Basic. The larger version is the default size for the drawing, and the smaller one is an example of changing the image size when the *Stretch* parameter is true. The Properties window shows (Metafile) for the Picture property when you select a metafile image.

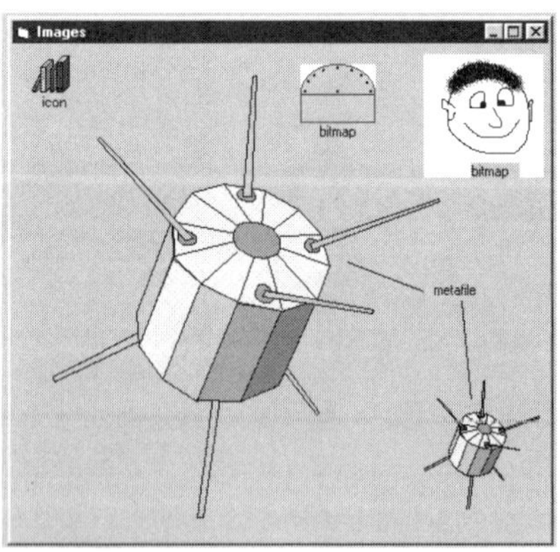

Figure L11-4 Some sample images

Putting Images in an Image Control

Visual Basic has several ways to get an image into an image control. The simplest is to select the Picture property and to open an image file, as the preceding examples did. Once you have an image control, you can copy and paste it to get a second version. When you paste, you'll be asked if you want a control array. If you say yes, then Visual Basic makes an array out of the original and the copy. (We'll cover an example with an array of picture controls soon.) If you say no, then Visual Basic assigns a new name to the copy.

You also can use the Clipboard. For instance, you can copy an image from Microsoft PaintBrush or from the drawing program for Microsoft Word and paste it into an image control. If the image-making program is bitmapped, such as PaintBrush and other paint programs, the image is pasted as a bitmap. If the program is vector-based, such as Microsoft Word's draw program and other drawing programs, the image is pasted as a metafile image.

You can use assignment in procedure codes. For instance, suppose you want to copy the image in the Image1 control to the Image2 control. You can do this:

```
Image2.Picture = Image1.Picture ' copying images
```

Finally, you can load images during run time by using the *LoadPicture* procedure. For instance, if you have an image in the C:\GRAPHICS\MYSTUFF\FLUFFY.BMP file, you can load the image into an image control with this code:

```
imgCat.Picture = LoadPicture("C:\GRAPHICS\MYSTUFF\FLUFFY.BMP")
```

The disadvantage of this approach is that the program will fail if you don't have that file available and in its indicated location when you run the program.

Where Do All the Pictures Go?

Unless you use the LoadPicture approach, placing a picture in an image control results in copying the picture data to your program. (Visual Basic creates an auxiliary file with an .FRX extension to hold the data.) Thus, the more images you have, the bigger your program gets. The advantage is that the program doesn't depend upon the presence of other picture files.

Image Control Limitations

Microsoft designed image controls to offer good graphics performance without placing excessive demands on the system. For this reason, they have a simpler feature set than many controls. In particular, image controls have the following properties:

- An image control can't get the focus.
- An image control can't go on top of another control.
- An image control, unlike a frame, can't hold another control.

So if you want to place a cute icon atop a command button, you can't. You can't have an image control respond to keystrokes because that would require the control getting the focus. These same limitations apply to shape controls and line controls, too.

Simple Animation

You can use image controls to implement simple forms of animation. For example, many of the icons supplied with Visual Basic come in complementary sets, such as identical arrows in different directions, or faces of varying degrees of happiness. (*The Programmer's Guide* that comes with Visual Basic includes an appendix showing pictures of all the icons.) You can create animation by having an image control display first one icon, then another, producing a changing image.

Let's try a simple example, one that features a hungry filing cabinet. The key elements are these:

- Store two filing cabinet images, one of an open cabinet, one of a closed cabinet, in two image controls with the Visible property set to False.
- Use a timer control to alternately copy first one, then the other image to a visible image control.
- To facilitate the process, use a control array for the first two image controls.

Table L11-2 shows the controls and properties you'll need. The closed file cabinet image is *Files05a.ico,* and the open file cabinet image is *Files05b.ico.* Both are found in the OFFICE subdirectory of the Icons subdirectory of the Visual Basic directory. Figure L11-5 shows the two icons.

OBJECT	PROPERTY	SETTING
Form1	Caption	Hungry Filing Cabinet
	Name	frmAnimate
Image1 (array)	Index	0,1
	Name	imgSource
	Picture	(Icon)
Image2	Name	imgFC
Timer1	Interval	500
	Name	tmrAnimate

Table L11-2 Properties for the Hungry Filing Cabinet program

Next, provide the following code:

```
Option Explicit

Private Sub tmrAnimate_Timer()
    Static Index As Integer
```

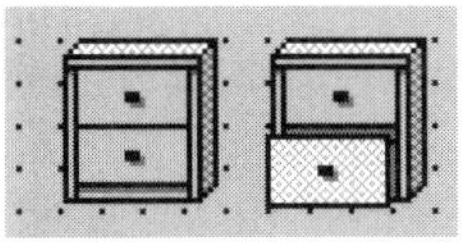

Figure L11-5 Two filing cabinet icons

```
    imgFC.Picture = imgSource(Index)
    Index = (Index + 1) Mod 2
End Sub
```

Using a static variable, recall, automatically sets the variable to 0 and lets the procedure remember the value of *Index* between events, so that the value can toggle between 0 and 1. Run the program, and the filing cabinet will appear to open and close its bottom drawer once a second.

Adding Movement

With a little more work, you can get the icon to move around the form. One way is to alter the Top and Left properties, which describe the location of the top left corner of the image with respect to the containing form or frame. For example, if you have a control named imgFC, you can cause it to move 100 twips to the right with code like this:

```
imgFC.Left = FC.Left + 100
```

To have the image keep moving, you can place that code inside a timer control so that the image is moved, say, every half second. However, you then have to monitor the motion so that the image doesn't move out of the form or frame. The frame's ScaleWidth property comes in handy for this purpose, for it gives the *inside* width of the frame. (The Width parameter gives the *outside* width, including the border.) The ScaleWidth property measures distances in twips by default. However, you can use the ScaleMode property to use other units, and you even can set up your own custom units. The next lesson will discuss those options. Meanwhile, let's stick to twips.

To keep the imgFC image control in the form horizontally, the Left property has to satisfy two constraints:

- VB *imgFC.Left* >= 0, that is, the image is to the right of the left form border
- VB *imgFC.Left + imgFC.Width < = frmAnimate.ScaleWidth,* that is, the right side of the image control is to the left of the right form border

If you just use the test *imgFC.Left <=frmAnimate.ScaleWidth,* you could have the left edge of the image control in the form, but the rest of it out of the form. To keep the whole image in the form, you need to include the width of the image. The expression *imgFC.Left + imgFC.Width* is the coordinate of the right edge of the image (see Figure L11-6).

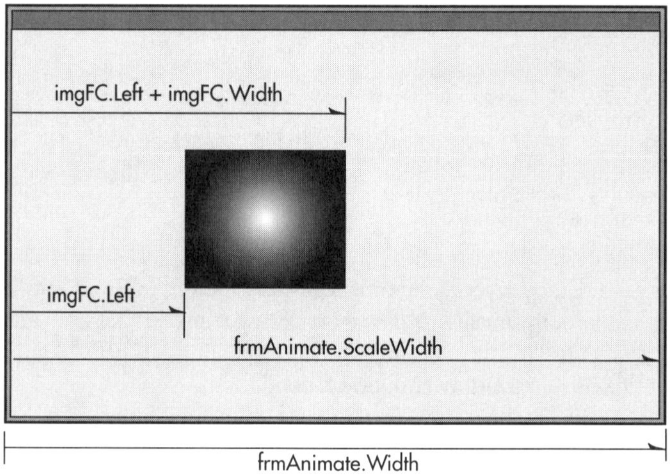

Figure L11-6 Horizontal positions and sizes

Similarly, you can use the Top and Height properties of the image and the ScaleHeight property of the form to move the image vertically in the form, keeping in mind that increasing the Top property moves the image downward on the screen.

To move the image both horizontally and vertically, you can modify both the Left and Top properties:

```
imgFC.Left = imgFC.Left + 100
imgFC.Top = imgFC.Top + 100
```

However, this creates a jerky movement because the image moves in two steps (horizontally, then vertically) instead of in one step. To smooth the movement, use the *Move* method instead. For instance, consider the following statement:

```
imgFC.Move 300, 600
```

This sets the *imgFC.Left* property to 300 and the *imgFC.Top* property to 600, and the image goes to that position directly, in one step. Note that the *Move* method uses absolute coordinates, not relative coordinates. That means the statement above moves the image to the coordinates (300,600) rather than adding 300 and 600 to the original position. Thus, to reproduce the effect of the previous statements that set the Left and Top properties separately, you can do this:

```
imgFC.Move imgFC.Left + 100, imgFC.Top + 100
```

See Figure L11-7.

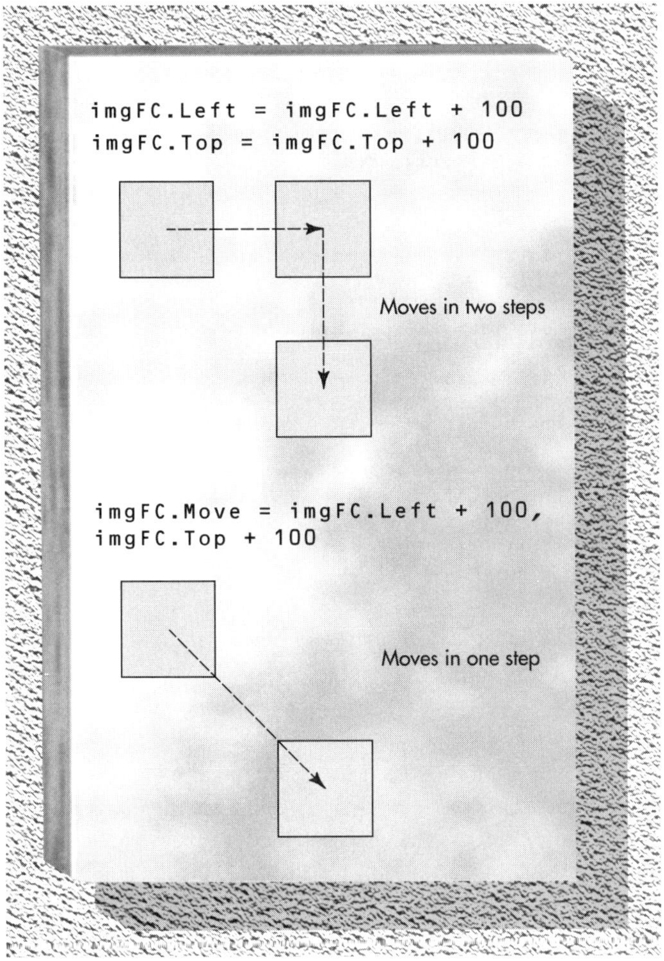

Figure L11-7 Using *Move* versus using the Top and Left properties

We now have the tools to create a simple animation in which the file cabinet image moves around the screen, changing direction when it reaches the edge of the form. The following modification of the code for the preceding example shows one way:

```
Option Explicit
Dim XMove As Integer     'x-move step size
Dim YMove As Integer     'y-move step size

Private Sub Form_Load()
    XMove = 100
    YMove = 100
End Sub
```

continued on next page

continued from previous page

```
Private Sub Timer1_Timer()
    Static Index As Integer
    Dim XNext As Integer
    Dim YNext As Integer
    imgFC.Picture = imgSource(Index \ 2)
    Index = (Index + 1) Mod 4   'cycle thru 0-3
    XNext = imgFC.Left + XMove
    If XNext < 0 Then  ' too far left
        XMove = -XMove ' change direction
        XNext = 0      ' place at border
    ElseIf (XNext + imgFC.Width) > frmMove.ScaleWidth Then
        XMove = -XMove 'change direction if too far right
        XNext = frmMove.ScaleWidth - imgFC.Width
    End If
    YNext = imgFC.Top + YMove
    If YNext < 0 Then  ' too far up
       YMove = -YMove  ' change direction
       YNext = imgFC.Top + YMove
    ElseIf (YNext + imgFC.Height) > frmMove.ScaleHeight Then
        YMove = -YMove ' change direction if too far down
        YNext = frmMove.ScaleHeight - imgFC.Height
    End If
    imgFC.Move XNext, YNext ' move to next position
End Sub
```

Let's examine this code. The basic instructions for moving the image are these:

```
XNext = imgFC.Left + XMove
YNext = imgFC.Top + Ymove
imgFC.Move XNext, YNext
```

Here *XMove* and *YMove* are module-level variables initialized to 100 by the *Form_Load* event procedure. However, one design goal is that the image reverse its direction when reaching a border. The approach here is to reverse the sign of *XMove* whenever the image bumps into a vertical border. This is done by comparing the next calculated position to the form boundaries:

```
If XNext < 0 Then   ' too far left
    XMove = -XMove  ' change direction
    XNext = 0       ' place at border
ElseIf (XNext + imgFC.Width) > frmMove.ScaleWidth Then
    XMove = -XMove  'change direction if too far right
    XNext = frmMove.ScaleWidth - imgFC.Width
End If
```

If the image goes beyond a border, this code repositions the image at the border and reverses the direction of motion. Similar code handles the vertical positioning.

The original example used this code to control which image is displayed:

```
imgFC.Picture = imgSource(Index)
Index = (Index + 1) Mod 2
```

The new version, however, uses this:

```
imgFC.Picture = imgSource(Index \ 2)
Index = (Index + 1) Mod 4
```

Notice the integer division. If *Index* is 0 or 1, *Index* \ 2 is 0, and if *Index* is 2 or 3, *Index* \ 2 is 1. This has the effect of changing the image every other timer cycle, while the image is repositioned every cycle. This is one way to get different change rates for things controlled by the same timer.

Try running the program. Try changing the form size as the program runs. The appearance of the animation movement depends on how big the movement steps are and how often the steps are taken. Using smaller steps makes the animation smoother but slower. Depending on the speed of your computer system, you can compensate for the smaller steps by making the timer interval smaller. You might experiment with different movement steps and timer intervals.

The Picture Object

Visual Basic 4 adds another picture-management tool by defining a Picture object to represent a Picture property, much as a Font object represents a Font property. You can, for instance, declare a variable of type *Picture:*

```
Dim MyPic as Picture
```

(For this to work, the Standard OLE Objects choice has to be check-marked in the References selection under the Tools menu. This is done automatically for new projects, but you may have to do so manually if you are converting a project created under an older version of Visual Basic.)

The variable *MyPic* acts as a label, or *reference,* that can be attached to an existing picture. For example, you can do either of the following:

```
Set MyPic = imgFC.Picture   ' Make MyPic refer to imgFC.Picture.
Set MyPic = LoadPicture("c:\graphics\jugglers.bmp") ' Make MyPic refer to
                                                      jugglers.bmp
```

Note the use of the word *Set.* As you'll see in Lesson 13, this is standard operating procedure when working with variables that refer to objects.

You can use Picture objects as an alternative to storing invisible images on a form, as the last example did. Instead, you can eliminate the two invisible image controls and do the following.

1. Create an array of Picture object references:

```
Dim FileCab(0 To 1) As Picture
```

2. Make these variables refer to the two filing cabinet images:

```
Private Sub Form_Load()
    ...
    Set FileCab(0) = LoadPicture("c:\vb\icons\office\files05a.ico")
    Set FileCab(1) = LoadPicture("c:\vb\icons\office\files05b.ico")
End Sub
```

3. Use the timer control to toggle between the two images:

```
Private Sub Timer1_Timer()
    ...
Set imgFC.Picture = FileCab(Index \ 2)
    ...
End Sub
```

With this approach, the images are loaded into memory when the program starts, and the timer then copies images from memory to the screen as the program runs. It's a bit more direct than creating an array of image controls which you then have to hide.

THE PICTURE BOX CONTROL

The picture box control is something like an enhanced frame control. You can place other controls, such as labels, command buttons, shapes, and image controls, in a picture box, just as you can place them in a frame. But you also can add a picture directly to a picture box, just as you can add a picture to an image control. Also, you can use the *Print* method to display text in a picture box, much as you can with a form. Furthermore, you can use Visual Basic graphics methods for drawing in a picture box, a topic explored in the next lesson. Actually, forms also provide all these facilities, so a picture box is a kind of mini-form.

To place a picture in a picture box, follow the same procedure you used for image controls. After creating a picture box, go to the Properties window and use the Picture property to select an image. The image can be in bitmap, icon, or metafile format.

There are some differences in how picture box and image controls handle pictures.

- An *image control* expands or contracts to the same size as an icon or bitmap image placed in it, while a *picture box* can be made larger than an icon or bitmap. In the latter case, the icon or bitmap appears in the upper-left corner of the picture box.
- The *image control* Stretch property allows you to expand and shrink a bitmap or icon image, and you can modify the horizontal and vertical dimensions independently of one another. The *picture box* has no Stretch property, and the size of an icon or bitmap in a picture box remains unchanged. You can, however, make the picture box smaller than a bitmap or icon image so that only part of the image shows.
- When you place a metafile image in an *image control,* the control, by default, expands to the dimensions of the original image. If, however, the image control Stretch property is set to True, the image is shrunk or expanded to fit the dimensions of the image control. A *picture box,* by default, acts like an image control with the Stretch property set to True; that is, the image is fitted to the dimensions of the picture box. A picture box has no Stretch property, but it does have an AutoSize property, which is set to False by default. If AutoSize is set to True, then the picture box adjusts to the size of the original image. If AutoSize is true, it may appear that you can manually resize the picture box in design mode, but the picture box will revert to the original size when you run the program.

Images in a picture box act as part of the background for the box, and any other controls you place in a picture box will appear to be on top of the picture. Figure L11-8, for example, shows two picture boxes. The top one contains a label on top of a metafile image, while the bottom one contains an icon, a label, and a command button. Notice how the image of the quarter has been distorted to fit the size and shape of the picture box.

Picture Box Text

Printing in a picture box is a lot like printing in a form—you use the *Print* method. The main difference is that you have to supply the name of the picture box. For instance, if the picture box is named picMe, then the command

```
picMe.Print "Visual Basic"
```

prints the string “Visual Basic” in the picture box. Aside from using the object name, you use the *Print* method the same way as you used *Print* in a form. Indeed, *Print* is the same method for both forms and picture boxes. If you omit the object name, Visual Basic assumes the destination object is the form, but you could use the form name explicitly if you wanted to (see Figure L11-9).

The picture box has some font properties. The Font property is the same as for other controls; that is, it is a Font object with its own properties. Selecting the Font property opens a dialog box that lets you set Font object properties like the font size, font name, and font style. There's also a FontTransparent property which, by default, is set to True. This lets you see through the text. If you set FontTransparent to False, then the entire rectangle containing the text becomes opaque. This is easier to see than describe, so let's create a short program illustrating how FontTransparent works. Open a new form, and add a picture box and a timer. For the picture, select the metafile *Satelit2.wmf*. Set properties as described in Table L11-3.

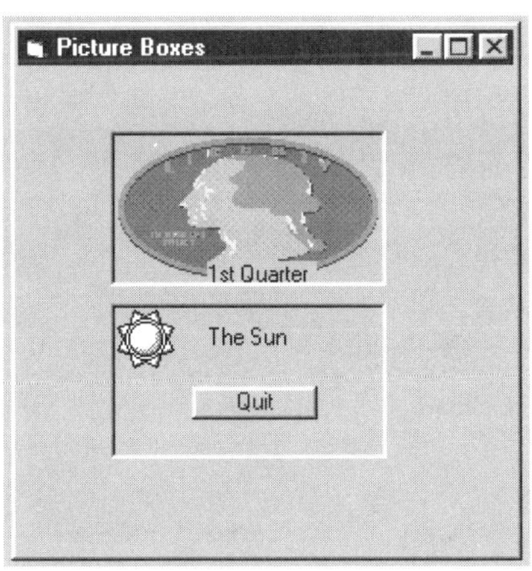

Figure L11-8 Two picture boxes

OBJECT	PROPERTY	SETTING
Form1	Caption	Satellite
	Name	frmSat
PictureBox1	Font.Font	Arial
	Font.Size	18
	Picture	*(Metafile) Satelit2.wmf*
Timer1	Interval	1000
	Name	tmrSat

Table L11-3 Properties for the Satellite program

Now use the Code window to add the following statements:

```
Private Sub tmrSat_Timer()
    Static Count As Integer
    picSat.Print "Satellite Alert!"
    picSat.FontTransparent = Not picSat.FontTransparent
    Count = Count + 1
    If Count = 5 Then tmrSat.Enabled = False
End Sub
```

The timer prints a new line each second until five lines have been printed. (Remember, static variables automatically start out with the value 0.) The *Not* operator negates the value it precedes, so the line

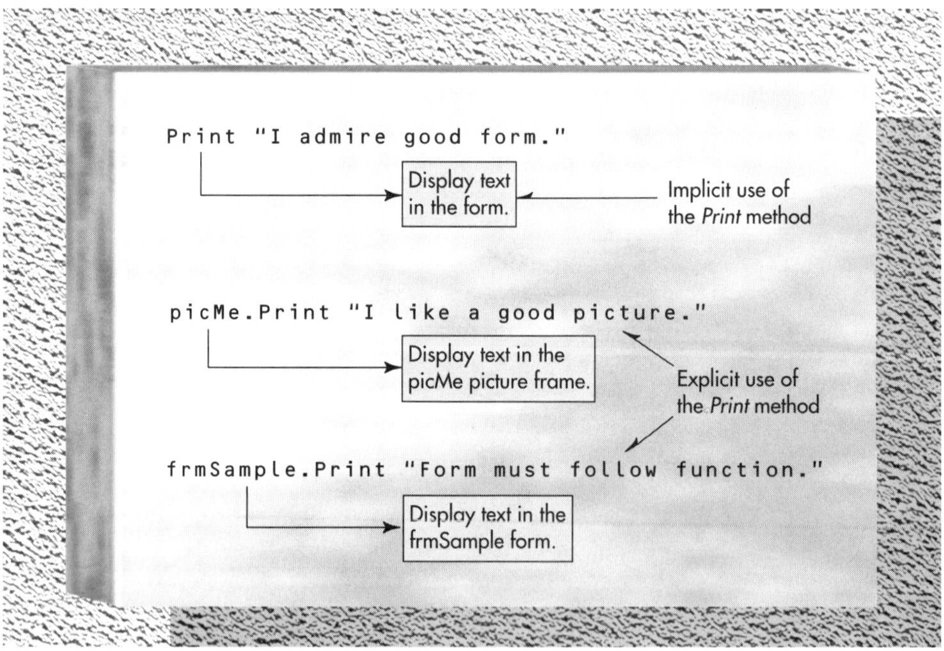

Figure L11-9 The *Print* method

```
picSat.FontTransparent = Not picSat.FontTransparent
```

toggles the FontTransparent value between False and True each timer cycle. Figure L11-10 shows the result of running the program. Note how the text overlies the picture, and note how setting FontTransparent to False causes the text to block the view of a rectangular section of the background.

Picture Box Color Properties

Picture boxes have four properties relating to color:

- BackColor
- ForeColor
- FillColor
- FillStyle

As you must expect by now, BackColor controls the background color for the picture box, and ForeColor controls the color of text displayed in the control. The FillColor and FillStyle properties work together, with the FillStyle describing a fill pattern and the FillColor specifying the color used for the pattern. In that respect, these two properties work just as they do for shape controls. However, if you fiddle around with these values, you'll notice they have no effect on the appearance of a picture box. That's because they don't affect the picture box itself. Instead, they control the appearance of graphic forms drawn in a picture box. Visual Basic has a family of methods that can be used to draw in a picture box or in a frame. Indeed, that's what the next lesson covers. But let's preview one of those graphic methods now, so you can see the role played by the FillColor and FillStyle properties.

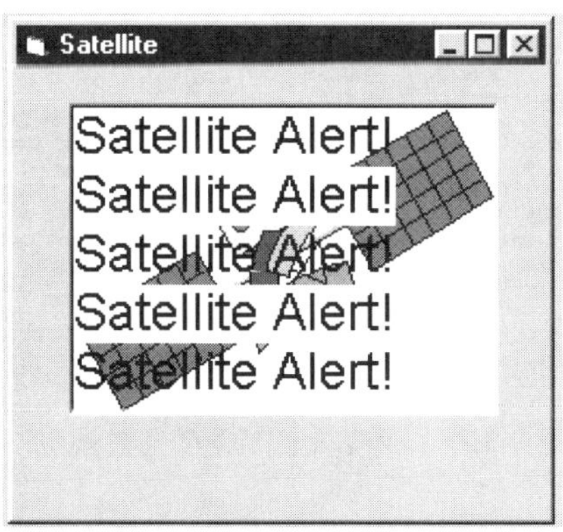

Figure L11-10 True and False values for FontTransparent

The *Circle* Method

Just as the *Print* method lets you display text in a picture box, the *Circle* method lets you draw a circle in a picture box. The simplest way to use *Circle* in a picture box named *picCircles* is like this:

```
picCircles.Circle (2000, 1800), 1000
```

Here the (2000, 1800) represents the horizontal and vertical distance of the center of the circle measured from the upper-left corner of the containing object. The third value is the radius of the circle. These distances are measured in terms of the picture box's ScaleMode property, which is set to twips by default. As with *Print,* if you omit an object name when using the method, Visual Basic uses the form as the object. That is, the statement

```
Circle (2000, 1800), 1000
```

would draw a circle on the form rather than in a picture box.

When drawing a circle in a picture box, Visual Basic uses the FillStyle and FillColor specified by the picture box for the interior of the circle. For drawing the circle's boundary, Visual Basic uses the picture box ForeColor value. However, you can override that setting by providing an additional argument for the boundary color. For example, the following code uses green instead of the ForeColor value:

```
picCircles.Circle (2000, 1800), 1000, vbGreen
```

You can't override the FillStyle and FillColor values however, so all the circles drawn in a particular picture box will have the same fill pattern and fill color.

To see how this all works, create a form with a picture box, setting properties as described in Table L11-4.

OBJECT	PROPERTY	SETTING
Form1	Caption	Circles in a Box
	Name	frmCircle
PictureBox1	BackColor	&H00C0C0C0& (gray)
	FillColor	&H00FF0000& (blue)
	FillStyle	7 - Diagonal Cross
	Font.Font	Arial
	Font.Size	28
	ForeColor	&H000000FF& (red)

Table L11-4 Properties for the Circles in a Box program

Next, create a *Click* event for the picture box with the following code:

```
Private Sub picCircles_Click()
    picCircles.Print "Here be circles!"
    picCircles.Circle (2000, 1600), 1000
    picCircles.Circle (2000, 1600), 500, vbBlack
End Sub
```

Figure L11-11 shows an annotated version of the result of running this program and clicking on the picture box. Note which properties control which colors.

Forms and Graphics

Forms provide the same graphics support that picture boxes do. You can use the Picture property to display a bitmapped image, an icon, or a metafile image in a form. You can use the BackColor, ForeColor, FillColor, and FillStyle properties of a form in exactly the same manner as you do for a picture box. You can use the *Print* and *Circle* methods, along with several other graphics methods in a form.

SUMMARY

The image control lets you display pictures from bitmap, icon, or metafile files. Normally, the image control is sized to match the size of the picture in it, but you can use the Stretch property to rescale a picture and to alter its proportions.

You can use the Move method of an image control to move a picture around a form, creating a form of animation. Or you can display alternating images to create another form of animation.

Picture boxes and forms also let you display images. Bitmapped images and icons can't be scaled, but you can size the picture box or frame to be larger or smaller than the displayed image. Windows Metafile images, by default, scale to fit the form or picture box size, but the AutoSize property scales the form or picture box to the original size of the picture.

Picture boxes act like forms in that you can create other controls in a picture box and you can use text and graphics methods such as *Print* and *Circle*.

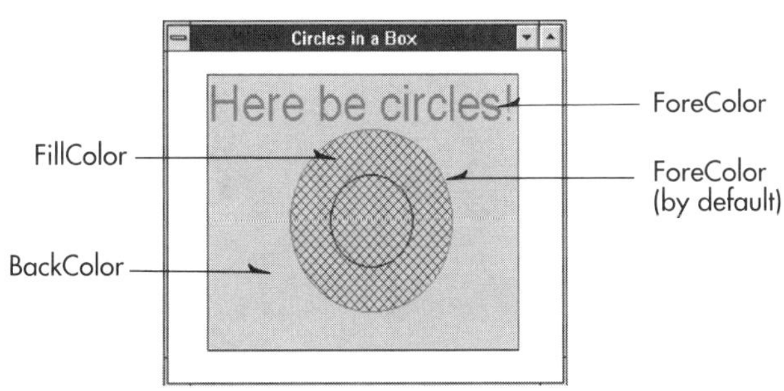

Figure L11-11 Color properties in a picture box

QUIZ 11

1. What kinds of images can you place in an image control?
2. What kinds of images can you place in a picture box control?
3. What must you do to resize a picture in an image control?
4. How many images can an image control hold? A picture box control?
5. How can you constrain a picture box to have the same size as the picture it holds?
6. How can you constrain a metafile picture to have the same size as the picture box into which it is placed?
7. For a picture box, what is the difference between the ForeColor property and the FillColor property?
8. What do you do to display text in a picture box?
9. What does the *Move* method do?
10. How is the *Circle* method similar to the *Print* method?

TRY IT YOURSELF

1. Sample the various icons, bitmaps, and metafile images available on your system.

2. Suppose you decide to use the *Click* and *DoubleClick* events instead of the *MouseDown* event to control the resizing example. That is, clicking the mouse will double the size, and double-clicking will halve the size.

   a. The following code doesn't work quite right. Why not?

```
Private Sub imgResize_Click()
        imgResize.Width = imgResize.Width * 2
        imgResize.Height = imgResize.Height * 2
End Sub

Private Sub imgResize_DblClick()
      imgResize.Width = imgResize.Width \ 2
      imgResize.Height = imgResize.Height \ 2
End Sub
```

   b. Modify this code so that it does work.

3. Add two scroll controls to the moving filing cabinet example. Have one control let you set the animation step size and the other control let you set the timer interval.

4. Write a program having a form containing a large picture box. When you click on the picture box, the program draws ten concentric circles.

LESSON

12

DRAWING ON A FORM

Graphics are important to modern programs. They attract and guide the eye. They allow for a more intuitive design for programs. They dazzle, please, and, sometimes, annoy. And because graphics often require considerable computer resources, their existence helps justify buying that new, more powerful, computer. Visual Basic has many ways to add graphics to your work. You've already seen the shape and line graphic controls that let you create geometric graphics in design mode. And you've seen how image and picture box controls let you import pictures into your work. This lesson looks at yet another family of graphical tools,

the *graphics methods*. These methods, like the *Circle* method introduced in Lesson 11, let you construct geometric graphics during run time. You'll also learn more about the graphical environment, for instance, about the different graphical layers in a form and about the coordinate systems you can use.

In particular, you'll learn about the following topics:

- **The *Circle* method for drawing circles and ellipses**
- **The *Line* method for drawing lines**
- **The *PSet* method for drawing a point**
- **The *Point* method for returning the location of a point**
- **The *Cls* method for clearing a form or picture box of graphics**
- **The *Paint* event**
- **Coordinate systems**
- **Graphical layering**
- **The AutoDraw property**
- **Clipping regions**

THE WAY OF THE CIRCLE

The *Circle* method, as you saw in Lesson 11, paints a circle on the display. You can use the *Circle* method, as well as the other graphics methods, in a form or in a picture box. As with other methods, the general syntax is the object name and the method name joined by a period, as in *picIt.Circle* or *frmLess.Circle*. However, you can omit the object when using a graphics method, and Visual Basic will then apply it to the form. Official documentation describes this part of the syntax as follows:

[*object.*]**Circle**

The brackets indicate an optional part. The italics indicate that *object* is a placeholder to be replaced by the name of a specific object. The boldface indicates that **Circle** is to be typed literally; it's not a placeholder.

The simplest way to use *Circle* is to tell it the location of the center of the circle and the radius of the circle:

```
Circle (2000,1500), 1000
```

Because no object is mentioned here, this means to draw a circle on the form. The "(2000, 1500)" part means place the center of the circle 2,000 twips to the right of upper-left corner of the form and 1,500 twips below that corner. The "1000" means draw a circle with a radius of 1,000 twips. At least, that's what these numbers mean if you haven't changed the default scaling. (You'll learn more about scaling options later in this lesson.)

Suppose you want to draw some concentric circles. Then you can do this:

```
Dim I As Integer
For I = 1 To 6
    Circle (2000, 1500), 200 * I
Next I
```

The first circle has a radius of 200 * 1, or 200, the second circle has a radius of 200 * 2, or 400, and so on. Since all the circles have the same center (2000,1500), they are concentric.

Try this code by placing it in the *Form_Load* event and seeing what happens:

```
Option Explicit

Private Sub Form_Load()
    Dim I As Integer
    For I = 1 To 6
        Circle (2000, 1500), 200 * I
    Next I
End Sub
```

Surprise! When you run this program, nothing gets drawn on the form! That's because Visual Basic doesn't execute graphic commands for items that aren't yet visible, and the form isn't visible until the *Form_Load* event procedure finishes.

The *Paint* Event

The *Paint* event can help you out of this awkward situation. This event is triggered when an object becomes visible. So graphic commands in a *Paint* event procedure will be executed when the form becomes visible. Let's try again to draw concentric circles, but this time use the *Form_Paint* event:

```
Option Explicit

Private Sub Form_Paint()
    Dim I As Integer
    For I = 1 To 6
        Circle (2000, 1500), 200 * I
    Next I
End Sub
```

This time running the program produces the concentric circles, as shown in Figure L12-1.

Tip

If you want a form to open showing graphics produced by graphic methods, place the code using the graphics methods in the *Form_Paint* event procedure. If you want a picture box to show graphics methods drawings, place the methods in the *Paint* event for the picture box.

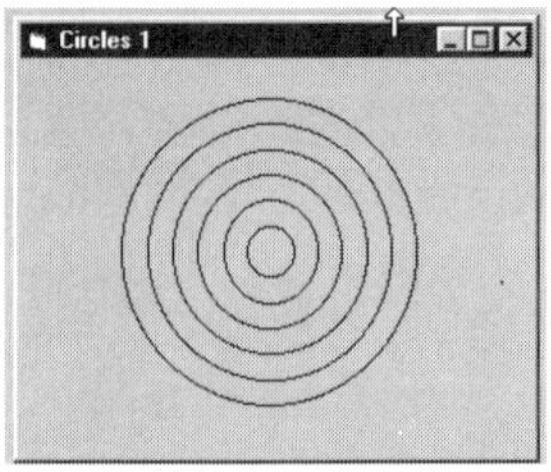

Figure L12-1 Concentric circles

The Full Circle

The *Circle* method has several optional settings. Its complete syntax is this:

[*object*.]**Circle** [**Step**] (*x*, *y*), *radius*, [*color*], [*start*], [*end*], [*aspect*]

Again, the brackets indicate optional parts, the boldface indicates words that are typed literally, and the italics indicate placeholders for which you substitute values. (So far the lessons have been rather informal about syntax, for the commands have been simple. The graphics methods, however, are sufficiently involved to require more care in describing the syntax.) The *color* parameter sets the color used to draw the circle; the *start* and *end* parameters let you specify an arc of a circle; and the *aspect* parameter lets you draw an ellipse instead of a circle. Table L12-1 summarizes each part of the *Circle* syntax:

TERM	MEANING
object	The name of the form or picture box in which to draw the circle. The form is used if the name is omitted.
Circle	The name of the method.
Step	If this keyword is used, the location of a circle's center is measured relative to the current X and Y positions (given by the CurrentX and CurrentY properties) instead of relative to the upper-left corner of the form or picture box.
(x, y)	The horizontal and vertical coordinates of the circle's center, measured in units of the current scale system (twips, by default).
radius	The circle's radius in units of the current scale system (twips, by default).
color	The color used to draw the circle. If omitted, the containing object's ForeColor value is used.
start	The starting angle in radians, measured counterclockwise from the horizontal axis, for drawing an arc.
end	The ending angle in radians, measured counterclockwise from the horizontal axis, for drawing an arc.

TERM	MEANING
aspect	The ratio of the vertical diameter to the horizontal diameter of the ellipse. The default value is 1, corresponding to a circle. When *aspect* is not 1, the *radius* value corresponds to the longer of the two diameters.

Table L12-1 *Circle* method elements

If you want to use, say, the *aspect* setting without using the *start* and *end* values, you can use commas to skip parameters. For instance, to draw a red ellipse, you can give the following command:

```
Circle (2000,3000), 1500, vbRed, , , 3
```

The commas indicate that you're skipping the *start* and *end* parameters.

The Current Position—Visual Basic Knows Where

The *Step* option causes coordinates to be measured relative to the current graphics position, which is measured relative to the top left corner of the object in which you're drawing. Where is the current position? If you haven't drawn anything yet, then the current graphics position starts out at the top left corner, so it has the coordinates (0,0). Otherwise, the current position depends upon the last graphics method you used, as set forth in Table L12-2. You can use the CurrentX and the CurrentY properties to obtain or to change the current position. For example,

```
Print "Current X position = "; CurrentX
```

displays the current horizontal position for a form while the command

```
CurrentY = 2000
```

resets the current vertical position for a form. For a picture box, you need to provide the picture box name, as in *picWoz.CurrentX*.

METHOD	CURRENTX, CURRENTY SETTING
Circle	The center of the circle or ellipse
Line	The endpoint of the line
PSet	The point drawn
Cls	0,0

Table L12-2 The current graphic position after a graphics method executes

The Elliptical Approach

Let's make a few ellipses. Open a new form, open the Code window, and add the following:

```
Option Explicit
```

```
Private Sub Form_Paint()
    Dim I As Integer
    Dim Aspect1 As Single
    Dim Aspect2 As Single
    Circle (3200, 3100), 2800, vbBlack
    For I = 1 To 20
        Aspect1 = 1 + I / 5
        Aspect2 = 1 / Aspect1
        Circle (3200, 3100), 2800, vbRed, , , Aspect1
        Circle (3200, 3200), 2800, vbBlue, , , Aspect2
    Next I
End Sub
```

The first *Circle* command draws a circle in black. The two *Circle* commands in the *For* loop draw ellipses. Initially, *Aspect1* is set to 1 + 1 / 5, or 1.2, so the first *Circle* command in the loop draws an ellipse with an aspect ratio of 1.2. Because the aspect ratio is the ratio of the vertical diameter to the horizontal diameter, this ellipse is taller than it is wide. This means the radius value (2800) applies to the vertical diameter.

The *Aspect2* variable, however, starts off with a value of *1 / Aspect1*, or about 0.833. This means the ellipse is wider than it is tall and that the radius value applies to its horizontal diameter.

Each loop cycle changes the two aspect ratios, producing two families of ellipses. The blue ellipses all have the same horizontal diameter and decreasing vertical diameters, while the red ellipses all have the same vertical diameter and decreasing horizontal diameters (see Figure L12-2).

Arcs Galore

The *Start* and *Stop* arguments let you draw an arc. For example, the command

```
Circle (2000,2000), 1000,,0,1
```

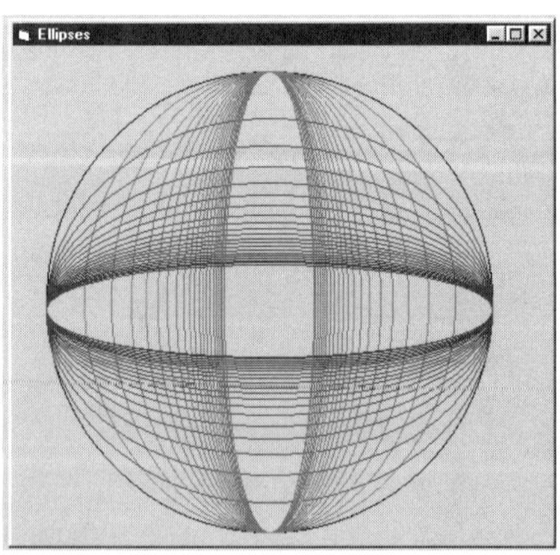

Figure L12-2 Two families of ellipses

draws an arc stretching from an angle of 0 to an angle of 1. Keep in mind that angles are measured counterclockwise from the horizontal axis (as shown in Figure L12-3) and that the angles are measured in a unit called a *radian.* A full circle (360°) is 2π radians, where π (pi) is the famous constant 3.1415926..., and so forth. So 1 radian is about 57.3°.

Table L12-3 shows the radian equivalents of some common angles. Clearly, it would be convenient to have the value of pi handy to make conversions. Visual Basic doesn't supply a symbolic representation of pi, but you can create one with the following magic formula:

```
Option Explicit
Dim Pi As Double

Private Sub Form_Load()
    Pi = 4 * Atn(1)
End Sub
```

Magic Explained

The *Atn()* function is the Visual Basic version of the trigonometric arctangent function. The function call *Atn(x)* returns the angle whose tangent is *x,* so *Atn(1)* returns the angle whose tangent is 1. That angle is 45°. However, Visual Basic measures angles in radians, and 45° is π / 4 radians. So multiplying this by 4 yields π itself.

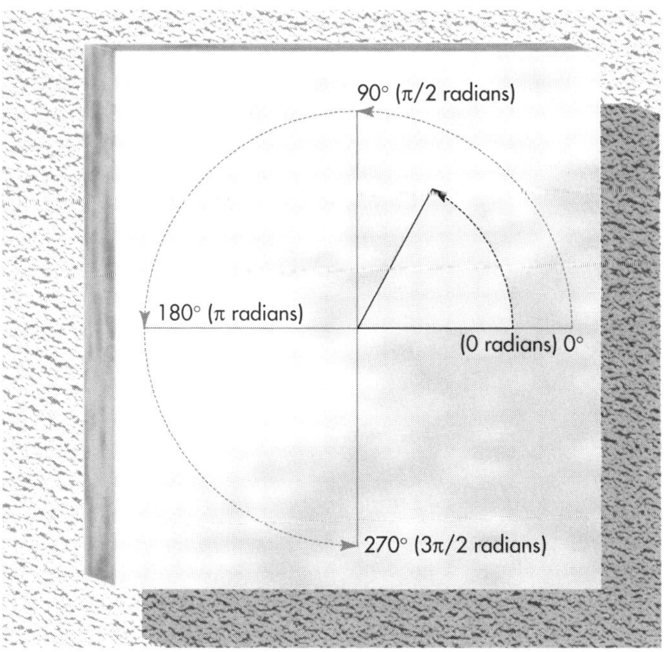

Figure L12-3 Arcs and angles

Or, if you don't need to wring the last bit of precision out of Visual Basic for pi, you can declare a constant:

```
Const Pi as Double = 3.1415926536
```

ANGLE IN DEGREES	RADIAN EQUIVALENT	APPROXIMATE VALUE
30	pi / 6	0.2618
45	pi / 4	0.7854
60	pi / 3	0.5236
90	pi / 2	1.5708
135	3 pi / 4	2.3562
180	pi	3.1416

Table L12-3 Degrees and radians

Suppose, then, you wanted to draw an arc from 45° to 135°. You could give a command like the following:

```
Circle (2000,2000), 1000, , 0.7854, 2.3562
```

If you want to specify the angles more precisely or want an angle not shown in Table L12-3, you can use the *Pi* variable we just defined to convert from degrees to radians. To convert, multiply the degrees by *Pi* and divide the result by 180:

```
Circle (2000,2000), 1000, , 45 * Pi / 180, 135 * Pi / 180
```

Either command yields an arc like that shown in Figure L12-4. (This and the next two figures were generated by the upcoming example program.)

Visual Basic always draws an arc counterclockwise. Suppose, for instance, that you reverse the order of the angles in the previous command:

```
Circle (2000,2000), 1000, , 135 * Pi / 180, 45 * Pi / 180
```

This would draw an arc from the 135 position counterclockwise all the way around through 180°, 270°, 0°, and back to 45°.

You can get some interesting effects by using the angle differently. For instance, if you use a negative angle, Visual Basic interprets it as a positive angle, but draws a line from the center of the circle to the endpoint of the line. For instance, the command

```
Circle (2000,2000), 1000, , -45 * Pi / 180, -135 * Pi / 180
```

draws the same arc as the preceding example, but joins both ends to the center of the circle, producing a pie slice, as shown in Figure L12-5.

Recall that Visual Basic always draws the arc in the counterclockwise direction, so if you list the larger angle first and use negative values, you can get a pie with a piece missing. For instance, the code

```
Circle (2000,2000), 1000, , -135 * Pi / 180, -45 * Pi / 180
```

generates the shape shown in Figure L12-6.

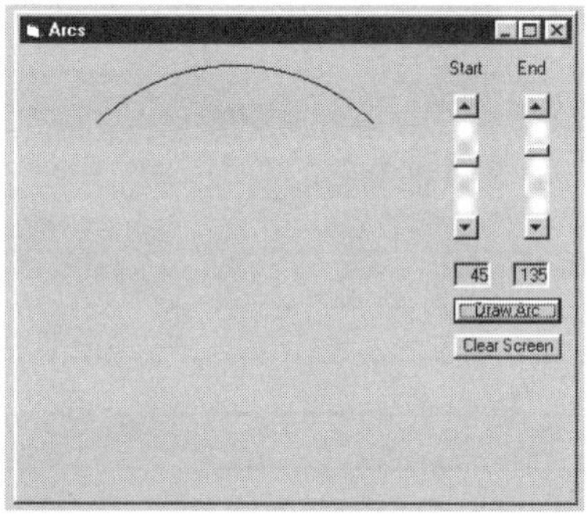

Figure L12-4 Using *Circle* to make an arc

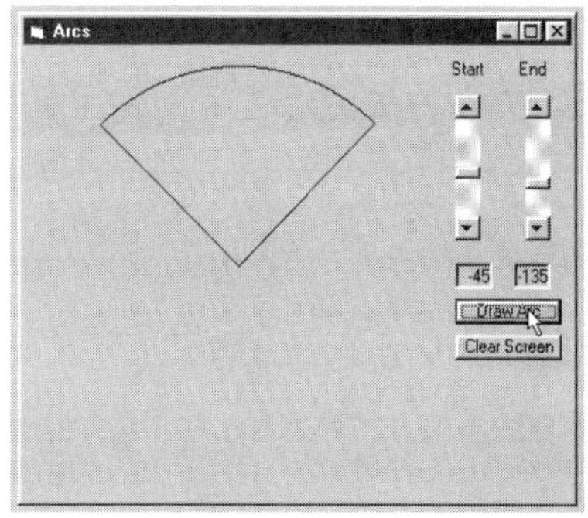

Figure L12-5 Using *Circle* to make a piece of pie

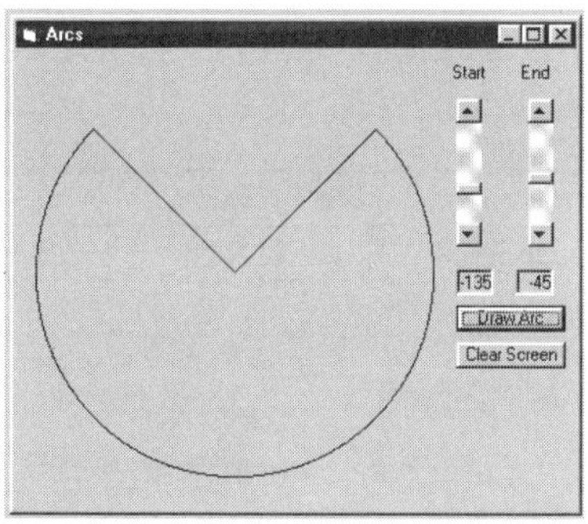

Figure L12-6 A pie missing a slice

Let's look at the program that produced the last three figures. Not only does it illustrate using the *Circle* command, but it also reviews some techniques, such as getting input from scrollbars. Open a new form, add four labels, two horizontal scrollbars, and two command buttons as shown in Figures L12-4 through L12-6 and as described in Table L12-4.

OBJECT	PROPERTY	SETTING
Form1	Caption	Arcs
	Name	frmArcs
Label1	Caption	Start
	Name	lblStart
Label2	Caption	End
	Name	lblEnd
Label3	BorderStyle	1 - Fixed Single
	Caption	0
	Name	lblStartVal

continued on next page

continued from previous page

OBJECT	PROPERTY	SETTING
Label4	BorderStyle	1 - Fixed Single
	Caption	0
	Name	lblEndVal
VScroll1	LargeChange	30
	Max	–360
	Min	360
	Name	vsbStart
	Value	0
VScroll2	LargeChange	30
	Max	–360
	Min	360
	Name	vsbEnd
	Value	0
Command1	Caption	Draw Arc
	Name	cmdDraw
Command2	Caption	Clear Screen
	Name	cmdClear

Table L12-4 The Arcs form

The program uses vertical scrollbars to let the user enter starting and ending values for angles for drawing arcs. For convenience, it accepts angles in degrees and converts degrees to radians internally. A vertical scrollbar reaches its maximum value when the scroll box is at the bottom. Setting the Max property to –360 and the Min to 360 makes raising the scroll box increase the value, which seems more natural in this case.

Next, Listing L12-1 shows the code. About the only new element here is the *Cls* method, which clears the form of any text or graphics you've drawn on it.

Listing L12-1
The Arcs program

```
Option Explicit
Dim Pi As Double
Dim DtoR As Double  'Convert degrees to radians.

Private Sub cmdClear_Click()
    Cls             'clear the form
End Sub

Private Sub cmdDraw_Click()
    Circle (2200, 2200), 2000, , vsbStart.Value * DtoR, vsbEnd.Value * DtoR
End Sub
```

```
Private Sub Form_Load()
    Pi = 4 * Atn(1)       'Calculate pi.
    DtoR = Pi / 180       'Calculate conversion factor.
End Sub

Private Sub vsbEnd_Change()
    lblEndVal.Caption = vsbEnd.Value          'Show value.
End Sub

Private Sub vsbStart_Change()
    lblStartVal.Caption = vsbStart.Value     'Show value.
End Sub
```

The *Cls* method clears a form or a picture window of graphics and text drawn during run time. It doesn't affect graphics added at design time, such as by using the Picture property of a form or picture window.

DRAWING-RELATED PROPERTIES

Suppose you want some variety in your circles—thicker lines, for example, or a solid interior. For a graphics *control* (a Shape or Line control), you can attain these goals by setting certain control properties, such as FillStyle. With a graphics *method*, however, there is a slight technical problem. The figures you draw using *Circle* and the other graphics methods are *not* objects, the way forms and controls are, so they don't have any properties. Instead, you modify the appearance of these graphic figures by using the properties of the object on which you draw. That is, if you draw on a form, you use properties of the form to modify the drawings. Similarly, if you draw in a picture box, you can use picture box properties. Table L12-5 lists the properties that come into play. You can use them to modify the output of the *Circle* method as well as of the other drawing methods (*Line* and *PSet*).

PROPERTY	DESCRIPTION
DrawMode	Controls how the drawing color combines with the background color
DrawStyle	Controls the appearance of lines (solid, dotted, etc.)
DrawWidth	Controls the width, in pixels, of drawn lines
FillColor	Controls the color used to fill drawn shapes
FillStyle	Controls the pattern used to fill drawn shapes

Table L12-5 Draw-related properties

When you use, say, *Circle* to draw a shape, Visual Basic uses the current setting of the various drawing properties to control the appearance. If you change a setting, currently drawn figures are not affected, but subsequent drawings are. So you can draw a circle with one fill pattern, change the FillStyle property, and draw a second circle with the new fill pattern.

Note

Figures drawn using the graphics methods are modified by the draw properties of the containing object, which would be a form or a picture box. Graphic controls, such as Shape and Line, however, have their own individual draw properties, and these draw properties modify the appearance of the graphics controls.

Let's take a closer look at the draw properties.

The DrawMode Property

You can think of draw commands such as *Circle* as drawing with a pen upon a background. The color you draw with is termed the *pen color.* The background consists of empty areas painted with the BackColor color plus previous drawings. Each new drawing lies atop previous drawings. The pen color is set to the ForeColor color unless you've explicitly changed it, for example, by using the *color* parameter to the *Circle* command. There are many possible interactions between the background color and the pen color. The simplest behavior, which is the default, is that the pen color opaquely covers the background. The DrawMode property offers many other alternatives, and Table L12-6 lists them.

SETTING	NAME	DESCRIPTION
1	Blackness	Draws in black
2	Not Merge Pen	Inverse of setting 15
3	Mask Not Pen	Combination of colors common to the background color and the inverse of the pen color
4	Not Copy Pen	Inverse of setting 13
5	Mask Pen Not	Combination of the colors common to both the pen color and the inverse of the background
6	Invert	Inverse of the background color
7	Xor Pen	Combination of the colors in the pen and in the background color, but not in both
8	NotMaskPen	Inverse of setting 9
9	Mask Pen	Combination of colors common to both the pen and the background
10	Not Xor Pen	Inverse of setting 7
11	Nop	No operation—drawing has no effect
12	Merge Not Pen	Combination of the background color and the inverse of the pen color
13	Copy Pen (default)	Color specified by ForeColor property or by drawing command

SETTING	NAME	DESCRIPTION
14	Merge Pen Not	Combination of the pen color and the inverse of the background color
15	Merge Pen	Combination of the pen color and the background color
16	Whiteness	Draws in white

Table L12-6 DrawMode settings

At first (or second) glance, this list of possibilities may seem rather bewildering. Note, however, that there are two popular themes:

- Inverting a color
- Combining two colors

Inverting a color means taking the binary representation of a color value and changing each 1 to a 0 and each 0 to a 1. Figure L12-7, for instance, illustrates inverting both a color represented by the Visual Basic constant vbBlue and a color that is a blend of red, blue, and green intensities.

Combining two colors means setting a bit in the resulting color to 1 if at least one of the combined colors has that bit set to 1. For instance, Figure L12-8 illustrates combining vbBlue with vbGreen as well as combining two color blends.

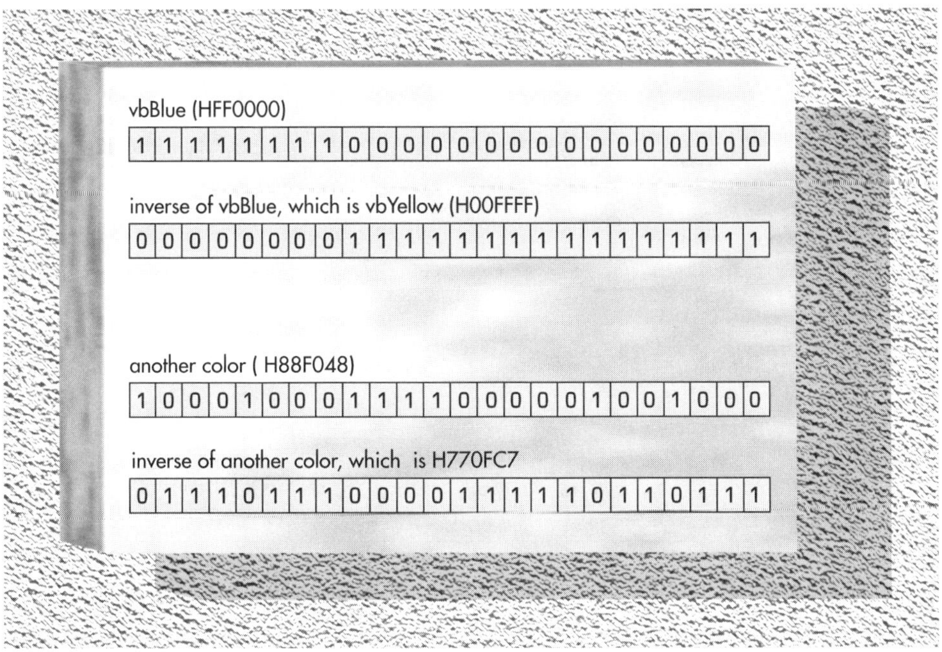

Figure L12-7 Inverting colors

You may have noticed the following:

- Inverting a color is the same as applying the *Not* operator (see Lesson 6) to the color value.
- The inverse of a color is what is termed the complement of a color (see Lesson 10).
- Combining two colors is the same as applying the *Or* operator (see Lesson 6) to the two color values.
- Xor Pen (number 7 in the list) is the same as applying the *Xor* operator (see Lesson 6) to the two color values. That is, the final value of a particular bit will be 1 only if one or the other (but not both) of the corresponding bits of the values being combined are 1.

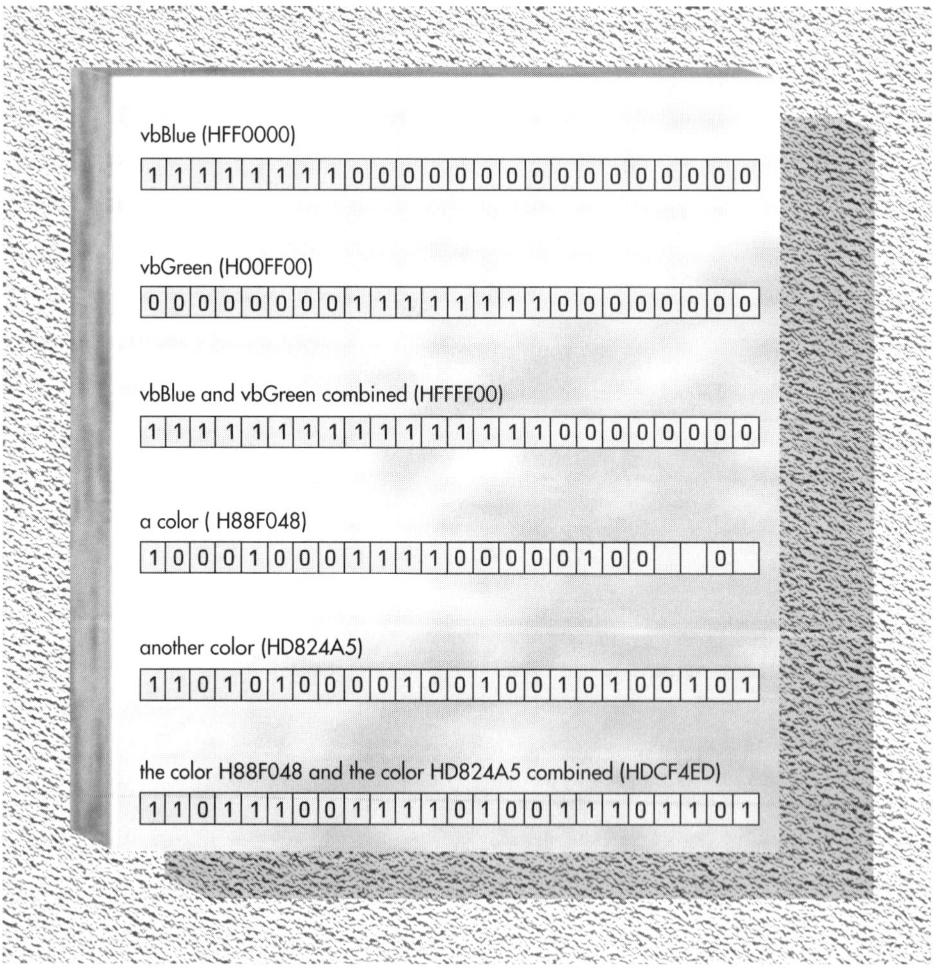

Figure L12-8 Combining two colors

The real question is, why all these modes? Consider the default mode. What happens if a red circle overlaps, in part, a red shape control? Red on red is a bit difficult to see, so that part of the circle becomes invisible. But mode 6, for example, would make the color of the circle be the inverse of the background, so no matter what the background color is, the color of the circle will be different, hence the circle will be visible against any background.

This book won't explore all the possibilities, but will look at some examples after cataloging the drawing properties.

The DrawStyle and DrawWidth Properties

The DrawWidth property specifies the width of a line in pixels. The default size is 1 pixel wide. The DrawStyle property specifies the style (solid, dashed, and so on) used to draw lines. Here the term "line" includes the curved lines produced by the *Circle* method as well as the straight lines produced by the *Line* method. Table L12-7 lists the DrawStyle choices. Note that some of them depend on the value of the DrawWidth property. The difference between settings 0 and 6 can be seen in the boundaries of closed figures, such as a box, drawn with a DrawWidth property greater than 1. For the default setting, the boundary line is centered on the perimeter, while for setting 6, the border is drawn inside the perimeter.

SETTING	DESCRIPTION
0	Solid (default)
1	Dash (solid if DrawWidth > 1)
2	Dot (solid if DrawWidth > 1)
3	Dash-dot (solid if DrawWidth > 1)
4	Dash-dot-dot (solid if DrawWidth > 1)
5	Transparent
6	Inside solid

Table L12-7 DrawStyle settings

It's simple to check out these styles. The code shown in Listing L12-2, for example, produces the circles shown in Figure L12-9. The loop cycles the DrawStyle property through its possible values. If you omit an object name from the DrawStyle property, as does this code, Visual Basic assumes you mean the DrawStyle property for the form.

Listing L12-2
Using the DrawStyle property

```
Option Explicit

Private Sub Form_Paint()
    Dim I As Integer
```

continued on next page

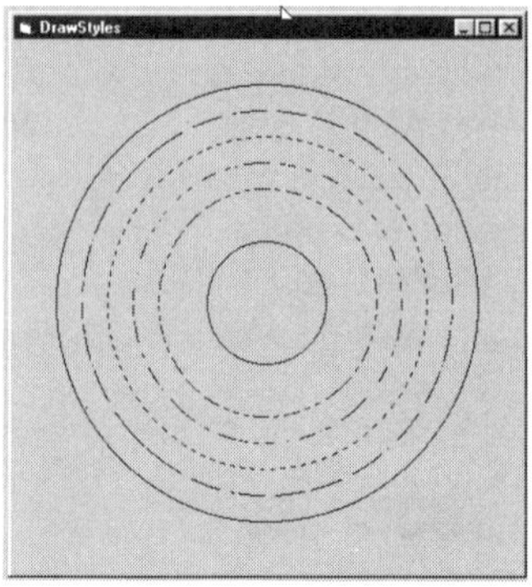

Figure L12-9 Results of using different DrawStyle values

continued from previous page

```
    For I = 0 To 6
        DrawStyle = I     ' property of the form
        Circle (3000, 3000), 2500 - 300 * I
    Next I
End Sub
```

The FillColor and FillStyle Properties

The FillColor and FillStyle properties control the appearance of the interior of a drawn shape. These can be shapes drawn with the *Circle* method or with the box variation of the *Line* method to be discussed soon. Just as with graphic controls, these properties control the color and pattern with which a shape is filled. The FillColor is used to draw the pattern, and the BackColor property controls the background color under the pattern. In short, these properties behave the same with drawn shapes as they do for the shape control (see Lesson 10). Table L12-8 lists the patterns available.

SETTING	DESCRIPTION
0	Solid
1	Transparent (default)
2	Horizontal line
3	Vertical line
4	Upward diagonal
5	Downward diagonal
6	Cross
7	Diagonal cross

Table L12-8 FillStyle settings

Listing L12-3 shows code using these different settings, and Figure L12-10 shows the corresponding output. The code uses two *For* loops to draw two rows of circles, each with a different value for the FillStyle. The variables *I* and *J* determine the position of the circles and the value of FillStyle. The circles are drawn using the ForeColor color, which is the default black, but the patterns are drawn using the FillColor color, which the code sets to red.

Listing L12-3
Using FillStyle settings

```
Option Explicit

Private Sub Form_Paint()
    Dim I, J As Integer
    frmFillStyle.DrawWidth = 4    'frmFillStyle. is optional.
    frmFillStyle.FillColor = vbRed
    For I = 0 To 3
        For J = 0 To 1
            frmFillStyle.FillStyle = I + 4 * J
            Circle (1000 + 1000 * I, 1000 + 1000 * J), 600
        Next J
    Next I
End Sub
```

THE LINE'S SHARE

The *Line* method lets you draw straight lines. It also has a box-drawing variant. In its simplest form, the *Line* method looks like this:

```
Line (x1,y1) - (x2,y2)
```

This command draws a line from the point having coordinates (*x1*,*y1*) to the point having coordinates (*x2*, *y2*).

Listing L12-4 uses this simple form to draw a few lines. It also illustrates the DrawWidth and DrawMode properties. Figure L12-11 shows the output. Note the varied ways in which the color of each line interacts with the background colors. Some details don't show up in the grayscale rendering of the original, so try running the program and matching the DrawMode results to their descriptions.

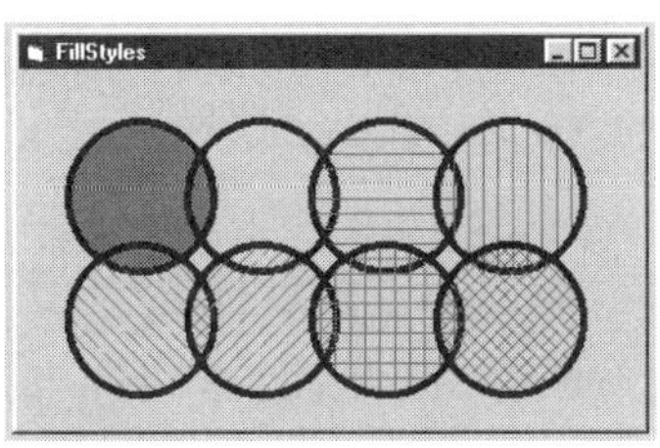

Figure L12-10 Different FillStyle settings

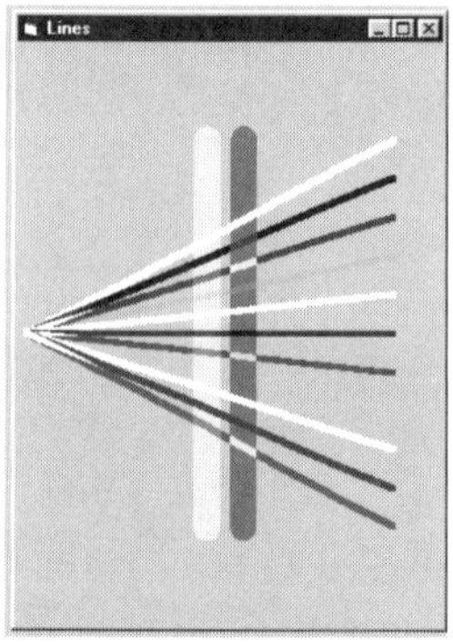

Figure L12-11 Some lines with different DrawMode settings

Listing L12-4
Using the Line method

```
Option Explicit

Private Sub Form_Paint()
     Dim I As Integer
     frmLines.ForeColor = vbCyan
     frmLines.DrawWidth = 20
     Line (2000, 1000)-(2000, 5000) ' vertical line
     frmLines.ForeColor = vbRed
     frmLines.DrawWidth = 20
     Line (2400, 1000)-(2400, 5000)     ' vertical line further to the right
     frmLines.ForeColor = vbBlue
     frmLines.DrawWidth = 4
     For I = 0 To 10
          frmLines.DrawMode = I + 4
          Line (100, 3000)-(4000, 1000 + 400 * I)   ' create fan of lines
     Next I
End Sub
```

The Rest of the Story

There's more to the *Line* method. Here's its full syntax.

[*object*.]**Line** [[**Step**](*x1*, *y1*)] - **Step** (*x2*, *y2*), [*color*], [**B**[**F**]]

If you wish to use the *Line* method in a picture box, then you should substitute the name of the picture box for *object*. If you omit the object name, the method draws in the currently active form.

Notice that the coordinates of the starting point are optional. If you omit them, Visual Basic takes the current graphic position as the starting point. If you use the optional *Step* keyword with the starting point, that means the coordinates are measured from the current graphic position, rather than from the coordinate system origin. Similarly, using *Step* with the endpoint coordinates means those coordinates are relative to the start of the line (see Figure L12-12).

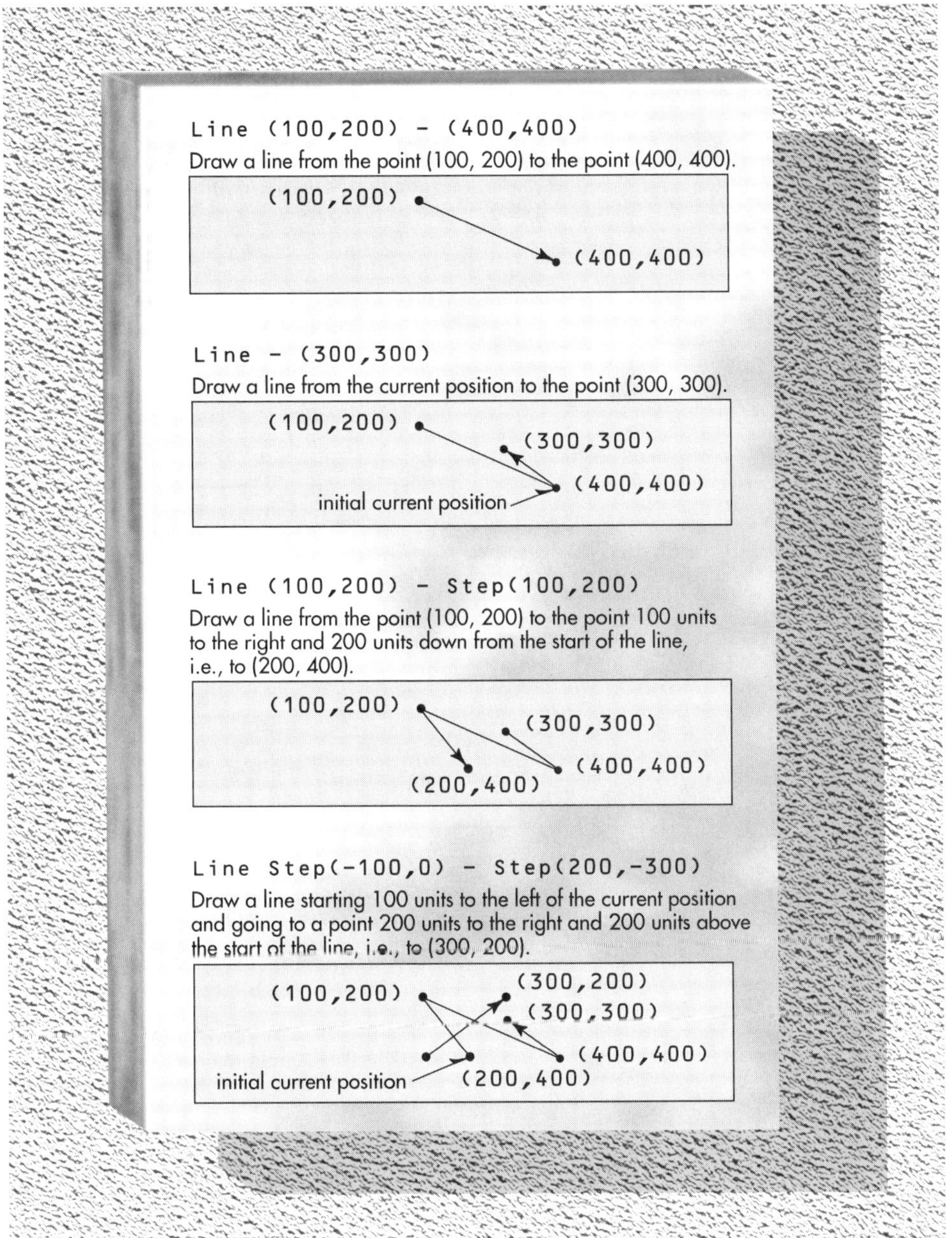

Figure L12-12 Variations on a line

By default, Visual Basic draws the line using the current ForeColor value, but you can use the *color* parameter to specify another color. For example, the command

```
Line -(500,100), vbCyan
```

means draw a line from the current position to the location (500,100) using the color cyan.

The final optional parameter means to draw a box instead of a line. In this case, the start and end coordinates represent the two diagonal corners of the box. If you use B, the box is drawn using the current FillStyle and FillColor for the interior. If you use the combination BF, the box interior is filled solid with the same color used to draw the box, which would be the ForeColor setting unless you used a color parameter. For example,

```
Line (100,100) - (500,500),vbBlue, BF
```

draws a box with a blue border and interior, with (100,100) being the upper-left corner and (500,500) being the lower-right corner. The command

```
Line (100,100) - (500,500), , BF
```

(notice the placeholding commas indicating the color parameter has been skipped) draws the same kind of box, but using the current ForeColor color.

Listing L12-5 shows a program that draws several filled boxes in graduated shades of gray, and Figure L12-13 shows the output.

Listing L12-5
Drawing boxes

```
Option Explicit

Private Sub Form_Paint()
    Dim I As Integer
    Dim P1, P2 As Integer
    Dim Color As Long
    For I = 0 To 7
        Color = RGB(0, 0, 32 * (I + 1) - 1)
        P1 = 100 + 300 * I
        P2 = 5000 - 300 * I
```

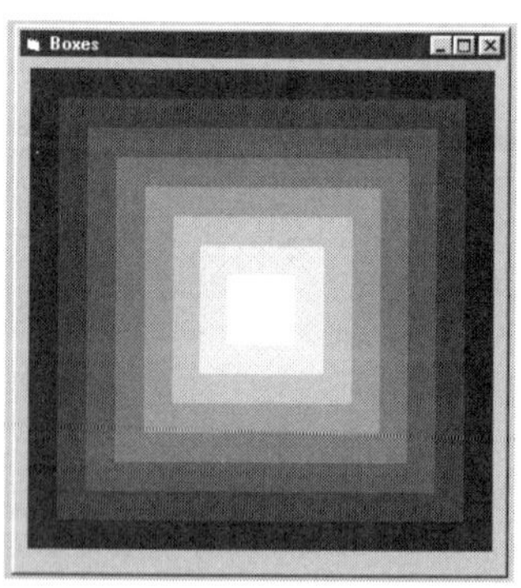

Figure L12-13 Using Line to draw boxes

```
        Line (P1, P1)-(P2, P2), Color, BF
    Next I
End Sub
```

GETTING TO THE POINT

The most basic drawing technique is to draw a single point, and that is what the *PSet* method does. In its simplest form, the command looks like this:

```
PSet (x,y)
```

This command sets the pixel at location *x, y* to the current ForeColor color. Here's the general syntax:

[*object*.]**PSet** [**Step**] (*x*,*y*) [*color*]

You can use *PSet* in a form or in a picture box. The *object* parameter should be replaced with the name of the form or picture box, and Visual Basic will use the current form if you omit that parameter. As usual, the optional *Step* keyword makes Visual Basic interpret the coordinates as being relative to the current graphics position instead of to the origin. And the *color* parameter, of course, overrides the ForeColor setting for painting the point.

The *PSet* method is affected by the DrawMode, DrawStyle, and DrawWidth properties. Of course, a dotted or dashed pixel doesn't make a lot of sense, so the only DrawStyle setting that makes a practical difference from the default is 5 (Transparent), which causes the *PSet* method to have no effect.

The DrawWidth property affects both dimensions of the point. That is, if DrawWidth is set to 3, you get a point 3 pixels tall and 3 pixels wide. If the DrawWidth setting is greater than 1, Visual Basic centers the fat point on the specified coordinates.

The *PSet* command is awkward to use if you use the default twip-based coordinates. For instance, consider the following loop:

```
For I = 1 to 100
    PSet (I, 200)
Next I
```

This may look as if it paints a row of 100 pixels as *I* varies from 1 to 100. But keep in mind that one pixel is several twips wide. For instance, there are 15 twips per pixel in the 800x600 pixel mode. Thus, increasing the *x*-coordinate by 1 only moves the current graphics position 1/15th of a pixel, and the above loop draws 15 pixels atop one another before moving another whole pixel to the right.

You can get around this awkwardness by using the TwipsPerPixelX and TwipsPerPixelY properties. For example, you can rewrite the previous loop this way:

```
For I = 1 to 100
    PSet (I * Screen.TwipsPerPixelX, 200)
Next I
```

But it's much simpler to switch units and to measure coordinates in pixels instead of twips. The next section examines this option.

SCALING NEW HEIGHTS (AND WIDTHS)

Forms and picture boxes feature the ScaleMode property, which lets you select the units used for coordinates. Table L12-9 lists your choices.

SETTING	DESCRIPTION
0	Custom
1	Twip (default) (1,440 per logical inch)
2	Point (72 per logical inch)
3	Pixel (smallest monitor or printer resolution)
4	Character (120 twips by 240 twips)
5	Inch
6	Millimeter (0.254 inch)
7	Centimeter (2.54 inches)

Table L12-9 ScaleMode settings

Let's try a *PSet* example using pixel coordinates. You can use a form's Properties window to set the ScaleMode property, or you can set it in code. Let's try the first approach. Create a form as described in Table L12-10.

OBJECT	PROPERTY	SETTING
Form1	Caption	Paint Pixels
	Name	frmPixel
	ScaleMode	3 - Pixel

Table L12-10 Properties for the Paint Pixels program

Next, open the Code window and enter the code from Listing L12-6.

Listing L12-6
The Paint Pixels program

```
Option Explicit

Private Sub Form_Paint()
    Dim I, J As Integer
    Randomize
    DrawWidth = 1
    For I = 21 To 120
        For J = 21 To 120
            PSet (I, J), RGB(256 * Rnd, 256 * Rnd, 256 * Rnd)
        Next J
```

```
    Next I
    DrawWidth = 10
    For I = 221 To 320 Step 10
        For J = 21 To 120 Step 10
            PSet (I, J), RGB(256 * Rnd, 256 * Rnd, 256 * Rnd)
        Next J
    Next I
End Sub
```

This program fills two squares with pixels painted with randomly selected colors. The first set of two For loops uses *I* and *J* to locate each pixel in the square. The *I* variable acts as the *x*-coordinate, and the *J* variable as the *y*-coordinate. You'll probably notice that filling in the first square is very sloooow. There are 100 rows and 100 columns, leading to 10,000 separate pixels to be addressed and painted individually.

The second set of *For* loops proceeds much faster, for setting DrawWidth to 10 means the box is now only 10 by 10 points in size, with each point using 100 pixels. Figure L12-14 shows the output of Paint Pixels.

Tip

Using *PSet* offers pixel-by-pixel control over the appearance of an image, but it's much slower than specialized methods such as *Line* or using a FillStyle property.

When you run the program, try this:

1. Resize the form so that the image is partially hidden.
2. Expand the form back to its original size.

You'll notice that when you return the form to its original size, Visual Basic redraws the two squares. Moreover, the colors are different this time. That's because uncovering the entire image triggers a *Paint* event, so the *Form_Paint* event procedure runs again using a new set of random colors.

Note

A Paint event occurs when you first open a form and whenever something occurs that requires repainting the form such as covering, and then uncovering a drawing on the form.

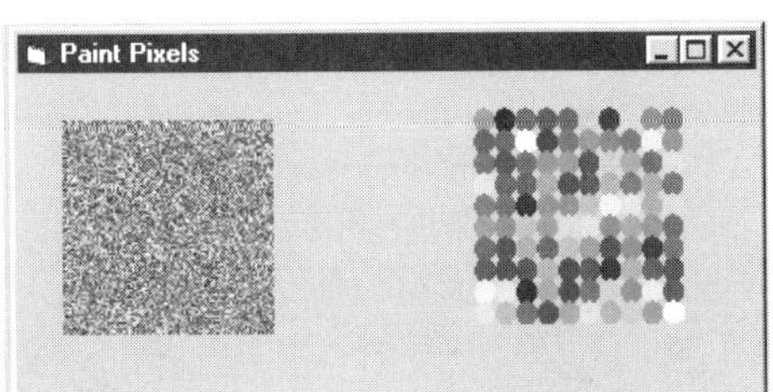

Figure L12-14 The Paint Pixels form

Scale-Related Properties

Several properties describe sizes and positions. Each form or control has Height, Width, Top, and Left properties describing the external size and position of the form or control. Also, each form or picture box control has ScaleHeight, ScaleWidth, ScaleTop, and ScaleLeft properties describing interior dimensions and locations.

Changing the ScaleMode value affects some of these properties. For instance, the Width of a form always is expressed in twips, while the ScaleWidth is expressed in the units specified by ScaleMode. Compare the two Properties windows shown in Figures L12-15 and L12-16. The two describe the same form, and you'll note that both show the same value for Width. But they show different values for ScaleWidth because the first figure uses twips and the second uses pixels.

More generally, the Height, Width, Top, and Left properties of a form are always measured in twips. The ScaleHeight, ScaleWidth, ScaleTop, and ScaleLeft properties, however, are measured in the ScaleMode units.

The situation is slightly different for controls. The Height, Width, Top, and Left properties for controls are measured in ScaleMode units of the container. That is, a command button in a form has its Height property measured in units specified by the form's ScaleMode value, while a command button in a picture box has its Height property measured in units specified by the picture box's ScaleMode value.

Tip

Controls within another object, such as a form or a picture box, use the containing object's ScaleMode units for specifying the control's Top, Left, Height, and Width properties.

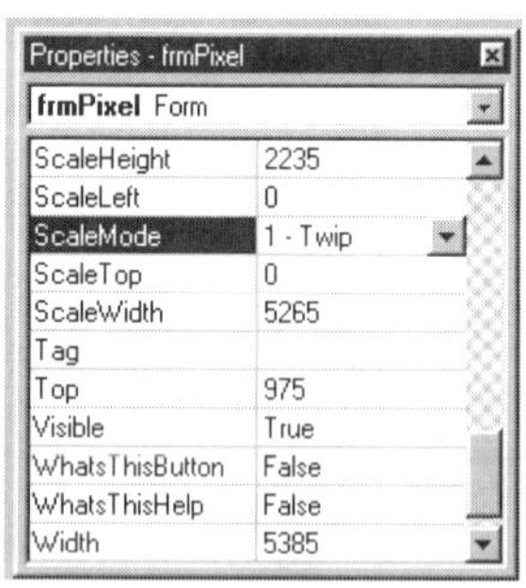

Figure L12-15 Properties using ScaleMode set to twips

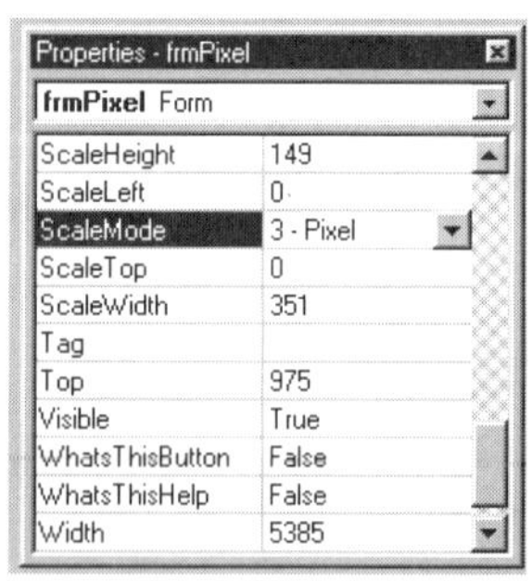

Figure L12-16 Properties using ScaleMode set to pixels

Custom Scaling

The most intriguing option for ScaleMode is 0 - User. When you select that mode, you then can use ScaleWidth, ScaleHeight, ScaleTop, and ScaleLeft to define a coordinate system. For example, if you set ScaleHeight to 100, you define the vertical unit to be 1/100th of the internal height, making 100 units equal to the internal height. Similarly, setting ScaleWidth to 100 makes the interior horizontal dimension of the form 100 units.

One advantage of using such a custom scale is that it can make it simpler to visualize locations when you use graphics methods. For instance, if you want a horizontal line 1/4 the way down from the top, use this command:

```
Line (0,25) - (100,25)
```

Since the ScaleHeight is 100, 1/4 the way down is 25. You can make the same sort of calculation if ScaleHeight is, say, 6453, but using a scale of 100 is simpler.

The ScaleTop and ScaleLeft properties let you redefine the origin of your custom coordinate system. By default, the upper-left corner of the form is (0,0). But the commands

```
ScaleTop = -50
ScaleLeft = -50
```

give the upper-left corner the coordinates (–50,–50). Combined with setting ScaleWidth and ScaleHeight to 100, this places the origin, that is, (0,0), at the center of the form.

The ScaleHeight, ScaleWidth, ScaleTop, and ScaleLeft settings define unit sizes in terms of the form dimensions at the time you make the settings. So if you later resize the form to half its previous width, the new value of ScaleWidth will be 50 instead of 100.

Note

If you use code or the Properties window to assign values to ScaleWidth, ScaleHeight, ScaleTop, or ScaleLeft, Visual Basic automatically sets ScaleMode to 0 - User, the custom mode.

The *Scale* Method

Rather than setting properties to define a scale, you can use the *Scale* method. The syntax looks like this:

[*object.*]**Scale** (*x1*,*y1*) - (*x2*,*y2*)

You can use this method with forms and picture boxes, and it applies to the current form if you omit the object name. The effect is to make (*x1*,*y1*) the coordinates of the upper-left corner and (*x2*,*y2*) the lower-right corner. This makes the horizontal width *x2 - x1*, and that defines the horizontal scale. Similarly, *y2 - y1* defines the vertical scale. For example, the command

```
Scale (-500,-500) - (500,500)
```

defines a scale for which the internal dimensions are 1000x1000 and which has an origin at the center of the form.

LAYERS

Playing around with Visual Basic, you may have noticed that if you overlap graphic controls with, say, command buttons, the command buttons always appear on top. And if you mix graphic controls and command buttons with graphics drawn using the graphics methods, the controls always appear on top of the drawings. The reason for this behavior is that Visual Basic uses three layers—front, middle, and back. Most controls go on the front layer, graphic controls go on the middle layer, and the output from graphics methods normally go on the back layer. Within any one layer, newer controls or drawing go over older ones. Table L12-11 indicates the normal arrangement.

LAYER	INHABITED BY
Front	All controls other than graphics controls and labels
Middle	Graphics controls and labels
Back	Output from graphics methods, background color

Table L12-11 What goes where (normally)

That "normal" qualifier suggests exceptions. Where things wind up depends on three factors:

- The AutoRedraw setting
- The ClipControls setting
- Whether graphics methods are used in a Paint event

Let's look further into this subject.

AutoRedraw, the *Paint* Event, and Persistent Graphics

Life in a Windows environment sometimes leads to a Visual Basic form becoming partially or entirely hidden for a while. For example, you might resize a form, hiding some of its controls. Or you might drag another window over the form or activate a window behind a form, bringing it to the front. What happens when you uncover the form again? For controls, the answer is simple—the controls reappear. Visual Basic maintains the description of each control in memory, so it can restore them whenever necessary. For output from the graphics methods and from the Print method, the situation is more complex, depending on the state of the AutoDraw property and upon which event contains the graphics methods. Both forms and picture boxes have the AutoRedraw property, which is False by default. As the name suggests, the AutoRedraw property describes whether graphics get redrawn automatically when they are covered and subsequently uncovered. However, AutoRedraw interacts with the location of graphics methods as described in Table L12-12.

AUTOREDRAW	SETTING	LOCATION OF GRAPHICS METHOD EFFECT
False	In a Paint event	Graphics are redrawn, graphics are in the back layer
True	In a Paint event	*Paint* events ignored, graphics never drawn
False	Outside a Paint event	Graphics not redrawn, back and mid layers mixed
True	Outside a Paint event	Graphics are recopied from memory

Table L12-12 Persistence of graphics drawn with graphic methods

Automatic Restoration

Controls on a form are restored to view automatically when any part of a form is hidden, then uncovered. Graphics drawn using graphic methods and text produced with Print are redrawn automatically only for the first and last options in Table L12-12.

Let's take a closer look at your options. The first option in Table L12-12 is the one all the examples so far in this lesson have followed. It's the usual way to handle graphics. When you do something that requires graphics to be refreshed, that act generates a *Paint* event. The *Paint* event runs the code in the *Paint* event procedure, and the code redraws the graphics. Note that if you cover, then uncover, 10 percent of a form, Visual Basic redraws the whole form because it executes all the code in the *Paint* event; it can't just regenerate the 10 percent. For graphics methods like *Circle* and *Line,* regenerating the graphics goes pretty fast with a modern computer. But the process can be pretty slow if you used *PSet* often.

The second option, setting AutoRedraw to True and placing graphics methods in a *Paint* event, is pretty useless, for enabling AutoRedraw causes Visual Basic to ignore Paint events entirely. Run any of the earlier examples in this chapter with AutoRedraw set to True, and you won't get any graphics at all. Of course, having no graphics does solve the problem of refreshing them.

The third option is leaving AutoRedraw set at False and placing graphics methods somewhere other than in a *Paint* procedure. In this case, graphics that get covered stay blank when uncovered. Let's try that Copy the Paint Pixels program (see Table L12-10 and Listing L12-6). Next, add a command button to the form, copy the code to the button's *Click* event, and erase the *Form_Paint* event. Run the program and click on the command button. Once the graphics are drawn, hide part of the form, then uncover it again. You should get something like Figure L12-17.

Finally, let's look at the case where AutoRedraw actually accomplishes something. Take the project just described, but set AutoRedraw to True. Again, start the program and click on the command button. If it appears that nothing is happening, don't panic! With AutoRedraw set to True, you don't get to watch as *PSet* paints each pixel. Instead, the form remains blank until the graphics methods are done, and then the entire image appears all at once!

Next, obscure part of the graphics area, and then uncover it again. The image is restored virtually instantaneously. Recall that restoring the image using the *Paint* event was rather slow. The reason for this difference is in how the AutoRedraw feature works. When AutoRedraw is True, Visual Basic maintains a bitmapped copy of the graphics in memory. When Visual Basic refreshes an image in this mode, it copies the image back to the screen. This is faster than executing the graphics method statement to redraw the image, but it makes heavier demands on memory.

The Paint Event Versus the AutoRedraw Property

Visual Basic provides two ways to refresh graphics automatically. Method 1 is setting AutoRedraw to False and placing graphics methods in a Paint event handler. This method regenerates graphics by reexecuting the original code that produced the graphics. Method 2 is setting AutoRedraw to True and placing graphics methods in locations other than in Paint event handlers. This method regenerates graphics by preserving a copy of the graphics image in memory and copying from that image back to the screen. In general, Method 1 takes more time and less memory, while Method 2 takes less time to restore an image but more memory.

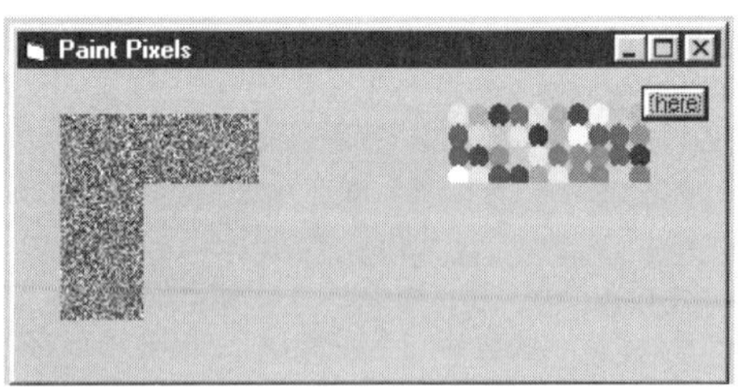

Figure L12-17 Graphics handling with AutoRedraw set to False

AutoRedraw, Forms, and Picture Boxes

The AutoRedraw property for a picture box is independent of the AutoRedraw property for a form. You can, for example, set AutoRedraw to False for a form while setting a picture box's AutoRedraw property to True. Regardless of the settings, Visual Basic restores a picture box because a picture box is a control. That means the picture box border and any controls in the picture box are restored. But the graphics contents of the picture box are restored only if you have an appropriate combination of AutoRedraw properties and of graphic method placement. For instance, each of the following combinations produces graphics in a picture box that are automatically redrawn.

- Set the picture box AutoRedraw property to False, and use the graphics methods in the picture box's *Paint* event procedure.
- Set the picture box AutoRedraw property to True, and use the graphics methods outside of the picture box's *Paint* event procedure.

A SideLight

The AutoRedraw setting affects how the *Cls* command works. Normally, *Cls* clears the output of Print and of the graphics methods. However, if you generate graphics or text output with AutoRedraw set to True, then set AutoRedraw to False, *Cls* won't affect that output. But it will clear any output you generate while AutoRedraw remains false. Thus you can produce a mixture of erasable and nonerasable graphics and text.

THE CLIPCONTROLS PROPERTY—NO GRAPHICS HERE

Each form and picture box has a ClipControls property that is set to True by default. In essence this setting excludes controls from the available drawing area on a form or picture window. That is, drawing is restricted to those parts of a form not covered by a control, providing the control is not a graphics control or a label. Setting ClipControls to False can remove that restriction, depending, yes, on the AutoRedraw settings and the location of the graphics methods. Let's look at a couple of cases before generalizing.

Begin by creating a form with a large button. Use Figure L12-18 to gauge the proportions and Table L12-13 to set properties. Note that you get a chance to use the custom scaling option.

OBJECT	PROPERTY	SETTING
Form1	Caption	Clipping
	ClipControls	True
	DrawWidth	10
	Name	frmClip
	ScaleHeight	100
	ScaleMode	1 - User
	ScaleWidth	100
Command1	Caption	Click Here
	Name	cmdHere

Table L12-13 Properties for the Clipping program

Now give it the following code, which places one graphics method in a *Paint* event and a second graphics method outside a *Paint* event.

```
Option Explicit

Private Sub cmdHere_Click()
    Line (0, 30)-(95, 30), vbBlue
End Sub

Private Sub Form_Paint()
    Line (0, 60)-(95, 60), vbRed
End Sub
```

Run the program, click on the button, and you get output like that shown in Figure L12-18. Note that both lines lie behind the button. Next, change the ClipControls setting to False, and run the program again. This time the output looks like Figure L12-19. The output from the *Paint* event remained under the button, but output from the *Click* event gets painted over the button. In short, when ClipControls is set to False, graphics methods outside a *Paint* event are free to draw anywhere on a form, but graphics methods inside a *Paint* event still are restricted.

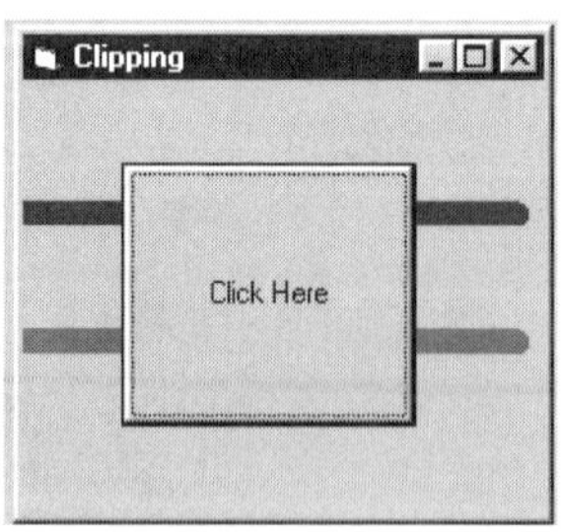

Figure L12-18 ClipControls set to True

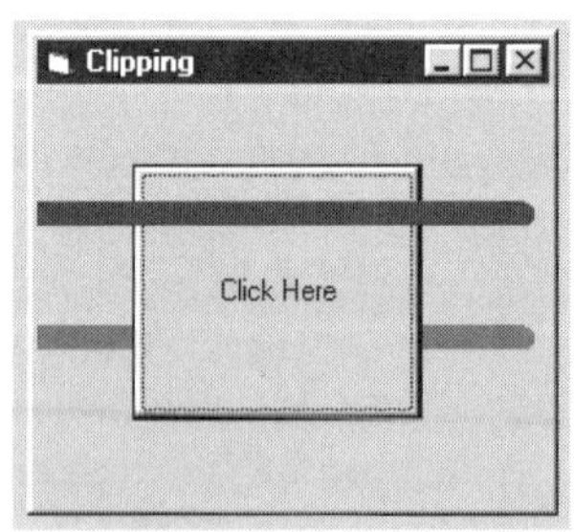

Figure L12-19 ClipControls set to False

All the possibilities won't be discussed, but Table L12-14 expands Table L12-12, summarizing the different behaviors you get with different combinations of AutoRedraw, ClipControls, and graphics methods placement. You can use the form settings for the Clipping program to try the different combinations yourself.

AUTOREDRAW	GRAPHICS METHOD	CLIPCONTROLS	EFFECT
False	In a Paint event	True	Graphics redrawn, graphics are in the back layer
False	In a Paint event	False	Graphics redrawn, graphics are in the back layer
True	In a Paint event	True	Paint events ignored, normal layering
True	In a Paint event	False	Paint events ignored, normal layering
False	Out of a Paint event	True	Graphics not redrawn, back and mid layers mixed
False	Out of a Paint event	False	Graphics not redrawn, all layers mixed
True	Out of a Paint event	True	Normal layering, graphics recopied from memory
True	Out of a Paint even	False	Normal layering, graphics recopied from memory

Table L12-14 Persistence of graphics drawn with graphic methods

Which of these combinations should you use? If you don't use a slow method like *PSet*, just use the default settings (AutoRedraw = False, ClipControls = True), and place your graphics methods in *Paint* event procedures. If you want to speed up redrawing, use AutoRedraw = True and place your graphics methods in non-*Paint* procedures. If you do use AutoRedraw = True, consider drawing your graphics in a picture box and using AutoRedraw = False for the form as a whole. That way, the program will only have to use enough memory to hold the picture box image rather than holding an image of the whole form. Another way to speed up the AutoRedraw feature is to set ClipControls to False. That's because AutoRedraw = True enforces normal layering so that controls will appear in front of graphics anyway, so there's no need for the program to calculate the boundaries of the clipping region.

SUMMARY

Visual Basic has many ways of getting graphics into a program. You can load images into a form, an image control, or a picture box. You can construct geometric shapes with the Shape and Line controls. And you can draw on a form or picture box by using graphics methods.

The *Circle* graphics method lets you draw circles and ellipses, the *Line* method lets you draw circles and boxes, the *PSet* method lets you paint individual pixels, and the *Cls* method lets you clear the effects of the other commands. As with other methods, you use these methods by prefixing them with the name of the object and a period, as in *picNose.Cls*. However, unlike most methods, you can omit the object, in which case Visual Basic applies the method to the current form.

In general, graphics methods are affected by the DrawMode, DrawStyle, DrawWidth, FillColor, and FillStyle properties of the object containing the drawing. That is, graphics drawn on a form are affected by the form properties, while graphics drawn in a picture box are affected by the picture box properties. The DrawMode property affects how the pen color (the color used to make the drawing) interacts with the background color. The DrawStyle property affects the appearance of lines—solid, dotted, dashed, and so on. The DrawWidth property affects the width of a line, and the width and height of a point. The FillColor and FillStyle properties control the appearance of the interior of circles, ellipses, and boxes drawn using the *Circle* and *Line* commands.

Usually, graphics methods are placed in the *Paint* event procedures for forms and picture boxes. Visual Basic generates a *Paint* event when a form or picture box first appears and whenever it needs to be redrawn—for example, when you cover and subsequently uncover a form or picture box. Thus, placing graphics in *Paint* events causes graphics images to be regenerated when they are concealed and later revealed.

The AutoRedraw property gives an alternative method for managing the redrawing of images. When AutoRedraw for a form or picture box is set to True, Visual Basic retains a bitmapped image of that object in memory, and it uses that copy to regenerate graphics images.

Normally, Visual Basic paints on three levels. The background and the output of graphics methods and of the *Print* method go on the back layer, graphics controls and labels go on the middle layer, and the remaining controls go on the front layer. However, the settings of the AutoRedraw and ClipControls properties and the location of graphics methods (in or out of *Paint* event procedures) can modify the normal behavior.

QUIZ 12

1. Compare a circle painted using the Circle method with a circle created with a Shape control in terms of the following characteristics:
   a. When they are created (design time or run time)
   b. Which object's properties affect them
   c. The layers they normally appear in
   d. The processes for restoring them when covered, then uncovered

2. What role does Step play in using the Circle method?
   a. It defines how many steps are used to draw a circle.
   b. It defines how many colors are used to draw a circle.
   c. It indicates that coordinates are relative to the current position.
   d. It creates a step-circle.

3. Where is the current position after
   a. Executing a Circle command?
   b. Executing a Line command?
   c. Executing a PSet command?

4. Describe what each of the following commands will do:
   a. Circle (2000,1000), 800
   b. Circle (2000,1000), 800, vbCyan
   c. Circle (2000,1000), 800, vbCyan, 1, 2
   d. Circle (2000,1000), 800, , , , 2
   e. Circle Step (2000,1000), 800

5. Describe what each of the following commands will do:
   a. Line (10,50) - (1000, 0)
   b. Line - (300,300)
   c. Line - Step (200,400)
   d. Line (50,50) - (2000, 000), vbBlue, B
   e. Line (50,50) - (2000,2000), vbBlue, BF

6. What effect does setting DrawWidth to 10 have on PSet?

7. What do you do to cause a circle painted on a form to have a solid red interior?

8. What do you do to cause a circle painted in a picture box to have a solid red interior?

9. What is the Paint event, and why is it the usual practice to place graphics methods in Paint event procedures?

10. How do you make a program measure coordinates in pixels instead of in twips?

11. What are the effects of setting AutoRedraw to True?

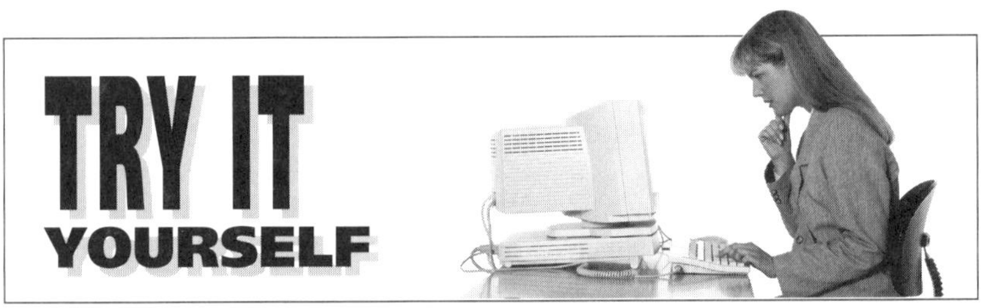

1. Modify the ellipse example by using a timer control to draw the ellipses with a time delay between each pair.

2. Set up a program that uses a list box to let you choose the DrawMode property during run time. The program displays a circle against a mixed background consisting of two boxes of different colors painted using *Line*. When you select a new mode, the program clears the screen, and redraws the background and the circle by using the new DrawMode setting. Use the program to investigate the visual effects of the different DrawMode values.

3. Write a program that uses *Line* to draw a triangle in a picture box. Define a user scale in which the ScaleWidth and ScaleHeight are set to 100. Since each side starts where the preceding side ends, once you paint the first side, you can use the *Line* format that omits the starting point for the remaining sides.

LESSON 13

A MOUSE AMID OBJECTS

It's time to return to some Visual Basic basics—the mouse and objects. The mouse is often the user's main tool in using a program, and objects are your main tools in building programs, so both are important elements of the Visual Basic experience. In this lesson, you'll learn more about using mouse events and more

about controls. In particular, you'll come to terms with the following:

- **The MouseMove event**
- **The DragMode and DragIcon properties**
- **The DragOver and DragDrop events**
- **The Control type variable**
- **The Controls collection**
- **The For Each In statement**

MOUSE TRAILS

Lesson 12 concentrated on painting forms. Let's try a picture box example, one that creates graphical tracking of the mouse. First, open a new project and draw a large picture box on the form. Use Figure L13-1 as a guide, and set properties as outlined in Table L13-1.

OBJECT	PROPERTY	SETTING
Form1	Caption	Painter Mouse
	Name	frmPmouse
Picture1	BackColor	&H00FFFFFF& (white)
	Name	picArena

Table L13-1 Properties for the Painter Mouse program

So far, this project is pretty simple. And it stays simple. To track the mouse, you can use the *MouseMove* event procedure for the picture box. Recall (from

Figure L13-1 The Painter Mouse project at work

Lesson 4) that moving the mouse generates the *MouseMove* event, and that the *MouseMove* event procedure has arguments that indicate, among other things, the location of the mouse. So all you have to do to mark the motion of the mouse is to use those coordinates with the *PSet* command. As the mouse moves, it generates *MouseMove* events, and each event will cause Visual Basic to paint the pixel marking the mouse's location at the instant the *MouseMove* event occurs. In short, just add the following code:

```
Private Sub picArena_MouseMove(Button As Integer, Shift As Integer, _
    X As Single, Y As Single)
    picArena.PSet (X, Y)
End Sub
```

Here the event procedure arguments *X* and *Y* are the coordinates of the mouse, and you can use them as arguments to *PSet*. Note that since this project is supposed to paint inside the picture box, it has to prefix the *PSet* method with the name of the picture box.

Can it be this easy? Yes, it can. Figure L13-1 shows the program in action. Try it yourself. If you move the mouse rapidly, the dots are widely spaced. If you move the mouse slowly, the dots are closely spaced. That's because *MouseMove* events are generated periodically, with a time lapse between successive events. Moving the mouse around should give you a good feel for how frequently the *MouseMove* events occur. Also, note that if you move the mouse outside the picture box, tracking ceases.

IMPROVED MOUSE TRAILS

Although it's exciting at first to have the screen track your mouse movements, it soon gets boring. You can't change colors. You can't change the size of the dots. You can't turn off the tracking. You can't clean up the picture box. All these deficiencies can be easily fixed. Make a copy of the Painter Mouse project and add the frames, option buttons, and command button described in Table L13-2 and illustrated in Figure L13-2. Note that the option buttons are organized into two control arrays. Don't forget that to place controls in a frame, you have to create the frame first, then draw the controls directly in the frame.

OBJECT	PROPERTY	SETTING
Form1	Caption	Painter Mouse 2
	Name	frmPmouse
Picture1	BackColor	&H00FFFFFF& (white)
	Name	picArena
Frame1	Caption	Color
	Name	fraColor
Frame2	Caption	PointWidth
	Name	fraWidth

continued on next page

continued from previous page

OBJECT	PROPERTY	SETTING
Option1	Caption	Red
	Index	0
	Name	optColor
	Value	True
Option2	Caption	Green
	Index	1
	Name	optColor
Option3	Caption	Blue
	Index	2
	Name	optColor
Option4	Caption	Black
	Index	3
	Name	optColor
Option5	Caption	Background
	Index	4
	Name	optColor
Option6	Caption	1
	Index	0
	Name	optWidth
	Value	True
Option7	Caption	2
	Index	1
	Name	optWidth
Option8	Caption	4
	Index	2
	Name	optWidth
Command1	Caption	Clear
	Name	cmdClear

Table L13-2 Properties for the Painter Mouse 2 program

First, let's solve the problem of providing color options. There are three steps. The first is creating a module-level variable called *Color*. The second is using this variable with *PSet* to specify the color used to paint pixels:

```
PSet (X, Y), Color
```

The third step is to use a *Select Case* statement in the *optColor_Click* event procedure to assign colors to the *Color* variable. As Table L13-2 suggests, the choices will be red, green, blue, black, and the background color. By selecting the background color, you can, in effect, erase pixels of other colors by setting them to the background color. Listing L13-1 shows this procedure along with the rest of the project procedures.

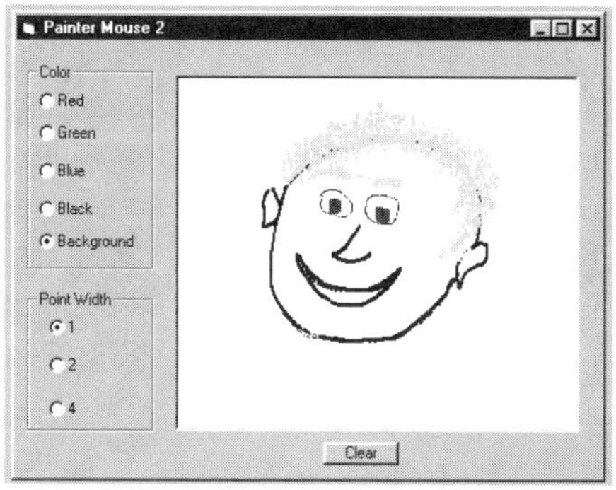

Figure L13-2 Using Painter Mouse 2

To set the size of the mark made by the mouse, use the picArena.DrawWidth property. This can be set using the optWidth array of option buttons. The buttons promise choices of 1, 2, and 4 pixels. One way to accomplish this is to set the DrawWidth property to the Caption property of the selected option button:

```
Private Sub optWidth_Click(Index As Integer)
    picArena.DrawWidth = optWidth(Index).Caption
End Sub
```

If you click on the first option button, Index is 0, and DrawWidth is set to OptWidth(0).Caption, which is 1. Note that if you add another option button choice for the width to the array, you don't have to change this code. There's one subtle point here—the Caption property is a string, while the DrawWidth property is an integer. As usual, however, Visual Basic makes the type conversion for you automatically.

To clear the picture box, use the *picArena.Cls* method in the *cmdClear_Click* event, as shown in Listing L13-1.

You can use the *Button* parameter to the *MouseMove* event procedure to make mouse painting take place only if the left mouse button is down:

```
Private Sub picArena_MouseMove(Button As Integer, Shift As Integer, _
    X As Single, Y As Single)
    If Button = vbLeftButton Then   ' paint when left button is down
        picArena.PSet (X, Y), Color
    End If
End Sub
```

Recall the *vbLeftButton* is a Visual Basic constant you can use.

So far, the mouse paints only if it is in motion. But it can be useful to paint a particular pixel just by clicking the mouse without moving it. You can't use the *Click* event for that purpose, for it doesn't know the *X* and *Y* coordinates. But the *MouseDown* event does know the mouse position, so you can use it:

```
Private Sub picArena_MouseDown(Button As Integer, Shift As Integer, X As
Single, Y As Single)
    picArena.PSet (X, Y), Color     ' paint single point
End Sub
```

One more point—you can use either the *Form_Load* or the *Form_Initialize* event to initialize the *Color* variable to red. Listing L13-1 shows this and the rest of the code used for the Painter Mouse 2 project.

Listing L13-1
The Painter Mouse 2 program

```
Option Explicit
Dim Color As Long    ' color used by mouse to paint

Private Sub cmdClear_Click()
    picArena.Cls      ' clear picture box of graphics
End Sub

Private Sub Form_Initialize()
    Color = vbRed    ' set initial value for color
End Sub

Private Sub optColor_Click(Index As Integer)
    Select Case Index    ' choose color based on option button
    Case 0
        Color = vbRed
    Case 1
        Color = vbGreen
    Case 2
        Color = vbBlue
    Case 3
        Color = vbBlack
    Case 4
        Color = picArena.BackColor
    Case Else
        Print "Ooops!"
    End Select
End Sub

Private Sub optWidth_Click(Index As Integer)
    picArena.DrawWidth = optWidth(Index).Caption
End Sub

Private Sub picArena_MouseDown(Button As Integer, Shift As Integer, X As
Single, Y As Single)
    picArena.PSet (X, Y), Color      ' paint single point
End Sub

Private Sub picArena_MouseMove(Button As Integer, Shift As Integer, X As
Single, Y As Single)
    If Button = vbLeftButton Then    ' paint when left button is down
        picArena.PSet (X, Y), Color
    End If
End Sub
```

Figure L13-2 shows an example of using Painter Mouse 2. As you can see, it hasn't taken a lot to create a simple paint program.

Suppose you want the mouse to draw a continuous line, more like what pencil tools for typical paint programs do. In that case, you would like for Visual

Basic to connect the location of the mouse at each mouse event to its location at the previous event. You can do that by replacing *PSet* with *Line*. That is, replace

```
picArena.PSet (X, Y), Color
```

with the following:

```
picArena.Line -(X, Y), Color
```

This syntax for *Line*, recall (from Lesson 12) draws a line from the current graphics position to the location (*X*,*Y*), and the current graphics position is the end of the previous line segment. Thus this links successive locations with a line, producing a continuous trace.

WHAT A DRAG IT IS

In design mode, you can drag controls around the form, placing them where you desire. Once a program is running, however, programmers usually like their controls to stay put, so that's the default behavior. But you can permit the dragging of controls during run mode, too, by using drag-related properties and event procedures. All the standard controls, other than the graphics controls, have two drag-related properties.

- DragMode—determines whether dragging is automatic
- DragIcon—determines what's shown when an object is dragged

The DragMode property has two possible settings. The default is 0 - Manual. With this setting, the control can't be dragged unless you use the control's *Drag* method, which will be discussed later in his lesson. Setting DragMode to 1 - Automatic for a control enables dragging for that control. Try it. Open a new project and place a frame control on it, as shown in Figure L13-3. Set properties as described in Table L13-3.

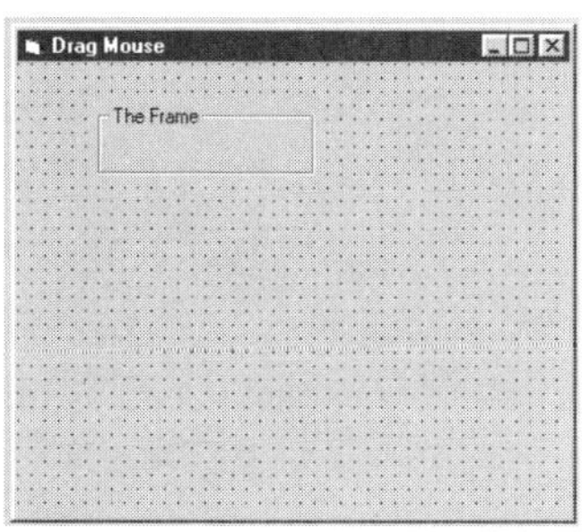

Figure L13-3 The Drag Mouse form, an early stage

OBJECT	PROPERTY	SETTING
Form1	Caption	Drag Mouse
	Name	frmDrag
Frame1	Caption	The Frame
	DragMode	1 - Automatic
	Name	fraDrag

Table L13-3 Properties for the Drag Mouse Program

Run the program and try dragging the frame. (To drag, locate the mouse pointer over the control, press the left mouse button, and drag the mouse pointer across the screen.) You'll notice the following:

- A grayed rectangular outline of the dragged control follows the mouse pointer.
- When you release the mouse button, the dragged outline disappears, and the control remains in its original location.

You can change this. The DragIcon control lets you alter the image dragged along with the mouse pointer, and the *DragDrop* event lets you do many things, including moving the dragged object.

> **Note**
>
> Enabling dragging does not in itself enable you to move the dragged control. You have to program the *DragDrop* event to get movement.

Enhanced Dragging—The *DragDrop* Event

Let's delve further into dragging methodology. In particular, let's investigate how to use dragging to set properties, how to change the drag icon, and how to have dragging move controls. First, we need more demonstration controls on the

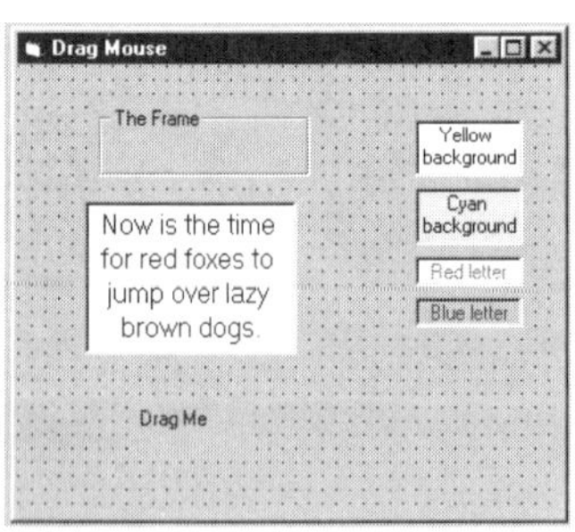

Figure L13-4 The mature Drag Mouse form

form, so modify Drag Mouse as indicated in Figure L13-4 and Table L13-4. Note that there are two control arrays of labels. Also note that the text box has its DragIcon property set. You do this by selecting the DragIcon property in the Properties window, clicking on the 3-dot button in the Setting box, and navigating to the DRAGDROP subdirectory of the Visual Basic ICONS directory. This directory holds several icons designed to be used with the dragging process. Select the *Drag1pg.ico* file. This project has three goals:

- The text box will display an icon when it's dragged.
- Dragging a control to one of the four labels on the right will change the BackColor or ForeColor property of the object.
- You'll be able to drag the Drag Me label to other locations on the form.

OBJECT	PROPERTY	SETTING
Form1	Caption	Drag Mouse
	Name	frmDrag
Frame1	Caption	The Frame
	DragMode	1 - Automatic
	Name	fraDrag
Text1	Alignment	2 - Center
	DragIcon	(Icon) drag1pg.ico
	DragMode	1- Automatic
	Font.Size	12
	MultiLine	True
	Name	txtDrag
	Text	Now is the time for red foxes to jump over lazy brown dogs.
Label1	Caption	Drag Me
	DragMode	1 - Automatic
	Name	lblDrag
Label2	Alignment	2 - Center
	BackColor	&H0000FFFF& (yellow)
	BorderStyle	1 - Fixed Single
	Caption	Yellow background
	Index	0
	Name	lblBack
Label3	Alignment	2 - Center
	BackColor	&H00FFFF00& (cyan)
	BorderStyle	1 - Fixed Single
	Caption	Cyan background
	Index	1
	Name	lblBack

continued on next page

continued from previous page

OBJECT	PROPERTY	SETTING
Label4	Alignment	2 - Center
	BorderStyle	1 - Fixed Single
	Caption	Red letter
	ForeColor	&H000000FF& (red)
	Index	0
	Name	lblFore
Label5	Alignment	2 - Center
	BorderStyle	1 - Fixed Single
	Caption	Blue letter
	ForeColor	&H00FF0000& (blue)
	Index	1
	Name	lblFore

Table L13-4 Properties for the enhanced Drag Mouse program

Okay, now we have three controls (fraDrag, txtDrag, and lblDrag) with automatic dragging enabled. You can't drag the four labels on the right because they don't have automatic dragging enabled. If you run the program now, you'll find that the frame and label show a moving gray rectangle when dragged, but the text box shows the selected icon, which turns out to be a hand holding a piece of paper (see Figure L13-5). Thus, by setting the DragIcon property to a particular icon, you've accomplished the first goal for this project.

The next step is to empower Visual Basic to take action when you release the left mouse button after dragging. The key is that this act (releasing the left mouse button after dragging) generates a *DragDrop* event. The event is sent to

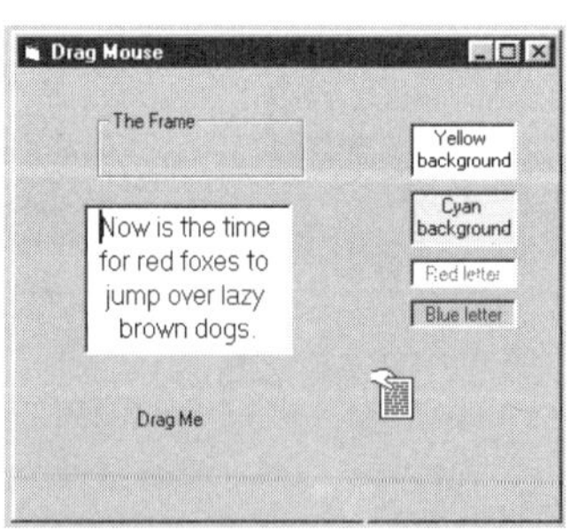

Figure L13-5 The text box shows the DragIcon when dragged

the object under the mouse pointer when the button is released. So, for example, releasing the button when the mouse is over the form triggers the *frmDrag_DragDrop* event procedure. Releasing the button when the mouse is over one of the members of the lblBack array triggers the *lblBack_DragDrop* procedure. By providing code to such a procedure, you can choreograph what happens when you drag a control and drop it over another control or form.

A couple of definitions should help clarify this discussion. The *source object* is the object being dragged, and the *target object* is the object under the mouse pointer when the left button of the dragging mouse is released. The *DragDrop* event procedure reflects these terms, for it includes a variable representing the source. Here, for example, is the format for the form's *DragDrop* event procedure:

```
Private Sub Form_DragDrop(Source As Control, X As Single, Y As Single)

End Sub
```

The event has three arguments. The final two (*X* and *Y*) should be familiar; as with several other mouse event procedures, they refer to the coordinates of the mouse pointer. In this case, they give the mouse coordinates at the instant the mouse button is released. The first argument, however, is something so new and so interesting that it deserves its own heading:

The *Control* Type

The first argument to a *DragDrop* event procedure is a variable of type *Control*. This variable represents whatever control is being dragged. For instance, if you drag the fraDrag control, then the value of the *Source* variable is the fraDrag control. If you drag the txtDrag control, *Source* is the txtDrag control. In general, a *Control* type variable can be set to any control.

A *Source* variable really is a control. That is, you can use *Source* the same way you would use a regular control. For instance, you can use control properties For example, the statement

```
Source.BackColor = vbYellow
```

sets the BackColor property of *Source* to yellow. If *Source* happens to be the fraDrag control, then fraDrag gets a yellow background. If *Source* is txtDrag, then the txtDrag control gets a yellow background.

There is a possible problem with a *Control* variable. Suppose you use the following code:

```
Source.Caption = "I've been dragged!"
```

This makes sense if *Source* is, say, a frame or a command button, but it is in error if *Source* is a text box because text boxes don't have Caption properties. This doesn't mean you can't use the Caption property with a *Control* variable. It does mean that you have to make sure that you don't use an expression like *Source.Caption* in the wrong place.

Using the *DragDrop* Event

Meanwhile, let's return to the second goal for this program, to have dragging a control to one of the labels change the properties of the dragged control. For example, consider the "Yellow background" and "Cyan background" labels. They are part of the lblBack control array, so you can use the *DragDrop* event for that array:

```
Private Sub lblBack_DragDrop(Index As Integer, Source As Control, _
    X As Single, Y As Single)
    Source.BackColor = lblBack(Index).BackColor
End Sub
```

Here, *Index* is the control array index, and it identifies which of the two labels received the *DragDrop* event. Thus *lblBack(Index)* is the target control. And, of course, Source is the source control. So the statement

```
Source.BackColor = lblBack(Index).BackColor
```

gives the source object (the dragged object) the same background color as the target object.

Similarly, the event procedure

```
Private Sub lblFore_DragDrop(Index As Integer, Source As Control, _
    X As Single, Y As Single)
    Source.ForeColor = lblFore(Index).ForeColor
End Sub
```

sets the ForeColor property of the dragged control to be the same as the ForeColor property of the target control.

Add these two procedures to the Code window and run the program. Drag the frame over to the "Yellow background" label and drop it there. The frame itself remains in its original position, but its background color turns yellow. Drag, say, the text box to the "Red letter" label and drop the icon on the label. Again, the control stays put, but its text color changes to red. You've achieved the second goal for this project.

Dragging to a New Location

The third goal is making it possible to drag an object to a new location on the form. To do this, you again use the *DragDrop* event for the form. The *DragDrop* event arguments include the position of the mouse when you drop the dragged object, so you can use them as arguments to a *Move* method. The *Move* method (see Lesson 10), recall, moves an object's top left corner to the indicated location.

```
Private Sub Form_DragDrop(Source As Control, X As Single, Y As Single)
    Source.Move X, Y
End Sub
```

This allows you to drag any of the three draggable controls around the form. When you release the mouse button, the control moves so that its upper-left corner is at the location of the mouse pointer. Note that this event lets you drag controls to other parts of the form. It doesn't let you drag them onto other controls. For instance, suppose you drag the Drag Me label over the text box and try to drop it there. In this case, the *DragDrop* event is sent to the text box, not to the form, so Form_DragDrop is not triggered.

Note

The *DragDrop* event goes to the control or form under the mouse pointer when you release the mouse button after dragging.

Using *Typeof Is*

As mentioned earlier, one problem with a *Control* type variable like *Source* is that you don't necessarily know what specific type of control *Source* has been set to. That needn't be a problem, for the Visual Basic *Typeof Is* expression can be used with *If Then* to check the type of control for you. For instance, suppose you want to modify the Drag Mouse project so that only labels can be moved by dragging. You can use this code:

```
Private Sub Form_DragDrop(Source As Control, X As Single, Y As Single)
    If TypeOf Source Is Label Then
        Source.Move X, Y
    End If
End Sub
```

If the dragged object is a label, the *TypeOf Is* expression is true, and the *Source.Move* method is executed. Otherwise, the expression is false, and nothing happens.

The *TypeOf Is* expression has this general form:

TypeOf *object-name* **Is** *object-type*

Here *object-name* is the name of an object, such as fraDrag, or a reference to an object, such as the *Control* type variable *Source*. And *object-type* is the name of a Visual Basic object type, such as TextBox, Form, Label, or CheckBox. If the particular object is of the indicated type, then the whole expression is true. Otherwise, the expression is false. It would be nice if this method could be generalized so you could, say, evaluate *TypeOf Offer Is Bogus* to help navigate through the hazards of daily life.

OBJECT TYPES

Let's get back to the subject of the *Control type*. It's one of several types that refer to controls and other objects. These *control types* come in two groups:

- Specific object types
- Generic object types

Specific object types restrict a variable to just one kind of object. For instance, to create a variable that can only be set to text box controls, you can do this:

```
Dim MyBox As TextBox
```

To set an object variable to a particular object, you use a special syntax using the *Set* statement. For instance, suppose there is a text box named *txtProse*. You would do this to set the *MyBox* variable to the txtProse text box:

```
Set MyBox  = txtProse   ' MyBox variable now refers to txtProse control.
```

Now you can use *MyBox* like a text box, for it is a text box. For instance, the statement

```
MyBox.Text = "You look fabulous!"
```

will set the text property of the txtProse box to "You look fabulous!"

Object type variables are *references*. That means a statement like

```
Dim MyBox as TextBox
```

doesn't create a new text box control. Instead, it creates a name that, through using the Set statement, can refer to an existing text box.

If you want to dissociate the *MyBox* variable from any control, you can use the special *Nothing* object:

```
Set MyBox = Nothing     ' MyBox variable now doesn't refer to anything.
```

You can create variables of any of the specific Visual Basic object types. For instance, Lesson 11 used a variable of the *Picture* type. Similarly, you can create a variable of a *Font* type, since Visual Basic treats a Font property as an object. Object variables are particularly useful when you write your own procedures, as Lesson 16 will discuss.

Generic object types are more general. The *Control* type is a generic type because it can refer to any kind of control, not just one specific type. Visual Basic has four generic object types, which are listed in Table L13-5. The MDI form and children forms refer to projects with multiple forms (see Lesson 19). Currently, such a project can have one MDI (Multiple Document Interface) form along with many children forms. Future Visual Basic versions may allow multiple MDI forms, so Microsoft threw in the MDIForm generic type in anticipation of that event.

GENERIC OBJECT TYPE	CAN REFER TO
Form	Any form in an application, including MDI and MDI children forms
Control	Any control in an application
MDIForm	Any MDI form in an application
Object	Any object, including controls and forms

Table L13-5 Generic object types

A COLLECTION OF CONTROLS

Edified and enriched by that short introduction to object types, let's return to a new dragging example. This project will illustrate two main points:

- Using a collection of controls
- Using manual dragging

First, a *collection* is new to Visual Basic. Like forms and controls, a collection is an object, meaning it is a unit combining data and code. (This lesson will talk more about the concept of an object later.) A collection is not an object that appears onscreen. That is, unlike a form or control, it doesn't have a visual representation. The neat feature of a collection is that it contains other objects or items of data. For instance, you can have a collection of forms, a collection of labels, or a collection of Strings. A collection is like an array, but a bit more loosely organized. For example, you can have more than one kind of control in it. Also, adding and deleting objects in a collection can change the order in which things in a collection are found. Although you can create your own collections, this lesson will work with a collection that automatically comes with a form. This collection is called *Controls,* and it is a collection of all the controls on a form. The *Controls* collection gives you a convenient way to treat all the controls as a single unit. In addition, as you'll soon see, one of the collection methods lets you access all the members of a collection individually. To see this in action, let's create a new project.

To create the Collections project, create a new form and place a label control, an image control, a text box control, a frame control, and two command button controls on the form, as indicated by Table L13-6 and Figure L13-6. These six controls all are placed in the *Controls* collection automatically. The *Rocket.ico* icon file is in Visual Basic's INDUSTRY subdirectory of the ICONS directory.

OBJECT	PROPERTY	SETTING
Form1	BackColor	&H00FFFFFF& (white)
	Caption	Collections
	Name	frmCollection
Frame1	BackColor	&H00000000& (black)
	Caption	The Black Hole
	ForeColor	&H00FFFFFF& (white)
	Name	fraHole
Text1	Alignment	2 - Center
	DragMode	1 - Automatic
	MultiLine	True
	Name	txtDrop
	Text	Don't take me out of context!

continued on next page

continued from previous page

OBJECT	PROPERTY	SETTING
Label1	Caption	Don't label me!
	DragMode	1 - Automatic
	Name	lblDrop
Image1	DragMode	1 - Automatic
	Name	imgDrop
	Picture	(Icon) ROCKET.ICO
Command1	Caption	Yellow
	DragMode	1 - Automatic
	Name	cmdYellow
Command2	Caption	Restore Controls
	Name	cmdRestore

Table L13-6 Properties for the Collections program

Here is what this project is supposed to do:

1. Let you drag the label, the image control, the text box, and the Yellow command button to other locations on the form
2. Let you drag those same four controls over the Black Hole frame and drop them there, the effect being to make a dropped control disappear from the screen
3. Let you restore missing controls to view by clicking on the Restore Controls command button
4. Highlight the label and the text box while they are dragged over the Black Hole

Goal #1 you already know how to do. Set the DragMode properties for those four controls to 1 - Automatic, and use the *Move* method in the *DragDrop* event procedure for the form:

```
Private Sub Form_DragDrop(Source As Control, X As Single, Y As Single)
    Source.Move X, Y
End Sub
```

Goal #2 is a slight variation. To make the control disappear, set its Visible property to False. Because the drop takes place over the Black Hole frame, you use the *DragDrop* event procedure for the frame instead of for the form:

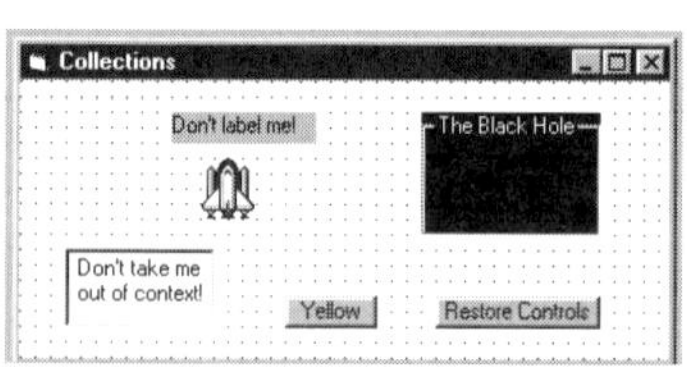

Figure L13-6 The Collections form

```
Private Sub fraHole_DragDrop(Source As Control, X As Single, Y As
Single)
    Source.Visible = False
End Sub
```

Where you drop a control determines which *DragDrop* event procedure is executed. If you drag a control and drop it over the form, Visual Basic moves the control to the drop point. If you drop it over the Black Hole frame, Visual Basic sets the control's Visible property to False.

Goal #3 is where you get to use the *Controls* collection feature, and that involves a new version of the *For* loop.

The *For Each In* Loop

The simplest way to make the invisible controls visible is to set the Visible property for *every* control on the form to True. That way, your program doesn't have to keep track of which controls are visible and which aren't. Since every control on the form is in the *Controls* collection, you need a way to say, "Set the Visible property to True for every control in the *Controls* collection." Visual Basic has a form of *For* loop that does just that. Here's how to code the Restore Controls command button:

```
Private Sub cmdRestore_Click()
    Dim Thing As Control          ' Create a Control type variable.
    For Each Thing In Controls
        Thing.Visible = True
    Next Thing
End Sub
```

First, this code creates a type *Control* variable, calling it *Thing*. (You can, of course, use any other name that's valid for a variable, such as *TheControl* or *Varitrol*.) Then it uses the new *For* loop version:

```
For Each Thing In Controls
    Thing.Visible = True
Next Thing
```

This form of *For* loop works for collections, and it does what it looks like it does—it sets the variable *Thing* to be the first control in the *Controls* section, executes a loop cycle, sets *Thing* to the next item in the collection, and so on, until it exhausts the collection. This example sets the Visible property to True for each control in the *Controls* collection. And because the *Controls* collection automatically contains every control on the form, this particular loop makes every control on the form visible. If you want to get a better view of what's happening, you can have the loop print the name of each control as it processes it; this will show you the order they're arranged in the collection:

```
For Each Thing In Controls
    Thing.Visible = True
    Print Thing.Name
Next Thing
```

More generally, the *For Each In* loop has this syntax:

For Each *element* **In** *group*

...

Next *element*

Here *group* can be the name of a collection or of an array. Also, *element* is a variable of a type appropriate to *group*. If *group* is an array, then element must be the *Variant* type. If *group* is a collection of data, such as of *Integer*, then element must be of the *Variant* type. If *group* is a collection of objects, then *element* must be an appropriate generic type, such as *Control*, *Form*, or *Object*.

The *DragOver* Event

Now let's move on to goal #4, highlighting the label and the text box while they are dragged over the frame control. To do this, use the *DragOver* event. Like the *MouseMove* event, the *DragOver* event is triggered continually. For instance, add this event procedure to the project.

```
Private Sub Form_DragOver(Source As Control, X As Single, Y As Single, _
     State As Integer)
     Beep
End Sub
```

This will cause your computer to beep (or the equivalent) as you drag a control across the form. However, the beeping will cease when the mouse pointer is over another control in the form, for in that case, the *DragOver* event is sent to the control, not to the form.

The *Source*, *X*, and *Y* arguments to the *DragOver* event have the same meaning as they do for the *DragDrop* event, namely, the control being dragged, and the *x*- and *y*- coordinates of the mouse pointer. The *State* argument is new. It has three possible values, which reflect the relationship between the *DragOver* event and the object being dragged over. Table L13-7 lists the values.

VALUE	MEANS
0	Enter—The source control has just entered the target object.
1	Leave—The source control has just left the target object.
2	Over—The source control moved from one place to another in the target.

Table L13-7 Values for the *State* argument to the *DragOver* event

Note

DragDrop and *DragOver* events are sent to the object (control or form) directly under the mouse pointer.

To highlight controls when they pass over the Black Hole frame involves writing a *DragOver* event procedure for the frame control. To highlight the source control, you can invert the foreground and background colors. In particular, you want to invert the colors when the source control enters the target, then invert them back to the original values when the object leaves. In other words, you want to invert the colors when *State* is 0 (object entering) and reinvert them when *State* is 1 (object leaving). You don't want to continually invert them while the source is over the target (*State* is 2). One way to accomplish this is with the following code:

```
Dim Color As Long
If State = 0 Or State = 1 Then
    Color = Source.BackColor
    Source.BackColor = Source.ForeColor
    Source.ForeColor = Color
End If
```

However, this has a problem, for the command button control doesn't have a ForeColor property, and the image control has neither ForeColor nor BackColor properties. (Remember, you have to be careful about that sort of mismatch.) The cure is to use the *TypeOf Is* expression to determine which controls get handled this way. That is, you can do the following:

```
Dim Color As Long
    If TypeOf Source Is Label Or TypeOf Source Is TextBox Then
        If State = 0 Or State = 1 Then
            Color = Source.BackColor
            Source.BackColor = Source.ForeColor
            Source.ForeColor = Color
        End If
    End If
```

Now the code is applied just to the controls in the project that do have both color properties.

Manual Dragging—The *Drag* Method

The project still has a problem, one which will become apparent if you add the following event procedure for the Yellow command button:

```
Private Sub cmdYellow_Click()
    frmCollection.BackColor = vbBlue Xor frmCollection.BackColor
    If cmdYellow.Caption = "Yellow" Then
        cmdYellow.Caption = "White"
    Else
        cmdYellow.Caption = "Yellow"
    End If
End Sub
```

The intent of this code is to toggle the background color between white and yellow. It's based on the fact that *vbBlue Xor vbWhite* is *vbYellow,* and *vbBlue Xor vbYellow* is *vbWhite*. Add this procedure, run the program, and try clicking on the button. Nothing happens. This is because of an important fact—setting the DragMode property to 1 - Automatic for a control screens it from other mouse events, such as *MouseClick* and *MouseDown!*

Note

When a control has its DragMode set to 1 - Automatic, that object is blocked from receiving other mouse events. The only interaction it has with the mouse is that you can use the mouse to drag the object.

If you want to be able to drag an object and have the object respond to other mouse events, you can use *manual dragging*. To do so, you first must have the DragMode property set to the default value, which is 0 - Manual. Then you must use the *Drag* method to turn dragging on and off. Typically, you use the *Drag* method in a *MouseDown* event procedure to turn dragging on, then use the *Drag* method in a *MouseUp* event procedure to turn dragging off.

You invoke the *Drag* method using the object you wish to drag. The syntax looks like this:

object.**Drag** *action*

Here *object* is the name of the object affected, and *action* describes what you want done. Table L13-8 lists the possible values for *action*. Omitting the *action* argument is the same as using 1; it enables dragging.

VALUE	SYMBOLIC CONSTANT	MEANS
0	vbCancel	Cancel the drag operation
1	vbBeginDrag	Enable dragging
2	vbEndDrag	Disable dragging and drop dragged object

Table L13-8 Values for the Drag method argument

For example, you can use the following code to activate and deactivate dragging manually for the cmdYellow button:

```
Private Sub cmdYellow_MouseDown(Button As Integer, Shift As Integer, _
    X As Single, Y As Single)
    cmdYellow.Drag vbBeginDrag
End Sub

Private Sub cmdYellow_MouseUp(Button As Integer, Shift As Integer, _
    X As Single, Y As Single)
    cmdYellow.Drag vbEndDrag
End Sub
```

The Collections project has used several procedures. Listing L13-2 gathers them in one place.

Listing L13-2
The Collections project

```
Option Explicit

Private Sub cmdRestore_Click()
```

```
    Dim Thing As Control
    For Each Thing In Controls
        Thing.Visible = True
    Next Thing
End Sub

Private Sub cmdYellow_Click()
    frmCollection.BackColor = vbBlue Xor frmCollection.BackColor
    If cmdYellow.Caption = "Yellow" Then
        cmdYellow.Caption = "White"
    Else
        cmdYellow.Caption = "Yellow"
    End If
End Sub

Private Sub cmdYellow_MouseDown(Button As Integer, Shift As Integer, _
    X As Single, Y As Single)
    cmdYellow.Drag vbBeginDrag
End Sub

Private Sub cmdYellow_MouseUp(Button As Integer, Shift As Integer, _
    X As Single, Y As Single)
    cmdYellow.Drag vbEndDrag
End Sub

Private Sub Form_DragDrop(Source As Control, X As Single, Y As Single)
    Source.Move X, Y
End Sub

Private Sub fraHole_DragDrop(Source As Control, X As Single, Y As Single)
    Source.Visible = False
End Sub

Private Sub fraHole_DragOver(Source As Control, X As Single, Y As Single, _
    State As Integer)
    Dim Color As Long
    If TypeOf Source Is Label Or TypeOf Source Is TextBox Then
        If State = 0 Or State = 1 Then
            Color = Source.BackColor
            Source.BackColor = Source.ForeColor
            Source.ForeColor = Color
        End If
    End If
End Sub
```

A CLOSER LOOK AT OBJECTS

Objects lie at the heart of Visual Basic. When you create a form, you create an object. When you add a control to a form, you create an object. Now that you've had some experience using objects, it's a good time to take a closer look at them.

An object combines code and data into a single unit. Let's review what this means by examining a specific object, such as a text box control. Suppose you create a text box named txtTile. It comes with a list of properties, such as Width, BackColor, Text, DragMode, Visible, and Top. This information comes in a variety of forms, including numbers, strings, and Boolean values. But all the information is tied together as part of a single object. The notation emphasizes this fact. For instance, the terms *txtTile.Width* and *txtTile.Name* indicate that both Width and Name are part of the txtTile object.

The code part of a text box object consists of its methods and its event procedures. For instance, every text box control has a *Move* method that you can use to move the object and a *Drag* method that you can use to turn dragging on and off. As with properties, you tie methods to the name of a particular object. For instance,

```
txtTile.Move 2000,3000
```

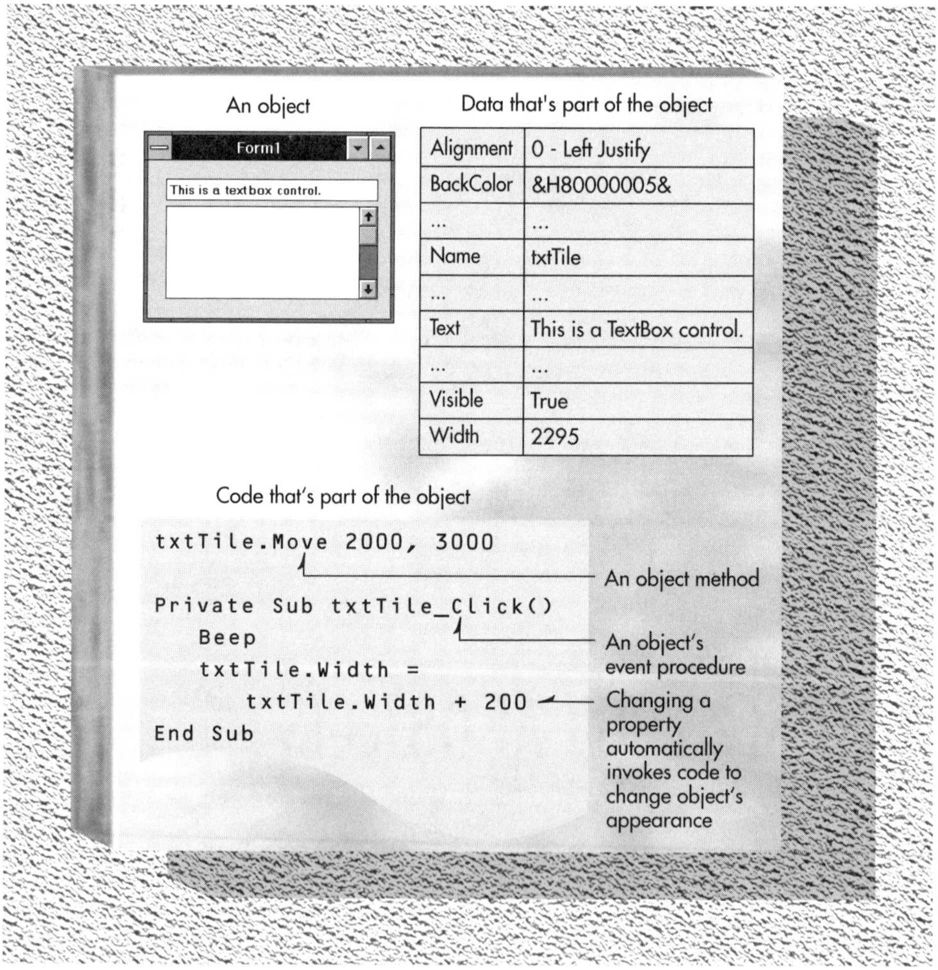

Figure L13-7 Code and data in a typical control

means move the txTile object so that its upper-left corner is at the coordinates (2000,3000). Note that you don't have to do anything to create the properties and methods for a text box. The mere act of creating a text box automatically supplies it with these packages of data and code.

The event procedures are a bit different from the methods. First, they define an object's interface with its environment—how, for instance, it responds to a mouse click or to being covered and uncovered. Second, although Visual Basic defines what events a control can respond to, you define what the response is. Third, you use a different syntax for event procedures than for methods. Nonetheless, you do associate events with particular objects. For instance, *txtTile_Click* indicates the *Click* event procedure invoked when you click on the txtTile control.

Actually, there's more to the code part of an object. For instance, the act of changing a property invokes the code that makes that change onscreen. For instance, setting the BackColor property to red invokes code that sets the pixels inside the object to red. Figure L13-7 summarizes the data and code components of a typical control.

Object Virtues

So what do objects give you? Conceptually, they let you think of a Visual Basic program in terms of building blocks. For instance, you might decide your project needs a text box, two vertical scrollbars, a command button, and an array of three option buttons. Then you simply drag those controls onto a form.

Another related conceptual plus is that objects offer a high level of abstraction. The very existence of these controls offers you guidance as to how to put an interface together. A few years ago, without such objects available, you would have to work out an interface plan from scratch. Visual Basic has designed its objects so that each kind of object corresponds to a useful programming unit. When, say, you create a command button, you don't need to think about the code needed to draw a button, you don't need to figure out how to have the program detect if the mouse has been positioned over the button, you don't need to design code to make the button respond visibly to a mouse click. Instead, you can concentrate on higher-level matters, such as what is the purpose of the button.

Practically, Visual Basic objects save you a tremendous amount of work. Someone else has done the work of designing and testing them. Visual Basic 4 also lets you design your own objects (see Lesson 20). In that case, you do have to do some of the design and testing work yourself, but once you complete the design, you can reuse it easily. The fact that an object bundles its data and code together is what makes reusing an object simple; you don't have to worry about forgetting some obscure code snippet or data value when you reuse an object in a new project.

Also, objects facilitate cooperation between programs. For instance, the Visual Basic OLE 2.0 control lets you import objects from other programs, such as spreadsheet objects from an Excel program. Your Visual Basic program then can use the property and methods of the imported object.

The Class-Object Relationship

It's useful to have a way to distinguish between the abstract design of an object, such as a command button, and particular instances of an object, such as a command button called cmdExit. In some circles, programmers use the word *object* to mean the abstract design and the term *object instance* to denote a particular object used in a program. Visual Basic, however, like C++, uses the word *class* to denote the abstract design and the word *object* to denote specific instances of the design. One way of looking at this is that a class is analogous to a type and an object is analogous to a variable. There is only one *Integer* type, but you can have as many *Integer* variables as you like. Similarly, there is only one command button class, but you can have as many command button objects as you like. Another way of looking at classes and objects is that a class is like a cookie cutter; it sets the pattern. Objects, then, are like cookies made to the pattern of the cookie cutter.

Visual Basic 4 is more dedicated to the class-object model than earlier versions. For instance, it has added the *Font* and *Picture* objects. Also, you now can create a module in which you define classes of your own. You then can add that module to a project and incorporate objects of those classes into your program.

You don't create objects in design mode. Rather, you build descriptions of all the objects you want. The objects come into being when you run the program. The various property values are loaded into the section of memory used to store data, and the code part is loaded into the section of memory used to store code. The objects come into being.

Let's take a closer look at what happens when objects are created. First, as a matter of terminology, you *instantiate* an object. Okay, then, what happens when you instantiate an object? The class definition tells Visual Basic what kinds of data are needed. For instance, if you instantiate a command button, you need to represent all the properties of a command button, such as BackColor, DragMode, and Visible. The list of properties, then, tells Visual Basic how much memory needs to be allocated to hold the data and how that memory should be divided into different data types. Next, Visual Basic needs to *initialize* the data. That is, each property should be set to a definite value. Here Visual Basic uses the values in the Properties window. The value for BackColor is copied to the section of memory reserved for the BackColor property of the object, and so on.

When it comes to initialization, forms are a bit different from controls. For a control, the control properties encompass all the data associated with a control. But with a form, you can add more data by defining module-level variables. With previous versions of Visual Basic, you would initialize these variables in the *Form_Load* event procedure. Conceptually, however, it's more satisfying to have the form completely initialized before you load it. Therefore, Visual Basic 4 provides a special event, the *Form_Initialize* event, that occurs before the *Form_Load* event. The purpose of this event is to give you the opportunity to initialize any module-level variables you've defined. However, you shouldn't use this event to set property values. That's because these values are initialized automatically using the settings in the Properties window. If you add code, say, assigning 3000 to *Form.Width,* you've really changing a property, not initializing it. Similarly, using the *AddItem* method to add items to a list box is modifying a list that has been initialized to being empty. This sort of code should go in the *Form_Load* event, not in the *Form_Initialize* event.

As a practical matter, you can initialize new variables in the *Load* event. However, that means that prior to the *Load* event, you have an incompletely defined form. Its built-in properties are set to the values provided by the Properties window, but its module-level variables aren't yet set. Also attempting to assign property values in the *Initialize* event leads to an error message, so don't bother trying to do so.

Tip

Use the *Form_Initialize* event procedure to initialize module-level variables you've defined on a form. Use the *Form_Load* event procedure to set values that affect the appearance of a form, such as properties of the form and of its objects and items to be added to list boxes. Use the *Form_Paint* event procedure for graphics methods and the *Print* method.

The Object Browser

Visual Basic 4 has added a new tool to help you navigate through the objects in your project. It's called the *Object Browser,* and you access it by selecting Object Browser from the Visual Basic View menu. You then get a window like that shown in Figure L13-8.

The Object Browser has three text-display areas: a combo box labeled Libraries/Projects, a list box labeled Classes/Modules, and a list box labeled

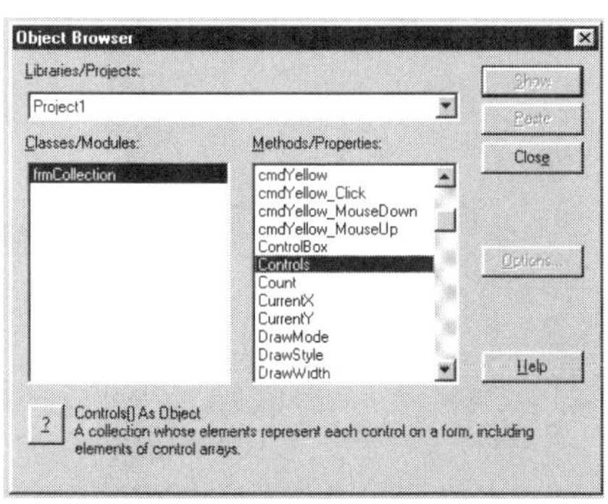

Figure L13-8 The Object Browser

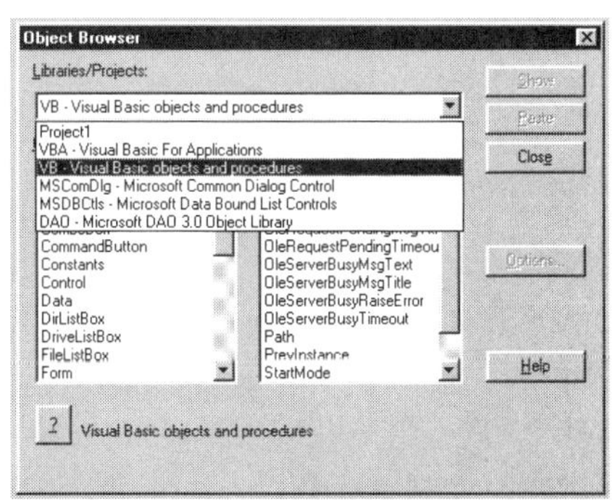

Figure L13-9 Selecting a library to browse

Methods/Properties. If you have an active project, it appears in the Libraries/Projects combo box, and the modules used in that project appear in the Classes/Modules list box. When you select a particular module, all the methods, objects, properties, and events used in that project appear in the Methods/Properties list. For instance, Figure L13-8, based on the Collections program, shows the components of that project. If you highlight an item from the Methods/Properties list, Visual Basic displays a brief description of that item at the bottom of the Object Browser window. If there is Help information about that item, the ? button at the bottom left of the window becomes active, and you can click the button to see the Help material. If you select an event procedure, you can double-click in the procedure to bring up the full procedure in the regular Visual Basic Code window. This is particularly handy for finding bits of code when you have a large program.

You can also use the browser to look through general libraries. For instance, if you open the combo box, you'll see a list of browsable projects and libraries, as shown in Figure L13-9. The "VB - Visual Basic objects and procedures" listing, for example, is the Visual Basic library of objects. If you select it, the left list box will show all the standard Visual Basic objects you can use. Many are the familiar controls, but the list also includes the Constants object. If you select it, the right list box will display all the Visual Basic constants, such as vbBlack, that you've used. You can select a constant, as in Figure L13-10, and get a brief description of it at the bottom of the window. If you select a control in the left window, the right window will list all the methods and properties for that control. In short, the Object Browser gives you a quick, convenient Visual Basic reference.

SUMMARY

Visual Basic programs are very mouse-aware. Earlier lessons discussed the *Click, DblClick, MouseMove, MouseDown,* and *MouseUp* events. This lesson presents the *DragOver* and *DragDrop* events. The *DragOver* event is sent continually to the object under the mouse pointer when you use the mouse to drag an object. The

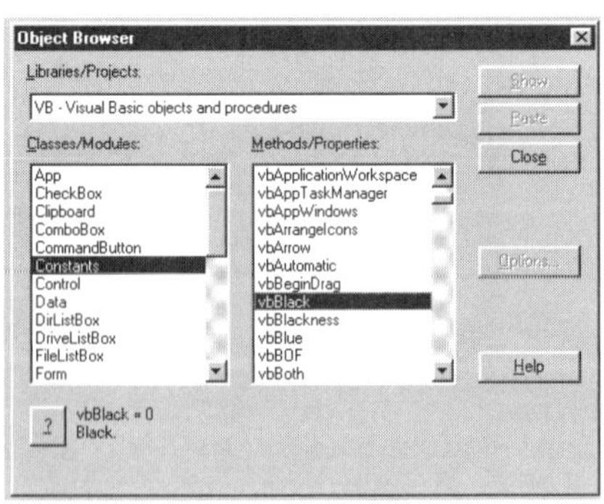

Figure L13-10 Browsing constants

DragDrop event is sent to the object under the mouse pointer when you release a dragged object by releasing the left mouse button.

You can enable dragging for a particular control by setting its DragMode property to 1 - Automatic. Or you can leave DragMode at its default setting (0 - Manual) and activate dragging by using the *Drag* method for the object. If, say, an object is named txtMost, you would use the *txtMost.Drag vbBeginDrag* command in the *MouseDown* event to turn dragging on and use the *txtMost.Drag vbEndDrag* command in the *MouseUp* event to turn dragging off. The main reason for using manual dragging instead of automatic dragging is that automatic dragging blocks an object from receiving any other mouse events.

The *DragDrop* and *DragOver* events are sent to the object over which the mouse pointer sits. These events need a way to identify the object that's being dragged. They do so by using an argument of type *Control*. A type *Control* variable can be set to any control, and you can use the variable in combination with the control's properties and methods.

A *Control* variable is a special example of an object variable, that is, a variable whose value is an object. Object variables can be specific. For instance, there's a specific type for each kind of control. Thus a type *Label* variable can be assigned a label control, and a type *Image* variable can be assigned an image control. Visual Basic also has some generic object types. A *Form* type variable can be assigned any form, a *Control* variable can be assigned any control, and an *Object* variable can be assigned any object, including forms and controls.

A collection is a type of object that can contain other objects or data items. Visual Basic creates some collections automatically. For instance, the collection called *Controls* contains all the controls on your form. A collection is similar to an array in that it gives you a way to treat a group of items as an entity. You can use the *For Each In* statement to access each element of a collection in turn.

Objects are central to Visual Basic. The term "class" refers to the abstract description of an object, and objects are concrete instantiations of a class. The class is the mold, objects are the results of using the mold.

The Object Browser gives you a quick way to inspect a project, seeing what objects, methods, and events it uses, and offering a way to navigate around large projects. It also lets you browse through libraries of objects that you can use.

QUIZ 13

1. What are the arguments to the *DragDrop* event, and what do they represent?

2. What are the arguments to the *DragOver* event, and what do they represent?

3. How do you enable automatic dragging?

4. How do you enable manual dragging?

5. Why would you use manual dragging when automatic dragging is so much simpler?

6. Suppose you want a control to move when you drag it, what must you do?

7. Suppose you have this declaration:

```
Dim Quiz As Control
```

Explain why each of the following is valid or invalid (assume that the various controls and forms exist):

```
Quiz = txtRitter
Set Quiz = cmdCenter
Set Quiz = Form1
Set Quiz = 99
```

8. Indicate whether each of the following variables can be set to a text box:

```
Dim Plip As Control
Dim Glip as Object
Dim Dlip as Form
Dim Mlip as TextBox
Dim Vlip as ListBox
```

TRY IT YOURSELF

1. Modify the Painter Mouse 2 project so that you can draw with a continuous line by pressing the left mouse button, or with points marking each *MouseMove* event by pressing the right mouse button. Also add a label control below the painting area that displays the current mouse coordinates relative to the picture box.

2. Modify the Collections project so that you can modify the contents of the text box while the program is running, but still retain the ability to drag the control.

3. Create a form with many objects on it, including a list box that lists the names of all the other controls on the form. Use the *For Each In* statement to set up the list.

LESSON 14 A WAY WITH WORDS

Visual Basic has a way with words. It can accept text input, it can manipulate text, and it can display and print text. You've seen many of these features already. For instance, you've used list boxes and text boxes for text input; you've used text boxes, labels, and the *Print* method for text output; you've used *Str* to convert numbers to strings; you've used & to combine strings; you've used font properties as well as properties like Alignment, ForeColor, and MultiLine to control the appearance of text; and you've used cut and paste methods with text selections—quite a lot! But there's more. In this lesson, you'll learn about the following:

- **Using the combo box for input**
- **Using Format to format the appearance of text**
- **Accessing information about the fonts installed on your system with the FontCount and Fonts properties**
- **Using the Print method**
- **Using the Format function**
- **Using the PrintForm method for printing on paper**
- **Using the Printer object for printing on paper**

HAVE IT YOUR WAY—THE COMBO BOX CONTROL

You remember the list box control—it shows you a list of items from which you can make a choice. That's nice, but it limits you to the choices in the list. The *combo box* control shows a list, too, but expands your options by also letting you type in your own choice. The default combo box has three parts (see Figure L14-1): an edit box, a down arrow, and a *drop list*. The drop list appears when you click on the down arrow and disappears when you make a selection from the list. The selection you make appears in the *edit box*. The edit box is like a small text box. If you select the contents of the box, you can replace them with your own typed input. So if you wondered why it's called a combo box, that's why—it combines features of a list box with features of a text box.

To see how combo boxes work, let's modify the Quick Author project from Lesson 3 to use combo boxes instead of list boxes. Now that you know about control arrays, it also makes sense to replace the three separate list boxes with a control array of three combo boxes. The easiest way to make the change is to open the original project, use Save As to make a copy of the project and its file, and to make a few modifications. For instance, on the form, delete the three list boxes and create a control array of three combo boxes using the name cboHelp.

Figure L14-1 The combo box control

(Use the same name for all three controls, and assign them Index properties of 0, 1, and 2.) Then, in the *Form_Load* procedure, replace lstAdjective with cboHelp(0), lstNoun with cboHelp(1), and lstVerb with cboHelp(2). You can use Copy and Paste to speed up the change, or use the Replace choice from the Edit menu. The result should look like this (comments added):

```
Private Sub Form_Load()
    ' Initialize the three combo box lists.
    cboHelp(0).AddItem "dweebish"
    cboHelp(0).AddItem "addled"
    cboHelp(0).AddItem "clamorous"
    cboHelp(0).AddItem "baleful"
    cboHelp(0).AddItem "execrable"
    cboHelp(1).AddItem "poet"
    cboHelp(1).AddItem "programmer"
    cboHelp(1).AddItem "politician"
    cboHelp(1).AddItem "prince"
    cboHelp(1).AddItem "pogoist"
    cboHelp(2).AddItem "sings"
    cboHelp(2).AddItem "waddles"
    cboHelp(2).AddItem "pirouettes"
    cboHelp(2).AddItem "flirts"
    cboHelp(2).AddItem "astounds"
    ' Have each combo box select the first item in the list.
    cboHelp(0).ListIndex = 0
    cboHelp(1).ListIndex = 0
    cboHelp(2).ListIndex = 0
    lblSentence_Click
End Sub
```

Using an array simplifies some of the code. First, you can replace

```
Private Sub lstAdjective_Click ()
    lblSentence_Click
End Sub

Private Sub lstNoun_Click ()
    lblSentence_Click
End Sub

Private Sub lstVerb_Click ()
    lblSentence_Click
End Sub
```

with a single event procedure:

```
Private Sub cboHelp_Click(Index As Integer)
    lblSentence_Click
End Sub
```

The *lblSentence_Click* event, you may recall, contains the code that writes the tremendous prose that appears in the lblSentence label.

Next, you can replace this

```
Private Sub lblSentence_Click ()
    lblSentence.Caption = "The " & lstAdjective.Text & " "
    lblSentence.Caption = lblSentence.Caption & lstNoun.Text & " "
    lblSentence.Caption = lblSentence.Caption & lstVerb.Text & "!"
End Sub
```

with the following:

```
Private Sub lblSentence_Click()
     Dim I As Integer
     lblSentence.Caption = "The"
     For I = 0 To 2
          lblSentence.Caption = lblSentence.Caption & " " &
cboHelp(I).Text
     Next I
     lblSentence.Caption = lblSentence.Caption & "!"
End Sub
```

Well, perhaps using a loop doesn't look that much simpler in this case, but it would be a big improvement if you'd had, say, ten words to combine.

These changes provide the code support for replacing the original list boxes with combo boxes. If you run the program at this point, you'll find that it works pretty much as before, except the combo box features a drop-down list. That is, you just see a single entry in the selection box until you click on the down arrow. Then the complete list drops down, and you can select from the rest of the list. See Figure L14-2, which shows two combo boxes in the initial state and one in the drop-down state. Once you select an item in the drop-down list, the choice appears in the edit box, and the drop-down list disappears.

Making Your Choice

Now let's see how you can enter your choice. Click on one of the boxes. That gives it the focus and highlights the choice showing in the selection box. Then type in a word of your choice. It replaces the former selection. However, the sentence displayed below the combo boxes doesn't change until you open another combo box drop list and click on a choice there. The reason for this is that Quick Author uses the Click event to trigger rewriting the sentence, and clicking on a list choice triggers that event. To have a change in the edit box take place immediately, take advantage of the fact that a combo box, like a text box, rec-

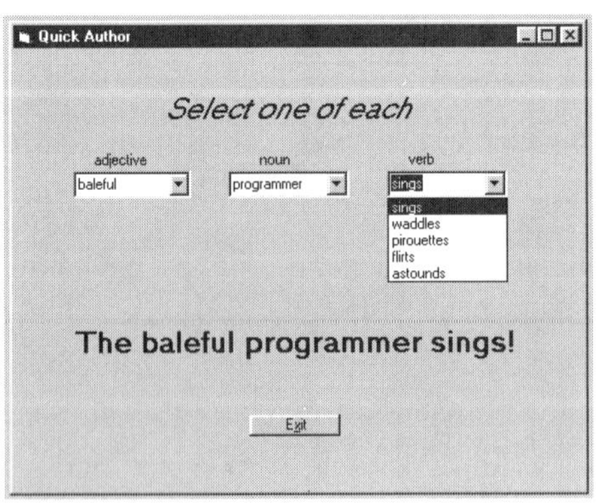

Figure L14-2 Combo boxes

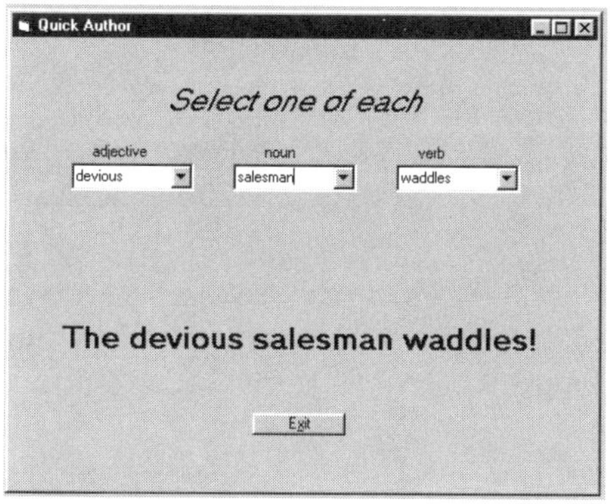

Figure L14-3 The Change event at work

ognizes the Change event. Changing anything in the combo box setting box triggers the Change event, so to rewrite the sentence immediately, add this code:

```
Private Sub cboHelp_Change(Index As Integer)
    lblSentence_Click    ' Send a click event.
End Sub
```

With this code in place, Visual Basic updates the output sentence immediately as you type in a new word (see Figure L14-3).

Tip

Use the *Click* event for a combo box to register selecting an item from the combo box list, and use the *Change* event to register changes made in the combo box edit box.

Some Combo Box Features

The list box and the combo box both have a Text property. For a list box, the Text property is initialized to an empty string (""), and it gets set to whichever item in the list is currently selected. You won't find Text in the Properties window for a list box because, to the user, it is a read-only value. You can change the value of Text by changing the selection, but you can't alter Text directly. For instance, for a list the following simply isn't allowed:

```
lstGroceries.Text = "sourdough bread"    ' not allowed
```

For the default combo box, however, Text is both read and write. The value of Text shows in the edit box, so if you alter the contents of the edit box, you alter the Text property. Also, Text shows up in the Properties window for a combo box. By default, it's set to the Name property. For instance, you may have noticed that in design mode, all three combo boxes displayed the word "cboHelp". If you set the Text property to some other value, that's what shows in design mode.

When you ran the program, however, each combo box showed the first item in its list. That's because the code

```
' Have each combo box select the first item in the list.
    cboHelp(0).ListIndex = 0
    cboHelp(1).ListIndex = 0
    cboHelp(2).ListIndex = 0
```

selects the first item in each list (ListIndex is the index of the selected item), and Text represents the selection. If you omit this code, each combo box will start up showing the text that appears in the Properties window for the Text property.

Note

The Text property for a combo box represents the currently selected text, and it corresponds to the text displayed in the edit box.

If you scan the Properties window for a combo box, you'll spot a property called Style. This property has three possible settings:

- 0 - Dropdown Combo
- 1 - Simple Combo
- 2 - Dropdown List

The Dropdown Combo style is the default, and it's the one that's been discussed. The Simple Combo replaces the drop-down list with a regular list. In design time, you size the combo box. During run time, Visual Basic uses that area to display the list. If the list is too long to fit in the box, Visual Basic adds a vertical scrollbar. Thus the Dropdown Combo displays the list only when you click on the arrow, while the Simple Combo displays the list at all times. On the other hand, when you display a drop list, Visual Basic shows the whole list, while the Simple Combo restricts the display area to the area you sketched out in design mode. Finally, the Dropdown List is similar to the Dropdown Combo, except that you can't edit the choices. So the Dropdown List functions like a regular list box, except that it saves space by not showing the list unless you click on the down arrow. A Dropdown Combo and a Dropdown List look alike. However, clicking in a Dropdown Combo text box selects the text, while clicking in a Dropdown List box causes the rest of the list to drop down.

Since Quick Author has three combo boxes, try setting one to each style. Figure L14-4 shows the result. To show the full contents of the Simple Combo, you have to resize the control in design mode first.

A VISIT TO FONT LAND

Have you added fonts to your Windows system? If you are a tinkerer, it's hard to resist the temptation. There are many inexpensive font packages out there,

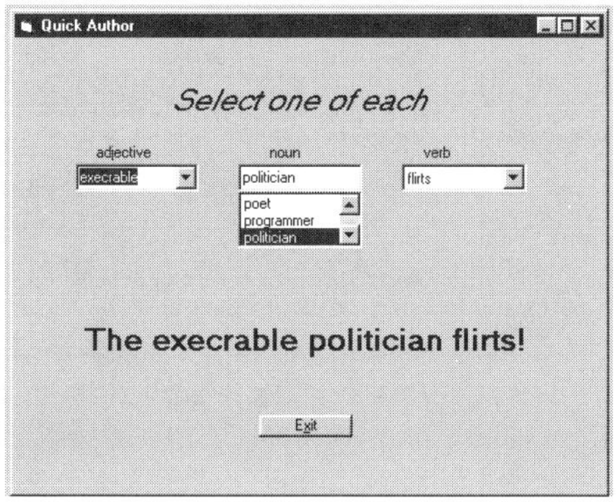

Figure L14-4 Three styles of combo boxes

and several products toss in a free font or two. You've already seen how you can use the Font object property and dialog box to set font properties in your projects. Visual Basic has a couple of other properties named Fonts and FontCount that let you investigate the full range of your fonts. Before going into that, however, let's take a brief look at fonts in general.

Screen Fonts, Printer Fonts, and Type Technology

Windows recognizes two categories of fonts—*screen* fonts and *printer* fonts. Screen fonts are used to display text on your screen, and printer fonts are used by your printer. Why two different fonts? One reason is that the two are displayed at different resolutions. Screen fonts typically are displayed at around 50–100 dots per inch, while laser printer fonts usually are around 300 or 600 dots per inch. Normally, you'll have matched sets. That is, if you have a screen Courier font, you'll also have a printer Courier font, and the screen font will match the printer font as closely as the different resolutions allow. Suppose, however, that a printer has some built-in fonts and that you don't install the corresponding screen fonts on your computer. Then you'll have fonts that you can print but which you can't display properly onscreen.

There are a couple of technologies that simplify the font situation. For example, TrueType technology uses *scaleable* fonts, fonts described by sets of mathematical curves. TrueType technology then generates both screen fonts and printer fonts from the same master plan. That way you get an automatic pairing of screen fonts and printer fonts. Also, the scaling feature means that the fonts can be generated in any size. (The older technology of bitmapped fonts required a separate data file for each font size.) Support for TrueType is built into Windows. Postscript fonts offer a similar technology. Windows doesn't fully support Postscript fonts directly, but font-managing programs like Adobe Type Manager (ATM) generate screen and printer fonts as needed from Postscript font files.

What Fonts Do You Have?

How many fonts do you have? The FontCount property reveals the answer. You can use this property with two objects, the Screen object and the Printer object. The Screen object (see Lesson 8) represents your display, and the expression Screen.FontCount is the number of screen fonts installed on your system. The Printer object, as you might expect, represents your printer. If you have more than one printer, the Printer object, by default, represents your default printer. And Printer.FontCount represents the number of printer fonts installed.

What are your fonts called? The Screen and Printer objects each have a Fonts property. Basically, it's an array, with an index running from 0 to FontCount −1. So *Screen.Fonts(0)* is the name of the first screen font, *Screen.Fonts(1)* is the name of the second screen font, and so on.

You can use these properties to create a project that counts your fonts, places them in a list box, and lets you display a selected font in the size of your choice. First, create a form with a list box, a combo box, four label controls, and a text box as shown in Figure L14-5 and described in Table L14-1. Note that Label3 is a blank label immediately to the right of Label2. The list box is for displaying the font names, and the combo box is for displaying the font size. Using a list box for the names makes sense, for there's no point to typing in a font name not in the list. Using a combo box for the font size also makes sense, for you may want to enter an unlisted size—the choice for size is open-ended, at least for scaleable fonts.

OBJECT	PROPERTY	SETTING
Form1	Caption	Font Show
	Name	frmFonts
Command1	Caption	List Fonts
	Name	cmdFonts
List1	Name	lstFonts
Combo1	Name	cboSize
Label1	Caption	Font Size
	Name	lblSize
Label2	Caption	Font index =
	Name	lblIndexIs
Label3	Caption	
	Name	lblIndex
Label4	Caption	Number of fonts =
	Name	lblCount
Text1	MultiLine	True
	Name	txtFonts
	Text	Just look at this font!

Table L14-1 Properties for the Font Show program

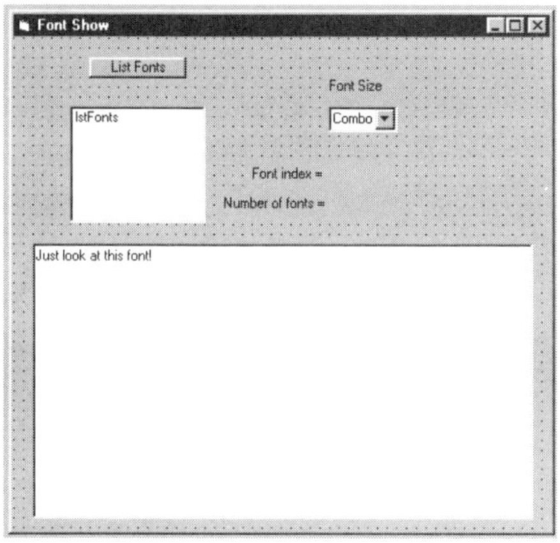

Figure L14-5 Font Show project (design mode)

Next comes the code. If you have a lot of fonts, filling the list can take awhile. For that reason, this program uses a command button instead of the *Form_Load* event to set up the list. That way, you don't have to wait for the list to fill before seeing the form. Here's the code for the button. The last statement in the procedure uses the *Str* function to convert the number of fonts to a string. It also uses the & operator to add the result to the initial caption, which is the string "Number of fonts =". (Remember, Str prefaces positive numbers with a space.)

```
Private Sub cmdFonts_Click()
    Dim I
    For I = 0 To Screen.FontCount - 1      ' Take each font in turn
        lstFonts.AddItem Screen.Fonts(I)   ' and add its name to the list.
    Next I
    lstFonts.ListIndex = 0                 ' Select the first font in the
                                           ' list.
    lblCount.Caption = lblCount.Caption & Str(Screen.FontCount)
End Sub
```

Clicking on a list entry should display the index number for the selected font and set the text box contents to that font. The following *Click* event takes care of these tasks:

```
Private Sub lstFonts_Click()
    txtFonts.Font.Name = lstFonts.Text     ' Set text box font.
    lblIndex.Caption = lstFonts.ListIndex ' Display font index.
End Sub
```

Next, let's turn to the font size. The following *Form_Load* event places a few common font sizes in the combo box list and sets the edit box to the first entry:

```
Private Sub Form_Load()
    cboSize.AddItem 8
    cboSize.AddItem 10
    cboSize.AddItem 12
    cboSize.AddItem 18
```

continued on next page

continued from previous page

```
    cboSize.AddItem 24
    cboSize.AddItem 36
    cboSize.ListIndex = 0
End Sub
```

Don't forget that you use the *Click* event to register a combo box choice made by selecting a list item, and that you use the *Change* event to register changes made by altering the text in the edit box. So, to register a choice made by clicking on a combo box list selection, use the *Click* event:

```
Private Sub cboSize_Click()
    txtFonts.Font.Size = cboSize.Text
End Sub
```

Here Visual Basic automatically converts *cboSize.Text,* which is a number in string form, to a numeric value.

To register a choice made by modifying the text in the edit box, use the *Change* event:

```
Private Sub cboSize_Change()
    If IsNumeric(cboSize.Text) Then
        txtFonts.Font.Size = cboSize.Text    End If
End Sub
```

The *If* statement offers a bit of protection. The *IsNumeric* function is a *Boolean* function that returns True if its argument is a number, a string that can be converted to a number, or a *Variant* that can be converted to a number. If you omit this check, you'll have problems when someone clears the box (the text property becomes the empty string) or enters something like "Tiny".

Tip

Use *IsNumeric* to screen text input that is intended to be used as a number.

That's all it takes. Figure L14-6 shows the project in run mode.

Figure L14-6 Font Show in run mode

USING THE *PRINT* METHOD

You can use the *Print* method with forms, with picture boxes, and (something you'll see later in this lesson) with the Printer object. Normally the *Print* method takes one argument, which can be text or numeric, and prints it on one line. For example, the commands

```
Dim Days as Integer
Days = 232
Print "There are"
Print Days
Print "shopping days until Valentine's Day."
```

display the following text on a form:

```
There are
232
shopping days until Valentine's Day.
```

You can, however, display different elements on the same line. One way is to build up a single string from different parts, using *Str* to convert numbers to strings and using *&* to combine strings. For instance, the command

```
Print "There are" & Str(Days) & " shopping days until Valentine's Day."
```

displays the following output:

```
There are 232 shopping days until Valentine's Day.
```

(Don't forget that *Str* adds a space in front of the number, a space that's replaced with a "–" if the number is negative.)

Actually, you don't need to use *Str* to concatenate a number with a string if you use & to concatenate, but you do need it if you use + to concatenate. The reason is that + does double duty as a concatenation operator and an addition operator. So an expression like *"845" + 9* could be interpreted as *convert "845" to a number and add*, or as *convert 9 to a string and concatenate.* In the face of such possible confusion, Visual Basic doesn't allow the expression. But *&* only means concatenate, so *"845" & 9* can only mean to convert 9 to a string and concatenate. You could use the following:

```
Print "There are " & Days & " shopping days until Valentine's Day."
```

The *Print* method itself has two ways of combining information. One is to separate items by semicolons, and the other is to separate them by commas:

```
Print "See"; "Spot"; "run!"
Print "See", "Spot", "run!"
```

Using a semicolon works much the same as using an *&* to join strings, running the elements together. Using a comma, however, causes each section to begin at the next *print zone:*

```
SeeSpotRun!
See             Spot            Run!
```

Print Zones, *Tab*, and *Spc*

What's a print zone? Back in DOS days, computers used simple fonts for which each character took up the same width on the screen. (The Courier font, for example, has that property.) Then you could divide text output into evenly spaced columns. For instance, EGA and VGA monitors normally display 80 characters per line, and you can divide the output line into 80 equal columns, numbering them from 1 through 80. In those days, Visual Basic's ancestors defined a print zone as beginning every 14 columns. The first print zone began at column 1, the second at column 15, the third at column 29, and so on. The statement

```
Print "See", "Spot"
```

would cause the program to proceed from the end of the word *See* to the first open print zone, which would be column 15. If the first phrase extended past column 15, then the next phrase would start at the next open print zone. For instance, the command

```
Print "See the handsome dog", "Spot"
```

would cause *Spot* to be printed starting at column 29.

Most Windows fonts, however, are *proportional fonts,* which means that a slim letter like *l* occupies less width than a fatty like *m*. Here the concept of column is not well-defined. What Visual Basic does is define a column width as the *average width for a character of the current font and current font size*. So the placement of the print zone changes with different fonts and different font sizes.

> **Note**
>
> With nonproportional fonts (called *monospaced* fonts), the number of characters needed to fill a print zone is 14, the width of a print zone. With proportional fonts, the number of characters that fill a print zone is not necessarily equal to the width of the print zone. It can be more or less than 14, depending on the characters used.

If you're not happy with the default print zones, you can use the *Tab* function to position the next output in the column of your choice. For example, the command

```
Print Tab(10); "Fritz"; Tab(20), "Fitz"
```

displays *Fritz* starting at column 10 and *Fitz* starting at column 20. As with the print zones, the column placement depends on the font and on the font size.

Similarly, the *Spc* function skips the indicated number of spaces. For example, the command

```
Print "Fritz"; Spc(20), "Fitz"
```

Figure L14-7 The Printing on a Form form

skips 20 spaces after *Fritz* before printing *Fitz*. As with Tab, each space is equal to the average character width for the current font selection.

Let's look at a project that illustrates some of these points. Open a new project, giving it two command buttons and a menu. (It's been a while since we've used a menu, so it's time to get a little practice.) Figure L14-7 shows the arrangement of controls, and Tables L14-2 and L14-3 describe the project and menu. If you don't have the Arial font, substitute another scaleable font, if you have one.

OBJECT	PROPERTY	SETTING
Form1	Caption	Printing on a Form
	Name	frmPF
Command1	Caption	Show Text
	Name	cmdShow
Command2	Caption	Clear Text
	Name	cmdClear

Table L14-2 Properties for the Printing on a Form program

LIST BOX ENTRY	CAPTION	NAME
Font Name	Font Name	*mnuFontName*
....Arial	&Arial	*mnuFontNameArial*
....MS Sans Serif	MS Sans Serif	*mnuFontNameMS*
Font Size	Font Size	*mnuFontSize*
....8	8	*mnuFontSize8*
....12	12	*mnuFontSize12*

Table L14-3 Initial menu entries for the Printing on a Form program

Next, let's add some code illustrating the use of semicolons, commas, and the *Tab* function. Listing L14-1 shows what you should add.

Listing L14-1
The Printing on a Form program

```
Option Explicit

Private Sub cmdClear_Click()
    frmPF.Cls
End Sub

Private Sub cmdShow_Click()
    Print "Sue Mi"; "Cataloger", "22"
    Print "Joe King", "Logger", 28
    Print "Stella Katt", "Catastrophysicist", 43
    Print "Sue Mi"; "Cataloger"; "22"
    Print "Joe King"; "Logger"; 28
    Print "Stella Katt"; "Catastrophysicist"; 43
    Print "Sue Mi", Tab(14), "Cataloger", Tab(28), 22
    Print "Joe King", Tab(14), "Logger", Tab(28), 28
    Print "Stella Katt", Tab(14), "Catastrophysicist", Tab(28), 43
    Print "Sue Mi"; Tab(14); "Cataloger"; Tab(28); 22
    Print "Joe King"; Tab(14); "Logger"; Tab(28); 28
    Print "Stella Katt"; Tab(14); "Catastrophysicist"; Tab(28); 43
End Sub

Private Sub mnuFontNameArial_Click()
    frmPF.Font.Name = "Arial"
    mnuFontNameArial.Checked = True
    mnuFontNameMS.Checked = False
    End Sub

Private Sub mnuFontNameMS_Click()
    frmPF.Font.Name = "MS Sans Serif"
    mnuFontNameMS.Checked = True
    mnuFontNameArial.Checked = False
End Sub

Private Sub mnuFontSize12_Click()
    frmPF.Font.Size = 12
    mnuFontSize12.Checked = True
    mnuFontSize8.Checked = False
End Sub


Private Sub mnuFontSize8_Click()
    frmPF.Font.Size = 8
    mnuFontSize8.Checked = True
    mnuFontSize12.Checked = False
End Sub
```

Figure L14-8 shows the output with the startup settings, and Figure L14-9 shows the output using Arial and a font size of 12.

Looking at the output, you can see how the position of the print zones changes with the font size selection. Also notice that following a *Tab* with a comma causes the next bit of output to appear at the designated column but on the next line. Yet a *Tab* followed by a semicolon normally stays on the same line. However, note that if the designated column lies inside text that's already been

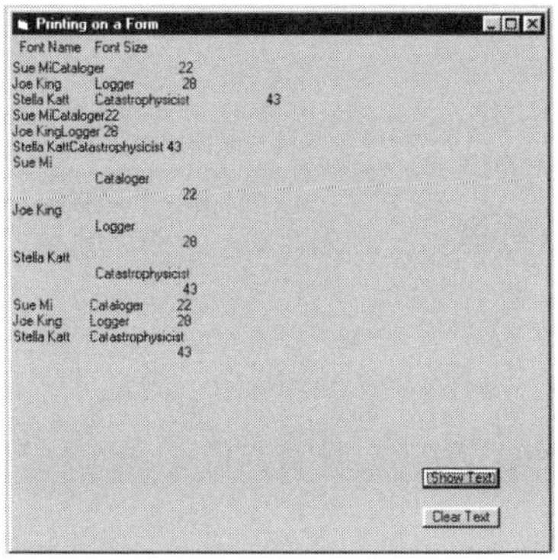

Figure L14-8 Output with MS Sans Serif and a font size of 8

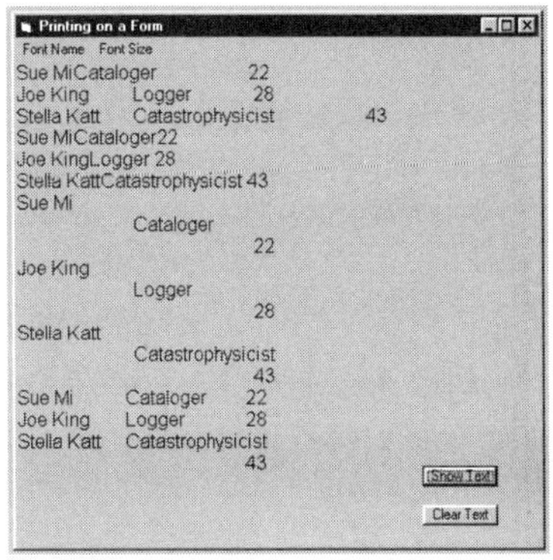

Figure L14-9 Output with Arial and a font size of 12

displayed, even the *Tab(28);* combination goes to the next line, as it did for the following command:

```
Print "Stella Katt"; Tab(14); "Catastrophysicist"; Tab(28); 43
```

(Whether a catastrophysicist is a cat specializing in astrophysics or a physicist specializing in catastrophies, we leave to the reader.)

Another thing to note is the difference between how Print handles a number versus a string. The combination *"Cataloger"; "22"* prints as *Cataloger22,* for Visual Basic joins strings. But *"Logger"; 28* prints as *Logger 28* because Visual Basic adds a space in front of positive numbers.

One other interesting feature you may wish to try is that a comma or semicolon at the end of the line causes the next *Print* command to continue on the same line. That is,

```
Print "Big",
Print "Dog"
```

is the same as

```
Print "Big", "Dog
```

A similar situation holds for a terminal semicolon.

Positioning Text

The *Print* method shares much in common with the graphics methods. For instance, the *Print* method prints on the same layer (the back layer, by default) that the graphics methods draw on. Also, if you use *Print* in places other than the *Paint* event, you can use the AutoRedraw property to cause newly uncovered text to be refreshed. Finally, a *Print* statement starts printing at the position given by the CurrentX and CurrentY properties. Those coordinates locate the

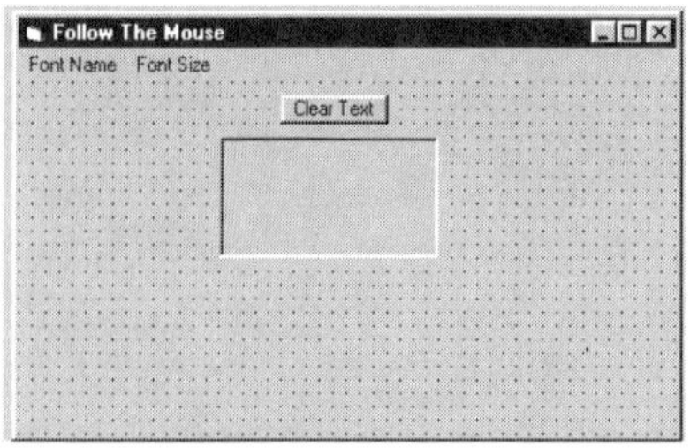

Figure L14-10 The Follow The Mouse form

upper-left corner of the block containing the text. The next example explores these properties. Create a form with a menu (the same menu as the last example), a picture frame, and a command button as shown in Figure L14-10 and described in Tables L14-4 and L14-5.

OBJECT	PROPERTY	SETTING
Form1	AutoRedraw	True
	Caption	Follow The Mouse
	Name	frmFM
Command1	Caption	Clear Text
	Name	cmdClear
rPicture1	AutoRedraw	True
	Name	picPrint

Table L14-4 Properties for the Follow The Mouse program

LIST BOX ENTRY	CAPTION	NAME
Font Name	Font Name	*mnuFontName*
....Arial	&Arial	*mnuFontNameArial*
....MS Sans Serif	MS Sans Serif	*mnuFontNameMS*
Font Size	Font Size	*mnuFontSize*
....8	8	*mnuFontSize8*
....12	12	*mnuFontSize12*

Table L14-5 Initial menu entries for the Printing on a Form program

This project has the following goals:

1. Clicking on the form causes the coordinates of the mouse to be displayed at the point at which the mouse is clicked.
2. Clicking in the picture box causes text to appear centered in the picture box.
3. The picture box can be dragged.

The first goal is simple to achieve. Just use the *MouseDown* event:

```
Private Sub Form_MouseDown(Button As Integer, Shift As Integer, _
    X As Single, Y As Single)
    CurrentX = X
    CurrentY = Y
    Print Str(X) & "," & Str(Y)
End Sub
```

This sets the current position to the mouse position, so printing will occur at that location. And why use the *MouseDown* event instead of the *Click* event? If you answer, "Because the *Click* event doesn't provide the *X* and *Y* values," you've earned the right to feel smug.

The second goal is made easier by two functions, *TextWidth* and *TextHeight*. *TextWidth* takes a string as an argument and returns its width in the current scale. Similarly, *TextHeight* returns the height of the string. To center the string "I'm centered!" in the picture box, you can do this:

```
Dim Msg As String
Msg = "I'm centered!"
picPrint.CurrentX = (picPrint.ScaleWidth - TextWidth(Msg)) / 2
picPrint.CurrentY = (picPrint.ScaleHeight - TextHeight(Msg)) / 2
picPrint.Print Msg
```

The expression *picPrint.ScaleWidth - TextWidth(Msg)* equals the width of the portion of the picture box not used by text, so dividing that value by 2 gives you the value of the left (or right) margin.

Finally, let's go to the third goal. As you learned in Lesson 13, if you want a control to be draggable and still be able to receive other mouse events, you have to use manual dragging. For example, use the *MouseDown* event for the picture box to display a centered string, and then turn dragging on. Use this code:

```
Private Sub Form_DragDrop(Source As Control, X As Single, Y As Single)
    picPrint.Move X, Y
End Sub

Private Sub picPrint_MouseDown(Button As Integer, Shift As Integer, _
    X As Single, Y As Single)
    Dim Msg As String
    Msg = "I'm centered!"
    picPrint.CurrentX = (picPrint.ScaleWidth - TextWidth(Msg)) / 2
    picPrint.CurrentY = (picPrint.ScaleHeight - TextHeight(Msg)) / 2
    picPrint.Print Msg
    picPrint.Drag vbBeginDrag
End Sub

Private Sub picPrint_MouseUp(Button As Integer, Shift As Integer, _
    X As Single, Y As Single)
    picPrint.Drag vbEndDrag
End Sub
```

For the menus and the command button, use the same code as in the last example.

Now try the program. You'll note that as you drag the picture box, you can cover and uncover text on the form. Setting the form's AutoRedraw property to True is

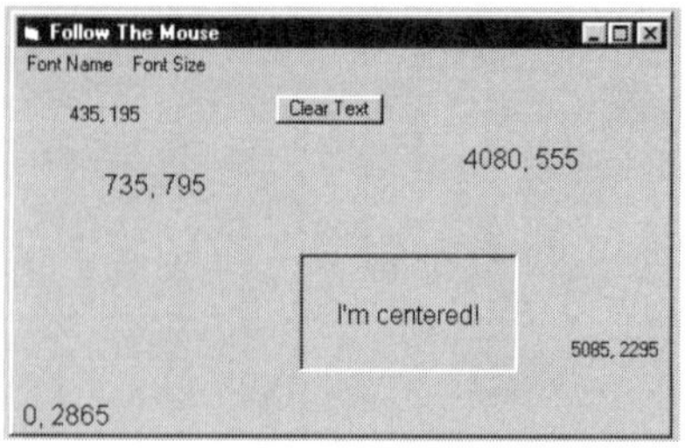

Figure L14-11 Follow The Mouse results

what allows uncovered text to be restored. Also, if you drag the picture box so that it's mostly outside the form, then extend the form to include the picture box, any text in the picture box is restored. That's because the AutoRedraw property for the picture box is true. Figure L14-11 shows a sample running of the program.

FORMATTING TEXT

Perhaps you want more options about how text is displayed. The versatile *Format* function gives you additional control over the appearance of text output. In its simplest form, Format has this syntax:

Format(*expression*)

If the *expression* part is a string, *Format* returns the string. If the expression part is a number, *Format* returns a string representing the number, much as *Str* does. The difference is that *Str* adds a space if the number doesn't have a minus sign, while *Format* does not. That is,

```
Print "I have";Str(5); " left."
```

displays

```
I have 5 left.
```

while

```
Print "I have";Format(5); " left."
```

displays

```
I have5 left.
```

The expression part can be things you can't print directly. For instance, Visual Basic has a *Date* function that returns the current date according to the computer's system clock. A date has different parts, such as the day, the month, and the year, and Visual Basic places it in a data form more complex than a number or a string. As a result, attempting to print a date directly doesn't work. The statement

```
Print Date  ' runtime error
```

leads to a runtime error because *Print* doesn't recognize the type of data used by *Date*. But *Format* does, so you can do the following:

```
Print Format(Date)  ' works
```

The output looks like this:

```
6/21/96
```

The same sort of situation holds for the *Time* function. It returns the time in a form that flusters *Print* but which can be tamed by format:

```
Print Format(Time)  ' works
```

The output looks like this:

```
9:24:51 AM
```

Actually, you can format the date and time several ways if you use the next simplest syntax for *Format:*

Format(*expression, format*)

Here *format* is a string describing the particular format to use. It can be a standard format provided by Visual Basic, or it can be a format you define. Table L14-6 lists the standard date formats you can use. In Windows 95, you select the system date and time formats by clicking on the Regional Setting icon in the Control Panel.

FORMAT EXPRESSION	MEANING	EXAMPLE
"General Date"	Display a date or time using your system settings	5/27/96 and 8:34:19 PM
"Long Date"	Display a date or time using your system	Monday, May 27, 1996
"Medium Date"	Display a date using the medium date format suitable to the language version of the host application (e.g., an Excel application using Visual Basic for Applications)	27-May-96
"Short Date"	Display a date in your system's short date format	5/27/96
"Long Time"	Display a time using your system's long time format	8:34:19 PM
"Medium Time"	Display a time in a 12-hour format	08:34 PM
"Short Time"	Display a time in a 24-hour format	20:34

Table L14-6 Predefined time and date formats

For example, to display a date using the long format, do this:

```
Print Format (Date, "Long Date")
```

To create your own format, concoct a string following the guidelines provided in Visual Basic Help under the User Defined Date/Time Formats heading. Table L14-7 lists some of the more common choices.

NOTATION	MEANING
:	Time separator, typically a :, but the exact characters used depend upon your system settings
/	Date separator, typically a /, but the exact characters used depend upon your system settings
d	Display day without a leading 0, as in 6
dd	Display day with a leading 0, as in 06
ddd	Display day as an abbreviation, as in Sat
dddd	Display day as a full word, as in Saturday
m	Display month as a number without a leading 0, as in 4
mm	Display month as a number with a leading 0, as in 04
mmm	Display month as an abbreviation, as in Mar
mmmm	Display month as a full name, as in March
yy	Display year as a two-digit number, as in 96
yyyy	Display year as a four-digit number, as in 1996
h	Display hour without a leading zero, as in 9
hh	Display hour with a leading zero, as in 09
m	Display minute without a leading 0, as in 5
mm	Display minute with a leading 0, as in 05
s	Display second without a leading 0, as in 5
ss	Display second with a leading 0, as in 05
AM/PM	Use 12-hour clock with uppercase AM and PM
am/pm	Use 12-hour clock with lowercase am and pm

Table L14-7 Some date and time format codes

How do you use these codes? You create a string including the codes and use it for the format argument to *Format*. You also can include other characters in the string, and they get used literally. For example, here are some possible date formats along with sample output.

```
Print Format(Date, "mm dd yy"}  07 05 96
Print Format(Date, "mmm d, yyyy")   Jul 5, 1996
Print Format(Date, "dddd, d mmmm yyyy") Friday, 5 July 1996
```

Let's see how *Date*, *Time*, and *Format* can be used in an application. We'll create a form that displays the date and time in a picture box. You can use option buttons in a frame to select from several display formats. Figure L14-12 shows the program in operation, and Table L14-8 shows the project properties.

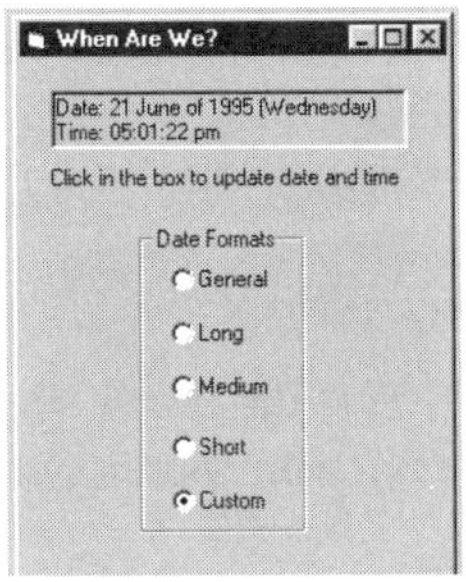

Figure L14-12 When Are We?

OBJECT	PROPERTY	SETTING
Form1	AutoRedraw	True
	Caption	When Are We?
	Name	frmDate
Picture1	AutoRedraw	True
	Name	picDate
Label1	Caption	Click in the box to update date and time
	Name	lblDate
Frame1	Caption	Date Formats
	Name	fraDate
Option1	Caption	General
	Index	0
	Name	optDate
Option2	Caption	Long
	Index	1
	Name	optDate
Option3	Caption	Medium
	Index	2
	Name	optDate
Option4	Caption	Short
	Index	3
	Name	optDate
Option5	Caption	Custom
	Index	4
	Name	optDate

Table L14-8 Properties for the When Are We? program

This is a good opportunity to review event management. This project displays the time and date. One question is, when should the information be displayed? The following list seems reasonable:

- When the program first starts
- Whenever the user wants to update the time
- Whenever the user changes the format
- Whenever the information gets concealed, then uncovered

You can meet the first goal a couple of ways. One is to place the code in the *Paint* event for the picture box. That also takes care of the redrawing aspect, providing you're careful. Here's the uncareful way:

```
Private Sub picDate_Paint()
' uncareful way
    picDate.Print "Date: " & Format(Date)
    picDate.Print "Time: " & Format(Time)
End Sub
```

This works fine when you start the program, but if you cover, then uncover the text, that triggers this event again, reprinting the information. That sounds fine, but remember that each *Print* command starts a new line, so the next text gets printed below the first two lines, effectively outside the visible portion of the picture box. If the text is redisplayed, it should be displayed at the same location. One fix is to use *Cls* to clear the picture box, resetting the current position to the top left corner:

```
Private Sub picDate_Paint()
'careful way -- resets current position to top left
    picDate.Cls
    picDate.Print "Date: " & Format(Date)
    picDate.Print "Time: " & Format(Time)
End Sub
```

A second way, and the one used here, is to make sure that picDate is the first control in the tabbing order and to use the *GotFocus* event instead of the Paint event to display the text.

```
Private Sub picDate_GotFocus()
    picDate.Print "Date: " & Format(Date)
    picDate.Print "Time: " & Format(Time)
End Sub
```

Then, to ensure redrawing, set AutoRedraw for the picDate control to True. This time you don't have to worry about repositioning the current position. That's because AutoRedraw doesn't reexecute the *Print* commands. Instead, it restores a bitmapped image from a saved copy.

Next, a simple way to let the user update the display on demand is to use the *Click* event for the picture box. That means the *Click* event will need to know which format choice has been selected. That's most easily accomplished by using module-level variables. So we can do the following:

```
Option Explicit
Dim DateFormat As String
Dim TimeFormat As String
```

```
Private Sub Form_Initialize()
    DateFormat = "General Date"
    TimeFormat = "General Date"
End Sub

Private Sub picDate_Click()
    picDate.Cls
    picDate.Print "Date: " & Format(Date, DateFormat)
    picDate.Print "Time: " & Format(Time, TimeFormat)
End Sub
```

The *Initialize* event is the choice for initializing module-level variables. Again, we use *Cls* so that each new display of data starts at the top left of the picture box.

Finally, the simplest way to have choosing a format also update the display is to use the *optDate_Click* event to select the format and to have that event call the *picDate_Click* event to redraw the display. The *optDate_Click* event, by the way, gives you a chance to review using the *Select Case* statement with a control array.

```
Private Sub optDate_Click(Index As Integer)
    Select Case Index
    Case 0
        DateFormat = "General Date"
        TimeFormat = "General Date"
    Case 1
        DateFormat = "Long Date"
        TimeFormat = "Long Time"
    Case 2
        DateFormat = "Medium Date"
        TimeFormat = "Medium Time"
    Case 3
        DateFormat = "Short Date"
        TimeFormat = "Short Time"
    Case 4
        DateFormat = "d mmmm of yyyy (dddd)"
        TimeFormat = "hh:nn:ss am/pm"
    End Select
    picDate_Click   'redraw display
End Sub
```

MORE FORMATTING

You also can use the format expression in a *Format* function to specify how numbers are formatted. For example, the "Standard" format displays numbers using a thousands separator and two places to the right of the decimal. Try the following code, for instance:

```
Print 4/3
Print Format(4/3)
Print Format(4/3, "Standard")
Print Format(40000/3)
Print Format(40000/3, "Standard")
```

You should get the following output:

```
 1.333333
1.333333
1.33
13333.3333333333
13,333.33
```

Note the following points:

- Printing 4/3 without using Format results in a leading space being added.
- Printing 4/3 without using a format argument displays a total of 7 digits; that's consistent with the precision of a type Single value, which is the type Visual Basic converts an Integer value when doing floating-point division.
- Printing 40000/3 without using a format argument displays a total of 14 digits; that's consistent with the precision of a type *Double* value. The reason that Visual Basic switches to type *Double* is that 40000 is bigger than the largest Integer value, so Visual Basic treats 40000 as *Long*, and when Visual Basic does floating-point division with a *Long* value, it converts values to *Double*.
- You can get quite a variation in the appearance of numeric output if you don't format it explicitly.
- Both of the values printed using the Standard format follow the description, using a comma for the thousands separator, if needed, and showing two places to the right of the decimal.

Incidentally, the thousands separator and the decimal marker depend on the Locale setting. The US setting uses a comma and decimal point, but some nations use a period and a decimal comma. Table L14-9 lists some of the more common named formats you have at your command.

FORMAT EXPRESSION	MEANING
"General Number"	Display a number as is, using no thousands separator.
"Currency"	Display a number as a currency, using a thousands separator and two places to the right of the decimal. The exact appearance depends upon the Windows Locale setting; the US setting adds a $ sign.
"Fixed"	Display two figures to the right of decimal.
"Standard"	Display two figures to the right of the decimal and also use a thousands separator
"Percent"	Display the value as a percent, multiplying the original value by 100, showing two places to the right of the decimal, and appending a % sign.

FORMAT EXPRESSION	MEANING
"Scientific"	Use standard scientific notation, as in 1.33E4, meaning 1.33 times 10 to the 4th power.

Table L14-9 Some predefined numeric formats

As with dates and time, you also can produce customized numerical formats. Table L14-10 lists the more common choices. You can use these symbols to construct format strings. For example, the string "0.00" means "always show two digits to the right of the decimal separator and show at least one digit to the left." The string "#,###.##" means "show the decimal separator and the thousands separator, and show two digits to the right of the decimal separator, but don't show trailing zeros." As with date formatting, you also can use regular characters in the string, such as dollar signs. Table L14-11 shows some examples.

FORMAT SYMBOL	MEANING
0	Display a digit, even if it is a leading or trailing 0
#	Display a digit, unless it is a leading or trailing 0
.	Display the decimal separator (environment-dependent)
,	Display the thousands separator (environment-dependent)

Table L14-10 Some numeric format symbols

FORMAT STATEMENT	OUTPUT
Format(2.1, "0.00")	2.10
Format(2.1,"#.##")	2.1
Format(1234.567, "#,###.00")	1,234.57
Format(2.4 , "$#,###.00")	$2.40
Format(2.4 , "$0,000.00")	$0,002.40

Table L14-11 Sample numeric formatting

In Search of the Missing $

If you've worked with previsual versions of Microsoft Basic, you may have used the Format$ function and be wondering what happened to the $ at the end of the function name. Well, Format$ still exists. The difference between Format$ and Format is that Format$ returns its information as a String type, while Format uses the newer Variant type, reflecting Visual Basic's use of the Variant type as a kind of universal catch-all type. Indeed, Visual Basic supports a whole host of new functions that return Variant types along with older String versions. For example, there are Str and Str$, functions that convert numbers to strings. Then there are function pairs that return parts of strings, such as Left and Left$, Mid and Mid$, Trim, and Trim$.

PRINTING

Let's turn to another form of displaying words—printing. You have a couple of choices in Visual Basic. One is using the *PrintForm* method. It prints a bitmapped copy of a form. Since screen resolution is usually in the range of 50–100 dots per inch (dpi), while laser printers typically have a resolution in the range of 300–600 dpi, *PrintForm* doesn't take full advantage of the resolution of many printers.

The second method is constructing an image on the *Printer* object, then printing that image. This method does take full advantage of your printer's resolution, but it only prints material produced by the Print method, by the graphics method, and by the PaintPicture method (to be discussed soon). If, say, you want to use the Printer object to print a form with some option buttons, you have to use the Circle method to draw semblances of the option buttons on the Printer object.

Let's put together a form with some graphics, text, and controls, and see how it prints using the two methods.

Using the *PrintForm* Method

First, create a form with a picture box, some text, some graphics, and a control button. Eventually, the form will look like Figure L14-13. Table L14-12 outlines the properties. The metafile image of a printer is from the BUSINESS subdirectory of the METAFILE subdirectory of the Visual Basic directory. The reason for setting AutoRedraw to True is that the *PrintForm* method doesn't print the output of *Print* and of graphics methods otherwise. (You'll have to admit that's a pretty good reason!)

OBJECT	PROPERTY	SETTING
Form1	AutoRedraw	True
	Caption	To Be Printed
	Name	frmPrinter

Figure L14-13 The To Be Printed form

OBJECT	PROPERTY	SETTING
Picture1	Name	picPrint
	Picture	(Metafile) Printer.wmf
Command1	Caption	Print Me
	Name	cmdPrint

Table L14-12 Properties for the To Be Printed program

The project will use code instead of the Properties window to set several properties, such as the font size and the DrawWidth property. This will make it simpler to convert the project to one using the Printer object, for the Printer object has properties but no entry in the Properties window. The project will use *Print* to display the text "Behold the Printer!" in the middle of the form, and it will use graphics methods to draw concentric ovals and a circle and a boundary box. Listing L14-2 shows the details. About the only new material is found in the *cmdPrint_Click* event, which uses the *PrintForm* method to print a copy of the form.

Tip

Remember that you need to set AutoRedraw to True if you wish to print the output of *Print* and of the graphics methods by using *PrintForm.*

The current position for a circle or ellipse is the center of the circle. Thus, using *Step (0,0)* in the *Circle* commands means each shape is centered on the same point, the point set by using *CurrentX* and *CurrentY* just before the *For Next* loop.

Listing L14-2
The To Be Printed program

```
Option Explicit

Private Sub cmdPrint_Click()
     ' Print the form.
     frmPrinter.PrintForm
End Sub

Private Sub picPrint_GotFocus()
     Dim MyStr As String
     Dim I As Integer
     Dim Radius As Single
     ' Set font and display string.
     Font.Name = "Arial"
     Font.Size = 24
     MyStr = "Behold the Printer!"
     ' Prepare to center string.
     CurrentX = (ScaleWidth - TextWidth(MyStr)) / 2
     CurrentY = (ScaleHeight - TextHeight(MyStr)) / 2
     Print MyStr
     ' Center ovals in the lower half of the form.
```

continued on next page

continued from previous page

```
    CurrentX = ScaleWidth / 2
    CurrentY = 3 * ScaleHeight / 4
    Radius = ScaleWidth / 3
    DrawWidth = 4
    ' Draw 5 concentric ovals centered on current position.
    For I = 1 To 5
       Circle Step(0, 0), Radius, , , , 0.4
        Radius = Radius * 0.8
    Next I
    FillStyle = 0
    ' Draw a solid circle.
    Circle Step(0, 0), 0.4 * Radius
    ' Return to transparent fill.
    FillStyle = 1
    ' Draw an inside border.
    DrawStyle = 6
    Line (0, 0)-(ScaleWidth, ScaleHeight), , B
End Sub
```

Figure L14-13 shows the form itself during run mode, and Figure L14-14 shows the result of clicking on the command button and printing the form. Note that the printout reproduces all the contents of the form, but it doesn't print the form boundary or title bar.

Using the Printer Object

The *Printer* object is a drawing space that matches the default printer as defined by the Windows Control Panel. As a drawing space, it has properties such as

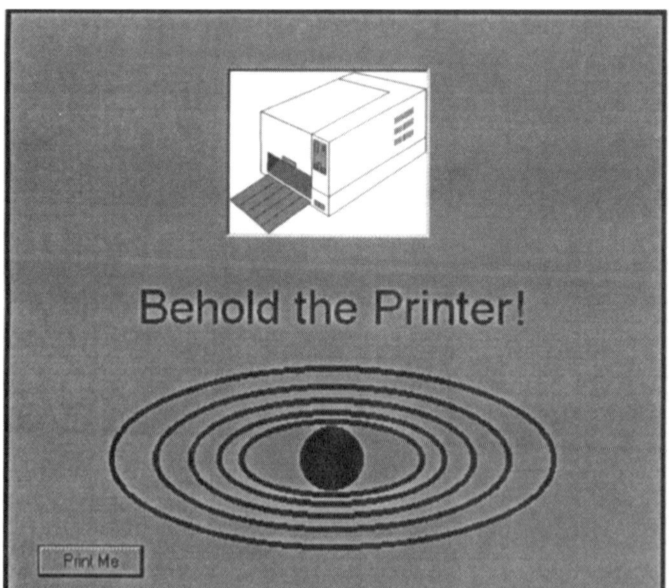

Figure L14-14 The output from using PrintForm

ScaleHeight, Font.Size, BackColor, and so on. Also, because it is a drawing space, you can use the *Print, Pset, Circle,* and *Line* methods to draw on the Printer object and the *PaintPicture* method (to be discussed in a moment) to copy images to the Printer object. Because the Printer object also matches a printer, it has properties such as DeviceName, PaperSize, and Orientation corresponding to the printer name, paper size, and orientation specified by the Control Panel.

The Printer object is not something you can look at. When you draw or print on it, nothing happens onscreen. Instead, you're creating an image on a kind of virtual page. Certain *Printer* methods, however, such as *EndDoc,* can copy that image to a real piece of paper in your printer. The Printer object is a *device-independent* drawing space. That means, for example, that you use Visual Basic methods to draw circles, not the internal methods used by a printer. Visual Basic and the Windows printer drivers then take care of translating the Visual Basic description of text and graphics to the language used by the printer. Thus the output will vary from printer to printer. If a printer has 150 dpi resolution, graphics will be printed at that resolution. If a printer has 600 dpi resolution, the graphics will be printed at that resolution.

There is no way to place controls in a Printer object, so you can print only what you can draw using the *Print, PSet, Circle, Line,* and *PaintPicture* methods. Because a printer has different resolution from a screen, output can look different. For example, the last example used a line width of 4 pixels. For a laser printer with 300 dpi, this translates to a much narrower line.

Using Print and the graphics methods with the Printer object is the same as using them with a picture box—just use Printer as the invoking object. For instance,

```
Printer.Print "See Spot cogitate!"
```

prints a phrase at the top left of the printer object. Similarly, you can set and use Printer properties using object notation. For example to center a string variable named *Msg* horizontally on the printer object, you can do this:

```
Printer.CurrentX = (Printer.ScaleWidth - Printer.TextWidth(Msg)) / 2
```

Incidentally, Visual Basic 4 has added a convenient way to lessen your typing load. If you have several properties of the same object in your code, you use a *With* statement to identify which object to use. For example, you can replace the last line with this:

```
With Printer
    .CurrentX = (.ScaleWidth -.TextWidth(Msg)) / 2
End With
```

Within the confines of this *With–End* With statement, expressions like *.Current* are interpreted as *Printer.Current.* Note that you still have to use the period. This example uses just one line, but you could have several lines of property-using code contained between *With Printer* and *End With.* Similarly, you could replace *With Printer* with *With picBox* and make all the code apply to an object named *picBox* instead. However, *With* works just with properties, not with methods, so you still have to write out commands like *Printer.Print* in full.

Tip

Use the *With* statement to simplify code in which you refer to many properties of the same object.

The PaintPicture Method

The *PaintPicture* method copies the contents of a graphics file to a form, picture box, or to a Printer object. The graphics file itself isn't named explicitly; instead, it must be the Picture property of a form or picture box. You have to specify where the top left corner of the graphic is placed, and you have the option of specifying the width and height of the graphic. The syntax to be used is:

object.**PaintPicture** *Picture, X, Y, [Width, Height]*

Here *object* refers to the object receiving the graphic; *Picture* is the picture property of a form, picture box, or Printer object; *X* and *Y* are the coordinates of the top left corner of the graphic; and *Width* and *Height* are the width and height to be used for the graphic. Dimensions are in terms of the ScaleMode units, which are twips, by default. The command

```
Printer.PaintPicture picNick.Picture 1000, 2000, 5000, 4000
```

copies the graphics specified by the *picNick.Picture* property to the Printer object. The graphic element will be sized so it's 5,000 twips wide, 4,000 twips tall, with its top left corner at (1000,2000). The method has several other optional arguments that won't be discussed.

Converting the To Be Printed Program

Now to convert the To Be Printed program to an example using the Printer object. We can leave the form itself unchanged and just change the code part. Listing L14-3 shows the new version of the code. Note the new code for printing:

```
Printer.EndDoc
```

This code says, "I'm done preparing the Printer object—go ahead and print it." If you omit this command, Visual Basic will print when you terminate the To Be Printed program. Figure L14-15 shows the output. You may not be able to tell from the reproduction, but the detail is finer than output from using *PrintForm*.

Listing L14-3
The modified To Be Printed program

```
Option Explicit

Private Sub cmdPrint_Click()
    Printer.EndDoc  'Print Printer object.
End Sub
```

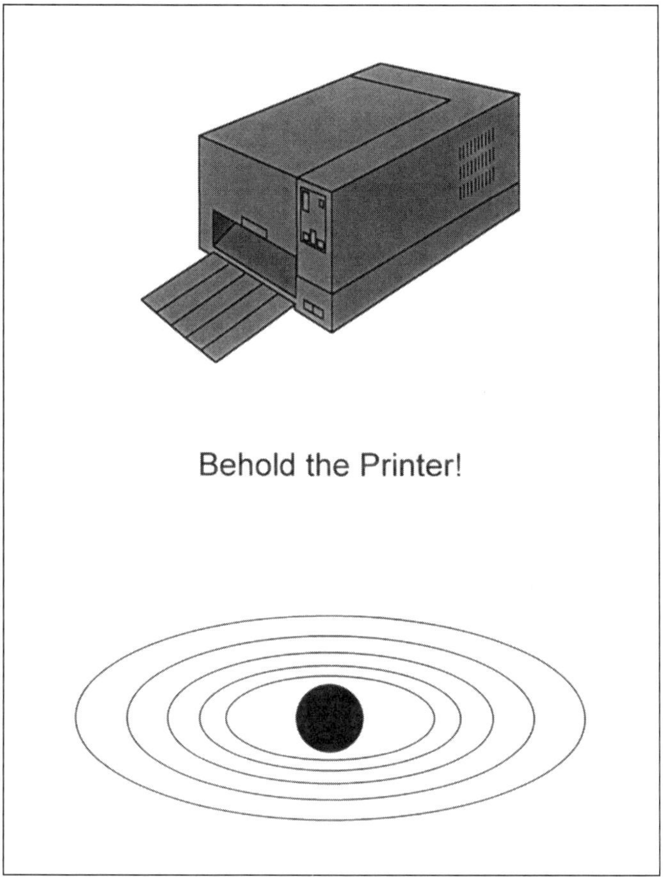

Figure L14-15 Printing from the Printer object

```
Private Sub picPrint_GotFocus()
    Dim MyStr As String
    Dim I As Integer
    Dim Radius As Single
    Dim Wd As Single
    Dim Ht As Single
    With Printer    ' Use printer as default object.
        Wd = .ScaleWidth    'Save typing later.
        Ht = .ScaleHeight   'ditto
        ' Copy picture from form to Printer object.
        Printer.PaintPicture picPrint.Picture, 0.25 * Wd, 0.1 * Ht, _
            0.5 * Wd, 0.3 * Ht
        .Font.Name = "Arial"
        .Font.Size = 24
        MyStr = "Behold the Printer!"
        .CurrentX = (Wd - .TextWidth(MyStr)) / 2
        .CurrentY = (Ht - .TextHeight(MyStr)) / 2
        Printer.Print MyStr
        .CurrentX = Wd / 2
        .CurrentY = 3 * Ht / 4
```

continued on next page

continued from previous page

```
        Radius = Wd / 3
        .DrawWidth = 4
        For I = 1 To 5
            Printer.Circle Step(0, 0), Radius, , , , 0.4
            Radius = Radius * 0.8
        Next I
        .FillStyle = 0
        Printer.Circle Step(0, 0), 0.4 * Radius
        .FillStyle = 1
        .DrawStyle = 6
        Printer.Line (0, 0)-(Wd, Ht), , B
    End With
End Sub
```

The *Printers* Collection

Version 4 of Visual Basic adds a collection called *Printers*. Just as *Controls* is a collection of all the controls on a form, *Printers* is a collection of all the printers on your system. Actually, Visual Basic doesn't know which printers are connected to your system, but it does know which printers appear in the Printers list of the Windows Printer Setup dialog box. It also knows which printer drivers each printer uses. Here is a short loop that displays the names and drivers for your system:

```
Dim Pr As Printer
For Each Pr In Printers
    Print Pr.DeviceName; Tab(30); Pr.DriverName
Next
```

The variable *Pr* is an example of a specific object type variable; it represents a Printer object. The loop makes *Pr* represent each of your installed printers in turn. The DeviceName property is the printer name, and the DriverName is the name of the driver used for that printer. Figure L14-16 shows the output from a program using this code.

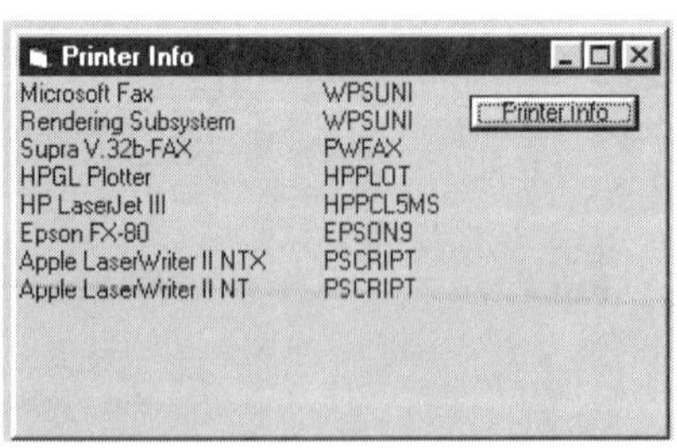

Figure L14-16 Listing printers and drivers

SUMMARY

Visual Basic has many tools for handling text. You can use text boxes, list boxes, and combo boxes for obtaining text input. The combo box combines features of a list box and a text box so that you can either enter a choice or select an item from a list. Entering a choice triggers the *Change* event for a combo box, while selecting an item triggers the *Click* event. You can use the Caption and Text properties for various controls for displaying text. You can use the *Print* method to display text in forms and picture boxes. The *Format* statement lets you prescribe the appearance of date, time, and numeric data.

Just as the Screen object represents your display, the Printer object represents your printer. Each of these objects has a FontCount property which gives the number of fonts available and a Fonts property, which essentially is an array of all the font names. Applying these properties to the Screen object yields information about screen fonts, while applying them to the Printer object yields information about printer fonts. Screen fonts are the fonts used to display text on your display, while printer fonts are used for printing.

To print a bitmapped image of a form, you can use the *PrintForm* method. To take advantage of a printer's resolution, you can construct images on the Printer object. You can use *Print* to place text on the Printer object, you can use the graphics methods to draw on the Printer object, and you can use the *PaintPicture* method to copy a graphics image to the Printer object. Then use the *EndDoc* method to print the images.

QUIZ 14

1. The combo box combines

a. A label with a list box

b. A text box with a list box

c. A pepperoni control with a sausage control

2. What's the difference between a screen font and a printer font?

3. What's the difference between a bitmapped font and a scaleable font?

4. Assuming the date is the day you read this, what would the following display?
   a. Print Format(Date)
   b. Print Format(Date, "Long Date")
   c. Print Format(Date, "Short Date")
   d. Print Format(Date, "dddd, yyyy mmmm dd")

5. What would the following statements display?
   a. Print "I have" & Str(10)
   b. Print "I have" & Str(-10)
   c. Print "I have " & Format(10)
   d. Print "I have " & Format(-10)
   e. Print Format(2.3456);
   f. Print Format(2.3456, "00.00");
   g. Print Format(2.3456, "##.##");

6. Describe the trade-offs between using the *PrintForm* method and the *EndDoc* method to print.

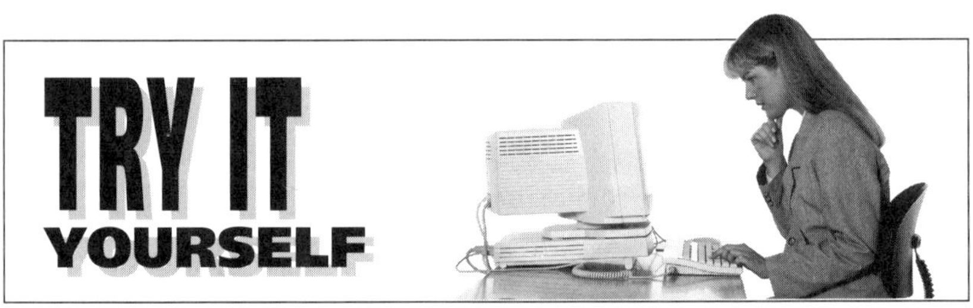

1. Modify the When Are We? project so it uses a timer to update the display once a second.

2. Produce a project similar to the When Are We? project, do something similar to the time display, but have it format numbers that you enter in a text box.

3. Write a program that prints a list (on your printer) of the names of all your screen fonts.

4. Write a program that prints a list (on your printer) of the names of all your printer fonts along with a sample of each printer font.

5. Create a program that produces output like that shown in Figure L14-16.

LESSON 15

THE MATH WHIZ

Computers were born to compute. Their inner beings long to crunch numbers. True, creative programmers have channeled that strength in many directions, such as games and morphing programs, but handling numbers is what computers do. Visual Basic, respecting the computer's nature, supports math in several ways, and you'll learn more about that support in this lesson. In particular, you'll learn about or review the following:

- **The built-in arithmetic operations: +, −, *, /, \, Mod, and ^**
- **The *Rnd* random-number function and the *Randomize* statement**
- **The number value functions: *Abs, Sgn, Fix,* and *Int***
- **The general math functions: *Sqr, Exp,* and *Log***
- **The trigonometric functions: *Sin, Cos, Tan,* and *Atn***

THE OPERATORS AND OPERATOR PRECEDENCE

You've seen and used all the arithmetic operators already, but let's take another look. This time, we'll take a longer look at *operator precedence*. It's a kind of pecking order among arithmetic operators that determines which operator gets to go first when two operators share a value. For instance, consider this statement:

```
F = 32 + 1.8 * C
```

Both the multiplication operator (*) and the addition operator (+) want to use the value 1.8. Visual Basic gives higher precedence to multiplication, and that means multiplication takes place first. Then 32 gets added to the result. This is the correct sequence for converting Celsius temperatures to Fahrenheit. Table L15-1 summarizes the arithmetic operators, listing them in order of decreasing precedence.

OPERATOR	MEANING	EXAMPLE
^	Exponentiation	5 ^ 3 means 5 to the 3rd power, or 5 * 5 *5, or 125
–	Negation	If X is 23, then –X is –23; if Y is –5, –Y is 5
*, /	Multiplication and division	2.2 * 5. 0 is 11.0, 14 / 5 is 2.8
\	Integer division	14 / 5 is 2, the integer part of regular division
Mod	Modulo arithmetic	14 Mod 5 is 4, the remainder from integer division
+, –	Addition and subtraction	34.2 + 4.2 is 38.4, 34.3 – 4.2 is 30.1

Table L15-1 Arithmetic operators in order of decreasing precedence

WORKING WITH OPERATORS

Visual Basic tells the difference between negation and subtraction by context. If the minus sign looks to the left, looks to the right, and sees a value in both directions, it means subtraction. If there's no value to the left, it means negation. For instance, the last two of the next three examples have an assignment operator instead of a value immediately to the left of the minus sign, so the minus sign is negation.

```
Net = Gross - Costs      ' subtraction
Yours = -Mine            ' negation
Net = -Costs + Gross     ' negation, followed by addition
```

Multiplication and division have the same precedence. In that case, precedence is decided by which one comes first, going left to right:

```
X = 12 * 4 / 5      ' is 48 / 5, or 9.6, not 12 / 0.8, or 15
```

Similarly, addition and subtraction have the same precedence and are applied in left-to-right order.

You can use parentheses to control the order of operations. Expressions within parentheses are evaluated first, then the result is used:

```
Nerficity = Q * 25 - V  ' Multiply Q and 25, then subtract V.
Nurficity = Q * (25 - V)    ' Subtract V from 25, multiply answer by Q.
```

The integer division (\) and Mod operators are defined just for integers. If you use them with floating-point values, Visual Basic rounds those value to the nearest integers first. For instance, the expression *22.6 Mod 7.2* would be converted first to *23 Mod 7*, which then is evaluated to 2, the remainder from dividing 23 by 7.

By the way, integer division and the *Mod* operator are handy for stuff like converting inches to inches and feet, or minutes to hours and minutes. For instance, suppose *HtInch* is someone's height in inches. Then you can make calculations like these:

```
HtFeet = HtInch \ 12        ' integer division
InchesLeft = HtInch Mod 12      ' modulus
```

For example, if *HtInch* is 79, the *HtFeet* is *79 \ 12,* or *6,* and *InchesLeft* is *79 Mod 12*, or *7*. So the 79" person is 6'7" tall.

RANDOM NUMBERS ON THE LOOSE

You've already used *Rnd* and *Randomize* several times. They are particularly useful for creating simulations and games. Let's review what these two functions do, then develop a couple of interesting examples.

The *Rnd* function returns a random number that is less than 1 and greater than or equal to 0. That is, it might return 0, or 0.5, or 0.99999, but it never returns the value 1. The function uses a particular *algorithm,* or recipe, to calculate random numbers. This recipe starts with a particular value, called the *seed,* that it uses to calculate the first random number. The first random number then leads to a new seed that's used to calculate the next random number, and so on. Starting with a particular seed always leads to the same sequence of random numbers. And by default, Visual Basic always starts with the same seed when you first start a program. Suppose, for example, you have a loop like this:

```
For I = 1 to 30
    Print Rnd
Next I
```

Each time you start the program and activate this loop, you'll get the same 30 random numbers. However, if you run the loop twice in a row without restarting the program, you'll get a different set of numbers the second time. The seed gets reset to the default only when you start up the program.

This default behavior is fine if all you need is a bunch of numbers spread more or less evenly, but it does lack the element of surprise. To make the behavior a bit less predictable, use the *Randomize* statement to set the seed to a different value. Its syntax is this:

Randomize [*number*]

If you supply the optional *number* argument, it's used as the starting seed. If you omit the number, Visual Basic uses the value returned by the *Timer* function as the seed. The *Timer* function, in turn, returns the time from the system clock. Because the time is always changing, using *Randomize* that way, in effect, randomizes the seed, making the output of *Rnd* unpredictable—just what you need for games.

Often, you want random numbers with a different range. There's a standard technique for accomplishing that. For example, suppose you want random integers in the range 0 to 9. Then you can use this expression:

```
Int(10 * Rnd)    ' a random integer in the range 0 to 9
```

Multiplying *Rnd* by 10 gives a floating-point number greater than or equal to 0 and less than 10. The *Int* function truncates a floating-point number, discarding the part after the decimal point. So *Int(9.9999),* for example, is 9.

To get a number in the range 1 to 10, add a 1:

```
Int(10 * Rnd + 1)    ' a random integer in the range 1 to 10
```

If you want an integer in the range *Low* to *High,* use this formula:

```
Int((High - Low + 1) * Rnd + Low)
```

Throwing Dice

Many role-playing games have players generate random numbers by rolling dice. Visual Basic, using *Rnd,* can do the job much faster. Let's see what's required. First, such games often use a variety of dice—4-sided dice, 6-sided dice, 8-sided dice, 10-sided dice, 12-sided dice, 20-sided dice, and 100-sided dice. (For the nit-picking, a 10-sided die is really a 20-sided die with each number appearing on 2 sides, and a 100-sided die really is 2 10-sided dice, with each die providing 1 digit.) Second, dice often are thrown in groups, for example, casting 3 6-sided dice. So your program should let the user select the kind of dice to use and the number of dice to be thrown. While you're at it, you may as well add the capacity to make several throws in a row.

So what should the interface be? If you have a small number of mutually exclusive choices, such as for the kind of dice to use, option buttons are a good bet. Let's place an array of option buttons in a frame. If you have a larger number of choices, you could use a list box or a text box, but a scrollbar works well for integer choices. That way, you don't have to worry about users accidentally entering the wrong kind of data. So let's use scrollbars and label controls to get the number of dice and the number of throws. To trigger the simulation, use a command button. To display the output, you could use a text box. But a picture box is nice for this purpose because then you can use the *Print* method to produce consecutive lines of output. All in all, let's go for the interface described by Table L15-2 and illustrated by Figure L15-1.

OBJECT	PROPERTY	SETTING
Form1	Caption	Throwing Dice
	Name	frmDice
Frame1	Caption	Number of Sides
	Font.Size	12
	Name	fraSides
Option1	Caption	4
	Font.Size	12
	Index	0
	Name	optSides
Option2	Caption	6
	Font.Size	12
	Index	1
	Name	optSides
	Value	True
Option3	Caption	8
	Font.Size	12
	Index	2
	Name	optSides
Option4	Caption	10
	Font.Size	12
	Index	3
	Name	optSides
Option5	Caption	12
	Font.Size	12
	Index	4
	Name	optSides
Option6	Caption	20
	Font.Size	12
	Index	5
	Name	optSides
	Value	True
Option7	Caption	100
	Font.Size	12
	Index	6
	Name	optSides
Command1	Caption	&Throw Dice
	Name	cmdThrow
Command2	Caption	E&xit
	Name	cmdExit

continued on next page

continued from previous page

OBJECT	PROPERTY	SETTING
Label1	Caption	Number of Dice
	Font.Size	12
	Name	lblND
Label2	Caption	2
	Font.Size	12
	Name	lblDice
Label3	Caption	Number of throws
	Font.Size	12
	Name	lblNC
Label4	Caption	1
	Font.Size	12
	Name	lbThrows
HScrollBar1	LargeChange	5
	Max	20
	Min	1
	Name	hsbDice
	Value	2
HScrollBar2	LargeChange	3
	Max	15
	Min	1
	Name	hsbDice
PictureBox1	AutoRedraw	True
	Name	picThrows

Table L15-2 Properties for the Dice Throw program

So much for the pretty face—now let's look at the computational heart, as shown in Listing L15-1.

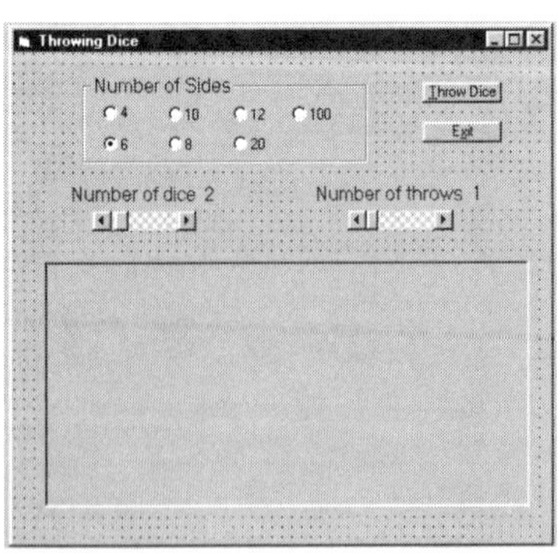

Figure L15-1 The Dice Throw form

Listing L15-1
The Dice Throw code

```
Option Explicit
Dim Sides As Integer
Const Format1 As String = "0 "
Const Format2 As String = "00 "

Private Sub cmdThrow_Click()
    Dim MyStr As String
    Dim Frmt As String
    Dim I, J As Integer
    Dim Total As Integer
    Dim Throw As Integer
    picThrows.Cls
    If Sides < 10 Then
        Frmt = Format1
    Else
        Frmt = Format2
    End If
    For I = 1 To hsbThrows.Value
        MyStr = Format(I, "00") & ": "
        Total = 0
        For J = 1 To hsbDice.Value
            Throw = Int(Sides * Rnd + 1)
            Total = Total + Throw
            MyStr = MyStr & Format(Throw, Frmt)
        Next J
        MyStr = MyStr & " : total =" & Str(Total)
        picThrows.Print MyStr
    Next I
End Sub

Private Sub cmdExit_Click()
    End
End Sub

Private Sub Form_Initialize()
    Sides = 6
    Randomize
End Sub

Private Sub hsbThrows_Change()
    lblThrows.Caption = hsbThrows.Value
End Sub

Private Sub hsbDice_Change()
    lblDice.Caption = hsbDice.Value
End Sub

Private Sub optSides_Click(Index As Integer)
    Sides = optSides(Index).Caption
End Sub
```

Much of the code should be familiar—for example, using the *Change* event for the scrollbars to update the labels displaying the values, using a command button to terminate the program, using *Randomize* in the *Form_Initialize* event to initialize the random number function, and using the captions of the option buttons to set the value for a variable:

```
Sides = optSides(Index).Caption
```

The *cmdThrow_Click* event contains the bulk of the code. The most significant part is this:

```
For I = 1 To hsbThrows.Value
    MyStr = Format(I, "00") & ": "
    Total = 0
    For J = 1 To hsbDice.Value
        Throw = Int(Sides * Rnd + 1)
        Total = Total + Throw
        MyStr = MyStr & Format(Throw, Frmt)
    Next J
    MyStr = MyStr & " : total =" & Str(Total)
    picThrows.Print MyStr
Next I
```

Each value of *I* corresponds to one line of output. The inner *For* loop (the one using *J* as a counter) builds a string of random values, one value for each die thrown. After that, the event procedure appends the total number of points cast to the end of each line, then prints the line in the picture box.

If the number of sides is under 10, the program prints the single-digit values. But to make the appearance a bit more regular, the program switches formats when the number of sides is 10 or greater, printing each number as a 2-digit value, for example, printing 2 13 as 02 13. Figure L15-2 shows a sample of the output.

Number-Value Functions

The previous project used the *Int* function, which converts a floating-point number to an integer by truncating the fractional part. Visual Basic also supplies an *Abs* function, which returns the absolute value of a value; a *Sgn* function,

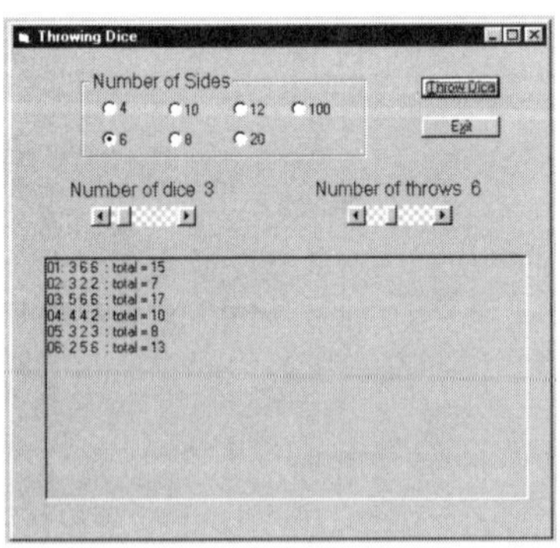

Figure L15-2 The dice are cast!

which indicates the sign of a value; and a *Fix* function, which is similar to *Int,* except it handles negative numbers differently. Table L15-3 summarizes these functions.

FUNCTION	RETURN VALUE
Int(x)	The largest integer less than or equal to *x*
Fix(x)	The largest integer whose absolute value is less than the absolute value of *x* and whose sign is the same as *x*
Abs(x)	The absolute value of *x*, i.e., the value shorn of its sign
Sgn(x)	1 if *x* is positive, –1 if *x* is negative, and 0 if x is 0

Table L15-3 Miscellaneous math functions

The *Int* and *Fix* functions work the same if *x* isn't negative. For positive *x,* both simply drop the fractional part of the number:

- VB *Int(2.32)* evaluates to 2
- VB *Fix(2.32)* evaluates to 2
- VB *Int(9.9999)* evaluates to 9
- VB *Fix(9.9999)* evaluates to 9

Note that these functions don't round to the nearest integer; instead they toss out the entire fractional part. If you want to round to the nearest integer, you can simply assign a value to a type integer variable:

```
Dim X as Single
Dim N as Integer
X = 5.67
N = X        ' 5.67 rounded to 6 and assigned to N
```

Tip

Use the *Int* function to convert numbers to integers by truncation; use assignment to an *Integer* value to convert numbers to integers by rounding.

The difference between *Fix* and *Int* shows up with negative numbers. Consider *Int(–2.3).* The largest integer less than –2.3 is –3. That's because 0 is less than 1, –1 is less than 0, –2 is less than –1, and so on. So *Int(–2.3)* is –3.

Now consider *Fix.* The rule looks complicated, but the outcome is simple. Let's try the rule with *Fix(–2.3).* The absolute value of –2.3 is 2.3. The largest integer less than 2.3 is 2. Giving it the same sign as –2.3 makes the result –2. One way of describing *Fix* is to say that it truncates in the direction of 0. That is, the truncated value is closer to 0 (or the same distance to 0) than the original value. *Int,* on the other hand, truncates towards negative infinity. Here are a few examples of *Fix* and *Int:*

- *Int*(–2.32) evaluates to –3
- *Fix*(–2.32) evaluates to –2
- *Int*(–9.9999) evaluates to –10
- *Fix*(–9.9999) evaluates to –9

VENTURING INTO THE LAND OF ODDS

Now let's get back to computational math functions. Some simulations make it a bit more difficult to use random numbers. For example, suppose you want to simulate shuffling a deck of cards. You could create an empty array of 52 elements, then fill the array with numbers selected randomly in the range 0–51. Each number would represent a different card. For example, if *N* is the number, you could use *N* Mod 13 to represent the card value (1 = ace, 2 = 2, and so on) and let *N* \ 13 represent the suit (0 = Clubs, 1 = Diamonds, 2 = Hearts, and 3 = Spades). However, once you select a particular card, you can't use it again; you're only allowed 1 Ace of Spades per deck!

That raises an interesting programming problem—how do you pick a series of random numbers if you're allowed only one of each kind? The most straightforward approach is to pick a random number and compare it with each of the random numbers you've already picked. If it's new, add it to the array; otherwise, pick again. This is not an efficient approach. Suppose, for example, that you've already picked 98 out of 100 numbers. Usually, it will take quite a few random picks before you randomly generate one of the two remaining choices.

But there is a better way. Suppose, for example, you need to pick 20 numbers in the range of 1–80 without generating any duplicates. First, create an array of 80 elements and fill it with the integers 1–80. Next, pick a number at random in the range 1–80. Let this number represent the *index* of an array element, and then switch the number at that location with the number at the top of the array. For instance, if you pick 8, switch element 8 (which happens to hold the value 8) with element 1 (which happens to hold the value 1). Now comes the clever part. Next time pick a random index in the range 2–80. Since you've placed the number you picked in element 1, picking an index in the range 2–80 guarantees that you won't pick that number again. And the number you displaced from the first position is now in the part of the array open for picking. Next, swap the number in the picked location with the number in element 2. Now the two picked values are in the two top slots, so pick an index at random in the range 3–80, and so on. Each time, you swap the contents of the selected element into the top of the list, then restrict the search to the remaining part of the array. By the time you've picked, say, 78 numbers, they'll occupy the top 78 positions of the array, and you'll be selecting a number at random from just the two remaining slots. In general, a particular index may be selected more than once, but every number in the array gets picked exactly one time (see Figure L15-3).

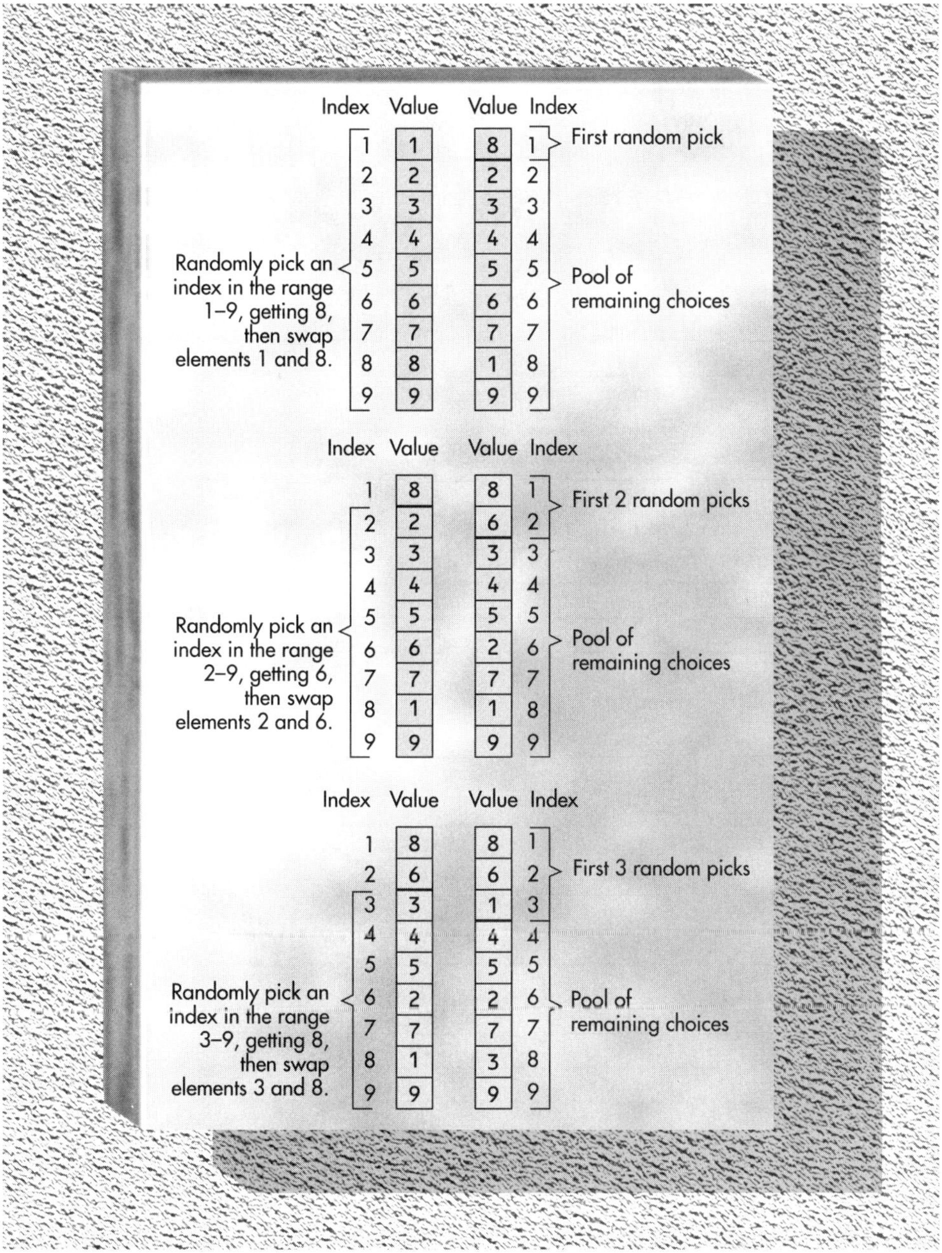

Figure L15-3 Random numbers when a number can be picked just once

Let's apply this technique to simulating a Keno or Lotto pick. A Lotto, for example, may select 6 numbers at random from the range 1–53, while Keno selects 20 numbers at random from the range 1–80.

First, consider the interface. The program should allow the user to select how many numbers are picked and what the range of choices is. For this, you can use the same scrollbar technique you used before. You can use a command button to initiate selection, and you can use a text box to show the results. In short, you can use the interface illustrated in Figure L15-4 and outlined in Table L15-4.

OBJECT	PROPERTY	SETTING
Form1	Caption	Lotto Picks
	Name	frmPicks
Command1	Caption	&Draw Numbers
	Font.Bold	True
	Name	cmdDraw
Command2	Caption	E&xit
	Font.Bold	True
	Name	cmdExit
Label1	Caption	Number of spots on game card
	Font.Bold	True
	Name	lblNs
Label2	Caption	1
	Font.Bold	True
	Font.Size	18
	Name	lblSpots
Label3	Caption	Number of picks
	Font.Bold	True
	Name	lblNP
Label4	Caption	1
	Font.Bold	True
	Font.Size	18
	Name	lblPicks
Label5	Caption	Results of the draw:
	Font.Bold	True
	Font.Size	12
VScrollBar1	LargeChange	10
	Max	100
	Min	1
	Name	vscSpots
VScrollBar2	LargeChange	5
	Max	20
	Min	1
	Name	vscPicks
TextBox1	AutoRedraw	True
	Font.Bold	True
	Font.Size	10

OBJECT	PROPERTY	SETTING
	Locked	True
	Name	txtLotto
	Text	

Table L15-4 Properties for the Lotto program

The program uses a text box instead of a label or picture box because it looks better in the Auto3D mode. However, you wouldn't want people altering the output, so the program sets the Locked property to True.

Tip

If you want to use a text box because of its properties and appearance but don't want users directly altering the contents, set the text box's Locked property to True. Then users can read the contents but they can't edit them.

There is one complication to this interface—the user should not be able to choose to pick more numbers than are available. That is, if the user decides to pick from the range 1–15, the program should make it impossible to choose to have, say, 18 picks in that range. What we need are *coupled controls,* that is, a pair of controls in which one control affects the behavior of a second control. We can do that by having the *Change* event for one scrollbar affect the Max property for the second scrollbar. For example, setting a value of 18 for the range scrollbar can reset the Max property to 18 for the Number of Picks scrollbar. The *vscSpots_Change* event in Listing L15-2 does that. It also limits the maximum number of picks to 20 in any case.

Dynamic Arrays

The listing also introduces a new kind of array, one that's allocated dynamically, that is, its size is set during run time, not design time. The idea is that if the user selects a game with, say, 80 values to choose from, you need an array with 80 elements. But if the user selects a game with only 20 values to choose from, you

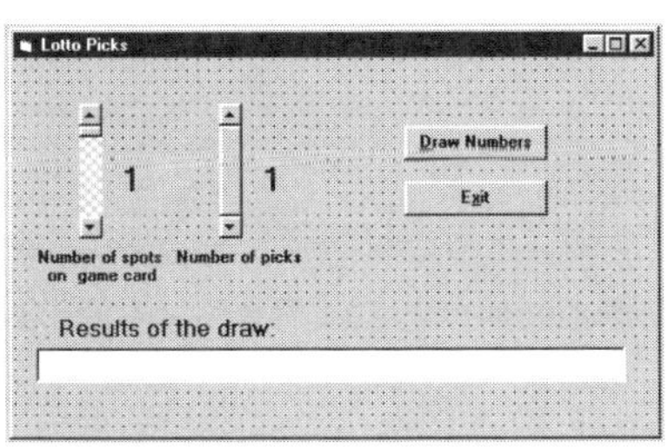

Figure L15-4 The Lotto form

only need an array with 20 elements. Up to now, we've used code like this to create an array:

```
Dim Cards (1 to 52) as Integer
```

Here the array limits are constants known at design time. If you want to use array limits that are determined at run time, use *ReDim* instead of *Dim*. For instance, Listing L15-2 uses this code:

```
ReDim spots(1 To vscSpots.Value) As Integer
```

Tip

Use *Dim* to create an array whose size is known at design time. Use *ReDim* to create an array whose size is determined during run time. Such an array is called a *dynamic array*.

Implementing Random Selection

The main point of this project is illustrating how to pick random values without repeating yourself. Here is the code that implements the plan just discussed:

```
' Pick index at random, then swap pick with
' an element at the beginning of the array.
' After N picks, the picks will fill first N
' elements of the array.
For I = 1 To Picks
    ThePick = Int((Max - I + 1) * Rnd + I)
    Temp = spots(I)
    spots(I) = spots(ThePick)
    spots(ThePick) = Temp
Next
```

After this loop ends, *Picks* values selected at random from the range 1–*Max* occupy the beginning of the *Spots* array. Listing L15-2 shows the entire code, and Figure L15-5 shows a sample run. (Who knows? That example may be worth $30,000,000 to someone!)

Listing L15-2
The Lotto program

```
Option Explicit
Private Sub cmdExit_Click()
    End
End Sub

Private Sub cmdDraw_Click()
    ' Create an array whose size is given by scrollbar.
    ReDim spots(1 To vscSpots.Value) As Integer
    Dim ThePick As Integer  'index for randomly selected value
    Dim Picks As Integer    'total number of picks to be made
```

```
    Dim Max As Integer       'total number of spots
    Dim Temp As Integer      'for swapping values
    Dim I As Integer         'FOR loop counter
    Dim Winners As String    'string of picked values
    Picks = vscPicks.Value
    Max = vscSpots.Value
    ' Initialize array of possible values.
    For I = 1 To Max
        spots(I) = I
    Next
    ' Pick index at random, then swap pick with
    ' an element at the beginning of the array.
    ' After N picks, the picks will fill first N
    ' elements of the array.
    For I = 1 To Picks
        ThePick = Int((Max - I + 1) * Rnd + I)
        Temp = spots(I)
        spots(I) = spots(ThePick)
        spots(ThePick) = Temp
    Next
    Winners = ""
    For I = 1 To Picks
        Winners = Winners + Str(spots(I))
    Next
    txtLotto.Text = Winners
  End Sub

Private Sub Form_Initialize()
    Randomize
End Sub

Private Sub vscSpots_Change()
    lbl1.Caption = vscSpots.Value
    If vscSpots.Value < 20 Then
        vscPicks.Max = vscSpots.Value
    Else
        vscPicks.Max = 20
    End If
End Sub

Private Sub vscPicks_Change()
    lbl2.Caption = vscPicks.Value
End Sub
```

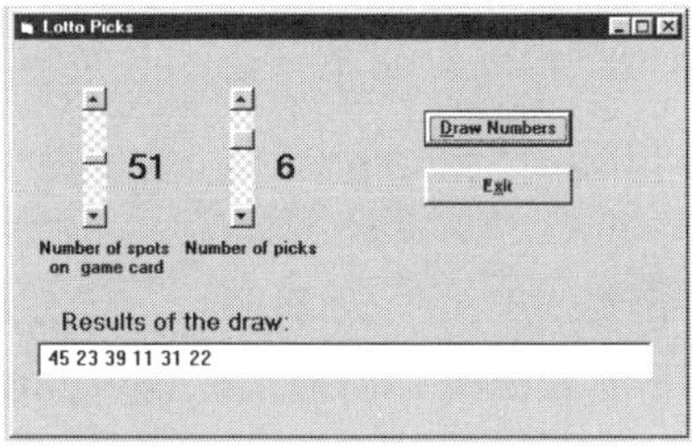

Figure L15-5 A sample Lotto pick

GENERAL MATH FUNCTIONS

If you've ever played around with math, you've probably run into square roots, exponentials, and logarithms. Visual Basic has functions to evaluate these quantities. Like functions in mathematics, these functions take a number as an argument and return another number. For instance, if you give the *Sqr* function a number, it returns the square root of that number. (The square root of a number is a number that, when multiplied by itself, gives you back the original number.) For example, *Sqr(49)* evaluates to 7, and *Sqr(6.25)* evaluates to 2.5. Table L15-5 summarizes Visual Basic's general math functions.

FUNCTION	RETURN VALUE
Sqr(x)	Square root of x
Exp(x)	e^x, where e is the base for natural logarithms, approximately 2.718282
Log(x)	Natural logarithm of x, base e, meaning $e^{Log(x)}$ is x

Table L15-5 General math functions

If you aren't familiar with math, these functions may seem meaningless (or worse) to you, but they can be handy. Let's look at three short examples.

Can You See for Miles and Miles and Miles?

On a clear day at a place with a level horizon, how far can you see? The answer depends on how high you are off the ground. Also, non-coincidentally, the answer involves taking a square root. Suppose *Distance* stands for how far you can see (the distance to the horizon), *Height* stands for how high your eyes are above the ground, and *Radius* stands for the radius of the Earth, (see Figure L15-6). Then the distance from you to the horizon can be calculated from the following formula:

Distance = Sqr(2 * *Radius* * *Height* + *Height* ^2)

Note to the Curious

For brevity, let's use D, R, and H for Distance, Radius, and Height. The angle between the D line and the R line is 90 degrees because a tangent line is perpendicular to the radius of a circle. According to Pythagoras, then,

R2 + D2 = (H + R)2

Algebra converts this to

R2 + D2 = H2 + 2HR + R2

Subtract R2 from both sides and take the square root. That gives the desired formula:

D = square root (2HR + R2)

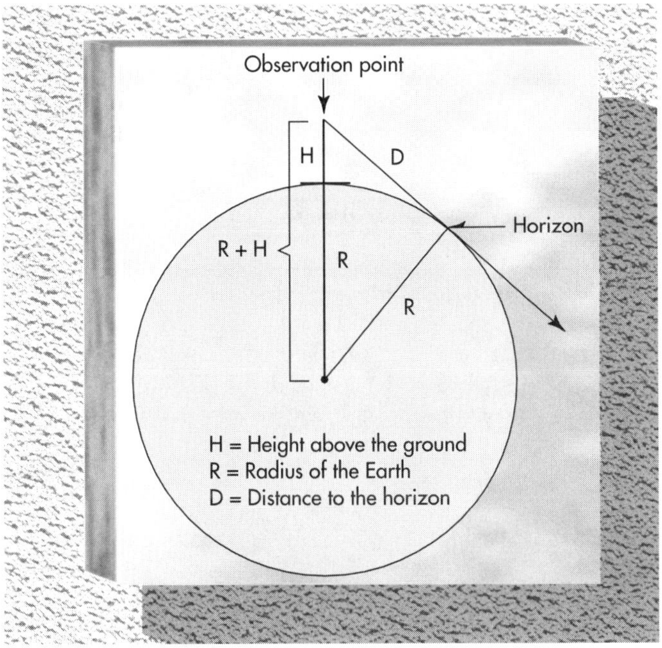

Figure L15-6 Distance to the horizon

Given the formula, it's short work to produce a Visual Basic program to do the calculations. Create a new form as described by Table L15-6 and as illustrated in Figure L15-7.

OBJECT	PROPERTY	SETTING
Form1	Caption	The Horizon
	Name	frmSqrt
Label1	Alignment	2-Center
	Caption	How far can you see? Enter your height in feet above the ground in the box below.
	Font.Size	12
	Name	lblfar
Label2	Caption	Height:
	Font.Size	12
	Name	lblHeight
Label3	Caption	feet
	Font.Size	12
	Name	lblFeet
Label4	Alignment	2 - Center
	AutoSize	True
	Caption	You can see 0 miles!

continued on next page

continued from previous page

OBJECT	PROPERTY	SETTING
	Font.Size	12
	Name	lblSee
TextBox1	Font.Size	12
	Name	txtHeight
	Text	0

Table L15-6 Properties for the Horizon program

Next, you have to use the formula in the *Change* event for the text box so that changing the height causes Visual Basic to recalculate the distance you can see. Try Listing L15-3 in the Code window.

Listing L15-3
The Horizon program

```
Option Explicit

Private Sub txtHeight_Change()
Private Sub txtHeight_Change()
    Dim Distance As Single
    Dim Height As Single
    If IsNumeric(txtHeight.Text) Then
        Height = CSng(txtHeight.Text)
        Distance = Sqr(41805000 * Height + Height ^ 2) / 5280
        lblSee.Caption = "You can see " & Format(Distance, "Standard") _
            & " miles!"
    Else
        lblSee.Caption = "Please enter a height in feet."
    End IfEnd Sub
```

Like an earlier example, this program checks to see if the Text property is numeric. If the string isn't numeric, the program prompts the user to enter a number. If the entry is a number string, the program then converts the number to a type *Single* value and calculates the distance. The value 41,805,000 is twice the Earth's radius in feet, using the same units as were used for the height. Then the 5,280 converts the final answer from feet to miles. Figure L15-7 shows the program in use. You might want to try some other values, such as 1,000 feet for a very tall building or 14,000 feet for a good-sized mountain.

Grow Time

Next, let's give the exponential function *Exp* a chance to display its stuff. As Table L15-5 states, *Exp(x)* evaluates to e^x, where e is one of those transcendental mathematical constants, like π, and has the approximate value 2.718282. That may not strike you as particularly useful, but exponentials turn up in many situations. For example, the formula for population growth with a constant growth

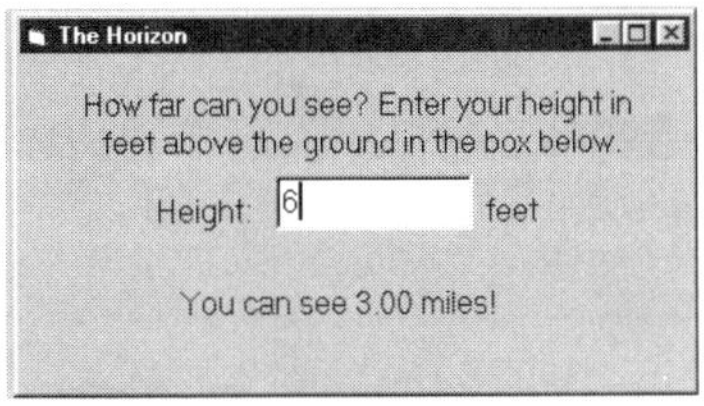

Figure L15-7 The Horizon program in use

rate uses an exponential. In particular, if *Rate* is the annual growth rate (birth rate minus the death rate) and if *T* is the time in years, then the following equation holds:

Population = (Starting Population) * Exp(Rate * T)

Let's try this in a program designed to model the worldwide population growth. Let the user enter a starting population, a starting time, a growth rate, and a time step, and have the program show the subsequent populations for 20 different times. A time step of, say, ten years, means the program will display the population at ten-year intervals. With 20 steps, that'll cover a 200-year period. Let's use combo boxes to provide some standard values for populations and starting times—for example, providing a population of 1,600,000,000 for the year 1900 and a population of 5,333,000,000 for 1990. You can use a third combo box to specify a time step. Combo boxes make sense for all these values, for they provide a set of standard values, yet they also allow a user to enter other choices.

With growth rates, users sometimes get confused as to whether they should enter a rate as a percent, as in 8%, or as a decimal fraction, as in 0.08. You can simplify matters by using a scrollbar along with a label that displays choices in the percent form. Figure L15-8 shows the layout, while Table L15-7 outlines the properties. Note the vertical scrollbar has a range from 1500. The idea is that 1500 will represent 15%, allowing the user to enter rates to the nearest 0.01%.

OBJECT	PROPERTY	SETTING
Form1	Caption	Population Growth
	Name	frmExp
Label1	Caption	Initial Population
	Name	lblPop
Label2	Caption	Starting Year
	Name	lblYear
Label3	Caption	Step Size in Years
	Name	lblStep
Label4	Caption	Growth Rate
	Name	lblGR

continued on next page

continued from previous page

OBJECT	PROPERTY	SETTING
PictureBox1	AutoRedraw	True
	Name	picGrow
Combo1	Name	cboPop
Combo2	Name	cboYear
Combo3	Name	cboStep
VScrollBar1	LargeChange	50
	Max	0
	Min	1500
	Name	vscRate
Command1	Caption	Calculate
	Name	cmdCalc

Table L15-7 Properties for the Population Growth form

Next, let's check the code. The *Form_Load* event can handle initializing the three combo boxes. You'll notice that when you enter a number like 5333000000, Visual Basic adds a # suffix. That indicates that the number is being stored as a type *Double* value. Smaller values, such as 1600000000, can be stored as a *Long* integer, but the larger populations exceed the *Long* limits, so Visual Basic switches to type *Double*.

```
Private Sub Form_Load()
    cboYear.AddItem 1650         'year
    cboPop.AddItem 550000000     'population in 1650
    cboYear.AddItem 1750
    cboPop.AddItem 725000000     'population in 1750
    cboYear.AddItem 1850
    cboPop.AddItem 1175000000    'population in 1850
    cboYear.AddItem 1900
    cboPop.AddItem 1600000000    'population in 1900
    cboYear.AddItem 1950
```

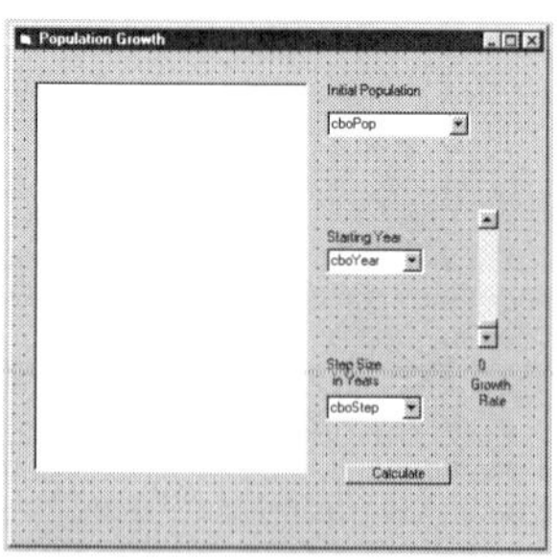

Figure L15-8 The Population Growth form

```
    cboPop.AddItem 2565000000#   'population in 1950
    cboYear.AddItem 1980
    cboPop.AddItem 4477000000#   'population in 1980
    cboYear.AddItem 1990
    cboPop.AddItem 5333000000#   'population in 1990
    cboYear.ListIndex = 3
    cboPop.ListIndex = 3
    cboStep.AddItem 5            'calculate in 5-year steps
    cboStep.AddItem 10           '10-year steps
    cboStep.AddItem 20           '20-year steps
    cboStep.ListIndex = 1
End Sub
```

Using combo boxes for the year and population raises an interesting programming problem. Can you arrange things so that selecting 1990 from the list in the year combo box also sets the population combo box to the corresponding population? Similarly, can you have selecting 5,333,000,000 from the population combo list automatically set the year combo box to 1990? In short, can you couple these two controls so that selecting a value from one sets the corresponding value in the other? The answer is yes. Is it hard to do? No. Remember, you select an item on a list by clicking on it, so you can use the *Click* event for one list to set the other list, and vice versa. The *Form_Load* event order simplifies matters by giving matched items the same index. That is, 1850 is the third item in one list, so *cboYear.ListIndex* is 2 for that item. The corresponding population is the third item in its list, so *cboPop.ListIndex* is 2 for that item. So all you have to do is the following:

```
Private Sub cboPop_Click()
    cboYear.Text = cboYear.List(cboPop.ListIndex)
    picGrow.Cls
End Sub
```

Here, for example, *cboPop.ListIndex* is the index of the item you've just clicked, so *cboYear.List(cboPop.ListIndex)* is the corresponding item in the Year list. The code then sets the Text property (displayed in the edit box) to that item. The second line clears the display area. That's to prevent a situation in which the display area shows the calculations made from a different set of givens than currently displayed. Similarly, you can do the following:

```
Private Sub cboYear_Click()
    cboPop.Text = cboPop.List(cboYear.ListIndex)
    picGrow.Cls
End Sub

Private Sub txtPop_Change()
    picGrow.Cls
End Sub

Private Sub txtYear_Change()
    picGrow.Cls
End Sub
```

The last two procedures clear the display area if you change parameters by entering them directly in the edit boxes.

Next, let's set the growth rate. The top value for the scrollbar has been set at 1500. To make that equal to 15%, or 0.15, divide by 10000. To display it as a percent, use *Format* and the "Percent" format string. Also let's clear the display when resetting the percent.

```
Private Sub vscRate_Change()
    lblRate.Caption = Format(vscRate / 10000, "Percent")
    picGrow.Cls
End Sub
```

The final task is to make the calculations. The following code begins by creating the relevant variables and initializing them to the values set by the other controls. Then it clears the display area and uses the exponential formula to calculate the population values for subsequent time steps. Figure L15-9 shows a sample run.

```
Private Sub cmdCalc_Click()
    Dim Year As Integer
    Dim StartYear As Integer
    Dim StartPop As Double
    Dim StepSize As Integer
    Dim Rate As Double
    Rate = vscRate.Value / 10000
    StartYear = cboYear.Text
    StartPop = cboPop.Text
    StepSize = cboStep.Text
    lblRate.Caption = Format(Rate, "Percent")
    picGrow.Cls
    picGrow.Print " Year", "Population"
    For Year = StartYear To (StartYear + 20 * StepSize) Step StepSize
        picGrow.Print Year,
        picGrow.Print _
            Format(StartPop * Exp(Rate * (Year - StartYear)), _ "#,###")
    Next Year
End Sub
```

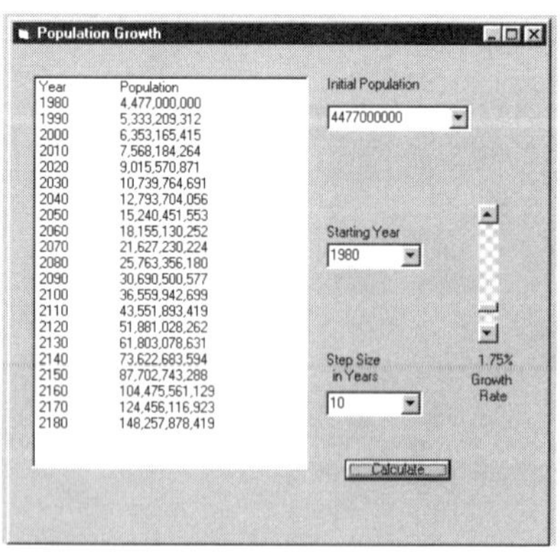

Figure L15-9 Exponential growth

Easy as Falling off a Log

The *Log* function is the inverse of the *Exp* function. That is, if you take a number and evaluate its exponential, you get a second number as a result. If you apply the *Log* function to that result, you get back the original number. Like the *Exp* function, the *Log* function turns up often in scientific and financial equations. For instance, suppose you have $1,000 and want an investment that will increase that to $3,000 in 10 years. What annual interest rate do you need? If the interest is compounded once a year, the answer is this:

rate = Exp((Log(3000/1000)/10) - 1)

So you need both the *Exp* and *Log* functions to get the answer. More generally, if *Initial* is the starting amount, *Final* is the amount you want, and if the interest is compounded *N* times a year for *T* years, the formula is this:

rate = N * (Exp((Log(Final/Initial))/(N*T)) –1)

Once you have the formula, it's simple to put together a short program to perform the calculation. You can use text boxes to get values for the initial amount, final amounts, and number of years. Interest usually is compounded for particular values, such as once a year, once a quarter, and so on, so it makes more sense to use a combo box listing common values. Table L15-8 shows the properties, and Figure L15-10 shows the program in operation. Incidentally, going from yearly to daily compounding reduces the required interest for tripling an investment in 10 years from 11.61% to 10.99%.

OBJECT	PROPERTY	SETTING
Form1	Caption	Interested?
	Name	frmLog
Label1	Caption	Initial Amount
	Name	lblInitial
Label2	Caption	Final Amount
	Name	lblFinal
Label3	Caption	Years
	Name	lblYears
Label4	Caption	Payments per Year
	Name	lblPPerYear
Label5	Caption	Annual Rate
	Name	lblRate
TextBox1	Name	txtInitial
	Text	1000
TextBox2	Name	txtFinal
	Text	2000
TextBox3	Name	txtYears
	Text	10

continued on next page

continued from previous page

OBJECT	PROPERTY	SETTING
TextBox4	Name	txtRate
	ReadOnly	True
	Text	
Combo1	Name	cboPayments
Command1	Caption	Compute Rate
	Name	cmdRate

Table L15-8 Properties for the Interested? form

The code doesn't do anything new other than use the formula. Listing L15-4 shows what to enter in the Code window.

Listing L15-4
The Interested? program

```
Option Explicit

Private Sub cmdRate_Click()
Dim A0 As Single     'initial amount
Dim A1 As Single     'final amount
Dim Rate As Single   'annual interest rate
Dim Years As Single 'years of payments
Dim NP As Single     'number of payments per year
NP = cboPayments.Text
A1 = txtFinal.Text
A0 = txtInitial.Text
Years = txtYears.Text
Rate = NP * (Exp(Log(A1 / A0) / (NP * Years)) - 1)
txtRate.Text = Format(Rate, "Percent")
End Sub

Private Sub Form_Load()
    cboPayments.AddItem 1   'yearly
```

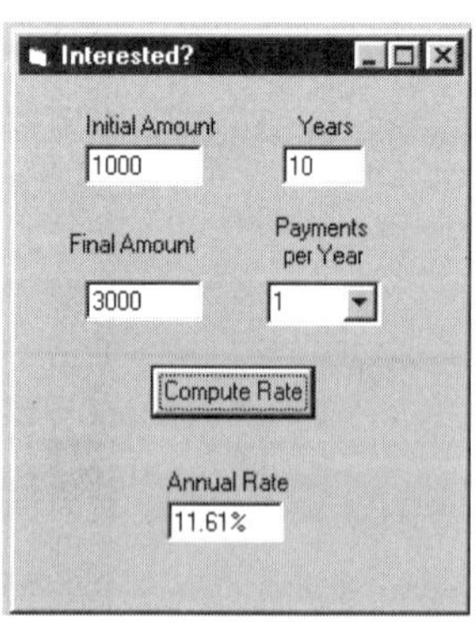

Figure L15-10 Making money

```
    cboPayments.AddItem 4   'quarterly
    cboPayments.AddItem 12  'monthly
    cboPayments.AddItem 365 'daily
End Sub
```

THE TRIGONOMETRY FUNCTIONS

Trigonometry has its roots in geometry and in the surveying of land, but its functions have many other applications. For instance, many music synthesizers work by combining sine waves in different ways to produce different tonal qualities. Visual Basic provides the trigonometric functions listed in Table L15-9. These functions can be defined in terms of the ratios of sides in a right triangle, as illustrated in Figure L15-11. Radians are a "natural" unit for measuring angles. A 180° angle is π (pi) radians, so one radian is about 57.3°.

FUNCTION	RETURN VALUE
Sin(x)	Sine of x (x measured in radians)
Cos(x)	Cosine of x (x measured in radians)
Tan(x)	Tangent of x (x measured in radians)
Atn(x)	Angle whose tangent is x (answer in radians)

Table L15-9 Trigonometric functions

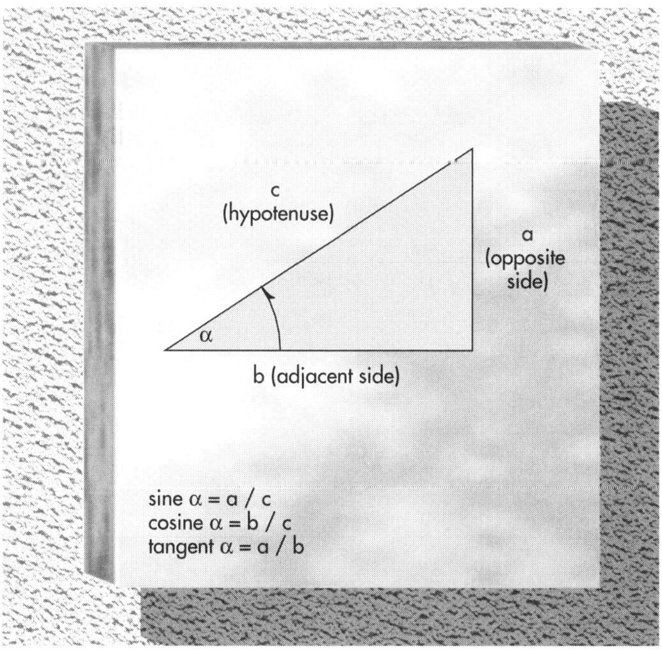

Figure L15-11 Trigonometric definitions

Rather than investigate all the wonderful calculations you can do using trig, let's look at a visualization of sound synthesis. A pure tone, such as a middle E produced by a tuning fork, can be represented by a sine wave that has the same *frequency* (number of oscillations per second) as the note. (A *sine wave* is the form you get when you plot the sine function.) More complex tones, such as a middle E produced by a singer, piano, or trombone, get their distinctive characters by blending in different ratios of *overtones* (*harmonics*), which are sine waves that are integer multiples of the basic frequency. For instance, a middle E has a *fundamental* frequency of 440 Hz (440 vibrations per second). The fundamental also is called the *first harmonic*. Its *first overtone* (or *second harmonic*) has a frequency of 880 Hz, its *second overtone* (*third harmonic*) has a frequency of 1320 Hz, and so on. These can be visualized as sine waves of increasing frequency and decreasing wavelengths.

Combining a fundamental frequency with its harmonics produces a *waveform* whose appearance relates to the tonal quality of the sound; different waveforms sound different, even when they represent the same fundamental tone. Synthesizers, for example, can try to duplicate the sound of a violin by combining sine waves in such a way as to duplicate the waveform of a violin sound.

With Visual Basic, it's relatively simple to put together a program that lets you select a blend of harmonics and see what they look like individually and combined. Prepare a program according to the recipe provided by Table L15-10 and Figure L15-12. Note that the program uses a control array of labels, a control array of horizontal scrollbars, and a control array of text boxes. In each case, the indices run from 2 to 5 because the controls correspond to the 2nd through the 5th harmonics. Use Copy and Paste to speed up adding these control arrays. The purpose of the scrollbars is to let you select how much of each harmonic to blend with the fundamental.

OBJECT	PROPERTY	SETTING
Form1	Auto3d	True
	Caption	Harmonic Waves
	Name	frmHarmonic
Label1	Caption	2nd harmonic
	Index	2
	Name	lblHarm
Label2	Caption	3rd harmonic
	Index	3
	Name	lblHarm
Label3	Caption	4th harmonic
	Index	4
	Name	lblHarm
Label4	Caption	5th harmonic
	Index	5
	Name	lblHarm

OBJECT	PROPERTY	SETTING
HScrollBar1	Max	10
	Index	2
	Name	hsbHarm
HScrollBar2	Max	10
	Index	3
	Name	hsbHarm
HScrollBar3	Max	10
	Index	4
	Name	hsbHarm
HScrollBar4	Max	10
	Index	5
	Name	hsbHarm
TextBox1	Alignment	1 - Right Justify
	Index	2
	Name	txtHarm
	ReadOnly	True
	Text	0.0
TextBox2	Alignment	1 - Right Justify
	Index	3
	Name	txtHarm
	ReadOnly	True
	Text	0.0
TextBox3	Alignment	1 - Right Justify
	Index	4
	Name	txtHarm
	ReadOnly	True
	Text	0.0
TextBox4	Alignment	1 - Right Justify
	Index	5
	Name	txtHarm
	ReadOnly	True
	Text	0.0
Command1	Caption	&Plot
	Name	cmdPlot
Command2	Caption	Clear
	Name	cmdClear
PictureBox1	Name	picHarm
	ScaleHeight	–3
	ScaleLeft	0
	ScaleMode	0 - User

continued on next page

continued from previous page

OBJECT	PROPERTY	SETTING
	ScaleTop	1.5
	ScaleWidth	6.283
PictureBox2	Name	picWhole
	ScaleHeight	–8
	ScaleLeft	0
	ScaleMode	0 - User
	ScaleTop	4
	ScaleWidth	6.283

Table L15-10 Properties for the Harmonic Waves form

Before going to the code, note the scale properties for the two picture boxes. The ScaleWidth of 6.283 is (approximately) 2π radians (360°). The reason for choosing this range is that the sine function repeats itself every 2π radians, so this range lets you see the full function. For the picHarm picture box, using a negative scale height of –3 means the *y*-coordinate increases from bottom to top, the usual way for graphs, instead of from top to bottom, the usual way for Visual Basic coordinates. Setting ScaleTop to 1.5 then makes the vertical range from 1.5 to –1.5. The picWhole picture box uses the same technique to make the vertical range go from 4 to –4. This scaling centers the sine waves on the horizontal axis.

The basic idea for plotting a function is to use the *PSet* method, using *X* and *Sin(X)* as coordinates, and using a *For* loop to march across the screen. Here *Start* and *Finish* represent the initial and final values for the *X*-coordinate:

```
For X = Start To Finish Step 0.01
    picHarm.PSet (X, Sin(X)), vbBlue
Next X
```

To plot the second harmonic, replace Sin(X) with Sin(X * 2). Similarly, use Sin(X * 3) to get the third harmonic. (That's how harmonics work. Multiplying

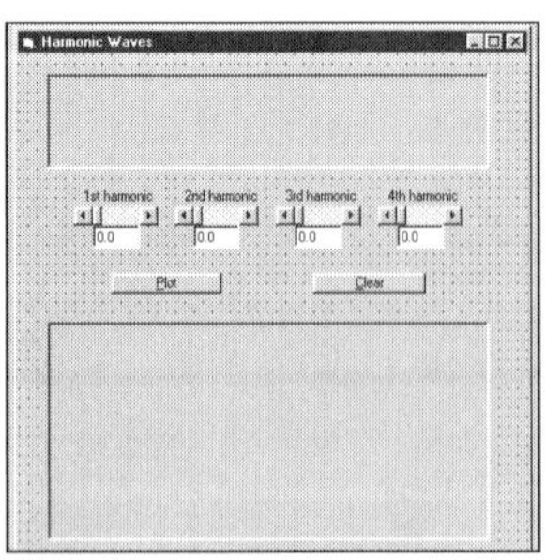

Figure L15-12 The Harmonic Waves form

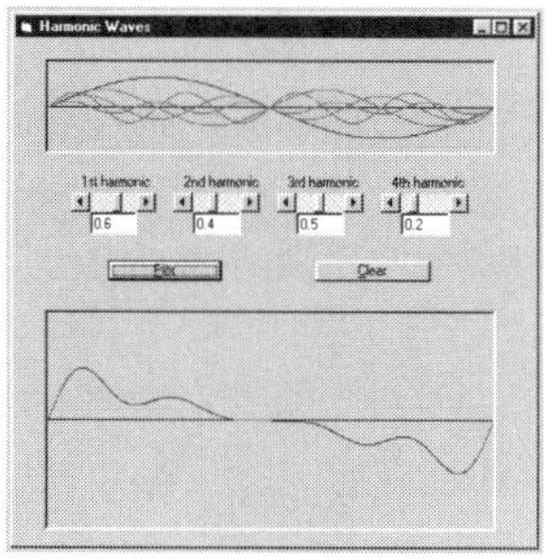

Figure L15-13 TA waveform blend

X by 2 makes the *Sin* function go through twice as many cycles. That is, if *X* ranges from 0 to 2π, then *x* ∗ 2 ranges from 0 to 4π.) The scrollbars let you set a coefficient that governs the vertical scaling for each harmonic. That represents how much harmonic gets blended in. The larger the coefficient for a harmonic, the more you get of that particular sound. The program stores these values in an array called *Coef* whose index range is 2 to 5, corresponding to the index values for the scrollbar controls. That is, the first scrollbar and the first *Coef* element have an *Index* value of 2, and so on. This means that we can use

```
Coef(Index) * Sin(X * Index)
```

to represent the *Y* value for each harmonic.

The picHarm box will show each sine curve separately, so it will use code like this:

```
For I = 2 To 5
    picHarm.PSet (X, Coef(I) * Sin(X * I)), vbRed
Next I
```

But the picWhole box will add all the components together, so it will use code like this:

```
Y = Sin(X)
For I = 2 To 5
    Y = Y + Coef(I) * Sin(X * I)
Next I
```

Listing L15-5 shows the complete code for the program. It starts out with *Coef* array values of 0 so that the opening graphs show just the pure sine function. By using the scrollbars, however, you can select new values and produce a blend, as shown by Figure L15-13.

Listing L15-5
The Harmonic Waves program

```
Option Explicit
Dim Coef(2 To 5) As Single
```

continued on next page

continued from previous page

```
Private Sub cmdClear_Click()
    picHarm.Cls
    picWhole.Cls
End Sub

Private Sub cmdPlot_Click()
    picHarm_Paint
    picWhole_Paint
End Sub

Private Sub Form_Initialize()
    Dim I As Integer
    For I = 2 To 5
        Coef(I) = 0
    Next I
End Sub

Private Sub hsbHarm_Change(Index As Integer)
    Coef(Index) = hsbHarm(Index).Value / 10
    txtHarm(Index).Text = Format(Coef(Index), "0.0")
End Sub

Private Sub picHarm_Paint()
    Dim X As Single
    Dim Start As Single
    Dim Finish As Single
    Dim I As Integer
    Start = 0
    Finish = picHarm.ScaleWidth
    picHarm.Line (Start, 0)-(Finish, 0), vbBlack
    For X = Start To Finish Step 0.01
        picHarm.PSet (X, Sin(X)), vbBlue
        For I = 2 To 5
            picHarm.PSet (X, Coef(I) * Sin(X * I)), vbRed
        Next I
    Next X
End Sub

Private Sub picWhole_Paint()
    Dim X As Single
    Dim Y As Single
    Dim Start As Single
    Dim Finish As Single
    Dim I As Integer
    Start = 0
    Finish = picWhole.ScaleWidth
    picWhole.Line (Start, 0)-(Finish, 0), vbBlack
    For X = Start To Finish Step 0.01
        Y = Sin(X)
        For I = 2 To 5
            Y = Y + Coef(I) * Sin(X * I)
        Next I
        picWhole.PSet (X, Y), vbBlue
    Next X
End Sub
```

SUMMARY

Math functions give Visual Basic the muscle to perform a variety of tasks, including recreational, scientific, financial, engineering, and graphical calculations. The *Rnd* and *Randomize* functions give you random number support, and the general math functions and trigonometric math functions come in handy in many situations. You can construct many other functions from these functions—look up "Derived Math Functions" in Visual Basic Help.

QUIZ 15

1. Evaluate the following expressions. (If you don't want to evaluate them yourself, see if you can talk Visual Basic into evaluating them for you.)

a. 2 + 5
b. 50 / 8
c. 50 \ 8
d. 3 ^ 2
e. 2 ^ 3

2. Suppose you have an urgent need for ten random numbers in the range 100–200. Write a loop that prints ten such numbers.

3. Evaluate the following expressions:

a. Abs(10-15)
b. Int(23.66)
c. Int(–23.66)
d. Fix(23.66)
e. Fix(–23.66)

4. Johannes Kepler discovered that the time (in years) taken by a planet to orbit the Sun equals the square root of the cube of the average distance (in Astronomical Units) of the planet from the Sun. If D is the average distance of a planet from the Sun, write an expression that evaluates to how long that planet takes to orbit the Sun.

5. How far is it to the horizon from a viewpoint 10 feet off the ground? 100 feet off the ground? 10,000 feet off the ground?

6. What interest rate, compounded quarterly, do you need to double your money in five years?

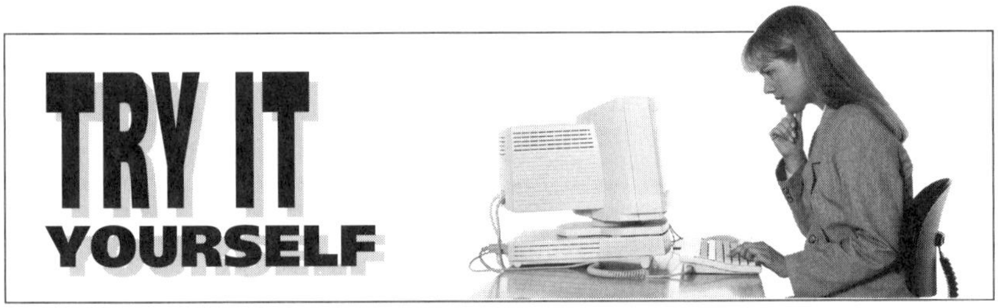

1. Write a program that asks you how many seconds it takes you to run a mile and which converts that to a time in minutes and seconds.

2. Try your graphics skills. Simplify the dice-throwing program so that it uses just two six-sided dice, but have it show the results graphically by showing two squares with the proper number of pips showing.

3. Write a program that shuffles a 52-card deck and displays the result. You can use a suffix to indicate the suit when you display it. For example, "10 H" could be the 10 of hearts. To keep things simple, you can use 1 for an Ace, 11 for a Jack, 12 for a Queen, and 13 for a King.

4. You've probably heard radioactive materials described in terms of a *half life*. The half life is how long it takes for half the sample to decay. You might think the whole sample would be gone after two half lives, but that's not how it works. Instead, half of what is left decays the next half life, and so on. So if you start with 64 pounds, you have 32 pounds left after one half life, 16 pounds after two half lives, 8 pounds after 3 half lives, and so. More generally, if A_0 is the amount you start with, if *A* is the amount after *T* time elapses, and if *THalf* is the half life, you have this relationship, where log is the natural (base e) logarithm:

$$A = A_0 e^{-(\log 2) * T / THalf}$$

Write a program that lets you provide a half-life value, an amount of radioactive material, and an elapsed time, and which then tells you the amount of radioactive material remaining.

LESSON

16 DOING IT YOUR WAY

An important principle of modern programming is to make things modular. Visual Basic's controls certainly fit the bill, and so do the myriad facilities built in to Visual Basic—functions such as *Sqr* and *Format* and methods such as *Circle* and *Print*. These functions and methods are preprogrammed modules for performing common tasks. But Visual Basic doesn't limit you to these built-in methods and functions. As you already know, it provides a framework—the event procedures—to provide your own responses to standard events. Beyond that, Visual Basic lets you name and write your own procedures and functions, and that's what this lesson's about. In particular, you'll learn about the following topics:

- **Creating procedures**
- **Procedures with arguments**
- **Procedures with objects as arguments**
- **Using the MsgBox message box**
- **Using the InputBox dialog box**
- **Creating functions**
- **Passing arguments by reference and by value**
- **Allowing for optional arguments**

PROCEEDING WITH PROCEDURES

Procedures do things. If you want an example of a procedure, think of methods. Methods, such as *Print, Circle,* and *AddItem,* are procedures attached to particular objects. They do things, such as display a message, draw a circle, or add "Cabbage" to a list. The procedures you'll work with now, however, are *general procedures,* meaning they aren't attached to any particular object. Let's look at two important questions:

- Why would you create a procedure?
- How do you create a procedure?

(If you don't have a good answer for the first question, you probably won't be interested in the second one.)

One good reason to write a procedure is if you find you're using the same chunk of code over and over. Rather than retype or copy the chunk each time, you can make a procedure out of it. Then, whenever you need that chunk of code, you call the procedure. Another reason to write procedures is to organize your code and make your programs more readable. For instance, suppose you had a command-button *Click* procedure that uses a few feet of code getting information, manipulating it somehow, then displaying a result. You could replace most of that code with three procedures, one called *GetInfo,* one called *MassageInfo,* and one called *ShowInfo.* Then the *Click* procedure would call these three procedures, making the *Click* procedure short and easily understood.

Making Diamonds

Let's look at an example that replaces repeated code with a procedure. Suppose you want to draw a diamond shape on a form. You can do that using the *Line* method four times:

```
Line -Step(500, 500)
Line -Step(-500, 500)
Line -Step(-500, -500)
Line -Step(500, -500)
```

This example starts from the current graphics position, then draws a line diagonally down to the right, diagonally down to the left, diagonally up to the left, and diagonally up to the right.

Now suppose you want to draw several diamonds. Then you can change the current graphics position and use the same code again. This is where your lazy-programmer circuit—er, efficient-programmer circuit—should kick in and say, why not use a procedure instead?

Let's do it. Open a new project and enter the code shown in Listing L16-1. To create the *Form_Paint* procedure, open the Code window and select the *Paint* procedure. (Recall that graphics drawn in a *Paint* procedure are redrawn automatically if the form is concealed, then revealed again.) To create the *Diamond0* procedure, just type it as shown after the *Option Explicit* statement at the top of the Code window. If you position the cursor in the *Diamond0* definition, the Code window Object box will identify the object as *(General)*, meaning it's not associated with any particular object. That is, the procedure is just *Diamond0*, not *Form_Diamond0* nor *cmdStrike_Diamond0*.

Listing L16-1
The Diamond0 program

```
Option Explicit

Sub Diamond0()                    'define a general procedure
    Line -Step(500, 500)
    Line -Step(-500, 500)
    Line -Step(-500, -500)
    Line -Step(500, -500)
End Sub                           'end of definition

Private Sub Form_Paint()
    Dim I As Integer
    CurrentY = 1000
    For I = 1 To 5
        CurrentX = 1000 * I
        Diamond0                  'call the procedure
    Next I
End Sub
```

The *Diamond0* procedure has this simple form:

Sub *Procedure_Name* ()
....[*statements*]
End Sub

Note the keywords **Sub** and **End Sub**. They mark the beginning and the end of the procedure definition. Also note the parentheses. More generally, they enclose arguments to the procedure, but you're beginning with a simple case with no arguments.

Public and Private

Visual Basic uses the keyword Private in declaring event procedures, as in the following:

Private Sub Form_Paint()

That means the procedure is private to the form module and can't be called by code in other modules. If you use the keyword *Public* instead of *Private* or omit using either, the procedure is a public procedure and can be called by code in other modules. So far, all the examples have been one-module programs, so the distinction hasn't been relevant. But the distinction will become important in Lessons 19 and 20, which discuss multiple-module projects.

To call this procedure, just use the procedure name as a line of code; note that no parentheses are used here:

```
Diamond0
```

We say that this procedure call takes place in the *calling procedure* and that *Diamond0* is the *called procedure*. When the program reaches the procedure call, it jumps from the call statement to the called procedure. After executing the statements in the called procedure, the program jumps back to the next line in the calling procedure. See Figure L16-1.

This example calls *Diamond0* five times, so it should draw five diamonds. Figure L16-2 shows the result of running this program.

Adding Arguments

The *Diamond0* procedure lacks ambition. It only draws one size of diamond. Usually, it's a good idea to make procedures more general than that. But if the procedure is to make diamonds of more than one size, it needs to get information about the desired size. And the way to do that is to supply the procedure with arguments. You already have a model for how that looks. For instance, the skeleton for a *KeyPress* event procedure looks like this:

```
Private Sub cmdMe_KeyPress(KeyAscii As Integer)

End Sub
```

The idea is that you declare arguments within the parentheses. This procedure, for instance, declares a type *Integer* argument named *KeyAscii*.

Let's apply this technique to a new diamond procedure called *Diamond1*. First, decide what information it needs. You could just give one argument that takes the place of the 500 value:

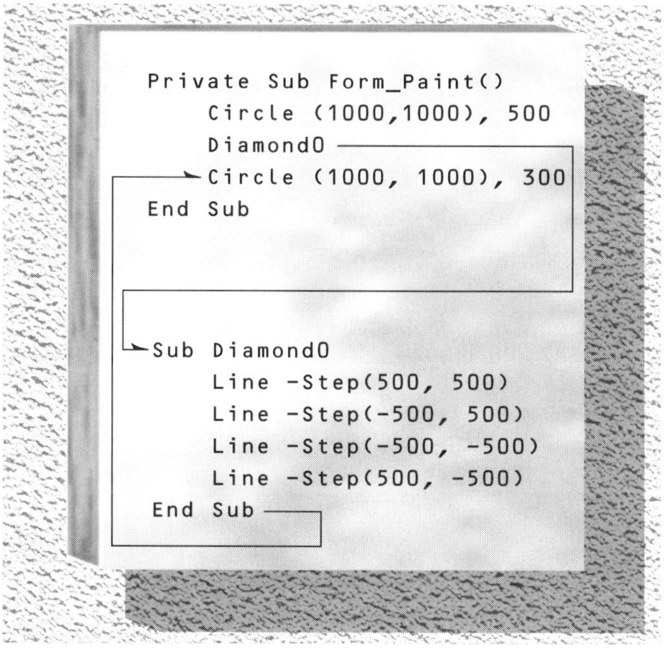

Figure L16-1 Calling a procedure

```
Sub Diamond1(Size as Single)     'first draft
    Line -Step(Size, Size)
    Line -Step(-Size, Size)
    Line -Step(-Size, -Size)
    Line -Step(Size, -Size)
End Sub
```

However, you can make this more general. First, you can add arguments specifying the starting point for drawing the diamond. Next, instead of limiting the diamond to one shape, you can add arguments representing the width and height of the diamond. Because the procedures you define aren't described in Visual Basic Help, it's a good idea to include some comments explaining the subroutine.

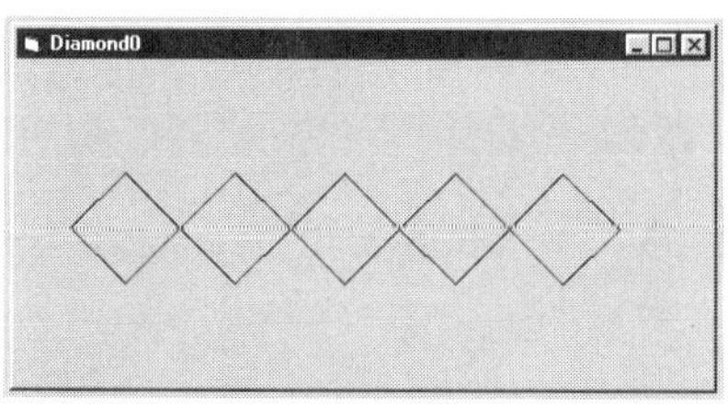

Figure L16-2 Output from the Diamond0 procedure

```
'Diamond1 draws a diamond shape on a form.
'X,Y are coordinates of top of diamond.
'W is width of diamond, H is height of diamond.
Sub Diamond1(X As Single, Y As Single, W As Single, H As Single)
    Line (X, Y)-Step(W / 2, H / 2)
    Line -Step(-W / 2, H / 2)
    Line -Step(-W / 2, -H / 2)
    Line -Step(W / 2, -H / 2)
End Sub
```

Note

As with ordinary variables, Visual Basic assumes a procedure argument is a Variant unless you give the type explicitly. So the definition

Sub Light (X)

...

End Sub

means *X* is a type *Variant* argument. If the context calls for a specific type, such as *Single* for specifying positions, you are better off explicitly declaring the type that should be used.

Listing L16-2 shows a program using this procedure. It uses a loop to draw a succession of diamond shapes:

```
For I = 1 To 5
    Diamond1 2000, 250, 250 * I, 500 * I
    Diamond1 4000, 1000, 500 * I, 1000
Next I
```

The first call produces diamonds of progressively greater width (*250 * I*) and height (*500 * I*) as *I* increases, while the second call produces diamonds of progressively greater width (*500 * I*) and of constant height (*1000*). Figure L16-3 shows the output.

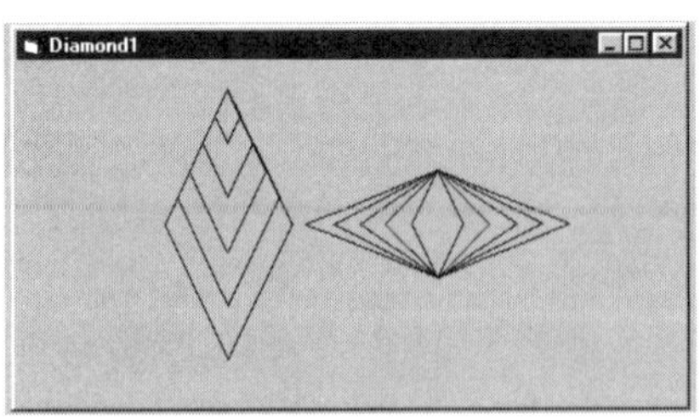

Figure L16-3 Using Diamond1

Listing L16-2
The Diamond1 program

```
Option Explicit

'Diamond1 draws a diamond shape on a form.
'X,Y are coordinates of top of diamond.
'W is width of diamond, H is height of diamond.
Sub Diamond1(X As Single, Y As Single, W As Single, H As Single)
    Line (X, Y)-Step(W / 2, H / 2)
    Line -Step(-W / 2, H / 2)
    Line -Step(-W / 2, -H / 2)
    Line -Step(W / 2, -H / 2)
End Sub

Private Sub Form_Paint()
    Dim I As Integer
    For I = 1 To 5
        Diamond1 2000, 250, 250 * I, 500 * I
        Diamond1 4000, 1000, 500 * I, 1000
    Next I
End Sub
```

Tip

When writing a procedure, consider if you can easily make it more general and useful by providing additional arguments.

Adding Flexibility—Object Arguments

Diamond1 is a nice improvement over *Diamond0.* But what if you want to draw diamonds in a picture box instead of on a form? *Diamond1* just does forms. You could modify it as follows:

```
Sub Diamond2(X As Single, Y As Single, W As Single, H As Single)
    picMe.Line (X, Y)-Step(W / 2, H / 2)
    picMe.Line -Step(-W / 2, H / 2)
    picMe.Line -Step(-W / 2, -H / 2)
    picMe.Line -Step(W / 2, -H / 2)
End Sub
```

This attempt would draw diamonds in a picture box named *picMe,* but not in a picture box by any other name. That's too restrictive to be useful. Remember, however, that you can have object variables (see Lesson 13), that is, variables that represent objects, such as picture boxes. You can use an argument of an object type to represent which object gets the diamond drawn. There are three object types that can represent a picture box. First, there's the specific type of *PictureBox.* Then there are the two generic types *Control* and *Object.* Using a *PictureBox* type argument would let the procedure work with any picture box, but only with picture boxes. Use of a *Control* type argument would let the procedure work with any kind of control. However, the only control that has a *Line* method is the picture box, so use of the more general *Control* type doesn't make sense. Use of the *Object* type, however, would let the procedure work with picture boxes and with forms, since both are objects. That suggests something along the following lines:

```
Sub Diamond2(X As Single, Y As Single, W As Single, H As Single, _
        PaintPlace As Object)
    PaintPlace.Line (X, Y)-Step(W / 2, H / 2)
    PaintPlace.Line -Step(-W / 2, H / 2)
    PaintPlace.Line -Step(-W / 2, -H / 2)
    PaintPlace.Line -Step(W / 2, -H / 2)
End Sub
```

If you have a form named *frmDiam2* and a picture box named *picDiam*, you now can use code like the following:

```
'Draw a diamond on a form.
Diamond2(1000, 2000, 500, 1000, frmDiam2)
'Draw a diamond on a form without bothering to remember the name.
Diamond2(1000, 2000, 500, 1000, Me) 'Me = the form containing this code
'Draw a diamond in a picture box.
Diamond2(500, 1000, 400, 600, picDiam)
```

In the first procedure call, the type *Object* argument *PaintPlace* is the form *frmDiam2;* in the second call, *PaintPlace* is *Me* (the shortcut name for the current form); and in the third call, *PaintPlace* is the picture box *picDiam.*

Tip

Use *Object* type arguments to tie a general procedure to specific objects.

However, you can abuse this version of *Diamond2*. Suppose cmdTest is a command button. What's to keep you from doing this?

```
Diamond2(500, 1000, 400, 600, cmdTest) 'misuse of procedure
```

The answer is that nothing keeps you from doing this. Of course, command buttons don't have a *Line* method, so Visual Basic will give you an error message to that effect. Still, it would be nice to make the procedure a bit more considerate. Here's one way:

```
Sub Diamond2(X As Single, Y As Single, W As Single, H As Single, _
        PaintPlace As Object)
    If (TypeOf PaintPlace Is Form) Or (TypeOf PaintPlace Is PictureBox) Then
        PaintPlace.Line (X, Y)-Step(W / 2, H / 2)
        PaintPlace.Line -Step(-W / 2, H / 2)
        PaintPlace.Line -Step(-W / 2, -H / 2)
        PaintPlace.Line -Step(W / 2, -H / 2)
    Else
        MsgBox "Diamond2 used with wrong kind of object", , "Diamond2"
    End If
End Sub
```

There are three things to note here. First, the procedure uses the *TypeOf Is* statement (see Lesson 13) to limit drawing to an approved list of objects.

Second, it uses a new function called *MsgBox* to tell you when you've misused the procedure. You'll learn a bit more about this function later. For now, suffice it to say that it displays a *dialog box*. The first string argument is the message displayed in the box, the second argument (skipped here) describes what buttons appear in the box, and the third argument is a string used to title the box. If you omit the second argument, as shown, the box displays an OK button which must be clicked on before you can return to the rest of the program. If you omit the third argument, Visual Basic uses the project name. The third thing to note is that the program uses the TypeOf function (see Lesson 5) to identify the type of the offending object.

To test *Diamond2*, create a new project as described by Table L16-1 and enter Listing L16-3 in the Code window.

OBJECT	PROPERTY	SETTING
Form1	Caption	Diamond2
	Name	frmDiam2
PictureBox1	Name	picDiam
	ScaleHeight	100
	ScaleWidth	100
Command1	Caption	Testing
	Name	cmdDiam

Table L16-1 Properties for the Diamond2 form

Listing L16-3
The Diamond2 program

```
Option Explicit

'Draws a diamond in object PaintPlace, which should be a form or picture box.
'X,Y are the coordinates of the top of the diamond.
'W is the width and H is the height.
Sub Diamond2(X As Single, Y As Single, W As Single, H As Single, _
        PaintPlace As Object)
    If (TypeOf PaintPlace Is Form) Or (TypeOf PaintPlace Is PictureBox)
Then
    PaintPlace.Line (X, Y)-Step(W / 2, H / 2)
        PaintPlace.Line -Step(-W / 2, H / 2)
        PaintPlace.Line -Step(-W / 2, -H / 2)
        PaintPlace.Line -Step(W / 2, -H / 2)
Else
       MsgBox "Diamond2 can't be used with a " & TypeName(PaintPlace), _
           , "Diamond2"
    End IfEnd Sub

Private Sub cmdTest_Click()
    Diamond2 100, 100, 50, 50, cmdTest
End Sub

Private Sub Form_Paint()
    Dim I As Integer
```

continued on next page

continued from previous page

```
    For I = 1 To 5
        Diamond2 2000, 500, 250 * I, 500 * I, frmdiam2
    Next I
End Sub

Private Sub picDiam_Paint()
    Dim I As Integer
    For I = 1 To 5
        Diamond2 50, 100 * (I - 1) / (2 * I), 100 / I, 100 / I, picDiam
    Next I
End Sub
```

Figure L16-4 shows the result of running this program, and Figure L16-5 shows the message box that appears after clicking the Test command button.

DIALOG BOXES—*MSGBOX* AND *INPUTBOX*

Visual Basic provides two dialog box functions. The first, *MsgBox*, puts a message box onscreen and presents one to three response buttons to the user. The second, *InputBox*, solicits the user for keyboard input.

You've already seen *MsgBox* used with the following syntax:

MsgBox *prompt* [, *buttons*] [, *title*]

Here *prompt* is a string representing the message to be displayed, *buttons* is an integer defining what response buttons will appear, and *title* is the string that will appear in the message box title bar. If *buttons* is omitted, just an OK button appears, and if *title* is omitted, the application name is used. There are two more possible arguments that can be used to associate the message box with Help references, but this book won't go into those. It will say more about the *buttons* variable. Table L16-2 lists the fundamental choices for this variable.

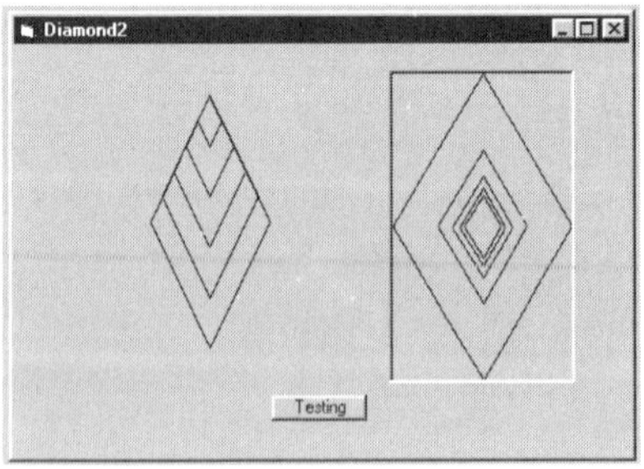

Figure L16-4 Drawing on a form and in a picture box

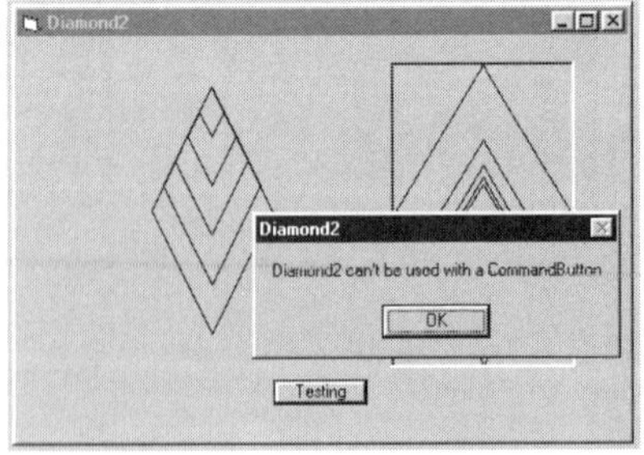

Figure L16-5 The *MsgBox* dialog box

VALUE	SYMBOLIC NAME	BUTTONS DISPLAYED
0	vbOKOnly	OK button
1	vbOKCancel	OK and Cancel buttons
2	vbAbortRetryIgnore	Abort, Retry, and Ignore buttons
3	vbYesNoCancel	Yes, No, and Cancel buttons
4	vbYesNo	Yes and No buttons
5	vbRetryCancel	Retry and Cancel Buttons

Table L16-2 Button choices for *MsgBox*

Use a value from this table to select which buttons appear in the message box. For example, the statement

```
MsgBox "Do you wish to continue?", vbYesNo
```

would give the user the choice of clicking on a Yes button or a No button. Of course, it would be nice to know which button got clicked. The *MsgBox* function returns a value that tells you the answer. Table L16-3 lists the possible return values.

VALUE	SYMBOLIC NAME	BUTTON CLICKED
1	vbOK	OK
2	vbCancel	Cancel
3	vbAbort	Abort
4	vbRetry	Retry
5	vbIgnore	Ignore
6	vbYes	Yes
7	vbNo	No

Table L16-3 Return values for *MsgBox*

You can get the *MsgBox* return value and compare it to the values in Table L16-3. For instance, you can do this:

```
Response = MsgBox ("Do you wish to continue?", vbYesNo)
If Response = vbYes Then
    ...
End If
```

There's a Visual Basic peculiarity you should notice. If you use *MsgBox* without obtaining the return value, as the earlier examples did, you don't enclose the arguments in parentheses. But if you do use the return value, as in the above code snippet, you do enclose the arguments in parentheses.

Rule

If you obtain the return value of *MsgBox*, enclose the *MsgBox* argument list in a pair of parentheses. Otherwise, omit the parentheses. The same rule applies to user-defined functions.

Let's look at a short example using message boxes. First, open a new project and follow the plan of Table L16-4.

OBJECT	PROPERTY	SETTING
Form1	Caption	Character Assessment
	Name	frmAssess
Command1	Caption	Assess
	Name	cmdAssess

Table L16-4 Properties for the Character Assessment Form

Then use the Code window to add the program shown in Listing L16-4. Note when parentheses are used and when they are omitted in using *MsgBox*.

Listing L16-4
The Character Assessment program

```
Option Explicit

Private Sub cmdAssess_Click()
    Dim Response As Integer
    Response = MsgBox("Do you wish to continue?", vbYesNo, "Assess")
    If Response = vbYes Then
        MsgBox "That was very foolish of you!", , "Assess"
    Else
        MsgBox "Perhaps next time...", , "Assess"
        End
    End If
End Sub
```

Clicking on the Yes button yields a character assessment. Clicking on No yields a comment and terminates the program. Figure L16-6 shows the appearance of the first dialog box. Note that the Yes button is highlighted, and hence is the default.

You can use the button argument to choose which button is the default choice by using the constants shown in Table L16-5. You add one of these constants to the constant used to specify the button choice. For example, to show the Yes and No buttons and to make No the default, use the following expression:

```
vbYesNo + vbDefaultButton2
```

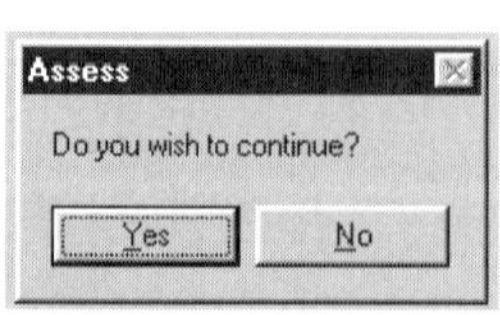

Figure L16-6 A message box with Yes and No buttons

VALUE	SYMBOLIC NAME	DEFAULT BUTTON
0	vbDefaultButton1	First button
256	vbDefaultButton2	Second button
512	vbDefaultButton3	Third button

Table L16-5 Default button choices for *MsgBox*

Also, you can modify the appearance of the message box by adding one of the values from Table L16-6 to the *buttons* argument. These choices add an icon to the message box. You can add only one icon. For instance, you could modify the second use of *MsgBox* in Listing L16-4 to read as follows:

```
MsgBox "That was very foolish of you!", vbOKOnly + vbInformation, "Assess"
```

Figure L16-7 shows how the information icon looks when this message box is displayed.

VALUE	SYMBOLIC NAME	ICON ADDED
16	vbCritical	Critical Message
32	vbQuestion	Warning Query
48	vbExclamation	Warning Message
64	vbInformation	Information Message

Table L16-6 Icon choices for *MsgBox*

Note

The *MsgBox* dialog box is an example of a *modal* dialog box. That means that once the dialog box comes up, you can't return to any other window until you respond to the box's needs, in this case, by clicking a button.

Getting Input with *InputBox*

The *MsgBox* function limits your input to clicking on one of the buttons displayed in the message box. The *InputBox* function is more open-ended, for it

Figure L16-7 The Information icon

supplies a text box for your input. Here's a somewhat simplified syntax, one that omits arguments relating to tying the box to a help file:

InputBox (*prompt* [, *title*] [, *default*] [, *xpos*] [, *ypos*])

Here *prompt* is a string displayed in the dialog box, *title* is a string used as the dialog box title, *default* is a string that appears as the default answer in the dialog text input box, and *xpos* and *ypos* are the horizontal and vertical coordinates of the top left corner of the dialog box. If *title* is omitted, Visual Basic uses the name of your program; if *default* is omitted, Visual Basic leaves the text input box empty. If *xpos* is omitted, Visual Basic centers the box horizontally; if *ypos* is omitted, Visual Basic centers the box vertically. Finally, when you press ENTER or click on the OK button, *InputBox* returns the string in the text input box, and the example assigns the string to the *Who* variable.

To see how this works, open a new project with a command button, as described in Table L16-7. Then endow the command button with the simple code shown in Listing L16-5. Running the program and clicking on the button then shows the input box illustrated in Figure L16-8. Enter a name, press ENTER, and you can see the response incorporated into a message box, as shown in Figure L16-9.

OBJECT	PROPERTY	SETTING
Form1	Caption	Dialog
	Name	frmDial
Command1	Caption	Query
	Name	cmdQuery

Table L16-7 Properties for the Dialog form

Listing L16-5
The Dialog program

```
Option Explicit

Private Sub cmdQuery_Click()
    Dim Who As String
    Who = InputBox("Hello, there! What's your name?", "Who are you?")
    MsgBox "Well, " & Who & ", I hope you are computer friendly!", ,
"Dialog"
End Sub
```

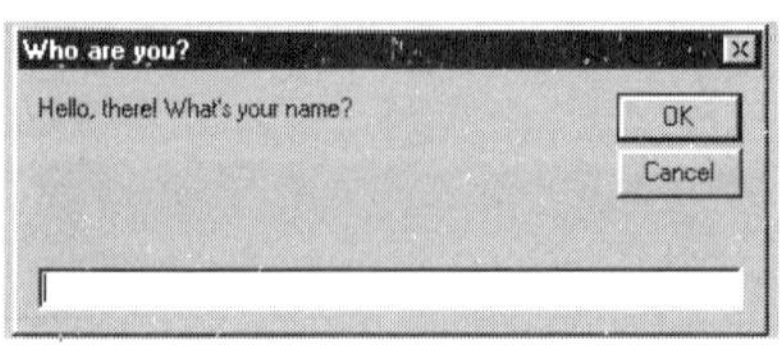

Figure L16-8 An input box

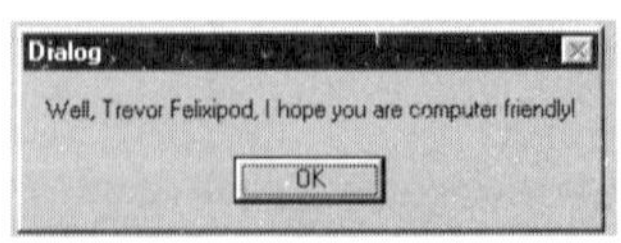

Figure L16-9 Using the return value of InputBox

FUNCTIONING ON YOUR OWN

Let's turn from the built-in *MsgBox* and *InputBox* functions to user-defined functions. A function is something that you can pass information to and which then returns a value to you. For example, you can pass a number to the *Sqr* function, and *Sqr* returns the square root of that number. The *InputBox* function returns the user's input string. The *Format* function returns formatted information as a *Variant* value. Visual Basic has a goodly supply of functions, and you can define your own functions, too.

Functions and procedures are quite similar to each other. The main difference is that a function returns a value. Thus, the syntax is similar to that for user-defined procedures, except that it allows for specifying a return value. Suppose, for example, you want a *Cube* function that calculates and returns the cube of a value. You can write it this way:

```
Function Cube (N as Double) as Double   ' takes a double, returns a double
      Cube = N * N * N   ' assign value to be returned to function name
End Function
```

Note that the body of the function assigns a value to the name of the function. This is how Visual Basic identifies the return value of a function. For that reason, a function definition declares a type for the function as well as for any arguments. The function type is the type of the return value (see Figure L16-10).

Once you have this function definition entered in your Code window, you can use the function in your project. Unlike the case for procedures, you use parentheses to enclose the arguments to a function in a function call. For example, you could display a table of numbers and their cubes, as shown in Listing L16-6 and Figure L16-11.

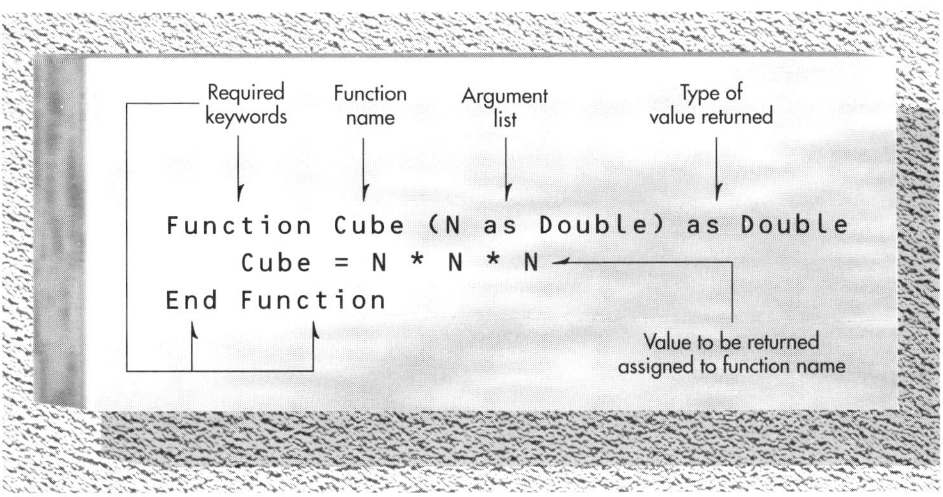

Figure L16-10 A function definition

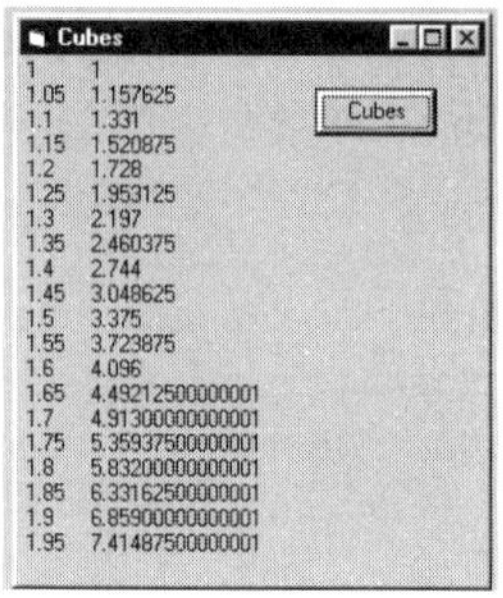

Figure L16-11 Displaying a table of cubes

Listing L16-6
The Cubes program

```
Option Explicit

Function Cube(N As Double) As Double
    Cube = N * N * N
End Function

Private Sub cmdCube_Click()
    Dim I As Double
    For I = 1# To 2# Step 0.05
        Print I; Tab(8); Cube(I)   'Cube(I), not Cube I
    Next I
End Sub
```

However, if you just call the function without using its return value, omit the parentheses. (But calling a function without using its return value only makes sense if the function has some side effect, such as displaying a message box.)

Rule

Function calls, unlike procedure calls, enclose the argument list in parentheses. The only exception is if you don't use the return value; then you omit the parentheses.

More generally, a function definition has this form:

Function *FunctionName* (*argument_list*) [**as** *Typename*]
  ...
  FunctionName = *value*
End Function

If you don't specify a type for the function, Visual Basic assumes it is a *Variant* type.

The *Exit Function* Statement

Sometimes functions require a more elaborate design than did the *Cube* example. For example, consider a function that takes the lengths of three sides of a triangle as arguments and returns the area of the triangle. Not all combinations of values correspond to triangles. For instance, suppose you specify sides of 10, 20, and 100. You can't draw such a triangle because one of the purported sides is longer than the other two put together. Let's look at one way to handle such a problem.

First, you need a formula for the area of a triangle in terms of the lengths of its sides. Suppose the three sides are s1, s2, and s3. First, calculate a value equal to half the perimeter:

sp = (s1 + s2 + s3) / 2

Given this value, you can calculate the area of the triangle as follows:

area = square root (sp * (sp – s1) * (sp – s2) * (sp – s3))

Next, you need a way to decide whether the values represent a real triangle. A simple way is to evaluate the expression sp * (sp – s1) * (sp – s2) * (sp – s3). This represents the square of the area, so if it's negative, the area would be an imaginary number. That's a pretty strong signal that the side values were invalid! It turns out that if the expression is positive, the sides do correspond to a genuine triangle.

Listing L16-7 follows up on this information to define a *TriArea* function along with a *Click* procedure that solicits values to use with the function. Here's the part that handles false triangles:

```
If A2 < 0 Then
    MsgBox "That's no triangle!", vbExclamation
    TriArea = -1
    Exit Function
End If
```

The *A2* variable represents the square of the area. If it's less than 0, the function puts up a message box telling you of the problem. Also, it sets *TriArea* to –1 as a sign that the area is not defined for this set of arguments. Finally, it uses the *Exit Function* statement. This causes the function to terminate immediately, returning the value –1.

The reason for using *Exit Function* is that if you have multiple assignments to the function name, the last assignment is the one that counts; a function doesn't terminate automatically the first time you assign to the function name. For instance, consider the following function:

```
Function Dumb( ) as Integer
    Dumb = 10
    Dumb = 3
    Dumb = 20
End Function
```

Visual Basic executes all three assignment statements, finally terminating and returning the value 20.

Listing L16-7
The Area of a Triangle program

```
Option Explicit

'returns area of a triangle having sides S1, S2, S3
Function TriArea(S1 As Single, S2 As Single, S3 As Single) As Single
     Dim SP As Single    'half the perimeter
     Dim A2 As Single    'square of the area
     SP = (S1 + S2 + S3) / 2
     A2 = SP * (SP - S1) * (SP - S2) * (SP - S3)
     If A2 < 0 Then
          MsgBox "That's no triangle!", vbExclamation
          TriArea = -1
          Exit Function
     End If
     TriArea = Sqr(A2)
End Function

Private Sub cmdTri_Click()
     Dim a As Single, b As Single, c As Single, Area As Single
     a = InputBox("Enter length of first side:", "Side A")
     b = InputBox("Enter length of second side:", "Side B")
     c = InputBox("Enter length of third side:", "Side C")
     Area = TriArea(a, b, c)
     If Area = -1 Then
          MsgBox "Try another set of values."
     Else
          MsgBox "Area of the triangle is " & Format(Area), , "Answer"
     End If
End Sub
```

By the way, if this were a program you planned for others to use, you also should use the *IsNumeric* function to check if the *InputBox* return values really represent numbers.

MORE ABOUT ARGUMENTS

There's more to function and procedure arguments than you might think. So far, the examples have contented themselves with giving each argument a name and a type. But there are other aspects and options. In particular, you can pass an argument by reference or by value, and you can have optional arguments. Let's examine these points.

Passing by Reference

By default, Visual Basic passes arguments *by reference*. This means that the argument variable in the called function or procedure is a reference to, or an alias for, the corresponding argument in the function or procedure call. For instance, consider the following function call from Listing L16-7:

```
Area = TriArea(a, b, c)
```

Passing by reference means that *S1* in the *TriArea* function definition becomes an alias for *a*, *S2* becomes an alias for *b*, and *S3* becomes an alias for *c*. That means that any changes to *S1* really are changes to *a*. For example, suppose *TriArea* had this code in it for some peculiar reason (such as to demonstrate this point):

```
S1 = 100 * S1
```

Because *S1* really is *a*, the variable *a* gets multiplied by 100. Thus, when the program returns to the *cmdTri_Click* event, the variable *a* would have a new value equal to 100 times its original value.

Note

The way passing by reference works internally is that Visual Basic passes the address (the location in memory) of the variable to the called function or procedure. The function or procedure then can use that address to access the contents of the original variable.

The alternative to passing by reference is *passing by value*, where a function or procedure creates a new variable that is a copy of the original variable. You'll get to that soon, but first let's look at reasons for passing by reference. One is if you want to use a procedure to modify its arguments. For instance, suppose you wanted to exchange the values of two variables. In that case, you really need the procedure to modify values in the calling program. You could write such a procedure like this:

```
Sub SwapDbl(X as Double, Y as Double)
    Dim Temp as Double
    Temp = X
    X = Y
    Y = Temp
End Sub
```

Suppose, now, that you used the following code:

```
Dim BobCash as Double, AnneCash as Double
BobCash = 3200.12
AnneCash = 2582.23
SwapDbl(BobCash, AnneCash)
```

Then, when *SwapDbl* swaps the values of *X* and *Y*, it's really swapping the values of *BobCash* and *AnneCash*. The *SwapDbl* procedure, by design, alters values in the calling procedure.

You also can use the reference property to write a procedure that usurps the role of a function. For instance, you could replace the *Cube()* function with the following procedure:

```
Sub ProCube (N as Double)
     Dim Temp as Double
     Temp = N
     N = Temp * Temp * Temp
End Sub
```

A procedure call like *ProCube(Ism)* would then reset the variable *Ism* to the cube of its original value. However, as you'll see shortly, this is a poor design. If you want to calculate a single value, it's better to use the function approach of returning that value than to use the procedure approach of altering an argument.

Another reason for passing by reference instead of by value is that it is more efficient in time and memory space when the argument is a data type that occupies a lot of space. For example, suppose the argument is a string of 2,000 characters. It's much simpler and quicker to pass the address of the string than to copy all 2,000 characters to a new location.

Finally, passing by reference is the way to go for object variables. Consider the program in Listing L16-8. The *ReScale* procedure changes the size of a control by multiplying its height and width by a scale factor. Clearly, this process only makes sense if you change the properties of the original control, so you want *Thing* to be a reference to the *imgSee* object rather than be a copy of the object. Also, you wouldn't want to spend the time and space needed to copy all the properties of an object.

Listing L16-8
The ByRef program

```
Option Explicit

Sub ReScale(Thing As Control, SF As Single)
     Thing.Height = SF * Thing.Height
     Thing.Width = SF * Thing.Width
End Sub

Private Sub cmdReSize_Click()
     Dim ScaleFactor As Single
     ScaleFactor = InputBox("Enter scale factor:", "Scaling")
     ReScale imgSee, ScaleFactor
End Sub
```

Problems with Passing by Reference

Passing by reference has some pitfalls. Consider the *Cube* function definition:

```
Function Cube(N As Double) As Double
     Cube = N * N * N
End Function
```

This says that *N* is a reference to a type *Double* variable. What happens, then, if you use the wrong kind of variable in a function call?

```
Dim X as Single, Y as Double
X = 5.2
Y = Cube(X)
```

Well, a *Single* is not a *Double*, and Visual Basic won't allow *N* to be a reference to *X*. You get a warning like that shown in Figure L16-12.

Note

When a variable is passed by reference to a procedure, it should have the same type as the corresponding procedure argument. Otherwise Visual Basic informs you that there is an argument type mismatch.

What if you use a number instead of a variable? That is, suppose you try this:

```
Dim Y as Double
Y = Cube (4)
```

This looks bad. First of all, 4 is type *Integer*, not *Double*. Second, 4 is not even a variable, and *N* is supposed to be an alias for a variable. So it looks like this function call shouldn't work. But it does! When the argument in the *Cube* function call is a value, Visual Basic creates an anonymous temporary variable of type *Double,* assigns the value to that variable, then makes *N* a reference to that nameless variable (see Figure L16-13).

In fact, Visual Basic performs that trick (making *N* refer to a temporary anonymous variable) when you use an expression of any sort rather than a variable when passing by reference. An expression is a combination of constants, variables, operators, and keywords that evaluates to a number, string, or object. So while

```
Cube (X)   ' X type Single
```

leads to an error, all the following examples are acceptable:

```
Cube (5)        ' 5 assigned to a temporary variable
Cube (W + 5)    'W type Double, W + 5 an expression
Cube (X + 5)       'X type Single, X + 5 an expression
Cube (Sqr(11)) 'Sqr a keyword, Sqr(11) an expression
Cube ((X))     ' X type Single, (X) an expression
```

Note that if *X* isn't type *Double* (to match the declared type for *N*), *Cube (X)* is an error, but *Cube ((X))* isn't. The parentheses are operators (order of evaluation), so placing them around a variable creates a variable-operator combination, which is an expression.

Figure L16-12 Result of passing the wrong kind of variable

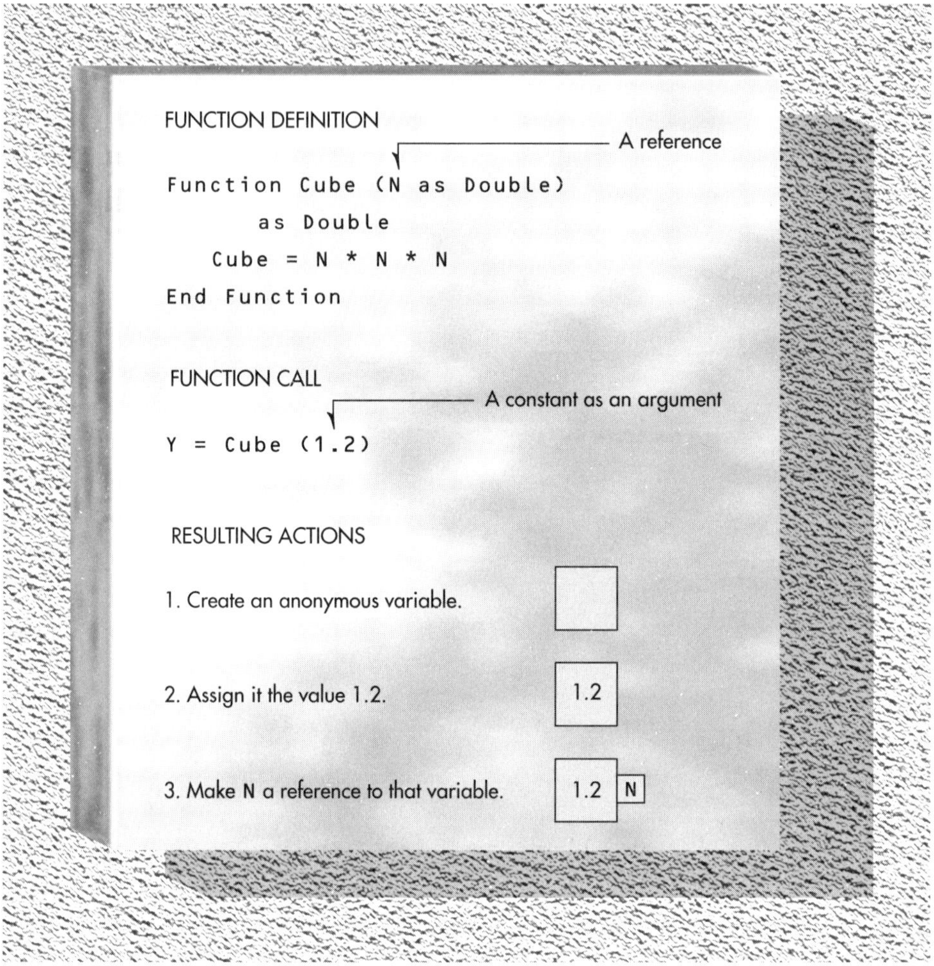

Figure L16-13 Passing by reference using a nonvariable argument

Note

When a procedure passes an argument by reference, the argument must either be a variable whose type is an exact match to the reference variable type or else an expression. In the latter case, Visual Basic generates a temporary, anonymous variable that's assigned the value of the expression, and the reference variable becomes an alias for that variable.

All this fancy work makes sense if the procedure or function uses the argument values without trying to change them. That's the case for the *Cube* definition. But consider the *ProCube* definition:

```
Sub ProCube (N as Double)
    Dim Temp as Double
    Temp = N
    N = Temp * Temp * Temp
End Sub
```

Consider the following code:

```
Dim X as Single, Y as Double
Y = 2.5
X = 3.5
ProCube(Y)
ProCube(X)
ProCube((X))
```

For the *ProCube(Y)* call, *N* becomes an alias for *Y* (both are *Double*), and *Y* gets reset to the cube of its original value. For the *ProCube(X)* call, you get an error because *X* is the wrong type of variable. For the *ProCube((X))* call, Visual Basic creates an anonymous variable, assigns it the value 3.5, finds the cube, and assigns that to the anonymous variable, not to *X*—all in all, a useless maneuver. The moral is that this is a poor design. If the intent is to calculate a single value, use a function that returns that value.

Passing by Value

In many cases, it makes more sense to pass by value than to pass by reference. When you pass by value, Visual Basic creates a new variable that is assigned the value of the procedure or function argument. That means the procedure or function works with a copy of the original data rather than with the original data itself (see Figure L16-14). To indicate that an argument is passed by value, use the keyword *ByVal* in the definition. For instance, here's yet another way to write a cube routine:

```
Function ValCube(ByVal N as Double) as Double
    ValCube - N * N ^ N
End Function
```

Here *N* is a local variable in the *ValCube* function. It's initialized to the value of whatever argument you use:

```
Dim X as Single, Y as Double, Z as Double
Y = 2.5
X = 3.5
Z = ValCube(Y)          'N set to 2.5
Z = ValCube(X)          'N set to 3.5
Z = ValCube(X + Y + 10) 'N set to 16.0
```

Note that when you pass by value, its okay if, say, the function uses a *Double* argument and you pass it a *Single* or an *Integer* value. The types don't have to match. All that is required is that it's legal to assign one to another. Since Visual Basic lets you assign from one numeric type to another, passing by value is a good choice for numeric arguments.

Let's summarize what you've learned. Passing by value has two advantages:

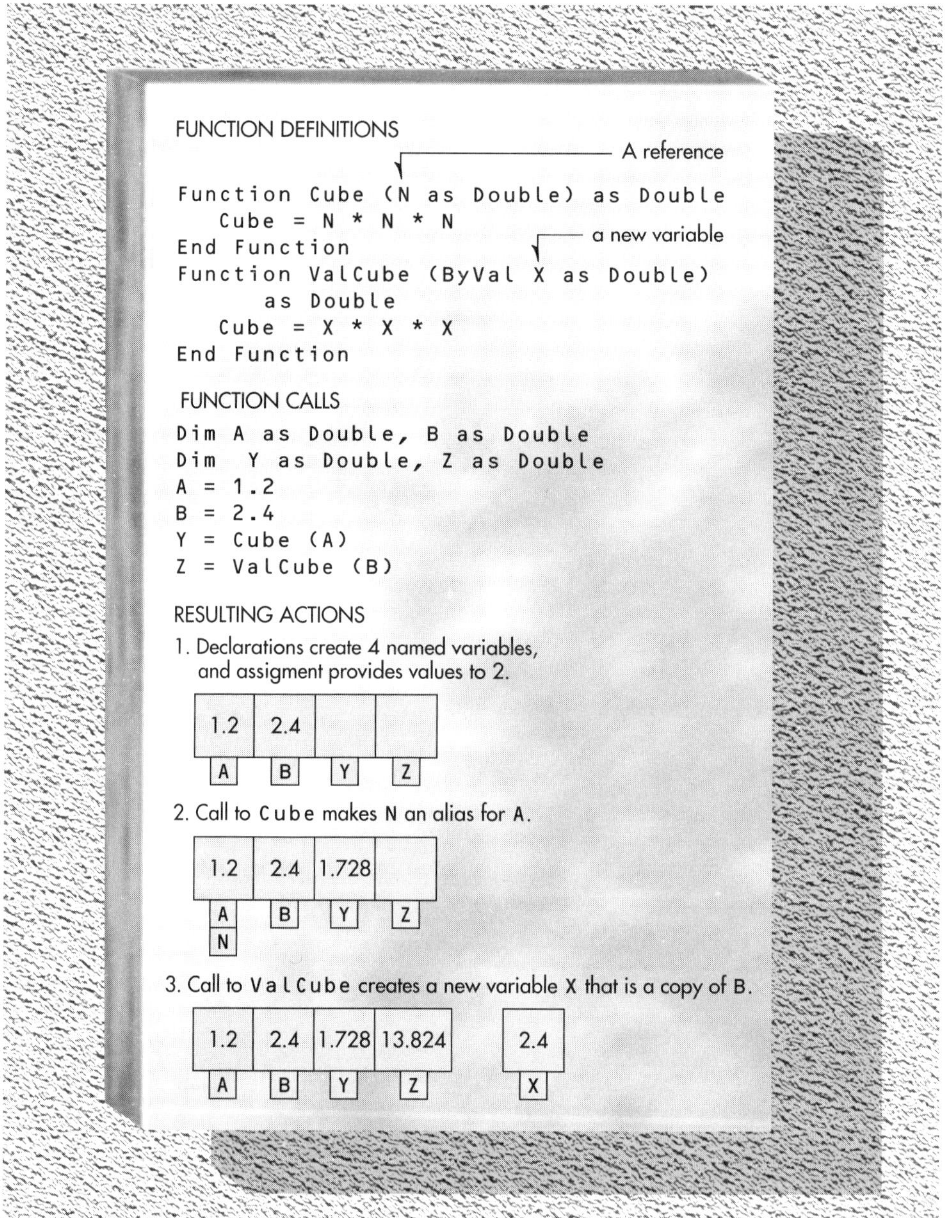

Figure L16-14 Passing by reference versus passing by value

- Because the procedure works with the copy of the original information, the original information is insulated from accidental change.
- As long as the passed value is of a type that can be assigned to the procedure argument, you don't have to worry about matching the argument types exactly.

Which should you use, the default passing by reference or the optional passing by value? The answer depends on the context. Here are some rules of thumb:

- If the purpose of the procedure is to modify its arguments, you have to pass by reference. Examples would be a procedure that capitalizes a string argument or a procedure that swaps two values.
- If the arguments are numbers that are used but not modified, pass by value. Examples would be a function that returns the larger of two arguments or a procedure that displays some numbers.
- If the arguments require larger chunks of memory than do numbers, pass by reference to avoid using time and memory to make copies. Examples would be procedures that operate on a string or on an object.

As mentioned earlier, passing by reference is the Visual Basic default. You can, however, use the keyword *ByRef* to clarify your intentions. For example consider a procedure definition that starts like this:

```
Sub Flark (ByVal X as Single, Y as Single)
```

In this case *X* is passed by value and *Y* is passed by reference (the default), but a careless reader might think both are passed by value. The following declaration, however, clarifies your intent:

```
Sub Flark (ByVal X as Single, ByRef Y as Single)
```

Optional Arguments

Visual Basic allows you to create procedures and functions with optional arguments, that is, arguments that you can choose to omit when calling a procedure or function. When defining a function or procedure with optional arguments, follow these rules:

- Precede the name of an optional argument with the keyword *Optional*.
- Use only the *Variant* type for optional arguments.
- Place optional arguments at the end of the argument list.

Let's see how this works. Suppose you were working on a program to generate memos. As part of that project, you wish to create a procedure that prints a *To:* line and a *Re:* line. Most of the memos in your company are about the Gandalf Project, so you'd like to make that the default entry for the *Re:* line, but you want to give the user the option of providing a different choice. You can start like this:

```
Sub Memo(NameTo As String, Optional Subject As Variant)
```

This states that the *Memo* function takes a string as its first argument and that it optionally has a *Variant* as its second argument.

When you write the code for *Memo*, you need some way of knowing whether the procedure call actually used a second argument. The *IsMissing* function gives the answer. It takes as its argument the name of an optional argument. If a procedure is called without using a particular optional argument, the *IsMissing* function returns True for that argument. Listing L16-9 shows how to use the *IsMissing* function to control what happens. If the user omits the argument, the *Memo* procedure prints the default subject line. Otherwise, *Memo* uses the subject provided by the user as the second argument.

Listing L16-9
The Optional Arguments program

```
Option Explicit

Sub Memo(NameTo As String, Optional Subject As Variant)
    Print "To: " & NameTo
    If IsMissing(Subject) Then
        Print "Re: The Gandalf Project"
    Else
        Print "Re: " & Subject
    End If
End Sub

Private Sub cmdTest_Click()
    Dim Name1 As String, Name2 As String
    Dim Subject As Variant
    Name1 = "Ronald Fellpepper"
    Name2 = "Annette Zogblat"
    Subject = "Giraffe Lore"
    Memo Name1, Subject 'override default subject line
    Print
    Memo Name2      'use default subject line
    Print
    Memo Name2, ""
End Sub
```

The command button in this listing invokes *Memo* three times, first with a second argument, then without a second argument, then with an empty string as the second argument. The output (see Figure L16-15) illustrates that passing an empty string still counts as passing an argument.

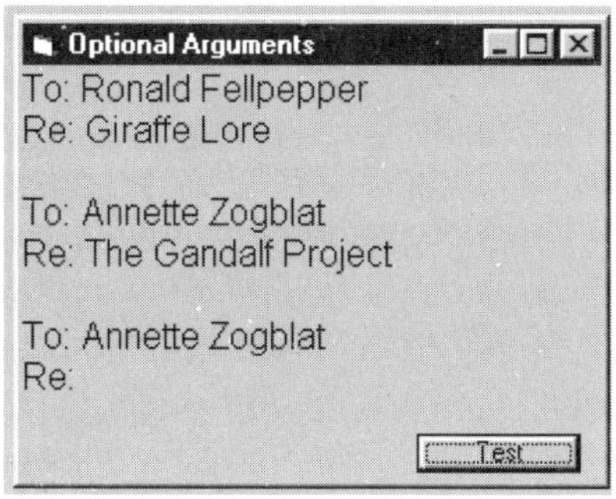

Figure L16-15 Using the *Memo* procedure

Using an Indefinite Number of Arguments

Procedures and functions normally take a fixed number of arguments. Optional arguments add some flexibility, but sometimes it's useful to have a function or procedure that takes an indefinite number of arguments. For example, suppose you want a function that returns the largest value in a series of values. For example, *Max(2,5)* would return 5 and *Max(40,60,-11,34)* would return 60.

To gain this capability, you use the keyword *ParamArray* along with a special syntax when declaring procedure or function arguments:

```
Function Max(ParamArray Nums()) As Variant
```

Essentially, this means that *Nums* is an array of parameters for the function. For flexibility, *ParamArray* array elements are type *Variant*. The simplest way to access the individual parameters is to use the *For Each* statement. (When you use *For Each* with an array, the array elements must be type *Variant*, and *Nums* meets that requirement.) For instance, the example in Listing L16-10 sets the variable *Maxi* to the first element of the array. Then it uses the *For Each* loop to compare each element with the current value of *Maxi*, updating *Maxi* whenever it finds a larger value.

Listing L16-10
The Maxi program

```
Option Explicit

Function Max(ParamArray Nums()) As Variant
    Dim N As Variant
    Dim Maxi As Variant
    Maxi = Nums(0)
    For Each N In Nums
        If N > Maxi Then Maxi = N
    Next N
    Max = Maxi
```

continued on next page

continued from previous page

```
End Function

Private Sub cmdTest_Click()
     frmMax.Font.Size = 18
     Print Max(3, 2, 5)
     Print Max(10, 11, 20, 14)
     Print Max("Cow", "Dog", "Cat")
End Sub
```

Figure L16-16 shows the result of running the example. Because the parameter array is type *Variant,* you can use *Max* with strings as well as with numbers, in which case the comparison is in terms of the ASCII code. (This is an example of a case where the *Variant* type is more suitable than a more specific type, such as *Integer.*)

SUMMARY

Procedures and functions help you to modularize your programs and to encapsulate common tasks. The procedure that uses another procedure is the calling procedure, and the procedure that's used is the called procedure. The same terminology holds for functions. In general, procedures and functions accept information from a calling procedure or function in the form of arguments. By default, these arguments are references, meaning they act as aliases for variables in the calling program. However, by using the *ByVal* keyword, you can have an argument passed by value, meaning that the value of an argument in a calling function or procedure is assigned to a new variable in the called function or procedure.

By using the *Optional* keyword in conjunction with the *IsMissing* function, you can create procedures or functions with optional arguments. These optional arguments must be *Variants*, and they must come at the end of the argument list.

Figure L16-16 Using an indefinite number of arguments

By using the *ParamArray* keyword in conjunction with a *For Each* loop, you can construct functions or procedures that take an indefinite number of arguments.

Functions can communicate, or return, a value back to the calling function or procedure. The technique is to assign the return value to the function name.

You can use the *MsgBox* and *InputBox* functions to create dialog boxes. The *MsgBox* function displays one to three response buttons that the user can select, while the *InputBox* function lets the user enter a response in a text box.

1. What, if anything, is wrong with the following procedure definition:

```
Sub Marine
    Print "Surfacing!"
End
```

2. What's a *calling procedure* and what's a *called procedure?*

3. Indicate whether each of the following is a valid type for a procedure argument:
   a. Double
   b. String
   c. Variant
   d. ListBox
   e. UnStable

4. If you wanted a procedure to be able to resize only labels, what would an appropriate argument type be?

5. If you wanted a procedure to be able to resize any control, but not forms, what would an appropriate argument type be?

6. How would you write a procedure that would be able to affect list boxes and combo boxes but no other kind of control?

7. In terms of having a dialog with a program, how is a message box different from an input box?

8. What would you use for the second argument to *MsgBox* to get the following conditions?

a. Show just the OK button.
b. Show the Yes, No, and Cancel buttons.
c. Show the Yes, No, and Cancel buttons with No being the default.
d. Show the Abort, Retry, and Ignore buttons accompanied by the Warning Message icon.

9. What's wrong, if anything, with the following function definition:

```
Sub Function Hypotenuse (X as Double, Y as Double)
    Double Hypo
    Hypo = X * X + Y * Y
End Sub
```

10. What's the difference between passing by value and passing by reference?

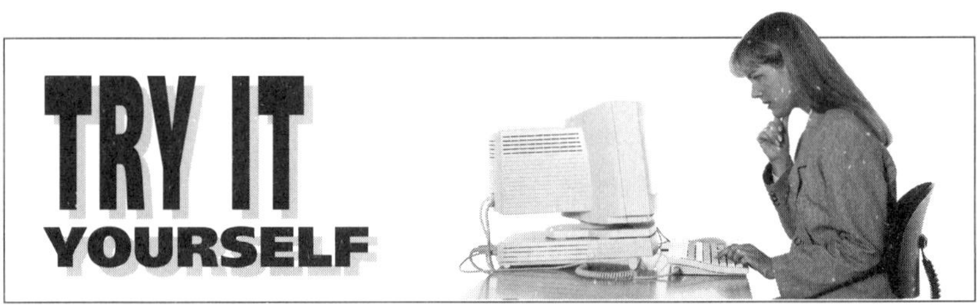

1. Modify the *Diamond2* procedure so that the coordinate arguments specify the center of the diamond instead of the top.

2. Write a procedure *PrintN* that takes a string and an integer as arguments and which prints the string a number of times equal to the value of the integer. For example,

```
PrintN "Viva Visual Basic", 5
```

would print the string *"Viva Visual Basic"* five times.

3. Write a function that returns the harmonic mean of two values. If *X* and *Y* are two values, the harmonic mean is 0.5 * *X* * *Y* / (*X* + *Y*). Have the function give a warning message if *X* equals -*Y*.

4. Write a function that returns the average of an indeterminate number of arguments.

5. Write a procedure that takes the name of a list box as its first argument plus an indeterminate additional number of arguments. The procedure adds each of the additional arguments to the specified list.

LESSON

17 WHAT'S WRONG?

Creating a program, even a Visual Basic program, is a marvelous opportunity for making mistakes. You can, for example, use a method incorrectly, try to use a nonexistent property, or lead the program to an untenable action, such as dividing by zero, or taking the square root of the string *"twenty"*. Or you can misorganize a program so that it does something different

from what you intended. Visual Basic does provide assistance to help you detect and fix such problems. In this lesson, you'll examine the following:

- **Compile errors, including syntax errors**
- **Runtime errors**
- **Logic errors**
- **The Debug window**
- **Watch values**
- **Breakpoints**
- **Error trapping**
- ***On Error***
- **The *Err* object**

By the time you complete this lesson, you'll be better prepared to deal with many of the vicissitudes of programming.

COMPILE ERRORS

Compile errors are the easiest to deal with. They occur when you write code unacceptable to the Visual Basic compiler. For instance, you might violate the official syntax for a command:

```
Line 100,100 - 2000,2000 'a syntax error
```

Here we've omitted the parentheses around each coordinate pair. What makes syntax errors easy to detect is that the compiler lets you know about them. If you type the preceding line of code in the Code window and try to go to the next line, Visual Basic turns the code to red (a sure sign of trouble) and displays

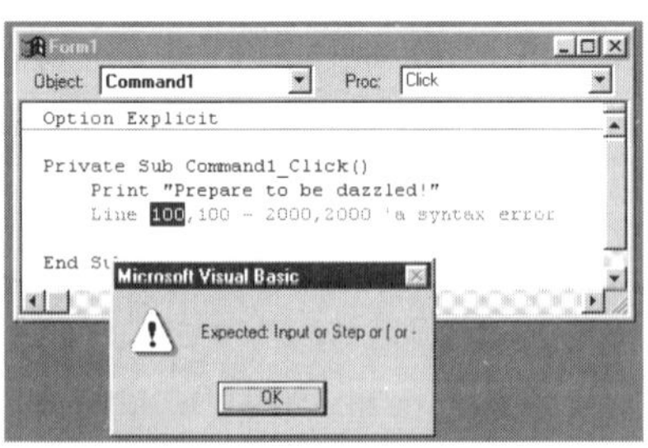

Figure L17-1 Visual Basic objects to syntax errors

a complaint in a message box, as shown in Figure L17-1. Visual Basic also highlights the part of the offending line that caught its attention. If you don't get this kind of service, select Environment Options from the Visual Basic Tools menu and make sure that the Display Syntax Errors check box is checked.

If the meaning of the complaint isn't clear to you, try pressing F1 while the message box is onscreen. This brings up Visual Basic Help. If you press F1 for the preceding example, for instance, you get a Help window headed "Expected: <various>." It discusses the various things that may have been expected in a statement, giving you guidance as to what the complaint was about.

Or you can click on OK, return to the Code window, select a method, property, or command, and press F1 to bring up help on that topic. In this case, for example, you would select the word *Line*, press F1, and consult Visual Basic Help about this method to see the proper syntax. (You can get help this way anytime, not just after blundering.)

Alternatively, you can use the Object Browser (under the View menu) to locate the *Line* method, then click on the question-mark icon to bring up Help. Or you can simply select Help from the main Visual Basic menu and use the Search feature to locate entries relating to *Line*. Perhaps the main point here is that you shouldn't forget about the large amount of information that Visual Basic makes available to you via Visual Basic Help.

Some compile errors don't show up until you try to run a program. One common kind of error is attempting to use a property or method with the wrong object. For example, suppose you have this code:

```
Private Sub cmdFine_Click()
    Text1.TEXT = "I'm fine!"
End Sub
```

The syntax itself is fine, but suppose you've forgotten to create a text box or that you created one and renamed it txtFine. Then there is no object called Text1.

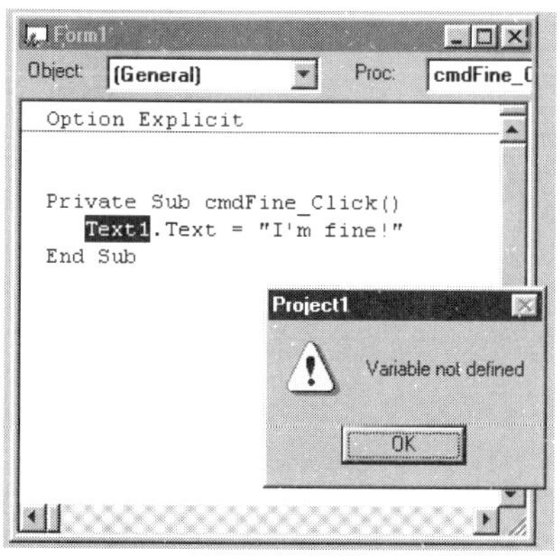

Figure L17-2 What happens when there's no Text1 object

Attempting to run the program then leads to a message box proclaiming "Variable not defined" (see Figure L17-2). Also it highlights Text1, identifying it as something that hasn't been defined.

You can get another kind of compiler error by associating a method or property with the wrong kind of object. For example, suppose you have a txtFine text box control and use this code:

```
Private Sub cmdFine_Click()
    txtFine.Caption = "I'm fine!"
End Sub
```

If you try to run a program with this code, Visual Basic highlights the word "Caption" and points out that "Method or Data Member not found." That's because a text box object doesn't have a Caption property. (A data member is the same as a property.) You'd get the same message if you, say, tried using *txtFine.Print "Hello"*, for text boxes don't have a *Print* method, either.

RUNTIME ERRORS

Runtime errors turn up while a program is running. These errors may turn up if the program tries to use values incorrectly, such as finding the square root of a negative number or trying to set the width of a control to "donkey." Or you may have made a logic error that sends the program off on a wild goose chase. Some errors cause a program to halt and tell you about the error, while others may have more subtle effects. Let's look at some examples now.

Type Problems

Some runtime errors occur when variables or properties acquire unexpected properties. For instance, consider the following procedure:

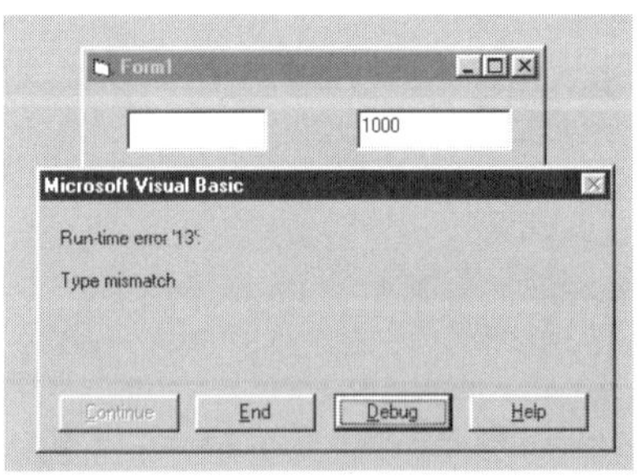

Figure L17-3 Result of attempting to cube an empty string

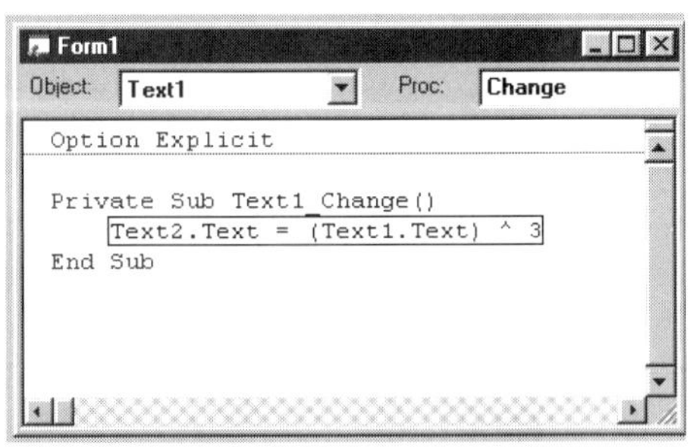

Figure L17-4 Selecting Debug points out the error's location

```
Private Sub Text1_Change()
    Text2.TEXT = (Text1.TEXT) ^ 3
End Sub
```

The intent is to display in the second text box the cube of whatever number is in the first text box. This works fine when, say, *Text1.TEXT* is 20. Even though the Text property is really the string "20", Visual Basic kindly converts the string to an integer. But suppose the user backs the cursor over the *20,* erasing the text. Then Text1.TEXT becomes the empty string, and Visual Basic doesn't convert that to a number. You can't really cube an empty string, so Visual Basic issues the runtime error message shown in Figure L17-3: "Type mismatch." As you would think, this means that you've mismatched a type to a proposed operation.

Note that this message box gives you some choices. *End* terminates the program, dumping you back into design mode. *Help* brings up a message explaining the nature of the error, in this case, the concept of the type mismatch. *Debug* brings up the Code window, which identifies the code that causes the problem. It also puts Visual Basic in break mode. Break mode will be discussed later. Right now, the main point is that selecting Debug helps pinpoint the problem (see Figure L17-4).

Once you find the problem, you can try to fix it. For example, you can fix the empty string problem this way:

```
Private Sub Text1_Change()
    If Text1.TEXT <> "" Then
       Text2.TEXT = (Text1.TEXT) ^ 3
    End If
End Sub
```

This is a bit lame, because it doesn't help if the user enters, say, "Duh," instead of a number. It does avoid the most likely input error, but you're better off thinking more generally. For instance, you can use the *IsNumeric* function, which returns True if its argument is a number or can be converted to a number. And you can tell the user what's wrong with the input:

```
Private Sub Text1_Change()
    If IsNumeric(Text1.TEXT) Then
        Text2.TEXT = (Text1.TEXT) ^ 3
    Else
        MsgBox "Please enter numbers only"
    End If
End Sub
```

Tip

When a program expects numeric input, use the *IsNumeric* function to check whether the input values are numbers, and use *MsgBox* to guide users to entering the correct type of data.

Zero Defects

Let's look at another example that invokes Debug. Let's construct a program that lets you enter a list of numbers and then displays their sum and average. One approach is the program outlined in Figure L17-5 and Table L17-1.

OBJECT	PROPERTY	SETTING
Form1	Caption	Average Finder
	Name	frmAve
Label1	Caption	Enter numbers here
	Name	lblHere
Label2	Caption	Sum
	Name	lblSum
Label3	Caption	Average
	Name	lblAve
Text1	Name	txtInput
	Text	
Text2	Name	txtSum
	Locked	True
	Text	
Text3	Name	txtAve
	Locked	True
	Text	
Picture1	AutoRedraw	True
	Name	picList
Command1	Caption	Done
	Name	cmdDone

Table L17-1 Properties for the Average Finder project

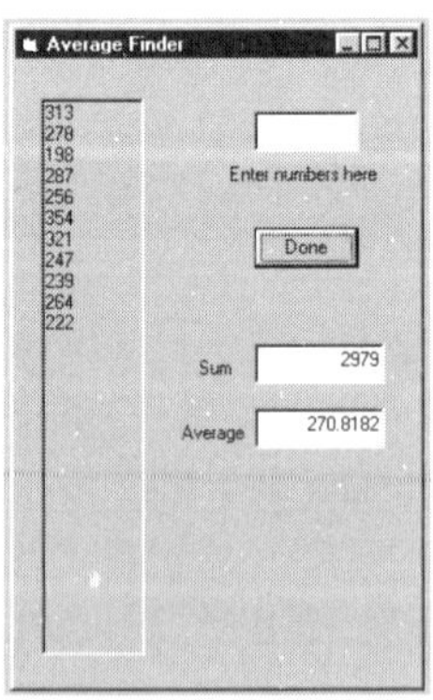

Figure L17-5 The Average Finder Project

The aim of this modest program is to let you enter numbers in the txtInput text box. Each number you enter is copied over to the picList picture box so that the box shows a list of all the numbers entered. When you click on the command button, the program calculates and displays the sum and average of the list of numbers. Listing L17-1 shows one possibility for the code. The key feature is using the *KeyPress* event to watch for ENTER. When the user presses ENTER, the *KeyPress* event then copies the txtInput text to the picList picture box, using picList.Print to print each new addition on a new line. So as not to treat the empty string as a number, the listing includes code to handle empty strings as well as any other nonnumeric strings.

Listing L17-1
The Average Finder project

```
Option Explicit
Dim Cnt As Integer
Dim Total As Single

Private Sub cmdDone_Click()
txtSum.TEXT = Total
    txtAve.TEXT = Total / Cnt
End Sub

Private Sub txtInput_KeyPress(KeyAscii As Integer)
    If KeyAscii = 13 Then
        If IsNumeric(txtInput.TEXT) Then
            Cnt = Cnt + 1
            Total = Total + CSng(txtInput.TEXT)
            picList.Print txtInput.TEXT
        Else
            MsgBox "Please enter numbers only", , "Average Finder"
        End If
        txtInput.TEXT = ""
    End If
End Sub
```

The program works fine until someone wonders, "What will happen if I click on Done without entering any numbers?" The answer is, you get a runtime error, as shown in Figure L17-6, which complains of an overflow. That means some number got too big to handle. If you then click on the Debug button, you find that the source of the error is this line:

```
txtAve.TEXT = "Average = " & Format(Total / Cnt)
```

The problem is that this line divides by *Cnt*, which starts out with the value 0. Dividing by 0 (even dividing 0 by 0) gets you in trouble with the computer hardware, so Visual Basic halts the program before that can happen.

There are three important points here:

- You shouldn't divide by 0.
- If you do, the Debugger helps you find the location of your error.

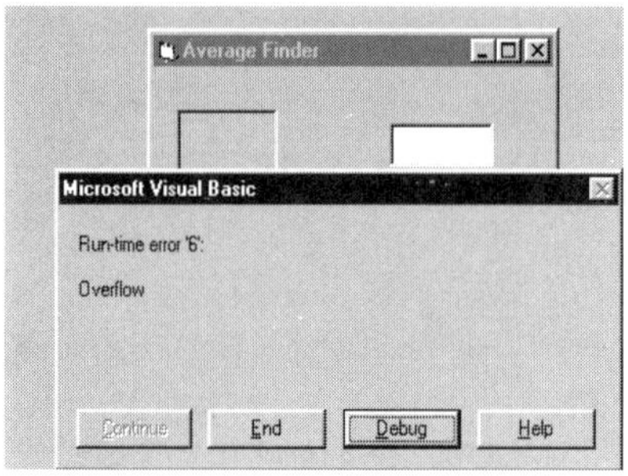

Figure L17-6 Overflow problem

Once you become aware of the potential error, you should try to eliminate it.

In many cases, you can fix things with a judiciously worded *If* statement. In this case, for example, you can replace the problem line with something like the following:

```
If Cnt <> 0 Then
     txtAve.TEXT = "Average = " & Format(Total / Cnt)
Else
     txtAve.TEXT = "Average not defined"
End If
```

Tip

Once you get a program to work the way you want with correct input, be sure to think about what happens when input doesn't meet the expectations of your program.

LOGIC ERRORS AND THE DEBUGGER

So far we've dealt with errors that the compiler can detect itself, either in design mode or in run mode. But there are other kinds of errors that you can make, errors that don't violate any language rules, that don't mismatch types, and that don't try to lead the hardware astray. For instance, there are *logic errors,* mistakes in the program design. A program with a logic error may bring your program to a crashing stop, or it may let the program run to completion, but doing the wrong things. For finding such errors, the Visual Basic debugging system is a valuable ally.

You're already familiar with Visual Basic's design mode and run mode. The debugging system works in a third mode, *break mode*. You can tell which mode you're in by reading the Visual Basic title bar. Break mode lets you step through a program statement-by-statement and examine the values of variables and properties, so it's excellent for sleuthing. There are several ways of getting into break mode:

- From run mode, choose Break from the Run menu.
- From run mode, click the Break icon on the Toolbar. (It's located between the Run and End icons and is marked with two vertical bars.)
- From run mode, press the CTRL-BREAK combination on the keyboard.
- Click the Debug button when you get a runtime error message box.
- From design mode, select Step Into from the Run menu (or press F8).
- From design mode, select Step Over from the Run menu (or press SHIFT-F8).
- From design mode, select a particular line of code, then select Step to Cursor from the Run menu (or press CTRL-F8).
- From design mode, enter the Stop command as part of the code. When the program reaches that statement while in run mode, it will switch to break mode.
- From design mode, use the Add Watch choice from the Tools menu to set a breakpoint, which will cause the program to go from run mode to break mode when a specified condition occurs.

As you can see, there are many ways to reach break mode, and you'll look at some of them more closely. First, however, what do you gain by going into break mode? Most importantly, you gain the following two facilities:

1. You can examine the value of any variable or property.
2. You can follow the program step-by-step through its execution.

The Debug Window

Entering debug mode opens the Code window and the Debug window. Debug mode uses the Code window to let you monitor step-by-step execution of the program, and the Debug window lets you monitor values. The Debug window has three parts, as shown in Figure L17-7. At the top a box displays the name of the procedure currently being executed. Below are two panes, or scrolling text boxes, for displaying text. The top pane is the *Watch pane*, which can be used to display values of variables and expressions. (The Watch pane might not show until you add watch values to it.) The bottom is the *Immediate pane*, which displays information you request by typing in the pane.

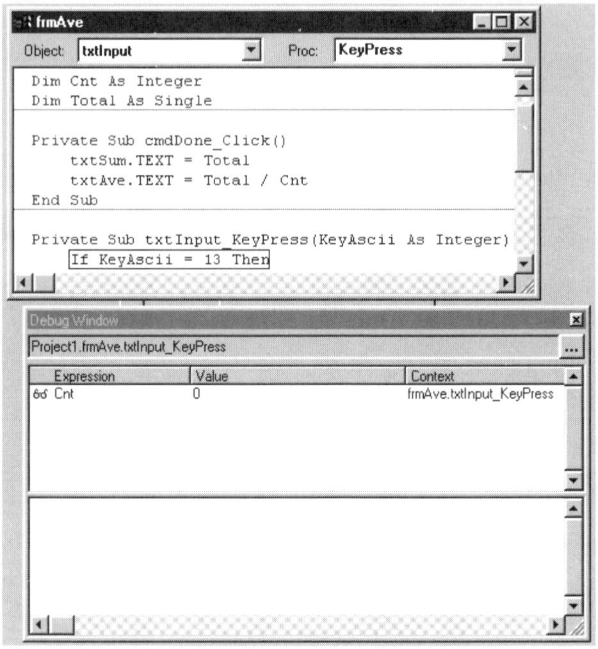

Figure L17-7 The Debug window

Let's start with the Immediate pane. Suppose you have a module-level variable called *Dollup* and you want to check its value. Then you can type the following in the Immediate pane:

```
Print Dollup
```

After you press ENTER, Visual Basic will display the value of *Dollup* on the next line. Or, to save a little effort on your part, you can use a question mark instead of typing out *Print:*

```
? Dollup
```

Again, after pressing ENTER, you'll see the value displayed.

You also can display information in the Immediate window by using the *Debug.Print* statement in the project code:

```
Print "Hello"         'prints Hello in the current form
picArd.Print "Enterprise"   'prints Enterprise in the picArd picture box
Debug.Print Q         'prints the value of Q in the Immediate pane
```

The Watch pane displays *Watch values*. These are variables, properties, or other expressions that you can select using the Add Watch selection from the Tools menu. One way to add an expression to the Watch window is to highlight the expression in your code (click and drag the mouse over the expression), and then select Watch. The highlighted expression will appear in a dialog box, and you can click on OK to accept it. When the Watch pane is showing in the Debug window, it will list the Watch expressions and show their values.

Let's look at a simple, yet dumb, example that will let you practice these skills. Create a project with a command button and the properties shown in Table L17-2.

OBJECT	PROPERTY	SETTING
Form1	Caption	30 to the 5th
	Name	frmDumb
Command1	Caption	Do It
	Name	cmdDumb

Table L17-2 Properties for the 30 to the 5th Project

Next, endow the project with the code shown in Listing L17-2. It uses a loop to compute the value of 30 to the 5th power. (Yes, using 30 ^ 5) would be much simpler, but this version gives us more variables to watch.)

Listing L17-2
The 30th to the 5th project

```
Option Explicit
Dim Wit As Integer

Private Sub cmdDumb_Click()
    Dim I As Integer
    Dim Power As Integer
    Power = 1
    For I = 1 To 5
        Power = Wit * Power
    Next I
    Print Power
End Sub

Private Sub Form_Initialize()
    Wit = 30
End Sub
```

If you run the program, you get a message box stating you have a runtime overflow error. Click on Debug, and the Debug window and Code window come up (If you don't see the Debug window, select Debug window from the View menu). The Code window shows a box around the following line:

```
Power = Wit * Power
```

This indicates that the overflow took place here. To get an idea of what's going on, type

```
Print I, Power
```

in the Immediate pane. You should see the result shown in Figure L17-8. Note that *Power* is 27,000. Multiplying it by 30 gives 810,000, which is far greater than the maximum integer value of 32,767. And that's why there's an overflow.

Figure L17-8 Using the Immediate pane

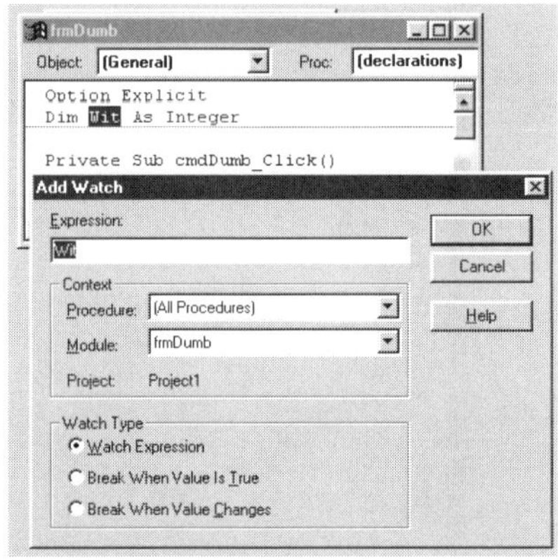

Figure L17-9 Adding a Watch value

Select End from the Run menu or click on the End button in the Toolbar. Let's use a slightly different approach to debugging the program. First, while in Design mode, select *Wit* in the Code window, and select Add Watch from the Tools menu. You should see a dialog box like that shown in Figure L17-9. Click on OK to accept this choice. Then do the same thing for the *I* and *Power* variables. Or you can open the Add Watch dialog box and type in the names directly. Now you've set the stage to use Step Into to watch these three variables evolve.

Stepping into a Program

It's time to run the program again. This time, instead of selecting Start, go to the Run menu and select Step Into. (Alternatively, press F8.) You'll see the Debug

Figure L17-10 The Watch pane

Figure L17-11 Advancing into the *cmdDumb_Click* procedure

window and Code window. The following line will appear boxed in the Code window:

```
Private Sub Form_Initialize()
```

That's because Step Into takes you to the beginning of the program, which, in this case, is the *Form_Initialize* procedure. Look at the Watch pane. You should see something like that shown in Figure L17-10. Each variable you added to the Watch list appears in the pane; the little pair of spectacles to the left of each name indicates that it is a Watch value. At this point, only the module-level variable is defined, and you can see that *Wit* is set to the default value of 0. The other two variables don't come into being until the program reaches the procedure in which they are defined. For now, they are labeled "Out of context." Note that the Context column shows where each variable can be used. The module-level variable *Wit* can be used in any procedure in the form, while the other two can be used just in the *cmdDumb_Click* procedure.

You may have noticed that the form itself hasn't appeared onscreen. Remember that the *Form_Initialize* procedure precedes the *Form_Load* procedure, which actually puts the form onscreen. So how do you progress? The simplest way is to press F8. Each keypress takes the program one statement further into its fate. Press it once, and the line

```
Wit = 30
```

gets boxed. But the Watch value for *Wit* remains at 0. That's because the boxed line is the statement about to be executed. The results don't take effect until you press F8 again and go to the next statement, so do so. That takes the program to the End Sub line, and now *Wit* in the Watch pane is 30.

Press F8 again, and the program form finally appears. Press F8 again, and nothing happens. That's because the next bit of code has to be activated by clicking on the command button. Do so. Now the program enters the *cmdDumb_Click* procedure, and the local variables come into context, as shown in Figure L17-11.

Keep pressing F8 and watch (in the Debug window Code pane) the program march through the code and watch (in the Watch pane) the variables change their values. This approach gives you an excellent view of what the program is doing. Eventually, when *I* is 4, the program gets to the point of multiplying 30 by 27,000, and you get the runtime Overflow message again. (At this point you may decide that perhaps you should have used *Double* instead of *Integer.*)

As you can see, combining the Step Into command with the Watch window gives you excellent tools for monitoring a program and seeing how its progress compares with your expectations.

Round Two

Let's try these tools with a more subtle problem. Return to design mode and start a new project. Let the form look like that of Figure L17-12, and give it the properties shown in Table L17-3.

OBJECT	PROPERTY	SETTING
Form1	Caption	Temperatures
	Name	frmTemp
Text1	Name	txtFahr
	Locked	True
	Text	
Text2	Name	txtCels
	Locked	True
	Text	
VScrollBar1	LargeChange	10
	Max	–100
	Min	500
	Name	vsbFahr
	Value	68
VScrollBar1	LargeChange	10
	Name	vsbCels
Label1	Caption	Fahrenheit
	Name	lblFahr
Label2	Caption	Celsius
	Name	lblCels

Table L17-3 Properties for the Temperatures project

The somewhat flawed idea behind this project is that one scrollbar will represent the temperature in Fahrenheit and the other scrollbar will represent the temperature in Celsius. The text boxes above the scrollbars will serve as readouts, and the controls will be coupled so that setting the temperature on one

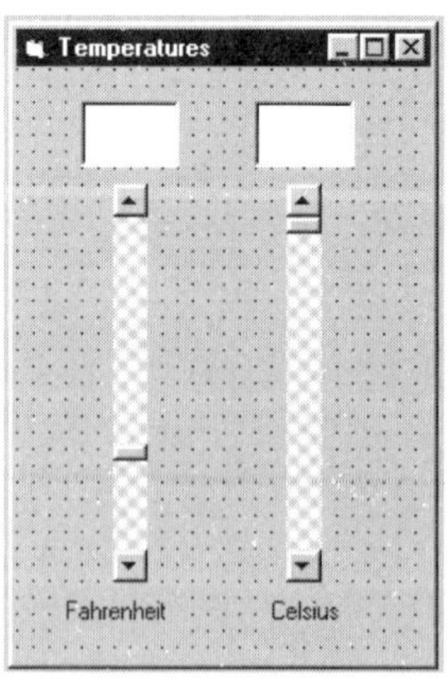

Figure L17-12 Yet another flawed program

scale automatically sets the other scale to the corresponding temperature. Listing L17-3 shows the code, which happens to contain an error.

Listing L17-3
The Temperature project

```
Option Explicit
' version with an error

Private Sub Form_Load()
    txtFahr.TEXT = vsbFahr.VALUE
    'convert Fahrenheit to Celsius
    vsbCels.Max = 5 * (vsbFahr.Max - 32) / 9
    vsbCels.Min = 5 * (vsbFahr.Min - 32) / 9
    vsbCels.VALUE = 5 * (vsbFahr.VALUE - 32) / 9
    txtCels.TEXT = vsbCels.VALUE
End Sub

Private Sub vsbCels_Change()
    txtCels.TEXT = vsbCels.VALUE
    'convert Celsius to Fahrenheit
    vsbFahr.VALUE = 9 * (vsbCels.VALUE + 32) / 5
End Sub

Private Sub vsbFahr_Change()
    txtFahr.TEXT = vsbFahr.VALUE
    'convert Fahrenheit to Celsius
    vsbCels.VALUE = 5 * (vsbFahr.VALUE - 32) / 9
End Sub
```

Try running this program, and you get the interesting error message shown in Figure L17-13. What the heck does "Invalid property value" mean? Perhaps selecting Debug and adding *vsbFahr.VALUE* and *vsbCels.VALUE* as Watch values might give us a clue. Figure L17-14 shows the results. Hmm. Apparently *vsbFahr.VALUE*

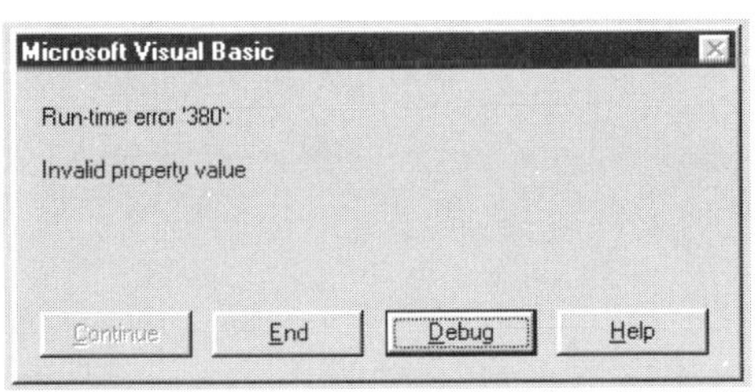

Figure L17-13 Unseemly disaster strikes

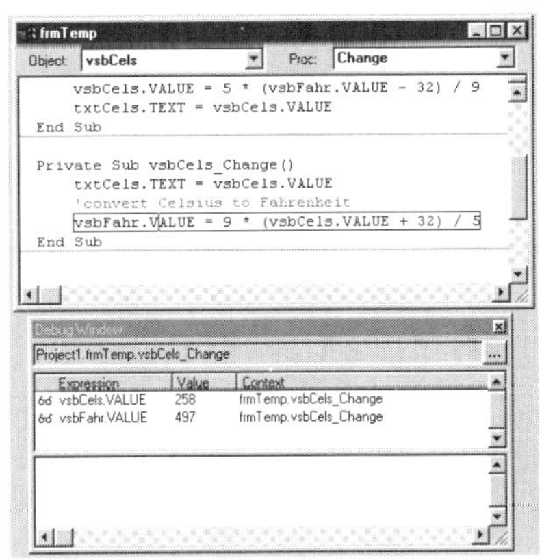

Figure L17-14 Unexpected temperatures

is 497 and *vsbCels.VALUE* is 258. Furthermore, if you calculate the next value of *vsbFahr.VALUE* using 258 for *vsbCels.VALUE* in the *vsbCels_Change* event, you get 522, which is outside the allowable limits (–100 to 500) established by the Min and Max properties. So you see the immediate cause of the invalid property value—the program tries to set *vsbFarh.VALUE* to 522. But the real question is, how can that happen? Table L17-3 shows that you set *vsbFahr.VALUE* to 68. How did it ever get to 497 without you doing anything? This sounds like a job for Step Into and the Watch pane.

End the program, add *vsbFahr.VALUE* and *vsbCels.VALUE* to the Watch list if you have not already done so. Press F8 to start the program, and you'll get the Code window and the Debug window. You'll note that *vsbFahr.VALUE* and *vsbCels.VALUE* start with the values of 68 and 0, respectively, which are the values they get from the Properties window. Press F8 a few more times and see the program set *vsbCels.VALUE* to 20, the Celsius equivalent of 68° F. So far, so good. Continue pressing F8. You'll see that the program skips the following line:

```
txtCels.TEXT = vsbCels.VALUE
```

Instead, the program jumps to the *vsbCels_Change* procedure. Why? Because *Form_Load* just changed *vsbCels.VALUE* from 0 to 20, which triggers the *Change* event for vsbCels, and that starts up the *vsbCels_Change* event procedure.

Proceed cautiously now. Pressing F8 again, you see that the *vsbCels_Change* procedure sets the txtCels.TEXT property to the proper value. Continuing with F8, you see that the procedure now calculates the corresponding *vsbFahr.VALUE*. Unfortunately, instead of converting 20°C to 68°F, it converts it to 94°F! Clearly, the program uses the wrong conversion formula. It should have been this:

```
'Convert Celsius to Fahrenheit correctly.
vsbFahr.VALUE = 9 * vsbCels.VALUE / 5 + 32
```

But what does that have to do with stack space, whatever that is? Continue pressing F8, and you'll begin to see the problem. The incorrect calculation *changes* the value of *vsbFahr.VALUE*, triggering the *vsbFahr_Change* event, which correctly converts 94°F to 38°C. That changes the value of *vsbCels.VALUE*, triggering another *vsbCels_Change* event, which incorrectly converts 38°C to 119°F, which triggers another *vsbFahr_Change*, which triggers another *vsbCels_Change* event, and so on ad infinitum, or, rather, until the program tries to set *vsbFahr.VALUE* to 522.

The Stack

Under somewhat different conditions, you can run into another error message—"Out of Stack Space." For example, you can change vsbFahr.Min to 30000 and do division first, then multiplication, as in the following:

```
vsbFahr.VALUE =((vsbCels.VALUE + 32) / 5 ) *9
```

This second change keeps the program from running into an overflow problem before getting to the stack problem. For example, *9 * 10000 / 5* evaluates to *90000 / 5*, and 90,000 overflows the Integer limits. But *(10000 / 5) * 9* evaluates to *2000 * 9*, or 18,000 without experiencing an overflow.

So what's a stack? The *stack* is a hunk of memory that Visual Basic uses to keep track of local variables and of procedure calls. Each time Visual Basic calls a procedure, it jumps to the computer memory location containing the code for that procedure. Visual Basic needs to keep track of where in the code to return to when the procedure terminates, so it stores that information (the return address) on the stack. If the new procedure has any parameters or local variables, those are added to the stack, too. To keep things in hand, when the program finishes a procedure, it frees up the memory used by the return address and the other values, and the stack gets smaller again (see Figure L17-15). To simplify the figure, it shows a user-defined procedure such as those discussed in Lesson 16.

Now let's look at what happened in our pathological example. When *vsbCels_Change* alters the value of *vsbFahr.VALUE*, that triggers the *vsbFahr_Change* event *before vsbCels_Change* finishes. So the *vsbCels_Change* values are still on the stack when *vsbFahr_Change* starts up. Similarly, *vsbFahr_Change* causes a new instance of *vsbCels_Change* to start *before vsbFahr_Change* changes, adding its information to the stack. None of these procedures gets to terminate because each one can't terminate until the other one does. Thus, they mutually cause the stack to grow larger and larger (see Figure L17-16). When the stack gets too big, Visual Basic halts the whole business, commenting that it is "Out of stack space." So the erroneous conversion formula led to a rather surprising failure, one that might have been hard to figure out without the use of the Visual Basic debugging facilities.

By the way, you can use the procedure box in the Debug window to confirm this picture. If you click on the button at the end of the box, a Calls message box opens, showing the list of active procedure calls. These are procedures which haven't terminated yet. Figure L17-17 shows an example. Reading from the bottom up, you see that *Form Load* has called *vsbCels_Change*, which has called *vsbFahr_Change*, which has called *vsbCels_Change*. (The "Non-Basic Code" part refers to the built-in Visual Basic code that manages event handling. It, too, contributes to the stack.) You can also open the Calls list by selecting Calls from the Tools menu or by clicking on the Calls icon in the Toolbar.

Fancy Stepping

Let's take a quick look at a few more debugging features. So far you've used Step Into F8 to cruise through a program. The Run menu also offers Step Over SHIFT-F8 and Step to Cursor CTRL-F8. The difference between Step Into and Step Over occurs when you're stepping through a procedure that calls another procedure. For instance, consider this example from Lesson 16:

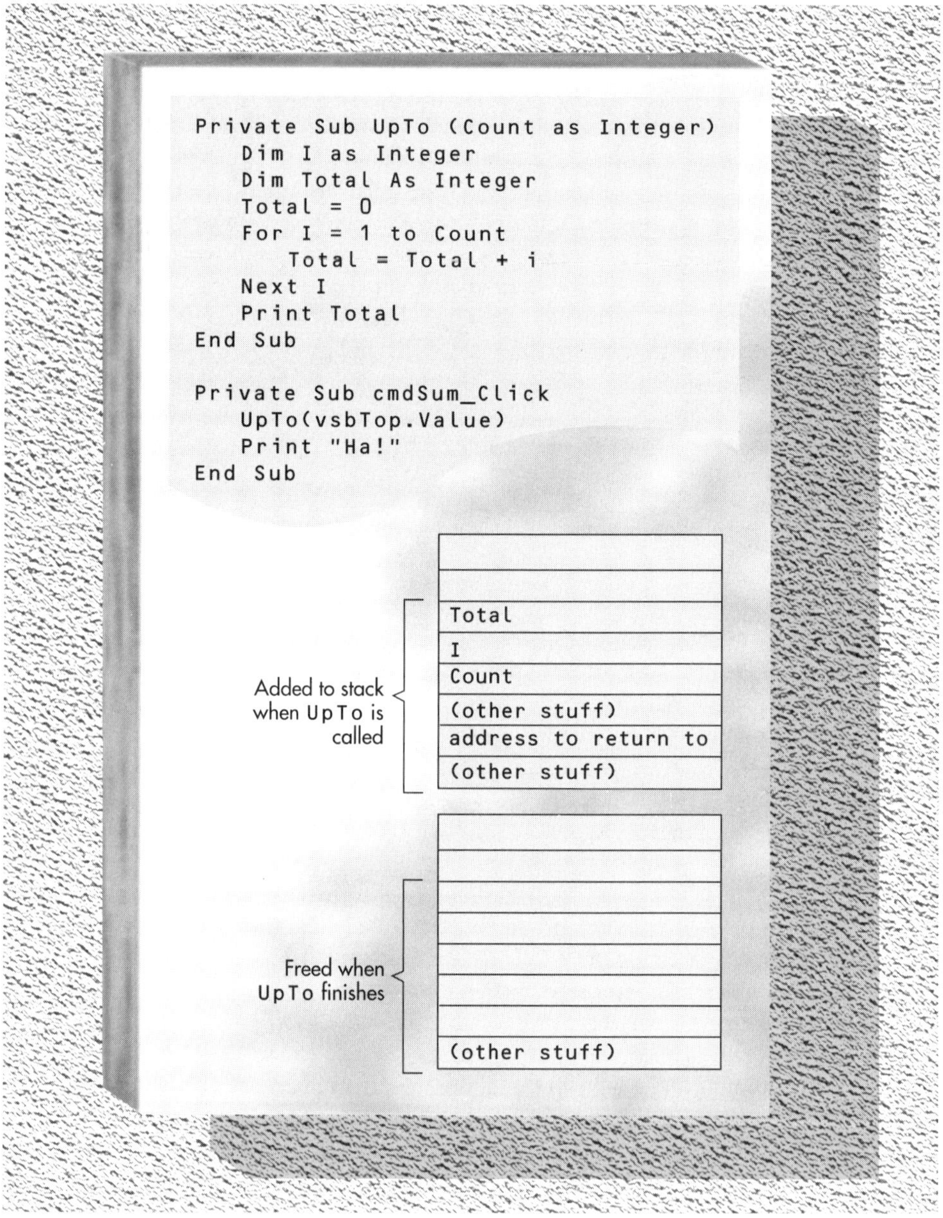

Figure L17-15 Adding and removing information from a stack

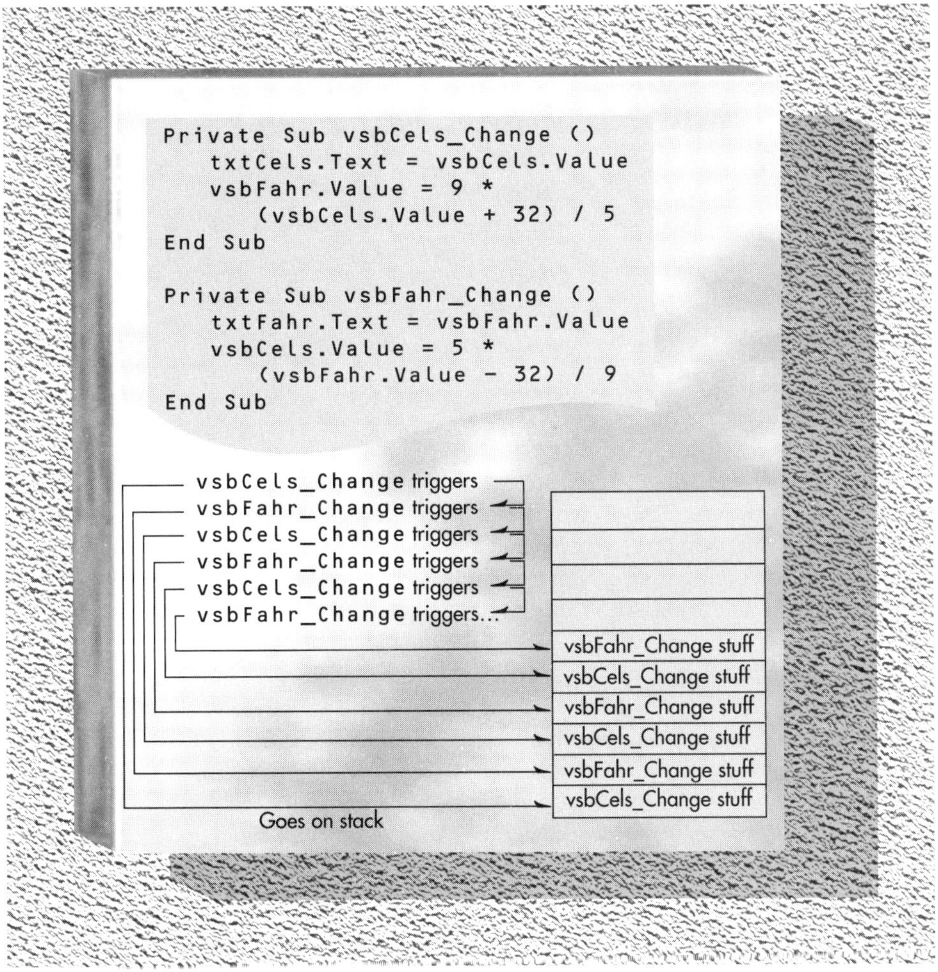

Figure L17-16 The ever-growing stack

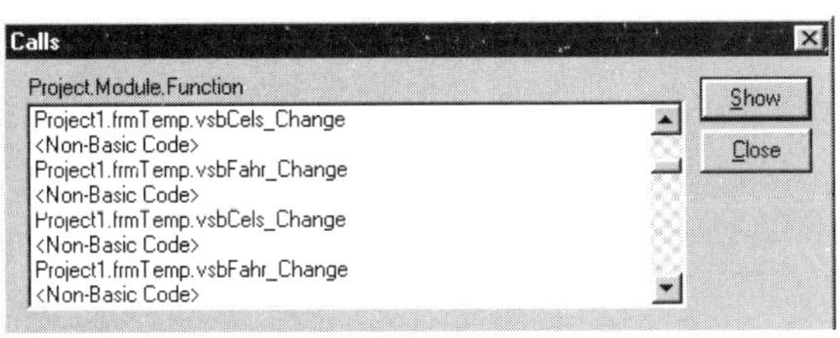

Figure L17-17 The Calls message box

```
Option Explicit

Function Max(ParamArray Nums()) As Variant
     Dim N As Variant
     Dim Maxi As Variant
     Maxi = Nums(0)
     For Each N In Nums
          If N > Maxi Then Maxi = N
     Next N
     Max = Maxi
End Function

Private Sub cmdTest_Click()
     frmMax.Font.Size = 18
     Print Max(3, 2, 5)
     Print Max(10, 11, 20, 14)
     Print Max("Cow", "Dog", "Cat")
End Sub
```

Suppose you start the program by pressing F8 (Step Into). Visual Basic will display the form, and you'll have to click the Test button. Continue pressing F8. Soon the *Print Max(3, 2, 5)* command is highlighted (boxed) in the Debug window. If you then press F8 once again, the debugger "steps into" the *Max* function. Continue to press F8, and eventually you get back to the *cmdTest_Click* procedure, with the next *Print* statement highlighted. In short, Step Into follows a program step-by-step into any called procedures, then back out again.

Now suppose you end the program, restart, and proceed using F8 until *Print Max(3, 2, 5)* is selected. This time choose Step Over (or press SHIFT-F8) instead of Step Into. Now the debugger executes the whole *Max* procedure without stepping through it with you, leaving you on the next *Print* line. In short, if you are debugging one procedure, Step Over lets you run a procedure called by the one you're debugging without stepping through it.

Tip

Suppose you are debugging a procedure step-by-step and it calls another procedure. If you want to step through that procedure also, use Step Into F8. If you just want to run that procedure and get to the next line in the procedure you're debugging, use Step Over SHIFT-F8.

It could happen that you've determined that there's a problem in the last third of a long procedure, and you don't want to spend the time stepping through the first two-thirds. In that case, when you are in design mode, position the cursor in the Code window at the line at which you want to start the step-by-step process. Then select Step to Cursor from the Run menu or press CTRL-F8. Visual Basic will run the program to that point, then kick into break mode. Then you can use Step Into or Step Over to investigate the rest of the code. Also, once you're in break mode, you can position the cursor in the Code pane and use Step to Cursor to run the program to that point.

Tip

To run a program to a particular line of code before starting debugging, locate the cursor at that line of code in the Code window and use Step to Cursor CTRL-F8 to execute the program to that point.

Watch Tricks

Suppose you're merrily stepping through a program and you see a variable whose value you want to know but which you haven't added to the Watch list yet. To find its value, you can select Instant Watch from the Tools menu (or press SHIFT-F9). That brings up a dialog box (see Figure L17-18) showing the value of the variable you've selected. If you want to add this variable to your Watch list, click on the Add button. If seeing the value this one time is all you need, then click on the Cancel button. Unlike the Add Watch menu selection, which is available in both design and break modes, the Instant Watch choice is available only in break mode.

You also can access Instant Watch by selecting a varible in the Code window and clicking the right mouse button. This brings up a menu which includes Instant Watch as a choice.

Earlier, you may have noticed that the Add Watch dialog box (see Figure L17-9) had three choices for Watch Type:

- Watch Expression (the default)
- Break When Value Is True
- Break When Value Changes

The final two choices are additional means of guiding a program into break mode. For example, the pathological Temperature project unexpectedly caused the temperatures to change. One way of seeing where this happens would be to highlight *vsbFahr.VALUE* in design mode, select Add Watch, and then choose Break When Value Changes. Then run the program. It will hum along until the *vsbFahr.VALUE* property changes, then switch to break mode.

The Watch expressions are not limited to variables and properties. You could, for example, enter the expression

```
vsbFahr.VALUE > 200
```

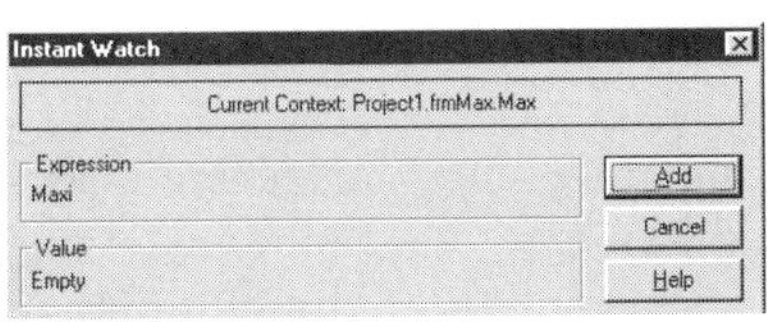

Figure L17-18 Instant Watch

in the Watch window and select Break When Value Is True. If you then ran the program, it would run until *vsbFahr.VALUE* exceeded 200, then switch to break mode.

DODGING BULLETS

Any interactive program is a target for unexpected input from a user. Your program asks how many lines of data to display, and the user enters –5. Your program asks the user to enter a color value in the range 0–255 and the user enters "Red" or "0–255". There are many opportunities for miscommunication. Your first line of defense should be to make it difficult or impossible for the user to provide wrong information. Let's look at a few suggestions.

Limit the User's Options

When feasible, don't give the user a blank check to use for input. Rather than use a text box or an input box to get information, use option buttons, check boxes, lists, scrollbars, and menu choices. That way, the user can only make choices from a predetermined set of options.

If you can limit the number of choices to, say, three or four mutually exclusive choices, use option buttons or a menu. For instance, you can offer the user a choice of four font sizes. If the choices are not mutually exclusive, for example, choosing from Bold, Italic, and Underlined, use check boxes or a menu.

If the number of choices is greater, such as a choice of 10 font sizes or of 50 fonts, consider using a list. If it's a long list, set its Sorted property to True. That makes it easier for a user to find a choice or to determine if a particular possibility is missing from the list.

If the user is supposed to select an integer in a particular range, consider using a scrollbar. For instance, examples in Lesson 10 used scrollbars to let users select RGB color values. You can also use scrollbars for floating-point values as long as they are evenly spaced. For instance, if you want a number to the nearest tenth in the range 0–10, you can make the scrollbar range 0–100, then divide by 10 to get the desired value.

Check the User's Input

Of course, you can't always limit the user to a set of canned responses. For example, if you ask for a name, date, income, or telephone number, you can't provide lists of all possible names, dates, incomes, and phone numbers for the user to select from. But you can check some forms of input for validity. Keep in mind that responses entered in a text box, combo box, or input box are strings. If you enter the number 234, you're really entering a string consisting of the 2,

3, and 4 characters. If you enter a date in the form 11/23/95, you're really entering a string consisting of digit characters and a couple of slash characters. So if you want a number, for example, you have the option of checking the characters in the string to see if they can be interpreted as a number. (You don't have to inspect the string personally; just use *IsNumeric*.) If so, you can assign the string to a numeric variable or property, and Visual Basic will do the string-to-number conversion for you.

The *Is* Family

The *Is* family of functions can help you examine *String* or *Variant* values to see if they fit the desired mode. Earlier, for instance, you saw the *IsNumeric* function, which returns True if its argument can be interpreted as a number. Table L17-4 lists several useful functions with similar natures. Not all of them relate to verifying input, but we might as well look at them all at once. Some, such as *IsArray* and *IsEmpty*, are most useful for *Variant* values.

FUNCTION	DESCRIPTION
IsArray	Returns True if argument is an array, False otherwise
IsDate	Returns True if argument can be interpreted as a date, False otherwise
IsEmpty	Returns True if argument is an uninitialized Variant variable or if it is explicitly set to the special value Empty
IsError	Returns True if argument is a *Variant* whose subtype is *vbError*
IsNull	Returns True if argument is the special value *Null* or contains the special value *Null*
IsNumeric	Returns True if argument can be interpreted as a number, False otherwise

Table L17-4 Functions that test their arguments

You've already learned about *IsNumeric*. Let's talk about the remaining functions in a little more detail, beginning with *IsArray*. The *Variant* type is remarkably adaptable. It can hold an integer, and it can hold an array of integers. For instance, the following sequence of steps, although odd, is acceptable.

```
Dim Arr(1 to 10) As Integer
Dim SuperVar As Variant
Dim I As Integer
For I = 1 to 10
    Arr(I) = I * I
Next I
SuperVar = 22    ' SuperVar is an integer
Print SuperVar   ' Print an integer
SuperVar = Arr   ' SuperVar is an array
For I = 1 to 10
    Print SuperVar(I)
Next I
```

Note that the command

```
Print SuperVar
```

makes sense when *SuperVar* holds an integer, but is an error when *SuperVar* holds an array. Similarly, the loop printing *SuperVar(I)* is an error if *SuperVar* holds an integer, but works when *SuperVar* holds an array. It's possible to create programs in which the contents of a *Variant* variable depend on choices made while the program runs. In such cases, you can use *IsArray* to check on the current state. For instance, you might have code along the following lines:

```
If IsArray(SuperVar) Then
    For I = 1 to N
        Print SuperVar(I)
    Next I
Else
    Print SuperVar
End If
```

Next, consider *IsDate*. Visual Basic supports a *Date* data type for holding dates. You can use the *Date* function to set a *Date* type variable, or you can assign a string to a *Date* type if it is in a format Visual Basic recognizes. To display a *Date* value, use *Format* as discussed in Lesson 14. For example, you can do the following:

```
Dim Day1 as Date, Day2 as Date
Day1 = Date ' Use Date function to get current date.
Day2 = "11 Aug 1999"
Print Format(Day1)
Print Format(Day2, "Medium Date")
```

Then you would see output like this:

```
4/12/96
11-Aug-99
```

Incidentally, instead of writing the date as a string, you can enclose it in # signs, as in the following:

```
Day2 = #18 Sep 1915#
```

When you use this form and move on to another line, the Visual Basic editor automatically rewrites the code in the standard general date format:

```
Day2 = #18/09/15#
```

The *IsDate* function lets you check to see if a value is a valid date before, say, you assign it to a *Date* type variable. If, for instance, you asked the user to enter a date into a text box, you could do something like this:

```
If IsDate(txtDate.TEXT) Then
    TheDate = txtDate.TEXT
Else
    MsgBox "Oops! I don't recognize that date format."
End If
```

The *IsEmpty* function lets you check to see if a *Variant* has been initialized. Uninitialized *Variant* variables have a special value represented symbolically by the keyword *Empty.* If you attempt to print an uninitialized *Variant* variable, you get an empty line, not the word *Empty*. Note that being uninitialized really means having no defined value. If you assign, say, the null string "" to a *Variant,* the variable is no longer *Empty.* For instance, consider the following code:

```
Dim Blob As Variant
Print "Empty is different from nothing"
Print Blob
Print IsEmpty(Blob)
Blob = ""
Print Blob
Print IsEmpty(Blob)
```

This produces the following input:

```
Empty is different from nothing

True

False
```

In short, the *IsEmpty* function lets you tell if a *Variant* variable has been initialized, and it lets you distinguish between an uninitialized variable and one that has been set to the null string.

The *IsError* function indicates whether its argument is an error value. More particularly, the argument should be a *Variant* that is classified as having a *vbError* type by the *VarType* function. We'll look at *IsError* and *VarType* in more detail later in this lesson.

The *IsNull* function, on the other hand, reveals if a *Variant* variable has been set to *Null*. *Null* is a Visual Basic keyword used to indicate that a variable does not contain valid data. How does a variable get such a value? By being assigned *Null*. For example, you could do something like this:

```
Dim Yips As Variant
...
If IsNumeric(txtCost.TEXT) Then
     Yips = txtCost.TEXT
Else
     Yips = Null ' Marks Yips as not containing valid data.
End If
```

Then other parts of the program can use the *Null* value as a test:

```
If IsNull(Yips) Then
     ...
End If
```

The *Null* value propagates, for any expression containing *Null* evaluates to *Null*. That is, suppose *Yips* is *Null* and that *Xips* is another *Variant* variable:

```
Xips = Yips * 12
```

This statement would make *Xips Null,* also. Similarly, a comparison such as *X<>Null* always evaluates to *Null,* and Visual Basic interprets *Null* as False in Boolean contexts. Anyway, you can use *IsNull* to check if data is valid before using it. Incidentally, unlike *Empty, Null* does print. That is, if *Yips* is *Null* and you print *Yips*, you'll see the word *Null* displayed.

Too Many Nothings?

Don't confuse *Empty* with *Null,* and don't confuse either with 0 or with the null string. The null string is a string with no characters, but it's still a valid string. Similarly, 0 is a valid number. A *Null* value, however, indicates a *Variant* variable doesn't have a valid value, while *Empty* means a *Variant* variable was created but never assigned any value.

When you use a *Variant* variable, the *VarType* function provides a convenient way to check the type of value stored in a *Variant*. Unlike *TypeName,* which returns a string, *VarType* returns a number indicating the type. You then can use the number in comparisons, *Select Case* statements, and the like. Table L17-5 lists the return values for *VarType*. If a *Variant* contains an array, the return value consists of *vbArray* plus the value for the type. For example, an array of *Long* values would produce a return value of *vbArray* + *vbLong*.

VALUE	SYMBOLIC NAME	VARIABLE TYPE
0	*vbEmpty*	*Empty* (uninitialized)
1	*vbNull*	*Null* (no valid data)
2	*vbInteger*	Integer
3	*vbLong*	Long integer
4	*vbSingle*	Single-precision floating point
5	*vbDouble*	Double-precision floating point
6	*vbCurrency*	Currency
7	*vbDate*	Date
8	*vbString*	String
9	*vbObject*	OLE automation object
10	*vbError*	Error
11	*vbBoolean*	Boolean
12	*vbVariant*	Variant (only used with vbArray)
13	*vbDataObject*	Non-OLE automation object
17	*vbByte*	Byte
8192	*vbArray*	Array

Table L17-5 *VarType* return values

Intercept and Take Corrective Action

A common strategy for handling possible errors is to anticipate where they might occur and then react to them before a runtime error occurs. If you determine, say, that a user has entered the wrong kind of input, you have options. You can have the program complain and quit:

```
Private Sub Text1_Change()
    If Not IsNumeric(txtScore.TEXT) Then
        MsgBox "I cannot accept that input!"
        End
    End If
End Sub
```

However, the sporting thing to do is to give the user another chance, as in this example from earlier in the lesson:

```
Private Sub Text1_Change()
    If IsNumeric(Text1.TEXT) Then
        Text2.TEXT = (Text1.TEXT) ^ 3
    Else
        MsgBox "Please enter numbers only"
    End If
End Sub
```

Using *CVErr* and *IsError*

Another approach to dealing with errors is to take advantage of the *IsError* function. This is a useful approach for functions that normally return numbers. The idea is to make the return value a *Variant*. If the function has no problems, have it return the correct number. If there is a problem, have the function return an error instead of a number. Then you can test the return value with *IsError* to see if the function worked.

To see in detail how this works, let's modify the *TriArea* function from Lesson 16. First, here is the original form:

```
'Returns area of a triangle having sides S1, S2, S3.
Function TriArea(S1 As Single, S2 As Single, S3 As Single) As Single
    Dim SP As Single   'half the perimeter
    Dim A2 As Single   'square of the area
    SP = (S1 + S2 + S3) / 2
    A2 = SP * (SP - S1) * (SP - S2) * (SP - S3)
    If A2 < 0 Then
        MsgBox "That's no triangle!", vbExclamation
        TriArea = -1
        Exit Function
    End If
    TriArea = Sqr(A2)
End Function
```

Now let's move the error handling to the calling function and modify *TriArea* to return an error if things don't work out. The key to returning an error is to use the *CVErr* function, which converts a number to an error value. In essence, this preserves the value of the number but tags it as being an error number. For example, suppose *TriArea* is a *Variant*. Then the line

```
TriArea = CVErr(5)  ' Tag 5 as being an error number.
```

makes *TriArea* be an error value; that is, *IsError(TriArea)* will be true.

So this is what to do (Listing L17-4):

- Make *TriArea* a type *Variant* function.
- Have *TriArea* return *CVErr(5)* if the sides don't make a triangle.
- Have the calling program use *IsError* to detect if there's been an error.

Listing L17-4
The Area of a Triangle project

```
Option Explicit

'Returns area of a triangle having sides S1, S2, S3.
Function TriArea(S1 As Single, S2 As Single, S3 As Single) As Variant
    Dim SP As Single
    Dim A2 As Single
    SP = (S1 + S2 + S3) / 2
    A2 = SP * (SP - S1) * (SP - S2) * (SP - S3)
    If A2 < 0 Then 'Not a triangle!
       TriArea = CVErr(5)  'Return an error number of 5.
        Exit Function
    End If
    TriArea = Sqr(A2)
End Function

Private Sub cmdTri_Click()
    Dim a As Single, b As Single, c As Single
    Dim Area As Variant
    a = InputBox("Enter length of first side:", "Side A")
    b = InputBox("Enter length of second side:", "Side B")
    c = InputBox("Enter length of third side:", "Side C")
    Area = TriArea(a, b, c)
    If IsError(Area) Then
        MsgBox CStr(Area) & ": That's no triangle!", , "Answer"
     Else
        MsgBox "Area of the triangle is " & Format(Area), , "Answer"
    End If
End Sub
```

Figure L17-19 shows the error message you get when you use wrong values. One point to notice is that you can use the *CStr* function (convert to string) to convert the error value to a string that you can incorporate into the message.

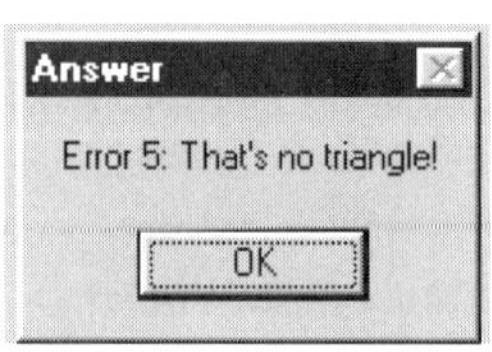

Figure L17-19 Using an error value

Why use an error value of 5? That choice was completely arbitrary. Note, however, that you can have a function use different error values for different errors. That's handy if there's more than one thing that can go wrong. For example, Listing L17-5 modifies the last example so that *TriArea* checks for nonnumeric arguments. If it finds any, the function returns an error value of 4. If the values are numeric but don't form the sides of a triangle, the function returns an error value of 5. The calling procedure, then, can check the error value to see which kind of error fouled things up.

Note the types and explicit type conversions. The new *TriArea* function definition doesn't specify types for its arguments, so they become *Variant* arguments by default. If the arguments pass the *IsNumeric* test, there's still the possibility that they are numbers in string form. That can cause a problem in an expression like

```
S1 + S2 + S3
```

because Visual Basic treats a + sign like an & operator when it comes between strings. So if the arguments were "3", "4", and "5" instead of 3, 4, and 5, the sum becomes "345" instead of 12. However, the new *TriArea* uses *CSng(S1)* to convert S1 to type *Single*, and so on, and all goes well.

Also note that the calling function uses *CInt(Area)* to convert an error value to a regular integer so that it can check the value in an *If* comparison.

Listing L17-5
The modified Area of a Triangle project

```
Option Explicit

'Returns area of a triangle having sides S1, S2, S3.
Function TriArea(S1, S2, S3) As Variant
    Dim SP As Single
    Dim A2 As Single
    If Not IsNumeric(S1) Or Not IsNumeric(S2) Or Not IsNumeric(S3) Then
        TriArea = CVErr(4)
        Exit Function
    End If
    SP = (CSng(S1) + CSng(S2) + CSng(S3)) / 2
    A2 = SP * (SP - S1) * (SP - S2) * (SP - S3)
    If A2 < 0 Then
       TriArea = CVErr(5)
        Exit Function
    End If
    TriArea = Sqr(A2)
End Function

Private Sub cmdTri_Click()
    Dim a, b, c, Area
    a = InputBox("Enter length of first side:", "Side A")
    b = InputBox("Enter length of second side:", "Side B")
```

continued on next page

continued from previous page

```
    c = InputBox("Enter length of third side:", "Side C")
    Area = TriArea(a, b, c)
    If IsError(Area) Then
        If CInt(Area) = 5 Then
            MsgBox "That's no triangle!", , "Answer"
        ElseIf CInt(Area) = 4 Then
            MsgBox "All sides must have numeric values", , "Answer"
        Else
            MsgBox "Unknown Error in TriArea", , "Answer"
        End If
     Else
        MsgBox "Area of the triangle is " & Format(Area), , "Answer"
    End If
End Sub
```

ERROR TRAPPING

Remember what happens if your program, say, tries to divide by 0? That causes a runtime error. By default, Visual Basic displays an error message, and you get a choice of quitting the program or of entering break mode and debugging. Clearly, runtime errors disrupt a program, and they may irritate or confuse users. The last few examples have concentrated on heading off trouble before a program generates a runtime error. Visual Basic provides an interesting alternative. Let the runtime error occur, and then have your code detect and respond to the error. In short, replace the default response to runtime errors with your own response. This process is called *error trapping* because you trap the error before Visual Basic begins its default response.

To use this approach, take the following steps:

1. Enable error trapping by using the *On Error* statement, which directs the program to go to a particular line of code if a runtime error occurs.
2. Write an error-handling routine to take care of the error if it occurs.
3. Exit the error-handling routine by using some form of the *Resume* statement.

Let's look at a simple example. First, start a new project as described in Table L17-6.

OBJECT	PROPERTY	SETTING
Form1	Caption	Trapping 101A
	Name	frmTrap1
Command1	Caption	Test
	Name	cmdTest

Table L17-6 Properties for the Trapping 101A project

Next, use the Code window to enter the code shown in Listing L17-6.

Listing L17-6
The Trapping 101A project

```
Option Explicit

Sub GoGet(M As Integer, N As Integer)
    M = InputBox("Enter an integer")
    N = InputBox("Enter another integer")
End Sub

Private Sub cmdTest_Click()
    Dim A As Integer, B As Integer, C As Integer
    GoGet A, B
    On Error GoTo Ooops 'Trapping starts here.
    C = A * B
    MsgBox A & " times " & Format(B) & " is " & Format(C)
    Exit Sub    'Skip errorhandling if not needed.
Ooops:  ' a label
    MsgBox "Error number = " & Err.Number
    MsgBox "Error description: " & Err.Description
    MsgBox "Enter smaller integers:"
    GoGet A, B  'Try to fix the problem.
    Resume  'Return to trouble-making statement.
End Sub
```

Now let's analyze the code. First, after declaring some variables, the *cmdTest_Click* procedure calls the *GoGet* procedure to set values for *A* and *B*. Then, with the following line, it turns on error trapping:

```
On Error GoTo Ooops 'trapping starts here
```

Here *Ooops* is a symbolic line label identifying where the program is supposed to go in the event of a runtime error. (You can use any reasonable word you want for the label.) In the event of a runtime error occurring in any part of the procedure following this statement, the program will stop what it's doing and go to the *Ooops* label. Later, the *Ooops* label appears just before the error-handler part of the code. (Note that you use a colon to indicate that *Ooops* is a label and not, say, a variable name.)

Suppose there is no runtime error. Then the *cmdTest_Click* procedure calculates and displays the product of two integers and terminates when it reaches the *End Sub* line.

Next, suppose there is a runtime error. For example, the product of *A* and *B* might be larger than the largest allowable integer value (32,767), generating an Overflow error. Then, instead of displaying the Overflow error message, the program jumps to the section of code headed by the *Ooops* label. At this point, our example displays some messages describing the error (more about *Err* in a moment), suggests the user try new values, uses *GoGet* to get the new values, and then issues the *Resume* statement.

The *Resume* statement means, "go back to the line that caused the problem and try again." That would be this line:

```
C = A * B
```

Because the program has obtained new values for *A* and *B*, there's a chance that the calculation will work this time.

Figure L17-20 shows the program flow for these two cases (no overflow and overflow).

Try running the program. First, after clicking the Test button, enter integers like 22 and 44. The program will display the answer. Then try entering 2000 and 4000. The product exceeds the allowable value for an integer, and this generates a runtime error. The program tells you so and lets you enter new values. Try 6 and 12, and you escape without crashing the program.

There's more to say about the error-trapping process, but first, let's take a look at the Err object.

The Err Object

The Err object, new with Visual Basic 4, is an object that keeps track of information about errors. When there's a runtime error, Visual Basic sets Err properties. For example, the Number property is the error number. For instance, if you get the default Overflow message, you'll see that it's labeled "Runtime error '6'". Visual Basic has an official runtime error number for each possible error type. Similarly, the Description property is a short description of the problem. For example, the Description property is set to the string *"Overflow"* if there is a runtime overflow.

The program in Listing L17-6 used these properties (*Err.Number* and *Err.Description*) to inform the user about the nature of the problem. Table L17-7 lists these and other properties for the Err object.

PROPERTY	DESCRIPTION
Description	Brief description of the error
HelpContext	A context ID for a topic in a Microsoft Windows Help file
HelpFile	Path name for a Microsoft Windows Help file
Number	Visual Basic error number for the error
Source	Name of the object or application that generated the error

Table L17-7 Properties of the Err object

The HelpFile and HelpContext properties identify where information about the particular error can be found. You can use this information, for example, with a message box, which optionally accepts Help file and Help context arguments (the fourth and fifth arguments). If you press F1 while a message box shows, Visual Basic will take you to the Help item specified by those arguments. For instance, you could replace the original error announcements in Listing L17-6 with this code:

```
Msg = "Error # " & Format(Err.Number) & " (" & Err.Description & ")" _
    & " was generated by " & Err.Source
MsgBox Msg, , "Error", Err.HelpFile, Err.HelpContext
```

Now a user can get the Visual Basic Help information about the overflow error.

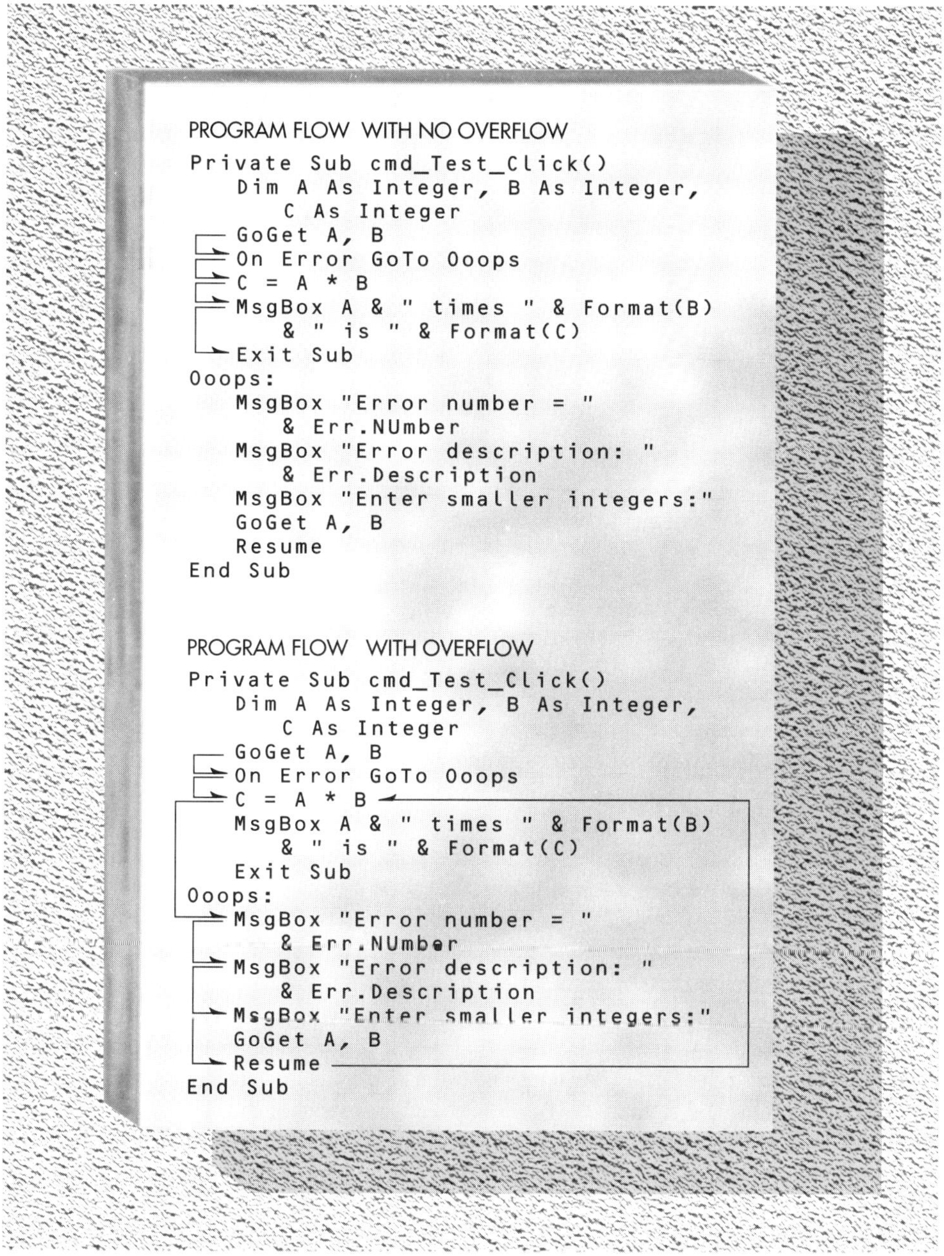

Figure L17-20 Error trapping

Back to Error Trapping

There are some points about error trapping that may not have been obvious from the example. First, once you enable error trapping with *On Error,* your program will trap all runtime errors. The error handler in the example assumed the error was an overflow produced by multiplying two large numbers. More generally, you should try to anticipate all errors that are likely to show up and have the handler deal with them separately. For example, suppose you expand the regular part of the program as follows:

```
C = A * B
MsgBox A & " times " & Format(B) & " is " & Format(C)
C = A / B
MsgBox A & " / " & Format(B) & " is " & Format(C)
```

Now there is the possibility of a second kind of error—division by zero (error number 11). One way to respond to more than one possible kind of error is to use a *Select Case* statement based on the Err.Number property:

```
Select Case Err.Number
    Case 6:    MsgBox "Enter smaller integers:"
    Case 11:   MsgBox "Don't use 0 for the second integer!"
    Case Else: MsgBox "I'm not prepared to deal with this! Bye."
                Stop 'Throw into break mode.
End Select
```

Another point to keep in mind is that error trapping only takes effect after the *On Error* statement has been executed. For example, consider the initial call to *GoGet* just before the *On Error* statement. If you generate a *Type Mismatch* runtime error there by entering, say, *Frog* and *Toad* instead of *4* and *10,* this program doesn't trap that error. Instead, you get the default runtime error behavior. On the other hand, if the program is executing the *GoGet* procedure call in the error-handling section (after the *Ooops* label) and you enter *Frog* and *Toad,* you generate a *Type MisMatch* runtime error, and that routes the program to the *Ooops* label again. In short, calling *GoGet* before the *On Error* statement executes will initiate the default runtime error handling, and calling *GoGet* afterwards initiates your runtime error handler.

Note that neither the program version in Listing L17-6 nor the *Select Case* example above anticipated the *Type Mismatch* error. At least the *Select Case* version routes you to the *Case Else* section in that eventuality.

One more thing to consider is where you want the program to go when it finishes handling the error. You have three choices, as described in Table L17-8.

STATEMENT	NEXT STATEMENT EXECUTED
Resume	The statement that caused the runtime error
Resume Next	The statement immediately following the runtime error
Resume ***Label***	The statement immediately following the symbolic line number *Label*

Table L17-8 Where execution resumes

Listing L17-7 modifies Listing L17-6 to illustrate some of these ideas. In particular, it responds to both overflow and division-by-zero errors, it provides Help information to a message box, and it uses *Resume* ***Label*** instead of *Resume*.

One interesting point this version emphasizes is that it is the time sequence of events, not the text sequence in the Code window, that determines when error trapping is in effect. For example, if you begin by entering *"Frog"* and *"Toad"*, you get the default error handling. That's because the program calls *GoGet* before reaching the *On Error* line. Suppose, however, that you enter *4* and *0* instead. When the program reaches the division statement, it jumps to the error handler, tells you what's wrong, then uses *Resume ReDo* to jump back up to the *GoGet* statement just above the *On Error* statement. But if you enter *"Frog"* and *"Toad"* this time, you get kicked into the error handler. That's because even though this line is *above* the *On Error* line, this time it was executed *after* the *On Error* line.

Listing L17-7
The modified Trapping 101A project

```
Option Explicit

Sub GoGet(M As Integer, N As Integer)
    M = InputBox("Enter an integer")
    N = InputBox("Enter another integer")
End Sub

Private Sub cmdTest_Click()
    Dim A As Integer, B As Integer, C As Integer
    Dim Msg As String
Redo:
    GoGet A, B
    On Error GoTo Ooops
    C = A * B
    MsgBox A & " times " & Format(B) & " is " & Format(C)
    C = A / B
    MsgBox A & " / " & Format(B) & " is " & Format(C)
    Exit Sub
Ooops:  ' a label
    Msg = "Error # " & Format(Err.Number) & " (" & Err.Description & ")" _
        & " was generated by " & Err.Source
    MsgBox Msg, , "Error", Err.HelpFile, Err.HelpContext
    Select Case Err.Number
        Case 6:    MsgBox "Enter smaller integers:"
        Case 11:   MsgBox "Don't use 0 for the second integer!"
        Case Else: MsgBox "I'm not prepared to deal with this! Bye."
                   Stop 'Throw into break mode.
    End Select
    Resume Redo 'Return to line with Redo label.
End Sub
```

These examples just touch the surface on error handling and error trapping, but they should help you start thinking about these topics.

SUMMARY

Computer programs provide ample scope for errors. You could mess up the syntax for a statement. Visual Basic catches syntax errors during design mode, making them easy to correct. Your code could lead to computational impossibilities, which, in turn, generate error messages. You could misguide a program, sending it into obvious or subtle errors. Often you can use the break mode to track down such runtime errors. The Step Into, Step Over, and Step to Cursor choices let you execute selected portions a step at a time, while the Watch window lets you inspect the values of variables, properties, and other expressions.

One common source of problems is input that doesn't conform to a program's expectations. You should try to anticipate such problems and minimize possible conflicts by fitting your choice of input tools to the needs of a program. Consider using option boxes, check boxes, menus, scrollbars, and lists to limit input to acceptable values.

It's not always possible to prevent the entry of bad values. Your next line of defense is to test for bad values. You can use *IsNumeric* and its cousins, as well as *VarType*, to see whether particular values are of the right type. If not, you can attempt to guide the user or your program to more suitable values.

You can use error trapping to detect runtime errors and to replace the default response to runtime errors (show a message, let you end the program, or go into break mode) with your own error-handling code. The *On Error* statement turns on error trapping, and you can use the properties of the Err object to learn more about which error occurred.

QUIZ 17

1. Identify syntax errors in each of the following lines:

```
Dim Single as Floor
Pirnt "I compute, therefore I compute."
Circle 100, 200, 50
If Floor > 3 Print "Everyone out!"
```

2. What is the easiest, most foolproof way of finding syntax errors?

3. What windows appear when you enter break mode?

4. What are the parts of the Debug window?

5. What's the difference between Step Over and Step Into?

6. Find the logic errors in the following code:

```
Bottles = 100
Do While Bottles < = 0
     Print Bottles & " of root beer on the wall"
Loop
```

7. What can you observe in the Watch window?

8. What's the difference between *IsError* and *On Error?*

9. What's the difference between *Resume* and *Resume Next?*

10. In Listing L17-7, what needs to be done to include the first call to *GoGet* in the error-trapping scheme?

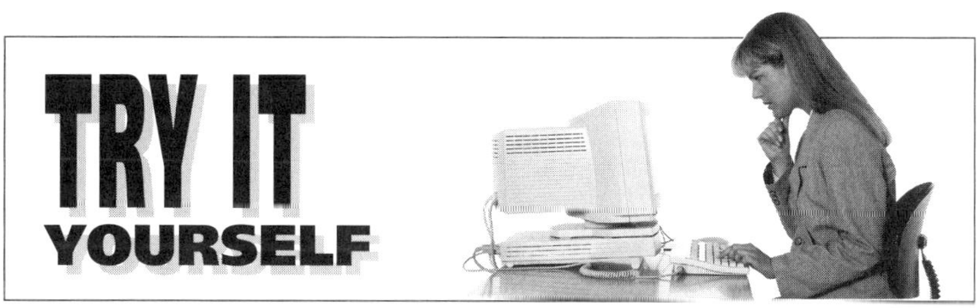

1. Fix Listing L17-1 so that it does handle the case of no numbers entered when the user clicks Done.

2. Redo step 1 using error trapping.

3. Redo Listing L17-4 using error trapping.

4. In Listing L17-7, bring *GoGet* into the error-trapping realm and expand the error handler to deal with the "Type mismatch" error.

LESSON 18

FILES

Programs interact with their environment. So far, you've seen programs interact with the user via the keyboard, mouse, display screen, and printer. And behind the scenes, programs constantly interact with the operating system. This lesson opens a new vista, the world of files. Files are a computer's repository of information. For example, the program examples for this book reside in files, as does the Visual Basic program itself, as well as the manuscript for this book. You can grant your Visual Basic programs the power to browse for file names,

to open a file, to create a new file, to read information from a file, and to save information to a file. In this lesson, you'll learn about the following topics:

- **Using the Drive List Box, Directory List Box, and File List Box controls**
- **Opening and displaying bitmapped and metafile image files**
- **Viewing text files**
- **Using the Common Dialog Box control**
- **Creating and saving text files**
- **Creating and saving random access files**

THE PATH TO SUCCESS—FINDING FILES

To open a file, a program needs to know where a file is. This involves identifying the drive containing the file (such as, C, D, and so on), the directory or chain of directories containing the file (such as, \BODYPART\HEAD\CHEEK\), and the name of the file itself (TONGUE). Together, these three parts constitute a complete *path name,* such as D:\BODYPART\HEAD\CHEEK\ TONGUE. Visual Basic provides three special-purpose list boxes designed to let you browse through your file system:

- The Drive List Box lists the available drives on your system and lets you select one.
- The Directory List Box lists the directories for a given drive, lets you move up and down different directory levels, and lets you select a particular directory.
- The File List Box lists the files in a particular directory and lets you select a file.

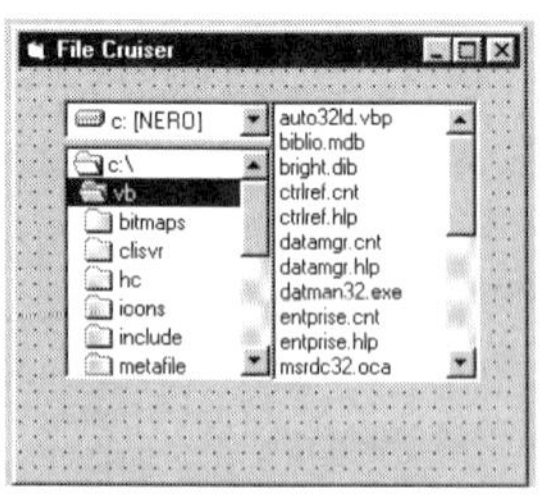

Figure L18-1 The File Cruiser form

By using these three controls, you can navigate to any file on your system. However, the process is not completely automatic. You need to link the controls together by using a few simple statements. To see what has to be done, let's start with the project described in Table L18-1 and illustrated in Figure L18-1.

OBJECT	PROPERTY	SETTING
Form1	Caption	File Cruiser
	Name	frmCruise
DriveListBox1	Name	drvCruise
DirListBox1	Name	dirCruise
FileListBox1	Name	filCruise

Table 18-1 The File Cruiser form

These list boxes are a little different from the standard list boxes. In particular, you don't initialize them by using *AddItem* in the *Form_Load* event. Instead, they are initialized when you draw them on the form. As you can see in Figure L18-1, they are initialized to the drive and directory containing Visual Basic. (If you made the program into a stand-alone application, as described in Lesson 19, the lists would be initialized to the drive and directory containing that application.)

OK, let's run this program and see what can be done. The drive list box is a combo box. First, click on the down arrow in the drive list box. You'll see a drop-down list of all your available drives. Click on a drive. The drop-down list disappears, and the drive you selected becomes the drive showing in the text box part of the combo box. Cool! You can navigate from one drive to another!

But there is a flaw. Even if you change the drive showing in the drive list, the directory window still shows directories in the original drive. Similarly, you can use the mouse to cruise the directory system, opening directories and subdirectories, but the file list box continues to show the files in the original directories. In short, the three list boxes are not yet coordinated with each other. But that can be fixed rather easily.

Getting File Cruiser into Gear

The way to synchronize the three list boxes, as with so many Visual Basic activities, is to use properties and events. Table L18-2 lists some useful properties for these three controls.

CONTROL	PROPERTY	VALUE	RUNTIME ONLY
DriveListBox	Drive	Drive letter	Yes
DirListBox	Path	Path of selected directory	Yes
FileListBox	FileName	Name of the currently selected file	Yes
	Path	Path of selected directory	Yes
	Archive	True if file has Archive attribute set	No

continued on next page

continued from previous page

CONTROL	PROPERTY	VALUE	RUNTIME ONLY
	Hidden	True if file has Hidden attribute set	No
	Normal	True if file has Normal attribute set	No
	Pattern	File matching pattern (*.* by default)	No
	ReadOnly	True if file has ReadOnly attribute set	No
	System	True if file has System attribute set	No

Table 18-2 Some useful properties

Right now you need the Drive and Path properties. The Drive property gets set to the drive letter. Actually, it gets set to the string that shows in the drive list box's text box, which includes the drive's volume name, if any, but only the first letter is important. Similarly, the Path property gets set to the directory path name, including the drive letter. So in the example showing in Figure L18-1, *drvCruise.Drive* is *"C: [NERO]"*, and *dirCruise.Path* and *filCruise.Path* both are *"c:\vb"*.

If you use the drive list box to change drives, you'd like the directory list box to display the directories on the new drive. The solution is one of those typical Visual Basic things—use an event to trigger the change, and use properties to make the change. In this instance, you can use the *Change* event for the drive list box and the Drive and Path properties:

```
Sub drvCruise_Change()
    dirCruise.Path = drvCruise.Drive 'Set path to drive.
End Sub
```

At first glance, this doesn't look all that helpful. For instance, suppose the Drive value is changed to *"d: [tana]"*. That isn't a valid path name value. Amazingly, however, this code doesn't assign the string *"d: [tana]"* to the Path property. Instead, Visual Basic uses the first letter of the string to identify the drive as the drive D and ignores the rest of the string. It then sets the Path property to the current directory on drive D, for example, to *"D:\danger\ducks"*.

Current Directories and Current Drives

DOS and Windows maintain the idea of the *current directory* and *current drive*. When you type *DIR* in DOS, it's the contents of the current directory on the current drive that get listed. In DOS, you change drives by typing a drive letter followed by a colon. For instance, typing *B:* takes you to drive B. To change directories, you use the CHDIR command (CD, for short). In Windows, when you open an application, Windows sets the current drive and directory according to the application's Working Directory value. (You can use the Properties selection in the Windows File Manager File menu to change the working directory for an application.)

Each drive has its own current directory. For instance, you can set the current directory in drive C to, say, c:\potato\chip, then change to drive D and set its current directory to, say, d:\harbors. If you then type DIR C:, you'll get a listing of the c:\potato\chip directory because the system remembers the current directory for each drive.

The next step is to bring the file list box up to date so that it shows the files in the directory currently showing in the directory list box. Changing the Path property for the directory list box triggers the *Change* event for that control, and you can use that event to update the Path property for the file directory box:

```
Sub dirCruise_Change()
    filCruise.Path = dirCruise.Path  'Set file path.
End Sub
```

Add these two event procedures to File Cruiser, and you can cruise your directory system, seeing your directories and files. This may be more thrilling for some than for others. Nonetheless, you now have learned the basic technique for allowing users of an application to select files.

Which Files Do You See?

By default, the file list box lists most, but not all files. In particular, it does not show hidden files and system files. That's because the file list box Hidden and System properties are set to False by default. But it does list normal files, archived files, and read-only files because the Archive, Normal, and ReadOnly properties are set to True. (Archived files are files that have been changed since being copied by a backup program, hidden files are files that don't normally show up when you list files, read-only files are files that can be read but not changed, and system files are certain files used by the operating system. You can change these properties for a file by using the DOS ATTRIB command or by using the Properties selection from the File menu of the Windows Explorer or My Computer.) Suppose you wanted to limit a program to viewing only read-only files. Then you could set the file list box's Archive, Hidden, Normal, and System properties to False, and the ReadOnly property to True.

You also can use the Pattern property to limit which files are displayed. By default, this property is set to *.*, a pattern that matches all file names. (The * is a "wildcard" character that stands for any combination of characters, including no characters at all. So *.* means a file with any name and any extension.) You might want to restrict viewing to just one kind of file. Often programs use particular file name extensions (the part after the period in a file name) to indicate a type. For example, Windows metafile files have a .WMF extension, ASCII text files often have a .TXT extension, and so on. So to restrict the view to text files, you could set the Pattern property to **.txt*. If you want to use more than one pattern, separate the patterns by semicolons, as in **.txt;*.bat;*.bak*. Then the file list box will show all files matching any one of the patterns in the list.

Selecting a File

The properties just discussed control which files are listed. How do you identify the file you actually select? The file list box FileName property is set to the name of the selected file. When you first open the file list box, no file is selected, and the FileName property is set to the empty string. When you select a file name by clicking on it in the list, Visual Basic then sets the FileName property to the name of that file.

You also can set the FileName property by code. For instance, you could have code like the following:

```
filCruise.FileName = "c:\dos\xcopy.exe"
```

If you do this, *filCruise.FileName* gets set to the file name part of the path name, and *filCruise.Path* gets set to the path name. That is, after this assignment statement, *filCruise.FileName* has the value *"xcopy.exe"*, while the property *filCruise.Path* has the value *"c:\dos"*.

If you do something like this, you'll want to coordinate the other two list boxes with this change. Changing the Path property for a file list box triggers a *PathChange* event, so you can do this:

```
Sub filCruise_PathChange()
   dirCruise.Path = filCruise.Path    'Set directory path.
End Sub
```

Changing the Path property for the directory list box, in turn, triggers the *Change* event for that control, and you can add code to that event to bring the drive list box in line:

```
Sub dirCruise_Change()
    filCruise.Path = dirCruise.Path  'Set file path.
    drvCruise.Drive = dirCruise.Path  'Synchronize drive.
End Sub
```

You could put a similar line in the *filCruise_PathChange* event instead, but placing the line here serves double duty. That is, you can also change *dirCruise.Path* directly in code. Placing the line here catches that case directly as well as catching a change in *filCruise.Path*.

Tip

Normally, you use the drive list box *Change* event to update the directory list box Path property, and the directory list box *Change* event to update the file list box Path property. If, however, your program allows you to change the file list box Path property directly, you also should use the file list box's *PathChange* event to update the directory list box Path property, and use the directory list *Change* event to update the drive list box's Drive property.

Graphic Improvements

Browsing through file names soon becomes tame. With just a few modifications, we can mutate File Cruiser into a much more exciting program, which we'll call Image Cruiser. This program will let you browse through graphical files that Visual Basic can recognize (bitmapped files and metafiles) and view their contents quickly and easily. The project will use the Pattern property to limit listed files to the bitmapped formats using the .BMP and .ICO extensions and the .WMF metafile extension. It will use the FileName property to identify which file you want to view, then load that image into an image control.

Before going into the details, let's think about image size. If we leave the image control Stretch property set to False, the control will expand or shrink to fit the image. That means the images will be very small for icons, while some metafile images may be too large to view in their entirety. Setting Stretch to True will result in the images being expanded or shrunk to fit the image control. That's good in some cases, but it won't give you a realistic view of icons. Therefore the program will use a couple of option buttons to select whether stretching is in effect. Thus the form will use the three file controls, an array of two option buttons, and an image control. Table L18-3 describes the controls and Figure L18-2 shows the design-mode layout.

OBJECT	PROPERTY	SETTING
Form1	Caption	Image Cruiser
	Name	frmImage
DriveListBox1	Name	drvImage
DirListBox1	Name	dirImage
FileListBox1	Name	filImage
	Pattern	*.bmp;*.ico;*.wmf
Option1(0)	Caption	Fit to View Frame
	Index	0
	Name	optStretch
	Value	True
Option1(1)	Caption	View As Is
	Index	1
	Name	optStretch
Image1	Name	imgImage
	Stretch	True

Table 18-3 The Image Cruiser form

Listing L18-1 shows the code. Here are the major points to note. First, if you set the Stretch property to False, then view an icon, the icon size becomes the new size of the image control. That means if you turn Stretch back on and next

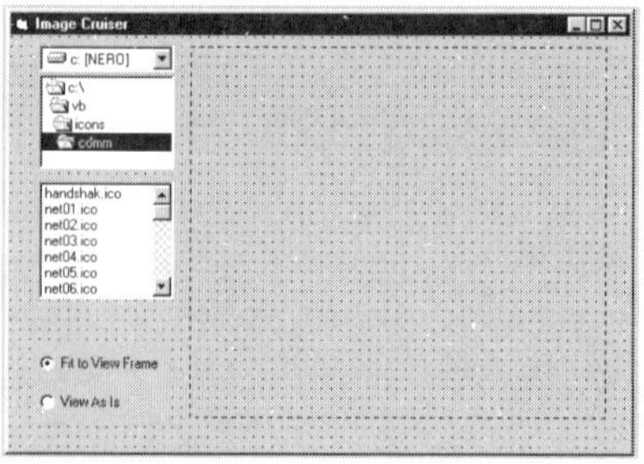

Figure L18-2 The Image Cruiser form

view a metafile, it will be squeezed down to icon size for viewing. Therefore the program uses the variables *Tall* and *Wide* to save the original dimensions of the image control. When you set Stretch to True, the program uses these values to reset the image control size to the original dimensions. Normally, you would view icons with Stretch set to False and metafiles with Stretch set to True, and the program uses those default settings by virtue of the following code:

```
' Set stretch option according to file type.
    If LCase(Right(filImage.filename, 3)) = "wmf" Then
        optStretch(0).VALUE = True
    Else
        optStretch(1).VALUE = True
    End If
```

The *Right* function takes a string and an integer as arguments and returns a string consisting of the indicated number of characters from the right end of the string. For example, *Right("think", 3)* returns the string *"ink"*. The *LCase* function, recall, converts a string to lowercase. So the *If* statement checks to see if a file name ends with the .WMF (windows metafile) extension.

Second, so you won't forget about *On Error,* the program adds a small error handler to the *drvImage_Change* event. This would be invoked, for example, if you tried to show the contents of drive A without first inserting a disk.

Third, the way you select a file for viewing is to double-click on the name in the file list, which triggers the following event procedure:

```
Private Sub filImage_DblClick()
    ChDrive drvImage.Drive
    ChDir filImage.Path
    ...
    imgImage.picture = LoadPicture(filImage.filename)
End Sub
```

This code uses the fact that you can load a picture into an image control during run time by using the *LoadPicture* command. Note that the code combines the path with the file name to build a complete path name. For instance, it would combine *c:\vb\icons\comm* with *handshak.ico* to build the path name *c:\vb\icons\comm\handshak.ico*.

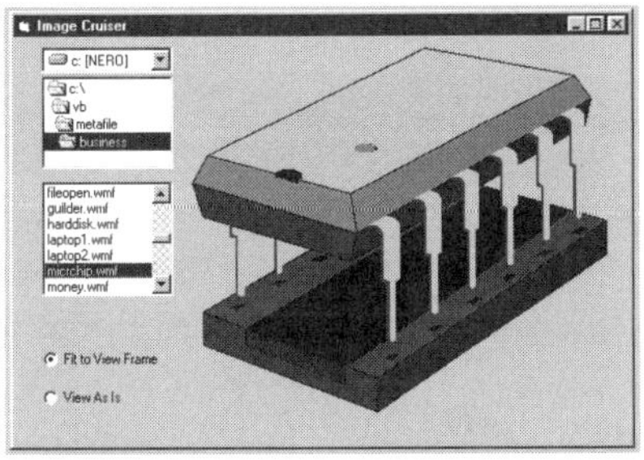

Figure L18-3 Viewing a metafile with Image Cruiser

Why, you may ask, can't you just use the file name alone? That's a good question. The reason is that using the file controls to browse through drives, directories, and files *does not change* the current path or the current drive as far as DOS or Windows is concerned. For a command like, say, *LoadPicture("handshak.ico")* to work, that file must reside on the current drive and in the current directory. Therefore the program uses the *ChDrive* and *ChDir* commands to change the settings. (The alternative is to use a full path name as the argument to *LoadPicture*.) Figure L18-3 shows a sample of Image Cruiser's talent.

Note

The three file controls let you view various drives, directories, and files, but changing the file control Drive and Path properties does not change the current drive and current directory values. To change the current drive and current directory, use the ChDrive and ChDir commands.

Listing L18-1
The Image Cruiser program

```
Option Explicit
Dim Tall As Integer, Wide As Integer 'original image size

Sub drvImage_Change()
    On Error GoTo NoCanDo
    dirImage.Path = drvImage.Drive 'Set path to drive.
    Exit Sub
NoCanDo:     ' Assume error is failure to open drive.
    MsgBox "Can't open that drive. Is it empty?"
    drvImage.Drive = dirImage.Path  ' Reset to old value.
End Sub

Sub dirImage_Change()
    filImage.Path = dirImage.Path  ' Set file path.
End Sub
```

continued on next page

continued from previous page

```
Private Sub filImage_DblClick()
     ChDrive drvImage.Drive
     ChDir filImage.Path
' Set stretch option according to file type.
     If LCase(Right(filImage.filename, 3)) = "wmf" Then
          optStretch(0).VALUE = True
     Else
          optStretch(1).VALUE = True
     End If
     imgImage.picture = LoadPicture(filImage.filename)
End Sub

Private Sub Form_Initialize()
     ' Save original size of image frame.
     Tall = imgImage.Height
     Wide = imgImage.Width
End Sub

Private Sub optStretch_Click(index As Integer)
     imgImage.Stretch = Not imgImage.Stretch 'toggle setting
     If index = 0 Then    ' Reset frame to original size.
          imgImage.Height = Tall
          imgImage.Width = Wide
     End If
End Sub
```

READING FILES

Now that you can browse graphics files, how about browsing text files? The basic ideas are similar. Use the file controls to browse through file names. Use the Pattern property so that only text files are displayed. But the details are different. There's no simple equivalent of the *LoadPicture* command for text. Instead, you have to follow the more traditional route of using the *Open* command to open a file, using *Input* or *Line Input #* to read the file contents, and using the *Close* command to close the file when you're done with it. Let's look at these commands.

Opening a File—*Open* and *FreeFile*

The Visual Basic command for opening a file is Open. Omitting some optional arguments, it has this form:

Open *pathname* **For** *mode* **As** *#filenumber*

The *pathname* parameter is the name of the file you wish to open. If it is in the current directory on the current drive, you can just use the file name without providing the complete path. The *mode* parameter describes the use you have in mind for the file. Table L18-4 lists the options. For instance, the browser program will use *input* mode since it will read the contents of the file.

FILE MODE	MEANING
Append	Open file in order to add data sequentially to the end of the file
Binary	Open the file in binary mode (uses binary instead of text representation of data)
Input	Open file in order to read from it sequentially
Output	Open file in order to write data sequentially to the file; previous contents are replaced
Random	Open file for random access

Table L18-4 Modes for opening files

Once a Visual Basic program opens a file, it doesn't refer to the file by name. Instead, it uses an integer, the *file number,* to identify the file. It should be in the range 1–511. For example, the statement

```
Open barney.txt For Input As #1
```

opens a file named *Barney.txt* and assigns a file number of 1. Later commands, then, will refer to the file as *1,* or *#1.*

Each file that's open needs its own unique file number, although when you close a file, you can reuse the same file number for a new file. If your program starts dealing with multiple files, you might have a problem keeping track of which file numbers are available. Fortunately, the Visual Basic function *FreeFile* takes care of the bookkeeping for you and returns a currently valid file number when you need one. So a better practice is to replace the preceding *Open* statement with these statements:

```
Dim FileNum As Integer
FileNum = FreeFile  'Obtain a valid file number.
Open barney.txt For Input As #FileNum
```

Reading a File—*Line Input #, EOF, Input, LOF,* and *Close*

There are several ways to read information from a file. If the file is a text file, you can use the *Line Input #* function, which reads one line at a time. It takes a file number identifying which file to read, and it returns the next line from that file. For instance, if *TheLine* is a *String* variable, the statement

```
TheLine = Line Input #Filenum
```

reads one line from the file opened with *FileNum* as its file number and assigns it to the variable *TheLine.* Visual Basic identifies lines in a file by the fact that each line ends in a carriage-return character (*Chr(13)*) or in a carriage-return and a line-feed character (*Chr(13) + Chr(10)*) combination. The combination is the standard DOS text format for marking lines. It turns out that although *Line Input #* reads the carriage-return/line-feed combination, it doesn't include it in the string it returns. That's because the function is designed to be used in concert with the *Print* method, which automatically adds a new line when it prints a string. That is, you might have code like this:

```
TheLine = Line Input #Filenum
picShow.Print TheLine
```

This would copy the line from the file to a picture box control.

To read more than one line from a file, you can use a loop. To terminate the loop, use the *EOF* function (End of File), which returns True when the *Line Input #* function reaches the end of a file. For instance, you could do this:

```
Dim TheLine As String
...
Do While Not EOF(FileNum)
     TheLine = Line Input #Filenum
     picShow.Print TheLine
Loop
```

However, you're not going to do that. Instead of using *Print* and a picture box, use a text box and its *Text* property. That way you can use the scrollbar options for a text box, which will facilitate viewing text. The idea is to set the Text property to the contents of the file, and you can do that most easily by using the *Input* function. It takes two arguments; the first is the number of characters to read, the second is a file number identifying which file to read. For example, the statement

txtText.Text = Input(10, #FileNum)

would read the next ten characters from the *FileNum* file and assign them, as a string, to the Text property of the txtText text box. The reason for using *Input* instead of *Line Input #* is that *Input* reads and passes on all the characters in the file, including carriage returns and line feeds. That way, the Text property winds up with all same formatting as the original text.

There's a slow way and a fast way to do this. The slow way is to use a loop to read one character at a time and add it to the Text property one character at a time:

```
txtText.Text = ""
Do While Not EOF(FileNum)
    txtText.Text = txtText.Text & Input(1, #FileNum)
Loop
```

The fast way is to read all the characters at once. You can do that if you know how many characters are in the file, and that's exactly what the *LOF* function (Length of File) tells you. Like the other file functions, it takes a file number as an argument to identify which file to use. So you can replace the loop with a single line of code:

```
txtText.Text = Input(LOF(FileNum), #FileNum)
```

That might be a pretty big string. Will it fit? There are several considerations here. First, can a single string hold the contents of a whole file? The Text property of a text box can accommodate a string up to about 32,000 characters. Text files tend to be short and simple. (Don't confuse text files with the more complex documents created by word processors.) Still, you might run into a file that challenges the limit, but let's not worry about that. If you insist on worrying, you can do something along the following lines:

```
FileLength = LOF(FileNum)
If FileLength < 32000 then
    txtText.Text = Input(FileLength, #FileNum)
Else
    txtText.Text = "Sorry, " & filText.FileName & " is too big to fit."
End If
```

Text Files

Text files contain text. The text is in the form of a series of characters, with each character stored using its ASCII code. The standard format for DOS text files uses the carriage-return/line-feed character combination to indicate the end of a line of text. Text files just contain the code for the characters. There's no font name information, no font size information, no font style information, no color information, no fancy symbols, just ordinary ASCII characters. This simple structure makes it easy to view text files.

Second, can a long string fit in a text box? The answer is yes. However, you need to help. First, set the MultiLine property of the text box to True. That will cause each line of text to appear on its own line in the text box. (Also, when MultiLine is False, the maximum number of characters in a text box is cut to about 2,000 characters.) Second, set the text box Scrollbars property to 3, which enables both horizontal and vertical scrollbars in the text box. That way, even if the lines are too long and numerous to fit in the display area of the text box, you can scroll around to see the whole file.

Finally, your program should close a file when it finishes with it. Just use the *Close* statement, using the file number to identify which file to close:

```
Close (FileNum)
```

Text Cruiser

Now you're nearly ready for the next project, browsing text files. First, however, let's fix a minor nuisance you may have noticed with Image Cruiser. Because it changes the current drive and current directory each time you view an image, these settings may be left with new values when you quit the program. It would be more polite to restore the original settings. You can do so in three steps:

1. Create module-level variables to store the original settings for current drive and current directory.

2. Use the *Form_Load* event to set these variables to the current values.
3. Use the *Form_Unload* event to use these variables to restore the original settings.

The one new element here is the *Form_Unload* event. It's triggered when you close a form by double-clicking on the left-hand box on its title bar. Or you can single-click on the box and select Close from the pop-up menu. It's not triggered when you select End from the Visual Basic run menu or click on the Visual Basic End icon. When a form is unloaded, it's removed from the screen and from memory.

Also, you can trigger the *Form_Unload* event manually with the *Unload* statement. For instance, the Text Cruiser project uses a command button *Click* procedure as follows:

```
Private Sub cmdExit_Click()
    Unload frmText
    End
End Sub
```

The *End* command alone won't trigger the *Unload* event, so this code uses the *Unload* statement to unload the form first, thus triggering the *Unload* event.

Table L18-5 shows the controls for the new Text Cruiser project, and Figure L18-4 shows the form layout. Listing L18-2 shows the project code. Most of it duplicates the Image Cruiser code because both programs share the same general design. One difference is the pattern. Many applications use a .TXT extension, so that is part of one of the patterns. But DOS batch files, which have the .BAT extension, are text files, as are Visual Basic 4 form files and project files, so the pattern includes them, too. Also note that the text box ScrollBars property is set to 3. This causes both horizontal and vertical scrollbars to be supplied with the text box.

OBJECT	PROPERTY	SETTING
Form1	Auto3D	True
	Caption	Text Cruiser
	Name	frmText
DriveListBox1	Name	drvText
DirListBox1	Name	dirText
FileListBox1	Name	filText
	Pattern	*.txt;*.bat;*.frm;*.vbp
Text1	MultiLine	True
	Name	txtText
	ScrollBars	3 - Both
Command1	Caption	E&xit
	Name	cmdExit

Table 18-5 The Text Cruiser form

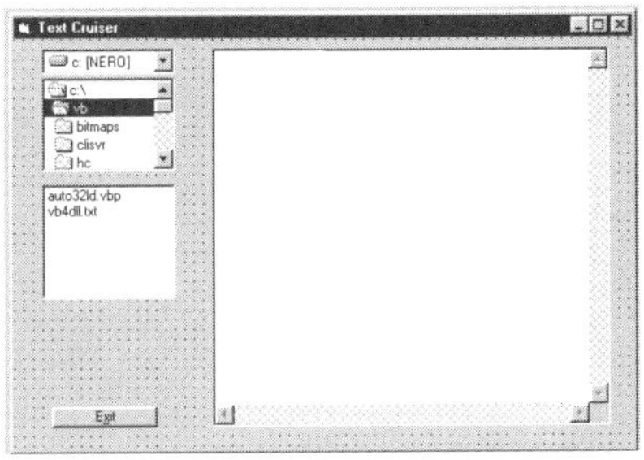

Figure L18-4 The Text Cruiser project

Listing L18-2
The File Cruiser program

```
Option Explicit
Dim StartDrive As String
Dim StartDir As String

Private Sub cmdExit_Click()
    Unload frmText
    End
End Sub

Private Sub drvText_Change()
    On Error GoTo NoCanDo
    dirText.Path = drvText.Drive 'Set path to drive.
    Exit Sub
NoCanDo:    ' Assume error is failure to open drive.
    MsgBox "Can't open that drive. Is it empty?"
    drvText.Drive = dirText.Path  ' Reset to old value.
End Sub
Private Sub dirText_Change()
    filText.Path = dirText.Path  ' Set file path.
End Sub

Private Sub filText_DblClick()
    ChDrive drvText.Drive
    ChDir filText.Path
    CopyToBox (filText.FileName) 'Place processing in a procedure.
End Sub

Private Sub filText_PathChange()
   dirText.Path = filText.Path  ' Set directory path.
End Sub

Sub CopyToBox(AFile As String)
    Dim FileNum As Integer
    FileNum = FreeFile
    Open AFile For Input As #FileNum
    txtText.Text = Input(LOF(FileNum), #FileNum)
    Close #FileNum
End Sub
```

continued on next page

continued from previous page

```
Private Sub Form_Load()
' Save initial setting for current drive and directory.
    StartDrive = drvText.Drive
    StartDir = dirText.Path
End Sub

Private Sub Form_Unload(Cancel As Integer)
  ' Restore initial setting for current drive and directory.
    ChDrive StartDrive
    ChDir StartDir
End Sub
```

With Text Cruiser, you now can inspect the contents of text files. Figure L18-5, for example, shows the result of loading one of the Visual Basic sample files and scrolling part way through it. Keep in mind that you are not viewing the file itself. Instead, you are viewing a *copy* of the file, a copy stored in the text box.

File Output

Text Cruiser is just a viewer. Suppose you want the power to edit text files. For instance, suppose you would like to be able to add text, delete text, and cut and paste text. Text Cruiser already lets you do that because those facilities are built in to text box controls. Once you get text in a text box control, you can edit it as you like. But keep in mind that you're working with a copy of the original material, and none of the changes you may make will have any effect on the original. Indeed, by the time you've seen the text appear onscreen, Visual Basic already has executed the Close command for the file.

If you want to save the changes you make, you can open the file again, but this time for output. Then you can copy the contents of the text box to the file. The way to open the file for output is this:

```
Dim FileNum As Integer
FileNum = FreeFile
Open filText.FileName For Output As #FileNum
```

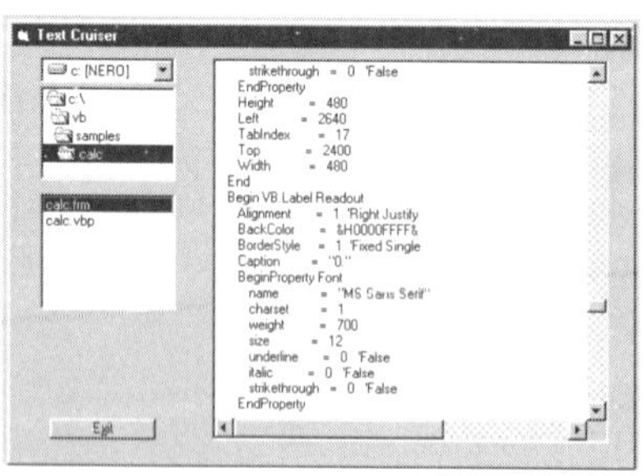

Figure L18-5 Viewing a form file

To write to a file, you can use the *Print #* statement. Its first argument is the file number of the file to which you wish to write. After that, you can provide the same sort of items to print as you do with the *Print* method. That is, you can print strings, numbers, and *Boolean* values. You can use *Tab, Spc,* and semicolons. In this case you want to print just one string, the string that represents the entire contents of the text box control:

```
Print #FileNum, txtText.Text
```

When you open a file in output mode, whatever you write replaces the prior contents of the file, wiping out the old contents. Therefore, you should exercise some care. In particular, you typically don't want changes to be saved to the file automatically. Instead, you want the user to make a conscious choice. One way to modify Text Cruiser so that it can save changes is to add a command button captioned Save Changes and to place the file-saving code in the *Click* procedure for that button. That way, the user has to take positive action to save, hence alter, a file. However, instead of modifying Text Cruiser, let's develop a different interface, one that utilizes Visual Basic's common dialog box controls.

THE COMMON DIALOG BOX CONTROL

Many Windows programs share an interface for common tasks such as opening and saving files, printing files, selecting fonts, and selecting colors. The common dialog box control brings that interface to Visual Basic programs. To create a common dialog box control, select the corresponding icon from the Toolbox and draw a control on a form. Like the timer control, the common dialog box control appears in design mode as a fixed-size icon and doesn't show on the form during run time. To get a dialog box, you have to use one of the common dialog box control methods. Each method initiates a different dialog box. Table L18-6 lists the methods and what they do.

METHOD	ACTION
ShowColor	Shows a color-setting dialog box
ShowFont	Shows a font dialog box
ShowHelp	Shows a help file
ShowOpen	Shows a dialog box for opening a file
ShowPrinter	Shows a printing dialog box
ShowSave	Shows a dialog box for saving a file

Table L18-6 Methods for the common dialog box control

These methods work well with a menu interface. For instance, you can use an Open selection in a File menu to invoke the *ShowOpen* method. With that in mind, let's revamp Text Cruiser into a menu-oriented program called Tiny Edit.

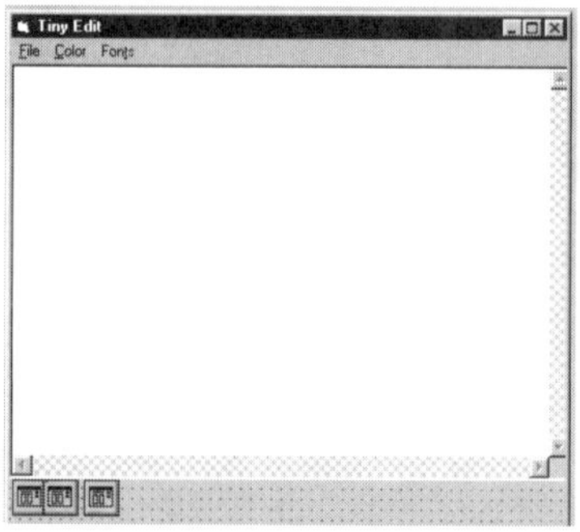

Figure L18-6 Tiny Edit in design mode

First, Table L18-7 shows the controls for the new project. (Properties will be discussed with the individual methods.) Next, Table L18-8 describes the menu setup, and Figure L18-6 shows the design mode layout. (In practice, you would let the text box fill the entire form, but the figure leaves some extra room on the bottom so you can see the three common dialog box control icons.) As you might guess from the names, the File menu will use a common dialog box control (dlgEdit) for opening and saving files, the Color menu will use a common dialog box control (dlgColor) for setting foreground and background colors in the text box, and the Fonts menu will use a common dialog box control (dlgFont) to set font properties.

OBJECT	PROPERTY	SETTING
Form1	Caption	Tiny Edit
	Name	frmEdit
CommonDialog1	Filter	Text (*.txt)|*.txt|Batch (*.bat)|*.bat
	Flags	&H2
	Name	dlgEdit
CommonDialog2	Flags	&H2
	Name	dlgColor
CommonDialog3	Flags	&H1
	Name	dlgFont
Text1	MultiLine	True
	Name	txtEdit
	ScrollBars	3 - Both

Table 18-7 The Tiny Edit form

LIST BOX ENTRY	CAPTION	NAME
&File	&File	*mnuFile*
....&Open	&Open	*mnuFileOpen*
....&Save As	&Save As	*mnuFileSave*

LIST BOX ENTRY	CAPTION	NAME
....&Close (Don't Save)	&Close (Don't Save)	*mnuFileClose*
....-	-	*mnuFileBar*
....E&xit	&Exit	*mnuFileExit*
&Color	&Color	*mnuColor*
....&Background	&Background	*mnuColorBack*
....&Foreground	&Foreground	*mnuColorFor*
Fon&ts	Fon&ts	*mnuFonts*
....&Settings	&Setting	*mnuFontsSettings*

Table L18-8 Menu entries for the Tiny Edit program

The Common Dialog Box and Files

The common dialog box control has two file-related methods: *ShowOpen* and *ShowSave*. Let's see how they work. First, let's see how to open a file-opening dialog box and how it looks. Enter the following event procedure in the Code window:

```
Private Sub mnuFileOpen_Click()
    dlgEdit.ShowOpen ' Show the dialog box for opening a file.
End Sub
```

This causes clicking on the Open choice in the File menu to open the dialog box. Run the program and try it. You should see something similar to that shown in Figure L18-7.

At the top, there's a drop-down list box labeled "Look in:". It displays an icon representing the current directory. If you're at the top level of a directory system, it displays an icon representing current drive. Icons to the right show standard Windows 95 directory controls. The first icon, if clicked, takes you up one directory level. The next icon lets you create a new directory. The third and fourth icons let you choose a list view (the default) or a more detailed view that shows file sizes, creation times, and the like.

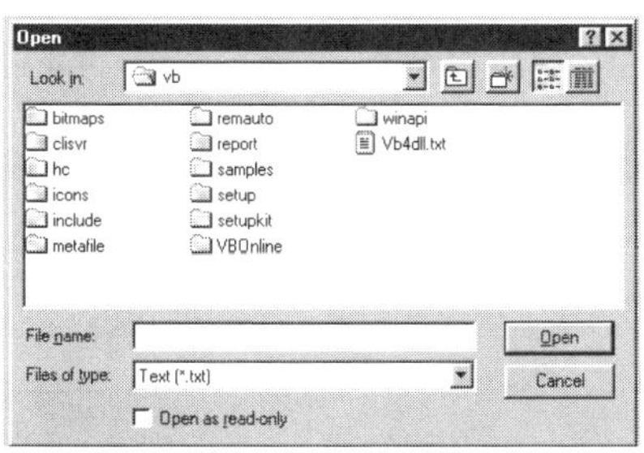

Figure L18-7 The Open dialog box

A box displaying the subdirectories and files occupies the bulk of the dialog box. Directories' names appear after a file folder icon. Beneath this box is a text box labeled "File name:" and a drop-down list box labeled "Files of type:". The entry in the "Files of type:" list box determines which files are listed in the large box. Here, for example, the list box contains the string "Text (*.txt)", meaning that only files having the .TXT extension are listed. Note the down arrow at the right of the list box. Click on it, and you'll see a list of other available patterns. In this case, you'll see "Batch (*.bat)". If you click on that selection, files with .BAT extensions will be listed.

If you click on a listed file, its name appears in the "File name:" box. You then can open the file by clicking on the Open button. Also, you can type the name of the file you want to open directly into the "File name:" box. Finally, if you type a pattern, such as *.* or *\.com*, into this box and press ENTER, the big box will show file names matching that pattern.

The Filter Property

Where did these file type choices come from? They came from the Filter property for the dlgEdit control. As Table L18-7 shows, this property has the following value:

```
Text (*.txt)|*.txt|Batch (*.bat)|*.bat
```

The Filter property consists of alternating descriptions and patterns separated by the pipe (vertical bar) symbol. Each description is paired with the following pattern. That is, the description "Text (*.txt)" is displayed in the Files of Type box, and the pattern is displayed in the File Name box and is used to match file names. The notation is a little confusing because the pipe is used for two purposes:

- To separate the description from the pattern within a pair
- To separate one pair from the next

Thus, the first pipe in the pattern above separates the "Text (*.txt)" description from the *\.txt* pattern, the third pipe separates the "Batch (*.bat)" description from the *\.bat* pattern, while the second pipe separates the text description-pattern group from the batch description-pattern group.

You can have spaces in the description part, but you should not have any spaces next to the pipe symbol, for the spaces would then become part of the description (not too bad an error) and part of the pattern (a bad error).

The pattern part can use multiple patterns separated by semicolons, just as in the Pattern property for a file list box. Also, showing the pattern in the description part isn't necessary; it just serves to clarify which files get matched. For instance, you can have a Filter property like this:

```
Text |*.txt|Bitmapped|*.ico;*.bmp
```

This gives the user two choices for the Files of Type box—*Text*, which will select files fitting the **.txt* pattern, and *Bitmapped*, matching icon and bitmapped files.

Note

If you omit the Filter setting, a common dialog box will list all files. However, if that's your intent, it's clearer to the user if you provide a suitable value for the Filter property. In that case, you need both a description and a pattern part separated by a pipe, as in the following:

```
All Files|*.*
```

The FileName Property

Okay, once you have the dialog box, you can select a file. How do you communicate that information to the program? When you select a file and click on the OK button, that sets the dialog box's FileName property to the path name of the file you selected. You then can open that file for input, just as Text Cruiser did. However, you also should allow for the possibility that the user doesn't enter a name or cancels. You can do the following, where *CopyToBox* is the same procedure used in Text Cruiser.

```
Private Sub mnuFileOpen_Click()
     Dim AFile As String
     dlgEdit.ShowOpen
     AFile = dlgEdit.FileName
     If AFile <> "" Then CopyToBox (AFile)
End Sub
```

Similarly, if you want to save a file, you can use the *ShowSave* method in the *Click* event for the Save As menu selection:

```
Private Sub mnuFileSave_Click()
     Dim AFile As String
     dlgEdit.ShowSave
     AFile = dlgEdit.FileName
     If AFile <> "" Then CopyToFile (AFile)
End Sub
```

Here *CopyToFile* is a procedure that copies the contents of the text box to the indicated file:

```
Sub CopyToFile(TheFile As String)
     Dim FileNum As Integer
     FileNum = FreeFile
     Open TheFile For Output As #FileNum
     Print #FileNum, txtEdit.Text
     Close #FileNum
End Sub
```

The *ShowSave* method shows a dialog box much the same as the ShowOpen box. The main difference is that the caption is Save As instead of Open.

The Flags Property

If you use the Save As feature, you can select an existing file or type in a new file name. If you type in a new file name, the *Open ... for Output* statement will create a new file with the chosen name. If you use an existing file, Visual Basic will replace the file contents with the new material. This sort of drastic change should be made with caution! You can use the Flags property to induce the Save As dialog box to give you a warning (see Figure L18-8) if you attempt to save material into an existing file. That is what Table L18-7 does when it sets the Flag property for dlgEdit to &H2. Table L18-9 lists some choices for the Flags property. (See Visual Basic Help for a complete list. Or else use the Object Browser; select the Microsoft Common Dialog Control library, and browse through the constants listed there.) You use the numeric constants in the Properties window, and you can use either the numeric or symbolic constants in code.

To set more than one flag in the Properties window, you can add them. For instance, to enable Overwrite confirmation (&H2) and to prevent someone from opening files that don't yet exist (&H1000), you can use the value &H1002. Or, if you are writing code, you can use the OR operator with the symbolic constants in Table L18-9.

```
dlgEdit.Flags = &H2 OR  &H1000
dlgEdit.Flags = cdlOFNOverwritePrompt OR cdlOFNReadOnly
```

FLAG VALUE	SYMBOLIC CONSTANT	MEANING
&H1	cdlOFNReadOnly	Causes the dialog box to open with the Read Only box checked
&H2	cdlOFNOverwritePrompt	Displays a message box prompting user to confirm overwrite operation
&H4	cdlOFNHideReadOnly	Hides the Read Only check box
&H8	cdlOFNNoChangeDir	Forces the dialog box to set the current directory to the directory that was current when the box opened
&H1000	cdlOFNFileMustExist	Allows user to enter only names of existing files in the File Name text box

Table L18-9 Some file-related flags for a common dialog box

Managing Colors

Next, let's examine the *ShowColor* method. Using it is similar to using the *ShowOpen* and *ShowSave* methods. Calling this method shows a color chooser dialog box. Setting the dlgColor.Flags property to 2 causes the optional Custom color section to be displayed automatically. (Visual Basic Help and the Object Browser list the other possible flag settings.) The control has a Color property that gets set to the user's selection. For example, you can start with this version of the *mnuColorBack_Click* procedure.

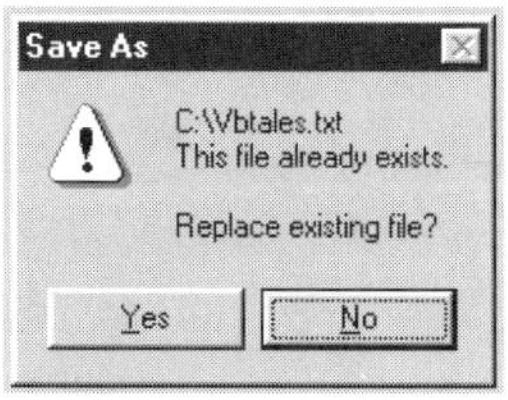

Figure L18-8 The overwrite warning

```
Private Sub mnuColorBack_Click()
    dlgColor.ShowColor
    txtEdit.BackColor = dlgColor.Color
End Sub
```

Similarly, you can use the same control for setting the foreground color:

```
Private Sub mnuColorFore_Click()
    dlgColor.ShowColor
    txtEdit.ForeColor = dlgColor.Color
End Sub
```

Clicking the corresponding menu choice shows the dialog box pictured in Figure L18-9, and selecting and accepting a color sets the text box background to the selected color. Note the box in the lower-right quadrant labeled Color|Solid. The part above "Color" shows what the selected color will look like in open space, and the "Solid" part shows how it will look as a background to text. What you see depends on the number of colors your video system displays.

As they stand, these two event procedures have a potential problem. If a user selects Cancel instead of OK, that leaves the Color property unchanged. But suppose you set a background color using *mnuColorBack_Click,* start to change the foreground color using *mnuColorFore_Click*, but cancel. Then the Color property will be the one you just set for the background. Unfortunately, the next

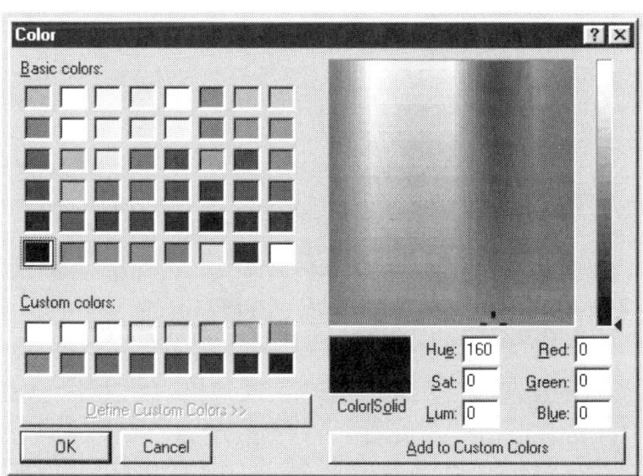

Figure L18-9 The common dialog box for color

statement in the *mnuColorFore_Click* procedure then sets the foreground color to the Color property, hence to the background color, making the text impossible to read.

This can be fixed if the dialog box can communicate the fact that the Cancel button was clicked. The way to do that is to set the CancelError property to True. That causes Visual Basic to generate an error (Error 32755, symbolic name *cdlCancel*) if the user clicks on the Cancel button, and the event procedure then can trap for that error:

```
Private Sub mnuColorBack_Click()
    On Error GoTo Cancelled
    dlgColor.ShowColor
    txtEdit.BackColor = dlgColor.Color
    Exit Sub
Cancelled:
    If Err.Number <> cdlCancel Then
        MsgBox Err.Description & " Bye!"
        End
    End If
End Sub
```

You can use similar code for the *mnuColorFore_Click* event.

Fonts Again

Next, let's investigate using a common dialog box to control font settings. To show the font dialog box, use the *ShowFont* method. However, you'll be disappointed unless you set the Flags property correctly first. You must specify whether to show screen fonts (1), printer fonts (2), or both (3). Table L18-7 uses the flag value of 1 since you're just displaying text onscreen. Table L18-10 shows a partial list of flag settings for a font dialog box. (You can find more values by using Visual Basic Help or by using the Object Browser.) As usual, you can combine values by adding them or, in code, by using the OR operator:

```
dlgFonts.Flags = &H20001        ' Show only scaleable screen fonts.
dlgFonts.Flags = cdlCFScreenFonts OR cdlCFScalableOnly 'ditto
```

FLAG VALUE	SYMBOLIC CONSTANT	MEANING
&H1	cdlCFScreenFonts	List screen fonts
&H2	cdlCFPrinterFonts	List printer fonts
&H3	cdlCFBoth	List printer fonts and screen fonts
&H100	cdlCFEffects	Enable color, strikethrough, and underline effect
&H20000	cdlCFScalableOnly	Only allow scaleable fonts to be selected
&H40000	cdlCFTTOnly	Only allow TrueType fonts to be selected

Table L18-10 Some font-related flags for a common dialog box

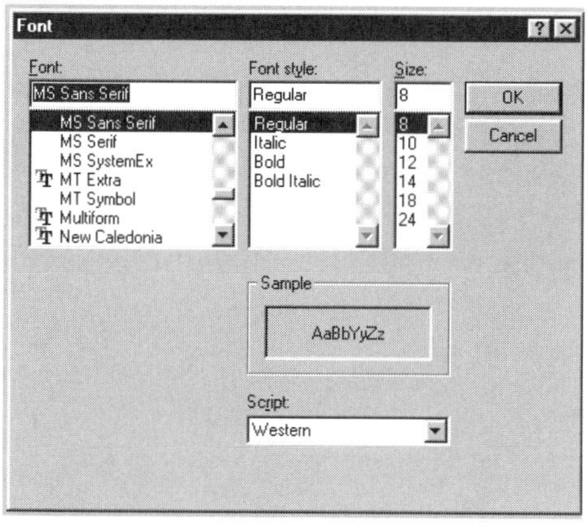

Figure L18-10 The Font common dialog box

The dialog box looks like that shown in Figure L18-10. Use it to make your selections. To communicate your choices to the program, use the Name, Size, and so on, properties of the Font object of the common dialog box to set the corresponding properties for the text box:

```
Private Sub mnuFontFont_Click()
    dlgFont.ShowFont
    txtEdit.Font.Name = dlgFont.FontName
    txtEdit.Font.Size = dlgFont.FontSize
    txtEdit.Font.Bold = dlgFont.FontBold
    txtEdit.Font.Italic = dlgFont.FontItalic
End Sub
```

You may have noticed that the dialog box in Figure L18-10 shows the standard Visual Basic MS Sans Serif font highlighted. That's because the program initializes the Font.Name property to the corresponding txtEdit.Font.Name property. You'll find that tidbit and the rest of the code in Listing L18-3. Figure L18-11 shows the program in run mode after some settings have been changed. Keep in mind that changes in colors and fonts are for your viewing pleasure only. When you save the file, only the characters themselves are saved.

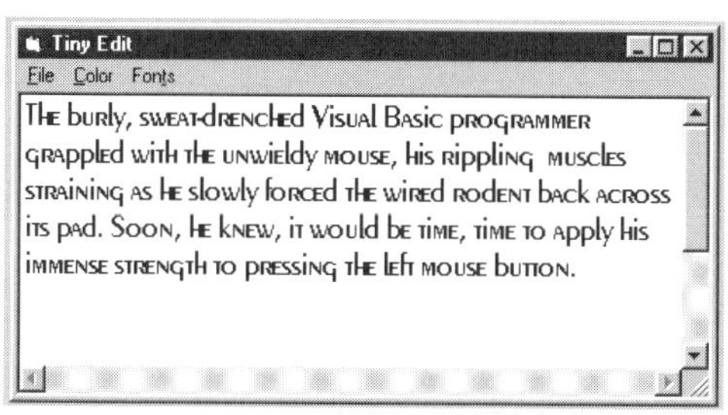

Figure L18-11 Tiny Edit in run mode

Listing L18-3
The Tiny Edit program

```
Option Explicit

Private Sub Form_Load()
    dlgFont.FontName = txtEdit.Font.Name
End Sub

Private Sub mnuColorBack_Click()
    On Error GoTo Cancelled
    dlgColor.ShowColor
    txtEdit.BackColor = dlgColor.Color
    Exit Sub
Cancelled:
    If Err.Number <> cdlCancel Then
        MsgBox Err.Description & " Bye!"
        End
    End If
End Sub

Private Sub mnuColorFore_Click()
    On Error GoTo Cancelled
    dlgColor.ShowColor
    txtEdit.ForeColor = dlgColor.Color
    Exit Sub
Cancelled:
    If Err.Number <> cdlCancel Then
        MsgBox Err.Description & " Bye!"
        End
    End If
End Sub

Private Sub mnuFileClose_Click()
    txtEdit.Text = ""
End Sub

Private Sub mnuFileExit_Click()
    End
End Sub

Private Sub mnuFileOpen_Click()
    Dim AFile As String
    dlgEdit.ShowOpen
    AFile = dlgEdit.FileName
    If AFile <> "" Then CopyToBox (AFile)
End Sub

Private Sub mnuFileSave_Click()
    Dim AFile As String
    dlgEdit.ShowSave
    AFile = dlgEdit.FileName
    If AFile <> "" Then CopyToFile (AFile)
End Sub

Sub CopyToBox(TheFile As String)
    Dim FileNum As Integer
    FileNum = FreeFile
```

```
    Open TheFile For Input As #FileNum
    txtEdit.Text = Input(LOF(FileNum), #FileNum)
    Close #FileNum
End Sub

Sub CopyToFile(TheFile As String)
    Dim FileNum As Integer
    FileNum = FreeFile
    Open TheFile For Output As #FileNum
    Print #FileNum, txtEdit.Text
    Close #FileNum
End Sub

Private Sub mnuFontFont_Click()
    dlgFont.ShowFont
    txtEdit.Font.Name = dlgFont.FontName
    txtEdit.Font.Size = dlgFont.FontSize
    txtEdit.Font.Bold = dlgFont.FontBold
    txtEdit.Font.Italic = dlgFont.FontItalic
End Sub
```

OTHER FILE CONSIDERATIONS

The examples of this lesson have dealt with sequential text files. *Sequential* means the file contents are read and written in sequence. That is, when a program reads a file, it starts at the beginning and reads the file through to the end. You can't back up in the file, and you can't skip ahead. In short, it's like playing a music tape on a tape recorder with no reverse or fast-forward controls. Being a text file means that all information is stored in text form, even numbers. How this works is obvious for strings. For instance, consider this statement:

```
Print #MyFileNum, "This file does nothing for your nails."
```

It copies the string to file. That is, it copies the ASCII code for the character *T* to the file, then copies the ASCII code for the character *h* to the file, and so on. After copying the ASCII code for the period character to the file, the print statement then writes the ASCII codes for the carriage-return character (13) and the line-feed character (10), for this combination is the standard marker for the end of a line in a DOS text file. In general, the file uses 1 byte of space for each character in the string.

But suppose you're saving numbers:

```
Dim Income As Double
Dim Shares as Integer
Income = 13520123.56
Shares = 21242
Print #MyFileNum, Shares; ":"; Income
```

Internally, the program stores *Shares* as a 2-byte binary integer, and it stores *Income* as an 8-byte floating-point binary number. But it prints them as strings. That is, when saving *Shares* to the file, the program first writes the ASCII code for the digit 2 character, then the ASCII code for the digit *1* character, and so on. In short, it uses 5 bytes of disk space to store the five digits in the number 21242. Similarly, it uses 11 bytes of disk space to store the ten digits and one decimal point in the *Income* value.

The advantage to this approach (converting numbers to text) is that it makes it easy to read the file. Any program that lets you read text files, including DOS Edit and Windows Write, will let you read the information.

The alternative to storing numbers as text is storing them in the same form that the computer stores them in memory. That is, store an *Integer* value in the same 2-byte format used for *Integer* variables in memory, and store a *Double* value in the same 8-byte format used for *Double* values in memory. A file that uses this technique is called a *binary* file. Storing numbers in binary format has two advantages over storing them in text format:

- Storage may take less space
- You don't lose precision

The above example shows how you can save space; a 2-byte binary integer surely occupies less space than a 5-character string. (Each character occupies 1 byte.) The precision issue is important for floating-point values. For instance, suppose you format *Income* to print rounded to the nearest dollar. Then the remaining digits in the value are printed and aren't saved. Also, because numbers are stored in binary (base 2) representation, there may not be an exact decimal representation of the binary value, just as you can't, say, write 1/3 exactly as a decimal fraction.

Note

A text file stores all values as text strings. A binary file stores information in the same format that a program uses to store the values in memory. Strings are still stored as text, but numbers are not. Binary files, in general, store numeric data in less space and with greater accuracy than do text files.

A Visual Basic program opens a file in sequential text mode when you use *For Input, For Output,* or *For Append* when opening the file. As mentioned earlier, opening a file *For Output* means that your *Print* statements will overwrite the preceding contents, if any, of a file, while opening a file *For Append* means your *Print* statements will add new output to the end of the file.

Random-Access and Binary-Access Files

If sequential text files don't meet your needs, you may find relief with random-access or binary-access files. Using *For Random* when opening a file gives you the random-access mode, while using *For Binary* gives you the binary-access mode. These modes share two characteristics:

- Random access (a program can jump directly to locations within a file)
- Binary format (numbers are stored in binary form)

So, despite the names, *both* types feature random access and binary formats. The main difference is that the random-access mode views files as a sequence of equal-sized chunks called *records,* while the binary-access mode views files as a sequence of bytes. So with a random-access file you can jump to a particular record, while with a binary-access file, you can jump to a particular byte. Random access is like a music CD player, which lets you jump directly to particular locations.

Historically, Basic programmers have used random mode for creating database applications, with each record representing a database record, holding, say, information about an employee or an inventory item. Basic programmers have used binary mode for the same purpose, investing a bit more programming effort to get smaller file sizes. With Visual Basic, it's often more convenient to use a Windows OLE database program like Access to provide the database power while using Visual Basic to provide a user interface. So the following is only a brief look at the random and binary access modes.

The Random-Access Mode and Records

If you use *For Random* when opening a file, the program reads and writes data in chunks called records. A *record* is a user-defined type that holds related information in a single unit. For instance, suppose you wanted to define a type to represent a member of a golf club. In particular, you would like to be able to store the member's first name, last name, golf handicap, and age. Then you could define a new type, called *Golfer,* by using the Visual Basic *Type* statement:

```
Type Golfer
     FirstName   As String * 15 'a string 15 characters long
     LastName    As String * 15
     Handicap    As Integer
     Age         As Integer
End Type
```

What's that *String * 15?* You'll look at that in a moment. But let's begin by seeing what this *Type* statement accomplishes. First, it defines a *Golfer* record as consisting of four *fields.* The first field is the *FirstName* field, the second is the *LastName* field, and so on, as described in the definition.

Second, you now can create record variables of the *Golfer* type. Just use the *Dim* statement as you would for built-in types:

```
Dim HotShot As Golfer   'Create a Golfer-type record.
```

Now *HotShot* is a record variable in which you can store a first name, a last name, a handicap, and an age, one item to each field.

Third, to access individual fields of a record, you use a period to join the name of a record to the name of a field:

```
HotShot.Age = 34    'Assign 34 to the Age field of the HotShot record.
```

This should look familiar, for it's the same syntax you use to specify a property of an object, as in *txtEdit.Text.*

Now let's get back to that *String * 15* thing. Visual Basic records require fixed-length fields. That is, if *HotShot* and *GraveDigger* are two records, then

HotShot.FirstName has to be the same size as *GraveDigger.FirstName*. Visual Basic strings, on the other hand, are variable-length by default. They adjust to fit the size of the string assigned to them. However, you have the option of creating fixed-length strings by following *String* with an asterisk and the size of the string:

```
Dim Veep as String * 20     'string 20 characters long
Dim Excuse as String * 200      'string 200 characters long
```

Suppose, then, you assign the name "Ace" to *HotShot.FirstName*. The *FirstName* field remains 15 characters long, but only the first three characters are used to hold the name "Ace." The rest of the field is filled with space characters.

That records have a fixed size is very important because of how they are used with random-access mode files. When you write to a file using the random-access mode, you write one record at a time. Thus the file consists of a sequence of equal-sized chunks, the records. When you read from a file, the program will read one record at a time. Since all the records are the same size, the program will read the same-size chunk of data each time, which is easy. If you want to skip to the 10th record, it's easy to compute where that begins.

When you open a file in the random-access mode, you should inform the program of the length of a record; that way, Visual Basic will know what size chunks to use when reading from and writing to the file. You can use the *Len* function to get the length of a record. For example, if *HotShot* is a *Golfer* type variable, you can do this:

```
RecSize = Len(HotShot)
```

Then you can open a file using this syntax:

```
Open "Golf.dat" For Random as #FileNum Len = RecSize
```

The *Len* = in this statement is part of the *Open* syntax for opening files in the random-access mode. This example sets up Visual Basic so that it can write *Golfer*-type records to the *Golf.dat* file.

Where's the File?

When the program first creates the Golf.dat file, where does it go? The answer is that it is placed in the current directory of the current drive. If you're using Visual Basic, this most likely is the Visual Basic directory. However, you can include drive letters and path information in the file name. That is, you can use the following:

```
Open "c:\golfdata\Golf.dat" For Random As #FN Len = RecSize
```

Once you open a file in random mode, you can both write to it and read from it. Visual Basic uses the *Put* statement to write records to a random-access file. For example, suppose you've opened a file in random-access mode as just described. Also, suppose *HotShot* is a *Golfer*-type record. Then, to copy the record to the first record position in the file, do this:

```
Put #FileNum, 1, HotShot
```

The first argument to *Put* is the file number assigned by the *Open* statement. The second argument is the record position in the file, and the third argument is the name of the record to copy to the file. To copy the same record to the third record position, use 3 as the second argument:

```
Put #FileNum, 3, HotShot
```

In general, the format is this:

Put #*filenumber*, *position*, *record-name*

However, you can omit the position argument (but not the comma) if you want to copy a record to the position immediately following the previous write:

```
Put #FileNum, , NoPar   'Write NoPar record after last record written.
```

Similarly, the *Get* statement reads a record from a file to a record variable. For example, the statement copies the second record in the file to the variable *Winner*.

```
Get #FileNum, 2, Winner 'Read 2nd record from file into Winner variable.
```

If you omit the record number (but not the comma, which must remain), the program will read the record following the one it just read.

Let's look at a very modest program showing how random-access files work. The first time you run the program, it will create a file named *Golf.dat* and write four golfer records to the file. When you run the program again, it will skip that step. Command buttons will let you open and close the file and move back and forth through the file. Text boxes will show the data for the most recently read record. Table L18-11 shows the properties, Figure L18-12 shows the layout, and Listing 18-4 shows the code.

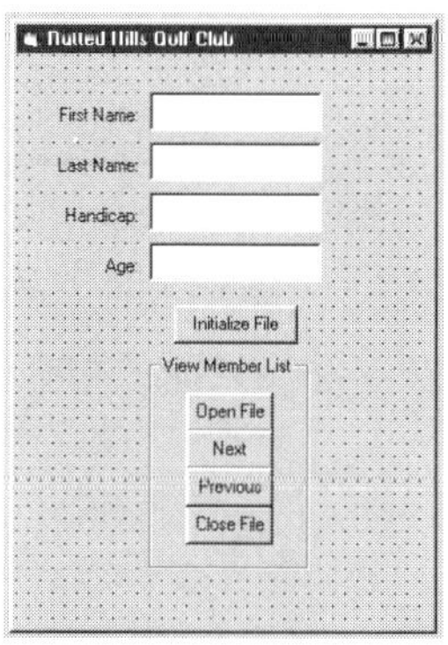

Figure L18-12 The Rutted Hills Golf Club form

A Random-Access Program

It helps if the program knows how many records are in a file. One way to find out is to divide the number of bytes in the file by the number of bytes in a single record. To get the file size, use the *LOF* function, which takes a file number as its argument and which returns the length of an opened file in bytes. To get the size of a single record, you can apply the *Len* function to a sample record:

```
RecSize = Len(FourSome(1))'length of 1st record in array
```

The program divides the length of the file by the length of a single record to find the number of records in the file:

```
NumRecs = LOF(FN) / RecSize ' Calculate number of records in the file.
```

Another useful thing to do is to determine if the *Golf.dat* data file exists and has data. For this, the program uses the *FileLen* function. It takes a file name as its argument, and you use it to find the length of an *unopened* file in bytes. Attempting to use this function on a nonexisting file generates error 53, so you can use error trapping to detect if the function call fails:

```
Private Sub Form_Load()
On Error GoTo NoFile
    If FileLen("Golf.dat") > 0 Then
        cmdInit.Visible = False
        cmdOpen.Enabled = True
    End If
    Exit Sub
NoFile:
    If Err.Number <> 53 Then     '53 = file not found
        MsgBox "Err.Description"
        End
    End If
End Sub
```

If the file exists and has nonzero size, the program hides the Initialize File button and enables the Open File button. Otherwise, the Initialize File button is visible and the Open File button is not enabled. If the *FileLen* function can't find the file, it generates error number 53. Ordinarily, that would terminate the program, but the *Form_Load* event procedure overrides that, terminating the program only if some other error shows up. Figure L18-13 shows the runtime appearance of the form the first time it's started. Clicking the Initialize File button then copies four records into the *Golf.dat* file.

The program uses the Enabled property to limit the user to sensible choices. For instance, you can't use the Open File button until a file has been created. You can't use the Next button to view a record until the file has been opened. You can't use the Previous button to view a record until you've gone past the first record. Figure L18-14 shows the situation after a couple of records have been viewed.

Note how *Get* and *Put* work with records as complete units. You can't read just part of a record; it's all or nothing.

Incidentally, you might want to look at the *Golf.dat* file with a program, such as DOS Edit or Windows Write, that can look at text files. (Be sure not to change

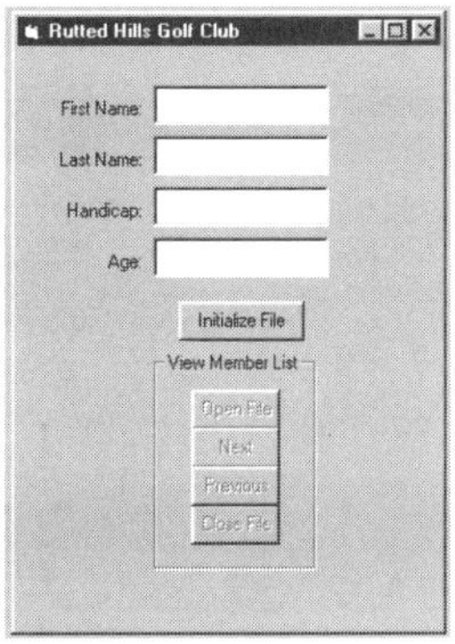

Figure L18-13 Before the data file is created

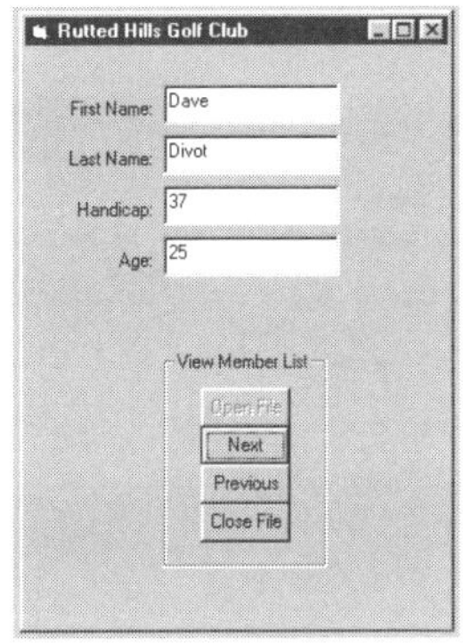

Figure L18-14 After the data file has been created and used

the file format, however.) You'll see that the text part of the records (the names) are still readable as text but that the numeric parts no longer are readable. That's because they're stored in binary format. To make complete sense of this file, you need a program that knows the exact record format used to write data to it.

OBJECT	PROPERTY	SETTING
Form1	Caption	Rutted Hills Golf Club
	Name	frmGolf
Label1	Alignment	1 - right
	Caption	First Name:
	Index	0
	Name	lblGolf
Label2	Alignment	1 - right
	Caption	Last Name:
	Index	1
	Name	lblGolf
Label3	Alignment	1 - right
	Caption	Handicap:
	Index	2
	Name	lblGolf
Label4	Alignment	1 - right
	Caption	Age:
	Index	3
	Name	lblGolf
Text1	Caption	""
	Index	0
	Locked	True
	Name	txtGolf

continued on next page

continued from previous page

OBJECT	PROPERTY	SETTING
Text2	Caption	""
	Index	1
	Locked	True
	Name	txtGolf
Text3	Caption	""
	Index	2
	Locked	True
	Name	txtGolf
Text4	Caption	""
	Index	3
	Locked	True
	Name	txtGolf
Frame1	Caption	View Member List
	Name	fraGolf
Command1	Caption	Initialize File
	Name	cmdInit
Command2	Caption	Open File
	Enabled	False
	Name	cmdOpen
Command3	Caption	Next
	Enabled	False
	Name	cmdNext
Command4	Caption	Previous
	Enabled	False
	Name	cmdPrev
Command5	Caption	Close File
	Enabled	False
	Name	cmdClose

Table 18-11 The Rutted Hills Golf Club form properties

Listing L18-4
The Rutted Hills Golf Club program

```
Option Explicit
Private Type Golfer
    FirstName   As String * 15 'a string 15 characters long
    LastName    As String * 15
    Handicap    As Integer
    Age     As Integer
End Type
```

```
Dim FourSome(1 To 4) As Golfer 'array of 4 golfer records
Dim FN As Integer
Dim RecSize As Integer
Dim NumRecs As Integer
Dim CurrentRec As Integer

Private Sub cmdClose_Click()
     Close #FN
     txtGolfer(0).Text = ""
     txtGolfer(1).Text = ""
     txtGolfer(2).Text = ""
     txtGolfer(3).Text = ""
     cmdOpen.Enabled = True
     cmdNext.Enabled = False
     cmdPrev.Enabled = False
     cmdClose.Enabled = False
End Sub

Private Sub cmdInit_Click()
     Dim I As Integer
     FN = FreeFile
     Open "Golf.dat" For Random As #FN Len = RecSize
     For I = 1 To 4
          Put #FN, I, FourSome(I)
     Next I
     Close #FN
     cmdInit.Visible = False
     cmdOpen.Enabled = True
End Sub

Private Sub cmdNext_Click()
     Dim Golfmember As Golfer
     CurrentRec = CurrentRec + 1
     Get #1, CurrentRec, Golfmember
     txtGolfer(0).Text = Golfmember.FirstName
     txtGolfer(1).Text = Golfmember.LastName
     txtGolfer(2).Text = Golfmember.Handicap
     txtGolfer(3).Text = Golfmember.Age
     cmdPrev.Enabled = True
     If CurrentRec = NumRecs Then cmdNext.Enabled = False
End Sub

Private Sub cmdOpen_Click()
     Dim Golfmember As Golfer
     FN = FreeFile
     Open "Golf.dat" For Random As #FN Len = RecSize
     NumRecs = LOF(FN) / RecSize ' Calculate number of records in the file.
     If NumRecs < 1 Then
          MsgBox "No Records in File"
          Exit Sub
     End If
     CurrentRec = 0
     If NumRecs > 1 Then cmdNext.Enabled = True
     cmdClose.Enabled = True
     cmdOpen.Enabled = False
End Sub

Private Sub cmdPrev_Click()
     Dim Golfmember As Golfer
     CurrentRec = CurrentRec - 1
     Get #1, CurrentRec, Golfmember
```

continued on next page

continued from previous page

```
    txtGolfer(0).Text = Golfmember.FirstName
    txtGolfer(1).Text = Golfmember.LastName
    txtGolfer(2).Text = Golfmember.Handicap
    txtGolfer(3).Text = Golfmember.Age
    cmdNext.Enabled = True
    If CurrentRec = 1 Then cmdPrev.Enabled = False
End Sub

Private Sub Form_Initialize()
    RecSize = Len(FourSome(1))
    FourSome(1).FirstName = "Gary"
    FourSome(1).LastName = "Gravedigger"
    FourSome(1).Handicap = 42
    FourSome(1).Age = 73
    FourSome(2).FirstName = "Harry"
    FourSome(2).LastName = "Hooker"
    FourSome(2).Handicap = 38
    FourSome(2).Age = 37
    FourSome(3).FirstName = "Dave"
    FourSome(3).LastName = "Divot"
    FourSome(3).Handicap = 37
    FourSome(3).Age = 25
    FourSome(4).FirstName = "Sally"
    FourSome(4).LastName = "Shanker"
    FourSome(4).Handicap = 40
    FourSome(4).Age = 73
End Sub

Private Sub Form_Load()
On Error GoTo NoFile
    If FileLen("Golf.dat") > 0 Then
        cmdInit.Visible = False
        cmdOpen.Enabled = True
    End If
    Exit Sub
NoFile:
    If Err.Number <> 53 Then     '53 = file not found
        MsgBox "Err.Description"
        End
    End If
End Sub
```

The Binary-Access Mode

This lesson won't develop a binary-access mode project. In general, this mode works similarly to random mode, except that the unit of access is a byte instead of a record. Thus you can access each byte in a file individually. If, say, you want to write a program that converts one graphic format to another, you need that level of control. To read a file created with binary mode, a program needs to know the exact rules by which the file was created. For instance, the first byte might hold a number equal to the number of bytes used to store the next item in a file. Files opened *For Binary* can be read from and written to. You use *Put* to write to a file, *Get* to read from it. The syntax looks similar to that for Random files. For instance, you could do the following:

```
Get #FN, 20, MyVariable
```

This copies the 20th byte from the file to the variable *MyVariable*.

File Sharing and Locking

In the Windows environment, you can have more than one program running at a time. A network environment can share files. Either situation can lead to two programs seeking to use the same file at the same time. What happens in that case? For a Visual Basic program, you can use an optional *lock* argument (just before the *As*) to the *Open* statement to specify behavior. (Because this argument can use more than one word, Visual Basic refers to it as a *clause*.) Table L18-12 lists the choices.

For instance, suppose you open a file as follows:

```
Open "Golf.dat" For Random Lock Write As #FN Len = RecSize
```

Then, while this program used the file, another program could open the file for reading but not for writing. However, the various lock choices can't override existing situations. That is, if another program already has opened a file for reading, a new program just starting up can't apply the *Lock Read* choice.

LOCK CLAUSE	MEANING
Shared	Other programs can read from the file or write to it
Lock Read	Other programs cannot read from the file
Lock Write	Other programs cannot write to the file
Lock Read Write	Other programs cannot read from or write to the program

Table L18-12 Controlling access to an open file

SUMMARY

Files are the data repositories for computers. They are organized in hierarchical directory systems, with a directory system for each drive. You can use the drive list box, directory list box, and file list box controls to navigate through your drives and directory systems. Alternatively, you can use the common dialog box control for the same purpose. This control also lets you select fonts and colors and control the printer.

You use the *Open* statement to open files. Typically, you open text files using input, output, or append mode. These modes are sequential, meaning a program reads data from a file or writes data to a file in sequential order. Being a text file means that all data, whether string or numeric, is stored in the text format, that is, as a string of characters. The *Open* statement associates a file number with a file. You can choose the number yourself or call upon the *FreeFile* function to provide a valid value. You can use the *Input* or *Line Input #* statements to read information from a sequential file and the *Print #* to write information to a sequential file. These commands use the file number to identify which file to use.

By using random or binary mode, you can open a file for random access and using the binary data format. Random access means you can directly read from or write to any location in the file without moving sequentially through the file.

The binary data format means the program uses the same format for storing data in a file as it does for storing data in memory. Strings look the same in text or in binary format, but numeric data is stored differently.

1. Suppose you have the following controls:

- A drive list box drvPony
- A directory list box dirPony
- A file list box filPony

What, if anything, must you do to accomplish each of the following?

a. Have selecting a drive in the drive list box change the drvPony.Drive property
b. Have selecting a drive in the drive list box change the current drive setting
c. Have selecting a drive in the drive list box change the directories showing in the directory list box
d. Have selecting a new directory in the directory list box update the file list box
e. Have selecting a new directory in the directory list box update the current directory setting
f. Have the program display in a txtPick text box the name of a file selected in the file list box

2. Suppose dlgDoAll is a common dialog box control. How would you do the following?

a. Display a dialog box for opening a file
b. Set the string variable MrFile to the name of the file selected in the dialog box
c. Set the frmDial form's background color to a color selected using the dialog box
d. Set the frmDial form's font to 24-point bold using the dialog box

3. Describe the errors, if any, in each of the following statements:

a. Open "dribble.txt" For Input As #1

b. Input NextChar
c. Close "dribble.txt"
d. Open "disand.dat" As Random Len = Len(Dabble)
e. Put #1, Dabble

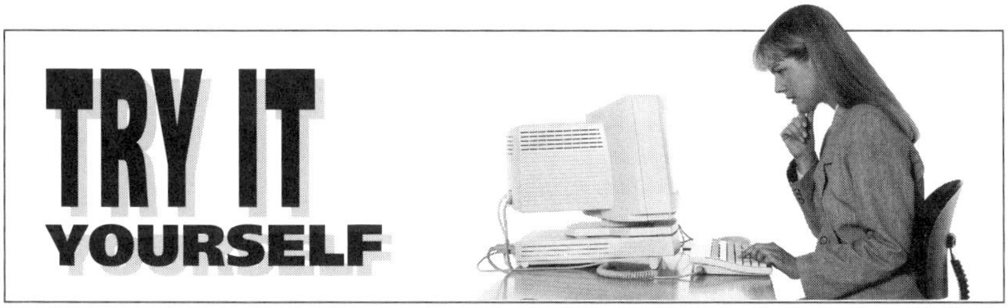

1. Modify Tiny Edit so that it has a label identifying the file being viewed.

2. The *Resize* event is triggered when you resize an object. Use the form's *Resize* event to make the Tiny Edit text box always fill the form, even if a user resizes the form during run time.

3. Modify the Rutted Hills Golf Club program so that a label and a scrollbar identify the number of the current record. Changing the scrollbar setting to a new number should cause the corresponding record to be displayed.

LESSON 19 VISUAL BASIC AND MULTIPLE FILES

As you move from smaller to larger programs in your Visual Basic programming achievements, you'll benefit from dividing your work into multiple files. This is just another expression of the value of modularizing programming tasks. On one level, you modularize by organizing a program into separate event procedures, other procedures, and functions. On the next level, you can organize the procedures and functions into separate modules that are stored in separate files. This has several advantages:

- Individual modules are kept to a small, more easily managed size.

- Grouping related procedures and functions into the same module helps you better visualize the organization of a program.
- The modular approach simplifies debugging and improving a program.
- You may be able to reuse some modules in other programs.

In this lesson you'll learn about the following:

- **Creating stand-alone application files**
- **The runtime dynamic link library file**
- **Code modules (.bas extension)**
- **Public and private procedures and variables**
- **Multiple forms**
- **Mother and child forms**

Lesson 20 will take you further and introduce class modules.

CREATING A STAND-ALONE APPLICATION

The first topic isn't so much about modularization as it is about an alternative way to run your Visual Basic programs. So far you've run all the examples in this book from within the Visual Basic environment. The programs have been stored in form files having the .frm extension. If you view a form file (perhaps by using Text Cruiser from Lesson 18), you'll see that it holds property settings for the form and its controls followed by the program code. All this information is text information, which is not what computers understand. Somewhere along the line, that information has to be translated into the binary data and binary code (machine language) that the computer's processor understands. So far, we've let the Visual Basic environment take care of that when the program runs. It interprets the text code in the form file and sends the corresponding binary code to the processor. Each time you run a program, Visual Basic translates it for you from scratch.

The alternative is to create a stand-alone file, one with an .exe extension. Once you do this, you can run the program without starting Visual Basic. Instead, you can run it directly from Windows, perhaps even place its icon in a program group. In short, your Visual Basic program becomes an independent Windows program—with one caveat that you'll encounter shortly.

How It's Done

Once you have a working program, creating a stand-alone version is quite easy. Let's use the Tiny Edit program from Lesson 18 as an example. Just follow these steps:

1. From Visual Basic, open the Tiny Edit project.

2. From the Visual Basic File menu, select Make EXE File.
3. In the dialog box (see Figure L19-1) enter a name (with an .EXE extension) for your application.
4. Optionally, click on the Options button, enter information (such as the icon and title to use) in the resulting dialog box (see Figure L19-2), and click on OK when you are done.
5. Click on OK in the Make EXE File dialog box.

That's it! Now you can use Run from the Windows File menu to run the application. Or you can use the TaskBar program to add the program to a program group. (Click on Start, select Settings, select TaskBar, click on the Start Menus tab, click on the Add button, and follow directions.) Then you can run the program by clicking on its icon.

By the way, the Options menu lets you embed comments and other information, such as copyright notices, in the executable file. Also, it lets you embed version information, a handy feature if you plan on continuing development of your application.

How It Works

If you examine the size of the stand-alone application file, you may be surprised at how small it is, particularly if you've worked with stand-alone DOS applications. After all, a rather short command such as *Print "Bison Power"* translates into quite a bit of machine language. And consider all the code that must be involved in, say, drawing a form, drawing the form's menu, and getting a menu to know when a mouse has been clicked over it. But the *Tinyedit.exe* file is only about 13K in size, much too small to contain all the necessary code.

The reason *Tinyedit.exe* can be so small is that it isn't a completely stand-alone application. All the code for doing standard Visual Basic tasks such as handling windows, keeping track of the mouse, and so on, is kept in a separate file, called a *runtime file*. If you are using the 16-bit version of Visual Basic 4, the file is called *Vb40016.dll*. For the 32-bit version, the file is called *Vb40032.dll*. When you install

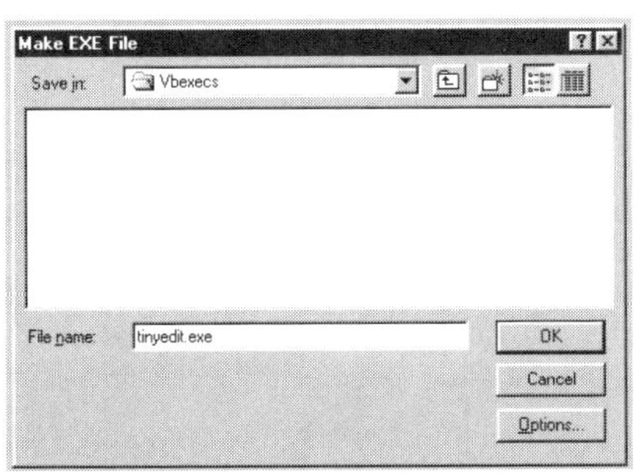

Figure L19-1 The Make EXE dialog box

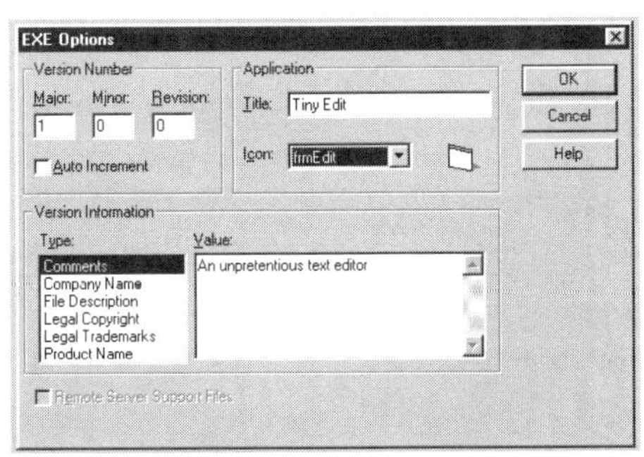

Figure L19-2 The Options dialog box

Visual Basic, the installation program places a copy of the appropriate runtime file in the SYSTEM subdirectory of the WINDOWS directory. You can run your stand-alone Visual Basic application without running the Visual Basic program, but you can't run it without having the appropriate runtime file present. Incidentally, earlier versions of Visual Basic had similar files. For instance, Visual Basic 3 used *Vbrun300.dll*. But to run a Visual Basic 4 program, you need the current runtime files.

Note

If you distribute a stand-alone version of an application you've created with Visual Basic, you should also distribute a copy of the appropriate runtime file so that those unfortunate people without a copy of Visual Basic on their system can still use your program.

The *Vb40016.dll* and *Vb40032.dll* files are examples of *dynamic link libraries*. Programming language compilers and translators come with libraries of code representing the standard procedures the language allows. The old-fashioned way of creating an executable program was to extract necessary code from these libraries and place it in the .EXE file. The process of combining library code with your code was (and is) called *linking*. Doing the linking when the executable program is created is called *static linking*. Figure L19-3 illustrates static linking. With static linking, the more features you used, the more code had to be added to your program. Windows programs, it turns out, require lots of supporting code, so static linking would add a tremendous amount of code even to a simple program like Tiny Edit. The real crunch comes when you create several applications. Static linking would produce a horde of huge applications, and most of the code in one application would duplicate the code in another. That is, each application would need code to draw windows, to track the mouse, to notice the mouse buttons, to represent a command button control, and so on.

Visual Basic takes a much more space-efficient approach. It gathers all that common code into one file, the runtime *Vb40016.dll* or *Vb40032.dll* file. When a stand-alone Visual Basic application needs, say, the code for drawing a command button, it links with the runtime file as the application runs. This is called *dynamic linking*. This enables a host of Visual Basic stand-alone applications to use the dynamic link library as a shared resource. That way, multiple applications don't need their own copies of the standard library code, and this keeps the application size way down. For instance, we mentioned that *Tinyedit.exe* was about 13K in size. However, it taps into a dynamic link library that is close to 1 MB in size. Figure L19-4 illustrates dynamic linking.

CODE MODULES AND .BAS FILES

The projects in these lessons have used two kinds of procedures and functions. One group, the event procedures, relates primarily to the user interface—what happens

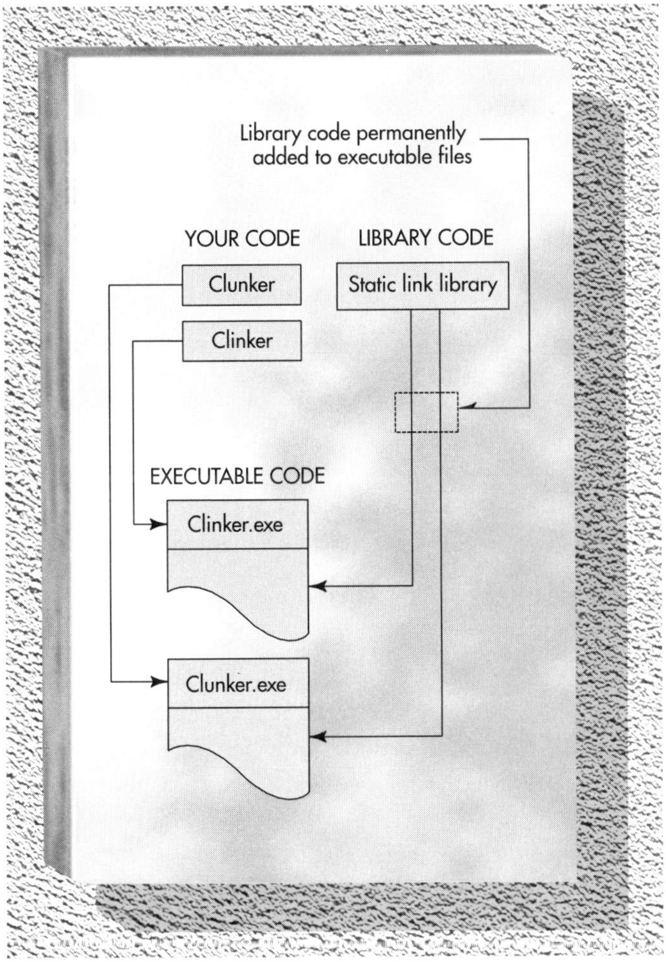

Figure L19-3 Static linking

when you click on a command button, enter text in a text box, slide a scrollbar box, and so on. The second group, the user-defined procedures and functions, relates more to the inner guts of a program—calculating a value, drawing a diamond, picking a random value, and so on. (At first we used event procedures for both kinds of work, but that was before we learned about user-defined procedures.)

Conceptually, it makes sense to separate interface programming from the real work of the program. For instance, consider the dice tossing and the Lotto picking programs from Lesson 15. The actual calculating of dice values or of Lotto picks has nothing to do with the form. The form merely provides a convenient interface for getting information from the user and for displaying the results. You could have fitted the same calculations to a more primitive DOS interface. Or, reversing that perspective, you could have taken the heart of an old Basic DOS program that made Lotto picks and fitted it with a new Visual

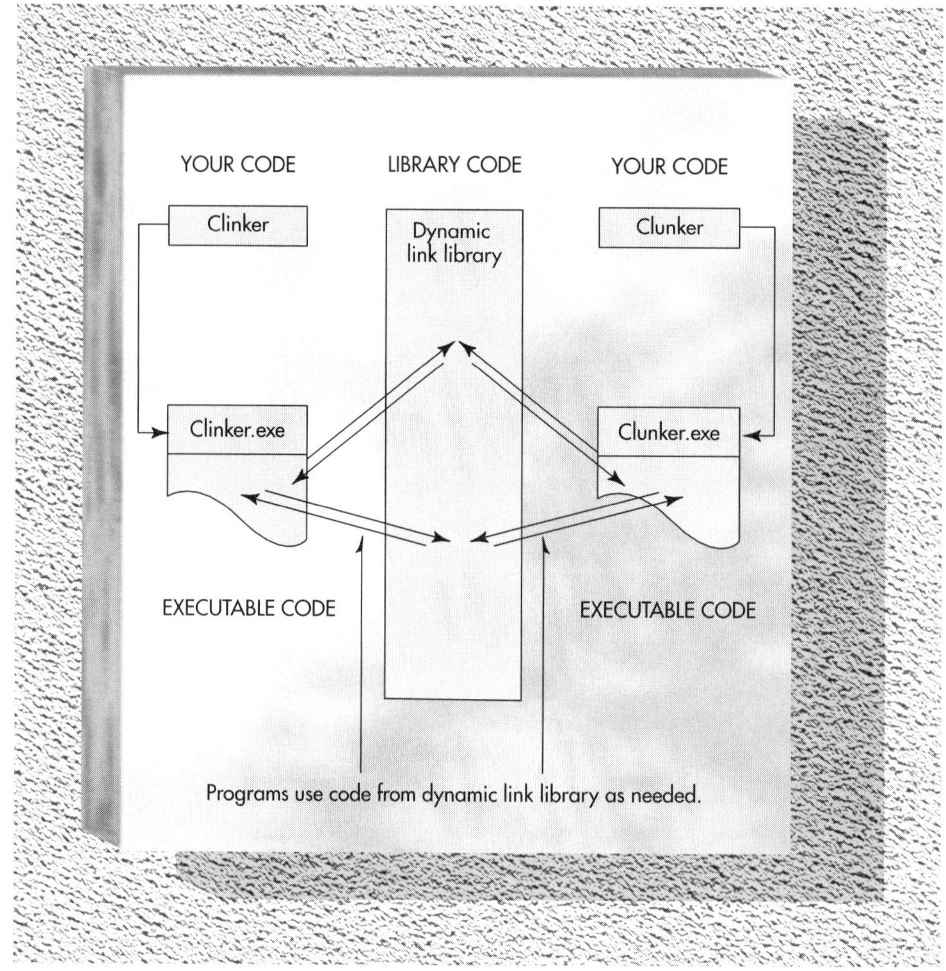

Figure L19-4 Dynamic linking

Basic interface. Then you could say that you've coupled a dynamic graphical front-end to the powerful computational engine of the older version. In fact, creating graphical "front ends" for older applications is the bread-and-butter work for professional Visual Basic programmers.

The way to implement this conceptual view is to use the form module (the one with the .frm extension) to describe the program interface. The form module contains controls and the properties and event procedures for those controls. This interface handles the transfer of information between you and the program. You then place the code for processing the information in a separate file, called a *code module,* and having a *.BAS* extension. Old Microsoft Basic hands will recognize that extension as the one used by QuickBasic and its ancestors for Basic code. With Visual Basic, you can use .bas files for the user-defined procedures and functions that process information. Thus, the .frm file will describe the outward appearance of a program, while the .bas files will determine its hidden workings.

> **Note**
>
> In a generic sense, forms and code (.bas) modules both are modules. However, because forms already have a unique name (forms), the term "module" is usually understood to be a code module.

Revising Lotto

To see how this approach works, let's revise the Lotto example of Lesson 15. The original version squeezes practically all the code into one event procedure, as Listing L19-1 reveals.

Listing L19-1

The original Lotto program

```
Private Sub cmdDraw_Click()
    ' Create an array whose size is given by scrollbar.
    ReDim spots(1 To vscSpots.Value) As Integer
    Dim ThePick As Integer      'index for randomly selected value
    Dim Picks As Integer        'total number of picks to be made
    Dim Max As Integer          'total number of spots
    Dim Temp As Integer         'for swapping values
    Dim I As Integer            'FOR loop counter
    Dim Winners As String       'string of picked values
    Picks = vscPicks.Value
    Max = vscSpots.Value
    ' Initialize array of possible values.
    For I = 1 To Max
        spots(I) = I
    Next
    ' Pick index at random, then swap pick with
    ' an element at the beginning of the array.
    ' After N picks, the picks will fill first N
    ' elements of the array.
    For I = 1 To Picks
        ThePick = Int((Max - I + 1) * Rnd + I)
        Temp = spots(I)
        spots(I) = spots(ThePick)
        spots(ThePick) = Temp
    Next
    Winners = ""
    For I = 1 To Picks
        Winners = Winners + Str(spots(I))
    Next
    txtLotto.Text = Winners
End Sub
```

Some of this code relates to the interface, for example, the vscPicks.Value and vscSpots.Value properties that get set by the scrollbar. Most of the code, however, consists of the algorithm for generating a random set of picks. Following the modular approach, let's delegate that stuff to a separate function, named *Winners*, that returns the string of winning values:

```
Private Sub cmdDraw_Click()
          ' Winners function takes number of spots, number of picks
          ' and returns a string of randomly selected values.
     txtLotto.Text = Winners(vscSpots.Value, vscPicks.Value)
End Sub
```

This certainly simplifies the *cmdDraw_Click* procedure! Note how it mainly deals with interface matters. It uses the interface to obtain two values to pass to the *Winners* function, and it uses the function's return value to set the Text property for a text box. If you just want to see how the program is organized without looking at the details of how the program makes its calculations, this version is much superior to the original.

Creating a New Module

Of course, there's still the matter of writing the *Winners* function. You could place the function in the form module, but it's now time to follow the separate module approach. Here's what you do:

1. Open the Lotto project.
2. While in design mode, select Module from the Insert menu. That opens a new Code window labeled Module1 (see Figure L19-5).
3. Save the module under the name of your choice, using the suggested *.BAS* extension.

If you look in the Project window, you'll see that the new module has been added to your project (see Figure L19-6). The Project window shows a kind of TinkerToy icon for the module, the module's file name, and the name of the module itself. By default the first module is called Module1, but you can use the

Figure L19-5 A new module

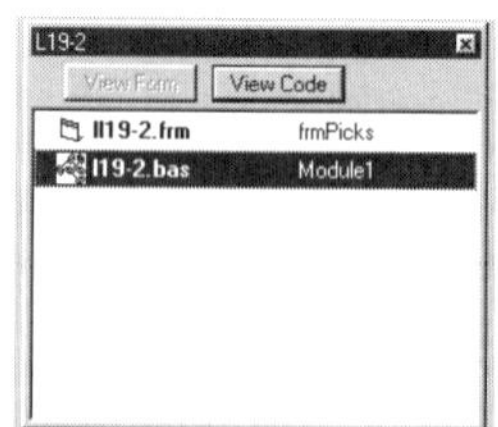

Figure L19-6 Modules are added to the project

Properties window for the module to assign it another name. (The module name, in fact, is the only property the module has.)

The program now has two modules—the original form module and the new code module. You can use the Project window to switch between the two. Use the mouse to highlight the module you want, and then click on the View Code button to show the Code window for the module you chose.

> **Tip**
>
> Use the Project window to select a particular module from a multimodule program, and use the View Code button to open the Code window for that module.

Using the New Module

The next step is to use this new module to hold the code for the Winners function. The simplest approach is to cut the original code from the *cmdDraw_Click* procedure in the form's Code window, paste it in the module's Code window, and do some editing. Also, you can type the new *cmdDraw_Click* code into the form's Code window.

Because we now know about user-defined functions and procedures, we can better modularize the code. For example, a look at the original code for *cmdDraw_Click* reveals that *Winners* needs to do the following:

- Create an array whose size equals the total number of spots on the game card
- Initialize the array elements to the corresponding numbers on the game card
- Rearrange the array so that the beginning of the array holds the random selections
- Combine the random selections into a string

We can accomplish these goals with a function definition like this:

```
Function Winners(TotalSpots As Integer, PickSpots As Integer) As String
    ReDim Spots(1 To TotalSpots) As Integer
    InitArray Spots        ' set to values 1 - TotalSpots
    FillArray Spots, PickSpots ' Put PickSpots random values into array.
    Winners = MakeString(Spots, PickSpots)
End Function
```

Here each task, aside from creating the *Spots* array, has been delegated to yet another procedure or function. The *Winners* function, in essence, acts as an outline, showing what gets done while regulating the details elsewhere. A relatively complex task is made simpler by breaking it into smaller parts. Also note how these procedures and functions don't directly involve the program's interface. They make no mention of control properties. *TotalSpots* and *PickSpots* are just ordinary integers. Of course, the function call in *cmdDraw_Click* connects those integers to control properties.

Now let's take on the new procedures and functions. First, the *InitArray* procedure takes an array argument. You indicate that this way:

```
Sub InitArray(Arr() as Integer)
     ....
End Sub
```

Here the () indicate that *Arr* is an array argument. Because Visual Basic passes arguments by reference, the procedure call

```
InitArray Spots
```

causes *Arr* to be an alias for *Spots*. Once you've declared the procedure correctly, you can proceed to the code:

```
Sub InitArray(Arr() As Integer)
    Dim I As Integer
    For I = 1 To UBound(Arr)
        Arr(I) = I
    Next I
End Sub
```

There's one new feature here. The *Ubound* (for upper-bound) function returns the index of the last element of an array, and the code uses that information to control the For loop. There's also an *Lbound* (for lower-bound) function that returns the index of the first element. However, in this case, the lower-bound for the index always is 1.

Next, the *FillArray* procedure does the randomizing work. Recall that only part of the array is randomized. For instance, if you pick six numbers on a 51-number card, the procedure uses the first six elements to hold the random selections. Therefore, you need to pass the number of picks as well as the array name to this procedure. This is essentially the same code you used in the original version with some of the variable names changed:

```
Sub FillArray(Arr() As Integer, n As Integer)
    ' Arr() is an array of Max elements, and N is the
    ' number of elements to be chosen.
    ' Pick index at random, then swap pick with
    ' an element at the beginning of the array.
    ' After N picks, the picks will fill first N
    ' elements of the array.
    Dim I As Integer            'for loop counter
    Dim Chosen As Integer       'index for randomly selected value
    Dim Temp As Integer         'for swapping values
    Dim Max As Integer          'array size
    Max = UBound(Arr)
    For I = 1 To n
        Chosen = Int((Max    I + 1) * Rnd + I)
        Temp = Arr(I)
        Arr(I) = Arr(Chosen)
        Arr(Chosen) = Temp
    Next I
End Sub
```

Finally, the *MakeString* function returns a string consisting of the random picks separated by spaces. Again, it merely transports the original code into a new function.

```
Function MakeString(Arr() As Integer, Lim As Integer) As String
    Dim I As Integer
    Dim Win As String
     For I = 1 To Lim
        Win = Win + Str(Arr(I))
    Next I
    MakeString = Win
End Function
```

All this code, of course, goes in the new code module.

Putting It Together

Actually, you don't have to do anything further to put the form code and module code together, for the fact that both are part of the same project takes care of that. However, now that you've gone modular, it's simple to add a couple more features. For example, you can sort the chosen numbers first so they appear in numerical order when displayed. Just write a sorting procedure and call it from the *Winners* function. Second, it's only fair to add an assessment of the odds of winning so that program users don't get overly optimistic. Just write a function to calculate the odds and use the function in *cmdDraw_Click* to set a Text property. The form code listing (see Listing L19-2) and the module code listing (see Listing L19-3) include these additions. You'll take a quick look at the techniques used in a moment.

To display the new odds information, you need to add a label and text box as described in Table L19-1. The text box has its MultiLine property set to True, even though it uses just one line. That's because the alignment options take effect only when MultiLine is True. For consistency, you can modify the original text box so that its text is centered, too. Figure L19-7 shows the new version in operation.

Listing L19-2
The Lotto form module

```
Option Explicit

Private Sub cmdExit_Click()
    End
End Sub

Private Sub cmdDraw_Click()
        ' Winners function takes number of spots, number of picks
        ' and returns a string of randomly selected values.
    txtLotto.Text = Winners(vscSpots.Value, vscPicks.Value)
        ' Odds function returns the total number of possible
        ' combinations of picks for the given number of spots.
    txtOdds.Text = "1 chance in " _
```

continued on next page

continued from previous page

```
        & Format(Odds(vscSpots.Value, vscPicks.Value), "#,###")
End Sub

Private Sub Form_Initialize()
    Randomize
End Sub

Private Sub vscSpots_Change()
    lblSpots.Caption = vscSpots.Value
    If vscSpots.Value < 20 Then
        vscPicks.Max = vscSpots.Value
    Else
        vscPicks.Max = 20
    End If
End Sub

Private Sub vscPicks_Change()
    lblPicks.Caption = vscPicks.Value
End Sub
```

OBJECT	PROPERTY	SETTING
Label1	Caption	Odds of winning:
	Font.Bold	True
	Font.Size	12
	Name	lblOdds
Text1	Alignment	2 - Center
	Font.Bold	True
	MultiLine	True
	Name	txtOdds
	Text	

Table L19-1 Additions to the Lotto project

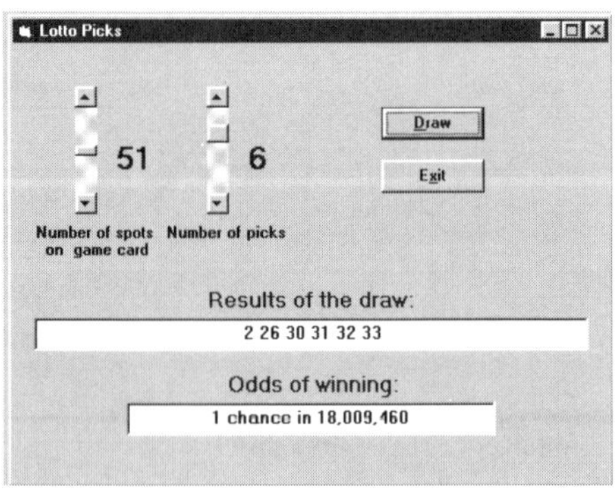

Figure L19-7 Lotto Picks with a truth-in-advertising feature

Listing L19-3
The Lotto code module

```
Option Explicit

Function Winners(TotalSpots As Integer, PickSpots As Integer) _
        As String
          ' Create an array whose size is given by TotalSpots.
    ReDim Spots(1 To TotalSpots) As Integer
          ' Initialize array of possible values.
    InitArray Spots
          'Fill first PickSpots elements at random.
    FillArray Spots, PickSpots
          'Arrange beginning of array in numerical order.
    Sort Spots, PickSpots
          'Make a string out of results.
    Winners = MakeString(Spots, PickSpots)
End Function

Sub InitArray(Arr() As Integer)
    Dim I As Integer
    For I = 1 To UBound(Arr)
        Arr(I) = I
    Next I
End Sub

Sub FillArray(Arr() As Integer, n As Integer)
    ' Arr() is an array of Max elements, and N is the
    ' number of elements to be chosen.
    ' Pick index at random, then swap pick with
    ' an element at the beginning of the array.
    ' After N picks, the picks will fill first N
    ' elements of the array.
    Dim I As Integer            'for loop counter
    Dim Chosen As Integer       'index for randomly selected value
    Dim Temp As Integer         'for swapping values
    Dim Max As Integer          'array size
    Max = UBound(Arr)
    For I = 1 To n
        Chosen = Int((Max - I + 1) * Rnd + I)
        Temp = Arr(I)
        Arr(I) = Arr(Chosen)
        Arr(Chosen) = Temp
    Next I
End Sub

Sub Sort(Arr() As Integer, Limit As Integer)
    Dim Top As Integer, Choice As Integer 'loop counters
    Dim Temp As Integer 'temporary variable for sorting
    For Top = 1 To Limit - 1
        For Choice = Top + 1 To Limit
            If Arr(Top) > Arr(Choice) Then
                Temp = Arr(Top)
                Arr(Top) = Arr(Choice)
                Arr(Choice) = Temp
            End If
```

continued on next page

continued from previous page

```
        Next Choice
    Next Top
End Sub

Function MakeString(Arr() As Integer, Lim As Integer) As String
    Dim I As Integer
    Dim Win As String
     For I = 1 To Lim
        Win = Win + Str(Arr(I))
    Next I
    MakeString = Win
End Function

Function Odds(TotalSpots As Integer, picks As Integer) As Double
    Dim result As Double
    Dim n As Double
    Dim p As Double
    result = 1#
    n = TotalSpots
    For p = picks To 1 Step -1
        result = result * n / p
        n = n - 1
    Next
    Odds = result
End Function
```

More Details

The sorting procedure should sort only the part of the array containing the picks, so the procedure call in *Winners* specifies the array and the number of elements to be sorted:

```
Sort Spots, PickSpots
```

The algorithm is a relatively slow but simple sorting routine, yet for arrays as small as these, speed is not an issue. The idea is to search through the array, find the smallest value, and place it in the first element of the array. One way to do that is to compare each element in turn with the first element, swapping them if the new element is smaller than the current occupant of the first element. At the end of this process, the smallest value will be in the first element. Next, repeat the process, but this time placing the smallest remaining value in the second element. Continue until the array is sorted. Here's one implementation:

```
Sub Sort(Arr() As Integer, Limit As Integer)
    Dim Top As Integer, Choice As Integer 'loop counters
    Dim Temp As Integer 'temporary variable for sorting
    For Top = 1 To Limit - 1
        For Choice = Top + 1 To Limit
            If Arr(Top) > Arr(Choice) Then
                Temp = Arr(Top)
                Arr(Top) = Arr(Choice)
                Arr(Choice) = Temp
            End If
        Next Choice
    Next Top
End Sub
```

To compute the odds of winning, you need to calculate the total number of possible combinations. For instance, on a card with 40 spots for which you get to pick 5 numbers, how many different choices are there for five picks? Let's see, there's 1,2,3,6,20 and 6,9,12,33,34 and ... clearly, we need a more systematic approach!

One way of looking at the process is that you have 40 choices for your first pick, 39 for the second pick, and so on. Altogether, for five picks, you'd have $40 * 39 * 38 * 37 * 36$ choices. But some of them are duplicates. That is, 2, 3, 4, 5, 6 is the same as 6, 5, 4, 3, 2 or 2, 3, 6, 5, 4. It turns out a selection of five choices can be arranged in $5 * 4 * 3 * 2 * 1$ different ways, so you have to divide that number into the first multiplication. The *Odds* function generalizes this recipe to *picks* selections out of *TotalSpots* spots:

```
Function Odds(TotalSpots As Integer, picks As Integer) As Double
    Dim result As Double
    Dim n As Double
    Dim p As Double
    result = 1#
    n = TotalSpots
    For p = picks To 1 Step -1
        result = result * n / p
        n = n - 1
    Next
    Odds = result
End Function
```

Further Thoughts

The Lotto example illustrates the separation of a program's interface from its processing duties. You can, for example, rewrite the interface while retaining the module unchanged. For another example, suppose you've devised procedures to draw diamonds, triangles, hexagons, and octagons. You could collect them in a module, then add this module to any project that needed these shapes. That raises a new question, how do you add an existing file to a project? The answer, assuming the project is current and that you're in design mode, is to select Add File from the Visual Basic File menu.

Tip

To add a new module to a project, use Module from the Visual Basic Insert menu. To add an existing module to a project, use Add File from the Visual Basic File menu.

Suppose you want to festoon the Lotto program with diamonds and hexagons? The modular approach is to use one module for the drawing routines and a second module for the computational routines. The guiding principle is to group related routines in the same module and unrelated routines in separate modules. This clarifies your program's organization. It also makes it simpler to reuse related blocks of routines in other programs.

Private and *Public*

You may have noticed that the event procedures in the form are preceded with the keyword *Private*, as in the following:

```
Private Sub cmdExit_Click()
```

But the functions and procedures in the Module1 module don't use the *Private* keyword:

```
Function Odds(TotalSpots As Integer, picks As Integer) As Double
```

The keyword *Private*, when used with a procedure or function, means the routine is private to the form or module in which it is defined. That means it can be called only by procedures or functions in the same form or module. In our example, this means that none of the procedures in the form can be used in the module. Is this a good thing? Yes. In programming, it's a good idea to follow the "need to know" principle. If a module has no need to know about particular functions, procedures, or variables, don't tell it about them. If the module can't use these routines or variables, then it can't misuse them. The Module1 module contains code for drawing numbers randomly and for calculating odds. Clearly, it doesn't need the ability to, say, generate a mouse click event. So it's quite reasonable to make the form's event procedures private. Private events in the form file also help avoid confusion when you create projects with several forms. For instance, because each procedure is private to its own form, each form can have its own *Form_Load* event without conflicts.

However, sometimes one module or form does need access to the procedures in another module. For example, the frmLotto form calls the *Odds* function in the Module1 module. That wouldn't work if the function were private. But if a function or procedure isn't declared with the *Private* keyword, it's public, meaning all parts of the project can use it. (If you really want to be explicit, you can use the keyword *Public* when defining a function or procedure.)

Incidentally, if you look again at the project, you'll see that the only module functions called by the form are *Winners* and *Odds*. All the other procedures and functions are there to help *Winners* do its job. Since only *Winners* and *Odds* need to be public, you really should make the rest of the functions and methods in the module private. That is, you should add Private to the procedure and function definitions:

```
Private Sub InitArray(Arr() As Integer)
    ...
End Sub

Private Function MakeString(Arr() As Integer, Lim As Integer) As String
    ...
End Function
```

Tip

Declare as *Private* any functions and procedures that are used only in the file in which they are defined. For purposes of documentation, you can declare as *Public* any functions or procedures that are to be shared across modules.

Public and Private Variables

Module-level variables also can be public or private. A private module-level variable is known just in the form in which it is defined, while a public module-level variable can be shared among modules. Unlike functions and procedures, which are public unless declared private, variables are private unless declared public.

To make a module-level variable public, use the keyword *Public* instead of *Dim:*

```
Public Offers As Integer    ' Offers is a public module-level variable.
```

Basic used to use the *Global* keyword for this purpose, but it has been phased out and replaced by *Public.*

To declare a private variable, use *Private* instead of the word *Dim* when declaring module-level variables. Since variables are private by default, both *Dim* and *Private* have the same effect, but using *Private* better documents your intent:

```
Dim Ex As Integer         ' Ex is private to a module by default.
Private Why As String     ' Why is declared private to a module.
```

Tip

Declare as *Public* any module-level variables that are to be shared across modules. As a matter of documentation, declare as *Private* any module-level variables that are to be used only in the file in which they are defined.

Note that the public concept applies to module-level variables, but not to procedure-level variables (local variables). Variables you declare within a procedure or function are local to that procedure or function, and you can't use the *Public* keyword when declaring them.

Public and Private Constants

When you define symbolic constants at the module level, you can declare them as public or private. Like variables, module-level constants are private by default:

```
Const DaysPerWeek As Integer = 7            'private by default
Private Const HoursPerDay As Integer = 24  'explicitly private
Public Const MilesPerLeague As Integer = 3 'public
```

There is an important restriction. Module-level constants declared in a form module or in a class module (see Lesson 20) cannot be declared public. But public constants are allowed in code modules.

FORMS UPON FORMS

When you used the Insert menu to add a module to a project, you may have noticed that you also had the option to add a form. There are many reasons to do so. For instance, you might design a program that uses a sequence of forms to inform or interview a user. Or you might want a supporting form to serve as a customized dialog box. Let's look at a few examples. You'll take the Quick Author program from Lesson 14 as a base example on which to build and add three new forms. The first will display a short message, the second will display a small real-time clock, and the third will be a custom dialog box that will let you add words to the three lists and remove words from them.

And Now for a Brief Message

Let's begin with a message window. First, open the Quick Author project from Lesson 14. Next, go to the Visual Basic Insert menu and select Form. You'll get a new form captioned Form1. You can set properties for this form and add controls to this form just as you've done all along. This time, set properties as described in Table L19-2.

OBJECT	PROPERTY	SETTING
Form1	BorderStyle	3 - Fixed Double
	Caption	Reward Yourself!
	Name	frmReward
Text1	Alignment	2 - Center
	MultiLine	True
	Locked	True
	Name	txtReward
	Text	Once you become rich and famous through the use of Quick Author, reward yourself with a vacation on a lush tropical isle!
		Write to the following address for more information:
		Quick Trip, a division of Quick Stuff
		1 Quick Way
		Quicksburg, CA 94999

Table L19-2 First Form added to the Quick Author project

You should note a few points about these properties. First, the Fixed Double setting for the form's border property means that the form can't be resized during run time and that it won't show the minimize and maximize click buttons during run time. Second, to enter multiple lines in the Properties window's text box, you have to press CTRL-ENTER at the end of each line. Simply pressing ENTER terminates input, and you have to click on the Text property setting box again to type the next line. But using CTRL-ENTER lets you continue from one line to the next. Third, size the text box to fit the text, and then size the form to fit the text box. The result should look like the form displayed in Figure L19-8. Use Save File from the File menu to save the new form. Both forms should now appear in the Project window, as shown in Figure L19-9.

If you try running the program at this stage, however, you won't see the new form; you'll just get the familiar Quick Author form. This figure raises a new question—how do you get the new form to appear when the program runs? The answer is to invoke the form's Show method. Let's add a control to frmQuickAuthor that does that. Table L19-3 describes the control.

OBJECT	PROPERTY	SETTING
Image1	Name	imgIsle
	Picture	(icon) (vb/icons/misc/misc42.ico)

Table L19-3 A new control for frmQuickAuthor

Image controls recognize *Click* events, so add this code to the frmQuickAuthor Code window:

```
Private Sub imgIsle_Click()
    frmReward.Show
End Sub
```

Now run the program and click on the new icon. You should see the new form onscreen (see Figure L19-10). You can't resize it, but you can move it around. And you can double-click on its Control box to get rid of it. Computer users, however, are accustomed to getting rid of this kind of message by clicking somewhere. You can accommodate that habit by adding the code in Listing L19-4 to the frmReward form's Code window. Use the Project window to select the new form, and then click the View Code button. The *Hide* method removes a form from display. Here are two ways to hide the form. First, you can click in the text box and activate its *Click* event. Second, you can click on the frmQuickAuthor form. That transfers the focus back to a control on that form, triggering the *LostFocus* event for the txtReward control.

Figure L19-8 The new form

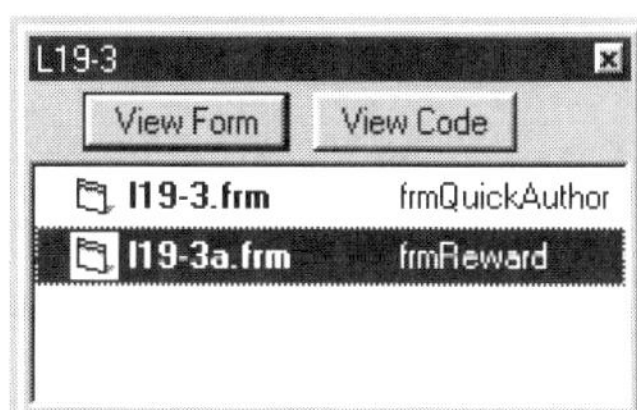

Figure L19-9 A project with two forms

Listing L19-4
Code for the Reward Yourself form

```
Option Explicit 'code for frmReward

Private Sub txtReward_Click()
    frmReward.Hide
End Sub

Private Sub txtReward_LostFocus()
    frmReward.Hide
End Sub
```

Reminder

To navigate between Code windows for different forms in the same project, use the Project window to select a form and the View Code button to view its code.

Form Metaphysics

The *Hide* method doesn't completely obliterate a form, it just removes it from the screen. But the hidden form continues to exist in memory. That is, the values of the form's properties as well as the values of any control properties remain stored in memory, as does the code for the form. Indeed, using the *Hide* method is the same as setting the form's Visible property to False. So you could, for instance, change a form's properties while it's hidden, then display the revised form.

Instead of using the *Hide* method, you could have used the *Unload* statement:

```
Unload frmReward
```

This is more drastic than hiding the form. It frees the memory used to hold the properties for the form and its controls, but it leaves the code for the form in memory.

Yet more extreme is using the following statement:

```
Set frmReward = NOTHING
```

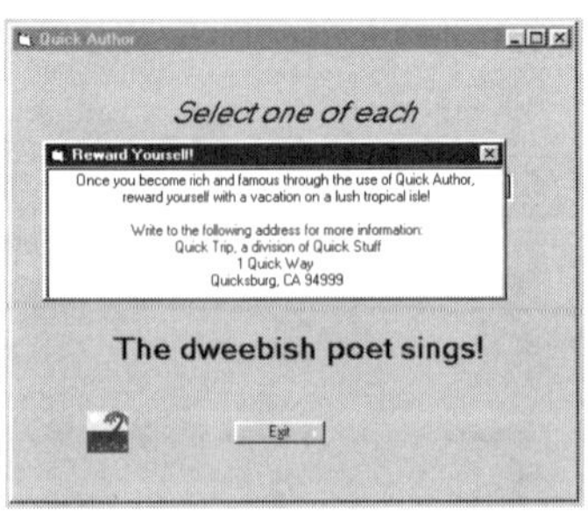

Figure L19-10 The new form in action

This eliminates all vestiges of the form from memory and invokes the Terminate event for the form.

This probably is a good time to summarize the processes that go on when you bring up a form.

1. The *Form_Initialize* event for the form occurs. Typically, you use the corresponding event procedure to initialize module-level variables defined in the form.
2. The *Form_Load* event for the form occurs. Code and property values are loaded into memory. You can use the corresponding event procedure to modify properties and to set up runtime control properties, such as the contents of a list box.
3. The *Form_Load* event automatically calls the *Show* method after the last statement in the event procedure; this draws the form on the display.

You can call the *Show* method earlier if you want the form to be drawn before, say, some lengthy initialization process takes place. Calling the *Show* method automatically invokes the *Form_Load* event if it hasn't already occurred, and the *Form_Load* event automatically invokes the *Form_Initialize* event first if it hasn't already occurred.

When you end a program, Visual Basic first unloads a form, reversing the work of loading, then terminates the form, reversing the work of initialization.

Which Form?

When you have more than one form, which form gets loaded first? Each project has a startup form. It's loaded automatically. To get the other forms onscreen, you use the *Show* method, like you just did. By default, the first form you create when designing a project becomes the startup form. However, you can use the Project Options choice from the Tools menu to select another form in the project to be the startup form.

A Timely Example

Just to see if you've got the right idea, let's add a second form. This time, however, let's give it something more active to do than displaying an advertisement. Let's make a clock! Once again, go to the Insert menu and select Form. Give it the properties described in Table L19-4. Don't forget to save the new form file and to save the project file.

OBJECT	PROPERTY	SETTING
Form1	Caption	Time
	Name	frmTime
Timer1	Interval	1000
	Name	tmrTime
TextBox1	Height	285
	Name	txtClock

continued on next page

continued from previous page

OBJECT	PROPERTY	SETTING
	Locked	True
	Text	
	Width	1095

Table L19-4 The second form added to the Quick Author project

Next, set the text to the time by using the *Time* and *Format* functions, as shown in Listing L19-5. The *Form_Load* event sets the time when the form first appears, and the *tmrTime_Timer* event updates the time each 1,000 milliseconds, that is, each second. Actually, because the system clock uses 18.2 clicks (approximately) per second, the updating doesn't occur at precisely 1-second intervals.

Listing L19-5
Code for the Time form

```
Option Explicit

Private Sub Form_Load()
    txtTime.Text = Format(Time, "Long Time")
End Sub

Private Sub tmrTime_Timer()
    txtTime.Text = Format(Time, "Long Time")
End Sub
```

To start up the clock display, you can add an icon to the frmQuickAuthor form, as described in Table L19-5. Then add the following code to the frmQuickAuthor form:

```
Private Sub imgClock_Click()
    frmTime.Show
End Sub
```

OBJECT	PROPERTY	SETTING
Image1	Name	imgClock
	Picture	(icon) (vb/icons/misc/clock02.ico)

Table L19-5 Another new control for frmQuickAuthor

Because this is a form you might want to leave onscreen as you work, there's no point in adding code to hide the clock. If you want to close it, you can double-click the form's control box. However, there is the matter of positioning the clock. Suppose you position the Time form over the Quick Author form, then click on the Quick Author form. That makes Quick Author the active form and brings it in front of the Time form, hiding it from view. But if you minimize or move the Quick Author form, you'll see that the Time form is still present. If you want the Time form to remain in view while you use the other form, you have to position it so that it's outside the Quick Author form. Figures L19-11 and L19-12 show one possible positioning. Notice how the title bar of the active form is highlighted.

> **Note**
>
> In a multiple-form project, the form that appears in the foreground with a highlighted title bar is the active form. The expression *Screen.ActiveForm* represents the active form. For instance, the expression *Screen.ActiveForm.Caption* would be the caption of whichever form was active at the moment.

An Interacting Form

So far the forms you've added have been independent of the main form other than being started by clicking icons on the main form. Now let's go a step further and develop a form that interacts with the frmQuickAuthor form. In Figures L19-11 and L19-12, you may have noticed a new button, one labeled *Modify a List.* You'll develop a form that delivers on that promise. First, to prepare for the new form, add the command button, as described in Table L19-6, to the frmQuickAuthor form. Then add the following code:

```
Private Sub cmdMod_Click()
    frmList.Show
End Sub
```

You've now committed yourself to deliver a form (frmList) that can modify the word lists in Quick Author.

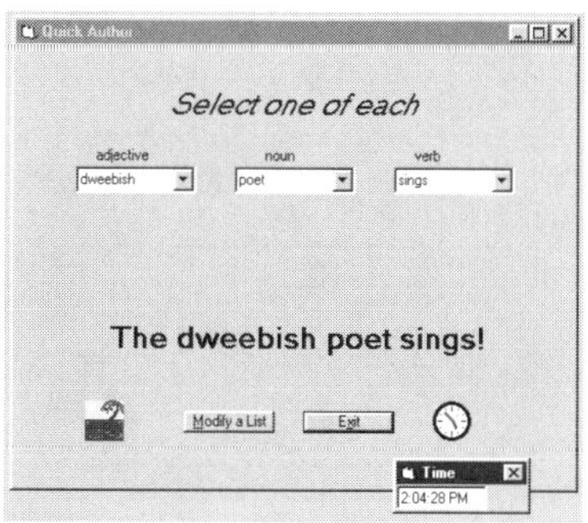

Figure L19-11 Two forms showing with frmTime active

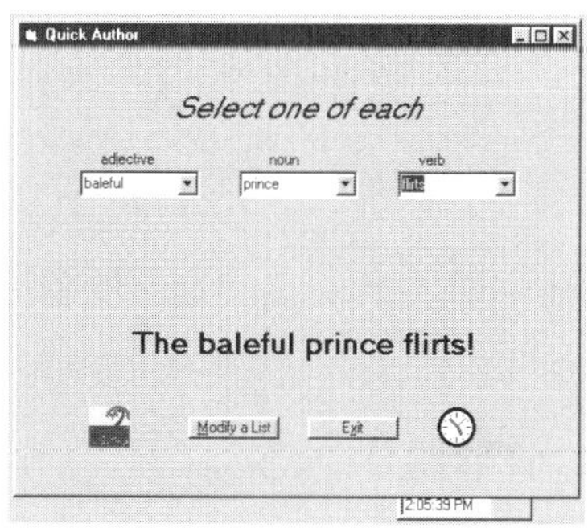

Figure L19-12 Two forms showing with frmQuickAuthor active

OBJECT	PROPERTY	SETTING
Command1	Caption	&Modify a List
	Name	cmdMod

Table L19-6 The final new control for frmQuickAuthor

Begin, as usual, by selecting Form from the Insert menu. Save the new form file and the project file. Next, a plan is needed. Here's one:

- Use option buttons to let the user select which word list to modify.
- Copy the selected list to the list box on the new form.
- Add command buttons to alter the copied list—one to clear the list, one to remove a selected item from the list, and one to add a word to the list.
- Add a command button that accepts the changes—it will copy the modified list back to the Quick Author form.
- Add a command button that cancels the changes—it will restore the copy to its original form.
- Add a command button that hides the form and returns to Quick Author—it will prompt the user if he or she has made changes without having accepted them.

Now that you have a plan, you can add the controls described in Table L19-7 and pictured in Figure L19-13.

OBJECT	PROPERTY	SETTING
Form1	Auto3d	True
	Caption	Change A List
	Name	frmList
Frame1	Caption	Choose a list:
	Name	fraList
Option1	Caption	adjectives
	Index	0
	Name	optList
Option2	Caption	nouns
	Index	1
	Name	optList
Option3	Caption	verbs
	Index	2
	Name	optList
ListBox1	Name	lstList

OBJECT	PROPERTY	SETTING
Command1	Caption	&Clear Whole List
	Name	cmdClear
Command2	Caption	&Remove Selected Item
	Name	cmdRemove
Command3	Caption	&Add a Word
	Name	cmdAdd
Command4	Caption	Accep&t Changes
	Name	cmdAccept
Command5	Caption	Ca&ncel Changes
	Name	cmdCancel
Command6	Caption	R&eturn to QA
	Name	cmdReturn

Table L19-7 The frmList form properties

All that's left to do is to write a little code. The keen foresight that comes from already having written the code suggests that you'll need a couple of module-level variables. One is to keep track of which list is being modified. That's because several different controls need that information, so a module-level variable will let the controls share that information. The second is to keep track of whether changes have been made but not accepted. The Return to QA button will need to know that information. Neither variable need be known to any other form in the project, so you can declare them using *Private:*

```
Option Explicit
Private WhichList As Integer    'Which list is being modified?
Private MadeChange As Boolean   'Have unsaved changes been made?
```

Let's take a closer look at the *WhichList* variable. In Quick Author, the three word lists are part of an array of list controls, so they can be identified by their index values, which run from 0 to 2. Similarly, the option buttons are part of a

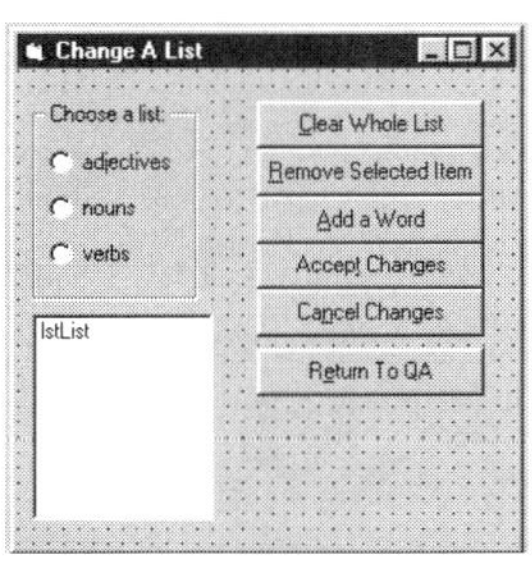

Figure L19-13 The frmList form

control array, and their index values also run from 0 to 2. So you can do the following to identify which list has been selected:

```
Private Sub optList_Click(Index As Integer)
    ...
    WhichList = Index
    ...
End Sub
```

Next, how do you handle copying the selected list to the list box in frmList? First, you need a way to identify the selected list box. If you check Lesson 15, you'll find that you used an array of combo boxes named cboHelp. So the individual combo boxes have names like *cboHelp(0)*. However, code in frmList can't use that name by itself because these combo boxes are in a different form. Instead, the code has to identify which form the boxes are in. The method, which should be familiar by now, is to add the form's name followed by a period. That is, within the frmList form, you can refer to a combo box in the frmQuickAuthor form by compound names like *frmQuickAuthor.cboHelp(0)*.

Note

If one form refers to a control in a second form, it should prefix the control name with the name of the second form followed by a period, as in *frmTango.picDance*.

To copy items from one list to the other, you can use the *AddItem* method in a loop. The ListCount property of a list tells how many items are in a list. Since indexing starts at 0, that means the index values in a list vary from 0 to ListCount - 1. If an item in a list has an index value of I, then the List(I) property represents that item. Using these facts, you can complete the *optList_Click* method as follows, where *Index* is the control array index representing which list is copied, and *I* is the combo box list index representing a particular item in the list:

```
Private Sub optList_Click(Index As Integer)
    Dim I As Integer
    WhichList = Index   'Save info on which list.
    lstList.Clear       'Start with an empty list.
    For I = 0 To frmQuickAuthor.cboHelp(Index).ListCount - 1
        lstList.AddItem frmQuickAuthor.cboHelp(Index).List(I)
    Next I
End Sub
```

This code adds each item from the frmQuickAuthor.cboHelp(Index) combo list box to the lstList box.

The command buttons make similar use of list properties and methods. For example, the *Clear* method clears a list box or combo box, removing each item. So the cmdClear button can use this code:

```
Private Sub cmdClear_Click()
    lstList.Clear
    MadeChange = True
End Sub
```

Similarly, the *Remove* method removes a single item if you provide its index value:

```
Private Sub cmdRemove_Click()
    If lstList.ListIndex >= 0 Then
        lstList.RemoveItem lstList.ListIndex
        MadeChange = True
    End If
End Sub
```

This code uses the fact that selecting an item in a list sets the ListIndex property to the index value for the selection. If nothing is selected, ListIndex is set to –1, so the code checks for that possibility.

To add a word, you can use the *InputBox* function to solicit user input. Then you can use the *AddItem* method to add the choice to the list:

```
Private Sub cmdAdd_Click()
    Dim NewWord As String
    NewWord = InputBox("Enter a word:", "New Word")
    If NewWord <> "" Then
        lstList.AddItem NewWord
        MadeChange = True
    End If
End Sub
```

Following the glorious plan, these event procedures just alter the list displayed in the list box on the new form. They also set the *MadeChange* variable to True, indicating that changes are pending. Clicking on the Accept Changes button, however, copies the changes to frmQuickAuthor and resets the *MadeChange* variable to False:

```
Private Sub cmdAccept_Click()
    Dim I As Integer
    frmQuickAuthor.cboHelp(WhichList).Clear
    For I = 0 To lstList.ListCount - 1
        frmQuickAuthor.cboHelp(WhichList).AddItem lstList.List(I)
    Next I
    frmQuickAuthor.cboHelp(WhichList).Text = lstList.List(0)
    MadeChange = False
End Sub
```

Listing L19-6 shows the complete listing for the frmList form. Note how the *cmdDone_Click* event procedure handles the case of a user making changes without accepting them. It uses a message dialog box to alert the user to the situation and to get the user's decision on whether to accept the changes.

Listing L19-6
Code for the Change a Form form

```
Option Explicit
Private WhichList As Integer     'Which list is being modified?
Private MadeChange As Boolean    'Have unsaved changes been made?
```

continued on next page

continued from previous page

```
Private Sub cmdAdd_Click()
    Dim NewWord As String
    NewWord = InputBox("Enter a word:", "New Word")
    If NewWord <> "" Then
        lstList.AddItem NewWord
        MadeChange = True
    End If
End Sub

Private Sub cmdCancel_Click()
    lstList.Clear
    optList_Click (WhichList)
End Sub

Private Sub cmdClear_Click()
    lstList.Clear
    MadeChange = True
End Sub

Private Sub cmdDone_Click()
    Dim Ans As String
    If MadeChange Then
        Ans = MsgBox("Save last change?", vbYesNo, "Save?")
        If Ans = vbYes Then cmdAccept_Click
    End If
    frmList.Hide
End Sub

Private Sub cmdRemove_Click()
    If lstList.ListIndex >= 0 Then
        lstList.RemoveItem lstList.ListIndex
        MadeChange = True
    End If
End Sub

Private Sub cmdAccept_Click()
    Dim I As Integer
    frmQuickAuthor.cboHelp(WhichList).Clear
    For I = 0 To lstList.ListCount - 1
        frmQuickAuthor.cboHelp(WhichList).AddItem lstList.List(I)
    Next I
    frmQuickAuthor.cboHelp(WhichList).Text = lstList.List(0)
    MadeChange = False
End Sub

Private Sub Form_Initialize()
    MadeChange = False
End Sub

Private Sub optList_Click(Index As Integer)
    Dim I As Integer
    WhichList = Index
    lstList.Clear
    For I = 0 To frmQuickAuthor.cboHelp(Index).ListCount - 1
        lstList.AddItem frmQuickAuthor.cboHelp(Index).List(I)
    Next I
End Sub
```

Having made all these changes, you should now run the program, adding new words to the lists, deleting words from the list, constructing new sentences, and so on. Figure L19-14 shows the new program in action.

FORMS WITHIN FORMS

Visual Basic offers yet another way to incorporate multiple forms. A project can have a *multiple document interface* (MDI) form. You can have only one MDI form, but an MDI form can have multiple child forms. These are forms that must stay inside the boundaries of the parent form. So an MDI parent form is a bit like a form that can treat other forms (the child forms) as controls. Let's examine some of the features of a child form.

First, start a new project. This should place a form captioned Form1 onscreen. Then select MDI form from the Insert menu. The new form will be called MDIForm1 by default. Next, make Form1 a child form by setting its MDIChild property to True. (You may first have to select Form1 in the Project window and click on the View Form button.) In design mode, you can move Form1 around. But try running the project. You'll see something like Figure L19-15. If you try to move Form1 around, you'll find you can see only the part of Form1 inside the parent MDI form. If you minimize it, its menu bar appears at the bottom of the MDI form, as shown in Figure L19-16. If you maximize a child, it expands to fill the interior of the MDI form, and the MDI form caption is merged with the child's caption, as shown in Figure L19-17. Also, a second bar is added below the title bar. It has a control icon for the child form at the left end and the usual set of minimize, maximize, and close boxes at the right end.

There are a couple of points that aren't apparent from just looking at the figures. First, the menu bar for a child form appears in the MDI form. Thus the menu changes when another child form becomes active. Second, in this example, Form1 is the startup form. When the startup form is a child form, as in this case, Visual Basic also automatically loads and shows the MDI form.

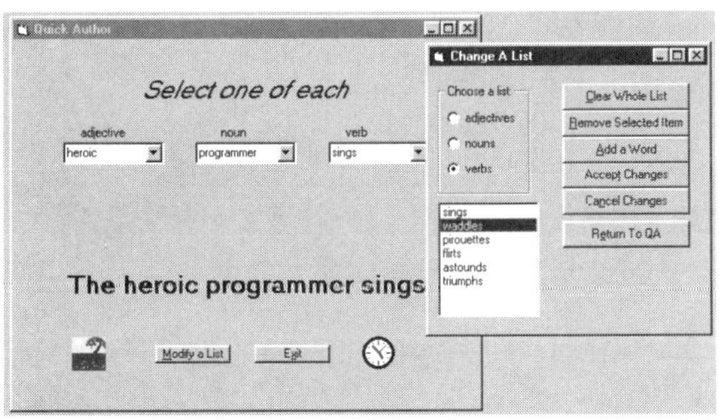

Figure L19-14 The revised Quick Author program

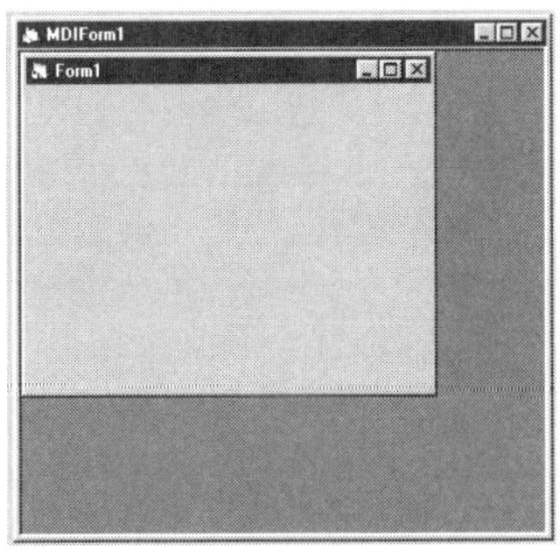

Figure L19-15 An MDI form with child

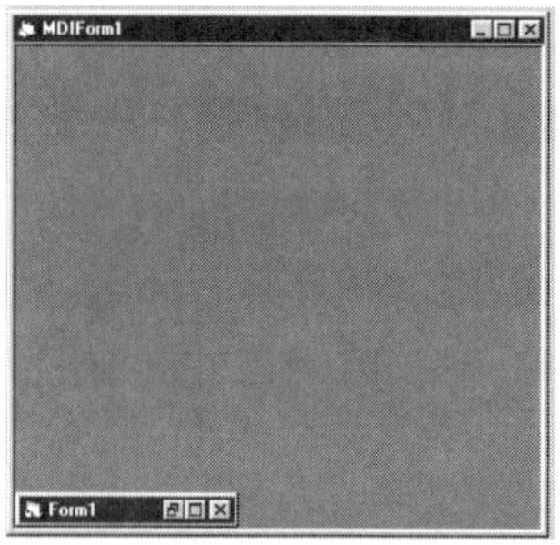

Figure L19-16 A minimized child form in an MDI form

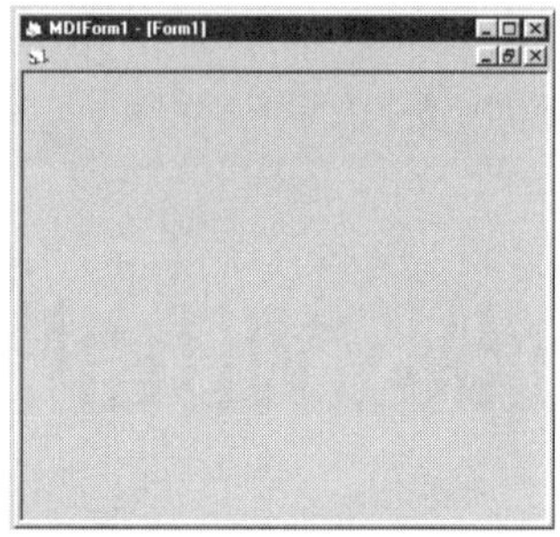

Figure L19-17 A maximized child form in an MDI form

However, if the MDI form is the startup form, child forms are not loaded until you explicitly load them, for example, by using the *Load* command or the *Show* method.

All My Children

Lesson 18 developed two related examples—Image Cruiser and Text Cruiser. You can make them children to the same MDI form and gain the convenience of having both available in the same application. First, copy the Image Cruiser form file (the one with the .FRM extension) and the Text Cruiser form file to the directory you're using for this project. Next, start up Visual Basic and begin a new project. Use the Insert menu to insert the MDI form. At this point you have an unneeded Form1 form in the project. Select it in the Project menu, and then use the Remove command from the File menu to remove that form. Actually, Form1 wasn't quite unneeded, for it was the startup form. So you need to make the MDI form the new startup form. To do so, select Options from the Tools menu, click on the Project tab, and select the MDI form in the Startup Form combo box. Then use Add File from the File menu to add the Text Cruiser form and the Image Cruiser form. Next, set a few properties as shown in Table L19-8.

OBJECT	PROPERTY	SETTING
MDIForm	Caption	SuperCruiser
	Name	frmMDICruise
frmImage	MDIChild	True
frmText	MDIChild	True

Table L19-8 Form properties for the MDI form project

Tip

To make an existing form a child to an MDI form, use Add File from the Visual Basic File menu to add the form's .FRM file to the project, and set the form's MDIChild property to true.

Next, you need a way to load these forms once the program starts. You can try using special icons, as in the Quick Author program. However, you'll find you can't add an image control to an MDI form. You'll also find you can't add a command button, a label, a text box—you get the picture. Actually, you do get the picture, for the one control you can add is a picture box. And then you can put whatever controls you like in the picture box. So add a picture box to the MDI form. You'll notice something interesting. It automatically snugs up to the top of the interior of the form, and it extends all the way from left to right. In fact, it's designed to facilitate creating a toolbar, which is why it has those properties. Next add two image controls to the picture box. Table L19-9 describes these additions to the SuperCruiser form.

OBJECT	PROPERTY	SETTING
Picture1	Name	picMDI
Image1 (in picMDI)	Name	imgImage
	Picture	(icon) (vb/icons/misc/misc41.ico)
Image2 (in picMDI)	Name	imgText
	Picture	(icon) (vb/icons/writing/note04.ico)

Table L19-9 Controls for the SuperCruiser program

Next add the following code to the MDI form:

```
Private Sub imgImage_Click()
    frmImage.Show
End Sub

Private Sub imgText_Click()
    frmText.Show
End Sub
```

Now you can use the MDI form to run Image Cruiser and Text Cruiser. Indeed, if you click on both icons, you can have both forms appearing simultaneously. Figure L19-18 shows an example after the two forms have been repositioned and resized.

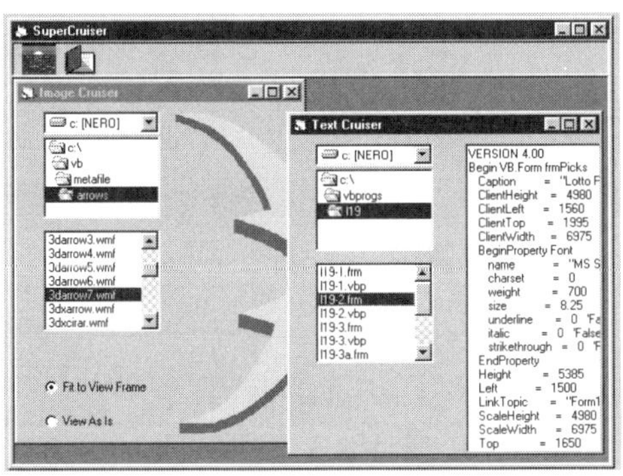

Figure L19-18 SuperCruiser, phase 1

Great! You now have a working MDI project. However, neither form was designed for this purpose, and they waste a lot of real estate with their file lists. You can spiff things up a bit by replacing the current file-selection interface with a menu interface using a common dialog box. Also, you can arrange things so that the display areas automatically resize themselves to match the size of the forms.

First, dispose of the controls that won't be needed. That means you should delete all the controls but the image control from frmImage and all the controls but the text box from frmText. Next, add a common dialog box to each of the forms, as outlined in Tables L19-10 and L19-11.

<table>
<tr><th>OBJECT</th><th>PROPERTY</th><th>SETTING</th></tr>
<tr><td>CommonDialog1</td><td>Filter</td><td>Bitmapped(*.bmp,*.ico)|*.bmp;*.ico|Metafile (*.wmf)|*.wmf</td></tr>
<tr><td></td><td>Flags</td><td>&H2</td></tr>
<tr><td></td><td>Name</td><td>dlgImage</td></tr>
</table>

Table L19-10 New control for the frmImage form

<table>
<tr><th>OBJECT</th><th>PROPERTY</th><th>SETTING</th></tr>
<tr><td>CommonDialog1</td><td>Filter</td><td>Text(*.txt,*bat)|*.txt;.*.bat|Forms(*.frm,*.vbp) |*.frm;*.vbp</td></tr>
<tr><td></td><td>Flags</td><td>&H2</td></tr>
<tr><td></td><td>Name</td><td>dlgEdit</td></tr>
</table>

Table L19-11 New control for the frmText form

The next step is to add menus to manage each form's features. Tables L19-12 and L19-13 show the menu design. The Windows menu is an interesting option available to MDI objects. When you check the WindowList property in the Menu dialog box, Visual Basic will list open child forms under the Window heading and place a check by the name of the active form.

LIST BOX ENTRY	CAPTION	NAME	CHECKED BOX
&File	&File	mnuFile	
....&Open	&Open	mnuFileOpen	
....&Hide	&Hide	mnuFileHide	
....&Close	&Close	mnuFileClose	
&Scale	&Scale	mnuScale	
....Fit to &Frame	Fit to &Frame	mnuScaleImage	
....Fit to &Image	Fit to &Image	mnuScaleFrame	
&Windows	&Windows	mnuWindow	WindowList

Table L19-12 Menu entries for the frmImage form

LIST BOX ENTRY	CAPTION	NAME	CHECKED BOX
&File	&File	mnuFile	
....&Open	&Open	mnuFileOpen	
....&Hide	&Hide	mnuFileHide	
....&Close	&Close	mnuFileClose	
&Windows	&Windows	mnuWindow	WindowList

Table L19-13 Menu entries for the frmText form

Finally, you have to empower the menu choices with suitable code. To do so, equip frmImage with the code shown in Listing L19-7 and frmText with the code shown in Listing L19-8.

Listing L19-7
Code for the frmImage form

```
Option Explicit

Private Sub Form_Load()
    imgImage.Width = frmImage.ScaleWidth
    imgImage.Height = frmImage.ScaleHeight
End Sub

Private Sub Form_Resize()
    If imgImage.Stretch = True Then
        imgImage.Width = frmImage.ScaleWidth
        imgImage.Height = frmImage.ScaleHeight
    End If
End Sub

Private Sub mnuFileClose_Click()
    Unload frmImage
End Sub

Private Sub mnuFileHide_Click()
    frmImage.Hide
End Sub

Private Sub mnuFileOpen_Click()
    dlgImage.ShowOpen
    If dlgImage.filename <> "" Then
        imgImage.picture = LoadPicture(dlgImage.filename)
    End If
End Sub

Private Sub mnuScaleFrame_Click()
    imgImage.Stretch = False
    mnuScaleImage.Checked = False
    mnuScaleFrame.Checked = True
End Sub

Private Sub mnuScaleImage_Click()
    imgImage.Width = frmImage.ScaleWidth
    imgImage.Height = frmImage.ScaleHeight
```

continued on next page

continued from previous page

```
     imgImage.Stretch = True
     mnuScaleImage.Checked = True
     mnuScaleFrame.Checked = False
End Sub
```

Listing L19-8
Code for the frmText form

```
Option Explicit

Sub CopyToBox(AFile As String)
     Dim FileNum As Integer
     FileNum = FreeFile
     Open AFile For Input As #FileNum
     txtText.Text = Input(LOF(FileNum), #FileNum)
     Close #FileNum
End Sub

Private Sub Form_Load()
     txtText.Width = frmText.ScaleWidth
     txtText.Height = frmText.ScaleHeight
End Sub

Private Sub Form_Resize()
     txtText.Width = frmText.ScaleWidth
     txtText.Height = frmText.ScaleHeight
End Sub

Private Sub mnuFileClose_Click()
     Unload frmText
End Sub

Private Sub mnuFileHide_Click()
     frmText.Hide
End Sub

Private Sub mnuFileOpen_Click()
     Dim AFile As String
     dlgText.ShowOpen
     AFile = dlgText.FileName
     If AFile <> "" Then CopyToBox (AFile)
End Sub
```

Figure L19-19 shows the program in operation after some rearrangement of the child windows. Note that the menu bar shows the menu for the active window.

Comments

The File menus give you the choice between hiding and unloading a form. Suppose, say, you've loaded an image into Image Cruiser. If you hide the form, then click on the Image icon again, you'll see Image Cruiser restored and still display-

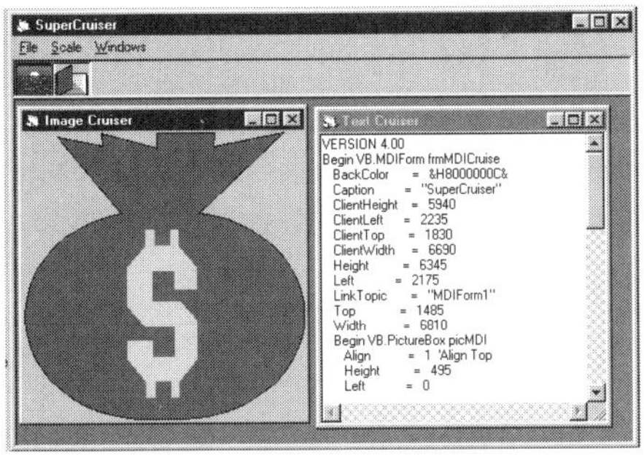

Figure L19-19 The revised SuperCruiser MDI program

ing that image. But if you unload the form, then click on the Image icon again, the form will be reloaded fresh, and no image will be shown until you load another one.

Conceptually, the *CopyToBox* procedure in frmText could have been placed in a separate module, but the form contained so little code that no further modularization is needed.

Both Image Cruiser and Text Cruiser use the *Form_Load* event to size the display area to fit the interior of the form. The *Form_Resize* event procedure is invoked if you resize the form, and both forms use that event to resize the display area to fill the interior of the form. However, the program doesn't resize the image control in Image Cruiser when the Stretch property is set to False. In that case the scaling is determined by the size of the original graphic.

AND NOW FOR SOMETHING NEW

Suppose you're using SuperCruiser to browse through some graphic images and you decide you want to view two images side-by-side. SuperCruiser already can display a graphics image and a text file simultaneously. Is there some way it can display two graphics images simultaneously? The answer is yes, and the method is to create a copy of the frmImage form to display the second image.

To create a duplicate of the frmImage form, you do this:

```
Dim NewForm As New frmImage
```

Here *NewForm* is a variable of type *frmImage*. The keyword New instructs Visual Basic to create a new form that is a duplicate of *frmImage*, and this statement makes the variable *NewForm* refer to the duplicate. More generally, the format is this:

Dim *variable_name* **As New** *form_name*

To see how this works, let's add some entries to *frmImage*'s Window menu. Table L19-14 shows the revised menu description. The entry to note now is New Window, but later you'll use the other two additions. Meanwhile, add this to *frmImage*'s Code window:

```
Private Sub mnuWindowNew_Click()
    Dim NewForm As New frmImage 'Create a new form.
    NewForm.Show          'Load and display it.
End Sub
```

If you run SuperCruiser, start up the Image Cruiser child form, and select New Window from the Windows menu, you'll get a second Image Cruiser. Each is capable of selecting and displaying graphics images.

Gee, you may exclaim, that is magnificently simple! Ah, but there is a slight catch. All the code in the original Image Cruiser form refers to frmImage. For instance, there are lines like this:

```
imgImage.Height = frmImage.ScaleHeight
```

So if you resize the new form, it will scale its imgImage control according to the size of the original frmImage form!

So there's a problem. How can you make the code refer to the new form instead of to the original? What about the *NewForm* variable? Could you do this, for instance?

```
imgImage.Height = NewForm.ScaleHeight   'a possibility?
```

The answer is no. First of all, NewForm is a local variable to the *mnuWindowNew_Click* event procedure, so it disappears when the event finishes. The form, however, doesn't disappear; that's what the *New* keyword accomplished. Anyway, once the *Click* event finishes, you are left with a form with no name! That makes it a little tricky to refer to the form.

But there is a solution. The *Screen* object has an ActiveForm property that evaluates to the currently active form. If *frmImage* is active, then *Screen.ActiveForm* is *frmImage*. If the copy is active, then *Screen.ActiveForm* is that form. So the solution to the problem is to replace references to frmImage with references to *Screen.ActiveForm*. (The one exception is that the *Dim As New* statement will still use *frmImage*.) For example, we can scale the image control this way:

```
imgImage.Height = Screen.ActiveForm.ScaleHeight    'the answer!
```

Tip

If you're writing code for a form that will be duplicated using *New*, use Screen.ActiveForm instead of a particular form name when referring to form properties.

LIST BOX ENTRY	CAPTION	NAME	CHECKED BOX
&File	&File	mnuFile	
....&Open	&Open	mnuFileOpen	
....&Hide	&Hide	mnuFileHide	
....&Close	&Close	mnuFileClose	
&Scale	&Scale	mnuScale	
....Fit to &Frame	Fit to &Frame	mnuScaleImage	
....Fit to &Image	Fit to &Image	mnuScaleFrame	
&Windows	&Windows	mnuWindow	WindowList
....&New Window	&New Window	mnuWindowNew	
....&Tile	&Tile	mnuWindowTile	
....&Cascade	&Cascade	mnuWindowCascade	

Table L19-14 Menu entries (revised) for the frmImage form

NEW ARRANGEMENTS

Once you have two or more child forms visible in an MDI form, it would be nice to have a quick way of rearranging the forms. Visual Basic helps out with this goal by having an *Arrange* method that can be used with an MDI form. Its syntax is this:

MDIFormName.**Arrange** *Style*

Note that it is the MDI form, not a child form, that invokes the method. You can choose the *Style* parameter from the constants listing in Table L19-15. For example, you can use the Cascade choice from the Windows menu to do this:

```
Private Sub mnuWindowCascade_Click()
    frmMDICruise.Arrange vbCascade
End Sub
```

VALUE	SYMBOLIC CONSTANT	MEANING
0	vbCascade	Cascade the child forms
1	vbTileHorizontal	Tile the child forms horizontally
2	vbTileVertical	Tile the child forms vertically
3	vbArrangeIcons	Arrange the icons for minimized child forms

Table L19-15 Parameters for the *Arrange* method

Listing L19-9 shows the revised code for frmImage, including the conversion to using *Screen.ActiveForm* instead of *frmImage*, and including code to cascade and tile open forms.

Listing L19-9
Code for the revised frmImage form

```
Option Explicit

Private Sub Form_Load()
     imgImage.Width = Screen.ActiveForm.ScaleWidth
     imgImage.Height = Screen.ActiveForm.ScaleHeight
End Sub

Private Sub Form_Resize()
     If imgImage.Stretch = True Then
          imgImage.Width = Screen.ActiveForm.ScaleWidth
          imgImage.Height = Screen.ActiveForm.ScaleHeight
     End If
End Sub

Private Sub mnuFileClose_Click()
     Unload Screen.ActiveForm
End Sub

Private Sub mnuFileHide_Click()
     Screen.ActiveForm.Hide
End Sub

Private Sub mnuFileOpen_Click()
     dlgImage.ShowOpen
     If dlgImage.FileName <> "" Then
          imgImage.Picture = LoadPicture(dlgImage.FileName)
     End If
End Sub

Private Sub mnuScaleFrame_Click()
     imgImage.Stretch = False
     mnuScaleImage.Checked = False
     mnuScaleFrame.Checked = True
End Sub

Private Sub mnuScaleImage_Click()
     imgImage.Width = Screen.ActiveForm.ScaleWidth
     imgImage.Height = Screen.ActiveForm.ScaleHeight
     imgImage.Stretch = True
     mnuScaleImage.Checked = True
     mnuScaleFrame.Checked = False
End Sub

Private Sub mnuWindowCascade_Click()
     frmMDICruise.Arrange vbCascade
End Sub

Private Sub mnuWindowNew_Click()
   Dim NewForm As New frmImage
   NewForm.Show
End Sub

Private Sub mnuWindowTile_Click()
     frmMDICruise.Arrange vbTileVertical
End Sub
```

SUMMARY

Visual Basic has several tools to help you organize and modularize your programs. If you want a Visual Basic program to operate as an independent Windows module without Visual Basic being active, use the Make EXE File option from the File menu. That creates a stand-alone version. However, it will require Windows and, in the WINDOWS/SYSTEM subdirectory, the runtime module (*Vb40016.dll* or *Vb40032.dll*).

You can separate interface-specific code from the processing parts of a program by placing the interface code in a form module (saved in a file having an .frm extension) and the processing code in a code module (saved in a file having a .BAS extension). You can use the Insert menu to add a new module to a project or use Add File from the File menu to add an existing module to a project.

Procedures and functions are public by default, meaning that a procedure or function defined in one module can be called from another module in the same project. You can use the keyword *Private* in a procedure or function definition to restrict the use of that procedure or function to the module in which it is defined. Similarly, you can use the keyword *Public* to document your intent that a procedure or function be sharable.

A module-level variable, on the other hand, is private by default, usable only in the module in which it is defined. You can replace *Dim* with *Public* when declaring a module-level variable to make it available to all the modules in a project. Similarly, constants are private by default. A constant in a code module (but not a form module) can be made public by replacing *Const* with *Public Const*.

You can use the Insert menu to add a new form to a project or Add File from the File menu to add an existing form to a project. If your project includes an MDI form, you make other forms child forms to the MDI form. That means they will be displayed within the confines of the MDI form and that the MDI form will display the menu of whichever child form is active.

By using the *Dim ... As New* statement, you can create a new form that is a copy of an existing form. In such cases, you should use Screen.ActiveForm instead of a particular form's name when referring to a form's properties in code. That way, the code will refer to whichever form is active instead of to the prototype form.

QUIZ 19

1. In which one(s) of the following environments will a stand-alone Visual Basic program run?
   a. A DOS environment
   b. A Windows environment without the Visual Basic runtime dynamic link library
   c. A Windows environment with the Visual Basic runtime dynamic link library
   d. A UNIX environment
   e. A mug of cola-coffee mix

2. Which one(s) of the following are reasons for having a code module (.BAS extension) as part of a project?
   a. To make old Basic hands feel more comfortable
   b. To help separate the interface of a program from its processing part
   c. To organize programs
   d. To make it simpler to read and debug programs
   e. To see how many modules you can add before your system breaks down

3. How do you add a new form to a project?

4. How do you add an existing form to a project?

5. What are some of the differences between constructing a project from several independent forms and constructing a project from one MDI form and several child forms?

6. What is a startup form, and how can you control which form is the startup form?

7. What's the difference between hiding a form and unloading a form?

8. How can you refer to an active form if it has no name?

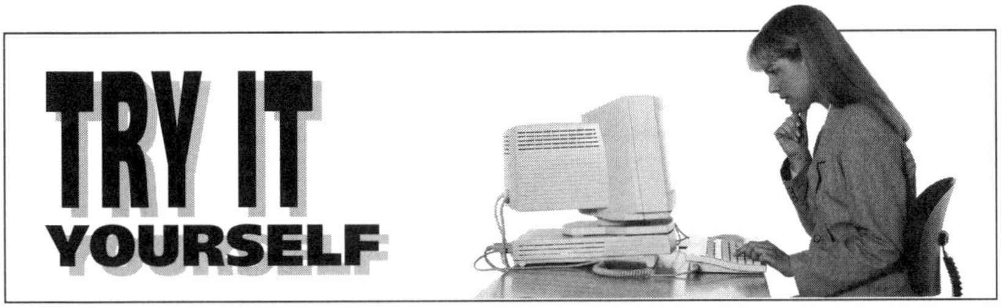

1. Make a stand-alone version of Lesson 18's Image Cruiser.

2. Design a new interface for the Lotto program that can use the computational module unchanged. For example, use combo list boxes or option buttons instead of scrollbars to get a more limited selection of input parameters.

3. Modularize the dice-throwing program of Lesson 15.

4. Create a multiform program that uses Lesson 18's Tiny Edit and Lesson 13's Painter Mouse 2 as elements.

5. Modify SuperCruiser so that it can open more than one Text Cruiser MDI child form.

LESSON 20 OBJECTS AND CLASSES

Objects are an integral part of the Visual Basic paradigm. (*Paradigm* means a guiding ideal or model. Books discussing objects are required to use this word at least once.) As you've seen, forms and controls are objects. Each object can be treated as a single unit, but each object comes with its own set of information (properties) and potential actions (methods). For instance, consider a picture box. It has properties describing its width, height, and background color, and it has built-in capabilities. Using a picture box's *Print* method, you can display text in the box. Using its graphics methods, you can draw in the box. Using

the picture box's *Hide* and *Show* methods, you can make it disappear and reappear. All you have to do to add such a marvel to your Visual Basic program is to click on the Picture Box icon in the Toolbox and draw a control on the form. The fact that the control is an object lets you treat it as a single entity, but that entity comes with a multitude of potentialities. A control such as a picture can be described as defining a picture box class. When you draw a picture box on a form, you create an instance of the class, or an object, having particular values for the properties (see Figure L20-1).

Visual Basic controls such as picture boxes are predefined objects, but Visual Basic also lets you define your own objects. In particular, you can create class modules. A class module defines an object, identifying its properties and methods. Once you have created a class module, you then can create objects as described by the class definition. Each object is an instance of the class. For example, you can think of the Visual Basic specification of the properties and methods of a picture box as the class definition of a picture box. Each picture box you put on a form, then, is a picture box object, and it is an instance of the picture box class. Roughly speaking, the relation of an object to a class is the same as that of a variable to a type.

The classes you define with a class module will have much in common with control classes. Both have properties and methods, and you can create multiple instances of both. One difference is that controls have a visual aspect—they appear on forms, and they are part of the program's visual interface with the user. Class module objects, on the other hand, don't have a visual element. You don't see a class module object. But you can use them. They are, in essence, a generalization of user-defined types.

In this lesson you'll do the following:

- **See how you can add properties and methods to forms**
- **Learn about *Property* procedures *(Let, Get,* and *Set)***
- **Create class modules**
- **Learn a bit about the philosophy of object-oriented class design**

FORMS AND PROPERTIES

Forms come with lots of properties, such as Top, Width, Visible, Caption, and so on. You can set many properties during design time by using the Properties window. But you also can set or alter properties during run time by using code. For instance, suppose a form has the name Form1 (as so many of them do). Then you can do any of the following:

```
Form1.Caption = "The Form1 Form"    // standard syntax
Caption = "Form Follows Function"   // can be used in form's Code window
Me.Caption = "Behold My Form!"      // me - a name I call myself
```

The first statement follows the standard syntax for identifying a property:

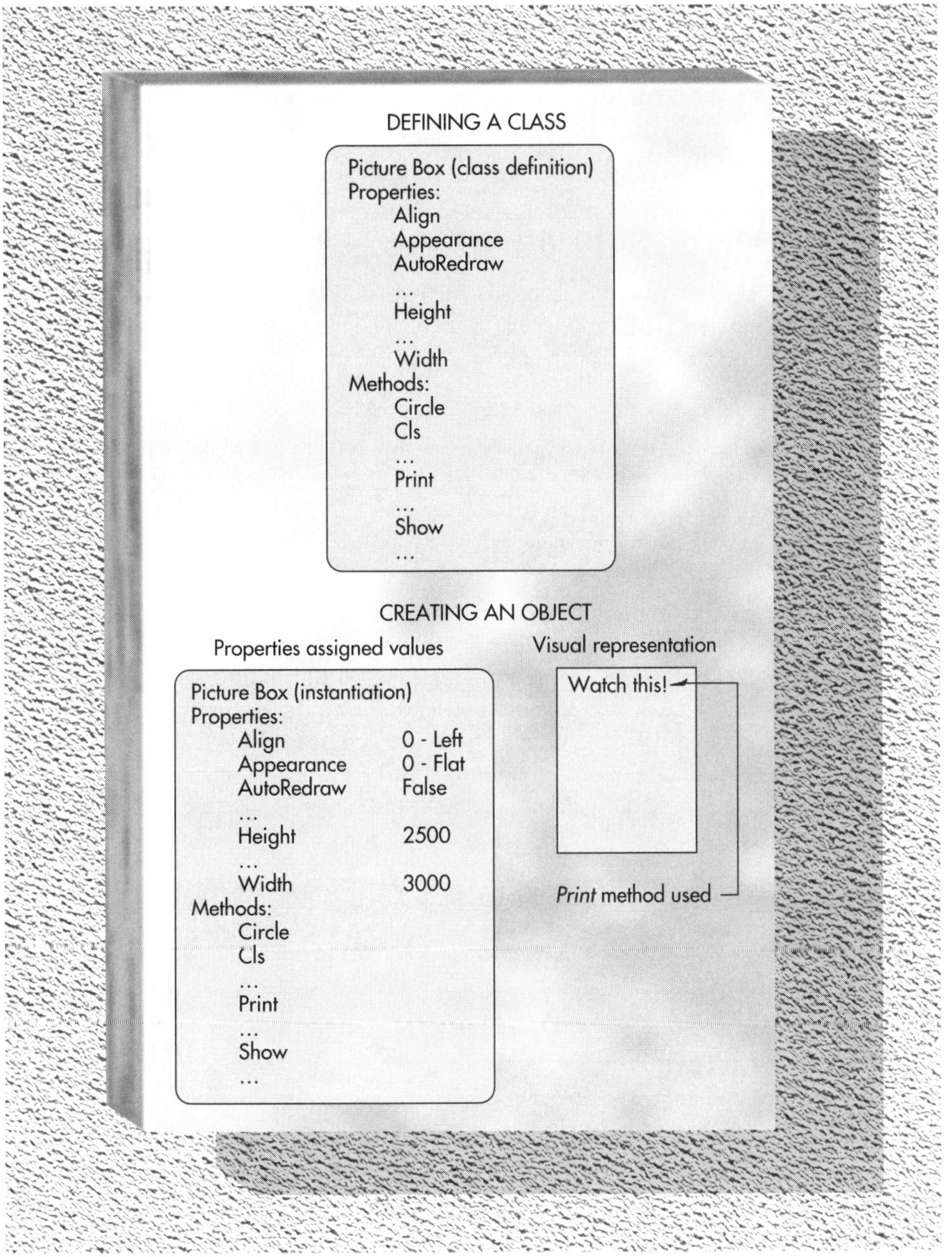

Figure L20-1 Class and object

objectname.propertyname

Here, of course, the object name is Form1 and the property name is Caption. However, when you write code in a form's Code window, you can omit the form's name, as in the second statement. You can only omit the form's name in the form's own Code window, however. If you referred to the form property in another module, you'd have to use the full name. The third statement uses a shortcut. Instead of using the actual form name, you can use the alias *Me*. One nice thing about using *Me* is that you don't have to change code if you change the form name. It's also handy when you create multiple instances of a form—more on that point later.

Adding a Property to a Form

Adding a property to a form can be as simple as adding a module-level variable to a form. For instance, suppose you place the following statement in the declarations section of a form's Code window:

```
Dim Tidy as Boolean
```

This creates a module-level variable called *Tidy*. You can use this variable anywhere in the form module as follows:

```
Form1.Tidy = True    // standard syntax
Tidy = False         // can be used in form's Code window
Me.Tidy = True       // Me an alias for Form1
```

The rules for identifying and using a form-level variable are the same as those for a form property, so the new variable really is a new property for the form.

Let's try this method of adding properties. Being adventurous, let's also try using an object variable as a property—that will provide some useful review.

First, create a form with an array of three text boxes, an array of three option buttons, a command button, and a fourth text box as shown in Figure L20-2 and described in Table L20-1. Next, enter the code shown in Listing L20-1 into the form's Code window.

OBJECT	PROPERTY	SETTING
Form1	Caption	Properties 1
	Name	frmProp1
Text1	Index	0
	Name	txtProp
	Text	One

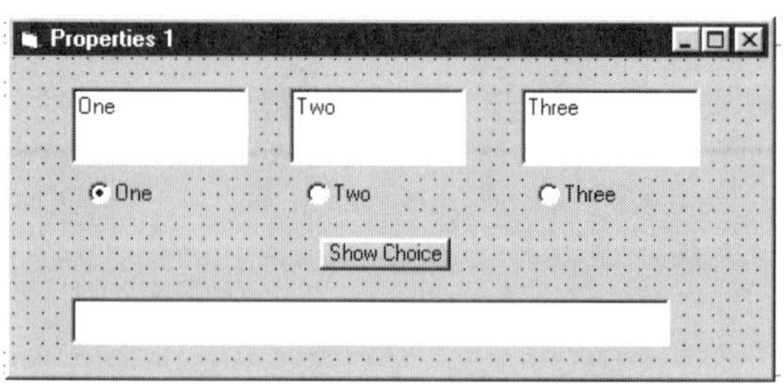

Figure L20-2 The Properties Form

OBJECT	PROPERTY	SETTING
Text2	Index	1
	Name	txtProp
	Text	Two
Text3	Index	2
	Name	txtProp
	Text	Three
Text4	Name	txtChosen
	Text	
Option1	Caption	One
	Index	0
	Name	optProp
	Value	True
Option2	Caption	Two
	Index	2
	Name	optProp
Option3	Caption	Three
	Index	2
	Name	optProp
Command1	Caption	Show Choice
	Name	cmdProp

Table L20-1 The Properties form properties

Listing L20-1
The Properties form code

```
Option Explicit
Dim TextPick As String
Dim BoxPick As TextBox

Private Sub cmdProp_Click()
     Dim I As Integer
     txtChosen.Text = TextPick
     For I = 0 To 2
          If BoxPick = txtProp(I) Then
               BoxPick.BackColor = vbYellow
          Else
               txtProp(I).BackColor = vbCyan
          End If
     Next I
End Sub

Private Sub Form_Load()
     Dim I As Integer
     TextPick = txtProp(0).Text
     Set BoxPick = txtProp(0)
     txtChosen = TextPick
```

continued on next page

continued from previous page

```
    For I = 0 To 2
        txtProp(I).BackColor = vbCyan
    Next I
End Sub

Private Sub optProp_Click(Index As Integer)
    TextPick = txtProp(Index).Text
    Set BoxPick = txtProp(Index)
End Sub
```

The New Properties at Work

The program design is simple. Selecting an option button selects the text box above it. The program uses two new form properties to keep track of the selection:

```
Dim TextPick as String
Dim BoxPick as TextBox
```

The *TextPick* variable acts as a type *String* property that keeps track of the text of the selected box, and the *BoxPick* variable is a type *TextBox* property that keeps track of which box is selected:

```
Private Sub optProp_Click(Index As Integer)
    TextPick = txtProp(Index).Text ' selected text
    Set BoxPick = txtProp(Index)       ' selected text box
End Sub
```

Clicking on the command button then uses these properties to display the chosen text in the fourth text box and to change the background color of the selected text box:

```
Private Sub cmdProp_Click()
    Dim I As Integer
    txtChosen.Text = TextPick
    For I = 0 To 2
        If BoxPick = txtProp(I) Then
            BoxPick.BackColor = vbYellow
        Else
            txtProp(I).BackColor = vbCyan
        End If
    Next I
End Sub
```

Now let's review a couple of points about objects and object variables. First, the declaration

```
Dim BoxPick as TextBox
```

does not create a text box! The *BoxPick* variable is a *reference* variable, much as arguments to Visual Basic procedures are by default. That means *BoxPick* can be used as an alias to refer to existing text boxes.

Note

Creating a control variable does not create a control; it creates a variable that can serve as a reference, or alternative name, to a control.

Second, the Visual Basic syntax for making a reference variable refer to a particular object is to use the *Set* keyword:

```
Set BoxPick = txtProp(Index)
```

For instance, if *Index* has the value 1, then this statement makes *BoxPick* an alias for the *txtProp(1)* text box control. Then an expression like *BoxPick.BackColor* will mean the *BackColor* property of the *txtProp(1)* text box.

Reminder

Use the assignment operator (=) to assign a value to a standard variable. Use *Set* and the assignment operator to assign a particular object to an object variable.

Third, you shouldn't leave reference variables like *BoxPick* unset. If you don't set *BoxPick* to refer to a specific control, then an expression like *BoxPick.BackColor* becomes meaningless. The Properties 1 program uses the *Form_Load* event to initialize the *BoxPick* property to a particular text box.

Something For Nothing

When you have a reference refer to a particular object, Visual Basic has to devote some resources to keeping track of that information. When you're done using a reference, you can recover those resources by assigning a special value, called *Nothing,* to the variable. For example, you can do this:

```
Dim Est As TextBox     'Create an object variable
Set Est As txtBondo    'Use resources
                       'Use Est for awhile
Set Est As Nothing     'Free resources
```

Deeper into Properties—*Property* Procedures

Simply declaring a new module-level variable may seem an informal way to add properties to a form. Visual Basic provides a more elaborate mechanism you can use instead—using *Property* procedures. Not only is the mechanism more elaborate, which really isn't a virtue, it's also more powerful, which may be a necessity. There are three kinds of *Property* procedures:

- *Property Get* procedures return the value of a property
- *Property Let* procedures assign a value to properties of the standard types
- *Property Set* procedures assign a value to properties of an object type

The way they are used is a bit circuitous, so let's look at the process a step at a time. Suppose you want a property called, say, *TextPick,* as in the previous example. Instead of defining a *String* variable called *TextPick,* you would define two *Property* procedures:

```
Property Get TextPick() As String   ' for returning the property's value
Property Let TextPick(txt as String)   ' for setting the property's value
```

What may take a little getting used to is that the *TextPick* property is represented by two property procedures instead of by a variable. That is, with this approach, there is no string variable called *TextPick*. Suppose, for example, you have a statement like this in your code:

```
TextPick = "A very nice string"
```

What happens is that this statement invokes the *Property Let TextPick* procedure, passing the *string* "*A very nice string*" as the *txt* argument to the procedure. Similarly, a statement like

```
txtChosen.Text = TextPick
```

actually calls the *Property Get TextPick* procedure, which is defined as returning a *String* value.

Of course, these procedures still need a place to store the string. You handle that by declaring a module-level variable that can be used by the two *Property* procedures. The *Let* procedure then will assign its argument to that variable, and the *Get* procedure will use the variable as its return value. Figure L20-3 illustrates this technique.

To convert the *TextPick* property in Listing L20-1 to using property procedures, replace

```
Dim TextPick as String
```

with the following:

```
Dim TPick As String    ' module-level variable to hold property value

Private Property Let TextPick(txt As String)   ' return value of property
    TPick = txt
End Property

Private Property Get TextPick() As String   ' assigns value to property
    TextPick = TPick
End Property
```

Similarly, you can use property procedures to replace the *BoxPick* variable. The only difference is that for objects, you use the *Property Set* procedure instead of the *Property Let* procedure. Thus you would replace

```
Dim BoxPick as TextBox
```

with the following:

```
Dim BPick As TextBox    ' module-level variable to hold property value

Private Property Set BoxPick(box As TextBox)   ' return value of property
    Set BPick = box    ' Use Set because BPick is an object.
End Property

Private Property Get BoxPick() As TextBox   ' assigns value to property
    Set BoxPick = Bpick' Use Set because Bpick is an object.
End Property
```

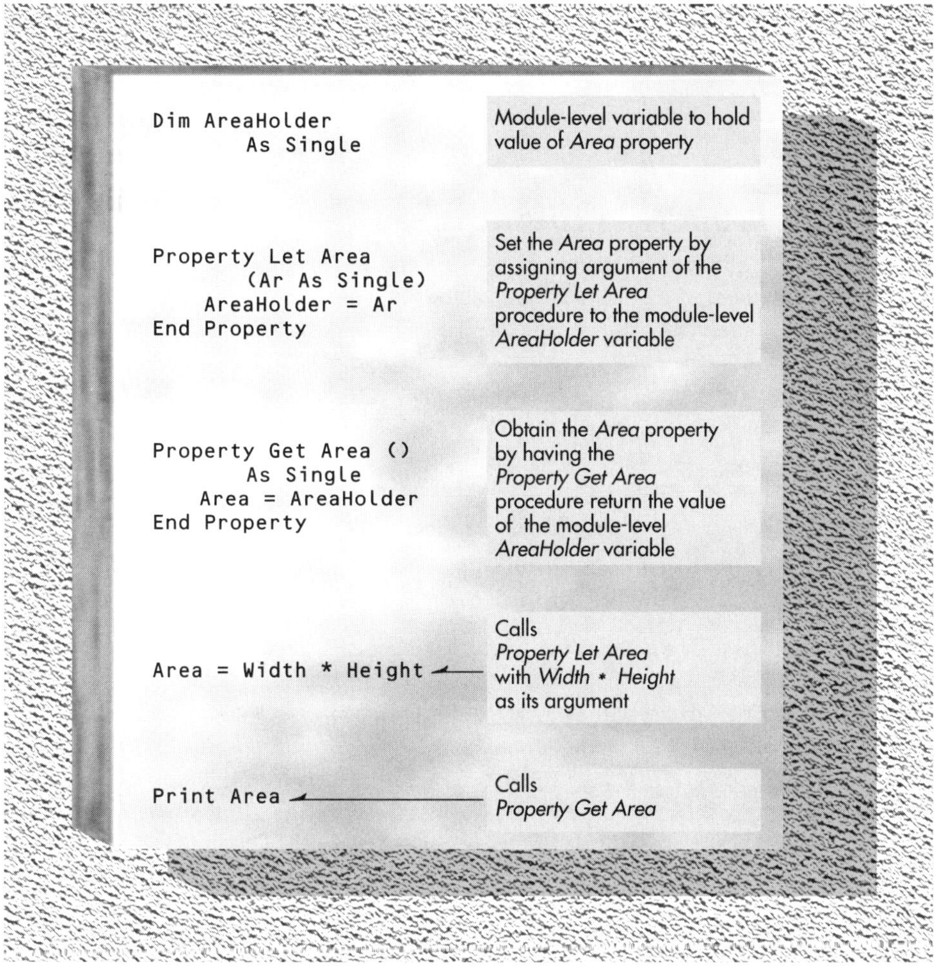

Figure L20-3 Using *Property Let* and *Property Get* with a module-level variable

Note

For a property that is a standard numerical or string type, use *Property Let* to set the property's value and *Property Get* to read the property's value. For a property that is an object, such as a control, use *Property Set* to set the property's value and *Property Get* to get the property's value. You pair a particular *Property Let* (or *Property Set*) to a *Property Get* by using the same property name in the procedure. For instance, *Property Let Area* and *Property Get Area* would describe the Area property, while *Property Set MrButton* and *Property Get MrButton* would describe a MrButton property. *Variant* variables occupy a special niche—you have your choice of using *Property Set* or *Property Let* with them. That's because a *Variant* variable can be set to a fundamental type or to an object type.

Go back to Listing L20-1 and make the two substitutions just described, leaving the rest of the code unchanged. Outwardly, the program will work exactly as before. However, all the uses of properties will be converted from directly accessing property variables to using *Property* procedures.

Why Use *Property* Procedures?

You undoubtedly noticed that the *Property* procedure approach is a bit roundabout. In the last example, there's no advantage to taking the *Property* procedure route. However, sometimes *Property* procedures are just the ticket. To see why, consider some of the standard properties of a form, such as the Width property. When you change the Width property, you do more than change the value of a variable. You also change the width of the form as displayed on the screen. This means that setting the Width property also invokes some code. Similarly, if you change the Visible property to False, you also invoke code that hides the form.

In general, then, changing a property also causes some code to be executed, and that's where property procedures come in. Since they are procedures, you can add code to perform actions beyond just setting the value of a variable.

To see how this works, let's add a new property to the last example. Call it TextVisible. It will be a *Boolean* property. If it is set to False, all text boxes will be hidden, and if it is set to True, all text boxes will be visible.

Make a copy of the original project and add a check box as described in Table L20-2 and shown in Figure L20-4.

OBJECT	PROPERTY	SETTING
CheckBox1	Caption	Hide Text
	Name	cmdHide

Table L20-2 A new control for the Properties form

Now let's create the TextVisible property. First, create a *Boolean* module-level variable to store the property's value:

```
Dim CanSee As Boolean   ' Value of TextVisible property
```

Next, create the *Property Get TextVisible* procedure. All it has to do is return the current value of the property, that is, the value of the *CanSee* variable:

```
Private Property Get TextVisible() As Boolean
    TextVisible = CanSee
End Property
```

Since TextVisible is a Boolean property, use *Let,* not *Set,* to set the value. In addition to setting the *CanSee* variable, this procedure has to identify all the text box controls on the form and set their Visible properties. We can use the *Controls* collection to identify all the controls and the *If Type Of* … *Is* statement to select just text box controls:

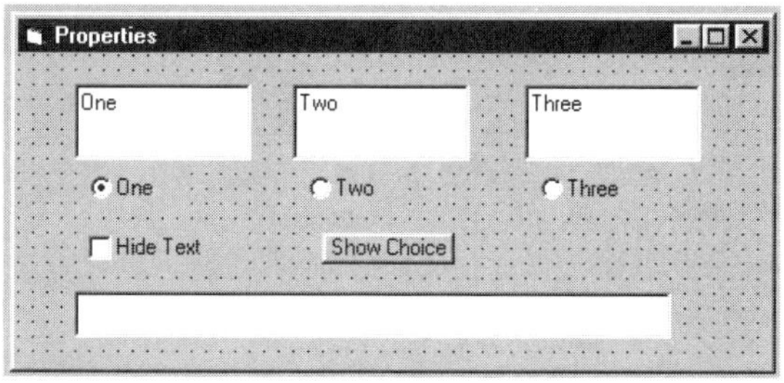

Figure L20-4 The modified Properties form

```
Private Property Let TextVisible(X As Boolean)
    Dim AControl As Control
    CanSee = X
    For Each AControl In Me.Controls()
        If TypeOf AControl Is TextBox Then
            AControl.Visible = X
        End If
    Next AControl
End Property
```

Suppose, now, that you add the following code to the program:

```
TextVisible = False
```

This statement calls the *Property Let TextVisible* procedure, setting the variable *CanSee* to False and setting the Visible property of every text box on the form to False. And that is how you create a property that does more than merely store a value. Listing L20-2 shows the complete listing, include the check box code for toggling the the TextVisible property.

Listing L20-2
The new Properties form code

```
Option Explicit
Dim TPick As String
Dim BPick As TextBox
Dim CanSee As Boolean

Private Property Get TextPick() As String
    TextPick = TPick
End Property

Private Property Let TextPick(X As String)
    TPick = X
End Property

Private Property Get BoxPick() As TextBox
    Set BoxPick = BPick
End Property
```

continued on next page

continued from previous page

```
Private Property Set BoxPick(X As TextBox)
     Set BPick = X
End Property

Private Property Get TextVisible() As Boolean
     TextVisible = CanSee
End Property

Private Property Let TextVisible(X As Boolean)
     Dim AControl As Control
     CanSee = X
     For Each AControl In Me.Controls()
          If TypeOf AControl Is TextBox Then
               AControl.Visible = X
          End If
     Next AControl
End Property

Private Sub chkHide_Click()
     If chkHide.Value = vbChecked Then
          TextVisible = False
     Else
          TextVisible = True
     End If
End Sub

Private Sub cmdProp_Click()
     Dim I As Integer
     txtWord.Text = TextPick
     For I = 0 To 2
          If BoxPick = txtProp(I) Then
               BoxPick.BackColor = vbYellow
          Else
               txtProp(I).BackColor = vbCyan
          End If
     Next I
End Sub

Private Sub Form_Load()
     Dim I As Integer
     TextPick = txtProp(0).Text
     Set BoxPick = txtProp(0)
     txtWord = TextPick
     For I = 0 To 2
          txtProp(I).BackColor = vbCyan
     Next I
     TextVisible = True
End Sub

Private Sub optProp_Click(Index As Integer)
     TextPick = txtProp(Index).Text
     Set BoxPick = txtProp(Index)
End Sub
```

Try the program. When you check the box, the text windows disappear, and when you uncheck the box, they reappear. Note that you can still use the option buttons to change selections while the text boxes are invisible. When you make the text boxes visible again, they reflect any changes you made in the meantime.

More about *Property* Procedures—Multiple Arguments

So far, the *Property* procedures you've used have followed these formats:

For numeric and string variables:

Dim *PropHolder* **As** *PropType*

Property Let *PropName*(*var* **as** *PropType*)
PropHolder = *var*
[more code if required]
End Property

Property Get *PropName*() **As** *PropType*
PropName = *PropHolder*
[more code if required]
End Property

For object variables:

Dim *PropHolder* **As** *PropType*
Property Set *PropName*(var **As** *PropType*)
Set *PropHolder* = *var*
[more code if required]
End Property

Property Get *PropName*() **As** *PropType*
Set *PropName* = *PropHolder*
[more code if required]
End Property

In short, each property uses a module-level variable to hold a value, a *Property Get* procedure to return the property value, and a *Property Set* (for objects) or *Property Let* (for regular variables) to set a property value. Each procedure can have additional code to implement any changes that accompany using a property value. All these features are true in general.

There are a couple of other features that have been true for the examples, but which are special cases of more general rules. The special cases are these:

- Each Property Get procedure took no arguments and had the property type as its return type.
- Each *Property Set* and *Property Let* procedure took one argument of the property type.

For instance, the *Property Get TextVisible* procedure returns a *Boolean* value, and the *Property Let TextVisible* procedure takes a *Boolean* argument.

More generally, each procedure can take multiple arguments, subject to the following rules:

1. The *Property Set* or *Property Let* procedure takes one more argument than the corresponding *Property Get* procedure.
2. The arguments to the *Property Get* procedure must correspond to (have the same names and types as) all but the last argument to the corresponding *Property Set* or *Property Let* procedure.
3. The last argument to a *Property Set* or *Property Let* procedure must be of the same type as the return type for the corresponding *Property Get* procedure.

These rules may sound more complicated than they really are. First, see that the special cases you've used comply. *Property Let TextVisible* takes 1 argument, which is 1 more than *Property Get TextVisible* takes. Next, the arguments of *Property Get TextVisible* (0 arguments to be precise) exactly match the names and types of all but the last *Property Let TextVisible* arguments—again a list of 0 arguments. Finally, the type of the last (and only) argument to *Property Let TextVisible* is the same as the *Property Get TextVisible* return type—*Boolean*.

Next, let's take a more complicated example. Suppose you have a procedure like this:

```
Property Get Bauble (X as Integer, Y as Single) As String
    ...
End Property
```

Then the corresponding *Let* procedure would have to look like this:

```
Property Let Bauble (X as Integer, Y as Single, Z as String)
    ...
End Property
```

But why would you need multiple arguments for a single property? One possibility is that the property depends on other values. For instance, the *Bauble* property could be a string constructed from some numbers.

Let's look at a short example. Construct the form described by Table L20-3 and illustrated by Figure L20-5.

OBJECT	PROPERTY	SETTING
Form1	Caption	Aspect
	Name	frmAspect
VScroll1	Large Change	10
	Max	30
	Min	5
	Name	vsbAspect

Table L20-3 The Aspect form properties

Let's endow this form with a new property, named *Aspect,* that describes the *aspect ratio* (the ratio of width to height) of the form. To set the aspect ratio, you'll provide two values: the height of the form and the desired aspect ratio.

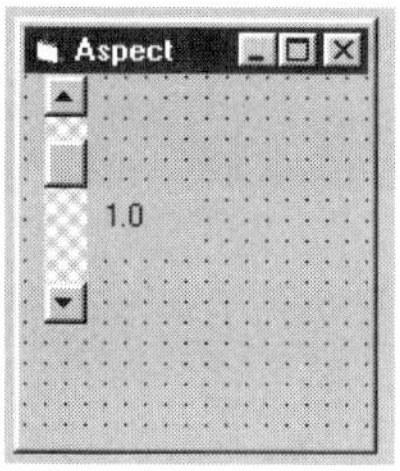

Figure L20-5 The Aspect form

The *Property Let Aspect* function, shown in Listing L20-3, then sets the form height to the first argument, the *AspectRatio* variable to the second argument, and the form width to the product of the two.

Listing L20-3
The Aspect form code

```
Option Explicit
Dim AspectRatio As Single

Property Let Aspect(H As Single, AR As Single)
    AspectRatio = AR
    Me.Height = H
    Me.Width = H * AR
End Property

Property Get Aspect(H As Single) As Single
    Aspect = AspectRatio
End Property

Private Sub Form_Load()
    Aspect(3000) = 1        'Syntax requires an argument for Aspect.
                            'Any number will do.
                            'See text for further explanation.
    vsbAspect.Value = 10
End Sub

Private Sub vsbAspect_Change()
    Aspect(Me.Height) = vsbAspect.Value / 10
    lblAspect.Caption = Aspect(1)
End Sub
```

When you run the program, you can use the scrollbar to change the Aspect property, causing the width of the form to adjust to the current setting. Figure L20-6 shows the program caught in the act.

One interesting feature to keep in mind is that when you use the *Property Let Aspect* function, you must provide it with the required argument even though it doesn't use it. For instance, the *Change* event procedure for the scrollbar uses this code:

```
lblAspect.Caption = Aspect(1)   '1 is an unused argument.
```

Figure L20-6 The Aspect program in progress

All the *Property Get Aspect* function does is return the value of the *AspectRatio* variable. However, because the *Property Let Aspect* function has arguments, the *Property Get Aspect* function *must* have one argument (rule #1), in this case, a *Single* value (rule #2). And that means you have to provide an argument to *Aspect* when retrieving the property value. It's pretty awkward, but having simple, clear-cut rules makes it easier for the Visual Basic program to deal with *Property* procedures.

REFERENCES, OBJECT INSTANCES, AND *NEW*

Let's go back to variables that refer to objects. As Lesson 16 discussed, you can declare variables that represent generic objects or specific objects, as in the following samples:

```
Dim MyForm As Form      ' MyForm can refer to any form.
Dim MyControl As Control    ' MyControl can refer to any control.
Dim MyTBox As TextBox   ' MyTBox can refer to any text box control.
```

None of these declarations creates new objects; they merely create aliases that can refer to existing objects. However, as discussed in Lesson 19, you can use the keyword *New* to create a new object when you create a reference variable. For example, suppose you have a form called *Form1*. You can do the following:

```
Dim NewForm As New Form1
```

This creates a new object, or instance, that is a copy of the original form. The new form will have all the property values, code, and controls of the original form. The variable *NewForm* will refer to the copy. Thus *NewForm.Caption* will be the caption property of the new form.

You can use *New* to create only certain kinds of objects. For example, you can use *New* to create a new form that's a copy of a specific form, and you can use *New* to create a new instance of a class defined in a class module (coming up soon!). But you can't use *New* to create a control, a fundamental data type, or a generic object. Table L20-4 summarizes the limits on *New*.

CREATING A	POSSIBLE	EXAMPLE	COMMENT
Fundamental data type	No	Dim Digit As New Integer	
Control	No	Dim Cheesehead As New Label	
Generic type	No	Dim AForm As New Form	
Specific control	No	Dim VB As New txtBook	
Specific form	Yes	Dim AForm As New frmHouse	frmHouse is a form
Class module object	Yes	Dim Rose As New Flower	Flower is a class module
OLE automation object	Yes	Dim SS As New Excel.Chart	Chart is an Excel object

Table L20-4 Constraints on New

Okay, let's look at an example. Create a new form as shown in Figure L20-7 and described by Table L20-5.

OBJECT	PROPERTY	SETTING
Form1	AutoRedraw	True
	Caption	Instances
	Name	frmInst
Command1	Caption	Dupe
	Name	cmdDup
Command2	Caption	List
	Name	cmdList
Command3	Caption	Clear
	Name	cmdClear

Table L20-5 The Instances form properties

Also, to keep track of all the forms you'll create, use the Insert menu to add a code module (*.BAS* file) to the project. Place this statement in the Code window for the code module:

```
Public Ct As Integer    ' number of forms created
```

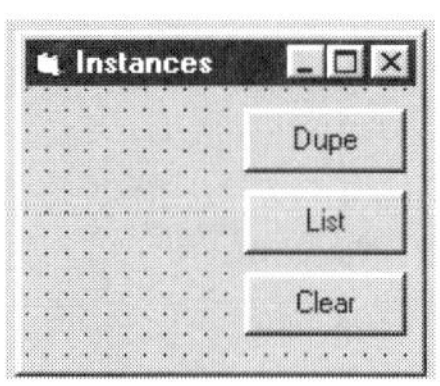

Figure L20-7 The Instances form

By placing *Ct* in a code module and declaring it public, you make it available to all forms in the project. Visual Basic variables automatically start with a value of 0, and you can have the project add 1 to *Ct* each time a new form is created.

You can set up things so that clicking the Dupe button produces a duplicate form. The basic code for creating and showing the form is this:

```
Dim NF As New frmInst    'Create new form.
NF.Show                  'Show new form onscreen.
```

Listing L20-4 does that and a few more things to help you follow the process.

Listing L20-4
The Instances form code

```
Option Explicit

Private Sub cmdClear_Click()
    Me.Cls
End Sub

Private Sub CmdDup_Click()
    Dim NF As New frmInst
    Ct = Ct + 1
    NF.TOP = Me.TOP + 800
    NF.Left = Me.Left + 500
    NF.Caption = "Copy #" & Ct
    NF.Show
    Me.Caption = Me.Caption & "!"
    Set NF = Me
    NF.Caption = NF.Caption & "?"
    Screen.ActiveForm.BackColor = vbRed
    frmInst.BackColor = vbBlue
End Sub

Private Sub cmdList_Click()
    Dim FI As Integer
    For FI = 0 To Forms.Count - 1
        Print "top = "; Forms(FI).TOP
    Next FI
End Sub
```

Program Notes

As promised, the *Click* event adds 1 to the *Ct* variable, keeping track of the number of forms created. Also, it offsets each new form so that it doesn't completely cover the one under it. Note the following code:

```
NF.Top = Me.Top + 800
```

Here *Me* refers to the form whose code is being executed. For instance, when you click the Dupe button on the original form, that executes the *CmdDup_Click* event in the original form, and *Me.Top* is the Top property of the original form. *NF*, on the other hand, refers to the new form, so *NF.Top* is the new form's Top property.

Note that *Me* always refers to the form whose code is executing. For instance, if you click on the Dupe button of the first copy of the original, *Me* will be the first copy, and *NF* will be the second copy. On the other hand, frmInst will always mean the original form, even though the copies inherit the same name for their Name properties. The program illustrates that with the following statement:

```
frmInst.BackColor = vbBlue
```

The only form that ever turns blue is the original form. But the statement

```
Me.Caption = Me.Caption & "!"
```

appends an exclamation mark to the caption of the form whose button has just been clicked, which will be the form just under the most newly created form.

The program also illustrates that *Screen.ActiveForm* refers to the form with the focus. The statement

```
Me.Caption = Me.Caption & "!"
```

changes the caption of the form whose button was clicked, but the statement

```
Screen.ActiveForm.BackColor = vbRed
```

changes the color of the newly created form, which became active when its *Show* method was invoked.

Typically, *Me* and *Screen.ActiveForm* refer to the same form. However, in this case, the executed code shifts the focus to a new form, changing what *Screen.ActiveForm* refers to, but not changing *Me*'s reference.

Let's look a bit more closely at the variable *NF*. First, as a variable, it doesn't have to remain attached to one particular value. For instance, the code

```
Set NF = Me                ' valid but ill advised
```

sets *NF* to refer to the clicked-upon form instead of to the newly created form. However, this is not a good idea, for now you don't have a reference to the new form.

Second, *NF* is a local variable to the *cmdDup Click* event. That means that each duplicate form gets its own copy of *NF* when you click the form's button. Also, being a local variable, it expires when the *cmdDup_Click* event terminates. Once that happens, the form has no name by which to refer to itself. However, other code in the form could use *Screen.ActiveForm* or *Me* to refer to the form.

The *Forms* Collection

The program uses the *Forms* collection, which is a collection of all forms currently part of a project. The List button uses the *Forms* collection to print the value of the Top property for each form that's open. There are a couple of ways of doing this. One, similar to how you used the *Controls* collection in Lesson 13, is to use a *For Each* loop:

```
Dim FormID As Form 'Declare a type Form variable.
For Each FormID In Forms   'Set FormID to each form in turn.
    Print FormID; "Top = "; FormID.TOP
Next FormID
```

The *FormID* variable gets set to each form in the collection, so *FormID.TOP* becomes the TOP property for each form in the collection.

For variety, however, there's a second approach based on the fact that *Forms.Count* is the total number of open forms. With this approach, you treat the collection like an array in which *FI* is an array index ranging from 0 to *Forms.Count* - 1 and in which *Forms*(FI) represents a form in the collection:

```
Dim FI As Integer
    For FI = 0 To Forms.Count - 1
        Print "top = "; Forms(FI).TOP
    Next FI
```

Note that *Forms.Count* doesn't necessarily equal the value of the public variable *Ct*. That's because *Ct* equals the number of forms created, while *Forms.Count* equals the number of forms open. If you create, say, ten forms, then close two of them, *Ct* would be 10 and *Forms.Count* would be 8.

Try the program. Notice that clicking on a button produces a copy of the form whose button you click. Each click creates a new instance of a *frmInst* object. Figure L20-8 shows the result of a few such clicks. Clicking on the close box on a form closes just that one form, even in the case of the original form. But clicking on the Stop button in the Visual Basic Toolbar terminates all the forms.

CLASS MODULES

An object is a self-contained entity comprised of data (properties) and code (methods). A *class* is a recipe for making an object. For instance, the PictureBox class specifies that a picture box has certain properties, such as Text, and certain methods, such as *Print*. When you place a picture box control on a form, Visual Basic uses the PictureBox class definition as its guide. Class modules let you define your own classes, which your program can use to create objects of those classes.

In the last example, frmInst was both an object (the first form displayed) and a pattern or template on which to base new instances of the form. Class mod-

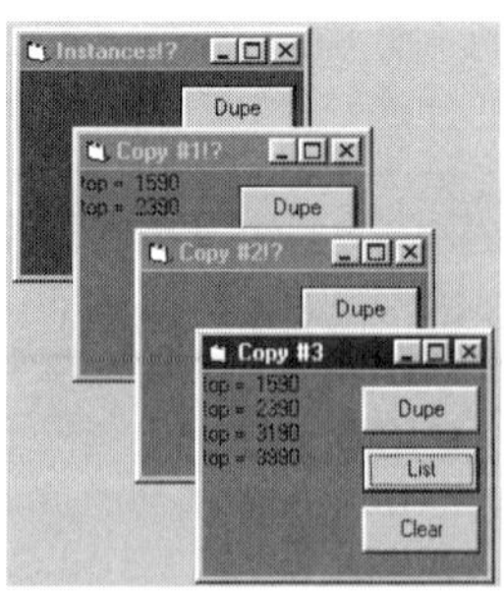

Figure L20-8 Multiple instances of a form class

ules make a cleaner distinction between a defining pattern and instances of the pattern. You create a class module by selecting Class Module from the Insert menu when you are in Visual Basic design mode. This adds a new file with a .CLS extension. For instance, you'll be doing an example in which the class module is named *Client.cls*. Class modules are a lot like code modules. You can define variables and procedures, but there is no visual aspect—you can't add controls to a code module.

The basic ideas behind the class module are pretty simple. By default, the base name of the module becomes the class name. Thus, the *Client.cls* module will define a *Client* class. (You can, if you choose, change the class name.) Any module-level variables you define for the class module become class properties. Also, you can use property procedures to define class properties. Any procedures you define in the class module become class methods. A class is not an object; instead, it is a recipe for making an object. Then you can use *New* to create actual object instances of a class:

```
Dim Debs as New Client   ' Debs refers to a new instance of the Client
                           class.
```

The process is pretty easy, but before plunging in, let's look a little at the philosophy behind classes and objects. That will help you get the best use out of class modules.

Object-Oriented Programming

One of the most important programming methodologies today is *object-oriented programming*, or OOP. Visual Basic is not a fully realized OOP language, but it does incorporate important elements of OOP technology.

One of the basic concepts of OOP is that a class is a user-defined type. Of course, Visual Basic already has a form of user-defined type—you can use the *Type* statement to define a type that can hold several items of data. But OOP takes the concept of user-defined type further, noting that a type is defined not only by the information it holds but also by the operations you can perform upon it. For instance, when you say a variable is type *Integer*, you're doing more than saying that it is an integer value. You also are saying that its something *you* can add to, subtract from, multiply by, divide by, and take the modulus of. Similarly, a *String* type variable has its own set of operations, such as concatenating two strings.

To define a type in OOP, then, you define information the type will represent, *and* you define the permissible operations. In Visual Basic, that translates into defining properties and defining methods for a class module. For instance, suppose you have to write a program to represent your bank account. You could begin by asking what data describes your account and come up with the following list:

- Name of bank
- Name of customer

- Account number
- Account balance
- Minimum balance for free checking
- Lowest balance during month

This may not be a complete list, but you get the idea. To represent this information, you could create a class module called *Account.cls*. Then you could add a property to represent each item of information.

Next, you could ask what operations could be performed on your account. Here are some possibilities:

- Initialize to customer name
- Set account number
- Display account information
- Deposit
- Withdraw
- Transfer into
- Transfer out of
- Incur penalty
- Check purchase

Again, there might be other possible actions, but you get the idea. As a class designer, you would add procedures to the class module to handle each of these actions.

Once you designed the class module, you could create a form that used it. For instance, the form could have buttons for opening a new account, for depositing money, and so on. To create a new bank account, you would have code like this:

```
Dim Sonya As New Account
```

To deposit, say, $50, you would use the *Deposit* method defined in the *Account.cls* module:

```
Sonya.Deposit 50 ' Add $50 to the Sonya account.
```

Access Control

A very important question is, who or what can change data in an object? For instance, it would be rather annoying if anyone could easily modify your account balance. The usual OOP approach is to allow access to an object's data *only* by that object's class methods. The class methods, then, form the public interface for the object. They (the methods) handle all transactions involving the object.

This approach is designed to protect the integrity of the data. This isn't security in the sense of protecting information from inimical intruders. Instead, it's security in the sense of protecting data from programming errors. For example, suppose Sonya withdrew $1,000 from her account. One way to code this is as follows:

```
Sonya.Balance = Sonya.Balance - 1000    ' simple but flawed
```

That's simple enough. In fact, it is too simple. Perhaps Sonya doesn't have that much in her account! Or perhaps that drops her below her minimum balance, triggering an additional charge. The way to handle these possibilities is with a well-designed Withdraw method that handles all these eventualities:

```
Sonya.Withdraw 1000 ' does error checking, etc.
```

If you compel users of the class to use your foolproof *Withdraw* method and you prohibit them from using the *Balance* property directly, you've reduced the possibility of messing up the account balance. That's the sort of protection OOP offers.

Visual Basic doesn't make you design your classes along these lines, but it does make it *possible* to do so. All you have to do is declare module-level variables as *Private* and to declare the methods (including *Property* procedures) that form the official interface as *Public*. Private variables can be used within the methods, but the outside world (a form or other module using the class module, for example) can only call upon the public methods.

A First Class Example

Let's try out these ideas. The Weight Loss Factory has hired you to write a program monitoring its clients. After studying the problem carefully, you decide you can represent a client by three values:

- The client's name
- The client's original weight
- The client's current weight

(To keep things simple, you've decided to ignore other data such as dates, trainers, and so on.) Open a new form, and select Class Module from the Insert menu. You'll see the Code window for the new class module. Press F4 to bring up the Properties window, as shown in Figure L20-9. You'll see a class module has three properties. Set the class name to *Client*. (You'll hear about the other properties later. For now, accept the default values.) Then select Save from the File menu to save the class module. Visual Basic will suggest *Client.cls* as the file name. Matching the file name to the class name makes it easier to keep track of class creations, so accept that suggestion.

Next add three module-level variables to represent the three data quantities:

```
Private StartWeight As Single
Private CurrentWeight As Single
Private ClientName As String
```

The keyword *Private* means that these variable are private to this particular module. You'd get the same effect if you used *Dim* instead of *Private*, but *Private* documents the intent better.

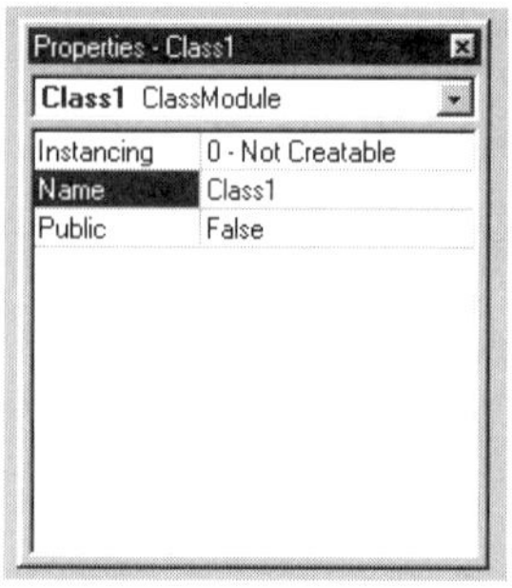

Figure L20-9 The class module Properties window

Now move on to the public interface for the *Client* class. There are many possibilities for methods. The following selection should be adequate:

- An *InitClient* method for initializing a *Client* object, setting values for the three private variables
- A *Property Let Weight* method for updating the current weight
- A *Property Get Weight* method for obtaining the current weight
- A *Property Get Name* method for obtaining the client's name
- A *WeightChange* function that returns the client's change in weight

The idea here is that the client's name and initial weight get set just once, by the *InitClient* method. Thus there are no *Property Let* methods for the name and initial weight, since they shouldn't be altered once set. (This oversimplification ignores legitimate changes of name and the need to correct data entry errors.) The *Property Get Name* method returns the value of *ClientName*. Because there is no *Property Set Name* method, the *Name* property is a read-only variable, in effect. The current weight needs to be changeable, so there is both a *Property Let Weight* and a *Property Get Weight* procedure. Listing L20-5 shows the complete code for the class module.

Listing L20-5
The Client.cls class definition

```
Option Explicit

Private StartWeight As Single
Private CurrentWeight As Single
Private ClientName As String

Public Sub InitClient(CName As String, SWt As Single)
    ClientName = CName
    StartWeight = SWt
    CurrentWeight = SWt
End Sub

Public Property Let Weight(Wt As Single)
```

```
    CurrentWeight = Wt
End Property

Public Property Get Weight() As Single
    Weight = CurrentWeight
End Property

Public Property Get Name() As String
    Name = ClientName
End Property

Public Function WeightChange() As Single
    WeightChange = CurrentWeight - StartWeight
End Function
```

Notice that the module definition follows the OOP guidelines. The actual variables used to store information are private, so they can be accessed from another module only by using the public interface, which is defined by the public methods and property procedures.

Now that you have defined a class, you can use it in a program. Go back to the form and give it the properties and controls described in Table L20-6 and Figure L20-10.

OBJECT	PROPERTY	SETTING
Form1	Caption	The Weight Loss Factory
	Name	frmClass
Command1	Caption	Show Bob
	Name	cmdShowBob
Command2	Caption	Show Babs
	Name	cmdShowBabs
Command3	Caption	Update Bob
	Name	cmdUpBob
Command4	Caption	Update Babs
	Name	cmdUpBabs
Command5	Caption	Review Bob
	Name	cmdRevBob
Command6	Caption	Review Babs
	Name	cmdRevBabs
TextBox1	Locked	True
	Name	txtBob
	Text	
TextBox2	Locked	True
	Name	txtBabs
	Text	

Table L20-6 The Weight Loss Factory form properties

You can give the form two class objects by declaring *Client* variables and using *New:*

```
Private Bob As New Client
Private Babs As New Client
```

Then you can use the *Form_Load* event to initialize the two objects:

```
Private Sub Form_Load()
    Bob.InitClient "Bob Snops", 266
    Babs.InitClient "Babs Snops", 188
End Sub
```

Note that you invoke a *Client* method the same way you invoke a control's method: join the object name to the method name with a period. So *Bob.InitClient* runs the *InitClient* method using the *Bob* object, and *Babs.InitClient* runs the *InitClient* method using the *Babs* object. Similarly, you use a period to join an object name to a property to identify a property of a particular object—*Bob.Name* is the Name property for the Bob object, and *Babs.Weight* is the *Weight* property for the *Babs* object.

Listing L20-6 shows the complete code for the form. Note how each event uses the public interface of the *Client* class to manipulate data for the two *Client* objects.

Listing L20-6
The Weight Loss Factory code

```
Option Explicit

Private Bob As New Client
Private Babs As New Client

Private Sub cmdRevBabs_Click()
    txtBabs.Text = Babs.Name & "'s weight change is " _
        & Babs.WeightChange & " lbs"
End Sub

Private Sub cmdRevBob_Click()
    txtBob.Text = Bob.Name & "'s weight change is " _
        & Bob.WeightChange & " lbs"
End Sub

Private Sub cmdShowBabs_Click()
    txtBabs.Text = Babs.Name & " weighs " & Babs.Weight & " lbs"
End Sub

Private Sub cmdShowBob_Click()
    txtBob.Text = Bob.Name & " weighs " & Bob.Weight & " lbs"
End Sub

Private Sub cmdUpBob_Click()
    Dim NewWeight As String
    NewWeight = InputBox("Enter new weight in pounds: ")
    If IsNumeric(NewWeight) Then
        Bob.Weight = CSng(NewWeight)
    Else
        MsgBox "Enter a number next time!"
```

```
    End If
    cmdShowBob_Click
End Sub

Private Sub cmdUpBabs_Click()
    Dim NewWeight As String
    NewWeight = InputBox("Enter new weight in pounds: ")
    If IsNumeric(NewWeight) Then
        Babs.Weight = CSng(NewWeight)
    Else
        MsgBox "Enter a number next time!"
    End If
    cmdShowBabs_Click
End Sub

Private Sub Form_Load()
    Bob.InitClient "Bob Snops", 266
    Babs.InitClient "Babs Snops", 188
End Sub
```

Class Properties

The Properties window for a class (see Figure L20-10) shows three properties: Instancing, Name, and Public. You've already seen that the Name property is the class name, and you use it when creating instances of the class. Now let's look at the rest.

The Instancing property has three possible values:

0- Not Creatable

1- Creatable SingleUse

2- Creatable MultiUse

The default value is 0 (Not Creatable), which sounds a bit odd, especially since the last example created instances of the class. However, this property describes your class's relationship to other applications. The settings relate to sharing objects between programs by using OLE. The default setting means that only the

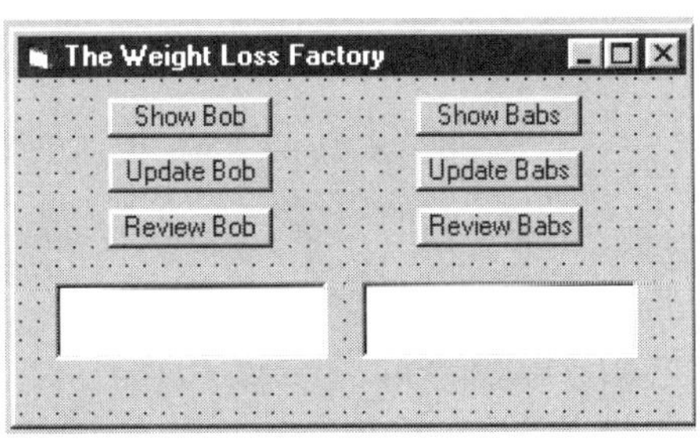

Figure L20-10 The Weight Loss Factory form

project containing the class module can create objects of that type. The other settings allow other applications to create instances of the class.

Similarly, the Public property (false by default) controls whether other applications can access an object of the class. If the Public property is false, the Instancing setting is moot, for you can't create an object belonging to a class you can't access. If Public is true, and Instancing is Not Creatable, then another application can use an object in the program containing the class module. If Public is true and Instancing is one of the Creatable values, then other programs also can create objects of the class.

Class Events

Classes have two events, a *Class_Initialize* event and a *Class_Terminate* event. These are analogous to the *Form_Initialize* event and *Form_Terminate* event. The *Class_Initialize* event takes place when a class object is first instantiated. You can use it, for example, to set default values. For instance, you could add the following to the *Client.cls* module:

```
Private Sub Class_Initialize()
     ClientName = "One Ton"
     CurrentWeight = 2000
     StartWeight = 2000
End Sub
```

These are the values an object would get if you failed to use the *InitClient* method. Similarly, the *Class_Terminate* event takes place when an object is terminated, for example, by assigning *Nothing* to the object's reference.

Class Comments

Class modules are one of Visual Basic 4's new features, so you won't find them used in older Visual Basic programs. But they are a very helpful addition toward modularizing code. Once you define a useful class module, you can reuse it in other projects. Instead of writing new code, you can just use the Add File command from the Visual Basic File menu to add a class to a project. Even if you don't choose to follow the OOP technique of private data and public methods, class modules can help your programming by making it more modular and easier to understand.

SUMMARY

Objects are a cornerstone of Visual Basic programming. Controls are objects, forms are objects, and you can create objects based upon class modules. To create a class module, select Class Module from the Visual Basic Insert menu. The Name property for the class module becomes the class name.

Procedures that you define in a form or class module become methods for that form or class. You can add properties to a form or class by adding module-level variables. However, *Property* procedures provide a more powerful way to add properties because you can incorporate code that's activated when you change a property. Typically, you use two paired *Property* procedures to establish a property. If the property is a fundamental type and the property name is, say, Beauty, use the *Property Let Beauty* procedure to set a property's value and the *Property Get Beauty* procedure to fetch the property's value. If the property is an object type and the property name is, say, Truth, use the *Property Set Truth* procedure to set a property's value and the *Property Get Truth* procedure to fetch the property's value.

Properties and methods, including property procedures, can be declared using the *Public* or *Private* keywords. Private properties and methods can be used freely within the defining module, but they are invisible to the outside world. Public properties and methods, on the other hand, can be used by other modules. For instance, a form can call a public method defined in a class module.

The object-oriented programming approach to class modules is to make class variables private so that the only way they can be modified is by using public methods (including *Property* procedures) defined in the class module. The public methods become the official programming interface for the object. This helps ensure that data gets modified only in predetermined ways, protecting the data from programming errors.

QUIZ 20

1. Below is some code for a form called frmDorf. Some of it is valid, but some of it is faulty. Spot the errors!

```
Dim Ajax As Form
Dim Comet As New Form
Dim Dolma As New frmDorf
Private Form_Load()
    Ajax = frmDorf
    Me.Caption = "Hampshire"
    Show Dolma
End Sub
```

2. Suppose you're defining a property called Dint. What determines whether you use *Property Set Dint* or *Property Let Dint*?

3. For variables of each of the following types, indicate whether you would use *Set* to set the variable's value and indicate whether you could use *New* to create new instances of the type. Assume frmA1 is the name of a form and that Torus is the name of a class.

TYPE	USE SET?	USE NEW?
Integer		
Label		
Control		
Torus		
Form		
frmA1		

4. The *Simple* class has a *Boolean* property called Happy that can be True or False. The Simple class has a *Howdy* method that returns the string "Howdy! It's a wonderful day!" if the Happy property is True, and returns the string "Lo. See ya later." if the Happy property is False.

a. Describe the steps you would go through to create the *Simple* class.
b. Show the code you would write to define the *Simple* class.
c. Show sample code for creating a *Simple* object.

5. When is the *Class_Initialize* event triggered?

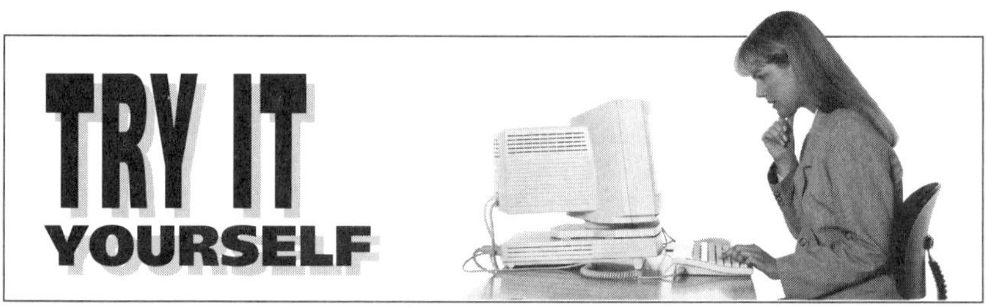

1. Create a form with an InvisibleInk property. When the property is True, the form's ForeColor is set to the form's BackColor property. When the property is False, the form's ForeColor property is set to its original value. Use the *Print* method to write some text on the form and use a check box to toggle the InvisibleInk property.

2. Create and test a BankAccount class along the lines discussed in this lesson.

MODULE 1

USING THE WINDOWS API

The beauty of Visual Basic is that it makes Windows programming easy. You tell Visual Basic you want a text window or a command button, and you get one, with Visual Basic taking care of all the messy details. Visual Basic lets you be the creative talent while it does the grunt work. However, Visual Basic does not encompass every possibility for Windows programming. (Doing so would make Visual Basic prodigiously large and cumbersome.) For example, suppose you want to rotate text or place an icon in a menu. Windows is capable of supporting such desires, while Visual Basic isn't, at least not directly. But, as a Visual Basic programmer, you have an incredible source of Windows power into which you

can tap—the *Windows Application Programming Interface* (API). The API is the collection of procedures and functions used as the building blocks for Windows applications. The Windows support built in to Visual Basic uses a subset of the API, but, with a little extra effort, you can use the whole thing.

In this module, you'll learn about the following:

- **What the Windows API is**
- **API libraries**
- **16-bit and 32-bit APIs**
- **How to use the API**
- **Some Windows programming concepts, such as device contexts**

THE HOW AND WHY OF THE API

The API consists of a large collection of functions and procedures that can be used to write Windows programs. You can call upon these functions from a variety of programming languages, including C, C++, Pascal, assembly, and Visual Basic. In layperson's terms, the Windows API is a pretty cool idea. Here are some benefits of the API:

- Provides a standard interface for users
- Saves duplication of effort
- Saves duplication of resources
- Provides a device-independent way of programming
- Provides added modularity

Let's look at these virtues.

A Standard Interface

One of Windows' selling points is that Windows programs have a common interface, making them easier to learn. A typical Windows program will have a file menu with selections like New and Open. When you use the menu to open a file, you'll typically see a dialog box that helps you navigate through the directory and file system. There are standard ways to close a window, to minimize a window, to resize a window, and so on. Typically, a program menu will have a Help heading, which accesses help files in a standard format. In addition to the standard user interface, there is a program's interface with the Windows operating system. Each program has to negotiate with Windows for resources, such as memory. Windows provides a standard toolbox of functions that access and manipulate resources. The API thus helps define a common user and system interface, supplying a common look and feel to Windows programs.

Saving Duplication of Effort

Suppose every Windows programmer had to start from scratch, designing code to show windows, exchange data, display menus, minimize a window, and do all the other things Windows programs commonly do. You'd wind up with dozens or hundreds of versions of common features and a colossal expenditure of time and effort. And the chances are that many of the versions would have bugs of some sort. But because the API already provides the basic features needed for a Windows program, Windows programmers can use the API instead and concentrate on higher-level design matters.

Save Duplication of Resources

If you have moved from DOS to Windows, you've probably noticed that Windows programs require more disk space to hold them and memory to run them. In part that's because a graphical interface such as Windows requires a lot more code than a simple text interface. The API helps keep the situation from being even worse by letting applications share API code. This code, which is already compiled, is kept separately in files called *dynamic link libraries* rather than in the programs that use the API. These library files have an *.EXE* (less common) or *.DLL* (most often) suffix and are found in the System subdirectory of the *Windows* directory. Each dynamic link library has a particular theme. For example, the *Gd32.dll* file is the Graphic Device Interface library for Windows 95 and has functions pertaining to screen and printer graphics. (Many Windows programs come with additional *.DLL* files, which may be located in other directories.)

When a program uses an API function, it goes to the appropriate dynamic link library, finds the function it needs, then executes the code in the library. One dynamic link library can provide a set of common services to all the Windows programs on your system, including Windows itself. Therefore you wind up with just one copy of that code, instead of 10 or 20 copies, one for each application. Sharing resources reduces the amount of disk space and memory that your Windows system would otherwise need.

Device-Independent Programming

Suppose a program wants to draw a window or other graphics element on your display screen. Eventually, this involves sending instructions to your computer's video card. There are a lot of video card designs as well as many video modes, such as 640x480 pixels (256 colors), 800x600 pixels (65,536 colors), and so on. This means that the same act (drawing a window, say) involves issuing different instructions for different combinations of video cards and video modes. The Windows API relieves application programmers from having to deal with all those possibilities. Instead, the API provides functions to perform specific acts, such as drawing a border around a region, drawing the cursor, or creating a window. The API calls you use are independent of the device you're drawing to, hence the expression device-independent.

Of course, at some point those device-independent commands have to lead to device-dependent commands to do the actual work. That's the responsibility of a special class of programs called *device drivers*. A device driver translates the device-independent language of the API to the device-dependent language of a particular video card or printer. The Windows setup program configures Windows to use the device drivers appropriate to your machine. Microsoft provides a large number of device drivers with Windows, and it also lets you install third-party device drivers.

This approach makes life easier for programmers all around. Application programmers don't have to worry about providing alternative code for different devices. Device makers don't have to worry about persuading various software companies to provide support for a new device; all they have to do is provide a Windows device driver based on the Windows API.

Added Modularity

By now you are familiar with the advantages of making programs modular. Modular programs are easier to understand, easier to fix, and easier to modify. Suppose, for example, that Microsoft programmers find a way to improve performance of a window-drawing routine. They can change the coding of an API while keeping the API interface unchanged. Then programs using the API will work better without any modification! Or suppose Microsoft wants to change the appearance of the standard windows, as they did in moving from Windows 3.1 to Windows 95. They can change the behavior of the standard API functions. A Windows program running under Windows 3.1 will display the old window design, and the identical program running under Windows 95 will show the new design.

In principle, the modular API approach can make programs more portable. Windows NT, for example, runs on several different hardware platforms. Vendors can write programs using the Windows NT API. Each platform would have its own version of the API, which would translate the standard API calls to the machine language of that platform.

API COMPLICATIONS

The API has been discussed as if there were just one of them. Unfortunately, that's not the case. Windows 3.1 is a 16-bit operating system, and it uses 16-bit APIs. Here 16-bit refers to the code model used for programs. The 8088 and 80286 processors used in earlier PCs can process code in 16-bit chunks. The 80386, 80486, and Pentium processors can process code in 32-bit chunks. Also, the newer processors can access more memory. In short, a 16-bit operating system keeps these processors from working at their full potential. Windows NT taps that potential and uses 32-bit code. Its API is similar to the Windows 3.1 API, but it assumes programs are 32-bit programs.

Windows 95 straddles the issue. It is a 32-bit operating system, but it retains the ability to run 16-bit programs. As a result, it has a 16-bit API and a 32-bit API. Usually, the API functions are similar, sometimes even identical, but there can be differences. In the context of Visual Basic, that means a project using API calls may have to be coded one way for 16-bit Visual Basic and slightly differently for 32-bit Visual Basic. However, this lesson will show you how to put together a program that will run under either Visual Basic version.

What Do You Have?

The Standard Edition of Visual Basic 4 is a 32-bit version. It runs under Windows 95 and Windows NT 3.51. If you use Make EXE to create a standalone executable file, it will run under Windows 95 and Windows NT 3.51. The Professional and Enterprise editions of Visual Basic 4 provide a 32-bit version and a 16-bit version. The 32-bit version has the same system requirements and capabilities as the Standard version. The 16-bit version can run under Windows 95, Windows NT 3.51, or Windows 3.1 and produces applications that can run in these three environments.

USING THE API

Before using an API function, you have to know its name, the dynamic link library file it's in, and how it works. You'll meet a few API functions as you go along, but this module won't attempt to survey them all. (Even a pithy summary of all the API functions would fill a large book.) Instead, let's concentrate on how to use them.

More About APIs

This module will introduce you to the Windows API. The Waite Group Press offers several books taking you deeper into the world of API. For instance, you can read *Windows 95 WIN32 Programming API Bible* by Simon, Gouker, and Barnes; *Windows 95 Database & Controls API Bible* by Simon; and *Windows 95 Multimedia & Networking API Bible* by Simon. *Visual Basic 4 How-To* by Thomas, et.al. presents many API examples in a Visual Basic context.

Using an API function in Visual Basic is a two-step process. First, you have to declare the function, indicating where to find the function and what arguments it takes. You may also have to define one or more user-defined types used by the function. Second, you call the function just as you would a built-in Visual Basic function.

To show how this works, let's try out a simple API function called *GetDriveType*. You tell *GetDriveType* which drive to look at, and it tells you what kind it is—removable media, fixed hard drive, and so on. You'll see the 16-bit version first, then the 32-bit version, then how to combine the two versions. The reason for beginning with the 16-bit version is that it is simpler; the 32-bit version adds an extra twist. If you're only interested in the 32-bit version, skim through the 16-bit section anyway for the ideas introduced there.

GetDriveType—Take 1 (16-bit)

The *GetDriveType* API function is part of the *Kernel.exe* dynamic link library. The Windows 3.1 SDK (Software Development Kit) documentation describes *GetDriveType* this way:

```
UINT GetDriveType(DriveNumber)
int DriveNumber;/* 0 = A, 1 = B, and so on*/
```

This is an old C-style function declaration. The *UINT* (for unsigned integer) is the function return type, *GetDriveType* is the function name, and *DriveNumber* is a type *int* (for integer) argument.

This looks a bit more familiar if you write the same information in the usual Visual Basic syntax for writing functions:

```
Function GetDriveType(ByVal DriveNumber As Integer) As Integer
```

Here *Integer*, the Visual Basic equivalent, replaces *UINT* and *int*. Figure M1-1 shows the logic behind this translation.

Using ByVal

C, the language used to develop the API, passes arguments by value, while Visual Basic, by default, passes arguments by reference. Therefore, to have Visual Basic pass information to an API function correctly, you normally have to use the *ByVal* keyword. However, C can pass *pointers* (addresses of variables), which corresponds to passing by reference. In that case (unless the API argument is a pointer to a string), omit *ByVal*.

To use *GetDriveType* in a Visual Basic program, you use a *Declare* statement. This statement combines a Visual Basic style description of the function with information about where to find this particular API function:

```
Declare Function GetDriveType Lib "kernel" (ByVal DriveNumber As Integer) _
          As Integer
```

The *Lib "kernel"* part tells Visual Basic that it will find the *GetDriveType* function in the *Kernel.exe* dynamic link library.

Where do you place this declaration? You can place it in a form module. In that case, you must preface it with the keyword *Private*, and the function can only be used in that module. Usually, however, API declarations are placed in a code module (.BAS extension) where they are, by default, public. Then all modules in the project can use the API function.

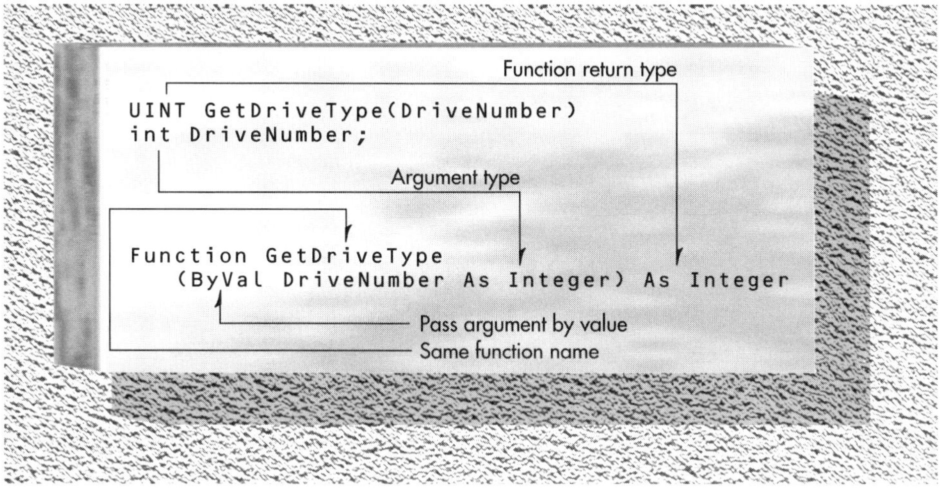

Figure M1-1 Translating a C declaration to Visual Basic

Once you've placed the declaration, you can use *GetDriveType* like any other Visual Basic function. Of course, it helps if you know what the function does. The SDK documentation reveals the following:

- You pass *GetDriveType* an integer representing the drive you wish to inquire about. The value 0 is drive A, 1 is drive B, and so on.
- *GetDriveType* returns *DRIVE_REMOVABLE* if the disk can be removed from the drive, *DRIVE_FIXED* if the disk cannot be removed, *DRIVE_REMOTE* if the drive is a remote, or network, drive, and 0 otherwise.

DRIVE_FIXED and pals are symbolic constants. Further research reveals that *DRIVE_REMOVABLE* is 2, *DRIVE_FIXED* is 3, and *DRIVE_REMOTE* is 4. These constants are defined in a C header file for use in C programs. You can define them manually in Visual Basic.

It's time to try an example. First, start a new project. Insert a code module and add the code shown in Listing M1-1. It defines some global constants and declares the *GetDriveType* function.

Listing M1-1
The code module (16-bit) for the Drive Types project

```
Option Explicit
' Define API constants.
Public Const DONT_KNOW = 0
Public Const DRIVE_REMOVABLE = 2
Public Const DRIVE_FIXED = 3
Public Const DRIVE_REMOTE = 4
```

continued on next page

continued from previous page

```
' Declare the API function.
Declare Function GetDriveType Lib "kernel" (ByVal DriveNumber As Integer) _
    As Integer
```

Tip

Place API declarations and constants in a code module, and make the constants *Public*. Then all the modules in the project can use the API functions and constants.

Getting all this information (declarations and constants) correct may seem like a difficult process, and it is. Visual Basic offers a supporting program called API Text Viewer that greatly simplifies the process, and you'll get to it later. But you wouldn't fully appreciate it if you didn't do things the hard way first.

Next, go back to the form module and endow it with the properties described in Table M1-1 and illustrated in Figure M1-2. One text box is for entering the drive label, and one is for reporting the drive type. The particular format for the drive label (C:\) will be compatible with the 16-bit and the 32-bit versions of this program.

OBJECT	PROPERTY	SETTING
Form1	Caption	Drive Types
	Name	frmDrivesType
Text1	Name	txtInput
	Text	"C:\"
Text2	Locked	True
	Name	txtOutput
	Text	
Label1	Caption	Drive Directory (i.e., C:\, etc.)
	Name	lblInput
Command1	Caption	Drive Type
	Name	cmdType

Table M1-1 The Drive Types form

Figure M1-2 The Drive Types project

To make the program work, you have to get the drive number from the drive letter. You can do this, for example:

```
DriveID = Asc(UCase(txtInput.Text)) - Asc("A")
```

The *UCase* function converts the input string to uppercase, and the *Asc* function returns the ASCII code value for the first letter in the string. Subtracting the ASCII code for the letter A then gives a value of 0 if the original string begins with an A, 1 if it begins with a B, and so on.

Next, you can pass the drive number as an argument to the *GetDriveType* function. Then you can use the return value with a *Select Case* statement to identify the drive type. Listing M1-2 shows the complete code. Note that it uses *GetDriveType* as it would any other Visual Basic function.

Listing M1-2
The Drive Types form (16-bit)

```
Option Explicit

Private Sub cmdType_Click()
    Dim DriveID As Integer
    Dim DriveType As Integer
    DriveID = Asc(UCase(txtInput.Text)) - Asc("A")
    DriveType = GetDriveType(DriveID)  ' Call the API function.
    Select Case DriveType
        Case DONT_KNOW
            txtOutput.Text = "Can't tell the drive type"
        Case DRIVE_REMOVABLE
            txtOutput.Text = "Removable-media drive"
        Case DRIVE_FIXED
             txtOutput.Text = "Fixed hard drive"
        Case DRIVE_REMOTE
            txtOutput.Text = "Remote network drive"
        Case Else
             txtOutput.Text = "Duh!"
      End Select
End Sub
```

Run this program using the 16-bit version of Visual Basic, and you'll be able to check out your drive types.

GetDriveType—Take 2 (32-bit)

If you try running the same program using the 32-bit version of Visual Basic, you'll have problems. That's because the 32-bit version of Visual Basic works with 32-bit DLLs, but not with 16-bit DLLs. So you have to look at the 32-bit definition of *GetDriveType*. The 32-bit API documentation looks a bit different. First, it declares *GetDriveType* this way:

```
UINT GetDriveType(
LPCTSTR  lpszRootPathName   // address of root path
   );
```

One change is cosmetic. This declaration uses the new C style for declaring functions instead of the old style. The new style places both the type and the variable name inside the parentheses. The old style would have looked like this:

```
UINT GetDriveType(lpszRootPathName)
LPCTSTR  lpszRootPathName;  // address of root path
```

The second change is significant. The function argument no longer is an integer. Instead, it is type LPCTSTR (long pointer to a C-type string). That certainly doesn't sound like any Visual Basic type! But it translates to passing a Visual Basic string by value. Thus, the corresponding Visual Basic description would be this:

```
Function GetDriveType (ByVal DrivePath As String) As Integer
```

The argument should be the root directory of the drive. For example, instead of passing 2 as an argument to indicate drive C, you would pass the string "C:\" as the argument. (The name of the variable is up to you; here the shorter *DrivePath* was chosen over *lpszRootPathName*.)

There's new information about return values, too. In addition to the previous choices, you now have *DRIVE_CDROM* (or 5) representing a CD-ROM player, *DRIVE_RAMDISK* (or 6) representing a ram disk, and 1 (no symbolic constant) representing a malformed directory path.

One more difference is that the 32-bit dynamic link library file is named *Kernel32.dll* instead of *Kernel.exe*.

Complications

Having this information at your disposal, you would conclude that the 32-bit declaration should look like this:

```
Declare Function GetDriveType Lib "kernel32" (ByVal DrivePath _
      As String) As Integer
```

Wrong! There is one more complication. The 32-bit API recognizes two kinds of strings. *ASCII strings* consist of 1-byte ASCII character codes. For instance the string "Crass" would contain the 1-byte ASCII code for the C character, the 1-byte ASCII code for the r character, and so on. *Unicode strings* use a 2-byte code for each character. (The extra space accommodates more extensive characters sets, such as those used in many Asian languages.) API functions that take string arguments or have string return values come in two varieties: ASCII versions and Unicode versions. The ASCII version adds an *A* to the end of the function name, so *GetDriveType* becomes *GetDriveTypeA*. The Unicode version adds a *W* to the end, so *GetDriveType* becomes *GetDriveTypeW*.

It turns out that 32-bit Visual Basic uses Unicode strings, but it also assumes that DLLs use ASCII strings, so it automatically converts strings to ASCII strings when passing them as arguments to DLLs. Therefore, you must use the ASCII version of *GetDriveType*. You can do this a couple of ways:

```
'Method 1 - use the modified name
Declare Function GetDriveTypeA Lib "kernel32" (ByVal DrivePath _
```

```
As String) As Integer

'Method 2 - use the Alias facility
Declare Function GetDriveType Lib "kernel32" Alias "GetDriveTypeA" _
     (ByVal DrivePath As String) As Integer
```

If you use the first method, you then must use the name *GetDriveTypeA* when you call the function. The second method lets you use the name *GetDriveType* when you call the function.

The Alias Facility

The alias facility lets you establish an alternative name for a DLL function. The syntax is a little misleading in that the string following the keyword *Alias* represents the real name of the function as it's recorded in the DLL file. The name you use in Visual Basic code (the real alias) is the name following the keyword *Function* in the *Declare* statement (see Figure M1-3). There are several reasons to use the alias feature. First, some DLL functions have names that are not legal Visual Basic identifiers. For instance, a DLL name might begin with an underscore character. Second, you may want a shorter name to use, for example, substituting *SetPal* for *SetSystemPaletteUse.* Third, when 16-bit and 32-bit DLLs use different names for the same function, you may want to use just one name in your code.

Drive Types Revised

Now you can revise the Drives Type project to work under 32-bit Visual Basic. First, revamp the code module as shown in Listing M1-3. The new version defines additional constants and uses the revised *Declare* statement.

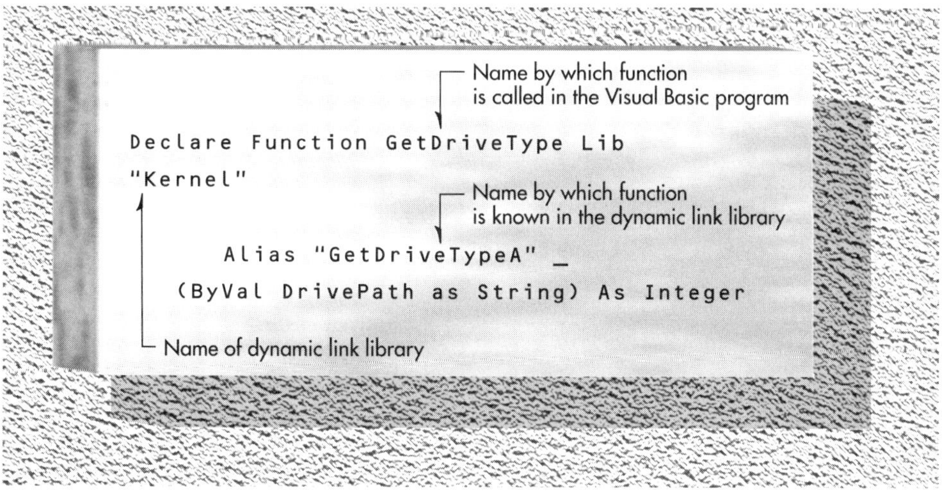

Figure M1-3 Using *Alias* in a *Declare* statement

Listing M1-3
The code module (32-bit) for the Drive Types project

```
Option Explicit
Public Const DONT_KNOW = 0
Public Const BAD_DIR_NAME = 1        '32-bit addition
Public Const DRIVE_REMOVABLE = 2
Public Const DRIVE_FIXED = 3
Public Const DRIVE_REMOTE = 4
Public Const DRIVE_CDROM = 5         ' 32-bit addition
Public Const DRIVE_RAMDISK = 6       ' 32-bit addition
'Declare 32-bit API function
Declare Function GetDriveType Lib "kernel32" Alias "GetDriveTypeA" _
    (ByVal DrivePath As String) As Integer
```

Next, revise the form module code as shown in Listing M1-4. The main change is passing the *txtInput.Text* string directly to the *GetDriveType* function instead of converting it to a number first. Second, the *Select Case* statement is expanded to include the new return value possibilities.

Listing M1-4
The Drive Types form (32-bit)

```
Option Explicit

Private Sub cmdType_Click()
    Dim DriveType As Integer
    DriveType = GetDriveType(txtInput.Text)
    Select Case DriveType
        Case DONT_KNOW
            txtOutput.Text = "Can't tell the drive type"
        Case BAD_DIR_NAME
            txtOutput.Text = "No such root directory"
        Case DRIVE_REMOVABLE
            txtOutput.Text = "Removable-media drive"
        Case DRIVE_FIXED
             txtOutput.Text = "Fixed hard drive"
        Case DRIVE_REMOTE
            txtOutput.Text = "Remote network drive"
        Case DRIVE_CDROM
            txtOutput.Text = "CD-ROM drive"
        Case DRIVE_RAMDISK
             txtOutput.Text = "RAM disk"
        Case Else
             txtOutput.Text = "Duh!"
       End Select
End Sub
```

GetDriveType—Take 3 (Conditional Compilation)

Ideally, you'd like to write Visual Basic projects that would work under both 16-bit and 32-bit versions of Visual Basic. The *GetDriveType* example presents three obstacles to overcome:

1. The 16-bit version uses the *kernel* library, while the 32-bit version uses the *kernel32* library.
2. The 16-bit version uses *GetDriveType,* while the 32-bit version uses *GetDriveTypeA.*
3. The 16-bit version uses an integer argument, while the 32-bit version uses a string argument.

Obstacle #1 (using different libraries) occurs whenever you go from the 16-bit to the 32-bit version. Obstacle #2 (different function names) occurs when string arguments or return values are involved. Obstacle #3 (different argument types) is relatively rare.

The way to hurdle these obstacles is to use *conditional compilation.* Conditional compilation is when the compiler (Visual Basic, in this case) can choose whether to compile particular statements depending upon some condition. For instance, you can ask the compiler to use one line of code for a 32-bit program and a different line of code for a 16-bit program. It looks like this:

```
#If Win32 Then
    ' place 32-bit code here
#Else
    ' place 16-bit code here
#End If
```

For example, you can do the following:

```
#If Win32 Then
    Declare Function GetDriveType Lib "kernel32" Alias _
        "GetDriveTypeA" (ByVal DrivePath As String) As Integer
#Else
    Declare Function GetDriveType Lib "kernel" _
        (ByVal DriveNumber As Integer) As Integer
#End If
```

The # prefixes identify *#If, #Else,* and *#End If* as conditional compilation directives. That means they are interpreted during *compile* time. If *Win32* is defined and nonzero, the compiler uses the first *Declare* statement; otherwise, the compiler uses the second Declare statement. (Normal *If* statements are interpreted during *run* time.)

And what is *Win32?* It's a *conditional compilation constant,* which means it's a value used by the *#If* conditional compilation mechanism. *Win32* is defined automatically by the 32-bit version of Visual Basic as being -1 (the numeric representation of True). Thus the 32-bit version of Visual Basic will use the first declaration, and the 16-bit version of Visual Basic will use the second declaration. Listing M1-5 shows how to write the code module so that it can be used with either version of Visual Basic.

Listing M1-5
The code module (universal) for the Drive Types project

```
Option Explicit
Public Const DONT_KNOW = 0
Public Const BAD_DIR_NAME = 1
```

continued on next page

continued from previous page

```
Public Const DRIVE_REMOVABLE = 2
Public Const DRIVE_FIXED = 3
Public Const DRIVE_REMOTE = 4
Public Const DRIVE_CDROM = 5
Public Const DRIVE_RAMDISK = 6
#If Win32 Then
    Public Declare Function GetDriveType Lib "kernel32" Alias _
        "GetDriveTypeA" (ByVal DrivePath As String) As Integer
#Else
    Public Declare Function GetDriveType Lib "kernel" _
        (ByVal DriveNumber As Integer) As Integer
#End If
```

Incidentally, you can use conditional compilation to solve other problems, too. If you select Options from the Tools menu and click on the Advanced tab, you'll see a text box labeled "Conditional Compilation Arguments." There you can enter conditional compilation constants that can be used by *#If* tests. You should set the name to -1 for True, 0 for False. For example, you can enter the following:

```
Blab = -1
```

Then code like

```
#If Blab Then
    Print "blah blah
#End If
```

will cause the *Print* statement to compile because *Blab* is defined as True. If you then remove the conditional compilation argument or define *Blab* as 0 (False), Visual Basic will skip that code. To create more than one conditional compilation constant, you can separate entries by a colon, as in the following:

```
Blab = -1:French=0:English=1
```

Also, you can use the *#Const* directive to create conditional constants directly in your modules:

```
#Const Verbose = -1
```

Returning to the project, you can solve the problem of two argument types by using conditional compilation in the form module, as shown in Listing M1-6. In general, you can use conditional compilation anywhere in your program.

Listing M1-6
The Drive Types form (universal)

```
Private Sub cmdType_Click()
    Dim DriveID As Integer
    Dim DriveType As Integer
    #If Win32 Then                  ' Use string argument.
        DriveType = GetDriveType(txtInput.Text)
```

```
    #Else                          ' Use integer argument.
        DriveID = Asc(UCase(txtInput.Text)) - Asc("A")
        DriveType = GetDriveType(DriveID)
    #End If
    Select Case DriveType
        Case DONT_KNOW
            txtOutput.Text = "Can't tell the drive type"
        Case BAD_DIR_NAME
            txtOutput.Text = "No such root directory"
        Case DRIVE_REMOVABLE
            txtOutput.Text = "Removable-media drive"
        Case DRIVE_FIXED
             txtOutput.Text = "Fixed hard drive"
        Case DRIVE_REMOTE
            txtOutput.Text = "Remote network drive"
        Case DRIVE_CDROM
            txtOutput.Text = "CD-ROM drive"
        Case DRIVE_RAMDISK
             txtOutput.Text = "RAM disk"
        Case Else
             txtOutput.Text = "Duh!"
      End Select
End Sub
```

There's one final step you may need to take. Select References from the Tools menu. If you see DAO 3.0 Library or DAO 2.5 Library checked, uncheck it. (DAO stands for Data Access Object.) The 32-bit version of Visual Basic automatically includes the first, and the 16-bit automatically includes the second. Neither is needed for this project, and including them can cause compatibility problems.

Some API Guidelines

Let's take a more general look at using Windows API functions. First, you need access to descriptions of the API functions so that you know what arguments they take, what values they return, and what they do. You also may need to know about defined constants and user-defined types used with a particular API function. You may have this information available in the form of a Windows help file, or you may have to obtain a book on the subject.

Once you identify an API function you wish to use, you have to use a *Declare* statement to make the function available to a Visual Basic program. If you place the *Declare* statement in a form module or class module, you must also use the keyword *Private*. The function you declare then can be used only in that module. Typically, however, you would place the *Declare* statement in a code module, making the function available to all modules in your program.

The *Declare* statement identifies the function name, indicates the API DLL file containing the function, specifies argument types, and specifies the function's return type. The fundamental syntax is this:

Declare Function | **Sub** *NameInProgram* **Lib** *"dllfile"* [**Alias** *"NameInFile"*] (*argument-list*)
[**As** *Type*]

If the API function has a return value, you use the keyword *Function* and the As *Type* portion, substituting the actual return type for *Type*. If the API function has no return value, use the keyword Sub and omit the As Type portion. API functions with no return type are prefixed with the C keyword void, as in the following:

```
void AnsiToOem(const char_huge *hpszWindows, char_huge *hpszOem);
```

And what type is *char_huge*? Don't worry, you'll take care of those details soon enough.

The keyword *Lib* precedes the name of the dynamic link library containing the function. For Windows API libraries, you just use the library name, as in "*Kernel*" and "*Kernel32*". However, you can use Declare with non-API dynamic link libraries, too. In that case, you use the complete file name, as in "*Mylib.dll*". In general, Visual Basic will search for a library in the current default directory, then in the *Windows* directory, then in the *Windows\System* subdirectory. You can use a path name for libraries in other locations, as in "*d:\tribbles\trouble.dll*".

Use *Alias* when the name in your program is different from the name in the library. In that case, the string following *Alias* represents the library name and the name after *Function* or *Sub* represents the name in your program.

API Types

API documentation describes types in a blend of fundamental C types, such as *int;* derived C types defined for the API, such as *UINT* and LPCTSTR; and C structures, which correspond to Visual Basic user-defined types. Table M1-2 summarizes some common type translations. Unfortunately, there is no one-to-one correspondence between API types and Visual Basic types. All the subtleties won't be discussed because the API Text Viewer (discussed shortly) will take care of them for you.

C-API DESCRIPTION	VISUAL BASIC ARGUMENT DECLARATION	CAUTIONS
Boolean x	ByVal x As Boolean	
int x, UINT x, WORD x	ByVal x As Integer	
long x, DWORD x	ByVal x As Long	
hWnd x, hDC x, hMenu x	ByVal x As Integer (16-bit)	
	ByVal x As Long (32-bit)	
LPSTR x, LPCTSTR x	ByVal x As String	
Pointer to a structure, such as:		
RECT * x	x As RECT	You must also define RECT
int * x, LPINT x	x As Integer	
void * x	x As Any	If passing a string S, pass ByVal S

C-API DESCRIPTION	VISUAL BASIC ARGUMENT DECLARATION	CAUTIONS
char * x	x As Byte	
Pointer to an array of integers:		
int X[]	X As Integer	Pass first element of array A, as in A[0]

Table M1-2 Some common argument type translations

API Libraries

The bulk of the API interface is found in three libraries. The Kernel library (*Kernel.exe* and *Kernel32.dll*) contains basic stuff such as functions for loading and executing programs, managing memory, and managing other resources. The User library (*User.exe* and *User32.dll*) contains functions managing features of the user interface, such as windows. The GDI (*Gdi.exe* and *Gdi32.dll*) is the graphics device interface and handles graphics. Unfortunately, the standard documentation of the API functions doesn't identify the relevant API module in the section that describes each function. Instead, you have to find that information in an appendix. However, you're probably better off using the shortcut described next.

The Easy Way

Getting all the types right can be difficult. The easy way to get the correct *Declare* statement is to use the *Win31api.txt* and *Win32api.txt* files that come with the 16-bit and 32-bit versions of Visual Basic. The *Win31api.txt* file contains Visual Basic *Declare* statements for the Windows 3.1 API, and the *Win32api.txt* file contains Visual Basic *Declare* statements for the Windows 32-bit API. You can use a text editor to open these files, copy declarations, and paste them into your Visual Basic application. Or you can use the API Text Viewer that comes with Visual Basic to search, copy, and paste declarations. These declarations will serve for most cases, but there are a few cases for which you'll need more information.

Figure M1-4 shows the Text API Viewer after the File menu has been used to open the *Win32api.txt* file. The drop-down list box labeled "API Type" gives you a choice of listing constants, declarations, or types. The Available Items list box lists all the choices for a given category. As shown in the figure, it lists all the API functions by name. By selecting a function name and clicking on the Add button (or double-clicking the name), you add the function name to the bottom list box, the one labeled Selected Items. You then can use the Copy button to copy the corresponding declaration to the Windows Clipboard, then paste the declaration into a Visual Basic Code window.

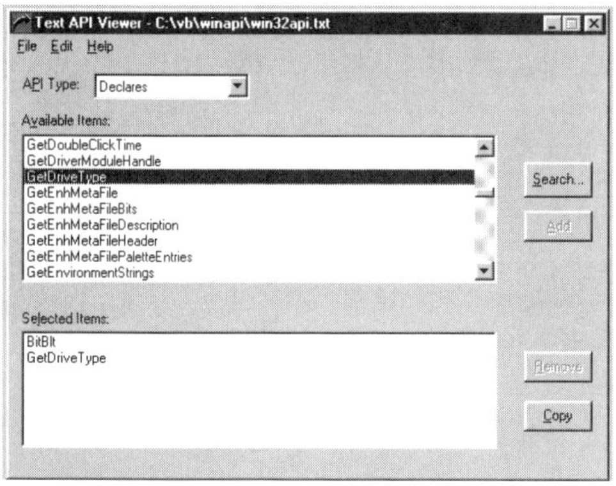

Figure M1-4 The Text API Viewer

API Constants

Many API functions, like *GetDriveType*, are described in terms of symbolic constants. Unfortunately, the documentation usually fails to specify the value of the constants. For instance, the *GetDriveType* documentation says the function returns *DRIVE_FIXED* for a nonremovable hard drive, but it doesn't say that this constant has the numeric value 3. For C programmers, this lack of information is no problem. They merely use *DRIVE_FIXED* in their code and let the compiler obtain the numeric information from special files called *header files*. Visual Basic doesn't use the C header files, so you have to either use the numeric value 3 or else define *DRIVE_FIXED* to be 3. The problem is, how do you know that the value is 3? The hard way to answer that question is to obtain copies of the C header files and search them for the correct definitions. The easy way is to use *Win31api.txt* and *Win32api.txt* files. In addition to containing *Declare* statements, they also define all the constants (using Visual Basic *Const* statements) used by the two APIs. Again, you can use a text editor or the API Text Viewer to locate, copy, and paste constant definitions.

API Structures

Many API functions use C structures as arguments or return values. A C structure corresponds to a Visual Basic user-defined type—one structure can hold several items of data of differing types. If an API uses a particular structure, your program needs to define the equivalent Visual Basic type. For example, several API functions use a *RECT* structure defined in C as follows:

```
typedef struct tagRect {
    int left;
    int top;
    int right;
    int bottom;
} RECT;
```

Your program would then have to define a type called *RECT* as follows:

```
Type RECT
    Left As Integer
    Top As Integer
    Right As Integer
    Bottom As Integer
End Type
```

Once again you can turn to the *Win31api.txt* and *Win32api.txt* files for help, for they contain Visual Basic Type definitions for the various structures used by the APIs.

EXPLORING THE API

The API lets you stretch the boundaries of Visual Basic. Let's look at two examples illustrating some of the things you can do. Noel Jerke kindly made these examples available for this book; you can glean more from his book *Visual Basic 4.0 Multimedia How-To.* The programs also illustrate some of the concepts used in Windows programming. You won't learn all about Windows programming, but you may see enough to appreciate how much Visual Basic does for you!

Spinning Text

The first example displays rotated text. It uses four API functions:

- VB *CreateFontIndirect* creates a logical font based on information provided by a LOGFONT structure argument.
- VB *SelectObject* selects an object into a given device context; for example, making a particular font object the selected font for a particular text box or picture box.
- VB *DeleteObject* deletes an object from memory, freeing the resources it used.
- VB *TextOut* writes a character string at a specified location in a particular device context using the currently selected font.

There are some new concepts here to explore. A *logical font* is a font description. It specifies things like the character height, character width, type style (Bold, Italic, and so on) and the name of the font. It may not be the actual font used. For instance, you might specify a logical font for printing that isn't supported by the printing device. In such cases, Windows tries to substitute the closest matching available font to the logical font.

A *device context* (DC, for short) is an abstract interface between a Windows application and an output device, such as a screen display or a printer. A device context holds information about the output device, such as the background color, text color, font, dimensions, and so on. A program printing text on the screen, for example, will use a device context associated with the screen. Windows identifies each device context with an integer value called a *handle*. In Visual Basic, the Printer object, each form, and each picture box has an associated device context. When you change the BackColor property for a form, for instance, you change the background color for the device context. These three kinds of objects (Printer object, forms, and picture boxes) have an hDC property, which is the handle for the associated device context. Many API calls require a device context handle to identify where a particular action takes place. For example, if you use the *TextOut* API function to display text in a picture box, you have to pass the picture box's handle (its hDC property) to the function. As you open and close various windows while in Windows, the value of the hDC property can change, so don't bother storing it for reuse.

By the way, handles are a common Windows technique for referring to objects of various kinds. Basically, a handle is a numeric index to a table of addresses of objects. So a handle of 4 would mean find the fourth address in a table and look for the object stored at that address. You can have handles for windows, logical fonts, device contexts, and so on.

Now let's talk about the design of the forthcoming example. Suppose you want to display text using a particular font in a picture box called *SpinPict*. The Visual Basic way would be to set the *SpinPict* font properties to the desired values and to use *SpinPict.Print* to display the desired text.

The API approach is more involved, but it also opens more possibilities. First, you can use *CreateFontIndirect* to create a logical font. At this point, you have a font description, but you have not yet given it a context. Also, the return value from *CreateFontIndirect* is a handle for the font.

Next, you call the *SelectObject* API function, which selects an object into a device context. What does that mean? Well, suppose *hFont* is a handle for the logical font you just created and *SpinPict.hDC* is the handle for the device context associated with the *SpinPict* picture box. Then the API call

```
SelectObject(SpinPict.hDC, hFont)
```

makes your logical font the current font for the picture box. In short, using *CreateFontIndirect* and *SelectObject* in this manner is equivalent to setting *SpinPict* font properties.

Then, to print a string in the text box, you can use *TextOut*. This function takes five arguments. The first is the handle of the device context in which the text is to appear, the second and third arguments are the *X*- and *Y*- coordinates where printing starts, the fourth is the string to be printed, and the fifth is the number of bytes in the string. *TextOut* uses the currently selected font.

Finally, when you're finished printing, you use *DeleteObject* to delete the font object. This function takes the font handle as its argument.

As you can see, this is much more involved than setting *SpinPict* properties and using *SpinPict.Print*. So why use the API functions instead? The answer is that the logical font object has more properties (*attributes* in the usual API terminology) than Visual Basic provides for fonts. In particular, there is an *escapement* attribute that describes the angle, in units of a tenth of a degree, between a line parallel to the base of the text and the horizontal x-axis. For instance, if you set this attribute to 300, the font will print at an angle of 30^0 from the horizontal. This fact lies at the core of the example. It uses the timer control to print a string 20 times. Each cycle the program creates a new font that is identical to the previous font except that the escapement attribute is increased by 180 (18^0), creating the appearance of spinning text.

To create this example, create a form with the properties described in Table M1-3.

OBJECT	PROPERTY	SETTING
Form1	Caption	Spinning Text Example
	Name	SpinExample
Picture1	Height	6270
	Name	SpinPict
	Width	8040
Timer1	Enabled	False
	Interval	10
	Name	Timer1

Table M1-3 The Spinning Text form

Next, insert a code module and add the code shown in Listing M1-7. Note that it defines the LOGFONT structure as well as declaring the four API functions used.

Listing M1-7
Spinning Text code module

```
'  The following type declaration describes the
'  Windows API LOGFONT structure.  THE LOGFONT
'  structure is used by several of the WIN API
'  text functions.

#If Win32 Then ' If 32-bit Windows, use this Declare.

Type LOGFONT
    lfHeight As Long
    lfWidth As Long
    lfEscapement As Long
    lfOrientation As Long
    lfWeight As Long
    lfItalic As String * 1
    lfUnderline As String * 1
    lfStrikeOut As String * 1
    lfCharSet As String * 1
    lfOutPrecision As String * 1
    lfClipPrecision As String * 1
```

continued on next page

continued from previous page

```
     lfQuality As String * 1
     lfPitchAndFamily As String * 1
     lfFaceName As String * 24
End Type


'  Declare the Windows API DeleteObject function.
Declare Function DeleteObject Lib "GDI32" (ByVal hObject As Integer) _
     As Integer

'  Declare the Windows API CreateFontIndirect function.
Declare Function CreateFontIndirect Lib "GDI32" Alias "CreateFontIndirectA" _
     (lpLogFont As LOGFONT) As Long

'  Declare the Windows API SelectObject function.
Declare Function SelectObject Lib "GDI32" (ByVal hDC As Integer, _
     ByVal hObject As Integer) As Integer

'  Declare the Windows API TextOut function.
Declare Function TextOut Lib "GDI32" Alias "TextOutA" (ByVal hDC As Long, _
     ByVal X As Long, ByVal Y As Long, ByVal lpString As String, _
     ByVal nCount As Long) As Long

#Else   ' If 16-bit Windows, use this Declare.

Type LOGFONT
     lfHeight As Integer
     lfWidth As Integer
     lfEscapement As Integer
     lfOrientation As Integer
     lfWeight As Integer
     lfItalic As String * 1
     lfUnderline As String * 1
     lfStrikeOut As String * 1
     lfCharSet As String * 1
     lfOutPrecision As String * 1
     lfClipPrecision As String * 1
     lfQuality As String * 1
     lfPitchAndFamily As String * 1
     lfFaceName As String * 24
End Type

'  Declare the Windows API DeleteObject function.
Declare Function DeleteObject Lib "GDI" (ByVal hObject As Integer) As
     Integer

'  Declare the Windows API CreateFontIndirect function.
Declare Function CreateFontIndirect Lib "GDI" (lpLogFont As LOGFONT) _
     As Integer

'  Declare the Windows API SelectObject function.
Declare Function SelectObject Lib "GDI" (ByVal hDC As Integer, _
     ByVal hObject As Integer) As Integer

'  Declare the Windows API TextOut function.
Declare Function TextOut Lib "GDI" (ByVal hDC As Integer, _
     ByVal X As Integer, ByVal Y As Integer, ByVal lpString As String, _
     ByVal nCount As Integer) As Integer

#End If
```

Next, add the code shown in Listing M1-8 to the form module. The CFONT variable is a LOGFONT structure and holds the information describing the font. If you don't have Arial on your system, substitute another scaleable font. Figure M1-5 shows the program in operation.

Listing M1-8
Spinning Text form module

```
Option Explicit
'  CFONT will be our font structure for the text.
Dim CFONT As LOGFONT

'  ESCAPE will hold the current ESCAPEMENT of the
'  displayed font.
Dim escape As Integer

'  ChangeX and ChangeY will hold the increment to move
'  the text to the upperleft corner.
Dim ChangeX As Integer
Dim ChangeY As Integer

Private Sub FontOut(Text$, Pict As Control, xx As Long, yy As Long, _
      FontStruct As LOGFONT)
Dim NewFont As Long
Dim OldFont As Long
Dim Throw As Long   'for return value not used here
'  Create the new font.
NewFont = CreateFontIndirect(FontStruct)

'  Select the new font into the picture
'  device context.
OldFont = SelectObject(Pict.hDC, NewFont)

'  Display the text.
Throw = TextOut(Pict.hDC, xx, yy, Text$, Len(Text$))

'  Select the font back for the original device context.
Throw = SelectObject(Pict.hDC, OldFont)

'  Delete the newly created font.
Throw = DeleteObject(NewFont)

End Sub

Private Sub Form_Load()

'  Move the picture to the origin of the form.
SpinPict.Move 0, 0

'  Set the scalemode to 3 (pixels) for the picture.
SpinPict.ScaleMode = 3

'  Set the form to be the same size as the picture.
SpinExample.Width = SpinPict.Width
SpinExample.Height = SpinPict.Height

'  Set up the initial font structure.  We will
```

continued on next page

continued from previous page

```
'   use a height of 30 and a width of 10.  The
'   weight will be medium (non-bold), and we will
'   use Arial.
CFONT.lfHeight = 30
CFONT.lfWidth = 10
CFONT.lfEscapement = 0
CFONT.lfWeight = 400
CFONT.lfItalic = Chr$(0)
CFONT.lfUnderline = Chr$(0)
CFONT.lfStrikeOut = Chr$(0)
CFONT.lfOutPrecision = Chr$(0)
CFONT.lfClipPrecision = Chr$(0)
CFONT.lfQuality = Chr$(0)
CFONT.lfPitchAndFamily = Chr$(0)
CFONT.lfCharSet = Chr$(0)
CFONT.lfFaceName = "Arial" + Chr$(0)


'   Locate the currentx and currenty for the first text display.
SpinPict.CurrentX = (SpinPict.ScaleWidth -
SpinPict.TextWidth("Introducing...")) / 2
SpinPict.CurrentY = (SpinPict.ScaleHeight -
SpinPict.TextHeight("Introducing...")) / 2

'   Caclulate the changes for 20 moves of "Introducing..." to the upper
    corner.
ChangeX = SpinPict.CurrentX / 20
ChangeY = SpinPict.CurrentY / 20

'   Start timer1.
timer1.Enabled = True

SpinPict.ForeColor = RGB(255, 0, 0)

End Sub

'Private Sub SpinPict_Paint()
     'timer1.Enabled = True
'End Sub

Private Sub Timer1_Timer()
Dim X As Long, Y As Long
'   Set the new escapement
CFONT.lfEscapement = CFONT.lfEscapement + 180

'   Calculate the center of the text.
X = (SpinPict.ScaleWidth - SpinPict.TextWidth("Spinning - Spinning")) / 2
Y = (SpinPict.ScaleHeight - SpinPict.TextHeight("Spinning - Spinning")) / 2

'   turn off after 360 degrees rotation.
If CFONT.lfEscapement = 3600 Then
     '   Turn off timer1.
     timer1.Enabled = False
End If

'   Call the FontOut procedure to display the text.
FontOut "Spinning - Spinning", SpinPict, X, Y, CFONT

End Sub
```

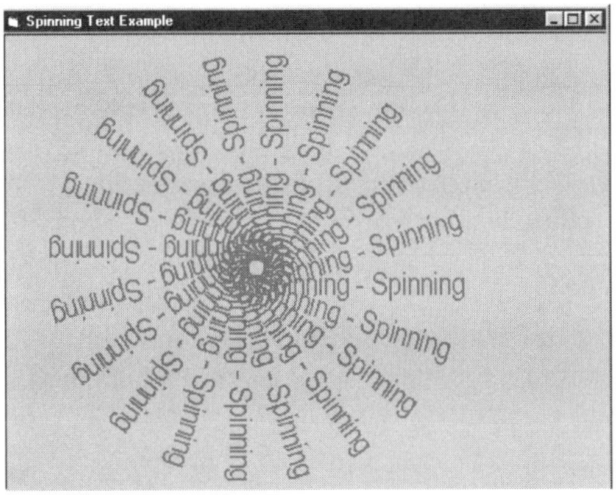

Figure M1-5 The result of running the Spinning Text example

A Transparent Bitmap Copy

The next example uses two powerful API graphics functions—*BitBlt* and *StretchBlt*. Both copy a bitmapped rectangular region from one device context to another. *BitBlt* (pronounced "bitblit" and short for bit block transfer) requires that the destination region have the same size as the source region, while *StretchBlt* allows you to copy from one region to one of a different size, stretching or shrinking the original image as necessary. These functions are part of the Graphics Device Interface (GDI) portion of the API. Here's the Visual Basic declaration (32-bit version) for *BitBlt:*

```
Declare Function BitBlt Lib "GDI32" (ByVal hDestDC As Integer, _
    ByVal x As Integer, ByVal y As Integer, ByVal nWidth As Integer, _
    ByVal nHeight As Integer, ByVal hSrcDC As Integer, ByVal XSrc As _
    Integer, ByVal YSrc As Integer, ByVal dwRop As Long) As Integer
```

Naturally, you'd like to know the meaning of all the arguments. The *hDestDC* argument is the handle for the destination device context. The *x* and *y* variables are the coordinates of the top left corner of the copied image relative to the top left corner of the context device. *nWidth* and *nHeight* are the width and height of the copied image. The *hSrcDC* argument is the handle for the source context device. Next, *XSrc* and *YSrc* are the coordinates of the top left corner of the source image in the source device context. Because the *BitBlt* doesn't change the image size, the source has the same height and width as the copy. Finally, *dwRop* is a raster operation code that describes the interaction between the source bitmap, the prior bitmap in the destination, and the destination's pattern property, which corresponds to the Visual Basic FillPattern property.

Three features make *BitBlt* very powerful. First, it is the fastest way in Windows to copy a rectangular bit pattern. Within Visual Basic, you could use the *Point* method, the *PSet* procedure, and nested *For* loops to copy an image point-by-point. That takes time. But *BitBlt* can copy the same information with a single function call.

Second, you can use source and destination device context flexibly. For instance, you could use *Form1.hDC* as both the source and destination device context handle to copy an image from one part of a form to another. Or if you have two picture boxes, picOne and picTwo, you can use the handles picTwo.hDC and picOne.hDC to copy an image from one picture box to another.

Third, the *dwRop* variable has 256 possible values describing 256 possible ways to blend the source pixels, destination pixels, and fill pattern. Many of these are represented by symbolic constants. Table M1-4 lists a few possibilities to give you an idea of what's available.

SYMBOLIC CONSTANT	DESCRIPTION
BLACKNESS	Turns all out-put black
DSTINVERT	Inverts destination bitmap
MERGECOPY	Combines source and pattern with Boolean AND operator
MERGEPAINT	Combines inverted source and pattern with Boolean OR operator
NOTSRCERASE	Combines source and destination with OR, then inverts
SRCAND	Combines source and destination pixels using Boolean AND
SRCCOPY	Copies source to the destination
SRCINVERT	Combines source and destination pixels using Boolean XOR

Table M1-4 Some ROP codes

StretchBlt is similar to *BitBlt* except that it takes two additional arguments specifying the width and height of the source rectangle. This information enables *StretchBlt* to expand or scrunch the source to fit the specified width and height of the destination region.

The project consists of a form with four picture boxes as described in Table M1-5 and pictured in Figure M1-6. Note that one small picture box contains a geometric pattern—the *Zigzag.bmp* bitmap is from the WINDOWS directory, but there's also a copy on the program disk. (Incidentally, the file is named Zigzag.bmp in Windows 3.1, but the Windows 95 version is named Zig Zag.bmp. A second picture box contains the image of a phonograph against a black background, and a third picture box contains a black-and-white mask of that image. The *Phono.bmp* and *Mask.bmp* files for these images come with this book's program disk.

OBJECT	PROPERTY	SETTING
Form1	Caption	Transparent Bitmap Copy
	Name	Transparent
Picture1	Name	BackPict
	ScaleHeight	385
	ScaleMode	3 - Pixel
	ScaleWidth	442

OBJECT	PROPERTY	SETTING
Picture2	Name	Mask
	Picture	(Bitmap) Mask.bmp
Picture3	Name	PrimaryImage
	Picture	(Bitmap) Phono..bmp
Picture4	Name	Flock
	Picture	(Bitmap) Zigzag.bmp
	ScaleMode	3 - Pixel
Command1	Caption	Click to See Transparent Picture
	Name	ClickButton

Table M1-5 The Transparent Copy form properties

The project also has a class module which defines a *TransBitBlt* class. Listings M1-9 and M1-10 show the code for the class module and the form module. Without dissecting the program in detail, let's summarize what it does.

The *Zigzag.bmp* file contains a 32 x 32 pixel geometric pattern. The form's *Paint* event uses *StretchBlt* to copy this bitmap to the *BackPict* picture box, expanding the bitmap to fit the box. This is a straight copy, so the program uses the *SRCCOPY* mode.

Next, the program uses *BitBlt* to copy the bitmap of the phonograph from the *PrimaryImage* picture box to *BackPict* transparently so that you can see the underlying Flock image through the portion of the phonograph image that is a black background. This is accomplished in two steps. First, the mask (a black-and-white copy of the phonograph image in which the background of the original is white in the mask) is copied to *BackPict* using the *SRCAND* mode. White *AND* any color is just the color, while black *AND* any color is black. So only the black parts of the mask show. Next, the program copies the phonograph image to *BackPict* using the *SRCINVERT* mode. The image *XORed* with the black parts

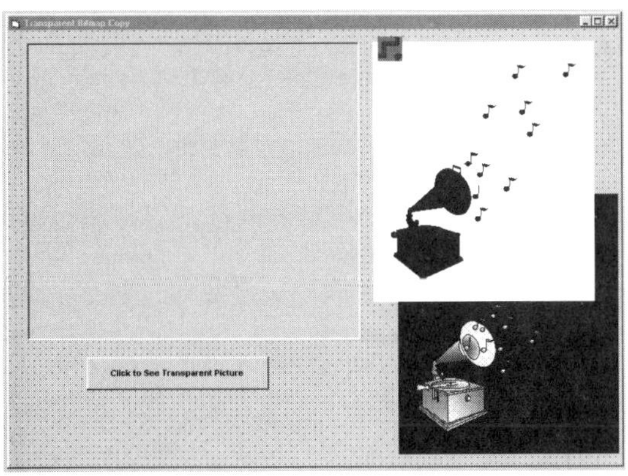

Figure M1-6 The Transparent Copy form

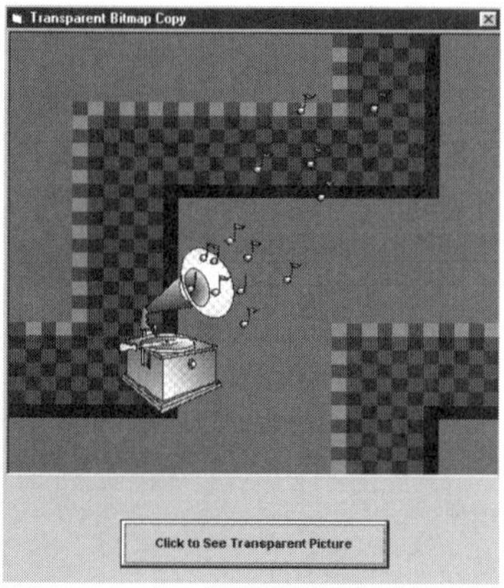

Figure M1-7 A transparent copy

of *BackPict* comes out unchanged, so you get the image of the phonograph. The black background of the phonograph picture *XOR*ed with the colored part *BackPict* leave the *BackPict* pixels unchanged, producing a transparent effect.

The transparent copy is a two-step process involving three images. The program uses a class module to handle this work, making the three images properties of the class and defining a class method (*showtrans*) to execute the two *BitBlt* commands. Figure M1-7 shows the result of running the program.

Listing M1-9
Transparent copy class module

```
Option Explicit
'  If 32-bit Windows, then these declares
'  will be used.
#If Win32 Then ' If 32-bit Windows, use this Declare.

'  BitBlt will be used to combine the mask and
'  primary image to make the transparent effect.
Private Declare Function BitBlt Lib "gdi32" (ByVal hDestDC As Integer, _
     ByVal X As Integer, ByVal Y As Integer, ByVal nWidth As Integer, _
     ByVal nHeight As Integer, ByVal hSrcDC As Integer, ByVal XSrc As _
     Integer, ByVal YSrc As Integer, ByVal dwRop As Long) As Integer

'  If 16-bit Windows, then these declares
'  will be used.
#Else

'  BitBlt will be used to combine the mask and
'  primary image to make the transparent effect.
Private Declare Function BitBlt Lib "GDI" (ByVal hDestDC As Integer, _
     ByVal X As Integer, ByVal Y As Integer, ByVal nWidth As Integer, _
     ByVal nHeight As Integer, ByVal hSrcDC As Integer, ByVal XSrc As _
     Integer, ByVal YSrc As Integer, ByVal dwRop As Long) As Integer

#End If
```

```
'  BitBlt Constants
Const SRCCOPY = &HCC0020
Const SRCAND = &H8800C6
Const SRCINVERT = &H660046

'  These are the three images
'  used in the transparent effect.
Private m_BackPict As Object
Private m_MaskPict As Object
Private m_PrimaryImg As Object

'  m_XOrgOrg and m_YOrgOrg are used to
'  place the origin of the transparent
'  image.
Private m_XOrg As Integer
Private m_YOrg As Integer

Public Property Set Background(Obj As Object)

'  Get the BackPict Picture.
Set m_BackPict = Obj

'  Ensure that the picture scalemode is Pixels.
m_BackPict.ScaleMode = 3

End Property

Public Property Set MaskPict(Obj As Object)

'  Get the Mask
Set m_MaskPict = Obj

'  Ensure the scalemode is set to pixels.
m_MaskPict.ScaleMode = 3

End Property

Public Property Set PrimaryImg(Obj As Object)

'  This is the original PrimaryImage to be transferred.
Set m_PrimaryImg = Obj

'  Ensure the scalemode is set to pixels.
m_PrimaryImg.ScaleMode = 3

End Property

Public Sub showtrans(xx As Integer, yy As Integer)
Dim Throw As Long   'for discarded return values
Dim m_XOrg As Integer, m_YOrg As Integer
'  X origin coord. to disp. picture
m_XOrg = xx

'  Y origin coord. to disp. picture
m_YOrg = yy

'  We will first transfer the black-and-white mask to the
'  BackPict pict.  We use the SRCAND constant to combine the bits
'  using the AND logic.
Throw = BitBlt(m_BackPict.hDC, m_XOrg, m_YOrg, m_MaskPict.ScaleWidth, _
    m_MaskPict.ScaleHeight, m_MaskPict.hDC, 0, 0, SRCAND)
```

continued on next page

continued from previous page

```
'  We now transfer the main PrimaryImage to the BackPict using the
'  SRCINVERT constant. Wherever there is a black pixel in
'  the mask, the original PrimaryImage will show through. Wherever
'  there is a white pixel in the mask and a black pixel in the
'  main PrimaryImage, the transparent effect will take place.
Throw = BitBlt(m_BackPict.hDC, m_XOrg, m_YOrg, m_PrimaryImg.ScaleWidth, _
    m_PrimaryImg.ScaleHeight, m_PrimaryImg.hDC, 0, 0, SRCINVERT)

End Sub
```

Listing M1-10
Transparent copy form module

```
Option Explicit
'  Globally declare the transparent
'  Bitblt class.
Dim Trans As TransBitBlt
' If 32-bit Windows, then these declares
'  will be used.
#If Win32 Then

'  StretchBlt will be used to copy the
'  ZigZag image onto the background
'  picture.
Private Declare Function StretchBlt Lib "gdi32" (ByVal hDC As Long, ByVal _
    X As Long, ByVal Y As Long, ByVal nWidth As Long, ByVal nHeight _
    As Long, ByVal hSrcDC As Long, ByVal XSrc As Long, ByVal YSrc As Long, _
    ByVal nSrcWidth As Long, ByVal nSrcHeight As Long, ByVal dwRop As Long) _
    As Long

' If 16-bit Windows, then these declares
'  will be used.
#Else

'  StretchBlt will be used to copy the
'  ZigZag image onto the background
'  picture.
'  Declaration uses old-style type suffixes.
Private Declare Function StretchBlt Lib "GDI" (ByVal hDC%, ByVal X%, _
    ByVal Y%, _ByVal nWidth%, ByVal nHeight%, ByVal hSrcDC%, _
    ByVal XSrc%, ByVal YSrc%, ByVal nSrcWidth%, ByVal nSrcHeight%, _
    ByVal dwRop&) As Long

#End If

'  Used for the StretchBlt copy
Const SRCCOPY = &HCC0020

Private Sub ClickButton_Click()
Dim XOrg As Integer, YOrg As Integer
'  x and y are calculated such that the arches PrimaryImage
'  will be centered on the BackPict.
XOrg = (BackPict.ScaleWidth / 2) - (mask.ScaleWidth / 2)
```

```
YOrg = (BackPict.ScaleHeight / 2) - (mask.ScaleHeight / 2)

'  Show the transparent PrimaryImage at x and y.
Trans.showtrans XOrg, YOrg

End Sub

Private Sub Form_Load()

'  Set the form width and height.
Transparent.Width = BackPict.Width + 70
Transparent.Height = BackPict.Height + 1800

'  Create the new class.
Set Trans = New TransBitBlt

'  Send in the three pictures.
Set Trans.Background = BackPict
Set Trans.MaskPict = mask
Set Trans.PrimaryImg = PrimaryImage

'  Move the BackPict.
BackPict.Move 0, 0

End Sub

Private Sub Form_Paint()
Dim Throw As Long
'  In order to use the StretchBlt, we have to have
'  the BackPict picture have a scalemode of 3.
BackPict.ScaleMode = 3

'  Stretch the zigzag.bmp PrimaryImage to fit in
'  the form.
Throw = StretchBlt(BackPict.hDC, 0, 0, BackPict.ScaleWidth, _
    BackPict.ScaleHeight, Flock.hDC, 0, 0, Flock.ScaleWidth, _
    Flock.ScaleHeight, SRCCOPY)
End Sub
```

SUMMARY

The Windows API (Application Programming Interface) is a collection of functions used to write Windows programs. Visual Basic accesses many of the API functions for you automatically as it does its stuff, but you can access them directly. To do so, you use a *Declare* statement that specifies an API function's name, arguments, return type, and location. Using API calls extends the range of what you can do with Visual Basic, but involves digging much more deeply into the details of Windows programming than does using Visual Basic's built-in capabilities.

MODULE 2 SOUND AND MULTIMEDIA

The advanced projects in this module feature MMControl, a multimedia control included with the Professional and Enterprise editions of Visual Basic 4.

For a long time, IBM PC compatibles have been sound-challenged. They come with a small, built-in speaker fit only for beeping when something goes wrong. With a little effort, you can program the speaker to play simple tunes. With a good deal of effort, you can coax more elaborate sounds from the system. On the whole, getting good sound from the standard PC is not quite as easy as rendering a convincing version of a Beethoven symphony on a lone kazoo.

Recently, however, PCs are appearing in greater numbers brandishing a multimedia claim. This means the PC has been equipped with a CD-ROM player and a sound

card. Sound cards add a lot to the computer's sonic abilities. They can reproduce complex sounds, such as voices and music, with reasonable verisimilitude. Although the sound card industry has yet to settle upon a single standard, most modern sound cards can function in a Windows system, and Visual Basic lets you use Windows-compatible cards. In this module, you'll learn about the following:

- **The nature of sound (just a little)**
- **WAV files**
- **MIDI files**
- **The MMControl**
- **Using the API in multimedia programming**

SOUND

Let's begin with a brief review of sound. It's produced by mechanical vibrations and transmitted through the air by pressure waves. A simple vibration or wave can be described by its *frequency,* which is the number of complete oscillations a second. For example, symphonic orchestras tune to a particular note (middle A) played on the oboe. This note is generated by air vibrating within the oboe 440 times a second; that vibration has a frequency of 440 Hz (short for Hertz). The vibration sends a wave traveling through the air at the speed of sound (about 1,100 ft/sec) and also having a frequency of 440 Hz. The *amplitude* of a wave describes the amount of energy carried by the wave, with a larger amplitude corresponded to more energy.

Sound also has a physiological component. Sound waves impinging upon the ear cause the eardrum to vibrate, relaying sounds to the inner ear, where different frequencies excite different nerves that transmit messages to the brain. Sounds with higher frequencies you hear as having a higher pitch. Sounds with higher amplitudes you hear as being louder.

A very pure sound, such as the one produced by a softly struck tuning fork, can be described as having a particular frequency and amplitude, but most sounds are a blend of many frequencies and amplitudes. These blends are what give sounds their character and richness. For example, suppose an oboe, piano, and trumpet all produce the middle A note. Each produces a sound having a frequency of 440 Hz, yet each sounds distinct from the others. It turns out each instrument also produces other frequencies at the same time. For musical instruments, these other frequencies are *overtones,* meaning that they are multiples of the basic frequency. In the case of middle E, the overtones would be 880 Hz, 1320 Hz, 1760 Hz, and so on. Blending these overtones in different amounts produces different sound qualities (or *timbres*), giving each instrument its distinct sound.

By using a microphone and oscilloscope or similar device, you can graph sound vibrations as a function of time. Such graphs visually describe the *waveform*. A pure sine wave waveform, such as that in Figure M2-1, corresponds to a pure tone. Mixing in overtones produces more complex waveforms, such as that shown in Figure M2-2. (You may recall that Lesson 15 discussed overtones and waveforms as examples of using the sine function.)

Other sounds, such as human voices, chicken squawks, pumpkin smashings, fingernails scratching a chalkboard, and so on, also are blends of many frequencies, but many or most of them aren't overtones, so the effect is less musical. The corresponding waveforms are more irregular in appearance.

Given that sounds are blends of various frequencies at various amplitudes, how can we store a sound in a computer? There's a basic mismatch of data style. Sound is a continuous phenomenon, with a continuous range of frequencies and amplitudes. But computers are equipped to deal with discrete data, where each item of data can be represented and stored as a binary number. For example, a computer can store text easily because text consists of a bunch of separate units (characters and symbols) that can be stored by storing the ASCII code for each character.

The solution is to digitize the data—that is, break up continuous data into individual chunks that can be represented and stored as numbers. This, for example, is how a computer displays images. What you see when you look out a window is continuous data, but a computer showing the same view displays a picture as a bunch of separate pixels; the image has been digitized. Also, the colors have been digitized, with a continuous variation of light intensity replaced by discrete steps in intensity. If the pixels are very small and if there are

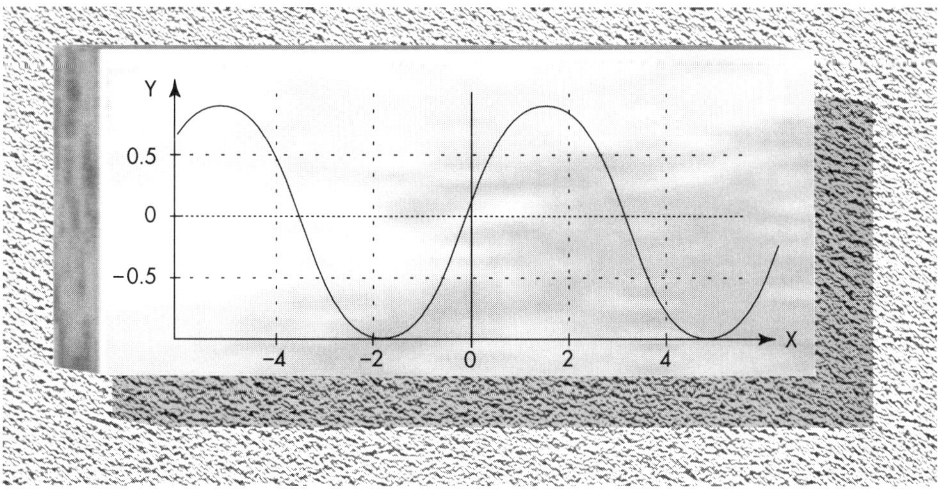

Figure M2-1 A pure tone

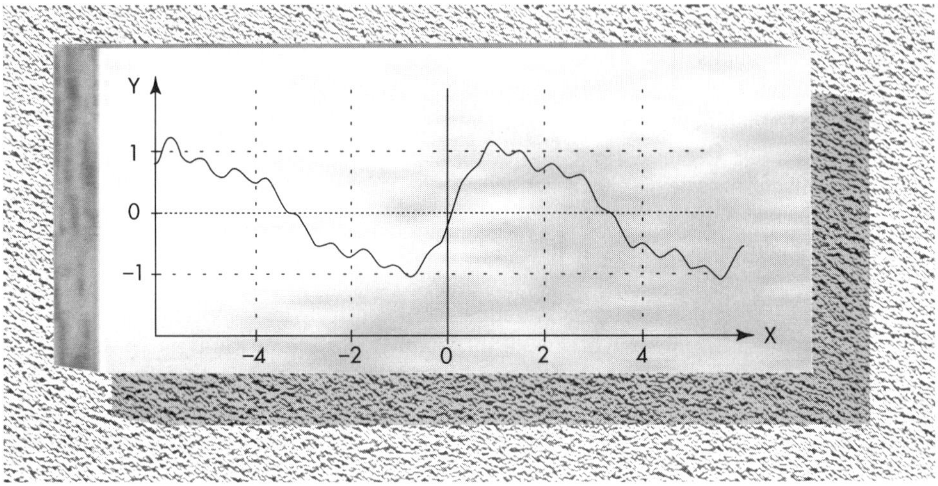

Figure M2-2 A sound with overtones

many color intensity steps, the image is close in appearance to the original, and we can describe the image as having high spatial and color resolution. If the pixels are large and you have a limited choice of intensity steps, the digital nature of the image is obvious, and you can describe the image as being low resolution.

Similarly, sound can be digitized. With images, you divide an image into discrete chunks of space and color values. With sound, you divide a sound into discrete chunks of time. Again, the result can be high resolution or low resolution. To get high resolution sound, you use a high *sampling rate,* meaning you divide a sound wave into very small chunks of time so that you have many samples of sound each second. Figure M2-3 shows a wave form digitized using two different time intervals. The more sound samples per second, the more closely the digitized sound will resemble the original sound. There are three common sampling rates used in Windows, as listed in Table M2-1. (A KHz is a kilohertz, or 1,000 Hz, so a sampling rate of 11 KHz means taking 11,000 sound samples per second.)

SAMPLING RATE	SOUND RESOLUTION
11 KHz	Low resolution (telephone quality)
22 KHz	Medium resolution (AM radio quality)
44 KHz	High resolution (music CD quality)

Table M2-1 Common sampling rates for digitizing sound

WAV Files

Once you digitize a sound, how do you make it available to a computer? One approach is to store the digitized sound in a file. Then a computer can read the file and feed

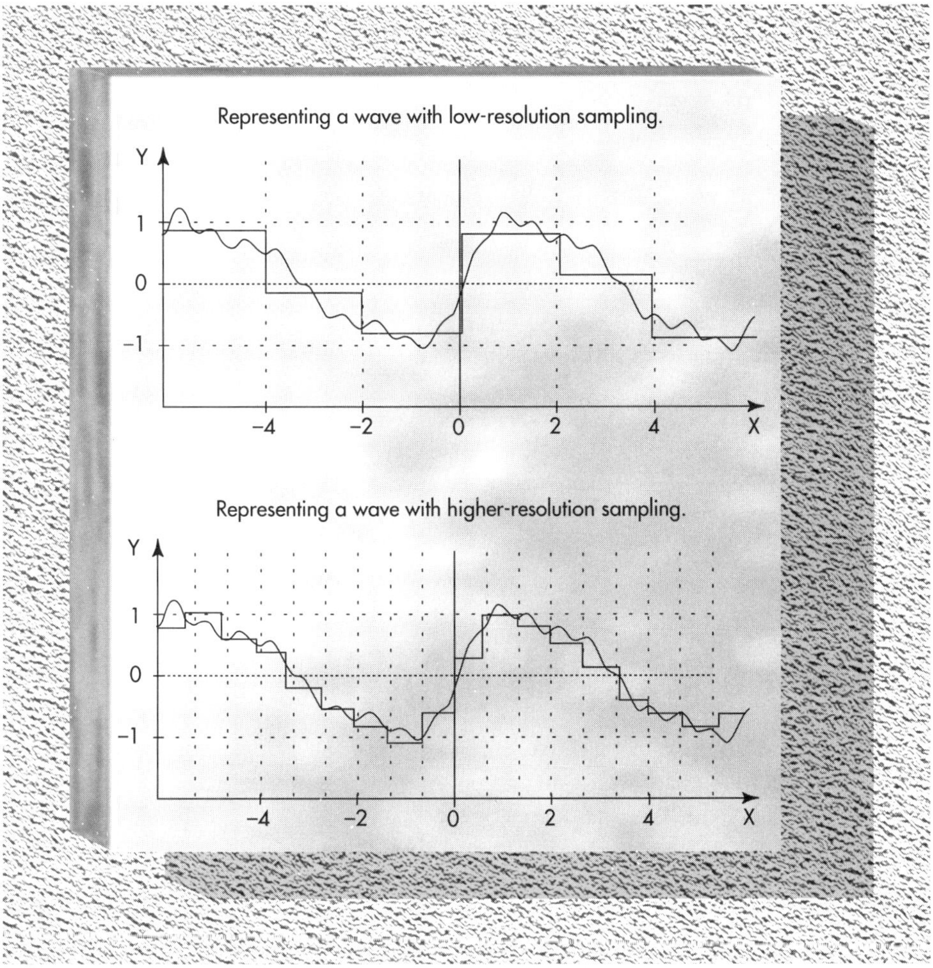

Figure M2-3 Digitized sounds

the data to a sound card, which then can generate the corresponding sounds. There are different formats for storing digitized sound. The standard format used in Windows is that used by files with the .WAV extension; they are called WAV files. For example, Windows itself uses WAV files for system sounds, such as warning chimes, that it uses instead of a beep if you have a sound card installed. Many sound cards come with hardware and programs that let you record sounds and store them as WAV files. Also, many vendors sell sound samples—the audio equivalent of clip art.

WAV files tend to be bulky, the more so the higher the quality. If, for example, the sampling rate is 44 KHz, then you need to store 44,000 data items per second. Compression techniques help, but WAV files are best suited for short sound bytes, such as "Beam me up, Scotty." Using medium or low resolution results in smaller file sizes.

MIDI Files

MIDI (Musical Instrument Device Interface) files, which have a .MID extension, use a different strategy for storing sounds. In fact, they don't store sounds at all. Instead, they store lists of notes to play, leaving it to the playback device to supply the correct sounds. An MIDI file is the computer analog to a musical score. For example, it will instruct a playback device to play a particular tune and sound like a banjo. Or it might instruct the device to play two musical lines, one sounding like a violin, and one sounding like a bagpipe. The playback device then uses its own built-in resources to carry out the command.

One advantage of an MIDI file is that it takes much less space to store a score than to store the actual sounds, so MIDI files are much smaller (per second of sound) than WAV files. On the other hand, the sound you hear depends on the playback device. Some sound cards, for example, do a reasonable job of impersonating a piano, while others don't.

One way of describing the difference between MIDI and WAV files is to say MIDI files are analogous to vector graphics (such as those found in .WMF files), while WAV files are analogous to bitmapped image files.

SOUND AND VISUAL BASIC

Visual Basic supports sound in a couple of ways. First, it has a control (the MMControl) for dealing with sound. Second, it can access API functions (see Module 1) that control sound. But for either of these approaches to work, you need to have a sound card installed that is compatible with Windows' sound drivers or which supplies its own Windows drivers. Windows 95 and some of the newer PCs support *Plug and Play,* a combination of hardware and software that simplifies the task of installing devices such as sound cards and CD-ROM players. Historically, however, installing sound cards or multimedia kits has been a troublesome and frustrating process for many users. Sound cards use many resources—port addresses, IRQs, DMA channels, perhaps ROM space, and TSAs—so the possibilities of hardware and software conflicts are great. (Even knowing what these terms mean is no guarantee of success!) The author, for example, lost the use of his hand scanner after installing a sound card even though they purportedly didn't have any conflicts. But changing a setting on the video card (for an unconnected reason) brought the hand scanner back on line. In short, the examples in this module definitely work on some computers, but there is no guarantee that they'll work on all systems.

THE MULTIMEDIA CONTROL

The Professional and Enterprise editions of Visual Basic provide a control called the *MMControl* (MM for *multimedia*) that lets you handle a variety of multimedia functions, including playing an audio CD, playing WAV files, and playing MIDI files.

Figure M2-4 The MMControl

An MMControl is a *custom control*, meaning that it normally doesn't show up in the Visual Basic Toolbox. So the first step in using the control is getting it in the Toolbox. Here's what you do:

1. Open the Visual Basic Tools menu.
2. Select Custom Controls.
3. In the Custom Controls dialog box that opens, scroll down the list of custom controls until you find Microsoft Multimedia Control.
4. Check the box to the left of the Microsoft Multimedia Control label.
5. Click on OK.

This should add the MMControl icon to the Toolbox. The addition is just for the current project. Click on the icon and draw a control on a form. You should see a row of buttons similar to buttons you might find on a tape recorder. Figure M2-4 shows the buttons along with labels identifying each button by name. (The labels are not part of the control; they were added as separate labels to create the figure.)

Using the MMControl

If you add an MMControl to a form, then run the program, all the buttons will be grayed out, reminding you once again that computers are not clairvoyant. You have to associate the control with a particular device and perhaps a particular file before you can use it. That's done the usual Visual Basic way, by using properties. Multimedia controls have lots of properties, and Table M2-2 lists a few of them.

PROPERTY	MEANING
AutoEnable	If True, let the control automatically determine which buttons are enabled (overrides individual button enabling settings).
Button Enabled	If AutoEnable is false, the individual *Button* Enabled settings control button enabling. The *Button* term is replaced by individual button names, such as Prev and Play.
CanEject, CanPlay, CanRecord, CanStep	Read-only properties describing device capabilities and set to True or False when a device is opened.
Command	During run time, specifies an MCI command, such as "Open" or "Play" to execute (see Table M2-3).

continued on next page

continued from previous page

PROPERTY	MEANING
DeviceType	Specifies type of MCI device to open (see Table M2-4).
FileName	The name of the file to be opened by an Open command or saved by a Save command.
Name	Name to be used in code to identify the control.
Shareable	If True, more than one application or control can access the device.
Wait	If True, MCI waits until the next MCI command finishes before returning control to the application.

Table M2-2 Some MMControl properties

COMMAND STRING	MCI COMMAND
"Open"	Opens a device
"Close"	Closes a device
"Play"	Plays a device
"Pause"	Pauses playing or recording; if the device already is paused, issues the MCI_RESUME command
"Stop"	Stops playing or recording
"Back"	Steps backward
"Step"	Steps forward
"Prev"	Goes to the beginning of the current track; if issued within three seconds of another "Prev" command, goes to the beginning of the previous track
"Next"	Goes to the beginning of the next track
"Seek"	If not playing, seek a position; if playing, continue playing
"Record"	Record
"Eject"	Eject media
"Sound"	Play a sound
"Save"	Save an open file

Table M2-3 Command strings for the MMControl Command property

DEVICE TYPE STRING	DEVICE
"AVIVideo"	Video for Windows files
"CDAudio"	An audio CD player
"DAT"	A DAT tape deck
"DigitalVideo"	Digital video
"MMMovie"	Multimedia movie

DEVICE TYPE STRING	DEVICE
"Other"	Other device
"Overlay"	Video overlay
"Scanner"	Scanner
"Sequencer"	An MIDI device
"VCR"	A VCR
"Videodisc"	A video disc player
"WaveAudio"	A WAV-compatible sound card

Table M2-4 Device types for the MMControl Device property

MCI

You'll notice that Table M2-2 frequently refers to MCI. *MCI* stands for Media Control Interface. It consists of a set of functions that use a standard interface to control a variety of media devices. MCI is part of the Windows API (Application Programming Interface, discussed in Module 1), which can be accessed from a variety of programming languages, including Visual Basic. The MMControl provides a Visual Basic interface to MCI so that you don't have to use the API directly. Thus the MMControl Command property is a way of issuing MCI commands without using API techniques. Table M2-3 lists the available commands. Clearly, not all commands make sense with all devices. You wouldn't, for example, eject a WAV file. The Multimedia Programmer's Reference from Microsoft's Windows Software Development Kit describes MCI in detail.

Let's look at how to use the control. Suppose, for example, you want to play a WAV file. Minimally, you would do the following:

1. Set the control's FileName property to the name of the file you want to play.
2. Set the control's DeviceType property to "WaveAudio."
3. Set the control's Command property to "Open."
4. Set the control's Command property to "Play."

The first three steps you have to write explicitly, but once you've opened the device, the appropriate buttons on the control become active. In particular, the Play button becomes active, and clicking on the Play button automatically issues the "Play" command. Indeed, each MMControl button issues the command having the same name as the button. For example, clicking on the Stop button is the same as setting the Command property to "Stop".

The Help menu contains even more information about the MMControl. However, the information is not in Visual Basic Help; rather, it is in Custom Control Reference Help. One way to get there is to start Visual Basic Help and use the Help File menu to open the *Ctrlref.hlp* file. Another is to highlight an MMControl in the Properties window's object box, and then press F1.

Meanwhile, let's try a simple example.

A Sound Example

Start a new project and use Custom Control from the Visual Basic Tools menu to add the MMControl to the Toolbox. Then draw the control onto the form along with two option buttons as shown in Figure M2-5. Set up properties as described in Table M2-5. Aside from the name, this program accepts all the default values for the multimedia control.

OBJECT	PROPERTY	SETTING
Form1	Caption	Sounds
	Name	frmMCI
MMControl1	Name	mciSimple
Option1	Caption	MIDI
	Index	0
	Name	optSource
Option2	Caption	WAV
	Index	1
	Name	optSource

Table M2-5 Properties for the Sounds program

The next step is to implement the simple approach. To do so, you need a sample MIDI file and a sample WAV file. For the MIDI file, use *Mcitest.mid* from the MCI subdirectory of the Visual Basic SAMPLES directory. (This directory contains a more elaborate MCI example you may wish to examine.) For the WAV sample, use the *Chimes.wav* file from the WINDOWS directory. These two files are about the same size (17K for the MIDI file, 15K for the WAV file), but, as you will soon hear, the WAV file provides about a second's worth of chimes while the MIDI file provides nearly 50 seconds of Bach. For convenience, the program will assume both files are in the same directory as the program, so you should copy them to that directory. (If you use the program disk that comes with this book, the two files already are in the same directory as the project.) Listing M2-1 shows the code.

Figure M2-5 A sound program

MIDI?

This program assumes your sound card can handle MIDI sound and that Windows is configured to use your sound card correctly. If you open the Multimedia choice in the Control Panel, you'll see a tab labeled MIDI. Click on the tab to see what MIDI drivers, if any, your system is configured to use.

Listing M2-1
The Sounds program

(This project requires the Professional or Enterprise edition.)

```
Option Explicit

Private Sub Form_Load()
On Error GoTo SORRY
    ' Set properties needed by MCI to open.
    mciSimple.Wait = True
    mciSimple.Shareable = False
    mciSimple.DeviceType = "Sequencer"
    mciSimple.FileName = App.Path & "\mcitest.mid"
' Open the MCI midi device.
    mciSimple.Command = "Open"
    Exit Sub
SORRY:
    MsgBox "Too bad: Error #" & Err.Number && " " & Err.Description
    End
End Sub

Private Sub Form_Unload(Cancel As Integer)
    mciSimple.Command = "Close"
End Sub

Private Sub optSource_Click(Index As Integer)
    If Index = 0 Then
        mciSimple.AutoEnable = True
        mciSimple.Command = "Close"
        mciSimple.DeviceType = "Sequencer"
        mciSimple.FileName = App.Path & "\mcitest.mid"
        mciSimple.Command = "Open"
    Else
        mciSimple.AutoEnable = False
        mciSimple.Command = "Close"
        mciSimple.DeviceType = "WaveAudio"
        mciSimple.FileName = App.Path & "\chimes.wav"
        mciSimple.Command = "Open"
    End If
End Sub
```

Program Notes

The program begins by opening the "Sequencer" device. Typically, this will be a sound card capable of playing MIDI sounds. The program sets the control FileName property to the MIDI file with this line:

```
mciSimple.FileName = App.Path & "\mcitest.mid"
```

Here the *App* object represents the application and the Path property is a string representing the drive and directory containing the application. Thus the combination *App.Path & "\mcitest.mid"* is the full path name of the MIDI file, assuming that it is in the same directory as the application. This way the code works regardless of where you keep the application and file as long as you keep them together.

Tip

Use *App.Path* to identify the drive and directory containing an application.

The program closes each device when finished with it. This happens when you quit the program (that triggers the *Form_Unload* event) and when you switch from using MIDI to WAV and back again. (Although a single sound card may handle both MIDI and WAV sounds, these are two separate functions integrated into a single card. Also, some computer users use separate devices for these two sound formats.)

The program makes one other change when switching between MIDI and WAV sources to modify the AutoEnable property. That's because some sound cards that handle WAV sources also have the ability to record WAV sources. If you have such a card, AutoEnable enables the record button. But that's inappropriate for this simple program. Setting AutoEnable to False gives you the option of enabling only those buttons you want. It turns out, however, that the default values for *Play.Enabled, Prev.Enabled,* and *Next.Enabled* are True, and those are the values needed for this example.

Try running the program. You'll note that to play a sound twice in succession, you have to click on Prev after the first play to reset the control at the beginning of the sound sample. Also note that if you first start the MIDI selection, you can switch to WAV mode and initiate the WAV sound without waiting for the MIDI selection to finish; Visual Basic doesn't have to wait for a sound to quit playing before resuming execution.

Note

Sound cards are asynchronous devices. That is, once a Visual Basic program sends a play command to a sound card, control returns immediately to the program, not waiting until the play selection finishes. Thus the program can go on to other things while a sound selection plays.

Can you play the MIDI sounds and WAV sounds simultaneously? If you use just one MMControl, the answer is no—a control can run only one device at a time. But by using two controls, you can control two devices.

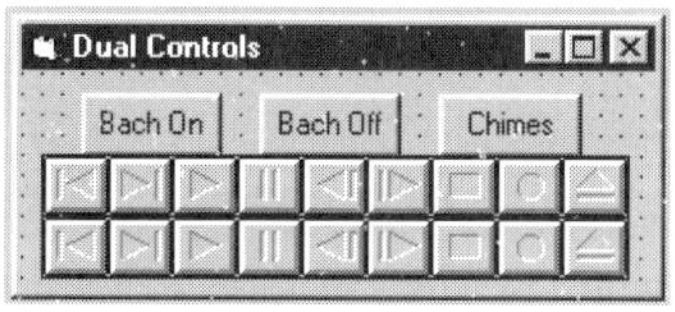

Figure M2-6 The Dual Controls form

Dual Controls

Let's explore using two controls to control two devices. Let's also experiment with using the control while keeping it invisible. Once again, start a new project and use the Tool menu to add the Microsoft Multimedia control to the Toolbox. This time, place two MMControl controls and three command buttons on the form, as illustrated in Figure M2-6 and described in Table M2-6.

OBJECT	PROPERTY	SETTING
Form1	Caption	Dual Controls
	Name	frmMCI
MMControl1	Name	mciMidi
	Visible	False
MMControl2	Name	mciWav
	Visible	False
Command1	Caption	Bach On
	Name	cmdBachOn
Command2	Caption	Bach Off
	Name	cmdBachOff
Command3	Caption	Chimes
	Name	cmdChimes

Table M2-6 Properties for the Dual Controls program

One multimedia control will be used to control the MIDI device and one to control the WAV device. Note that both controls have their visible properties set to False. So how can you play the sounds without using the button controls? The answer is to use the Command property instead. Listing M2-2 shows how.

Listing M2-2
The Dual Controls program

(This project requires the Professional or Enterprise edition.)

```
Option Explicit

Private Sub cmdBachOff_Click()
```

continued on next page

continued from previous page

```
    mciMidi.Command = "Stop"
End Sub

Private Sub cmdBachOn_Click()
    mciMidi.Command = "Prev"
    mciMidi.Command = "Play"
End Sub

Private Sub cmdChimes_Click()
    mciWav.Command = "Prev"
    mciWav.Command = "Play"
End Sub

Private Sub Form_Load()
On Error GoTo SORRY
    ' Set properties needed by MCI to open.
    mciMidi.Wait = True
    mciMidi.Shareable = False
    mciMidi.DeviceType = "Sequencer"
    mciMidi.FileName = App.Path & "\mcitest.mid"
    mciMidi.Command = "Open"
    mciWav.Wait = True
    mciWav.Shareable = False
    mciWav.DeviceType = "WaveAudio"
    mciWav.FileName = App.Path & "\chimes.wav"
    mciWav.Command = "Open"
    Exit Sub
SORRY:
    MsgBox "Too bad: Error #" & Err.Number & " " & Err.Description
    End
End Sub

Private Sub Form_Unload(Cancel As Integer)
    mciMidi.Command = "Close"
    mciWav.Command = "Close"
End Sub
```

For example, notice the code for the Bach On command button:

```
Private Sub cmdBachOn_Click()
    mciMidi.Command = "Prev"
    mciMidi.Command = "Play"
End Sub
```

It issues the command to reset the selection (in case it's been partially or fully played already), then issues the command to play the selection. When you run the program, just the command buttons show, as shown in Figure M2-7. Once you start the MIDI sound playing, you can click on the Chimes control to sound the chimes simultaneously.

Tip

If you want the capabilities of the multimedia control but don't want to use the MMControl pushbutton interface, make the control invisible and use the control's Command property to issue media commands.

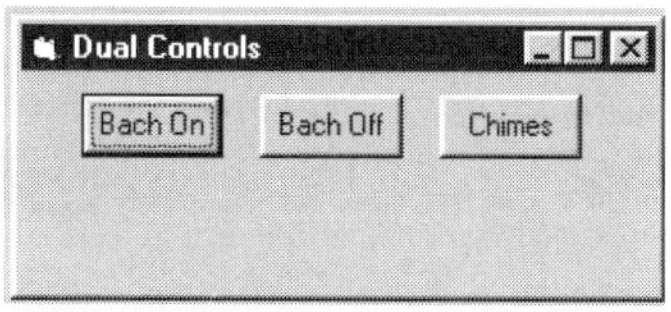

Figure M2-7 Dual Controls in run mode

BEYOND THE MMCONTROL CONTROL

The MMControl control provides a Visual Basic interface to the Windows MCI facilities. With a little bit of knowledge, you can have your Visual Basic program access MCI facilities directly. The secret is to use the API approach outlined in Module 1. That is, you use the *Define* statement to link your program to Windows functions found in dynamic link libraries. To show how that works, let's look at a sound-and-light program created by Mitch Waite, Gregg Irwin, and Mark Pruett. To simplify the presentation, let's look at the program at two stages—early and late—in its development.

The aim of these Visual Basic tinkerers was to simulate a fireworks display. This has two design elements:

- An audio representation of the sound of fireworks
- A visual representation of the appearance of fireworks

Let's pick up their work in progress, slightly altered to fit the programming style of this book.

Round 1.1—The Sound

At this stage in its development, the program plays a single WAV file to portray the sound. In particular, the 32-bit version uses the *sndPlaySound* function from the *Winmm.dll* dynamic link library. That entails the following declaration:

```
Declare Function sndPlaySound Lib "winmm.dll" Alias "sndPlaySoundA" _
    (ByVal lpszSoundName As String, ByVal uFlags As Long) As Long
```

The 16-bit version uses the MMSystem library instead:

```
Declare Function sndPlaySound Lib "MMSystem" (ByVal lpsound As String, _
    ByVal flag As Integer) As Integer
```

In either case, the *lpsound* variable identifies the file to be played, and the *flag* variable describes the play mode. For asynchronous play, the flag should have the value 1, so the authors provided this definition:

```
Public Const SND_ASYNC = &H1
```

The *Public* keyword indicates that the constant will be available to all modules in the project. Such global constants must be declared in a code module, and thus this definition and the declaration were placed in a module named *Globals*.

To play the sound, the program uses (in another module) the following API call:

```
Retcode = sndPlaySound(App.Path & "\" & "Explode3.wav", SND_ASYNC)
```

Note that this uses the same *App.Path* approach the earlier examples used to locate a sound file. Again, this assumes the sound file is in the same directory as the application.

... and the Fury

The visual portrayal of the fireworks burst is more involved. The idea is to start with a tightly bunched group of colored dots (all at the same place, actually) and have them expand outwards. Each dot then can be described by its horizontal and vertical position, along with its horizontal and vertical velocity. To keep track of the data describing a dot, the program defines a *vector* data type that holds both the position and the velocity of a dot. This definition also goes into the Globals module. Listing M2-3 shows the complete Globals module.

Listing M2-3

Code for the Globals code module

(This project requires the Professional or Enterprise edition.)

```
' define types, API function calls
Type vector
   X As Single   ' x-coordinate
   Y As Single   ' y-coordinate
   vx As Single  ' velocity in the x direction
   vy As Single  ' velocity in the y direction
End Type
#If Win32 Then
    Declare Function sndPlaySound Lib "winmm.dll" Alias "sndPlaySoundA" _
        (ByVal lpszSoundName As String, ByVal uFlags As Long) As Long
#Else
    Declare Function sndPlaySound Lib "MMSystem" (ByVal lpsound As String, _
        ByVal flag As Integer) As Integer
#End If
Public Const SND_ASYNC = &H1
```

To represent the various points that form the starburst, the program uses a *vector*-type array named *p* with 75 elements. If *N* is an array index, then *p(N)* represents point number *N*, *p(N).X* is its *X* position, *p(N).vx* is its horizontal velocity, and so on. Initially, all the points in the array are set to the same random location, and each is given its own random initial velocity. Then the points are allowed to spread apart according to the size and direction of their velocities. The program uses the following code for that:

```
p(N).X = p(N).X + p(N).vx
p(N).Y = p(N).Y + p(N).vy - 0.1
```

The -0.1 is to add a falling component to the *Y* motion. This code is placed in a *For* loop to handle all 75 points, and the *For* loop is in a *While* loop to advance the starburst through successive time steps. Listing M2-4 shows the procedure that plots the points. It resides in the second code module, which the project names BoomMake. The procedure is defined to take a Form object as an argument, so it's not restricted to a single form.

Listing M2-4
Code for the BoomMake code module

(This project requires the Professional or Enterprise edition.)

```
Option Explicit

Sub MakeBoom(AForm As Form)
    Dim N As Integer
    Dim Num As Integer
    Dim T As Integer
    Dim Lifetime As Integer
    Dim s As Integer, a As Integer, b As Integer
    Dim r1 As Single, r2 As Single, r3 As Single, r4 As Single
    Dim d As Single
    Dim FrColr As Long
    Dim Retcode As Integer
    Static Clr As Integer 'QB-style color value
    Num = 75
    ReDim p(Num) As vector

    AForm.DrawMode = 7  'XOR mode
    AForm.Scale (16, 8)-(-16, -16)

    s = 10
    a = 10 * (Rnd - 0.5)
    b = 10 * (Rnd - 0.5)
    Lifetime = 50 + (40 * Rnd)
    T = 1
    Clr = (Clr + 1) Mod 7

    For N = 1 To Num
        ' random direction
        r1 = Rnd - 0.5
        r2 = Rnd - 0.5
        r3 = Rnd - 0.5
        ' random velocity
        r4 = 4 + Rnd

        ' Start at a random position on the screen.
        p(N).X = a
        p(N).Y = b

        d = (r1 ^ 2 + r2 ^ 2 + r3 ^ 2) ^ 0.5

        If d < 1 Then
           p(N).vx = r4 * r1 / (d * s)
```

continued on next page

continued from previous page

```
            p(N).vy = r4 * r2 / (d * s)
        Else
            Stop
        End If
    Next N

    ' the damping factor.  This sets the length of time the
    ' particles expand.  A value of 1 means they just keep going.

    d = 0.9

    AForm.ForeColor = QBColor(Clr + 9)
    FrColr = AForm.ForeColor

    'Start the sound before you show the image.
    Retcode = sndPlaySound(App.Path & "\" & "Explode3.wav", SND_ASYNC)

    AForm.PSet (p(1).X, p(1).Y)'first point (same for all points)
    Do While T < Lifetime
        For N = 1 To Num
            If N Mod 10 = 0 Then
                DoEvents
                AForm.ForeColor = FrColr
            End If
            AForm.PSet (p(N).X, p(N).Y)

            ' Reposition each particle according to its velocity.
            ' Superimpose a constant -.1 downward velocity on the motion.
            ' Assume each particle has reached its terminal velocity.

            p(N).X = p(N).X + p(N).vx
            p(N).Y = p(N).Y + p(N).vy - 0.1

            ' Damp the motion each pass.
            p(N).vx = p(N).vx * d
            p(N).vy = p(N).vy * d

            AForm.PSet (p(N).X, p(N).Y)
        Next N
        ' clock tick
        T = T + 1
    Loop
    AForm.Cls
    AForm.DrawMode = 13 'back to default
End Sub
```

There are some points of graphic interest. For instance, the program uses the *PSet* command to draw the points. Note that the program calls *PSet* twice, once before updating the position and once after:

```
AForm.PSet (p(N).X, p(N).Y) 'same X, Y as at end of preceding cycle
' reposition each particle according to its velocity
...
AForm.PSet (p(N).X, p(N).Y) 'new X, Y values
```

Thus, once the loop gets going, the first call to *PSet* in a cycle overwrites the second call from the preceding cycle. Drawing each point may seem useless, but also note that the program uses the XOR drawing mode. Using the XOR mode results in toggling the painted point between the background and foreground color. Drawing the same point twice with *PSet* in the XOR mode makes the point appear, then disappear. Thus the effect of the two *PSet* calls in the loop is to erase the previous point and draw a new, relocated point. This produces an animation effect, making the point appear to move.

Another interesting aspect is the following code:

```
If N Mod 10 = 0 Then
    DoEvents
    AForm.ForeColor = FrColr
End If
```

The *DoEvents* function, recall, suspends an event temporarily to allow other events to be processed, such as mouse clicks on the Boom command button. These other events conceivably could change the foreground color, so this code segment restores the original value. The *If* statement causes *DoEvents* to be called every tenth cycle of the inner loop, which is often enough to catch other actions.

Finally, we need a context in which to place this code. For this, construct the form pictured in Figure M2-8 and described by Table M2-7. (For print clarity, the figure shows the form with a white background instead of the black one prescribed by the table.)

OBJECT	PROPERTY	SETTING
Form1	BackColor	&H00000000 (black)
	BorderStyle	1 - Fixed Single
	Caption	Boom
	Name	frmBoom
Command1	Caption	BOOM
	Name	cmdBoom
Command2	Caption	Exit
	Name	cmdExit

Table M2-7 Properties for the Boom program, phase 1

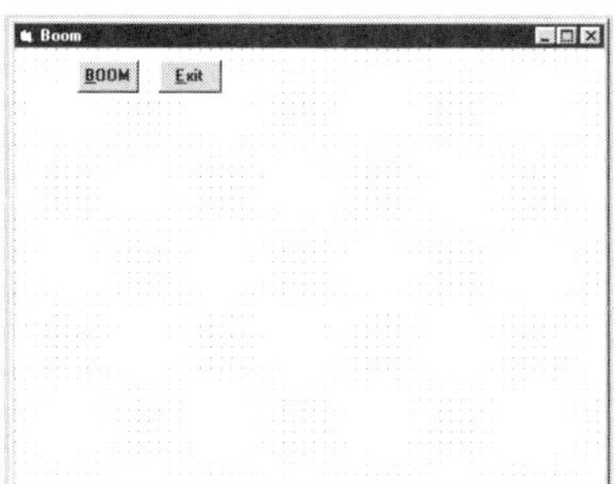

Figure M2-8 The Boom program, phase 1

The code for the form is short, as shown in Listing M2-5. It simply calls the *MakeBoom* procedure defined in Listing M2-4. That procedure requires the name of the form as an argument, so you could use the following call:

```
MakeBoom frmBoom
```

However, the Visual Basic term *Me* stands for the form whose Code window uses *Me*. By using *Me*, the program works without alteration if, at some time, you decide to change the form's name.

Note that the project should contain three modules: the frmBoom module, the code module containing the code for MakeBoom, and the code module containing the global definitions.

Listing M2-5
The code for the frmBoom form module

```
Option Explicit

Private Sub cmdBoom_Click()
    MakeBoom Me ' Me is an alias for the form holding this code
End Sub

Private Sub cmdExit_Click()
    End
End Sub
```

Running the Program

Try running the program. Click the Boom button to initiate the sounds (sort of) and sight (sort of) of fireworks. You can get an interesting effect by clicking Boom again before the first starburst finishes. The *DoEvents* statement causes a new starburst to interrupt the first starburst. When the new starburst finishes, the program goes back to complete the first starburst. But the last line of code in MakeBoom is this:

```
AForm.DrawMode = 13 'back to default
```

This turns off the XOR behavior, and points don't get erased. As a result, instead of getting moving dots, you get a growing tail of dots, for a different visual effect.

All in all, this is an interesting program, but it still is exploratory in nature. The sound of the explosion isn't all that convincing, and it's terribly demanding upon the user to have to click on the Boom button. The next version to be examined addresses these concerns.

Round 2

Let's look at the new version of the program. (Again, the original has been modified a bit to fit the programming style—such as it is—used in this book.) It has four modules, as described in Table M2-8. Each of these modules will be discussed next.

NAME	TYPE	PURPOSE
Boom	Form	Managing the controls and program
GlobalX2	Code Module	Declare global variables and API functions
SoundWorks	Code Module	Sound code
BoomWorks	Code Module	Graphics code

Table M2-8 Modules in the Boom program, phase 2

The Boom Module

First, let's look at the form. Table M2-9 lists the controls, and Figure M2-9 shows its appearance. (Again, the figure uses a white background instead of the form's black background for better visibility.) Note that the check boxes are part of a control array, as are the timers.

OBJECT	PROPERTY	SETTING
Form1	BackColor	&H00000000 (black)
	BorderStyle	1 - Fixed Single
	Caption	Boom
	Height	6835
	Name	frmBoom
	Width	8655
Command1	Caption	Start Tune
	Name	cmdStart
Command2	Caption	Stop Tune
	Name	cmdStop
Command3	Caption	E&xit
	Name	cmdExit
Picture1	BorderStyle	1 - Fixed Single
	Name	picSource
MMControl1	Name	mciTune
	Visible	False

Table M2-9 Properties for the Boom form, phase 2

The purposes of the first two command buttons are to turn an MIDI tune on and off. The third command button exits the program, first closing the MIDI device. The multimedia control manages the MIDI playing.

The picture box is part of a new strategy to use the Windows API instead of Visual Basic's *PSet* command to draw the starbursts. In the original version of the program, this control is hidden, but, for educational purposes, this version places it out in the open.

Listing M2-6 shows the code for the form.

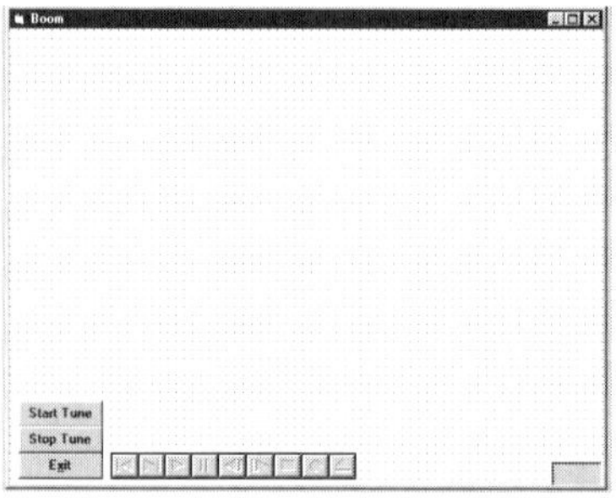

Figure M2-9 The Boom form, phase 2

Listing M2-6
The Boom form

```
'frmBoom -- alias Me
Option Explicit

Private Sub cmdExit_Click()
    Unload Me
    End
End Sub

Private Sub cmdStart_Click()
        mciTune.Command = "Prev"
        mciTune.Command = "Play"
End Sub

Private Sub cmdStop_Click()
        mciTune.Command = "Stop"
End Sub

Private Sub Form_Load()
' Set up sound.
    MidiInit Me
    InitWaves
' Set up graphics.
    ghDestDC% = Me.hdc          ' Copy destination is the form.
    ghSrcDC% = picSource.hdc    ' Copy source is the picture box.
' Set up form.
    Me.Scale (-Me.ScaleWidth, -Me.ScaleHeight)-(0, 0)
    Me.Show
    BoomMain Me        ' Start fireworks.
End Sub

Private Sub Form_Unload(Cancel As Integer)
' Turn off MIDI.
    mciTune.Command = "Close"
End Sub
```

Rather than discuss this code in detail, let's look at the main points. The event procedures in frmBoom provide the overall design for the program, managing the sound and graphic resources. It calls some sound-related functions, which are defined in the SoundWorks module, and the *BoomMain* procedure, defined in the BoomWorks module, which initiates the graphics.

How the Form Handles Sound

Let's take a closer look at the form's involvement with sound. The program plays up to four sounds—3 WAV files and one MIDI file. To play the MIDI file, the program uses a multimedia control in the same fashion it's used in the Double Controls program function, which is defined in the SoundWorks module (to be discussed later). The *Form_Load* event calls a *MidiInit* procedure (defined in the Soundworks module) to initialize the control. Three WAV files are used to produce the fireworks sound—you'll notice a significant improvement in realism. The *InitWaves* procedure (also defined in SoundWorks) initializes an array to the names of the three files.

The Globalx2 Module

The program uses Windows API function calls to control the MIDI sound and to handle the graphics. The Globalx2 module declares the API functions along with some global constants. Also, the graphics use a couple of user-defined types—*vector* and *TBoom*—which are defined here. The variables *ghDestDC%* and *ghSourceDC%* will be used to identify a destination device (the form) and a source device (the picture box) used by the API graphics routines. These variables get set in the Boom form and used in the BoomWorks form.

Listing M2-7 shows the contents of the Globalx2 module. The module uses a couple of variable-naming techniques we haven't been using. The line

```
DefInt A-Z
```

means that any variables whose names begin with letters in the range A–Z will be integer variables by default. The % suffix, as in *ghDestDC%,* also means the variable is type *Integer.* These methods predate using *Dim* with an explicit type name.

Listing M2-7
The Globalx2 form

```
Option Explicit
DefInt A-Z
'
' Declare Windows API functions used.
'
' Sound
Declare Function sndPlaySound Lib "winmm.dll" Alias "sndPlaySoundA" _
    (ByVal lpszSoundName As String, ByVal uFlags As Long) As Long
Public Const SND_ASYNC = &H1

' Graphics
Declare Function SetPixel Lib "gdi32" (ByVal hdc As Long, ByVal x As _
    Long, ByVal y As Long, ByVal crColor As Long) As Long
Declare Function BitBlt Lib "gdi32" (ByVal hDestDC As Long, _
    ByVal x As Long, ByVal y As Long, ByVal nWidth As Long, ByVal nHeight _
    As Long, ByVal hSrcDC As Long, ByVal xSrc As Long, ByVal ySrc As Long, _
    ByVal dwRop As Long) As Long
```

continued on next page

continued from previous page

```
Public Const SRCINVERT = &H660046       ' (DWORD) dest = source XOR dest

Type vector
    x   As Single
    y   As Single
    vx  As Single
    vy  As Single
End Type

Type T_Boom
    status              As Integer
    TickCount           As Integer
    NumParticles        As Integer
    Lifetime            As Integer
    Color               As Long
    nLiveParticles      As Integer
End Type

Public Const NUM_BOOMS = 2 '(actually = number of booms - 1)
Public Const NUM_PARTICLES = 90

Public ghDestDC%     '-- Form DC
Public ghSrcDC%      '-- Source Picture DC

Public Const BOOM_STATUS_DONE = 0
Public Const BOOM_STATUS_BOOMING = 1
Public Const BOOM_STATUS_READY = 2

Public gbDone%

Public WaveFiles(0 To NUM_BOOMS) As String
```

The SoundWorks Module

The SoundWorks module (see Listing M2-8) contains the sound-related code. The *InitWaves* procedure initializes an array to the names of three WAV files. The *playChan* function uses the *sndPlaySound* API call to play a WAV file. The argument to *playChan* is an integer representing an array index that identifies which file to play. The *MidiInit* procedure sets up the multimedia control. Since the control is in another module, you need to specify the form when naming the control. Rather than coding in a particular form name, the procedure uses a *Form* variable argument to identify the form. Thus the procedure call *MidiInit Me* causes *TheForm* to refer to *Me*, which, in turn, refers to *frmBoom*.

Listing M2-8
The SoundWorks module

```
' WAV stuff
Sub InitWaves()
    WaveFiles(0) = App.Path & "\giboom1q.wav"
    WaveFiles(1) = App.Path & "\giboom2q.wav"
    WaveFiles(2) = App.Path & "\giboom3q.wav"
End Sub
```

```
Function playChan(I As Integer) As Integer
    Dim Result As Integer
    Result = sndPlaySound(WaveFiles(I), SND_ASYNC)
    playChan = Result
End Function

Sub MidiInit(TheForm As Form)
    TheForm.mciTune.Wait = True
    TheForm.mciTune.Shareable = False
    TheForm.mciTune.DeviceType = "Sequencer"
    TheForm.mciTune.filename = App.Path & "\L2005_02.mid"
    TheForm.mciTune.Command = "Open"
End Sub
```

The BoomWorks Module

Finally, you get to the graphics portion (see Listing M2-9). It has two main improvements over the earlier version. First, it uses three starbursts instead of one. It accomplishes this by using a two-dimensional array:

```
Dim p(NUM_BOOMS, NUM_PARTICLES)  As vector
```

Earlier, the GlobalX2 module defined *NUM_BOOMS* as 2 and *NUM_PARTICLES* as 90. Since default array numbering starts at 0, this two-dimensional array represents three starbursts of 91 particles each.

The second improvement is that this version speeds up performance by using the Windows graphics API instead of *PSet* to draw the starbursts. More exactly, it uses *PSet* to draw a point in the picture box, then uses the API function *BitBlt* (see Module 1) to copy the point to 91 different locations on the form, drawing the starburst.

The Boom form calls *BoomMain* to start things off. *BoomMain,* in turn, uses a *Select Case* statement in a *While* loop to call either *BoomInit* or *BoomExpand.* The program is set up to call *BoomInit* three times in succession. *BoomInit* plays a WAV file and creates new starbursts, so calling it three times sets up the three starbursts and plays the three WAV file sounds. Then the program calls *BoomExpand* to expand the three starbursts. Each call expands one starburst one step. The loop and *Select Case* statement are set up so that *BoomExpand* expands each of the three starbursts one step, then each a second step, and so on. When the starbursts are expanded as far as they go, the program erases them, then returns to run *BoomInit* three more times to create three more starbursts, and so on.

Listing M2-9
The BoomWorks module

```
' graphics code (does call sound functions)
Option Explicit
Dim gtarrBoom(NUM_BOOMS)          As T_Boom    ' gtarr = Global Type Array
Dim p(NUM_BOOMS, NUM_PARTICLES)   As vector

Private Sub BoomExpand(TheForm As Form, iBoom As Integer)
```

continued on next page

continued from previous page

```
    Dim n%
    Dim d As Single
    Dim bOK%
    Dim BoomOffset%
    DoEvents
    ' the damping factor.  This sets the length of time the
    ' particles expand.  A value of 1 means they just keep going.
    d = 0.95

    BoomOffset% = iBoom% + 1

    gtarrBoom(iBoom%).TickCount = gtarrBoom(iBoom%).TickCount + 1

    If gtarrBoom(iBoom%).TickCount > gtarrBoom(iBoom%).Lifetime Then
        '-- Erase the blast (this does the same thing as CLS).
        For n% = 1 To NUM_PARTICLES
            bOK% = BitBlt(ghDestDC%, p(iBoom%, n%).x, p(iBoom%, n%).y, 1, 1, _
                ghSrcDC%, BoomOffset%, 1, SRCINVERT)
        Next n%
        gtarrBoom(iBoom%).status = BOOM_STATUS_DONE
        Exit Sub
    End If

    For n% = 1 To gtarrBoom(iBoom%).nLiveParticles 'NUM_PARTICLES

        '-- Erase the last particle.
        bOK% = BitBlt(ghDestDC%, p(iBoom%, n%).x, p(iBoom%, n%).y, 1, 1, _
              ghSrcDC%, BoomOffset%, 1, SRCINVERT)

        ' Reposition each particle according to its velocity.
        ' Superimpose a constant -.1 downward velocity on the motion.
        ' Assume each particle has reached its terminal velocity.

        p(iBoom%, n%).x = p(iBoom%, n%).x + p(iBoom%, n%).vx
        p(iBoom%, n%).y = p(iBoom%, n%).y + p(iBoom%, n%).vy + 1

        ' Damp the motion each pass.
        p(iBoom%, n%).vx = p(iBoom%, n%).vx * d
        p(iBoom%, n%).vy = p(iBoom%, n%).vy * d

        bOK% = BitBlt(ghDestDC%, p(iBoom%, n%).x, p(iBoom%, n%).y, 1, 1, _
            ghSrcDC%, BoomOffset%, 1, SRCINVERT)

    Next n%
End Sub

Private Sub BoomInit(TheForm As Form, iBoom As Integer)
    Dim n%
    Dim s%
    Dim a!, b!
    Dim r1!, r2!, r3!, r4!, d!
    Dim t%
    Dim Lifetime%
    Dim NumParticles%
    Dim bOK%
    Dim retcode
    DoEvents
' ---- Play a channel.
    If playChan(iBoom%) = 0 Then Exit Sub
```

```
'-------
    Static c3
    Randomize '-- Add a little variety.

     c3 = (c3 + 1) Mod 7
     s = 1 '10

    '-- I increased a and b (multiplier was 10)
    '   to cover a wider area of the form.
    a = (TheForm.ScaleWidth - 50) * Rnd + 25 '24 * (Rnd - .5)
    b = (TheForm.ScaleHeight - 50) * Rnd + 25 '16 * (Rnd - .5)

    n% = 1
    Do While n% <= NUM_PARTICLES
        ' random direction
        r1 = Rnd - 0.5
        r2 = Rnd - 0.5
        r3 = Rnd - 0.5
        ' random velocity
        r4 = 4 + Rnd

        ' Start at a random position on the screen.
        p(iBoom%, n).x = a
        p(iBoom%, n).y = b

        '-- The lower the value of d the higher the
        '   deltas and the faster the expansion.
        d = (r1 * r1 + r2 * r2 + r3 * r3) ^ 0.5

        p(iBoom%, n).vx = r4 * r1 / d '(d * s)
        p(iBoom%, n).vy = r4 * r2 / d '(d * s)

        n% = n% + 1
    Loop

    gtarrBoom(iBoom%).status = BOOM_STATUS_READY
    gtarrBoom(iBoom%).TickCount = 1
    gtarrBoom(iBoom%).Lifetime = 10 + (60 * Rnd)
    gtarrBoom(iBoom%).Color = QBColor(c3 + 9)
    gtarrBoom(iBoom%).nLiveParticles = NUM_PARTICLES

    TheForm.picSource.PSet (iBoom% + 1, 1), gtarrBoom(iBoom%).Color
    If NUM_PARTICLES Mod 2 Then
        bOK% = BitBlt(ghDestDC%, p(iBoom%, 1).x, p(iBoom%, 1).y, 1, 1, _
             ghSrcDC%, iBoom% + 1, 1, SRCINVERT)
    End If
End Sub

Sub BoomMain(TheForm As Form)
    Dim iBoom%  '-- Boom Index

    Do While Not (gbDone%)
        Select Case gtarrBoom(iBoom%).status
            Case BOOM_STATUS_BOOMING
                Call BoomExpand(TheForm, iBoom%)
            Case BOOM_STATUS_DONE
                Call BoomInit(TheForm, iBoom%)
            Case BOOM_STATUS_READY
                    DoEvents
                    gtarrBoom(iBoom%).status = BOOM_STATUS_BOOMING
```

continued on next page

continued from previous page

```
                Case Else
            End Select

            iBoom% = iBoom% + 1
            If iBoom% > NUM_BOOMS Then
                iBoom% = 0
            End If
        Loop
        Unload TheForm
End Sub
```

WHAT NEXT?

If you want to voyage further into the world of multimedia, you'll want to learn more about the Windows Multimedia API. You've used *sndPlaySound,* but that is just one of many functions and procedures. Two Waite Group Press sources of more information are *Windows 95 Multimedia & Networking API Bible,* by Richard Simon and *Visual Basic 4.0 Multimedia How-To,* by Noel Jerke. Also, Microsoft has a new Win95 Games SDK (software developers' kit) that includes multimedia tools.

SUMMARY

Computers have moved from a text-based interface to a graphics interface, and they will increasingly have an audio interface, too. Also, computers are becoming more integrated with video systems. With the Microsoft Multimedia control, you gain a relatively simple entry into this multimedia world. For a more intense involvement, you can turn to Windows API functions and to third-party libraries.

MODULE 3 INTRODUCING DATABASES

The advanced projects in this module require the Data Access Object (DAO) library and/or the Masked Edit control, which are included with the Professional and Enterprise editions of Visual Basic 4.

Databases store, manage, and analyze information. They lie at the heart of countless business, governmental, scientific, and educational programming efforts. Computers do many things—word processing, simulations, engineering and scientific calculations, drafting, accounting, gaming, desktop publishing, and so on—but, in this, the Information Age, managing information may be the computer activity that affects everyone the most.

Since nearly the dawn of history (that is, since the advent of MS-DOS) people have used Basic for database programming. For instance, the example in Lesson 18 on random-access files is a simple database. The bulk of database construction, however, is carried out by dedicated database programs, such as dBASE, FoxPro, Paradox, and Microsoft Access. Visual Basic has been designed to interact with databases produced by these programs, letting you create a customized Visual Basic interface to such databases. Microsoft Access, in particular, is closely tied to Visual Basic. The newest Access version even incorporates a version of Visual Basic (Visual Basic for Applications) as its built-in programming language. And Visual Basic can use the Microsoft Jet database engine, the core technology for Microsoft Access.

This module will introduce you to Visual Basic database capabilities, concentrating on the data control, available in the Professional and Enterprise editions.

DATABASES—A QUICK LOOK

Since Visual Basic and Microsoft Access are so closely related, let's take Access as a model for what to expect in a database. The fundamental unit for a database is the *record,* which is a collection of related data treated as a single entity. For instance, if you were describing your book collection, you might design a record that held the title, author, publisher, copyright date, page count, purchase price, and current value of a book. Each record would correspond to one book. Each individual data item in the record is a *field.* So a record in the example would have a title field, an author field, a publisher field, and so on.

A *table* is a collection of records, all of one type. For instance, if your library consists of 384 books, you could represent it by a table of 384 records. Each record would have the same set of fields. You can visualize a table as being organized so that each row is a record and each column is a particular field (see Figure M3-1).

A database file can contain more than one table. The tables can be independent of one another. For example, you might have a database representing possessions with one table for books, another table for compact disks, another table

Table: Books

Book ID	Author First Name	Author Last Name	Title	Copyright
1	Jack	Salt	The Pirate and the Monk	1939
2	Hilda	Gill	Last Rights	1948
3	Freda	Anthorpe	Drizzle	1945
4	Hinton	Cale	Darkstone Manor	1927
5	Theo	Bagalio	Warm Bait	1949
6	Dilford	Cramshaw	Knuckleheads on Broadway	1927
7	Annette	Queensong	Love Without a Net	1933
8	Gerard	Fitzmaster	A Soldier's Say	1931
9	Hilda	Gill	Hostile Makeover	1988

Record: 4 of 9

Figure M3-1 A table of records

for gardening tools, and so on. You also can have related tables. For instance, in addition to a table representing your books, you could have a table of authors with biographical fields, such as birth date and nationality, and you could have a table of publishers. The Jet database engine supports relational databases, which can keep track of relationships among various tables.

You also can have queries in a database file. A *query* is a subset of data defined by a set of criteria. For instance, you could define a query representing all books in your collection that were copyrighted before 1957. A query can be based on more than one table. For instance, you could ask for all books copyrighted before 1957 written by authors born after 1934. The database program then would scan your table of books and your table of authors to find which books fit the bill. (Technically, the query consists of an object that defines the criteria, and the extracted information constitutes a *recordset*.)

Database programs typically can generate *forms* and *reports*. Forms provide an alternative way to view and modify data from a table; they often are used for data input. The report organizes data for printing, adding spreadsheet-like facilities such as computing sums of fields.

The Microsoft Jet database engine is a set of dynamic link libraries that acts as an intermediary between a Visual Basic program and a database. For example, you might use the *Delete* method in a Visual Basic program to delete a record from a database. Visual Basic doesn't delete the record itself; instead, it passes this command on to the Jet database engine, and Jet does the work. Because Jet knows about different database file formats, you and your Visual Basic application don't have to know those details.

This module will concentrate on tables, which you'll access via the Visual Basic data control and, later, through data access objects.

THE DATA CONTROL AND BOUND CONTROLS

Now that you know all about databases, let's turn to the Visual Basic connection. The *data control* is just that—a connection. It connects a Visual Basic application to a database. Using a data control is the easiest way to access databases. Its simplicity comes at the price of relatively limited options, but that's no handicap when you are first learning about the subject.

When you place a data control on a form, it appears as a modified horizontal scrollbar, as shown in Figure M3-2. Once you associate it with a database, you can use the data control to move through the records. Clicking on a button with a single arrowhead moves you one record forward or one record back. Clicking on a button with an arrowhead and a vertical bar moves you to the first or last record of the database.

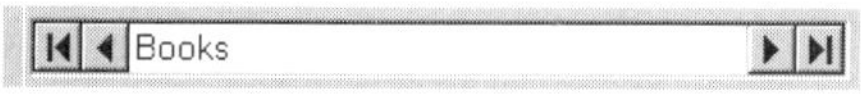

Figure M3-2 The data control

The data control works hand in hand with *bound controls*. These are controls such as text boxes that can be bound to particular fields in a database. You can create a data control and associate it with a particular database, and then you can bind a particular text box to a particular field so that the text box always displays that field for the current record. For instance, you could bind a text box to the Title field in the book inventory example. Then, as you used the data control to go from record to record, the text box automatically would display the title field of each record. Together, the data control and bound controls let you access a database without requiring you to write much code. In fact, you can get away with using no code at all! This is so easy, you've got to try it.

A Simple Example

Before starting the project, use the Tools menu to select References and make sure the *Data Access Object* (DAO) library is checked as active. The 32-bit version of Visual Basic uses version 3.0 of the library, while the 16-bit version uses version 2.5.

Next, you need a database file. The CD that comes with this book includes a small Access database file named *Simple.mdb*. It's the database illustrated in Figure M3-1, and this example will use that file. Begin, as usual, by opening a new project and adding some controls. In this case, add three labels, four text boxes, and one data control as shown in Figure M3-3.

The next step is to assign the properties shown in Table M3-1. Some of these properties have to be assigned in a particular sequence, so you're best off following the step-by-step description that follows the table.

Figure M3-3 The Books program

OBJECT	PROPERTY	SETTING
Form1	Caption	Books
	Name	frmBooks
Data1	Caption	Books
	Connect	Access
	DatabaseName	C:\VBProgs\M3\simple.mdb
	Name	datBooks
	RecordSource	Books
Label1	Alignment	1 - Right Justify
	Caption	Author:
Label2	Alignment	1 - Right Justify
	Caption	Title:
Label3	Alignment	1 - Right Justify
	Caption	Copyright:
Text1	DataField	Author First Name
	DataSource	datBooks
	Name	txtFName
	Text	
Text2	DataField	Author Last Name
	DataSource	datBooks
	Name	txtLName
	Text	
Text3	DataField	Title
	DataSource	datBooks
	Name	txtTitle
	Text	
Text4	DataField	Copyright
	DataSource	datBooks
	Name	txtCR
	Text	

Table M3-1 Properties for the Books program

Step 1: Set the form properties.

Step 2: Set the Caption for the data control.

Step 3: Next, set the DatabaseName property. This identifies the file that holds the database. The table assumes the file is in the C:\VBPROGS\M3 directory. If you've placed the file in a different location, enter the path name for that location instead. If you like, you can select the DataBaseName property, click on the three-dot button that appears in the Settings box, and bring up a dialog box that lets you browse through your directory system. Then you can click on the file when you locate it, and its full path name appears in the Settings box (see Figure M3-4).

Step 4: Once you've set the DatabaseName property, you can set the RecordSource property to Books. The RecordSource property identifies which table or query in the database will be the one associated with the data control. When you select the RecordSource property, you'll get a 3-dot button at the right end of the Settings box. Click on this button to get a list of all the available tables and queries in the database. In this case, there's just one item in the list, the Books table, so select it. Note that you can't set this property until after you've set the DatabaseName property. (Visual Basic has to know which database to search for the requested table.)

Step 5: Make sure that the Connect property is set to the default value, which is Access. This means the Data control will be connected to an Access-format database, which is the case. Also check that the RecordsetType is set to its default, 1- Dynaset. We'll look at the meaning of this property later.

Step 6: Set all the label properties.

Step 7: Set the txtFName properties. You're already familiar with the Name and Text properties, so set them first. Then set the DataSource property to datBooks, the name of the data control. This binds the text box to the data control, allowing the text box to access the data provided by the data control. After setting the DataSource property, set the DataField property to the field you want displayed in the text box. When you select the DataField property, a 3-dot button appears at the right end of the Settings box. Click on it, and a drop-down list will display the names of all the fields in the table identified by the data control's RecordSource setting (see Figure M3-5). Select the Author First Name field.

Step 8: Set the properties for the remaining three text boxes, following the same procedure as outlined in Step 7.

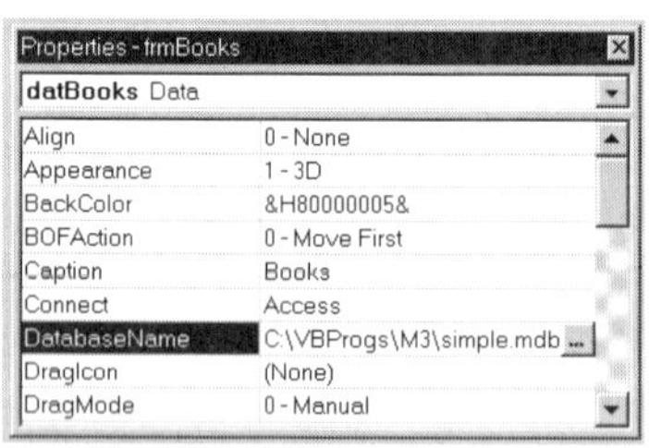

Figure M3-4 Setting the database file

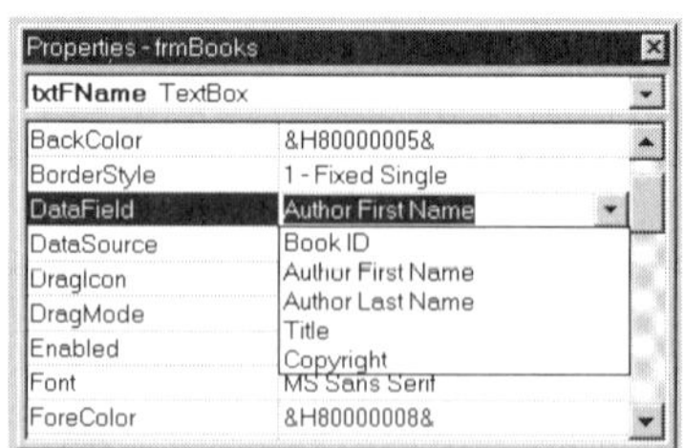

Figure M3-5 Setting the data field for a bound control

Normally, the next step after designing the form and setting the properties is to add the code, but in this case, the project is complete. Run it, and you'll be able to scan the entire database by clicking the buttons on the data control (see Figure M3-6).

A Bonus

This example illustrates how simple it is to create a program that scans the contents of a database. Now try something more daring and edit the contents of one of the text boxes. For example, change *Queensong* to *Quoonseng*. Then advance to the next record, then return. You'll see the field still contains *Quoonseng*. Quit the Books program, then restart it. The field still reads *Quoonseng!* Yes, you also can use this program to edit the database.

There are a couple of limitations. As it stands, this program only updates a field if you move to a different record. If you change a field, then quit without changing fields, your changes are not saved. Also, you can't add or delete records. How much can you expect without writing any code? A little later, you'll see an example that adds to the program's capabilities by adding a bit of code. First, however, let's look a bit further into the data control and bound controls.

Reprise

Let's review the process of using a data control and bound controls.

1. You associate a data control to a database by setting the data control's DatabaseName property to the name of the file containing the database.
2. You set the data control's Connect property to the type of database.
3. You set the data control's RecordSource property to a particular table or query in the database.
4. You bind a display control (such as a text box) to a database by setting the control's DataSource property to the name of the data control connected to that database. The bound control must be on the same form as the data control.

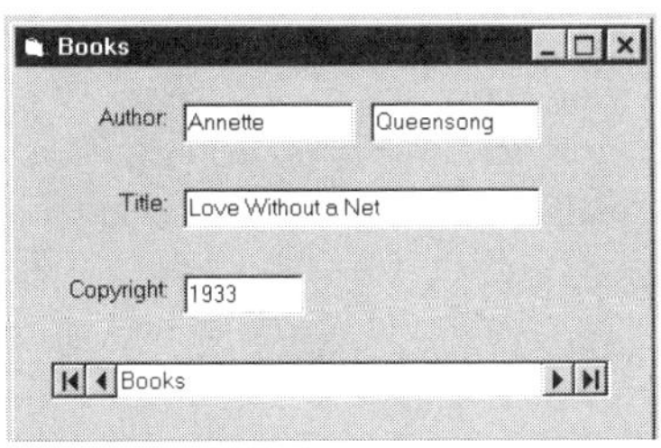

Figure M3-6 Using the data control and bound controls

5. You bind a display control (such as a text box) to a particular field in a table by setting the control's DataField property to the name of the field.

Once you do this, you can use the data control to move through records in the chosen table in the chosen database, and the bound control will display the contents of the chosen field. You can display several fields in a table by binding a control to each field. If a database has, say, two tables, you can use one data control to manage one table and a second data control to manage a second table.

What Can You Bind?

The text box is not the only kind of control you can bind, although it is the one most commonly used. Table M3-2 lists others that you can use. Intrinsic controls are built into Visual Basic, while custom controls can be added via the custom control choice in the Tools menu. Any control you wish to bind to a data control must be on the same form as the data control.

CONTROL	TYPE	STANDARD EDITION
Check box	Intrinsic	Yes
Image	Intrinsic	Yes
Label	Intrinsic	Yes
Picture box	Intrinsic	Yes
Text box	Intrinsic	Yes
List box	Intrinsic	Yes
Combo box	Intrinsic	Yes
OLE container control	Intrinsic	Yes
Data-bound list box	Custom	Yes
Data-bound combo box	Custom	Yes
Data-bound grid	Custom	Yes
Masked edit	Custom	No
3D panel	Custom	No
3D check box	Custom	No

Table M3-2 Controls that can be bound

Without going into detail, let's note a few facts about some of these controls. The label, like the text box, can be used for text and numbers. Because it is a read-only control, you can't use it to edit a database. The check box is suitable only for *Boolean* values or Yes/No values, since it offers only two settings. The list box and combo boxes are useful for entering data into a field that has a limited number of choices. For example, suppose you have a database record with a Quarter field that can be set to First, Second, Third, or Fourth. Rather than allow a mischievous user to enter Fifth, you can use a bound list box whose list items are limited to the valid values. The image box and picture box controls can be used to display images for databases that allow you to store graphic images in a field.

All the bound controls have a DataSource and a DataField property. The Books example set these properties in the Properties window, but they can be set in code as well. All bound controls also have a DataChanged property, which is set to True if a value displayed in a bound control changes. This is a runtime property, so it doesn't appear in the Properties window.

Recordset Objects and the RecordsetType Property

When Visual Basic retrieves a set of database records, it represents them as a type *Recordset* object, which is an object type defined by the Microsoft Jet database engine (the core technology of Microsoft Access). Specifically, it is an example of a data access object, and it's part of the DAO library mentioned earlier. The data control has a Recordset property that refers to the *Recordset* object. For example, the datBook data control has a datBooks.Recordset property that refers to the *Recordset* object representing the Books table of the *Simple.mdb* database file. The *Recordset* object comes equipped with a variety of properties and methods that can be used to manage the data. For example, the *Delete* method can be used to delete a record. You'll see some of these methods and properties soon.

Recordset objects come in three varieties, and the RecordsetType property determines which one you get. Table M3-3 summarizes your choices. The Dynaset (for dynamic set) is the default.

RECORDSET TYPE	EDITABLE	CAN DISPLAY FIELDS FROM MORE THAN ONE TABLE
0 - Table	Yes	No
1 - Dynaset	Yes	Yes
2 - Snapshot	No	Yes

Table M3-3 Recordset types

There is an enormous amount of information about Visual Basic and databases, and one module can't do the work of a complete book. So rather than expound all the ins and outs, let's move on to a more advanced example and see what can be learned from it.

A MEMBERSHIP LIST EXAMPLE

Your vehicle for further study is a Visual Basic program that lets you maintain a membership list. With it, you can edit records, delete records, and add records. In overall design, it's similar to the Books example, but it uses code to add the new features. This particular example was developed by Don Kiely, coauthor (with Stuart Bloom) of the Waite Group Press' *Visual Basic 4.0 Database How-To.*

It makes extensive use of the methods and properties of the data control object and of the data control's Recordset object property.

Controls and Properties

As usual, begin by creating a new form and add the controls pictured in Figure M3-7 and described in Table M3-4. This form has several elements, so let's note some of the main elements.

The form uses the 3 - Fixed Dialog setting for the BorderStyle, so the form's size remains fixed when you run the program. That's because the form size has been set to fit the controls within.

The program uses three frames to group information. Don't forget to create the frames first and then to add controls directly on to the frames.

The program uses the masked edit box control for phone numbers. If you are using the Standard Edition and don't have access to this control, use a text box instead. The advantage of the masked edit box is that it can format telephone numbers automatically. The Format property works much like the *Format* command and formats information displayed in the control. In this case, the form is (###) ###-####. Here the parentheses and hyphen are printed literally, and the # represents a digit. So a phone number stored in the database as the string "8005555555" is displayed in the form as (800) 555-5555. The Mask property works much like Format, except that it forces input to fit the format. That is, to enter the phone number form (800) 555-5555, you type 8005555555, and the masked edit box places the 800 in parentheses, and so on. Also, the masked edit box won't let you enter keystrokes that don't fit the pattern. For instance, if you press K, nothing happens. Only numbers are accepted.

The text boxes, check box, and masked edit boxes have the TabIndex properties set so that pressing TAB takes you through the corresponding fields in order.

The cmdPanel command button has Enabled set to False. It's used simply as a visual element on which to mount the other command buttons. If you have the Professional or Enterprise Edition, you may wish to try the panel control instead for a more subtle effect.

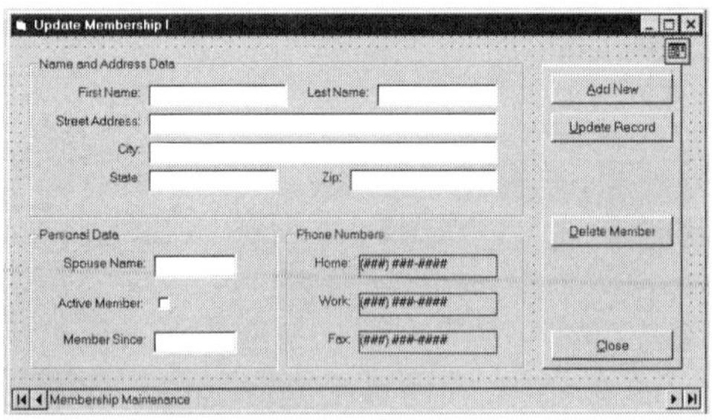

Figure M3-7 The Update Membership I form

The program operates upon the *Members.mdb* database file, which contains a table entitled Members. As with the previous example, you should substitute the path name appropriate to your system for the DatabaseName property.

OBJECT	PROPERTY	SETTING
Form1	BorderStyle	3 - Fixed Dialog
	Caption	Update Membership I
	Name	frmMembers
Data1	Caption	Membership Maintenance
	Connect	Access
	DatabaseName	C:\VBProgs\M3\members.mdb
	Name	dataMembers
	RecordSource	Members
Frame1	Caption	Name and Address Data
Frame2	Caption	Personal Data
Frame3	Caption	Phone Numbers
Label1	Alignment	1 - Right Justify
	Caption	Last Name:
Label2	Alignment	1 - Right Justify
	Caption	First Name:
Label3	Alignment	1 - Right Justify
	Caption	Street Address:
Label4	Alignment	1 - Right Justify
	Caption	City:
Label5	Alignment	1 - Right Justify
	Caption	State:
Label6	Alignment	1 - Right Justify
	Caption	Zip:
Label7	Alignment	1 - Right Justify
	Caption	Spouse Name:
Label8	Alignment	1 - Right Justify
	Caption	Member Since:
Label9	Alignment	1 - Right Justify
	Caption	Home:
Label10	Alignment	1 - Right Justify
	Caption	Fax:
Label11	Alignment	1 - Right Justify
	Caption	Work:
Text1	DataField	First Name
	DataSource	dataMembers
	Name	txtFirstName
	TabIndex	1

continued on next page

continued from previous page

OBJECT	PROPERTY	SETTING
	Text	
Text2	DataField	Last Name
	DataSource	dataMembers
Text2	Name	txtLastName
	TabIndex	2
	Text	
Text3	DataField	Address
	DataSource	dataMembers
	Name	txtAddress
	TabIndex	3
	Text	
Text4	DataField	City
	DataSource	dataMembers
	Name	txtCity
	TabIndex	4
	Text	
Text5	DataField	State
	DataSource	dataMembers
	Name	txtState
	TabIndex	5
	Text	
Text6	DataField	Zip
	DataSource	dataMembers
	Name	txtZip
	TabIndex	6
	Text	
Text7	DataField	Spouse Name
	DataSource	dataMembers
	Name	txtSpouseName
	TabIndex	7
	Text	
Text8	DataField	Member Since
	DataSource	dataMembers
	Name	txtMemberSince
	TabIndex	9
	Text	
Checkbox1	Caption	Active Member:
	DataField	Active
	DataSource	dataMembers

OBJECT	PROPERTY	SETTING
	Name	chkActiveMember
	TabIndex	8
mskEdBox1	DataField	Home Phone
	DataSource	dataMembers
	Format	(###) ###-####
	Mask	(###) ###-####
	Name	mskHomePhone
	TabIndex	10
mskEdBox2	DataField	Work Phone
	DataSource	dataMembers
	Format	(###) ###-####
	Mask	(###) ###-####
	Name	mskWorkPhone
	TabIndex	11
mskEdBox3	DataField	Fax Phone
	DataSource	dataMembers
	Format	(###) ###-####
	Mask	(###) ###-####
	Name	mskFaxPhone
	TabIndex	12
Command1	Caption	
	Enabled	False
	Name	cmdPanel
Command2	Caption	&Add New
	Name	cmdAddNew
Command3	Caption	&Update Record
	Name	cmdUpdate
Command4	Caption	&Delete Member
	Name	cmdDelete
Command5	Caption	&Close
	Name	cmdClose
CommonDialog1	Name	cdDataBase

Table M3-4 Properties for the Update Membership I form

Procedures

Okay, now you have the form drawn and the properties set. Unlike the Books example, however, this program requires some code to be added. Listing M3-1 shows what's needed.

Listing M3-1
The Update Membership I program

(This project requires the Professional or Enterprise edition.)

```
Option Explicit

'Form globals to maintain the current and total record number.
Dim TotRec As Integer
Dim CurrRec As Integer

'Stores the path and name of the database file for use throughout
'the application.
Dim strAppFile As String

Sub SetRecNum()
    'This procedure updates the caption of the data control to maintain
    'our location accurately.

    dataMembers.Caption = "Member " & CurrRec & " of " & TotRec
End Sub
Sub cmdAddNew_Click()
    'Add a new record. If default data needs to be entered in any fields,
    'make those entries between the AddNew and Update lines.
    dataMembers.Recordset.AddNew
    dataMembers.Recordset.Update

    'The new record will be at the end of the recordset, so move there.
    dataMembers.Recordset.MoveLast

    'Move to the first field for immediate editing.
    txtFirstName.SetFocus
End Sub

Private Sub cmdClose_Click()
    'End the program, after updating the current record.
    dataMembers.UpdateRecord

    'Since this application has only one form, Unload ends the app.
    Unload Me
End Sub

Sub cmdDelete_Click()
    Dim response As Integer

    'Delete the current record. First, make sure that's what we want.
    response = MsgBox("Are you sure that you want to delete this member?", _
               vbCritical + vbYesNo, "Verify Delete")

    If response = vbYes Then
        'Delete the record. This triggers the Validate event first.
        dataMembers.Recordset.Delete

        'Rebuild the recordset so that we have a clean copy.
        dataMembers.Recordset.Requery

        'If that was the last record in the recordset, add a new record
        'so that we don't have an empty recordset.
        If dataMembers.Recordset.BOF And dataMembers.Recordset.EOF Then
```

```
                dataMembers.Recordset.AddNew
                dataMembers.Recordset.Update
                dataMembers.Recordset.MoveLast
            Else
                'If that wasn't the last record, move to the first record
                'so that the current record is a valid record (not deleted).
                dataMembers.Recordset.MoveFirst
            End If
        End If
    End Sub

    Private Sub cmdUpdate_Click()
        'Save the contents of the bound control to the database. This way,
        'the user can save the data without moving the record pointer.
        dataMembers.UpdateRecord
    End Sub

    Sub dataMembers_Validate(Action As Integer, Save As Integer)
        'This procedure maintains the current record number and total number
        'of records, depending on what action is being taken.

        Select Case Action
            Case vbDataActionMoveFirst
                CurrRec = 1
            Case vbDataActionMovePrevious
                If CurrRec <> 1 Then CurrRec = CurrRec - 1
            Case vbDataActionMoveNext
                If CurrRec <> TotRec Then CurrRec = CurrRec + 1
            Case vbDataActionMoveLast
                CurrRec = TotRec
            Case vbDataActionAddNew
                TotRec = TotRec + 1
            Case vbDataActionUpdate
                'Do nothing
            Case vbDataActionDelete
                TotRec = TotRec - 1
            Case vbDataActionFind
                'Do nothing
            Case vbDataActionBookmark
                'Do nothing
            Case vbDataActionClose
                'Do nothing
            Case vbDataActionUnload
                'Do nothing
        End Select
        SetRecNum
    End Sub

    Private Sub Form_Activate()
        'This event triggers when the Form first becomes visible, in this
        'case after Form_Load. Move to the end of the recordset, so that
        'we have accurate starting numbers for TotRec and CurrRec.

        dataMembers.Recordset.MoveLast
        TotRec = dataMembers.Recordset.RecordCount
        dataMembers.Recordset.MoveFirst
        CurrRec = 1
        SetRecNum

    End Sub
```

continued on next page

continued from previous page

```
Private Sub Form_Load()
    'If the Members.mdb database is not in the application directory,
    'prompt the user to point us at its location, using a common dialog
    'control.

    strAppFile = App.Path
    If Right(strAppFile, 1) <> "\" Then strAppFile = strAppFile & "\"
    strAppFile = strAppFile & "Members.mdb"

    If Len(Dir(strAppFile)) = 0 Then
        'The length of the name is 0, so the file wasn't found. Set up the
        'file open common dialog and get the file's location.
        cdDatabase.InitDir = App.Path
        cdDatabase.filename = "Members.mdb"
        cdDatabase.Filter = "Access files (*.mdb)|*.mdb|All files (*.*)|*.*"
        cdDatabase.CancelError = True

        On Error GoTo CancelError
        cdDatabase.Action = 1
        On Error GoTo 0

        strAppFile = cdDatabase.filename

        If Len(Dir(strAppFile)) Then
            'The user pointed us at the database.
            dataMembers.DatabaseName = cdDatabase.filename
        Else
            'No file selected - canceled out of the file open dialog.
            MsgBox "No file selected. Ending application.", vbCritical, _
                "No Database Selected"
            End
        End If
    Else
        dataMembers.DatabaseName = strAppFile
    End If

    'Use an SQL statement so that the records are sorted by Last, First names.
    dataMembers.RecordSource = "SELECT * FROM Members ORDER BY [Last Name], _
        [First Name]"
    dataMembers.Refresh

    'There needs to be at least one record in the file.
    'If BOF and EOF are both
    'true, there are no records, so add one.
    If dataMembers.Recordset.BOF And dataMembers.Recordset.EOF Then
        dataMembers.Recordset.AddNew
        dataMembers.Recordset.Update
    End If

    'Center the form on the screen.
    Me.Move (Screen.Width - Me.Width) / 2, (Screen.Height - Me.Height) / 2

    Exit Sub

CancelError:
    End
End Sub
```

Using Properties and Methods

Listing M3-1 contains a lot of code. Rather than dissect it line by line, let's concentrate on the main points, starting with the *Form_Load* event. The first part of the procedure checks whether the database file is in the same directory as the application. If not, it uses a common dialog box to prompt you to locate the file. This could happen if you've moved the application or the database after creating the project. Once the file is found, the program begins using properties of the dataMembers data control. First, it sets the DatabaseName to the file name:

```
dataMembers.DatabaseName = strAppFile
```

At this point the *dataMembers.Recordset* object is initialized using the database specified by the DatabaseName property and the table specified by the RecordSource property, which was set to the Members table in the Properties window. This initialization is termed *populating* the recordset.

Next comes this pair of statements:

```
dataMembers.RecordSource = "SELECT * FROM Members ORDER BY [Last Name], _
    [First Name]"
dataMembers.Refresh
```

The RecordSource property, recall, determines the source of information displayed in the bound controls. The Properties window set this to the Members table. This code, however, overrides that setting by using an *SQL* (Structured Query Language) string. The *SELECT * FROM Members* part means "select all the fields from the Members table." The *ORDER BY [Last Name], [First Name]* part means "and arrange them in alphabetical order according to last name, then first name." The RecordSource property describes what data to use, but you have to use the *Refresh* method to update the *Recordset* object to make this change.

Without this code, the bound controls would show the records in the same order in which they are found in the database, while with this code, the records are shown in alphabetical order. This reordering affects just the Recordset object, not the original database. In summary, the program begins by using the Members table as the RecordSource and initializes the data control's Recordset object to the records in the Members table. It then uses the SQL statement and the *Refresh* method to sort the records alphabetically in the recordset, but not in the original data file.

SQL

SQL is an industry-standard language for managing relational databases. In fact, there is an ANSI (American National Standards Institute) definition of SQL. In practice, the versions of SQL individual database vendors may differ slightly from the standard, but not so much as to make it difficult to make a transition from one version to another. The Jet database engine supports SQL, and Microsoft recommends using SQL for better performance.

The Recordset object has properties of its own, which are used in the next block of code:

```
If dataMembers.Recordset.BOF And dataMembers.Recordset.EOF Then
    dataMembers.Recordset.AddNew
    dataMembers.Recordset.Update
End If
```

The BOF property stands for *B*eginning *o*f *F*ile, and it is true if the current record position is before the first record in the Recordset. The EOF property stands for *E*nd *o*f *F*ile, and it is true if the current record position is after the last record in the Recordset. The only way both can be true simultaneously is if there are no records in the Recordset. In that case, the program uses the *AddNew* method to add a new (blank) record to the Recordset, and then it uses the *Update* method to update the original database.

Note

The Recordset's Refresh method rebuilds the Recordset, while its Update method updates the database.

As you can see, the *Load_Form* event procedure use the properties and methods of the data control and of its Recordset object property to add capabilities that would otherwise be missing from the program.

Once the form is loaded, it becomes visible, and that triggers the *Activate* event:

```
Private Sub Form_Activate()
    dataMembers.Recordset.MoveLast
    TotRec = dataMembers.Recordset.RecordCount
    dataMembers.Recordset.MoveFirst
    CurrRec = 1
    SetRecNum

End Sub
```

The *MoveLast* method sets the current record to the last record in the Recordset object. The RecordCount property equals the number of records accessed, so when you reach the last record, this property equals the total number of records in the Recordset object. The program uses this value to initialize the *TotRec* variable. Next, it uses the *MoveFirst* method to move to the first record. Then it sets the *CurrRec* variable to 1. (The program uses *CurrRec* to keep track of which record is the current record.)

Suppose you want to edit an existing record. As with the Books example, you use the bound controls to enter the new information. If you then move to another record, Visual Basic automatically updates the database with the new information. However, this program gives you another option, which is to click on the Update button without changing records. That invokes the data control's *UpdateRecord* method:

```
Private Sub cmdUpdate_Click()
    'Save the contents of the bound control to the database. This way,
    'the user can save the data without moving the record pointer.
    dataMembers.UpdateRecord
End Sub
```

The effect of using the control's *UpdateRecord* event is similar to the effect of using the Recordset object's *Update* control except that *UpdateRecord* doesn't trigger the *Validate* event, which is discussed later.

What if you want to add a new record? Then you click on the Add New button, which uses the *AddNew* method to create a new record and the *Update* method to add it to the database. The new record is a blank record and is added at the end of the Recordset object, so the program also uses the *MoveLast* method to move to the end of the Recordset:

```
dataMembers.Recordset.AddNew
dataMembers.Recordset.Update
dataMembers.Recordset.MoveLast
```

To delete a record, the program uses the *Delete* method, which deletes the current record from the database. Then it uses the *Requery* method to update the Recordset based on the current contents of the database table, which reflects the deletion.

```
dataMembers.Recordset.Delete
dataMembers.Recordset.Requery
```

The *Requery* method uses the current query parameters, which, in this case, are the conditions set up by the SQL string used earlier. Most of the time, using Requery isn't necessary, for the Recordset and database are in sync. However, its presence seems to fix a possible runtime error that can occur if you delete every record from the database, then try to update the blank record showing. More typically, Requery is used to ensure the Recordset is up to date when there is a possibility that another user on a multiuser system may have modified the original database.

The Validate Event

Certain operations—moving to a different record, using *Delete, Update, Unload,* and *Close*—trigger a *Validate* event for a data control. This event takes place before the operation (moving, deleting, and so on) takes place. The data control responds to this event with an event procedure with the following syntax:

Private Sub *datacontrolname*_**Validate**(*action* **As Integer**, *save* **As Integer**)

The *action* variable represents the action triggering the *Validate* event, and the *save* variable is set to True if the record has been changed and to False otherwise. Table M3-5 lists constants representing the possible values for the *action* parameter. The methods are *Recordset* methods.

CONSTANT	VALUE	DESCRIPTION
0	vbDataActionCancel	Cancel the operation when the Sub exits.
1	vbDataActionMoveFirst	*MoveFirst* method.
2	vbDataActionMovePrevious	*MovePrevious* method.
3	vbDataActionMoveNext	*MoveNext* method.
4	vbDataActionMoveLast	*MoveLast* method.
5	vbDataActionAddNew	*AddNew* method.
6	vbDataActionUpdate	Update operation (not UpdateRecord).
7	vbDataActionDelete	*Delete* method.
8	vbDataActionFind	*Find* method.
9	vbDataActionBookmark	The Bookmark property has been set.
10	vbDataActionClose	The *Close* method.
11	vbDataActionUnload	The form is being unloaded.

Table M3-5 Actions that trigger the *Validate* event

The program maintains a variable (*CurrRec*) that keeps track of the current record and another variable (*TotRec*) that keeps track of the total number of records. It uses the *Validate* event to update these variables when required. For instance, using the *AddNew* method causes the action variable to be set to *vbDataActionAddNew*. When that's the case, the code adds 1 to *TotRec*.

Tip

Never use a method in a *Validate* event handler that triggers the *Validate* event. For example, suppose you used the *Update* method in a *Validate* event. Calling that method would trigger another *Validate* event, which could call *Update,* which would trigger *Validate,* and so on.

The *SetRecNum* procedure uses the values of *CurrRec* and *TotRec* to set the caption of the data control to something of the form "Member 2 of 6."

Commentary

It's very easy to combine a data control with bound controls to construct a simple interface to a database. If you want to add more features, however, such as the capabilities to add and delete records, you're in for a bout of code writing. Also, you need to learn more about the Recordset object and how to use its methods and properties. This object has many properties and methods beyond those used in the Update Membership I example.

Since Microsoft Access produced the original database and is perfectly capable of maintaining it, you might wonder what the point is to writing a Visual Basic interface. One reason is that an executable version of the Update Membership I program is much smaller than Access, only 20K instead of 2 MB.

There's little point in using a huge truck-and-trailer to deliver a pint of sour cream to your neighbor when you can just carry it over by hand. You can easily store the database file and your Visual Basic interface on a floppy or transmit them by modem. Thus, you can readily share your database project with others, even if they don't own a database program. (But they will need the Visual Basic runtime module.)

More generally, you can use Visual Basic to add capabilities to the basic database skills. For instance, you might add some sounds or pictures. Or you can use Visual Basic to integrate a variety of applications into one application. For example, a Visual Basic program could display data from a database of laboratory instrument data, offer a graphical view of the data on a simulated instrument panel, and co-opt a word processing program (via OLE) for making notes. One of the most common uses for Visual Basic is creating an integrated application from off-the-shelf applications, adding the last 10 percent of functionality and providing a consistent, friendly user interface.

THE NEXT STEP—DAO

The data control is relatively limited in what you can do with it directly. To gain more power and flexibility, you can move on to DAO (Data Access Objects). However, you need the Professional Edition or Enterprise Edition to take that step. The DAO approach is based on a set of class definitions. The set is referred to as a *class hierarchy* because of the way in which the definitions are related to each other. Each class comes with a set of properties and methods. The class hierarchy provides all the tools you need to create, modify, and otherwise work with databases. Before looking at an example, let's look at the DAO class hierarchy.

DAO Classes

The complete DAO class hierarchy is far too grand to be described completely by this humble module, but let's look at some of the main features. First, what does the expression "class hierarchy" mean? The DAO classes are designed in such a way that objects can contain other objects. There's a strict pecking order in this arrangement. For instance, a Recordset object can contain a Field object, but a Field object can't contain a Recordset object. Figure M3-8 illustrates this hierarchical order. Without exploring the full hierarchy, let's look at enough members to allow the creation of a new version of the Update Membership I program.

At the top of the hierarchy is the *DBEngine* class, which represents the Jet database engine. If your Visual Basic program uses Jet, it automatically creates an object of the *DBEngine* class; this object also is named DBEngine. Like other objects, the *DBEngine* has properties and methods. It also has a collection as a member. The collection is a special kind of object that can contain other objects. This is where the hierarchy concept comes in. The collection part of

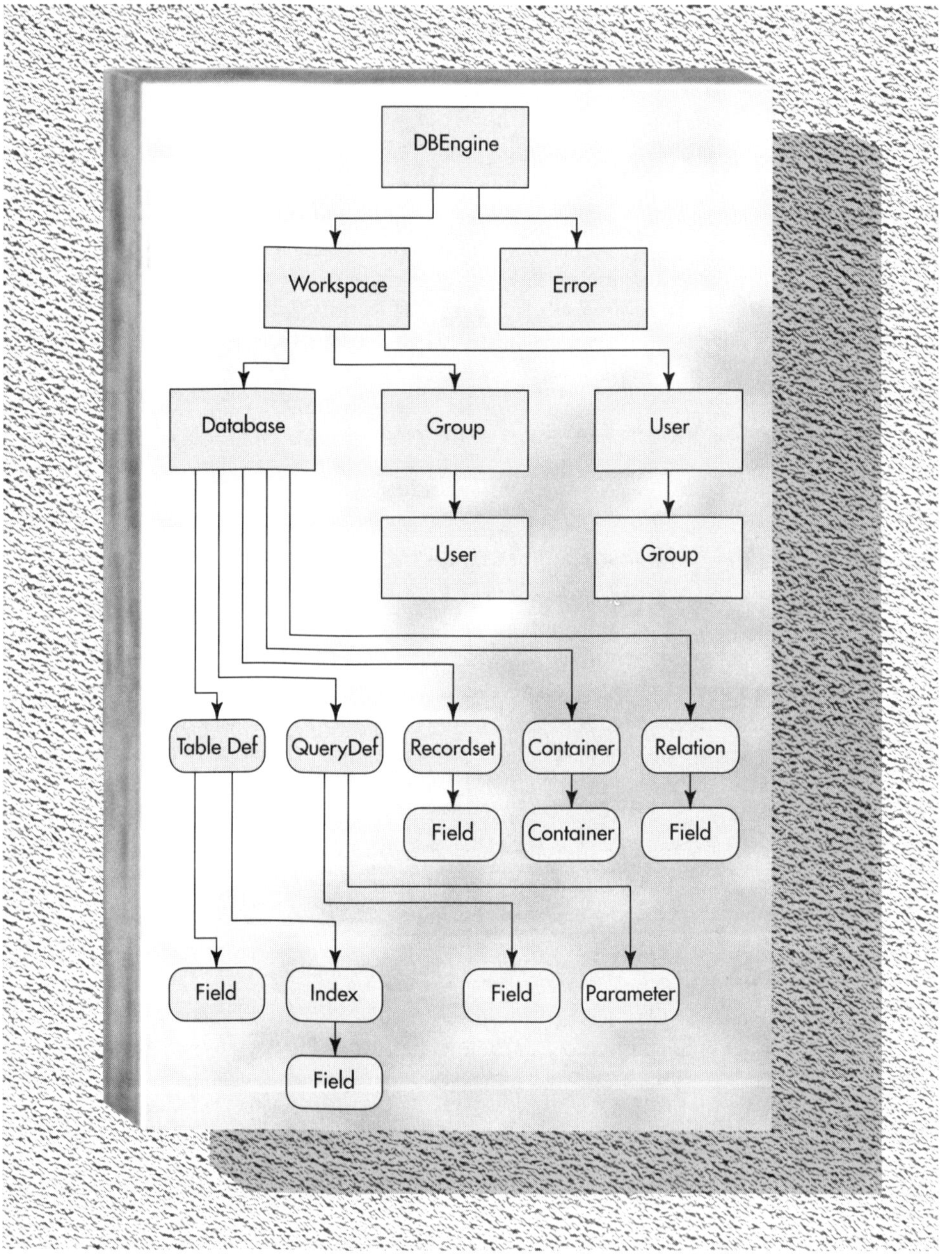

Figure M3-8 The DAO class hierarchy

a *DBEngine* can hold other objects, which in turn can have collections that hold other objects, and so on.

For the *DBEngine* class, the collection is named *Workspaces*. The *Workspaces* collection, in turn, can hold objects of the *Workspaces* class, much as the *Controls* collection holds objects of the *Control* type. When a program uses the Jet database engine, the *Workspaces* collection of the DBEngine object automatically gets a Workspace object. Since it is the first object in the collection, you can call the object Workspace(0).

A Workspace object lets you support several databases simultaneously. Toward that end, it has the *Databases* collection, which, following the same pattern as the *Workspaces* collection, contains objects of the *Database* class. So you could set up a *Workspace* object to manage two databases, and its *Databases* collection object would contain two *Database* objects, one for each database. A Workspace object also has properties and methods that let you open databases, create new databases, and provide a password. Beyond that, a Workspace object has additional collections that won't be discussed. Instead, let's follow just one path down through the hierarchy, the path through the *Databases* collection.

A Database object corresponds to a particular database. It has several collections, including a *Recordsets* collection that contains Recordset objects. (This is the same *Recordset* class that appears as a property of a data control.) A Recordset object represents a table or query viewed as a sequence of records. As you've seen, a Recordset object has many useful methods, such as *AddNew, MoveFirst, Update,* and other examples from the Update Membership I program. It also has a *Fields* collection, which contains objects of the *Field* class. These objects represent particular fields in a record.

Visual Basic uses the usual period notation to indicate objects or collections that are contained in other objects. For instance, consider the following expression:

```
DBEngine.Workspaces(0).Databases(1)
```

DBEngine is the top-level object. It has the *Workspaces* collection, and Workspaces(0) is the first Workspace object in that collection. Next, that object has a *DataBases* collection, and *DataBases(1)* is the second DataBase object in that collection. (Remember that collection numbering starts with 0.)

These classes, along with those not mentioned, provide a complete representation of databases and database processing. Using the properties and methods of the various classes, you can create databases, open databases, modify databases, and analyze databases.

USING DAO

You've already used data access objects when you used the data control. Basically, a data control is just a simple interface to the data access objects. For example, a data control has a DataBase property, which wasn't used, and a Recordset property, which was. The data control hides some of the details. For example, when you bind a text box control to a particular data control and data field, you're really setting up a correspondence between the text box Text property and a particular Field object in the Recordset object, but you're doing so without explicitly mentioning the Field object.

Instead of using a data control to access data access objects indirectly, you can create them directly (providing you have the Professional or Enterprise Edition of Visual Basic). This gives you full access to the complete database-handling package. The cost is the usual one of having more details to attend to. For instance, without using the data control, you can't use bound controls. So instead of having Visual Basic connect database fields to text boxes for you, you'll have to code that connection explicitly.

Revising the Update Membership Program

Let's see what's involved in converting the data control application Update Membership I to a DAO-based version Update Membership II. (This example, too, comes from Don Kiely.)

First, you need a new form. Figure M3-9 shows the new form, and Table M3-6 lists the properties. The main changes are replacing bound controls with unbound controls (that is, the DataField and DataSource properties aren't used), adding a command button to undo changes, eliminating the data control, and replacing the data control's visual interface with an array of four command buttons and a text box.

OBJECT	PROPERTY	SETTING
Form1	BorderStyle	3 - Fixed Dialog
	Caption	Update Membership II
	Name	frmMembers
Frame1	Caption	Name and Address Data
Frame2	Caption	Personal Data
Frame3	Caption	Phone Numbers

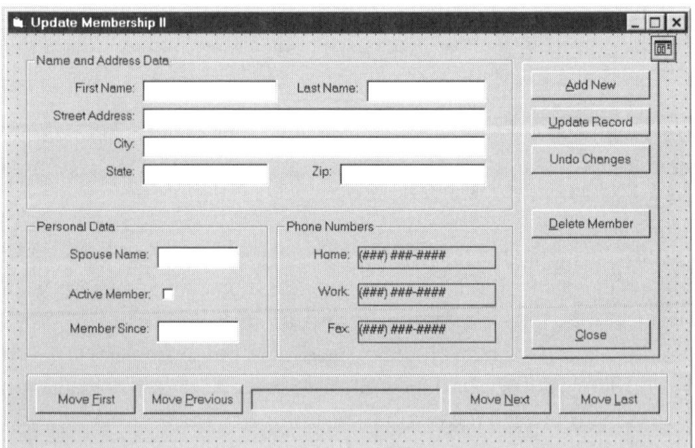

Figure M3-9 The Update Membership II form

OBJECT	PROPERTY	SETTING
Label1	Alignment	1 - Right Justify
	Caption	Last Name:
Label2	Alignment	1 - Right Justify
	Caption	First Name:
Label3	Alignment	1 - Right Justify
	Caption	Street Address:
Label4	Alignment	1 - Right Justify
	Caption	City:
Label5	Alignment	1 - Right Justify
	Caption	State:
Label6	Alignment	1 - Right Justify
	Caption	Zip:
Label7	Alignment	1 - Right Justify
	Caption	Spouse Name:
Label8	Alignment	1 - Right Justify
	Caption	Member Since:
Label9	Alignment	1 - Right Justify
	Caption	Home:
Label10	Alignment	1 - Right Justify
	Caption	Fax:
Label11	Alignment	1 - Right Justify
	Caption	Work:
Text1	Name	txtFirstName
	TabIndex	1
	Text	
Text2	Name	txtLastName
	TabIndex	2
	Text	
Text3	Name	txtAddress
	TabIndex	3
	Text	
Text4	Name	txtCity
	TabIndex	4
	Text	
Text5	Name	txtState
	TabIndex	5
	Text	
Text6	Name	txtZip
	TabIndex	6
	Text	

continued on next page

continued from previous page

OBJECT	PROPERTY	SETTING
Text7	Name	txtSpouseName
	TabIndex	7
	Text	
Text8	Name	txtMemberSince
	TabIndex	9
	Text	
Text9	Name	txtRecordNumber
	Text	
Checkbox1	Caption	Active Member:
	Name	chkActiveMember
	TabIndex	8
mskEdBox1	Format	(###) ###-####
	Mask	(###) ###-####
	Name	mskHomePhone
	TabIndex	10
mskEdBox2	Format	(###) ###-####
	Mask	(###) ###-####
	Name	mskWorkPhone
	TabIndex	11
mskEdBox3	Format	(###) ###-####
	Mask	(###) ###-####
	Name	mskFaxPhone
	TabIndex	12
Command1	Caption	
	Enabled	False
	Name	cmdPanel
Command2	Caption	&Add New
	Name	cmdAddNew
Command3	Caption	&Update Record
	Name	cmdUpdate
Command4	Caption	&Delete Member
	Name	cmdDelete
Command5	Caption	&Close
	Name	cmdClose
Command6	Caption	Undo Changes
	Name	cmdUndoChanges
Command7	Caption	Move &First
	Index	0
	Name	cmdMove

OBJECT	PROPERTY	SETTING
Command8	Caption	Move &Previous
	Index	1
	Name	cmdMove
Command9	Caption	Move &Next
	Index	2
	Name	cmdMove
Command10	Caption	Move &Last
	Index	3
	Name	cmdMove
CommonDialog1	Name	cdDataBase

Table M3-6 Properties for the Update Membership II form

Prerequisite Objects

Once you have a new form, you need some objects to represent the database:

- A *DBEngine* object to represent the database engine
- A *Workspace* object to represent your database workspace
- A *Database* object to represent the database you open
- A *Recordset* object to represent the Members table
- *Field* objects to represent the fields in each record

With the Standard Edition, the only way to get Database and Recordset objects is as part of a data control. With the Professional and Enterprise editions, however, you can declare object variables of these types. You don't have to declare a DBEngine object because you automatically get one when you open a database. For the Workspace object, you can use the one that's created automatically along with the DBEngine object—Workspaces(0), the first object in the *Workspaces* collection. The full name for this object is DBEngine.Workspaces(0). However, because there is just one DBEngine object, you can just use the name Workspaces(0), much as you can use *Print* instead of Form1.Print.

Workspaces(0) is a long name, so programmers often prefer to declare a type *Workspace* variable and set it to refer to Workspaces(0):

```
Dim ws As Workspace     ' Declare variable (not allowed in Standard Edition).
Set ws = Workspace(0)   ' Have it refer to the default workspace.
```

Remember, when you declare an object variable, you don't create a new object; you create a name that can be used to refer to an existing object.

Similarly, you can declare variables of the *Database* and *Recordset* types:

```
Dim db As Database
Dim rs As Recordset
```

Like the *ws* variable, these don't refer to real objects until you take further action. For example, you can use the *OpenDataBase* method of the *Workspace* class to create a Database object, then let *db* refer to that object:

```
Set db = ws.OpenDatabase(strAppFile)
```

Here *strAppFile* is a string variable representing the name of the database file. You also could refer to the db object as ws.Databases(0), assuming it's the first database object you've added to the *Databases* collection.

Similarly, you can use the *OpenRecordset* method of the *Database* class to create a Recordset object. The new example, for instance, will use the following code:

```
strSQL = "SELECT * FROM Members ORDER BY [Last Name],[First Name]"
Set rs = db.OpenRecordset(strSQL)
```

The SQL string is the same one used last time; it requests the information be alphabetized by last name, then first name. The *OpenRecordset* method of the *Database* class then creates a new recordset, populating it as directed, and the program makes *rs* a reference to the new recordset. The object referred to by *rs* also can be called *db.Recordsets(0)*, or *ws.Databases(0).rs*, or *DBEngine.Workspaces(0).Databases(0).Recordsets(0)*. You can see why programmers prefer to declare an object variable like *rs* to use as an alias!

Finally, you need a Field object for each field in the Recordset. Fortunately, these Field objects are created automatically when the Recordset is constructed. They are in the *Fields* collection of the *rs Recordset* object. As a convenience, you can access members of this collection by using the name of the field. For example, the Zip field is represented by the *rs.Fields("Zip")* object. That is, instead of using a numeric index, you use a string consisting of the field name as index to the *Fields* collection.

Revising Code

With this arsenal of objects, you are ready to convert Update Membership I to Update Membership II. First, the code will include the object declarations and assignments just covered. Then you can use these objects to duplicate the effects of the first version.

For example, consider the code to add a new record. The first version did this:

```
dataMembers.Recordset.AddNew
dataMembers.Recordset.Update
dataMembers.Recordset.MoveLast
```

That is, it used the *AddNew, Update,* and *MoveLast* methods of the *Recordset* class, applying them to the Recordset object associated with the *datamembers* data control. The new version will use the same methods, but applying them to the *rs* Recordset object:

```
rs.AddNew
rs.Update
rs.MoveLast
```

Much of the program can be converted in this fashion, replacing *dataMembers.Recordset* with *rs*.

Replacing the Bound Controls

Reproducing the functionality of the bound controls is more involved. One approach is to add a *ReadRecord* procedure that copies fields to the controls and a *SaveRecord* procedure that copies the information in the controls to the database fields. The basic code for copying information from a field to a text box is this:

```
txtLastName.Text = rs.Fields("Last Name")
```

However, there's a possibility that the field hasn't yet been defined, in which case the field will have the special value NULL. In that case, the text box should be assigned the empty string:

```
If IsNull(rs.Fields("Last Name")) Then
    txtLastName.Text = ""
Else
    txtLastName.Text = rs.Fields("Last Name")
End If
```

This can be shortened a bit by using the IIf function, which has this syntax:

IIf(*expr, truepart, falsepart*)

If the *expr* argument is true, the function returns the value of the *truepart* argument; otherwise, it returns the value of *falsepart*. Using this function, you can rewrite the code in this manner:

```
txtLastName.Text = IIf(Not IsNull(rs.Fields("Last Name")), _
    rs.Fields("Last Name"), "")
```

The *ReadRecord* procedure, then, would contain similar code for all the fields.

The basic code for copying information from a text box to a field is this:

```
rs.Edit
rs.Fields("Last Name") = txtLastName.Text
rs.Update
```

The *Edit* method copies the current record to a memory workspace called the *copy buffer*. The changes you make are made in this temporary copy, and the *Update* command saves the changes in the database and Recordset. The *SaveRecord* procedure, then, would have similar code for all the fields. Since the *Edit* and *Update* methods operate upon the entire record, they can be called once to handle all the fields.

Once you've defined *SaveRecord* and *ReadRecord*, you can use them in the other procedures to update and display records. For example, the *cmdClose_Click* event can be rewritten this way:

```
Private Sub cmdClose_Click()
    'End the program, after updating the current record.
    SaveRecord
     Unload Me
End Sub
```

Similarly, the *Click* event for the new cmdUndoChanges button can be written like this:

```
Private Sub cmdUndoChanges_Click()
    'Undo the changes to the controls by reloading the record.
    ReadRecord
End Sub
```

Replacing the Data Control

The objects you've defined replace part of the functionality of the data control. However, you also have to replace the user interface, the data control buttons that moved through the records. The program can do that with an array of four command buttons. One will move to the first record, one to the previous record, one to the next record, and one to the last record. For instance, the button going to the first record can use this code:

```
'Before moving from the current record, save any changes.
    SaveRecord
'Move to the first record.
    If CurrRec = 1 Then
        Beep
    Else
        rs.MoveFirst
        CurrRec = 1
    End If
'Load the contents of the current record, after moving.
    ReadRecord
'Update the current record number.
    SetRecNum
```

The main points to notice are that it's the programmer's responsibility to update the current record before moving to another record, and it's the programmer's responsibility to update the text boxes and other controls to reflect the new record. The project uses an array of command buttons for positioning, so it incorporates parts of this code into a *Select Case* statement.

The End Result

Now that you've seen the kinds of changes that need to be made, you're in a position to understand the code for Update Membership II, which appears in Listing M3-2.

Listing M3-2
The Update Membership II program

(This project requires the Professional or Enterprise edition.)

```
Option Explicit

'Form globals to maintain the current and total record number.
Dim TotRec As Integer
Dim CurrRec As Integer
```

```
'Store the path and name of the database file for use throughout
'the application.
Dim strAppFile As String

'Form globals to hold the Workspace, Database, and Recordset objects.
Dim ws As Workspace
Dim db As Database
Dim rs As Recordset

Sub ReadRecord()
    'Load the contents of the current record into the form's controls.
    'But, only do it if there is a current record.

    If Not (rs.BOF Or rs.EOF) Then
        txtLastName.Text = IIf(Not IsNull(rs.Fields("Last Name")), _
            rs.Fields("Last Name"), "")
        txtFirstName.Text = IIf(Not IsNull(rs.Fields("First Name")), _
            rs.Fields("First Name"), "")
        txtAddress.Text = IIf(Not IsNull(rs.Fields("Address")), _
            rs.Fields("Address"), "")
        txtCity.Text = IIf(Not IsNull(rs.Fields("City")), _
            rs.Fields("City"), "")
        txtState.Text = IIf(Not IsNull(rs.Fields("State")), _
            rs.Fields("State"), "")
        txtZip.Text = IIf(Not IsNull(rs.Fields("Zip")), _
            rs.Fields("Zip"), "")
        mskHomePhone.Text = IIf(Not IsNull(rs.Fields("Home Phone")), _
            rs.Fields("Home Phone"), "")
        mskWorkPhone.Text = IIf(Not IsNull(rs.Fields("Work Phone")), _
            rs.Fields("Work Phone"), "")
        mskFaxNumber.Text = IIf(Not IsNull(rs.Fields("Fax Number")), _
            rs.Fields("Fax Number"), "")

        If IsNull(rs.Fields("Active")) Then
            chkActiveMember.VALUE = 2 'Grayed
        ElseIf rs.Fields("Active") Then
            chkActiveMember.VALUE = 1 'Checked
        Else
            chkActiveMember.VALUE = 0 'Unchecked
        End If

        txtMemberSince.Text = IIf(Not IsNull(rs.Fields("Member Since")), _
            rs.Fields("Member Since"), "")
        txtSpouseName.Text = IIf(Not IsNull(rs.Fields("Spouse Name")), _
            rs.Fields("Spouse Name"), "")
    End If
End Sub

Sub SaveRecord()
    'Save the contents of the form's controls to the current record,
    'but only if there is a current record.

    If Not (rs.BOF Or rs.EOF) Then
        rs.Edit

        rs.Fields("Last Name") = txtLastName.Text
        rs.Fields("First Name") = txtFirstName.Text
        rs.Fields("Address") = txtAddress.Text
        rs.Fields("City") = txtCity.Text
        rs.Fields("State") = txtState.Text
```

continued on next page

continued from previous page

```
        rs.Fields("Zip") = txtZip.Text
        rs.Fields("Home Phone") = mskHomePhone.Text
        rs.Fields("Work Phone") = mskWorkPhone.Text
        rs.Fields("Fax Number") = mskFaxNumber.Text

        If chkActiveMember.VALUE = 0 Or chkActiveMember.VALUE = 2 Then
            rs.Fields("Active") = False
        Else
            rs.Fields("Active") = True
        End If

        rs.Fields("Member Since") = txtMemberSince.Text
        rs.Fields("Spouse Name") = txtSpouseName.Text

        rs.Update
    End If
End Sub

Sub SetRecNum()
    'This procedure updates the caption of txtRecordNumber to maintain
    'our location accurately. This does not execute if we are editing
    'a new record, since we won't have the correct information.

    If rs.EditMode <> dbEditAdd Then
        If rs.BOF = True Then
            txtRecordNumber = "Member BOF of " & TotRec
        ElseIf rs.EOF = True Then
            txtRecordNumber = "Member EOF of " & TotRec
        Else
            txtRecordNumber = "Member " & CurrRec & " of " & TotRec
        End If
    End If

End Sub

Sub cmdAddNew_Click()
    'Add a new record. If default data needs to be entered in any fields,
    'make those entries between the AddNew and Update lines.
    rs.AddNew
    rs.Update

    'The new record will be at the end of the recordset, so move there.
    rs.MoveLast

    'Load the form's controls with the current record. They are empty, of
    'course, but this is a quick way to clear the controls.
    ReadRecord

    'Move to the first field for immediate editing.
    txtFirstName.SetFocus

    'Update the record counter and display.
    TotRec = TotRec + 1
    CurrRec = TotRec

    SetRecNum
End Sub

Private Sub cmdClose_Click()
    'End the program, after updating the current record.
```

```
    SaveRecord

    'Since this application has only one form, Unload ends the app.
    Unload Me
End Sub

Sub cmdDelete_Click()
Dim response As Integer

    'Delete the current record. First, make sure that's what we want.
    response = MsgBox("Are you sure that you want to delete this member?", _
        vbCritical + vbYesNo, "Verify Delete")

    If response = vbYes Then
        'Delete the record. This triggers the Validate event first.
        rs.Delete

        'Rebuild the recordset so that we have a clean copy.
        rs.Requery

        'Update the total record count.
        TotRec = TotRec - 1

        'If that was the last record in the recordset, add a new record
        'so that we don't have an empty recordset.
        If rs.BOF And rs.EOF Then
            rs.AddNew
            rs.Update
            rs.MoveLast

            'Update the current record number.
            TotRec = TotRec + 1
            CurrRec = TotRec
        Else
            'If that wasn't the last record, move to the first record
            'so that the current record is a valid record (not deleted).
            rs.MoveFirst

            'Update the current record number.
            CurrRec = 1
        End If
    End If

    'Load the form's controls with data from the current record.
    ReadRecord

    'Update the record counter display.
    SetRecNum
End Sub

Private Sub cmdMove_Click(Index As Integer)
    'Before moving from the current record, save any changes.
    SaveRecord

    Select Case Index
        Case 0 'Move to the first record
            If CurrRec = 1 Then
                Beep
            Else
                rs.MoveFirst
                CurrRec = 1
```

continued on next page

continued from previous page

```
            End If

        Case 1 'Move to the previous record.
            rs.MovePrevious
            CurrRec = CurrRec - 1

            'Make sure that we aren't before the first record.
            'If so, move back to the first record.
            If rs.BOF Then
                Beep
                rs.MoveFirst
                CurrRec = 1
            End If

        Case 2 'Move to the next record.
            rs.MoveNext
            CurrRec = CurrRec + 1

            'Make sure that we aren't beyond the last record.
            'If so, move back to the last record.
            If rs.EOF Then
                Beep
                rs.MoveLast
                CurrRec = TotRec
            End If

        Case 3 'Move to the last record.
            If CurrRec = TotRec Then
                Beep
            Else
                rs.MoveLast
                CurrRec = TotRec
            End If

    End Select

    'Load the contents of the current record, after moving.
    ReadRecord

    'Update the current record number.
    SetRecNum
End Sub

Private Sub cmdUndoChanges_Click()
    'Undo the changes to the controls by reloading the record.
    ReadRecord
End Sub

Private Sub cmdUpdate_Click()
    'Save the contents of the form's control to the database. This way,
    'the user can save the data without moving the record pointer.
    SaveRecord
End Sub


Private Sub Form_Activate()
    'This event triggers when the Form first becomes visible, in this
    'case after Form_Load.

    'Move to the end of the recordset, so that
```

```
    'we have accurate starting numbers for TotRec and CurrRec.
    rs.MoveLast
    TotRec = rs.RecordCount
    rs.MoveFirst
    CurrRec = 1
    SetRecNum

    'Load the form's controls with data from the current record.
    ReadRecord

End Sub

Private Sub Form_Load()
Dim strSQL As String

    'If the Members.mdb database is not in the application directory,
    'prompt the user to point us at its location, using a common dialog
    'control.

    strAppFile = App.Path
    strAppFile = IIf(Right(strAppFile, 1) = "\", strAppFile, strAppFile & "\")
    strAppFile = strAppFile & "Members.mdb"

    If Len(Dir(strAppFile)) = 0 Then
        'The length of the name is 0, so the file wasn't found. Set up the
        'file open common dialog and get the file's location.
        cdDatabase.InitDir = App.Path
        cdDatabase.filename = "Members.mdb"
        cdDatabase.Filter = "Access files (*.mdb)|*.mdb|All files (*.*)|*.*"
        cdDatabase.CancelError = True

        On Error GoTo CancelError
        cdDatabase.Action = 1
        On Error GoTo 0

        strAppFile = cdDatabase.filename

        If Len(Dir(strAppFile)) = 0 Then
            'No file selected   canceled out of the file open dialog
            MsgBox "No file selected. Ending application.", vbCritical, _
                "No Database Selected"
            End
        End If
    End If

    'Open the database and set the global Database object variable.
    Set ws = Workspaces(0)
    Set db = ws.OpenDatabase(strAppFile)

    'Create the recordset object; this holds the actual records that we'll use.
    strSQL = "SELECT * FROM Members ORDER BY [Last Name],[First Name]"
    Set rs = db.OpenRecordset(strSQL)

    'There needs to be at least one record in the file. If BOF and EOF
    'are both true, there are no records, so add one.
    If rs.BOF And rs.EOF Then
        rs.AddNew
        rs.Update
    End If

    'Center the form on the screen.
```

continued on next page

continued from previous page

```
    Me.Move (Screen.Width - Me.Width) / 2, (Screen.Height - Me.Height) / 2

    Exit Sub

CancelError:
    End
End Sub
```

Commentary

The Update Membership II program mainly illustrates how to access a database without using the data control. The only new functionality it added was the Undo Changes button. However, you could use DAO to add other features. For example, there could be buttons to sort by name, sort by city, sort by ZIP code. The sorting techniques involve creating new recordsets. For example, you could do this to get a recordset sorted by ZIP code:

```
Dim rsByZip as Recordset
rs.Sort = "[Zip]"
Set rsByZip =rs.OpenRecordSet()
```

The Sort property tells Visual Basic how to sort data in the recordset when you use the *OpenRecordSet* method to create a new Recordset object. Then you could use *rsByZip.Fields* instead of *rs.Fields* to determine what gets displayed. The main point here is not how to sort, but that there are many possibilities.

Using DAO and data controls are not mutually exclusive. Indeed, the data control is an interface to DAO. It may turn out that you might wish to use both in an application. For instance, you could use a data control and bound controls to display the contents of a record, and use DAO to provide additional features.

SUMMARY

Database applications are among the most common, the most important, and, in many cases, the most challenging uses of the computer. Visual Basic, particularly the Professional and Enterprise editions, has been designed to support database work. The key element is the Jet database engine, which provides an interface between Visual Basic programs and a variety of database products.

The simplest way to tap into the power of the Jet database engine is to use the data control and bound controls. The data control links the program to a database and allows you to move from record to record. The bound controls, in turn, display the information in the current record.

You can use the data control and bound controls to display and edit records without having to write any code. By adding code, you can make the application able to add and delete records. This much you can do with any of the Visual Basic editions.

Going to the Professional Edition adds the ability to create new data access objects and to create new databases. The methods and properties of data access objects give you full programming control over databases.

The Enterprise Edition adds tools for creating client and server applications. In networked situations, it's useful to have one application (the server) maintain the primary database information and let other applications (the clients) send queries to the server to obtain and update information.

Clearly, there's much more to databases than what this module covers. The Waite Group Press has a couple of books that can take you much further. One is *Visual Basic 4 OLE, Database, & Controls SuperBible* by Michael Hatmaker, Bill Potter, C. Woody Butler, David Jung, John Murphy, and Ibrahim Malluf, which primarily is a reference. The second is *Visual Basic 4 Database How-To,* by Stuart Bloom and Don Kiely, which is example-laden. If you prefer to work things out on your own, you can study the database projects found in the SAMPLES directory of your Visual Basic installation. Don't forget that Visual Basic Help can help you understand things you find in those projects.

APPENDIX A NUMBER BASES

Our method for writing numbers is based on powers of ten. For instance, consider the number 2,468. The 2 represents 2 thousand, the 4 represents 4 hundreds, the 6 represents 6 tens, and the 8 represents 8 ones:

$$2{,}468 = 2 \times 1000 + 4 \times 100 + 6 \times 10 + 8 \times 1$$

One thousand is 10 x 10 x 10, which can be written as 10^3, or 10 to the third power. Using this notation, you can write the preceding relationship this way:

$$2{,}468 = 2 \times 10^3 + 4 \times 10^2 + 6 \times 10^1 + 8 \times 10^0$$

(Note: 10^0 is 1, as is any nonzero number to the zero power.)

Because our number notation is based on powers of 10, we refer to it as *base ten,* or *decimal,* notation. You can just as easily pick another number as a base. Visual Basic lets you use *base 16 (hexadecimal)* notation for writing integer numbers.

HEXADECIMAL NUMBERS

Hexadecimal numbers are based on powers of 16. That means 10 in hexadecimal represents the value 16 + 0, or 16. To represent the values between 9 and hexadecimal 16, we need a few more digits. Standard hexadecimal notation uses the letters a–f for that purpose. Visual Basic accepts either lowercase or uppercase versions of these characters, as shown in Table A-1.

HEXADECIMAL DIGITS	DECIMAL VALUE	HEXADECIMAL DIGITS	DECIMAL VALUE
a or A	10	d or D	13
b or B	11	e or E	14
c or C	12	f or F	15

Table A-1 Hexadecimal digits

Visual Basic uses an *&h* or an *&H* prefix to indicate hexadecimal notation. Thus *&H2B3* is a hexadecimal value. To find its decimal equivalent, you can evaluate the powers of 16:

$$\text{\&H2B3 (hex)} = 2 \times 16^2 + 11 \times 16^1 + 3 \times 16^0 = 2 \times 256 + 11 \times 16 + 3$$
$$= 691 \text{ (decimal)}$$

You can check this conversion by using *Print:*

```
Print &H2B3
```

You'll find that this prints the value 691.

Hardware documentation often uses hexadecimal notation to represent values such as memory locations and port numbers. Visual Basic usually represents color constants as hexadecimal values.

BINARY NUMBERS

Whether you use decimal or hexadecimal notation for writing an integer, the computer stores it as a *binary,* or base 2, value. Binary notation uses just two digits, 0 and 1. As an example, 10011011 is a *binary* number. Note, however, that Visual Basic doesn't provide for writing a number in binary notation. Binary numbers are based on powers of 2:

$$10011011 = 1 \times 2^7 + 0 \times 2^6 + 0 \times 2^5 + 1 \times 2^4 + 1 \times 2^3 + 0 \times 2^2 + 1 \times 2^1 + 1 \times 2^0$$
$$= 128 + 0 + 0 + 16 + 8 + 0 + 2 + 0$$
$$= 154$$

Binary notation makes a nice match to computer memory, in which each individual unit, called a *bit,* can be set to Off or On. Just identify the Off setting with 0 and the On setting with 1. Memory commonly is organized in units called *bytes,* with each byte being eight bits. The bits in a byte are numbered corresponding to the associated power of two. Thus the rightmost bit is bit number 0, the next bit is bit 1, and so on. Figure A-1, for example, represents a 2-byte integer.

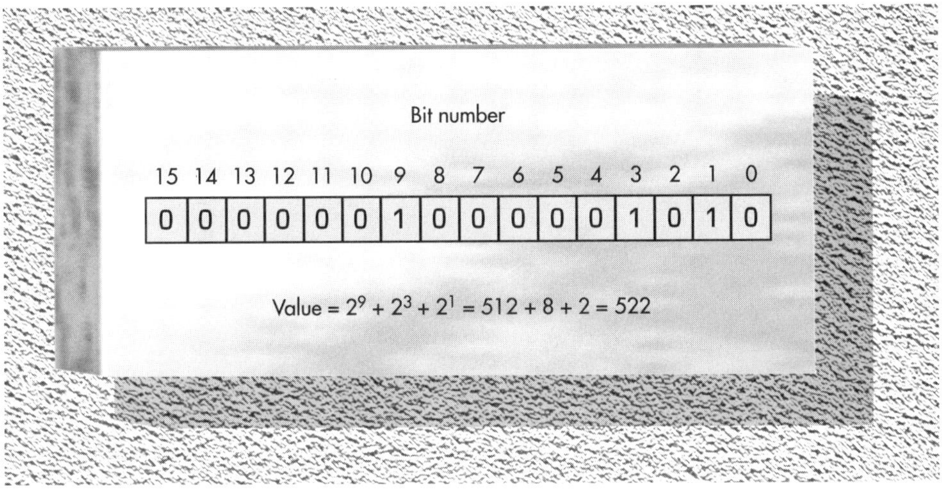

Figure A-1 A 2-byte integer value

Visual Basic sometimes uses individual bits in an integer as *flags,* that is, as values that can be set to on or off, yes or no. For instance, the common dialog control has a Flags property. If you examine the constants used to define flags, you'll see that they are powers of 2. The connection is that each power of 2 corresponds to a particular bit, or to a particular flag. Thus, setting a flag to 2 turns on bit 1, setting a flag to 8 turns on bit 3, and setting a flag to 2 + 8, or 10, turns on both bits 1 and 3.

APPENDIX

B BITS AND BYTES

The fundamental unit of computer memory is called the *bit*. It has two possible values, or settings, which are represented by the values 0 (or Off) and 1 (or On). Everything stored in a computer has to be stored as a combinations of 0s and 1s. Since 0s and 1s are the digits used for binary numbers (see Appendix A), the natural way to store an integer in a computer is as a binary number. Items other than integers have to be represented by some sort of binary code. Characters like the letter *V*, for example, are represented by the ASCII code (Appendix C). Similarly, computer instructions are represented by a binary code. Also, floating-point numbers are represented by a binary code in which some binary digits represent a value and other binary digits represent an exponent. In short, if you could see into computer memory, all you would see are 0s or 1s, regardless of what sort of information that memory represented.

Bits are organized into larger units called *bytes*, with each byte containing eight bits. Since there are two possible values for each bit in a byte, there are 2^8, or 256, possible settings for a byte. These can be used to represent, say, the values 0 to 255 or the values –128 to 127. Visual Basic uses a 2-byte unit to represent the *Integer* type. This allows 2^{16}, or 65,536, possible values, which are used to represent the integers in the range –32,768 to 32,767. Similarly, the *Long* type uses four bytes, allowing it to represent the range –2,147,483,648 to 2,147,483,647.

Normally, the *kilo* prefix means a thousand. For instance, a *kilometer* is a thousand meters. In the computer world, however, a kilo means 1,024, which is the power of 2 closest to 1,000 in value. Thus a *kilobyte* of memory is 1,024 bytes. Similarly, a megabyte is not a million bytes. Instead it is 1,024 x 1,024 bytes, or 1,048,576 bytes. Incidentally, the notations *Kb* and *Mb* mean kilobits and megabits, while *KB* and *MB* mean kilobytes and megabytes.

APPENDIX C

THE ASCII CHARACTER SET

Computers store characters using a numeric code. The ASCII code is the most commonly used code in the United States. Visual Basic lets you represent most single characters directly, by including the character in double quotation marks, as in "*A*" for the A character. You can also represent a single character by applying the *Chr* function to the ASCII value. For example Chr(13) is the carriage return character. Similarly, the function returns the ASCII value of a character. For example, *Asc*("*B*") is 65.

When used as a prefix in the following table, the ^ character denotes using CTRL.

DECIMAL	HEX	BINARY	CHARACTER
0	0	00000000	^@
1	&H1	00000001	^A (alert character)
2	&H2	00000010	^B
3	&H3	00000011	^C
4	&H4	00000100	^D
5	&H5	00000101	^E
6	&H6	00000110	^F
7	&H7	00000111	^G
8	&H8	00001000	^H (backspace)
9	&H9	00001001	^I (horizontal tab)
10	&HA	00001010	^J (line feed)
11	&HB	00001011	^K
12	&HC	00001100	^L
13	&HD	00001101	^M (carriage return)
14	&HE	00001110	^N
15	&HF	00001111	^O

continued on next page

continued from previous page

DECIMAL	HEX	BINARY	CHARACTER
16	&H10	00010000	^P
17	&H11	00010001	^Q
18	&H12	00010010	^R
19	&H13	00010011	^S
20	&H14	00010100	^T
21	&H15	00010101	^U
22	&H16	00010110	^V
23	&H17	00010111	^W
24	&H18	00011000	^X
25	&H19	00011001	^Y
26	&H1A	00011010	^Z
27	&H1B	00011011	^esc
28	&H1C	00011100	^\
29	&H1D	00011101	^]
30	&H1E	00011110	^^
31	&H1F	00011111	^_
32	&H20	00100000	space
33	&H21	00100001	!
34	&H22	00100010	"
35	&H23	00100011	#
36	&H24	00100100	$
37	&H25	00100101	%
38	&H26	00100110	&
39	&H27	00100111	'
40	&H28	00101000	(
41	&H29	00101001	)
42	&H2A	00101010	*
43	&H2B	00101011	+
44	&H2C	00101100	,
45	&H2D	00101101	-
46	&H2E	00101110	.
47	&H2F	00101111	/
48	&H30	00110000	0
49	&H31	00110001	1
50	&H32	00110010	2
51	&H33	00110011	3
52	&H34	00110100	4
53	&H35	00110101	5

DECIMAL	HEX	BINARY	CHARACTER
54	&H36	00110110	6
55	&H37	00110111	7
56	&H38	00111000	8
57	&H39	00111001	9
58	&H3A	00111010	:
59	&H3B	00111011	;
60	&H3C	00111100	<
61	&H3D	00111101	=
62	&H3E	00111110	>
63	&H3F	00111111	?
64	&H40	01000000	@
65	&H41	01000001	A
66	&H42	01000010	B
67	&H43	01000011	C
68	&H44	01000100	D
69	&H45	01000101	E
70	&H46	01000110	F
71	&H47	01000111	G
72	&H48	01001000	H
73	&H49	01001001	I
74	&H4A	01001010	J
75	&H4B	01001011	K
76	&H4C	01001100	L
77	&H4D	01001101	M
78	&H4E	01001110	N
79	&H4F	01001111	O
80	&H50	01010000	P
81	&H51	01010001	Q
82	&H52	01010010	R
83	&H53	01010011	S
84	&H54	01010100	T
85	&H55	01010101	U
86	&H56	01010110	V
87	&H57	01010111	W
88	&H58	01011000	X
89	&H59	01011001	Y
90	&H5A	01011010	Z
91	&H5B	01011011	[
92	&H5C	01011100	\

continued on next page

continued from previous page

DECIMAL	HEX	BINARY	CHARACTER
93	&H5D	01011101	]
94	&H5E	01011110	^
95	&H5F	01011111	_
96	&H60	01100000	'
97	&H61	01100001	a
98	&H62	01100010	b
99	&H63	01100011	c
100	&H64	01100100	d
101	&H65	01100101	e
102	&H66	01100110	f
103	&H67	01100111	g
104	&H68	01101000	h
105	&H69	01101001	i
106	&H6A	01101010	j
107	&H6B	01101011	k
108	&H6C	01101100	l
109	&H6D	01101101	m
110	&H6E	01101110	n
111	&H6F	01101111	o
112	&H70	01110000	p
113	&H71	01110001	q
114	&H72	01110010	r
115	&H73	01110011	s
116	&H74	01110100	t
117	&H75	01110101	u
118	&H76	01110110	v
119	&H77	01110111	w
120	&H78	01111000	x
121	&H79	01111001	y
122	&H7A	01111010	z
123	&H7B	01111011	{
124	&H7C	01111100	|
125	&H7D	01111101	}
126	&H7E	01111110	~
127	&H7F	01111111	del, rubout

APPENDIX D VISUAL BASIC FUNDAMENTAL TYPES

DATA TYPE	STORAGE SIZE	RANGE
Byte	1 byte	0 to 255
Boolean	2 bytes	True or False.
Integer	2 bytes	–32,768 to 32,767.
Long	4 bytes	–2,147,483,648 to 2,147,483,647.
Single	4 bytes	–3.402823E38 to –1.401298E-45 for negative values; 1.401298E-45 to 3.402823E38 for positive values.
Double	8 bytes	–1.79769313486232E308 to –4.94065645841247E-324 for negative values; 4.94065645841247E-324 to 1.79769313486232E308 for positive values.
Currency	8 bytes	–922,337,203,685,477.5808 to 922,337,203,685,477.5807.
Date	8 bytes	January 1, 100 to December 31, 9999.
Object	4 bytes	Any Object reference (hold the address of object).
String (variable-length)	10 bytes + string length	0 to approximately 2 billion characters
String (fixed-length)	Length of string	1 to approximately 65,400.
Variant (with numbers)	16 bytes	Any numeric value up to the range of a *Double*.

continued on next page

continued from previous page

DATA TYPE	STORAGE SIZE	RANGE
Variant (with characters)	22 bytes + string length	Same range as for variable-length *String*.
User-defined (using *Type*)	Number required by elements	The range of each element is the same as the range of its data type.

APPENDIX E ANSWERS TO QUIZZES

Lesson 1

1. b, 2. b, 3. b, 4. b, 5. b, 6. b

Lesson 2

1. An Object box identifies the object whose properties are listed. A Settings box lets you enter new settings for a property. A properties list lists each property and its current settings.

2. b, 3. c, 4. c, 5. a, 6. b, 7. c, 8. b, 9. a, 10. b

Lesson 3

1. b, 2. b, 3. c, 4. a, 5. c, 6. b, 7. b, 8. b

Lesson 4

1.c, 2. b, 3. b, 4. b, 5. c

6. MouseUp is caused by releasing a mouse button. LostFocus is caused by pressing TAB when a text box has the focus. Change is caused by typing M when a text box has the focus.

7. c, 8. b

Lesson 5

1. Indicate whether each of the following is a valid variable name or not:

a. Bigfoot	Valid
b. 2Much	Invalid

c. End — Invalid

d. ThisIsALongName — Valid

e. ButThisIsEvenALongerName!AlbeitAVeryStupidOne — Valid

f. Hot-Pink — Invalid

g. ClassOf99 — Valid

2. You can create variables without declaring them explicitly. True
   Microsoft recommends declaring variables explicitly. True
   The default type for a new variable is *String*. False
   The *Option Explicit* statement converts implicit declarations to explicit declarations. False
   A variable declared in one procedure automatically is available to other procedures in the same module. False
   You must be over 17 to use explicit declarations False

```
Andy = 1054                    Andy is assigned the integer value 1054
Bitsy = 1054                   Bitsy is assigned the string "1054"
Colinda = 1054                 Colinda is a Variant holding the integer 1054
Bitsy = TypeName(Colinda)      Bitsy is assigned the string "Integer"
Andy = "10" + "54"             Andy is assigned the integer 64
Bitsy = 10 + 54                Bitsy is assigned the string "54"
Colinda = "10" + Str(56)       Colinda is assigned the string "10 56"
Bitsy = TypeName(Colinda)      Bitsy is assigned the string "String"
Colinda = "The Crab Nebula"    Colinda is assigned the string "The Crab Nebula"
Andy = "The Crab Nebula"       causes an error message
```

4. a. *String*
   b. Integer
   c. Long
   d. Single
   e. Currency
   f. Double
   g. Single

Or you could use *Variant* for all of them.

Lesson 6

1.
```
3 = 4                             False
3 < = 4                           True
10 >= 6 + 4                       True
10 > 5 And 10 < 12                True
10 > 5 Or 10 > 14                 True
"house" > "castle"                True
Len ("house") > Len ("castle")    False
```

2. a.
```
If Guests > 12 Then Print "Too many!"
```
   b.
```
If Computer = "Cray" Then
Print "What's this program doing here?"
End If
```

c.
```
If X = 7 Then
Print "Seven is correct!"
Else
Print "Sorry, that's wrong."
End If
```

3. a. `Const InchesPerFoot As Integer = 12`
   b. `Const Dozen As Integer = 12`
   c. `Const Pi as Single = 3.14159`
   d. `Const People as Integer = 42`

4. d

5. Add either

```
cmdClear.VALUE = True
```

or

```
cmdClear_Click
```

to each of the option button *Click* events.

Lesson 7

1.
```
1
6
11
```

2. This loop would print nothing unless you added *Step –1* to the *For* statement.

3.
```
1
2
3
4
```

4.
```
1
2
3
4
5
```

5. This loop would print 1 indefinitely, for nothing in the loop changes the value of I.

6. Visual Basic loops use a *Boolean* test condition to determine whether to loop for another cycle. An entry-condition loop is based on the philosophy of looking before you loop. The test is evaluated at the beginning of each loop cycle, and if the result is false, the loop terminates. The exit-condition loop, however, loops before looking, testing the loop condition at the end of each cycle.

7. The Value property represents the value corresponding to the scroll box position, *Min* and *Max* represent the minimum and maximum values represented by the two extreme positions of the scroll box. *SmallChange* represents how much the value changes if you click on one of the arrows. *LargeChange* represents how

much the value changes if you click near the end of a scrollbar just before the arrow boxes.

Lesson 8

1. c
2. e
3. For a menu title, or for a control, an access key has you press a key while ALT is depressed. So if the access key is G, you press ALT-G. For a menu item, you first have to open the menu, then you can type the access key without pressing ALT. A hot key takes you directly to the result of clicking on a menu item, even if the menu itself is closed. Hot keys typically involve using CTRL or a function key.
4. The Checked property of a menu item is true if the menu item has a check mark showing. Clicking on a menu item alternately checks and unchecks the item.
5. Open the menu editor. Enter Dessert in the menu Caption box. Choose a name such as mnuDes for the name box. Click on the Next button and click on the right-pointing arrow to make the next item an entry under the Dessert menu title. Enter Pudding for the Caption and a name such as mnuDesPud for the Name. Click on the Next button. Enter Mousse for the Caption and a name such as mnuDesMous for the Name. Click on the Next button. Enter Flan for the Caption and a name such as mnuDesFlan for the Name. Click on the OK button.
6. c

Lesson 9

1. b
2. You can use the *Index* argument to the event procedure to determine which control received the event, and you can use an *If* statement or a *Select Case* statement to treat different values of *Index* differently.
3. b
4. You would place option buttons in a frame to group them visually and so that they would not interact with other option buttons on the same form.
5. a. `Dim Ari(1 to 20) As Integer`

   b. `Dim Stores(0 to 14) As String`

   c. `Dim GoodYear(1985 to 1994) As Boolean`
6.
```
Dim Scores (0 to 19) As Integer
Dim Sum As Integer
Dim I As Integer
Sum = 0
For I = 0 to 19
     Sum = Sum + Scores(I)
Next I
```

7. Typically, you would initialize a module-level array in the *Form_Initialize* or *Form_Load* event.

Lesson 10

1. c, 2. c, 3. d
4. BackColor represents the background color. ForeColor is used for text and drawing. FillColor is used for the FillStyle pattern.
5. The meaning of 8-bit, 16-bit, and 24-bit color is that 8-bit color uses 8 bits (1 byte) to describe the color of each pixel, 16-bit color uses 16 bits (2 bytes), and 24-bit uses 24 bits (3 bytes) to describe the color of each pixel. This means that 8-bit color supports 256 simultaneous colors, 16-bit color supports 65,736 colors, and 24-bit color supports 16.7 million colors.
6. Rectangle, square, rounded rectangle, rounded square, circle, oval
7. You set the Interval property to 2000.
8. You can set the Interval property to 0 or set the Enabled property to False.
9. b, 10. c

Lesson 11

1. Bitmapped images (.BMP and .ICO extensions) and Windows Metafile images (.WMF extension)
2. Bitmapped images (.BMP and .ICO extensions) and Windows Metafile images (.WMF extension)
3. You must set the image control Stretch property to True to resize an image.
4. An image control can hold one image, and a picture box control can hold one image directly. However, a picture box also can hold image boxes and other picture boxes.
5. Setting the picture box AutoSize property to True causes the picture box to take the size of the picture.
6. Metafile pictures placed in a picture box automatically conform to the size of the picture box unless the AutoSize property is set to False.
7. A picture box uses the ForeColor for output from the *Print* and graphics methods and uses FillColor for the FillStyle pattern.
8. To display text in a picture box, use the picture box's *Print* method.
9. The *Move* method moves a control on a form.
10. Both the *Print* and the *Circle* methods apply to both forms and picture boxes. One draws text, and the other draws circles.

Lesson 12

1. a. A circle created with a Shape control that appears at design time, and a circle painted using the *Circle* method is drawn during run time.

   b. A Shape control has its own properties, while a circle drawn using *Circle* is affected by the properties of its container (the form or picture box in which it is drawn).

   c. Both a Shape circle and a circle drawn using *Circle* normally appear on the back layer.

   d. A Shape control, like other controls, is redrawn automatically. A circle drawn with *Circle* is redrawn if (a) the *Circle* command is in a *Paint* event and AutoRedraw for the container is False, or if (b) the *Circle* command is in an event other than a *Paint* event and the AutoRedraw for the container is True.

2. c

3. a. At the center of the circle

   b. At the end of the line

   c. At the point

4. a. Draw a circle of radius 800 centered at (x,y) = (2000,100) using the current ForeColor.

   b. Draw a circle of radius 800 centered at (x,y) = (2000,100) using the color vbCyan.

   c. Draw an arc of a circle of radius 800 centered at (x,y) = (2000,100) using the color vbCyan. The arc runs from an angle of 1 radian to an angle of 2 radians.

   d. Draw a circle of a radius 800 centered at (x,y) = (2000,100) using the current ForeColor with an aspect ratio of 2.

   e. Draw a circle of radius 800 centered at point 2000 units to the right and 1000 units below the current graphics position using the current ForeColor.

5. a. Draw a line from (10,50) to (1000, 50).

   b. Draw a line from the current graphics position to (300, 300).

   c. Draw a line from the current graphics position to a point 200 units to the right and 400 units down.

   d. Draw a box with one corner at (50, 50) and the opposite corner at (2000, 2000) using the color vbBlue. The box will be filled with the current FillColor using the FillStyle.

   e. Draw a filled box with one corner at (50, 50) and the opposite corner at (2000,2000) using the color vbBlue to both draw and fill the box.

6. Setting DrawWidth to 10 causes *PSet* to paint points that are 10 pixels to the side.

7. To draw a circle with a solid red interior on a form, set the form's FillColor to red and the form's FillStyle to solid.

8. To draw a circle with a solid red interior in a picture box, set the picture box's FillColor to red and the form's FillStyle to solid.
9. Forms and picture boxes have a *Paint* event, which is triggered when the object becomes visible. Graphics painted using a *Paint* event get repainted if the form or picture box becomes concealed, then appears again.
10. Set the form's ScaleMode property to 3 - pixel to have measurements made in pixels.
11. Setting AutoRedraw to True causes graphics produced by graphics methods and text produced by the *Print* method never to appear if drawn from a *Paint* event and to reappear whenever uncovered if drawn from a non-*Paint* event. The text and graphics are stored in memory so they can be redrawn quickly.

Lesson 13

1. The arguments to the *DragDrop* event are *Source*, a type *Control* variable representing the control being dragged, and *X* and *Y*, two type *Single* variables representing the *X* and *Y* position of the mouse.
2. The arguments to the *DragOver* event are *Source*, a type *Control* variable representing the control being dragged, *X* and *Y*, two type *Single* variables representing the *X* and *Y* position of the mouse, and *State*, an *Integer* variable representing whether the object is entering, over, or leaving the object receiving the event.
3. To enable automatic dragging, set the DragMode property of a control to 1 - automatic.
4. To enable manual dragging, set the DragMode property of a control to 0 - manual. (This is the default setting.)
5. The reason for using manual dragging when automatic dragging is so much simpler is that a control with automatic dragging doesn't respond to other mouse events, such as mouse clicks.
6. To have a control move when you drag it, use the *DragDrop* event to reset the Top and Left properties of the dragged object to the new position.
7.

```
Quiz = txtRitter           ' invalid because you have to use Set
Set Quiz = cmdCenter       ' valid because a command button is a control
Set Quiz = Form1           ' invalid because a form is not a control
Set Quiz = 99              ' invalid because 99 is not a control
```

8.

```
Dim Plip As Control        ' Yes, because a text box is a control
Dim Glip as Object         ' Yes, because a text box is an object
Dim Dlip as Form           ' No, because a text box is not a form
Dim Mlip as TextBox        ' Yes, because a text box is a text box
Dim Vlip as ListBox        ' No, because a text box is not a list box
```

Lesson 14

1. b
2. The difference between a screen font and a printer font is that a screen font is used to display text on a display monitor, while a printer font is used by a printer.
3. A bitmapped font consists of a collection of bitmapped images of each character in a font. Each font size requires a separate set of bit images. A scaleable font describes each character mathematically, and the same description can be used to create fonts of any size (within limits).
4. a. 7/4/96

   b. Thursday, July 4, 1996

   c. 7/4/96

   d. Thursday, 1996 July 4
5. a. I have 10

   b. I have –10

   c. I have 10

   d. I have –10

   e. 2.3456

   f. 02.35

   g. 2.35
6. The *PrintForm* method reproduces the contents of a form, but it doesn't take advantage of the printer's resolution. The *EndDoc* approach using the Printer object utilizes the full resolution of the printer, but it only prints what you can draw on the Printer object by using the *Print* and graphics methods.

Lesson 15

1. a. 2 + 5 is 7

   b. 50 / 8 is 6.75

   c. 50 \ 8 is 6

   d. 3 ^ 2 is 9

   e. 2 ^ 3 is 8
2.

```
Dim I as Integer
For I = 1 To 10
    Print Int(101 * Rnd) + 100
Next I
```

3. a. Abs(10-15) is 5
   b. Int(23.66) is 23
   c. Int(-23.66) is -24
   d. Fix(23.66) is 23
   e. Fix(-23.66) is -23
4.

```
Dim P as Double ' time to orbit Sun
Dim A as Double ' average distance from Sun
P = Sqr(D^3)
```

5. 10 feet: see 3.87 miles
   100 feet: see 12.25 miles
   10,000 feet: see 122.47 miles
6. 14.11%

Lesson 16

1.

```
Sub Marine ()          ' add parentheses
    Print "Surfacing!"
End Sub                ' add Sub
```

2. If you have a statement like

```
Grub 25
```

then Grub is the called procedure and the procedure containing this statement is the calling procedure.

3. a. *Double* is a valid argument type
   b. *String* is a valid argument type
   c. *Variant* is a valid argument type
   d. *ListBox* is a valid argument type
   e. *UnStable* is a not valid argument type unless it is the name of a user-defined type
4. Use a type *Label* argument
5. Use a type *Control* argument
6. Use a type *Control* argument (call it MyControl, for example), then use

```
If TypeOf MyControl Is Listbox Or TypeOf MyControl Is ComboBox Then
```

to limit application of code to list boxes and combo boxes.

7. A message box displays a message and accepts input in the form of clicking on a button. An input box displays a message and accepts input in the form of a string entered by the user.
8. a. vbOKOnly

b. vbYesNoCancel

c. vbYesNoCancel + vbDefaultButton2

d. vbAbortRetryIgnore + vbExclamation

9.

```
Sub Function Hypotenuse (X as Double, Y as Double) As Double
    Double Hypo
    Hypo = X * X + Y * Y
    Hypotenuse = Sqr(Hypo)
End Sub
```

10. When a function passes by value, the function argument is a new variable that is assigned the value of the argument in the function call. When a function passes by reference, the function argument is an alias for the variable used as an argument in the function call.

Lesson 17

1.

```
Dim Floor As Single
Print "I compute, therefore I compute."
Circle (100, 200), 50
If Floor > 3 Then Print "Everyone out!"
```

2. The easiest, most foolproof way of finding syntax errors is to let the Visual Basic program find them for you while you are in design mode.
3. The Code window and the Debug window appear when you enter break mode.
4. The Debug window contains a box displaying the name of the procedure being executed, a Watch pane, and an Immediate pane.
5. Step Over "steps over" a procedure call, executing it without comment, and proceeding to the following statement. Step Into transfers to the called procedure and steps through it, returning to the original procedure when the called procedure finishes.
6. First, the *Bottles <= 0* is immediately false. Probably the intended test is *Bottles >= 0*. Second, nothing in the loop changes the value of the *Bottles* variable.
7. The Watch window displays the values of variables and expressions that you've added as watch expressions.
8. The *IsError* function returns True if its argument (typically a *Variant* return value from a function) is an error value, that is, a Variant of *VarType vbError. On Error* is a statement that directs program execution to an error handler when certain kinds of errors occur.
9. *Resume* means to resume program execution with the statement that originally caused the error, while *Resume Next* means to resume program execution with the statement following the statement that originally caused the error.
10. Place the *GoGet* call after the *On Error* statement.

Lesson 18

1. a. Selecting a drive in the drive list box automatically changes the drvPony.Drive property.

   b. Selecting a drive in the drive list box changes the current drive setting if you place the following command in the *drvPony_Change* event:

```
ChDrive drvPony.Drive
```

   c. Selecting a drive in the drive list box changes the directories showing in the directory list box if you place the following code in the *drvPony_Change* event:

```
dirPony.Path = drvPony.Drive
```

   d. Selecting a new directory in the directory list box updates the file list box if you place the following code in the *dirPony_Change* event:

```
filPony.Path = dirPony.Path
```

   e. Selecting a new directory in the directory list box updates the current directory setting box if you place the following code in the *dirPony_Change* event:

```
ChDir dirPony.Path
```

   f. A program will display in a txtPick text box the name of a file selected in the file list box if you place the following code in the *filPony_PathChange* event:

```
txtPick.Text = filPony.FileName
```

2. a. To display a dialog box for opening a file, use the following statement:

```
dlgDoAll.ShowOpen
```

   b. To set the string variable *MrFile* to the name of the file selected in the dialog box, use the following statement:

```
MrFile = dlgDoAll.FileName
```

   c. To set the frmDial form's background color to a color selected using the dialog box, use the following code:

```
dlgDoAll.ShowColor
' select color in dialog box
frmDial.BackColor = dlgDoAll.Color
```

   d. To set the frmDial form's font to 24-point bold using the dialog box, use the following code:

```
dlgDoAll.ShowFont
' select font size in dialog box
frmDial.Font.Size = dlgDoAll.FontSize
```

3. a. Open "dribble.txt" For Input As #1 is valid.

   b. Input NextChar should be NextChar = Input(1, #1).

   c. Close "dribble.txt" should be Close #1.

   d. Open "disand.dat" As Random Len = Len(Dabble) should be.

   Open "disand.dat" For Random As #1 Len = Len(Dabble).

e. Put #1, Dabble should be Put #1, , Dabble or else Put #1, Pos, Dabble with Pos being the record number where the Dabble record should be placed.

Lesson 19

1. c
2. b, c, d
3. Select Form from the Insert menu.
4. Select Add File from the File menu.
5. With one MDI form and several child forms, the only part of a child form visible is the part within the MDI form. Independent forms are sized independently of one another. If you minimize an MDI child, it appears as a menu bar at the bottom of the MDI form. If you minimize an independent form, it appears as a button on the Windows taskbar. If you maximize an MDI child, it fills the parent. If you maximize an independent form, it fills the screen. Child forms use the MDI form's menu bar. Each independent form has its own menu bar.
6. A startup form is the form that appears when you start a program. Select Options from the Tools menu, click on the Project tab, and enter your choice in the Start Up Form box.
7. Hiding a form removes its image from the screen, but all its properties are still in memory. Unloading a form erases the form description from memory.
8. You refer to an active form if it has no name by the term *Screen.ActiveForm.*

Lesson 20

1. First, the syntax errors.

```
Dim Ajax As Form
Dim Comet As New Form      ' New can be used with a specific form
                           ' not with a generic form.
Dim Dolma As New frmDorf
Private Form_Load()        ' Private Sub Form_Load ()
    Ajax = frmDorf         ' Must use Set
    Me.Caption = "Hampshire"
    Show Dolma             ' Should be Dolma.Show
End Sub
```

Second, this code sets up an infinite loop, for each new form has its own variable called *Dolma,* which it attempts to show, triggering a new *Form_Load* event, which attempts to show a new *Dolma* form, which triggers another *Form_Load* event, and so on.

2. Use *Property Set Dint* if *Dint* is an object variable, and use *Property Let Dint* if *Dint* is a fundamental type, like *Integer.*
3. For variables of each of the following types, indicate whether or not you would use Set to set the variable's value and indicate whether you could use New to

create new instances of the type. Assume fmA1 is the name of a form and that Torus is the name of a class.

TYPE	USE SET?	USE NEW?
Integer	No	No
Label	No	No
Control	Yes	No
Torus	Yes	Yes
Form	Yes	No
frmA1	Yes	Yes

4. a. First, start a new project and select Class Module from the Insert menu. For the name property, use *Simple*.

   b. Next, use *Property Let* and *Property Get* to define a Happy property and create a *Howdy* function:

```
Option Explicit

Private HappyVal As Boolean
Property Let Happy(HV As Boolean)
    HappyVal = HV
End Property

Property Get Happy() As Boolean
    Happy = HappyVal
End Property

Function Howdy() As String
    If Happy Then
        Howdy = "Howdy! It's a wonderful day!"
    Else
        Howdy = "Lo. See ya later."
    End If
End Function
```

   c. Use New to create a Simple object:

```
Dim Grump As New Simple
Grump.Happy = False
Print Grump.Howdy
```

5. The *Class_Initialize* event is triggered when an object of a class is created.

APPENDIX F
CERTIFICATION AND COURSE CREDIT

Waite Group Press and the University of Phoenix (UoP) are pleased to offer you the opportunity to obtain a two-level certification for the Visual Basic knowledge you've gained from completing *Certified Course in Visual Basic 4*. After you complete the first level, UoP will recognize your achievement by awarding a certificate. Completion of the first level allows you to move on to the second level, where you can earn three undergraduate course credits by passing a more thorough final exam, which involves programming in Visual Basic.

To become eligible for the first-level certification, you must take the final exam with the testing program included on the enclosed CD-ROM. When you have completed the exam, the program will prompt you to save it to a disk as file FINAL.XAM. You then need to copy it to a separate 3.5-inch floppy disk and label the disk with your name, phone number, and the title "Certified Course in VB: Final Exam." Submit this disk, the completed original (not a photocopy) of the University of Phoenix Certification Application found in the back of this book, and a $10 ($15 for orders outside of North America) processing fee (make check payable to University of Phoenix) to:

University of Phoenix
Technology Programs Department
7800 East Dorado Place
Englewood, CO 80111

Attn: Certified Course in VB Exam

Within two weeks of receipt, the University of Phoenix will grade your answers to the exam and return the results. To pass this exam, you must achieve a score of 75 percent or better.

If you do not achieve a 75 percent score, you will receive your score, a list of chapters you should emphasize when you review the material in the book, and a new card that entitles you to retake and resubmit the exam. Each time you submit your final exam for evaluation, you must pay the $10 ($15) processing fee. You may attempt to pass the final exam from the book a maximum of three times.

If you do achieve a 75 percent score, you will be awarded a certificate. In addition, you will receive an application to attempt the second-level exam. The second-level exam requires you to write one or more Visual Basic programs. Upon achieving a 75 percent or better score, you will be awarded three undergraduate college credits. The processing fee for the second-level exam is $35 ($45 for orders outside of North America), and you may attempt it only once. Both passing and failing candidates will receive brief comments from a University of Phoenix grader. The second-level exam application will explain the application, testing, and fee details more thoroughly.

The Final Exam Program

A Visual Basic program on the CD-ROM administers a 50-question final exam. The ready-to-run version is called VBFINAL.EXE, and it uses questions stored in the VBFINAL.DAT file. Once you have completed all 50 questions, the Make Answer file is enabled, and you can save your work in a file called FINANS.TXT. A text file on the CD (README.TXT) provides more information about the final examination program.

Copying the Exam

Because CD-ROMs are read-only drives, you cannot save test answers to the CD-ROM; however, you can copy the program to the hard disk or a floppy and run it from there. For information on copying these files refer to "Using the CD," in the Preface of this book.

Running the Exam

When you are ready to run the final examination program, click on the application file icon labeled "Vbfinal." When the program loads, you'll see a text box containing the first multiple choice question. Below this text box, you'll see option buttons corresponding to the answers. Initially, the option button labeled "(not answered)" is selected. The Next button moves you to the next question, and the Previous button returns to the last question, so you can review or alter earlier answers. The program automatically highlights the Next button after you click on an option button, so you can simply press ENTER to proceed. A small text box keeps track of the total number of questions you've answered.

INDEX

E

L

M

N

ENVIRONMENTAL AWARENESS

Books have a substantial influence on the destruction of the forests of the Earth. For example, it takes 17 trees to produce one ton of paper. A first printing of 30,000 copies of a typical 480 page book consumes 108,000 pounds of paper which will require 918 trees!

Waite Group Press™ is against the clear-cutting of forests and supports reforestation of the Pacific Northwest of the United States and Canada, where most of this paper comes from. As a publisher with several hundred thousand books sold each year, we feel an obligation to give back to the planet. We will therefore support organizations which seek to preserve the forests of planet Earth.

This is a legal agreement between you, the end user and purchaser, and The Waite Group®, Inc., and the authors of the programs contained in the disk. By opening the sealed disk package, you are agreeing to be bound by the terms of this Agreement. If you do not agree with the terms of this Agreement, promptly return the unopened disk package and the accompanying items (including the related book and other written material) to the place you obtained them for a refund.

SOFTWARE LICENSE

1. The Waite Group, Inc. grants you the right to use one copy of the enclosed software programs (the programs) on a single computer system (whether a single CPU, part of a licensed network, or a terminal connected to a single CPU). Each concurrent user of the program must have exclusive use of the related Waite Group, Inc. written materials.

2. The program, including the copyrights in each program, is owned by the respective author and the copyright in the entire work is owned by The Waite Group, Inc. and they are therefore protected under the copyright laws of the United States and other nations, under international treaties. You may make only one copy of the disk containing the programs exclusively for backup or archival purposes, or you may transfer the programs to one hard disk drive, using the original for backup or archival purposes. You may make no other copies of the programs, and you may make no copies of all or any part of the related Waite Group, Inc. written materials.

3. You may not rent or lease the programs, but you may transfer ownership of the programs and related written materials (including any and all updates and earlier versions) if you keep no copies of either, and if you make sure the transferee agrees to the terms of this license.

4. You may not decompile, reverse engineer, disassemble, copy, create a derivative work, or otherwise use the programs except as stated in this Agreement.

GOVERNING LAW

This Agreement is governed by the laws of the State of California.

LIMITED WARRANTY

The following warranties shall be effective for 90 days from the date of purchase: (i) The Waite Group, Inc. warrants the enclosed disk to be free of defects in materials and workmanship under normal use; and (ii) The Waite Group, Inc. warrants that the programs, unless modified by the purchaser, will substantially perform the functions described in the documentation provided by The Waite Group, Inc. when operated on the designated hardware and operating system. The Waite Group, Inc. does not warrant that the programs will meet purchaser's requirements or that operation of a program will be uninterrupted or error-free. The program warranty does not cover any program that has been altered or changed in any way by anyone other than The Waite Group, Inc. The Waite Group, Inc. is not responsible for problems caused by changes in the operating characteristics of computer hardware or computer operating systems that are made after the release of the programs, nor for problems in the interaction of the programs with each other or other software.

THESE WARRANTIES ARE EXCLUSIVE AND IN LIEU OF ALL OTHER WARRANTIES OF MERCHANTABILITY OR FITNESS FOR A PARTICULAR PURPOSE OR OF ANY OTHER WARRANTY, WHETHER EXPRESS OR IMPLIED.

EXCLUSIVE REMEDY

The Waite Group, Inc. will replace any defective disk without charge if the defective disk is returned to The Waite Group, Inc. within 90 days from date of purchase.

This is Purchaser's sole and exclusive remedy for any breach of warranty or claim for contract, tort, or damages.

LIMITATION OF LIABILITY

THE WAITE GROUP, INC. AND THE AUTHORS OF THE PROGRAMS SHALL NOT IN ANY CASE BE LIABLE FOR SPECIAL, INCIDENTAL, CONSEQUENTIAL, INDIRECT, OR OTHER SIMILAR DAMAGES ARISING FROM ANY BREACH OF THESE WARRANTIES EVEN IF THE WAITE GROUP, INC. OR ITS AGENT HAS BEEN ADVISED OF THE POSSIBILITY OF SUCH DAMAGES.

THE LIABILITY FOR DAMAGES OF THE WAITE GROUP, INC. AND THE AUTHORS OF THE PROGRAMS UNDER THIS AGREEMENT SHALL IN NO EVENT EXCEED THE PURCHASE PRICE PAID.

COMPLETE AGREEMENT

This Agreement constitutes the complete agreement between The Waite Group, Inc. and the authors of the programs, and you, the purchaser.

Some states do not allow the exclusion or limitation of implied warranties or liability for incidental or consequential damages, so the above exclusions or limitations may not apply to you. This limited warranty gives you specific legal rights; you may have others, which vary from state to state.

About the University of Phoenix

Technological Leadership Begins with Educational Leadership

The University of Phoenix (UoP) was founded in 1976 by Dr. John Sperling. Concerned that American business was losing its competitive edge in the global marketplace, Dr. Sperling built a university dedicated to making a difference. Sperling's vision was to recapture our entrepreneurial and technological leadership and forge new paths in creative and innovative management through continual education of the American workforce.

More than 150,000 students have attended the University of Phoenix. Its programs are acclaimed by employers for their role in providing students with timely and relevant education that combines theoretical knowledge and practical applications to the real world.

Every Program Is Geared for Working Adults

More than 60 percent of UoP students have 11 years or more of full-time work experience. This profile is different from that of traditional college programs—and it is a profile the University understands. Each of its degree programs is constantly evaluated and updated in light of this profile. Concrete objectives are set for each course, so students and faculty have a clear road map of what they need to accomplish. As the nation's leader in adult education, the University of Phoenix continues to set educational standards that are emulated by both traditional and nontraditional institutions alike.

Courses are designed and taught by working professionals who are recognized leaders in their field. Classes usually meet for four hours, one night per week, allowing students to complete their degree programs without delay. UoP provides students with a variety of options for meeting course objectives outside of the classroom.

Master of Science in Computer Information Systems (MSCIS)

The MSCIS program provides students with a thorough grounding in key technologies so that they can effectively deal with system integration issues. Even if a student's primary interest is object-oriented programming and design, he or she will understand the concepts of telecommunications, operating systems, and databases—the key elements of most systems with which the student will be involved. The bridges between each of these key technologies consist of effective management principles and techniques.

All students must complete a common set of foundation courses consisting of project management, CIS management, effective oral and written communications, data communications and local area networks, file and database concepts, software engineering, and

Open Systems computing (UNIX and C programming). Upon completion of the foundation courses, students must complete their degrees by taking a series of elective courses from the management (such as strategic planning, risk management of CIS assets, and CIS economics) and/or technology (such as object-oriented design, reengineering the software development process, and enterprise-wide networking) areas. A practical, work-related project completes the degree program.

Bachelor of Science in Business/Information Systems (BSB/IS)

Keeping in step with today's evolving business climate requires keeping up with information systems technology. The University of Phoenix BSB/IS degree is designed to bridge the gap between a traditional business education and a working knowledge of computer information systems. The degree supports students by providing the necessary skills to design, develop, and implement a successful integrated business information system.

When a student enrolls in the BSB/IS program, the Core Curriculum consists of business courses including: Organizational Behavior, Business Communications, Computers and Information Processing, Marketing, Business Statistics, and Finance and Accounting for Managers. A series of information systems classes is then required to complete the major course of study. These courses include Introduction to Software Engineering, Project Planning and Implementation, Computer Architecture, Data Design and Information Retrieval, Database Management Systems, Telecommunications, Programming Concepts, Structured Programming Techniques Using the C Language, and Information Resource Management.

It is not necessary to be an experienced information systems professional to enroll in the University of Phoenix MSCIS and BSB/IS programs. Students with diverse backgrounds and skill levels are able to benefit from these programs.

Accreditation

The University of Phoenix is accredited by the Commission on Institutions of Higher Education of the North Central Association of Colleges and Schools (NCA). Institutional accreditation ensures that UoP and its programs meet the stringent standards set by the NCA.

To Obtain More Information

You may request more information about the University of Phoenix by writing, calling, or sending email.

University of Phoenix Technology Programs
7800 E. Dorado Place
Englewood, CO 80111
(303) 755-9090, ext. 116
Internet: moreinfo@hawaii.uopcol.uophx.edu

CERTIFIED COURSE IN VB

Certification Application

I have read and completed *Certified Course in Visual Basic 4* by Waite Group Press, have taken the final exam on the enclosed disk, and wish to apply for the first-level certification (described in Appendix F of this book). I understand that only the original form from the book (not a photocopy) can be accepted as an official application by the University of Phoenix.

I understand that the University of Phoenix will grade my exam and notify me of my score within two weeks (allow longer for orders outside of North America). Additional information about the second level of certification will also be sent at that time.

Name ______________________________

Address ______________________________

City ______________ State ________ Zip ________

Daytime phone ______________________________

Signature ______________________________

❑ I have enclosed one 3.5" floppy disk containing my completed FINANS.TXT
I have labeled the disk with my name, phone number, and the title "Certified Course in Visual Basic 4: Final Exam." (Disk will not be returned.)

❑ I have enclosed a check (made payable to University of Phoenix) for $10 ($15 for orders outside of North America) the exam processing fee.

Send to:

University of Phoenix
Technology Programs Department
7800 East Dorado Place
Englewood, CO 80111
Attn: Certified Course in Visual Basic 4 Exam

SATISFACTION REPORT CARD

Please fill out this card if you wish to know of future updates to *Certified Course in Visual Basic 4*, or to receive our catalog.

First Name: ____ **Last Name:** ____

Street Address: ____

City: ____ **State:** ____ **Zip:** ____

E-mail Address ____

Daytime Telephone: ( ) ____

Date product was acquired: Month ____ **Day** ____ **Year** ____ **Your Occupation:** ____

Overall, how would you rate *Certified Course in Visual Basic 4*?

☐ Excellent ☐ Very Good ☐ Good
☐ Fair ☐ Below Average ☐ Poor

What did you like MOST about this book? ____

What did you like LEAST about this book? ____

Please describe any problems you may have encountered with installing or using the disk: ____

How did you use this book (problem-solver, tutorial, reference...)?

What is your level of computer expertise?

☐ New ☐ Dabbler ☐ Hacker
☐ Power User ☐ Programmer ☐ Experienced Professional

What computer languages are you familiar with? ____

Please describe your computer hardware:

Computer ____ Hard disk ____
5.25" disk drives ____ 3.5" disk drives ____
Video card ____ Monitor ____
Printer ____ Peripherals ____
Sound Board ____ CD ROM ____

Where did you buy this book?

☐ Bookstore (name): ____
☐ Discount store (name): ____
☐ Computer store (name): ____
☐ Catalog (name): ____
☐ Direct from WGP ☐ Other ____

What price did you pay for this book? ____

What influenced your purchase of this book?

☐ Recommendation ☐ Advertisement
☐ Magazine review ☐ Store display
☐ Mailing ☐ Book's format
☐ Reputation of Waite Group Press ☐ Other

How many computer books do you buy each year? ____

How many other Waite Group books do you own? ____

What is your favorite Waite Group book? ____

Is there any program or subject you would like to see Waite Group Press cover in a similar approach? ____

Additional comments? ____

Please send to: Waite Group Press
200 Tamal Plaza
Corte Madera, CA 94925

☐ **Check here for a free Waite Group catalog**

SATISFACTION CARD

STOP!

BEFORE YOU OPEN THE DISK OR CD-ROM PACKAGE ON THE FACING PAGE, CAREFULLY READ THE LICENSE AGREEMENT.

Opening this package indicates that you agree to abide by the license agreement found in the back of this book. If you do not agree with it, promptly return the unopened disk package (including the related book) to the place you obtained them for a refund.